Author of "The Law of God"
Archpriest Seraphim Slobodskoy
1912–1971

The Law of God

For Study at Home and School

Compiled by
Archpriest Seraphim Slobodskoy

First English Edition

Printshop of St. Job of Pochaev
Holy Trinity Monastery
Jordanville, N.Y.
1996

Printed with the Blessing of Archbishop Laurus
of Syracuse and Holy Trinity Monastery

Published 1993, 1996 in the United States of America
by Holy Trinity Monastery, Jordanville, N.Y. 13361-0036.

ISBN 0-88465-044-8

First printing: 1993
Second printing: 1996

TABLE OF CONTENTS

PART IV   CHRISTIAN FAITH AND LIFE

PART V THE DIVINE SERVICES OF THE ORTHODOX CHURCH

FOREWORD TO THE SECOND (RUSSIAN) EDITION

The need to have extensive material for the teaching of the Law of God is dictated by the following contemporary conditions, unique and unprecedented for the Orthodox:

1. The Law of God is not taught in the majority of schools, but all the natural sciences are taught, and from an intensely materialistic point of view.

2. The majority of Orthodox young people find themselves in the midst of foreign surroundings, amid differing confessions of faith and rationalistic sects.

3. The first (Russian) edition of this textbook is already out of print. Furthermore, the old editions of such textbooks cannot completely answer the needs and questions of contemporary youth.

All of the conditions indicated and other circumstances in our difficult times impose on parents, on all educators, and especially upon the teachers of the Law of God an **immense responsibility**. In addition, no one knows what tomorrow will bring. Will a child learn the Law of God or not? Perhaps tomorrow his family will move to a place where there will be **neither church schools, churches, nor priests**. This possibility alone prevents us from restricting ourselves, in the primary courses, to simply narrating to the child (without any explanation) the events of sacred history, as this was done earlier by a program that extended over many years.

In our time it is necessary to avoid relating the Law of God in the form of naive stories (as they say, "for children"), for the child will accept them only as stories. When grown, he will experience a rift between the Law of God and his perceptions of the world, which he will have during his lifetime. With many educated people today, knowledge of religion remains obtained only in the classrooms of the first years of school, in the most primitive form. This of course cannot satisfy the demands of the mind of a mature individual. Indeed, even among children growing up under present conditions and developing faster than ever, the most serious and agonizing questions arise — questions which many parents and adults simply cannot answer.

All of these circumstances pose a task of the first order — to put into the hands not only of children in church schools, but also of parents, and teachers, **the school of the Law of God**. In order to achieve this goal, experience has proved it necessary to provide one book comprising **all the fundamental points of the Orthodox Christian faith and way of life.**

In view of the fact that many of those studying may never take up the Holy Bible, but will be satisfied with the textbook alone, such a situation demands absolute correctness in transmitting the Word of God. Distortion and even the slightest inaccuracy in presenting the Word of God cannot be permitted.

We have had occasion to see many textbooks, especially for classes of younger children, in which there were many inaccuracies, even errors in translating the Word of God. We introduce here a few examples starting with the least important.

In textbooks they often write: *The mother of Moses wove from reeds a basket* .... In the Bible it says: *She took a basket out of the reeds and covered it with pitch and tar* (Ex. 2:3 Septuagint). At first glance this may seem like a minor "detail," but this detail later reveals itself in more important matters.

Likewise, most of the textbooks write that Goliath *mocked and reviled the name of God*. In fact the Word of God says: *Am I not a Philistine, and ye servants of Saul?... Today I will put to shame the regiments of the Israelites; send out a man to me, and the two of us will meet in battle....* And the Israelites: *Seest thou this man who has come forth? He hath come forth to mock Israel....* David himself witnesses this point when he says to Goliath: *Thou comest against me with sword, spear, and shield, but I come against thee in the Name of the Lord of Sabaoth, the God of the warriors of the Israelites, whom thou hast mocked* (I Kg. 17:8, 10, 25, 45, Septuagint). It is clearly stated that Goliath in no way laughed against God, but at the ranks of the Israelites.

However, there are also mistakes and distortions that have been fatal for many people, e.g., in the narration of the **flood**. In the overwhelming majority of textbooks, the authors are content to say that it rained forty days and forty nights, and the land was filled with water which covered all the high mountains.

In the Holy Bible it is stated differently: *...the same day were all the fountains of the great deep broken up, and the windows of heaven were opened; and the rain was upon the earth for forty days and forty nights...And the waters prevailed upon the earth a hundred and fifty days* (Gen. 7:11-12, 24). In the next chapter it says *...and after the end of the hundred and fifty days the waters were abated...in the tenth month, on the first day of the month, were the tops of the mountains seen.* (Gen. 8:3,5).

With utmost clarity Divine Revelation says that the flood intensified **for almost half a year**, not merely for forty days. Then the water began to abate and only after ten months did the mountain peaks appear. This means that the flood extended over no less than one year. This point is especially important and essential to know in our rationalistic age, for even scientific geology completely supports these biblical facts.

Let us point out one more very important example. All textbooks, with very few exceptions, take the **days of creation** to be our usual twenty-four hour days. Most textbooks begin thus: "God created the world in six days...", i.e., in one week. It is no wonder that in our time **such words, which do not exist in the Bible**, seem very strange to students. The atheists always make use of such terms, but these words are a complete distortion of Divine Revelation. These words evoke doubts in the person who is not firm in the faith, who then might reject the remaining Scriptures considering them superfluous and the fruit of human fantasy. The author of these lines himself experienced this temptation after hearing unavoidable anti-religious lectures in school. The question of the days of creation, considering our times, can in no way be left without comment — even more so, since we already find the explanation to this question in the fourth century in **St. Basil the Great's** book *The Six Days*, in **St. John Damascene**, and in the writings of **St. John Chrysostom, Clement of Alexandria, St. Athanasius the Great, Blessed Augustine** and others.

Our (twenty-four hour) days depend on the sun, and the sun did not yet exist during the first three days, hence they were not like our days. What kind they were is unknown, for *one day is with the Lord as a thousand years, and a thousand years as one day* (II Pet. 3:8). Judging from the gradual succession in the process of creation we can certainly assume that these days did not occur instantaneously. The Holy Fathers term the entire period, from the creation of the world to our days and extending to the end of the world to be the "seventh day." Therefore, we Orthodox Christians experience a spiritual crisis when we find ourselves confronted by criticism and doubts. The talented writer Mintslov in his book *The Sleep of the Earth*, describes his days of doubt and uncertainty.

Like so many others, Mintslov, in describing the disagreements among the students at the Petersburg Ecclesiastical Seminary, says through the mouth of the student Krestovozdvizhensky:

" 'One cannot close one's eyes to the achievements of science in researching the Bible: it is seventy-five percent clerical falsification.'

"For example, although in the history of the exodus of the Hebrews from Egypt the Bible relates that when they departed from Egypt the armies of the Egyptians perished with Pharaoh Mernephta in the Red Sea, yet not long ago they found in Egypt the sepulchre of this very pharaoh and from the inscription on it, it is clear that he did not die anywhere but in his own house.' "

We do not wish to quarrel with Mr. Mintslov regarding whether or not Pharaoh Mernephta is in fact that pharaoh under whom the Hebrews left Egypt. This is a matter for historians, and all the more since the Bible does not indicate the name of the pharaoh. We only want to point out that on this question Mr. Mintslov has shown himself to be completely ignorant, and at the same time he did not hesitate to presume to plant the "poison" of doubt on the reliability of the Word of God. In the Holy Scriptures there is no definite historical indication that Pharaoh himself perished.

In the Book of Exodus, in which the historical description of the crossing of the Red Sea by the Israelites is to be found, there are only references to the Egyptians, their chariots, and their horsemen (Ex. 14:23-28). As is clear, if one reads the text, it is nowhere stated that Pharaoh himself perished. At the same time, it is clearly stated that all the army of Pharaoh perished. Thus speaks Moses, as well as do other places in the Bible.

Only in the 135th Psalm in which the omnipotence of God is glorified does it say, *And He overthrew Pharaoh and his host in the Red Sea, for His mercy endureth for ever* (Ps. 135:15, Septuagint). This verse is not meant to be a historical description of the events. This is a psalm-hymn in which the overthrow of Pharaoh himself is used descriptively and symbolically to explain the final overthrow of his power and authority over the Israelite people. Insofar as the Israelites were concerned, Pharaoh perished, **"drowned."**

Likewise in the preceding verses of this psalm the power of God is figuratively and symbolically expressed when it says that the Lord led out Israel *with a strong hand and a lofty arm; for His mercy endureth for ever* (Ps. 135:12, Septuagint).

In exactly this way the Church also sings symbolically-figuratively about Pharaoh perishing in the sea. In the historical description in the book of Exodus, Pharaoh himself did not drown. In a similar manner the Church extols the victorious power of Christ on Sundays: "Thou hast crushed the **bronze** gates, and the **iron** chains Thou hast broken..." (Tone 2, verses on "Lord, I have cried"). No one would begin to understand these words literally, for everyone knows that in the spiritual, heavenly world there is no bronze nor iron, but to each person it is clear and understandable that these words are symbolic, figurative.

Christians believe and know that *all Scripture is given by inspiration of God* (II Tim. 3:16) and is **indisputable truth.**

Atheists often utilize the ignorance of the faithful about the Word of God when they begin to ridicule something about which in fact the Holy Scriptures say nothing. Thus they like to assert that the Bible claims that the earth is standing on four whales, that God molded man out of clay, and so forth. The writer Mintslov has, perhaps unknowingly, done the same. Therefore, if atheists attempt to disprove God's truth in the name of "science," then let each of us be sure whether this atheist knows what he is talking about and what he wants to refute.

Regrettably, in the retelling of the Holy Scriptures there are many inaccuracies. These, in large part, are the "stumbling blocks" which play a fatal role for the uninformed. In the composition of our textbook we have striven, with the help of the Lord, to eliminate all these "stumbling blocks" and to transmit, as much as possible, the precise words of Divine Revelation.

Our times require special attention and care in setting forth the Word of God. In contemporary circumstances it is profitable to demonstrate **the existence of God, the truth of the Law of God, and the spiritual-ethical basis of the life of man**. It is necessary to instruct the faithful how to answer questions in accordance with the instructions of the Apostle Peter: *Be ready always to give an answer to every man that asketh you a reason for the hope that is in you, with meekness and fear* (I Peter 3:15). It is especially necessary in our day to answer the cunning questions of the atheistic world which leads the attack on the truth of God in the name, as it were, of science. But it is exactly in this regard that they suffer continual defeat. Authentic science not only does not contradict, but on the contrary indubitably confirms God's truth.

In our days it is unavoidable in teaching of the Law of God that there be a place for elements of **apologetics** (defense of the Faith). Formerly this was not required, because of the constant confirmation of the Faith in the way of life. The narratives from the Law of God should consequently be supported by examples from the lives of the saints and other examples from ordinary life so that the child understands and assimilates the fact that the **Law of God** is not theory, not a science, but is life itself.

In conclusion one must comment on a most strange, incomprehensible, and completely impermissible distortion found in all textbooks we have seen so far. This distortion concerns the **sign of the cross**. In these textbooks it is said that the sign of the cross is made with the right hand thus: from the forehead, to the chest, then from the right to the left **shoulders**.

Imagine thus, that in the course of many years one has incorrectly made the sign of the cross. Instead of that victorious sign of Christ's victory over the devil, the Cross of Christ, one has distorted this holy sign. This can only be to the joy of the demons.

This drawing gives a complete visual explanation:

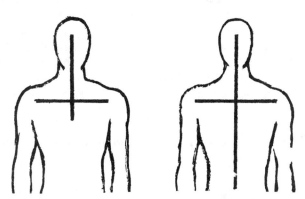

In the sacred book, the Psalter, from which Orthodox people were educated from ancient times, it is said in the "Brief Instruction": "about how it becometh the Orthodox Christian, according to the ancient tradition of the Holy Apostles and Fathers, to form on himself the sign of the cross... I shall state: first on our **foreheads**, which touches the highest part of the cross, second on the **stomach**, which touches the lowest point of the cross, third on our **right shoulder** and fourth on the **left**, by which the crossbeam is signed by the extended arms of the cross, on which our Lord Jesus Christ was crucified, His hands extended to gather all the nations scattered to the ends of the earth into one."

May the Lord preserve us from even the slightest deviation from the authentic Orthodox faith of Christ! May He help us to lighten the labor of educating children and the younger generation in eternal truth, righteousness, and love of God. And if this modest work brings some benefit to the Christian soul, then it will be a great joy to us.

May the Lord God, by the prayers of His Most-pure Mother, render herein His mercy to us and may He, through the power of His honored and life-creating Cross, guard us from all evil.

In compiling this book we have utilized the following works:

1) *First Book of the Law of God*, compiled by the noted Moscow catechetical teachers and reissued under the editorship of Archpriest Kolcheva; 2) *Precepts in the Law of God*, Archpriest A. Temnomerov; 3) *The Law of God*, Archpriest G. Cheltsov; 4) *A Short Sacred History*, Archmandrite Nathaniel; 5) *Precepts in the Law of God*, Archbishop Agathodor; 6) *A Sacred History of the Old and New Testaments*, Archpriest D. Sokolov; 7) *A Sacred History of the Old and New Testaments*, Priest M. Smirnov; 8) *A History of the Earthly Life of the Saviour*, A. Matviyev; 9) *A History of the Orthodox Christian Church*, Archpriest P. Smirnov; 10) *A Handbook for the Study of the Orthodox Christian Faith*, Archpriest P. Mazanov; 11) *Orthodox Christian Catechesis*, Archmandrite Averky; 12) *A Trial Orthodox Christian Catechesis*, Metropolitan Antony; 13) *A Brief Orthodox Catechesis*, Russian School ed. by the Church of "The Joy of All Who Sorrow," Paris. 14) *Studies in Orthodox Divine Services*, Archpriest N. Perekhvalsky; 15) *Brief Studies in the Divine Services of the Orthodox Church*, Archpriest A Rudakov; 16) *Studies in Orthodox Divine Services*, Archpriest B. Michailovsky; 17) *An Anthology of Precepts*, Archpriest L. Kolchev; 18) *In the Imperial Garden*, T. Shore; 19) *The Authenticity of the Biblical Miracles*, Arthur Hook; 20) *Did Jesus Christ Really Live?* Archpriest G. Shorets; 21) *Anthropology (The Science of Man)*, Prof. B. Nesmelov; 22) *Abstract for the Study of the Old Testament Bible*, Archbishop Vitaly; 23) *Lessons and Examples of the Christian Faith*, Archpriest George Dyachenko and others.

Finally, some sources are indicated in the text itself.

Archpriest Seraphim Slobodskoy
1966

INTRODUCTION TO THE FIRST ENGLISH EDITION

For thirty five years *The Law of God* by Father Seraphim Slobodskoy has been accessible only to Orthodox readers with a knowledge of Russian. After many years of preparation the first English edition of this valuable work is now available. The need for such a complete and diverse catechism in English has long been acutely felt by all those who instruct or seek instruction in the Orthodox Faith. The subject matter presented by the author is eternal; it covers all aspects of Orthodoxy including the Old and New Testaments.

When the first Russian edition of *The Law of God* appeared, Orthodox readers were still receptive to a traditional approach to catechisis. In the past three or four decades popular secular journals and even religious textbooks published by various Christian denominations have presented ancient Christian teachings in a spirit of scepticism and hostility. The directness and simplicity with which Father Seraphim presents the eternal Truths of our faith may seem inconsistent with recent trends, seeking to harmonize Christian teaching with so-called 'correct' worldly thinking, with modernism in theology and with the latest scientific sophistry. Under the influence of this liberal spirit some readers might find the attitudes expressed in *The Law of God* disquieting.

Our desire in publishing the present edition is to nurture souls in a true Orthodox Christian spirit. The material is presented in such a way as to be edifying and to give children and adults an intellectual foundation of support for their faith. While living in an environment which undermines the authority of the Church, *The Law of God* will supply the reader with support and defence for his beliefs, uncompromised to liberal trends. We can assure all Orthodox Christians that the spirit of this book reflects the mind of the Church. If we cannot supply the Christian flock with the pure, untainted water of salvation, then we have become like the salt of which the Saviour speaks ...*if the salt has lost its taste, how shall its saltness be restored? It is no longer good for anything except to be thrown out and trodden under foot by men* (Mt. 5, 13).

May our efforts in publishing this first English edition of *The Law of God* aid believers in cultivating this grace-filled 'saltness,' so that they might be able to answer for their faith to those who ask, and that they might inherit the Kingdom prepared by our Lord for His faithful servants.

Holy Trinity Monastery 1992

ACKNOWLEDGMENTS

We are very grateful to Mrs. Susan Price for her many years of labor in this translation from the Russian text. We also acknowledge all those who edited, advised, typeset, and printed the present edition of *The Law of God*. May the Lord bless all those who contributed their labor or helped with their donations in order to make this book available to the Orthodox world.

The Brotherhood of Holy Trinity Monastery

PART I

BASIC CONCEPTS

CHAPTER 1

The World

All that we see: heaven, the sun, the moon, stars, clouds, the earth on which we live, the air we breathe, the earth on which we live, including the grass, trees, mountains, rivers, seas, fish, birds, beasts, animals, and finally people —

God created all of this. Yes indeed, **the world is the creation of God**! When we see God's world then we understand how beautifully and wisely it was made.

Here we are in a meadow. Overhead, the blue sky with white clouds is stretched out like a tent, and on the earth there is thick, green grass, sprinkled with flowers. In the grass we can hear the sounds of various insects, butterflies fluttering around the flowers, and bees and gnats of different kinds flying through the air. The whole earth is like a huge, beautiful carpet. But there is no carpet woven by the hand of man that can be compared with the beauty of God's meadow.

Let us take a walk in the woods. There we can see a multitude of different kinds of trees, the mighty oak, the lordly pine, the spotted birch, the fragrant linden, the maple, the tall fir tree and the thick chestnut tree. There are little clearings with bushes and all kinds of herbs. Everywhere we hear the voices of birds, the buzzing and chirping of insects. Hundreds of different kinds of animals live in the forest. And how many different kinds of berries, mushrooms, and flowers there are! The forest is like a great world unto itself.

And here is the river. It quietly flows, sparkling in the sun, among the forests, fields, and meadows. How much fun it is to go for a swim! All around it is hot, but in the water it is cool and pleasant. How many different kinds of fish, frogs, waterbugs, and other living creatures there are! It has its own life, its own little world.

How magnificent the ocean is, with its huge and rich under-water world of living creatures.

How beautiful the mountains are with their lofty peaks covered with eternal snow and ice, high above the clouds.

The world is marvelous in its beauty, and all that is in it is full of life.

It is impossible to count all the plants and animals that populate the earth, from the very smallest, which are invisible to our eyes, to the very largest. They live everywhere — on the land, in the water, in the air, in the soil, and even deep beneath the earth. It is God Who gave all this life to the world.

The world of God is rich and varied! At the same time, in all this vast variety there reigns a marvelous and definite order established by God, or, as we often say, the "laws of nature." All the plants and animals are distributed throughout the world in keeping with this order. What each one is supposed to eat, that is what it eats. And there is a definite and logical purpose given to everything. Everything in the world is born, grows, and dies — one thing is replaced by another. God gave a special time and place and purpose to everything.

Man alone lives everywhere on the earth and has dominion over everything. God granted him reason and an immortal soul. He gave man a special and great purpose: to know God, to be like Him, that is, to become constantly better and inherit eternal life.

In their external appearance people are different, but they all have the same reasonable and immortal soul. Through this soul people are lifted above the animal world and become like God.

Now let us look into the deep, dark night, from earth up to heaven. How many stars we see scattered there. There is an infinite number of them! Many of the stars are just like our star, the sun. There are some that are many times larger than ours, but they are so far away from the earth that they seem to us to be

tiny, twinkling pinpoints of light. They are all in motion in an orderly and harmonious manner, according to definite paths and laws. Our earth amid the heavenly vastness seems like a tiny speck of light.

The world of God is vast, uncontainable! We can neither account for nor measure it all, for only God, Who created everything, knows the measure and weight and number of all things.

God created the entire world for the life and benefit of people, for each of us. God's love for us is infinite!

If we love God and live according to His law, then much that is unintelligible in the world will become understandable and clear to us. Let us love God's world and live in friendship, love, and joy with everyone. Then this joy will never end, and no one will take it away from us, for God Himself will be with us.

In order to remember that we belong to God, to be closer to Him and to love Him, that is, to fulfill our purpose on earth and to inherit eternal life, we must know more about God, know His holy will, that is, **GOD'S LAW.**

QUESTIONS: Who created the world and gave it life? Who made definite order in the world (or as we often say, established the laws of nature), and what does this consist of? What purpose did God give to man? For whom did God create the world? Why is it necessary for us to know God's Law?

CHAPTER 2

About God

God created the whole world **out of nothing**, by His Word alone. God can do all that He wishes. God is the highest existence. There is no one nor anything equal to Him anywhere, neither on earth nor in Heaven. We, mankind, cannot fully comprehend Him by our reason. We would know nothing about Him unless He Himself had not revealed it to us. What we know about God has all been revealed to us by God Himself.

When God created the first people, Adam and Eve, He appeared to them in Paradise, revealing Himself to them, revealed how He created the world, and how people must believe in the One True God and fulfill His will. This teaching of God was first passed on orally from generation to generation, but later, at the inspiration of God, it was written down by Moses and by the other prophets in the sacred books.

Finally, the **very Son of God, Jesus Christ**, appeared on earth and revealed all that mankind needs to know about God. He revealed to mankind a great mystery: **God is One** but a **Trinity in Three Persons**. The first Person is **God the Father**; the second Person is **God the Son**, the third Person is **God the Holy Spirit**. These are not three gods but one God in three Persons, **the Trinity in one essence and indivisible**.

All three Persons have the same divine dignity; there is not a senior one among them nor a junior; as **God the Father** is true **God**, so also **God the Son** is true **God**, and likewise, the **Holy Spirit** is true **God**.

They are different only in that **God the Father** is not begotten and does not proceed from anyone; **God the Son is begotten** of God the Father; the **Holy Spirit proceeds** from God the Father.

Jesus Christ through the revelation of the mystery of the All-holy Trinity taught us not only to worship God truly, but also to love God as all three Persons of the Most-holy Trinity — the Father, Son, and Holy Spirit. All eternally abide with one another in unceasing love and make up one Being. God is all-perfect love.

The great mystery, which God revealed to us concerning Himself, is **the mystery of the Holy Trinity**, which our weak mind cannot contain or understand.

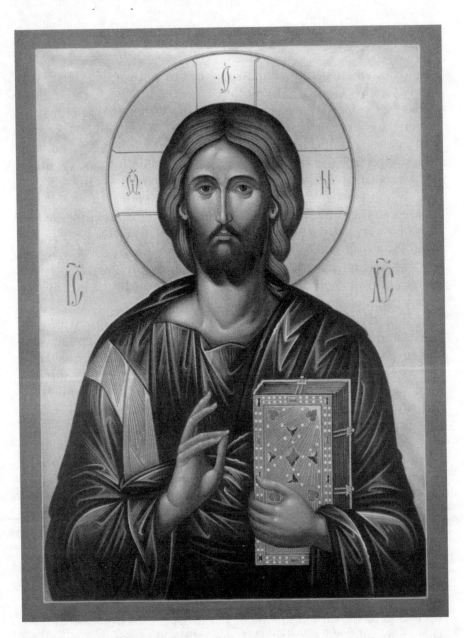

Our Lord Jesus Christ the Son of God

St. Cyril, the teacher of the Slavs, tried to explain the mystery of the Most-holy Trinity. He said, "Do you see in the heavens the brilliant sphere of the sun and how from it light is begotten and warmth proceeds? God the Father is like the sphere of the sun, without beginning or end. From Him is eternally begotten God the Son, like light from the sun; just as there comes

The Holy Trinity

warmth together with light from the sun, the Holy Spirit proceeds. Each one is distinguished separately: the sphere of the sun and the light and the warmth — these are not three suns, but one sun in the heavens. So also, in the Holy Trinity: there are three

Persons but God is one and indivisible." Blessed Augustine says: "You see the Trinity if you see love." This means that we can understand the mystery of the Holy Trinity more readily with the heart, that is by love, than with our feeble mind.

The teaching of Jesus Christ, the Son of God, was written down by His disciples in a sacred book, which is called the **Gospel**. The original word for Gospel is the Greek word *Evangelion*, which means glad tidings or good news.

The sacred books, gathered together into one book, are called the **Bible**. This is from Greek word which means **"book."**

QUESTIONS: Can we completely comprehend with our mind what God is and by ourselves learn about Him? Where do we learn about God and how He is the Creator of the world? Who revealed the teaching about God, that He is One but a Trinity in Persons? How are the Persons of the Holy Trinity called? How are They distinguished from One Another? What is the Gospel and what is the Bible?

CHAPTER 3

The Attributes of God

God revealed to us concerning Himself that He is *a bodiless and invisible spirit* (John 4:24).

What does it mean that God has neither a body, nor bones, as we have, and does not have in Himself anything that makes up our visible world, and therefore we cannot see Him?

In order to explain this, let us take an example from our earthly world. We do not see the air, but we see its actions and results; the movement of the air has great power which can move huge ships and complex machines. We feel and we know that we cannot live without the air that we breathe. So also we do not see God, but we see His activity and its results, His wisdom and power are everywhere in the world, and we feel them in ourselves.

The invisible God, out of love for us, at various times appeared to righteous people in a visible form — in images, or, reflections of Himself, that is to say, in such a form that they could behold Him. Otherwise they would have perished from directly beholding His majesty and glory.

God said to Moses, *There shall no man see Me, and live* (Ex. 33:20). If the sun blinds us with its brilliance, and we cannot look upon this creation of God lest we be blinded, then how much more so, on God Who created it. For *God is light, and in Him is no darkness at all* (I John 1:5), and He dwells in unapproachable light (I Tim. 6:16).

God is Eternal
(Ps. 89:3, Ex. 40:28)

All that we see in the world began at one time or another. It was born, and at some time it will also come to an end, it will die, it will be destroyed. All that is in the world is temporal; everything has its beginning and its end.

Once there was no Heaven, there was no earth, no time, but there was God, because He has no beginning. Having no beginning, He has no end. God always was and always shall be. God is outside time. **God always is.**

Therefore, He is called eternal.

God is unchanging
(James 1:17, Mal. 3:6)

There is nothing in the world constant or unchanging; everything constantly changes, grows, ages and disintegrates. One thing is replaced by another.

Only God is constant; there is no change in Him. He does not grow, does not age. He in no way, and on no account and at no time ever changes. Just as He always was, so He is now, and so He shall remain forever. God is always the same.

Therefore He is called unchanging.

God is omnipotent
(Gen. 17:1, Luke 1:37)

If a man wants to make something, he needs material; without material he cannot make anything. With paint and canvas man can paint a beautiful picture; from metal he can make a complex and useful machine. But he can never make, for instance, the earth on which we live, or the sun which gives light and warmth, and many other things.

Only for God is everything possible; there is nothing that He cannot do. He wished to create the world and He created it out of nothing by His word alone. God can do all that He wishes.

Therefore He is called omnipotent.

God is omnipresent
(Ps. 138:7-12)

God always, throughout all time, is present everywhere. There is no place in the world where He is not present. No one can hide from Him anywhere. God is everywhere.

Therefore, He is called omnipresent.

God is omniscient
(I John 3:20, Heb. 4:13)

Man can learn many things, know a great deal, but no man can know everything. Moreover, man cannot know the future, and cannot hear everything and see everything.

Only God alone knows everything, what was, what is, and what will be. For God there is no difference between day and night. He sees and hears everything at all times. He knows each of us, and not only what we do and say, but also what we think and what we want. God always hears everything, sees everything, and knows everything.

Therefore, He is called omniscient (knowing all things).

God is all-good
(Matt. 19:17)

People are not always good. It often happens that a person does not love someone else.

Only God loves all of us and loves us perfectly, not as man loves. He gives all that we need for life. All that we see in the heavens and on the earth was created by the Lord for the good and benefit of man.

This is how one bishop teaches about God's love for us: "Who gave us life? The Lord! From Him we received a rational soul that can think and learn. From Him we received a heart that is able to love. Around us is the air, without which we cannot live.

"We are always supplied with water which is as necessary for us as the air. We live on the earth which supplies us all the food that is necessary for the maintenance and preservation of our life. We are supplied with light without which we could not do anything for ourselves. We have fire with which we can keep ourselves warm when it is cold and with which we can prepare the food we eat. All this is the gift of God. We have a father, mother, brothers, sisters, and friends. How much joy, help, and consolation they provide for us! But we would not have any of these were it not pleasing to the Lord to give them to us."

God is always prepared to give us everything that is beneficial to us, everything good, and He takes more care for us than the best father does for his children.

Therefore God is called all-good, or Most-merciful.

We call God our **Heavenly Father**.

God is all-righteous
(Ps. 7:12, Ps. 10:7)

Men often tell lies and are unjust. But God is perfectly just. He always preserves righteousness, and He judges people justly. He does not punish a righteous man without a reason, and He does not leave a man unpunished for any evil deed, unless the man himself corrects his life by repentance and good deeds.

Therefore, God is called all-righteous and all-just.

God is all-sufficient
(Acts 17:25)

Man is always in need of something, therefore he is often dissatisfied.

God alone has everything and is not in need of anything for Himself; on the contrary, He gives everything to all.

Therefore, He is called all-sufficient.

God is all-blessed
(I Tim. 6:15)

God is not only all-sufficient, but He always has within Himself the very highest joy — complete blessedness, the very greatest happiness.

Therefore, God is called all-blessed. We can never find true joy in life, except in God alone.

We call God **creator**, or **maker**, because He created all things, visible and invisible.

We likewise call God **almighty, master, and king**, because He, by His almighty will, rules and reigns and directs all that was created by Him, holding them in His power and authority.

We call God Divine **provider**, because He provides for all things and takes care of all things.

QUESTIONS: What are the attributes of God? Why do we call God a spirit, eternal, unchanging, omnipotent, omnipresent, omniscient, all-good, all-righteous, all-sufficient and all-blessed? Why do we call Him creator and maker? Why do we call Him almighty, master, king, and provider?

CHAPTER 4

Prayer

God loves His creation; He loves each of us. *And I will be a Father unto you, and ye shall be My sons and daughters, saith the Lord Almighty* (II Cor. 6:18).

Therefore we can always at any time turn to God, to our Heavenly Father, as if to our own father or mother. Our turning to God is prayer.

This means that **prayer** is **conversation or speaking with God**. It is as necessary for us as air and food. Everything we have is from God, we have nothing of our own. Life, abilities, health, food: all these things are given to us by God.

Therefore, in times of both joy and sadness, whenever we need anything, we must turn to God in prayer, for the Lord is extremely good and merciful to us. If we ask from a pure heart, with faith and fervor concerning our needs, He will unfailingly fulfill our wish, and grant all we need. We must completely rely on His holy will and patiently wait, for God alone knows what we need and when to give it to us, what is useful and what is harmful.

People who are slothful about praying to God do great harm to their souls; for as they depart from God, God departs from them.

Without prayer man ceases to love God, he forgets about Him, and he does not fulfill His purpose on earth, he sins.

QUESTIONS: What does it mean to pray to God? Is it necessary to pray to God? When does God answer our prayer? Is it good for people not to pray to God?

CHAPTER 5

Sin

Sin, or **Evil**, is a violation of God's law. Transgression, or sin, is **violating the will of God**.

How did people begin to sin, and who was the first to violate the will of God?

Before the creation of the visible world and man, God created **angels**. Angels are bodiless **spirits**, invisible and immortal. All the angels were created good and God gave them complete freedom to love God or not, and to live with God or without God.

The Holy Angels

One of the most radiant and powerful angels did not wish to love God, to depend on Him, and fulfill the will of God, but desired to become like God Himself, to live independently. This angel ceased to obey God and began to resist God in everything. Thus he became the enemy of God, and many other angels went with him.

For such a rebellion against God these angels were all deprived of the light and blessedness that had been given to them, and they became evil, dark spirits.

All these dark, evil spirits are now called **demons or devils**. The main devil who was once the most radiant of the angels is called Satan, the enemy of God.

The Devil inspires people not to obey God, but to sin. The Devil deceives. By cleverness and deceit he taught the first people created by God, Adam and Eve, to violate the will of God.

All people come from Adam and Eve, who first fell into sin, and therefore we are born with an inclination to sin. Being constantly committed from generation to generation, sin has taken power over all men and has submitted everyone to itself. All men — to a greater or lesser degree — are sinners.

It is sin that constantly separates man from God and leads to suffering, illness, and death — temporal and eternal. It is for this reason that mankind began to suffer and die. Men alone, by their own efforts, could not overcome the evil that had spread throughout the world, or destroy death. God in His compassion gave help to men, sending to earth His Son, our Saviour, Jesus Christ.

QUESTIONS: What is sin? Who was the first to violate the will of God? Who is the Devil, or Satan? Who are the angels, and when were they created? Who are the evil spirits, and how are they called? Who taught men to sin, and how? Why are all of us born sinners? From Whom does sin separate mankind, what does it lead to, and why do all men die? Can men by themselves, by their own efforts, conquer evil and destroy death? How did God help people overcome evil and eternal death?

CHAPTER 6

The Sign of the Cross

We call ourselves **Christians** because we believe in God as we were taught to believe by the Son of God Himself, our Lord **Jesus Christ**.

Jesus Christ not only taught us to believe in God correctly, but He also **saved us from the power of sin and eternal death**.

The Son of God, Jesus Christ, out of love for us sinners came down from Heaven and, as a man, suffered instead of us for our sins: He was **crucified, He died on the Cross**, and on the third day **He resurrected**. As the sinless Son of God, **by His Cross** (that is, by suffering and death on the Cross for the sins of all men and of all the world), He conquered not only sin but also death itself — **He arose from the dead**, and He made the Cross the weapon of His victory over sin and death.

As the vanquisher of death, Who arose on the third day, He saved us also from eternal death. He will resurrect all of us, all the dead, when the last day of the world comes; He will resurrect us for joyful, eternal life with God.

The **Cross** is the **weapon**, or the **sign, of Christ's victory over sin and death**.

One teacher gave the following example in order to explain to his students how Jesus Christ could conquer evil in the world by His Cross:

For many years the Swiss fought against their enemies, the Austrians. Finally the opposing armies met in a certain valley for a decisive battle. The Austrian soldiers, wearing their armor, were drawn up in battle array with their lances extended forward, and the Swiss, beating them with their maces (heavy clubs with weights on the end), tried without success to break the ranks of the enemy. Several times the Swiss threw themselves on the enemy with blind courage, but every time they were thrown back. They were not strong enough to break through the thick row of lances.

Then one of the Swiss soldiers, Arnold Winkleried, sacrificed himself, ran ahead, grabbed with both arms several of the spears pointed at him, and allowed them to pierce his chest. In this way an opening was made for the Swiss and they broke into the ranks of the Austrians and won a decisive and final victory over their enemies.

So the hero, Winkleried, sacrificed his own life and died, but he made it possible for his people to conquer the enemy.

In the same way, our Lord Jesus Christ received in His breast the terrible spears of sin and death which were invincible for us. He died on the **Cross**, but He also **arose**, as the vanquisher of sin and death, and thus opened for us the way to eternal victory over evil and death. That is, He opened the way to eternal life.

The Cross of Our Lord

Now everything depends on us: if we wish to be delivered from the power of evil, sin and eternal death, then we must **follow** Christ, that is, **believe** in Christ, **love** Him, and fulfill His holy will, being obedient to Him in everything, live with Christ.

This is why, in order to express our faith in Jesus Christ our Saviour, we wear a Cross on our body, and during prayer we form the Cross over ourselves with our right hand, or make the **sign of the Cross**.

For the sign of the Cross we put the fingers of our right hand together as follows. We bring the tips of the first three fingers together (the thumb, index and middle ones), and bend the last two (the "ring" and little fingers) against the palm.

The first three fingers together express our faith in God the Father, God the Son, and God the Holy Spirit, as the Trinity one in essence and indivisible, and the two fingers bent show how the Son of God, when He came down from Heaven, being God, became man; that is, they signify His two natures — divine and human.

In order to make the sign of the Cross, with our fingers in this position, we touch our **forehead**, for the blessing of our mind, our **stomach**, for the blessing of our internal feelings, then our right and left **shoulders,** for the blessing of our bodily strength.

The sign of the Cross gives us great strength to repel and conquer evil and to do good, but we must remember to make the sign of the Cross correctly and without haste, otherwise it will not be the sign of the Cross, but just waving our hand around, which only gladdens the demons. By making the sign of the Cross carelessly we show a lack of reverence for God. This is a sin. This sin is called **sacrilege**.

We make the sign of the Cross, or "cross ourselves," at the beginning of prayer, during prayer, at the end of prayer, and when we draw near to anything holy: when we enter the church, when we reverence the Cross or an icon. We should cross ourselves at every important moment in our life: in danger, in sorrow, in joy, and so on.

When we cross ourselves, mentally we say, "In the name of the Father, and of the Son, and of the Holy Spirit." Thus we express our faith in the All-holy Trinity and our desire to live and labor for the glory of God.

The word "**amen**" means in truth, truly, let it be so, so be it.

QUESTIONS: What do we express when we make the sign of the Cross? How do we arrange our fingers in order to make the sign of the Cross, and what does this mean? When we make the sign of the Cross why do we touch our forehead, stomach and shoulders? Why is it important to make the sign of the Cross correctly and without haste? When should we make the sign of the Cross? What sin do we commit if we make the sign of the Cross carelessly?

CHAPTER 7

Standing and Bows During Prayer

In order to express to God our reverence before Him and our worship of Him, during prayer we **stand**, and do not sit; only the sick and elderly are allowed to pray sitting down.

Standing while at prayer is an ancient and God-ordained tradition. In Old Testament times, the congregation of Israel **stood** in the Temple (Neh. 9:4,5; 8:7, II Chron. 20:5,13), the Saints **stand** in Heaven before the Throne of God (Is. 6:2, I Kings 22:19, Dan. 7:10, Rev. 7:11), and even Jesus Christ Himself said, *When ye stand praying* (Mark 9:25). Therefore Christians, according to apostolic teaching, **stand** through the Divine Services, where it is often proclaimed: "Let us stand aright."

In recognizing our sinfulness and unworthiness before God, and as a sign of our humility, we make **bows** during our prayers. There are bows **from the waist**, when we bow from the waist, and **to the ground**, when we bow down on our knees and touch our head to the ground (a prostration).

QUESTIONS: Why should we stand and not sit during prayer? Why do we make bows during prayer? What kinds of bows are there?

CHAPTER 8

Different Types of Prayer

If we and those close to us are healthy and safe, if we have a place to live, clothes to wear, food to eat, then we ought to give praise and give thanks to God in our prayers.

Such prayers are called **praise** and **thanksgiving**.

St. Seraphim at Prayer

If some kind of misfortune, sickness, or woe happens or if we need something, then we must ask for God's help.

These prayers are called **petitions**.

If we do something wrong, sin, and we are guilty before God, then we must ask His forgiveness — repent.

These prayers are called **penitential**.

Since we are sinful before God (we constantly sin), we must always, before we ask God for anything, first repent and then ask God concerning our needs. This means that penitential prayer must always precede our petitions in prayer.

QUESTIONS: What must we offer to God when He sends us blessings? What are the prayers called when we praise and thank God? What do we offer God in prayer when some misfortune befalls us or we do something wrong?

CHAPTER 9

When God Hears Our Prayer

When we prepare to pray, we must first make peace with everyone to whom we have done evil, and even with those who have anything against us, and after that, with reverence and attention, stand for prayer. During prayer we must direct our mind so that it does not think about anything else, so that our heart wishes only one thing: to pray better and please God.

If we pray without making peace with our neighbors, if we pray hurriedly, if we talk or laugh during prayer, then our prayer will not be pleasing to God. God will not hear such a prayer, and He might even punish us.

For more diligent and intense prayer, and for a good pious life, **fasting** has been established.

The time of fasting, or lent, is the period when we must think more about God, about our sins before God, when we must pray more, repent, not get upset or hurt anyone, but rather, help everyone, read God's law, and so on. And to make it easier to fulfill all this we must first of all eat less — not eat any meat, eggs, or milk, that is, animal and dairy products, but eat only "lenten" food, that is, from plants: bread, vegetables, fruit, and fish (if allowed). We fast because the rich foods from animal and dairy products call forth a desire not to pray, but to sleep, or to act foolishly. When we develop the habit of not giving in to our desires for more or rich foods it makes it easier to fight against sin.

The greatest and longest fast comes before Pascha. It is called "Great Lent."

QUESTIONS: When can we hope that God will hear our prayer? What must we do to make our prayer reverent and fervent? Will God hear our prayer if we pray with haste and distraction? What has been established for diligent and intense prayer? What is fasting?

CHAPTER 10

Where and How We Can Pray to God

Prayer at Home

We can pray to God everywhere because God is everywhere: at home, in church, on every path. The Christian must pray every day, morning and evening, before and after eating, before and after every kind of work.

This kind of prayer is called **prayer at home** or **private prayer**.

On **Sundays** and **holy days**, and also on weekdays when we are free from work, we should go to church, where other Christians like us gather. There we all pray together.

Prayer in Church

This kind of prayer is called **public prayer** or **prayer in church**.

QUESTIONS: Where can we pray to God? Why can we pray to God everywhere? What is prayer called when we pray at home? What is prayer called when we pray in church?

CHAPTER 11

The Church Building

The church ("temple") is a special house consecrated to God — "the House of God," in which the Divine Services are conducted. In the church there abides the special grace or mercy of God, which is given to us through those who conduct

the Divine Services, namely, the clergy (bishops, priests and deacons).

The external appearance of the church differs from other

The Altar

buildings in that there is a **dome** which symbolizes Heaven rising over the church. At the top of the dome is its **peak,** where the **Cross** stands, to the glory of the Head, Jesus Christ. Over the entrance to the church there is usually built a **bell tower** where the bells are hung. The ringing of the bells serves to summon the faithful to prayer — to the Divine Services, and to give notice of the most important parts of the service taking place in the church.

At the entrance to the church there is a **porch** (courtyard, or entrance way). The inside of the church is divided into three parts: 1) the **narthex**, 2) the **church** itself, or the **nave, or middle part** of the church, where the people stand, 3) the **Altar**, or Sanctuary, where the services are conducted by the clergy and where the most important part of the whole church is located — **the Holy Table** (altar table), on which the Mystery of the Holy Eucharist is celebrated.

The altar is separated from the central part of the church by the **iconostasis**, which consists of several rows of **icons** and has

The Iconastasis

three doors. The central doors are called **the Royal Doors**, because through them the Lord Jesus Christ Himself, the King of glory, passes invisibly in the Holy Gifts (in Holy Communion). Therefore, no one may pass through the Royal Doors except the clergy.

The reading and chanting of prayers that are served in the church by the clergy are called **Divine Services**.

The most important divine service is the **Liturgy**. It is conducted before noonday. During this service the entire earthly life of the Saviour is commemorated, and the **Mystery of the**

Eucharist (Holy Communion), which Christ himself instituted at the Mystical Supper, is celebrated.

The Mystery of Holy Communion is the consecration of bread and wine by God's Grace, when they become the true Body and true Blood of Christ. In appearance they remain bread and wine, but we receive **the true Body and true Blood of the Saviour**, under the appearance of bread and wine, in order to enter the Kingdom of Heaven, have eternal life and change ourselves.

Receiving Holy Communion

Since the church is a **very holy place**, where **God Himself** is present invisibly by special mercy, we must enter it with prayer, and conduct ourselves quietly and reverently. During the Divine Services it is forbidden to talk, and even more so to laugh. It is forbidden to stand with your back to the Altar. Each person **stands** in his place and does not walk from one place to another. Only in case of sickness is it permitted to sit down and rest. It is wrong to leave the church before the end of the Divine Service.

We must approach Holy Communion **calmly** and **without haste, with our arms crossed over our breast**. After Communion we kiss the chalice without making the sign of the Cross, in order not to strike the chalice accidentally.

QUESTIONS: What is the church? What is its outside appearance like? How is the church divided inside? What is the iconostasis? Where are the Royal Doors? What is the Holy Table and what is celebrated on it? What is the most important Divine Service? What is commemorated at the Divine Liturgy? What is the Mystery of Holy Communion? Who instituted this Mystery? How should we conduct ourselves in church?

CHAPTER 12

The Priest's Blessing

The clergy (that is, specially ordained people who celebrate the Divine Services) are our spiritual fathers. Bishops and priests sign us with the sign of the Cross. This is called a **blessing**.

When the priest blesses us, he forms the Greek letters **IC XC**, that is, Jesus Christ, with the fingers of his hand. This means that through the priest our Lord Jesus Christ Himself blesses us. Therefore, we must receive the blessing of the clergy with reverence.

When we hear in the church the words of blessing, "Peace unto all" and others, in reply to them we should bow without making the sign of the Cross. In order to receive a personal blessing from a bishop or a priest, we

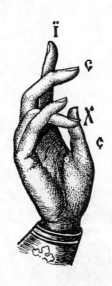

should place our hands in the form of a cross: the right hand on the left with the palms upward. When we have received the blessing we kiss the hand that blesses us — we kiss, as it were, the invisible hand of Christ the Saviour Himself.

QUESTIONS: Who signs us with the sign of the Cross? What is this called? What does the priest form with the fingers of his hand when he gives a blessing? What does this mean? How should we place our hands when we ask for a blessing? What should we do when we have received a blessing?

CHAPTER 13

Icons

In the church on the iconostasis, along the walls, and at home in the corners are the **holy icons**, before which we say our prayers.

An **icon** or **image** is what we call the representation of God Himself, the Mother of God, the angels, or the saints. This representation is consecrated with Holy Water and prayer. Through this blessing the Grace of the Holy Spirit is imparted to the icon, and we reverence the icon as being holy. There are icons,

The Icon Not-Made-by-Hands

through which the Grace of God that abides in them is revealed even by miracles, for instance in the healing of the sick.

The Saviour Himself gave us His portrait. Moved to compassion, He wiped His sacred face with a towel and miraculously depicted His face on this towel for the sick prince Abgar. When the sick prince prayed before this icon of the Saviour, that had not been made with hands, he was healed of his illness.

When praying before an icon, we must remember that the icon is not God Himself or a saint of God, but only the depiction of God or His saint. Therefore, we must not pray to the icon, but to God or the saint who is depicted on it.

The holy icon is a sacred book. In a sacred book we reverently read the words of God, and on a holy icon we reverently behold the holy faces which, like the Word of God, lift up our mind to God and His saints, and inflame our heart with love for our Creator and Saviour.

QUESTIONS: What do we call the holy icons? Where are the holy icons placed at home and in the church? Why are they called holy icons? Who blessed the use of holy icons by His example? What do we remember when we pray before the holy icons? What icon of the Saviour is named the Icon Not-Made-by-Hands?

How God Is Portrayed in the Holy Icons

God is an invisible Spirit. However, He appeared to holy men in a visible image. Therefore, we depict God in the icons in the form in which He appeared.

We depict the **Most-holy Trinity** in the form of three angels sitting at a table. This is because the Lord once appeared to Abraham in the form of three angels. In order to represent more clearly the spirituality of the angels that appeared to Abraham, we represent them with wings.

God the Son is represented in the form in which he appeared when he came down from heaven for our salvation and became man: an infant in the arms of the Mother of God, teaching the people and working miracles, transfigured, suffering on the Cross, lying in the tomb, resurrecting and ascending.

God the Holy Spirit is represented in the form of a dove, as He revealed Himself at the time of the Baptism of the Saviour in the Jordan by John the Baptist; and in the form of **tongues of fire**, as He descended visibly on the holy Apostles on the fiftieth day after the resurrection of Jesus Christ.

The Holy Trinity

QUESTIONS: If God is an invisible Spirit, how can He be depicted in the holy icons in a visible form? How do we depict the All-holy Trinity in the holy icons, and why do we depict Him in this way? How do we depict God the Father, God the Son, and God the Holy Spirit in the holy icons, and why do we depict Them in this way?

Others Besides God Who Are Depicted in the Holy Icons

Besides God we depict in the holy icons **the Mother of God, the holy angels and holy people**.

The Miraculous Myhrrstreaming Iveron Icon of the Mother of God

We should pray to them not as to God, but as being close to God, as having pleased Him by their holy life. Out of love for us they pray for us before God, and we should ask for their help

and intercession because the Lord for their sake will more speedily hear our sinful prayers.

It is worthy of note that the first icons of the Mother of God

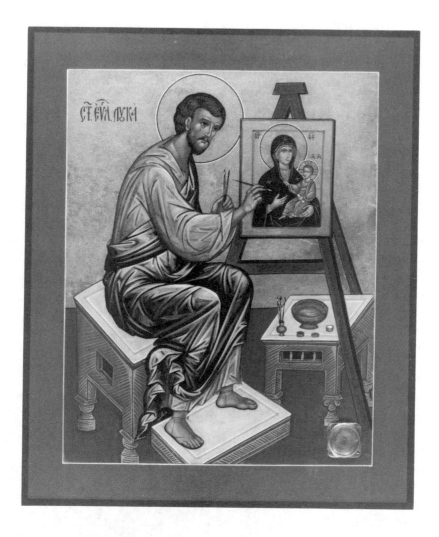

St. Luke Paints the First Icon of the Mother of God

painted by the disciple of the Lord, St. Luke, have been preserved down to our time. There is a tradition that when the
Mother of God saw Her portrait, she said, "The Grace of My Son

will dwell with this icon." We pray to the Mother of God because She is closest of all to God, and at the same time, She is also close to us. Because of Her motherly love and Her prayers God forgives us many things and helps us in many ways. She is a great and compassionate intercessor for all of us!

QUESTIONS: Besides God, who is depicted in the holy icons? How should we pray to the Mother of God, the holy angels and holy people? Who painted the first icon of the Mother of God? Why do we pray to the Mother of God more than to the other saints?

The Holy Angels

In the beginning when neither the world nor men existed yet, God created **the holy angels**.

Angels are bodiless spirits, therefore invisible and immortal. The Lord God granted to them loftier powers and abilities than to mankind. Their mind is more perfect than ours. They always fulfill the will of God. They are without sin, and now they are so filled with the Grace of God in doing good, that they do not desire in any way to sin.

Many times the angels have appeared in visible form, taking on a physical appearance, when God sent them to people to relate or to announce His will. The word "**angel**" means "**messenger**."

Every Christian is granted by God at his Baptism a **Guardian Angel** who invisibly protects him during all his earthly life from misfortunes and dangers; he warns against

The Guardian Angel

sin, guards us at the terrible hour of death, and does not depart after death.

The angels are depicted in icons in the form of handsome youths, as a sign of their spiritual beauty. Their wings show that they speedily fulfill the will of God.

QUESTIONS: When were the holy angels created? What are angels? What powers and abilities did God grant them? Can the holy angels sin? When did angels appear visibly and what does the word "angel" mean? How do we call the holy angels that God gives us at Baptism? Why are the holy angels depicted in the form of youths and with wings?

St. Mary Magdalene

About the Saints

On the icons also we represent **holy people** or **the saints of God**. We call them by this name because when they lived on earth, they pleased God by their righteous life. And now, dwelling in Heaven with God, they pray for us to God and help us who live on earth.

St. Tatiana

The saints have different titles: **prophets, apostles, martyrs, hierarchs, holy monks, unmercenaries, blessed ones, and the righteous**.

The prophets are the saints of God who, by the inspiration of the Holy Spirit, foretold the future, primarily about the Saviour. They lived before the coming of the Saviour.

The **apostles** were the closest disciples of Jesus Christ, whom He sent during His earthly life to preach. After the coming of the Holy Spirit upon them, they preached the Christian faith in all lands. At first there were twelve of them, and later, seventy more.

Two of the apostles, **Peter and Paul**, are called **leaders of the apostles**, because they labored in preaching the faith of Christ more than the others. Four of the apostles, **Matthew, Mark, Luke, and John the Theologian**, who wrote the Gospels, are called **Evangelists**.

Saints who spread the Christian faith in various places like the apostles, are called **Equal-to-the-Apostles**, as for example, **Mary Magdalene**, the first woman-martyr **Thecla**, the pious monarchs **Constantine** and **Helen**, the pious Russian prince **Vladimir**, Saint **Nina**, the Enlightener of Georgia, and others.

The martyrs are those Christians who accepted terrible tortures and even death for their faith in Jesus Christ. If they died in peace, that is, not as an immediate result of their sufferings for Christ, then we call them **confessors**.

The first to suffer for the Holy Faith after especially terrible sufferings for faith in Christ were **Archdeacon Stephen** and **St. Thecla**, and therefore they are called the **first martyrs**.

Those who died for the Holy Faith after especially cruel tortures, such as not all the martyrs were subjected to, are called

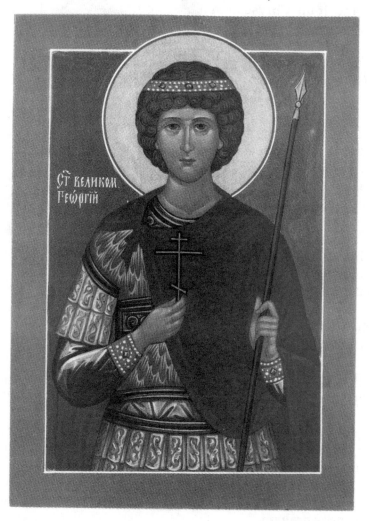

St. George

great martyrs, as for example, holy **Great Martyr George**, and the holy **Great Martyrs Barbara** and **Catherine**.

The confessors on whose faces the persecutors branded or tattooed blasphemous words are called **branded**.

Hierarchs are bishops and prelates who pleased God by a righteous life, such as **St. Nicholas** the Wonderworker, **St. Alexis**, Metropolitan of Moscow, and others.

Hierarchs and priests who suffered persecution for Christ are called **hieromartyrs**.

The hierarchs **Basil the Great, Gregory the Theologian**, and **John Chrysostom** are called **ecumenical teachers**, teachers of the entire Christian Church.

Holy monks and nuns are righteous people who abandoned the life of the world in society and pleased God by preserving their virginity (not entering into marriage), by fasting and prayer, and dwelling in the wilderness or in monasteries. Some examples are **Sergius of Radonezh, Seraphim of Sarov, St. Anastasia**, and others.

St. Kyra

Holy monks that endured suffering for Christ are called **Monk Martyrs**.

Unmercenaries are saints who served their neighbors with the unmercenary healing of illnesses; that is, without payment they healed illnesses, both physical and spiritual. They include **Cosmas** and **Damian**, the **Great Martyr and Healer Panteleimon**, and others.

The **Righteous** led a righteous life that was pleasing to God, living as we do in the world, with a family, as for example, **Joachim** and **Anna** and others.

The first righteous people on the earth were the patriarchs of the human race, who are called **forefathers**. They include **Adam, Noah** and **Abraham**.

QUESTIONS: Who are depicted in the holy icons, apart from God and the Mother of God and the holy angels? What names do they have? Whom do we call prophets, apostles, martyrs, hierarchs, holy monks, unmercenaries and righteous?

About Haloes on the Icons

Around the heads of the Saviour, the Mother of God and the holy saints of God, in the icons and pictures of them there is depicted a radiance or a circle of light which is called a **halo**.

In the halo of the Saviour there are three letters: ʿO ʾ῾ΩN, which translated from Greek into English mean "**Being**," or "**He Who Is**," for God alone always exists.

Over the head of the Mother of God are placed the letters: MP ΘV. These are the first and last letters of the Greek words which mean "Mary, Mother of God."

A halo is the depiction of the shining of light and glory of God which transfigure a man who is united with God.

This invisible shining of the light of God in the saints sometimes becomes visible for people around them.

Thus, for example, the holy Prophet Moses had to hide his face with a veil so that people would not be blinded by the light that proceeded from his face.

Also the face of St. Seraphim of Sarov shone like the sun during his talk with Nicholas Motovilov about the acquisition of the Holy Spirit. Motovilov himself wrote that it was not possible for him to look at the face of St. Seraphim.

Thus the Lord glorified His holy saints, who shine with the light of His glory even here on earth.

QUESTIONS: What do we call the circle of light which is depicted around the head of the Saviour, the Mother of God and the saints? What does the halo signify?

CHAPTER 14

Why We Call Ourselves Orthodox Christians

We call ourselves Orthodox Christians because we believe in our Lord Jesus Christ exactly as is written in the "**Creed**," and belong to the **One, Holy, Catholic and Apostolic Church** that was founded by the Saviour Himself on earth and which is directed by the Holy Spirit in preserving correctly, gloriously, and without change the teaching of Jesus Christ. That is, we belong to the Orthodox Christian Church.

All the other Christians who confess a faith in Christ which is not the same as the Orthodox Church, do not belong to her and are called the non-Orthodox or heterodox. This includes Catholics (the Roman Catholic Church) and Protestants (Lutherans, Baptists, and sectarians).

QUESTIONS: What do we call ourselves and why? What are other Christians called, who do not belong to the Holy Orthodox Church?

PART II

PRAYERS

CHAPTER 1

Short Prayers

Every Orthodox Christian is obliged to pray every day, morning and evening, before and after eating, before and after work, before and after lessons, etc.

In the morning we pray in order to thank God that He has kept us through the night, and to ask for His Fatherly blessing and help for the day that is beginning.

In the evening, before going to sleep, we also give thanks to the Lord for the day that has successfully concluded and we ask Him to keep us during the night.

In order to do our work successfully and safely we also, before all else, should ask God to bless and assist the work that lies before us, and upon finishing, to give thanks to God.

For the expression of our feelings to God and to His holy saints, the Church has given us different prayers. Here are some which are most commonly used:

IN THE NAME OF THE FATHER, AND OF THE SON, AND OF THE HOLY SPIRIT. AMEN.

In the name — by the name, to the honor, to the glory; **amen** — in truth, truly, let it be so, so be it.

This prayer is called the beginning prayer, because we say it before all the other prayers when we begin to pray.

In it we ask God the Father, God the Son, and God the Holy Spirit, that is the All-holy Trinity, invisibly to bless us by His name for the work that is before us.

QUESTIONS: What is this prayer called? Whom do we call upon in this prayer? What do we want when we say the prayer: "In the name of the Father, and of the Son, and of the Holy Spirit"? What is the meaning of "Amen?"

BLESS, O LORD!

We say this prayer at the beginning of all work.
QUESTION: What do we ask for in this prayer?

LORD, HAVE MERCY!

Have mercy — be merciful, forgive.
This is an ancient prayer and is used by all Christians. Even a little child can easily remember it. We say it when we remember our sins. For the glory of the Holy Trinity, we Christians say this prayer three times. We also say it twelve times, asking for God's blessing on every hour of the day and night, and we also say it forty times, for the sanctification of our entire life.

Prayer of Praise to the Lord God

GLORY TO THEE, OUR GOD, GLORY TO THEE.

Glory — praise.
In this prayer, we do not ask God for anything, but only glorify Him. We can also say a shorter prayer: **GLORY TO GOD**. We say this prayer at the end of work, as a sign of our thankfulness to God for His mercy to us.

The Prayer of the Publican

GOD BE MERCIFUL TO ME A SINNER.

This is the prayer of the publican (tax collector) who repented of his sins and received forgiveness. It is taken from the parable of the Saviour which He once told people for their instruction. Here is the parable. Two men went to the Temple to pray. One of them was a pharisee, the other a publican. The pharisee stood in front of everyone and prayed to God in this way: "I give Thee thanks, O God, that I am not such a sinful person as that publican. I give a tenth of my possessions to the poor, I fast twice a week." But the publican, realizing that he was a sinner, stood at the entrance to the Temple and did not even dare to lift his eyes to Heaven. He struck himself on the breast and said: **"God be merciful to me a sinner!"** The prayer of the publican was more acceptable and pleasing to God than that of the proud pharisee because the publican was humble and remembered to ask for forgiveness.

QUESTIONS: What is this prayer called? From where is it taken? Recount this parable. Why was the prayer of the publican more pleasing to God than that of the pharisee?

The Jesus Prayer

LORD JESUS CHRIST, SON OF GOD, HAVE MERCY ON ME, A SINNER!

This prayer contains the whole message of Christianity within it. It is directed to our Saviour Jesus Christ,

The Lord Jesus Christ Our Saviour

acknowledging Him as the Son of God and humbly asking His
mercy upon us. We should try to repeat this prayer at all times,
for it brings great benefit to the soul.

Another Prayer to the Lord Jesus

**O LORD JESUS CHRIST, SON OF GOD, THROUGH THE
PRAYERS OF THY MOST PURE MOTHER AND ALL THE
SAINTS, HAVE MERCY ON US. AMEN.**

Have mercy on us — be merciful to us, forgive us. **Jesus** —
Saviour; **Christ** — the Anointed; **through the prayers** — for the
sake of the prayers, or in answer to the prayers.

Jesus Christ is the Son of God, the second Person of the Holy
Trinity. As Son of God, He is our True God, as is God the Father
and God the Holy Spirit.

We call Him Jesus, which means **Saviour**, because He saved
us from sins and eternal death. For this, He, being the Son of
God, dwelt in the all-immaculate Virgin Mary, and in His incarnation through the Holy Spirit, **took flesh and became man of
Her**. That is, He accepted a human body and soul — **He was
born** of the Most-holy Virgin Mary, became the same kind of
man as we are, except that He was without sin — **He became
God-man**. And instead of us suffering and being tormented for
our sins, He, out of love for us sinners, suffered for us, died on
the Cross, and on the third day He rose, conquering sin and
death, and He gave us eternal life.

Realizing our sinfulness and not relying on the power of our
own prayers, in this prayer we ask all the saints and the Mother
of God, Who has special grace to save us sinners by Her intercession for us before Her Son, to pray for us sinners before our
Saviour.

Our Saviour is called Christ, the Anointed One, because He
had in full measure those gifts of the Holy Spirit, which were
given to the kings, prophets, and high priests in the Old Testament by anointing. Anointed also signifies the Lord's divine
mission of salvation.

QUESTIONS: Who is the Son of God? What else do we also
call Him? Why do we call Him Saviour? How did He accomplish
our salvation?

Prayer to the Holy Spirit

O HEAVENLY KING, COMFORTER, SPIRIT OF TRUTH, WHO ART EVERYWHERE PRESENT AND FILLEST ALL THINGS, TREASURY OF GOOD THINGS AND GIVER OF LIFE. COME AND DWELL IN US, AND CLEANSE US OF ALL IMPURITY, AND SAVE OUR SOULS, O GOOD ONE.

In this prayer we pray to the Holy Spirit, the third Person of the Holy Trinity.

In it we call the Holy Spirit **Heavenly King**, because He, as true God, equal to God the Father and God the Son, invisibly reigns over us, is over us and over the whole world. We call Him **Comforter**, because He comforts us in our sorrows and misfortunes, as He comforted the Apostles on the tenth day after the ascension of Jesus Christ into Heaven.

We call Him **Spirit of truth** (as our Saviour Himself called Him), because He, as the Holy Spirit, teaches all of us only truth and righteousness, only what is beneficial for us and serves for our salvation.

He is God, He is everywhere present and fills all things with Himself; **Who art everywhere present and fillest all things**. He, as the ruler of the entire world, sees all things and, where something is needed, He gives it. He is the **Treasury of good things**, that is, the keeper of all good works, the source of everything good that we could ever need.

We call the Holy Spirit the **Giver of life**, because all that lives and moves in the world does so by the Holy Spirit. That is, everything receives life from Him; especially people receive spiritual life from Him, holy and eternal life beyond the grave, being cleansed by Him of their sins.

Since the Holy Spirit has such marvelous qualities — is present everywhere, fills all things with His Grace and gives life to all — we turn to Him with special requests: **come and dwell in us**, that is, constantly abide in us, as in His temple; **cleanse us of all impurity**, that is, of sin; make us holy, worthy of His abiding within us. **Save our souls, O Good One** from sins and those punishments which follow for sins, and by this grant us the Kingdom of Heaven.

QUESTIONS: Whom do we address in this prayer? Which person of the Holy Trinity is the Holy Spirit? What is He called in this prayer? Why is He called Heavenly King, Comforter, Spirit of truth, Who is everywhere present, and Who fillest all things? What do we ask Him for? What does this mean: "Come and dwell in us and cleanse us of all impurity, and save our souls, O Good One"?

The Angelic Hymn to the Most-holy Trinity, or, the "Trisagion"

HOLY GOD, HOLY MIGHTY, HOLY IMMORTAL, HAVE MERCY ON US.

Mighty — powerful; **Immortal** — never dying, eternal.

This prayer is to be repeated three times in honor of the three Persons of the Holy Trinity.

The Boy Raised to the Sky During the People's Prayer

It is called the **Angelic Hymn**, because the holy angels sing it as they surround the Throne of God in Heaven. People who believe in Christ began to use this prayer some four hundred years after the Birth of Christ. In Constantinople there was a tremendous earthquake that destroyed homes and other buildings. The frightened King, Theodosius II, and the people turned to God with prayer. During this general prayer, a certain pious youth in sight of all was lifted up to Heaven by an invisible force, and then by the same invisible force let down again to earth. He told the people around him what he heard in Heaven, how the angels were singing: **Holy God, Holy Mighty, Holy Immortal**. The people, moved to compunction, repeated this prayer and added: **have mercy on us**, and the earthquake stopped.

In this prayer, we call the first Person of the Holy Trinity **God**, that is God the Father; **mighty** is God the Son, because He is also almighty, as is God the Father, even though as a man He suffered and died; **immortal** is the Holy Spirit, because He not only is eternal as is the Father and the Son, but He grants life to all creatures and eternal life to people.

Since in this prayer the word **holy** is repeated three times, it is also called the **Thrice Holy** or **Trisagion Hymn**.

QUESTIONS: Whom do we address in this prayer? How many times should we repeat it? What is it called? Why is it called the angelic prayer? What do we know about the origin of this prayer? Why is it also called the "Thrice-holy"?

Doxology of the Holy Trinity

GLORY TO THE FATHER, AND TO THE SON, AND TO THE HOLY SPIRIT, BOTH NOW AND EVER, AND UNTO THE AGES OF AGES. AMEN.

In this prayer we do not ask anything of God, but only glorify Him Who appears to men in three Persons: Father, Son and Holy Spirit, to Whom there belongs, both now and eternally, the same honor of glorification.

QUESTION: Whom do we glorify or praise in this prayer?

Prayer to the Most-holy Trinity

O MOST-HOLY TRINITY, HAVE MERCY ON US. O LORD, BLOT OUT OUR SINS. O MASTER, PARDON OUR INIQUITIES. O HOLY ONE, VISIT AND HEAL OUR INFIRMITIES FOR THY NAME'S SAKE.

Most holy — holy in the highest degree; **Trinity** — the three Persons of God, God the Father, God the Son, and God the Holy Spirit; **sins and iniquities** — our deeds that are against the will of God; **heal** — make well; **infirmities** — weaknesses, sins; **for Thy name's sake** — for the glorification of Thy name.

This prayer is a prayer of petition. In it we turn first to all the three Persons together, and then to each Person of the Trinity separately: to God the Father, that He might cleanse our sins; to God the Son, that He might forgive our iniquities; to God the Holy Spirit that He might visit and heal our infirmities.

The words: **for Thy name's sake** again apply to all three Persons of the Holy Trinity together, and just as God is One, so also His name is one, and therefore we say "for Thy name's sake" and not "for Thy names' sakes".

QUESTIONS: What kind of prayer is this? Whom do we address in it? What do the words mean: " blot out our sins, pardon our iniquities, visit and heal our infirmities"? To Whom do we turn when we say: "for Thy name's sake"? What do these words mean?

The Lord's Prayer

OUR FATHER, WHO ART IN THE HEAVENS,
1. HALLOWED BE THY NAME.
2. THY KINGDOM COME.
3. THY WILL BE DONE, ON EARTH, AS IT IS IN HEAVEN.
4. GIVE US THIS DAY OUR DAILY BREAD.
5. AND FORGIVE US OUR DEBTS, AS WE FORGIVE OUR DEBTORS.
6. AND LEAD US NOT INTO TEMPTATION.
7. BUT DELIVER US FROM THE EVIL ONE.

FOR THINE IS THE KINGDOM AND THE POWER AND
THE GLORY OF THE FATHER, AND OF THE SON, AND OF
THE HOLY SPIRIT, NOW AND EVER, AND UNTO THE
AGES OF AGES. AMEN.

This prayer is called the **Lord's prayer**, because the Lord
Jesus Christ Himself gave it to His disciples when they asked
Him to teach them how to pray. Therefore, this prayer is most
important for everyone.

In this prayer we address God the Father, the first Person of
the Holy Trinity.

It is divided into **an address, seven petitions**, or seven requests, and a **doxology**.

**The address: OUR FATHER, WHO ART IN THE
HEAVENS.** By these words we call on God, and calling Him the
Heavenly Father, we call on Him to hear our requests or peti-
tions.

When we say that He is in the Heavens, then we must understand the **spiritual, invisible Heavens**, and not the visible,
blue vault that is stretched out above us and which we call
"heaven."

1st petition: HALLOWED BE THY NAME, that is, help us
live in righteousness and holiness and by our holy deeds to glorify Thy name.

2nd: THY KINGDOM COME, that is, make us worthy even
here on the earth of Thy Heavenly Kingdom, which is **righteousness, love and peace**. Reign over us and rule us.

**3rd: THY WILL BE DONE, ON EARTH, AS IT IS IN
HEAVEN**, that is, may everything be not as we want but as is
pleasing to Thee, and help us to submit to this, Thy will, and to
fulfill it on the earth just as obediently, without complaining, as
the holy angels fulfill it in Heaven, with love and joy. Thou alone
knowest what is useful and needful for us, and desirest good for
us, more than we ourselves.

4th: GIVE US THIS DAY OUR DAILY BREAD, that is
grant us on this day, for today, our daily bread. By the word
"bread" here we mean all that is necessary for our earthly life:
food, clothing, a dwelling, but most important of all, the all pure
Body and precious Blood in the Mystery of Holy Communion,
without which there is not any salvation or eternal life.

The Lord commanded us to ask not for wealth nor luxury,
but only for the essential things,' and to hope in God for all

things, remembering that He, as a Father, is attentive and cares for us.

5th: AND FORGIVE US OUR DEBTS AS WE FORGIVE OUR DEBTORS, that is, forgive us our sins just as we forgive those who wrong or hurt us.

In this petition, our sins are called "our debts," because the Lord gave us the strength and ability in order to do good deeds, but we often use them for sin and evil and become "debtors" before God. We are constantly in debt to God. And so, if we ourselves will not sincerely forgive our "debtors," that is, people who have committed sins against us, then God will not forgive us. Our Lord Jesus Christ Himself told us about this.

6th: AND LEAD US NOT INTO TEMPTATION. Temptation is the state when someone or something tries to get us to commit a sin, attempts to get us to do something wrong or foolish. Here we ask: do not let us fall into temptations which we cannot overcome; help us to overcome temptations that come to us.

7th: BUT DELIVER US FROM THE EVIL ONE, that is, deliver us from every evil in this world and from the father of evil, from the Devil, who is always ready to destroy us. Deliver us from this conniving, evil power and its deceptions, which are nothing before Thee.

Doxology: FOR THINE IS THE KINGDOM, AND THE POWER, AND THE GLORY OF THE FATHER, AND OF THE SON, AND OF THE HOLY SPIRIT, NOW AND EVER, AND UNTO THE AGES OF AGES. AMEN.

For unto Thee, our God, the Father and Son and Holy Spirit, belong the kingdom and the power and eternal glory. All this is right, truly so.

QUESTIONS: Why is this called the Lord's prayer? Whom do we address in this prayer? How is it divided? What does it mean: "Who art in the Heavens"? Explain the petitions: 1st, "Hallowed be Thy Name"; 2nd, "Thy Kingdom come"; 3rd, "Thy will be done on earth as it is in Heaven"; 4th, "give us this day our daily bread"; 5th, "And forgive us our debts as we forgive our debtors"; 6th, "And lead us not into temptation"; 7th, "But deliver us from the evil one." What does the word "amen" mean?

The Angelic Salutation to the Mother of God

O THEOTOKOS AND VIRGIN, REJOICE, MARY, FULL OF GRACE, THE LORD IS WITH THEE; BLESSED ART THOU AMONG WOMEN, AND BLESSED IS THE FRUIT OF THY WOMB, FOR THOU HAST BORNE THE SAVIOUR OF OUR SOULS.

The Archangel Gabriel Greets the Mother of God

Theotokos — the Birthgiver of God (Who gave birth to God); **full of grace** — filled with the Grace of the Holy Spirit; **blessed** — glorified or worthy of glorification; **the fruit of Thy womb** — He who was born of Thee, Jesus Christ.

This is a prayer to the Most-holy Theotokos, Whom we call full of Grace, that is, filled with the Grace of the Holy Spirit, and blessed above all women, because from Her our Saviour, Jesus Christ, the Son of God, was so pleased to be born.

This prayer is also called the angelic greeting, because in it are the words of the angel (Archangel Gabriel): **Rejoice, Mary full of Grace, the Lord is with Thee: blessed art Thou among women**, which he said to the Virgin Mary when he appeared to Her in the city of Nazareth, announcing to Her the great joy, that of Her the Saviour of the world would be born. Also **blessed art Thou among women, and blessed is the fruit of Thy womb** was spoken to the Virgin Mary by the righteous Elizabeth, the mother of John the Baptist, when she met with Her.

The Virgin Mary is called **Theotokos** or "Birthgiver of God," because Jesus Christ, Who was born from Her, is true God.

She is called **virgin**, because She was a Virgin before the birth of Christ, at the birth and after the birth, for She had given a vow to God not to be married, and She remained forever Virgin, giving birth to Her Son by the Holy Spirit in a miraculous way.

QUESTIONS: To Whom do we pray when we say this prayer: "O Theotokos and Virgin, rejoice"? What do we call the Virgin Mary in this prayer? What do these words mean: "full of Grace," and "blessed art thou among women"? How do we explain the words: "for thou hast born the Saviour of our souls"? Why is this prayer called the angelic greeting? What do these words mean: "Theotokos," "Virgin"?

Hymn of Praise to the Theotokos

IT IS TRULY MEET TO BLESS THEE, THE THEOTOKOS, EVER-BLESSED AND MOST-BLAMELESS, AND MOTHER OF OUR GOD. MORE HONORABLE THAN THE CHERUBIM, AND BEYOND COMPARE MORE GLORIOUS THAN THE SERAPHIM, WHO WITHOUT CORRUPTION GAVEST BIRTH TO GOD THE WORD, THE VERY THEOTOKOS, THEE DO WE MAGNIFY.

It is truly meet — it is worthy, correct, proper; in truth, in all righteousness; **to bless thee** — to beatify, to glorify Thee; **ever blessed** — always having the highest joy, worthy of constant praise; **most-blameless** — completely innocent, pure, holy; **Cherubim and Seraphim** — the very highest angels who are closest to God; **God the Word** — Jesus Christ, the Son of God (as He is called in the Holy Gospel); **very** — real, true.

The Icon "It Is Truly Meet"

In this prayer, we praise the Theotokos as the Mother of our God, ever blessed and completely pure, and we magnify her, saying that She in Her honor and glory excels even the highest of the angels, the Cherubim and Seraphim; that is, the Mother of

God in Her perfection stands higher than all, not only people, but even the holy angels. In a miraculous way, and without pain She gave birth to Jesus Christ, by the Holy Spirit. Christ, Who became man through Her, is at the same time the Son of God come down from Heaven, and therefore She is the true Birth-giver of God, the Theotokos.

QUESTIONS: Whom do we glorify in this prayer? How do we glorify Her? What do these words mean: "ever-blessed, most-blameless, Mother of our God"? What do these words mean: "More honorable than the Cherubim and beyond compare more glorious than the Seraphim," "...without corruption gavest birth to God the Word," "...very Theotokos,..."?

A Short Prayer to the Mother of God

MOST HOLY THEOTOKOS, SAVE US!

In this prayer we ask the Mother of God to save us sinners by Her holy prayers before Her Son and our God.

Prayer to the Life-giving Cross

SAVE, O LORD, THY PEOPLE, AND BLESS THINE INHERITANCE, GRANT THOU VICTORY TO ORTHODOX CHRISTIANS OVER ENEMIES, AND BY THE POWER OF THY CROSS, DO THOU PRESERVE THY COMMONWEALTH.

Bless — make happy, send mercy; **Thine inheritance** — what belongs to Thee; **Thy commonwealth** — Thy home, that is, the society of the truly faithful, among whom God invisibly dwells; **by the power of Thy Cross, do Thou preserve** — protect by the power of Thy Cross.

In this prayer we ask God to save us, His people, and to bless us with great mercies; that He give victories to Orthodox Christians over their enemies and in general that He protect us by the power of His Cross.

QUESTIONS: What is the prayer to the Cross? What do the words mean: "Save, O Lord, Thy people"? "And bless Thine inheritance"? "Grant Thou victory to Orthodox Christians over enemies"? "And by the power of Thy Cross do Thou preserve Thy commonwealth"?

Prayer to the Guardian Angel

O ANGEL OF GOD, MY HOLY GUARDIAN, GIVEN BY GOD FROM HEAVEN TO PRESERVE ME, I FERVENTLY PRAY THEE: DO THOU ENLIGHTEN ME TODAY, AND PRESERVE ME FROM EVERY EVIL, DIRECT ME IN DOING GOOD, AND GUIDE ME ON THE PATH OF SALVATION. AMEN.

God grants to every Christian at his Baptism a Guardian Angel who invisibly guards a person from every evil. Therefore, we must pray every day to the Guardian Angel to preserve and have mercy on us.

Prayer to our Saint

PRAY UNTO GOD FOR ME, ST. (NAME), FOR I FERVENTLY FLEE UNTO THEE, THE SPEEDY HELPER AND INTERCESSOR FOR MY SOUL.

Apart from prayer to the Guardian Angel, we must also pray to the saint whose name we bear because he prays to God for us.

Every Christian, as soon as he is born into God's light at Holy Baptism, receives a **saint** as his patron and protector in the Church. The patron saint cares for the newly-born Christian like a most loving mother and preserves him from all misfortune and woe which meet a person on earth.

We should know when the yearly **feast day** of our patron saint (our "name's day") is and know the story of the life of this saint. On our name day we should dedicate the day to prayer in church and receive Holy Communion. If we cannot be in church on that day for some reason, we should pray very fervently at home.

Prayer for the Living

We must think not only of ourselves but of others, love them and pray to God for them, because we are all children of the same Heavenly Father. Such prayers are beneficial not only to those whom we pray for, but also for ourselves, because we show **love** for them in this way. The Lord told us that without love, no one can be a child of God.

We must pray for our homeland, for the land in which we live, for our spiritual father, parents, benefactors, Orthodox Christians, and for all people, both **for the living** and also **for the reposed**, *because all men are alive before God* (Luke 20:38).

SAVE, O LORD, AND HAVE MERCY ON MY SPIRITUAL FATHER (NAME), MY PARENTS (NAMES), MY RELATIVES, TEACHERS, BENEFACTORS AND ALL ORTHODOX CHRISTIANS.

Spiritual father — the priest to whom we go for confession; **benefactors** — those who do good to us, who help us.

Prayer for the Reposed

GIVE REST, O LORD, TO THE SOULS OF THY SERVANTS WHO HAVE FALLEN ASLEEP (NAMES) AND ALL MY RELATIVES AND BENEFACTORS WHO HAVE FALLEN ASLEEP, AND FORGIVE THEM ALL THEIR SINS, BOTH VOLUNTARY AND INVOLUNTARY, AND GRANT THEM THE HEAVENLY KINGDOM.

Give rest — in a quiet place, that is, together with the saints in the eternal, blessed dwelling; **reposed** — fallen asleep. We refer to the dead in this way, because people are not destroyed after death, but their souls are separated from the body and pass from this life into another heavenly life. There they abide in the spiritual world until the time of the general resurrection, which will occur at the second coming of the Son of God, when, according to His word, the souls of the dead will again unite with the bodies; people will come to life, will arise. Then each will receive according to what he deserves: the righteous — the Kingdom of Heaven, blessed, eternal life; but the sinners — eternal punishment.

voluntary sins — sins that were committed through one's own will; **involuntary** — committed unintentionally; **heavenly kingdom** — eternal, blessed life with God.

Prayer for the Reposed

Prayer Before Lessons

O MOST GOOD LORD! SEND DOWN UPON US THE GRACE OF THY HOLY SPIRIT, GRANTING US UNDERSTANDING AND THE STRENGTHENING OF OUR MENTAL POWERS, THAT ATTENDING TO THE TEACHING GIVEN US, WE MAY GROW TO THE GLORY OF THEE, OUR CREATOR, TO THE COMFORT OF OUR PARENTS, AND TO THE BENEFIT OF THE CHURCH AND OUR HOMELAND.

Most good — most compassionate, gracious; **Grace of the Holy Spirit** — the invisible power of the Holy Spirit; **our mental powers** — our mental abilities (mind, heart, will); **the church** — the society of all Orthodox Christians; **homeland** — the nation, the land where we live.

This prayer is directed to God the Father, Whom we call the Creator. In it we call upon Him to send down the Holy Spirit, so that by His Grace He might strengthen the powers of our soul (mind, heart, will) and so that we, listening with attention to the teaching that is being put before us, might grow up to be devoted sons and daughters of the Church and faithful servants of our homeland and a consolation for our parents.

Instead of this prayer we can also use the prayer to the Holy Spirit, "O Heavenly King," before lessons.

QUESTIONS: What kind of prayer is this? To Whom is it directed? What do we ask for in this prayer? What is the Church and our homeland?

Prayer After Lessons

WE THANK THEE, O CREATOR, THAT THOU HAST VOUCHSAFED US THY GRACE TO ATTEND INSTRUCTION. BLESS THOSE IN AUTHORITY OVER US, OUR PARENTS AND INSTRUCTORS, WHO ARE LEADING US TO AN AWARENESS OF GOOD, AND GRANT US POWER AND STRENGTH TO CONTINUE THIS STUDY.

That thou has vouchsafed us — that Thou hast found us worthy; **of thy Grace** — of Thy invisible help; **to attend** — to listen and understand with attention; **bless** — send mercy; **strength** — health, eagerness, energy.

This prayer is to God the Father. In it we first give thanks to God that He sent His help so that we might understand the teaching set before us. Then we ask Him for His mercy towards those in authority over us, our parents and teachers, who give us the possibility of learning everything good and useful and, in conclusion, we ask that He grant us health and inclination so that we might continue our studies successfully.

Instead of this prayer we can also say the prayer to the Mother of God, "It is truly meet," after lessons.

QUESTIONS: To Whom is this prayer directed? What do we thank God for at the beginning? What do we ask for in this prayer?

Prayer Before Eating

THE EYES OF ALL LOOK TO THEE WITH HOPE, AND THOU GAVEST THEM THEIR FOOD IN DUE SEASON. THOU OPENEST THY HAND AND FILLEST EVERY LIVING THING WITH THY FAVOUR (Ps. 144:16-17).

In this prayer we express trust that God will send us food at the proper time, as He grants not only to people but to all living creatures all that is necessary for life.

Instead of this prayer we can use the prayer of our Lord "Our Father" before eating.

QUESTIONS: To whom do we pray   before eating? What do we express in this prayer? How does God relate to living creatures?

Prayer before Eating

Prayer After Eating

**WE THANK THEE, O CHRIST OUR GOD, THAT THOU
HAST SATISFIED US WITH THINE EARTHLY GIFTS;
DEPRIVE US NOT OF THY HEAVENLY KINGDOM, BUT AS
THOU CAMEST AMONG THY DISCIPLES, O SAVIOUR,
AND GAVEST THEM PEACE, COME TO US AND SAVE US.**

Satisfied — filled, nourished; **earthly gifts** — earthly good
things, that is, what we ate and drank at the table; **Thy Heavenly
Kingdom** — eternal blessedness, which the righteous are
granted after death.

In this prayer we give thanks to God that He has nourished
us with food. We ask Him not to deprive us after our death of
eternal blessedness; we should always remember this when we
receive good things from the earth.

QUESTIONS: What prayer is used after eating? What do we
thank God for in this prayer? What do we mean by good things
of the earth? What is called the Kingdom of Heaven?

Morning Prayer

**HAVING RISEN FROM SLEEP, I HASTEN TO THEE, O
MASTER, LOVER OF MANKIND, AND BY THY LOVING-
KINDNESS, I STRIVE TO DO THY WORK, AND I PRAY TO
THEE: HELP ME AT ALL TIMES, IN EVERYTHING, AND
DELIVER ME FROM EVERY WORLDLY, EVIL THING, AND
EVERY IMPULSE OF THE DEVIL, AND SAVE ME, AND
LEAD ME INTO THINE ETERNAL KINGDOM. FOR THOU
ART MY CREATOR, AND THE GIVER AND PROVIDER OF
EVERYTHING GOOD, AND IN THEE IS ALL MY HOPE,
AND UNTO THEE DO I SEND UP GLORY, NOW AND
EVER, AND UNTO THE AGES OF AGES. AMEN.**

Lover of mankind — lover of people; **strive to do** — hurry,
try to do; **in everything** — in every deed; **worldly, evil thing** —
evil of the world (deeds that are not good); **impulse of the Devil**
— the temptation of the devil (evil spirit), temptation to do
wrong; **provider** — the one who looks ahead, who provides,
takes care.

Evening Prayer

O LORD OUR GOD, AS THOU ART GOOD AND THE
LOVER OF MANKIND, FORGIVE ME WHEREIN I HAVE
SINNED TODAY IN WORD, DEED, OR THOUGHT. GRANT
ME PEACEFUL AND UNDISTURBED SLEEP; SEND THY
GUARDIAN ANGEL TO PROTECT AND KEEP ME FROM
ALL EVIL. FOR THOU ART THE GUARDIAN OF OUR
SOULS AND BODIES, AND UNTO THEE DO WE SEND UP
GLORY: TO THE FATHER, AND TO THE SON, AND TO
THE HOLY SPIRIT, NOW AND EVER, AND UNTO THE
AGES OF AGES. AMEN.

Thought — imagination; **good** — merciful; **undisturbed** — restful; **protect and keep** — cover and keep safe.

Evening Prayer

PART III

THE SACRED HISTORY OF THE OLD AND NEW TESTAMENTS

THE OLD TESTAMENT

*In the beginning God created
the heavens and the earth
(Gen 1:1)*

Introduction to the Sacred History of the Old and New Testaments

God always abides in love. As God the Father loves God the Son and God the Holy Spirit, so God the Son loves God the Father and God the Holy Spirit, and so God the Holy Spirit loves God the Father and God the Son.

God is love (I John 4:8).

Living in love is a great joy, the highest blessing, and God wished that all other living beings should receive this joy. For this, He created the world. God first created the angels and then our earthly world.

To us men, God gave intellect and an immortal soul and gave us a special purpose: to know God and to become ever better and more virtuous, that is, to be perfected in love for God and for one another and to receive from this ever greater joy in life.

But people violated the will of God — they sinned. By their sin they darkened their mind and will, and introduced sickness and death into the body. They began to suffer and die. By their own efforts people were not able to conquer sin and its result in themselves, to set aright their mind, will, and heart, and to destroy death. Only Almighty God could do this. The all-knowing Lord knew all things before the creation of the world.

When the first people sinned, He said to them that He would come into the world as Saviour — the Son of God, Jesus Christ, Who would conquer sin, save people from eternal death, and return them to love, to eternal life — to blessedness.

The period from the creation of the world to the coming of the Saviour to earth is called the **Old Testament**, that is, the covenant or agreement of God with men, according to which God prepared men for the reception of the promised Saviour. Men were to remember the promise of God, to believe, and await the coming of Christ.

The fulfillment of this promise, the coming to earth of the Saviour, the Only-begotten Son of God, our Lord Jesus Christ, is called the **New Testament**, since Jesus Christ, having appeared on earth and vanquished sin and death, made a new covenant with men. According to this agreement, everyone may again receive the blessedness that was lost: eternal life with God, through the Holy Church which He founded on earth.

CHAPTER 1

Creation of Heaven, the Invisible World

In the beginning, before the creation of any of the visible world and of man, God created **Heaven**, that is, the **spiritual, invisible world** of the **angels**, out of nothing.

Angels are bodiless and immortal **spirits**, gifted with a mind, will and strength. God created an innumerable multitude of them. They differ among themselves according to degrees of perfection and types of service and are divided into a number of orders. The highest of these are called the seraphim, cherubim, and archangels.

All the angels were created good, so that they would love God and one another and might have from this life of love continual and great joy. God did not will to make them love Him by force, and, therefore He allowed the angels to decide for themselves whether or not they wished to love Him and live in God.

One, the highest and mightiest angel whose name was Lucifer, became proud of his might and power and did not wish to love God and fulfill the will of God, but desired to become like God. He began to whisper against God, to oppose Him, and he became a **dark, evil spirit** — **the Devil, Satan**. The word "Devil" means "slanderer," and the word "Satan" means the "opposer" of God and all that is good. This evil spirit tempted and took with him many other angels who also became **evil spirits** and are called **demons**.

Then one of the highest archangels, Archangel Michael, came forth against Satan and said: "Who is equal to God? There is none like God!" There was a war in Heaven: Michael and his angels made war against Satan, and Satan and his demons made war against them.

However, evil power could not endure the angels of God, and Satan, together with his demons, fell like lightning down into the **nether regions, Hades.** "Hades," and "the nether regions," are names for the place of separation far from God, where the evil spirits now dwell. There they are tormented in their malice, beholding their powerlessness against God. All of them, because of their refusal to repent, have become so confirmed in evil that they can no longer be good. They strive by deceit and cunning to tempt every man, whispering false ideas and evil desires in order to bring him to damnation.

In this way **evil** appeared in God's creation. By evil we mean all that is done contrary to the will of God, all that violates the will of God.

All the angels that remained faithful to God, dwelling from that time in unceasing love and joy, live with God, fulfilling the will of God.

They have been so confirmed in good and love of God that they can no longer in any way wish to do evil. Therefore are called **holy angels**. The word "angel" means "messenger." God sends them to make His will known to men; for this, the angels take on a visible human form.

God grants to every Christian a **Guardian Angel** at Baptism, an angel that invisibly guards a person during his entire earthly life and does not leave his soul even after death.

NOTE: This brief account of the creation of the heavenly-angelic

The Creation of the Angelic World

world is based on the accounts in Sacred Scripture and the teachings of the Holy Fathers and Teachers of the Orthodox Church.

A detailed account of the life of the angelic world was set forth by **St. Dionysius the Areopagite**, a disciple of St. Paul and first bishop of Athens, in his book, *The Heavenly Hierarchy*, which was written on the basis of all the places in the Holy Scriptures that speak of the angels.

CHAPTER 2

Creation of the Earth, the Visible World

After the creation of Heaven, the invisible, angelic world, God created out of nothing, by His word alone, **earth**, that is, the material from which He gradually made our visible, physical world, the visible sky, earth and all that is in them.

God could have created the world in a single instant, but since He wished from the very beginning that this world should live and develop step by step, He created it not in an instant, but over several periods of time, which in the Bible are called "days."

These "days" of creation were not the usual days that we know, consisting of twenty-four hours. Our days depend on the sun. However, during the first three "days" of creation there was no sun yet in existence, which means that the days described in Genesis could not have been the kind of days as we understand them. The Bible was written by the Prophet Moses in the ancient Hebrew language, and in this language both "day" and a period of time are called by the same word *Yom*. It is impossible for us to know exactly what kind of days these were, even more so since we know that *one day is with the Lord as a thousand years, and a thousand years as one day* (II Peter 3:8; Ps. 89:5).

The Holy Fathers of the Church consider the seventh "day" of the world to be continuing even at the present time, and that after the resurrection of the dead there will begin the **eighth eternal day**, that is, eternal future life. Thus **St. John of Damascus** (VIII century) writes concerning this: "The seven ages of this world are reckoned from the creation of Heaven and earth to the general conclusion and resurrection of men. For even though there is a personal ending, there is also a general, complete ending when there will be the general resurrection of men. The eighth age is the age to come."

St. Basil the Great in the fourth century wrote in his book *Hexaemeron*: "Therefore whether you call it a day or an age, you express one and the same idea."

Therefore, in the beginning, the matter created by God did not have any definite shape or form; it was formless and undeveloped (like fog or water) and covered with darkness, and the Spirit of God was borne upon it, imparting to it life-bearing power.

NOTE: The Holy Bible begins with the words: *In the beginning God created Heaven and the earth* (Gen. 1:1).

In the beginning in Hebrew is *bereshit* and means "first of all" or "at the beginning of time," that is, before *bereshit* there was only eternity.

Created here is expressed by the Hebrew word *bara*, which means **"created out of nothing."** It is distinguished from the Hebrew word *assa*, which means "to make, to form, to shape out of matter." The word *bara* (created out of nothing) is used three times in the account of the creation of the world: 1) in the beginning — the first act of creation, 2) at the creation of "living souls" — the first animals, and 3) at the creation of man.

Strictly speaking, nothing more is said concerning Heaven, that is, it was finished in its formation. This is, as was said above, the spiritual, angelic world. Later in the Bible the Holy Scriptures speak of the heavenly **firmament**, called "heaven" by God, as a reminder of the higher, spiritual Heaven.

The earth was without form, and void; and darkness was upon the face of the deep. And the spirit of God moved upon the face of the waters (Gen. 1:2). "Earth" here is understood to mean the original matter, still not put into form, from which the Lord God during the six "days" formed and made the visible world — the universe. This unformed matter or chaos is called the **deep**, as being unfathomable and unlimited space and water, as a water-like or mist-like matter.

Darkness was **upon the face of the deep**, that is, the entire chaotic mass was submerged in darkness, due to the complete absence of light.

And the Spirit of God was borne above the water: here began the creative work of God. By this expression "was borne" (the Hebrew word used here has the following meaning: "to embrace everything with oneself as a bird with its wings spread out embraces and warms its fledglings"), the action of the Spirit of God upon the first-created matter should be understood as the imparting to it of the living power which was necessary for its formation and development.

All three Persons of the Most-holy Trinity participated in the creation of the world equally, as the Triune God, One in essence and Indivisible. The word "God" in this place is written in the plural *Elohim*, that is **Gods** (the singular is *Eloah* or *El*— God), and the word **"created"** (*bara*) — is in the singular. In this way the original Hebrew text of the Bible, from its very first lines, points to the singular essence of the Persons of the Holy Trinity, saying as it were, "In the beginning Gods (the three Persons of the Holy Trinity) created Heaven and earth."

The Psalms also clearly speak of this: *By the Word of the Lord the Heavens were established, and all the might of them by the Spirit of His mouth* (Ps. 32:6). Here "Word" means the **Son of God,** "Lord" means **God the Father** and "the Spirit (breath) of His mouth" means **God the Holy Spirit**.

The Son of God, Jesus Christ, is plainly called "Word" in the Gospel: *In the beginning was the Word...and the Word was God...all things were made by Him, and without Him was not anything made that was made* (John 1:1-3).

It is especially important for us to know this, because the creation of the world would have been impossible if there had not first been the voluntary will of the Son of God to endure the sacrifice of the Cross for the salvation of the world. *All things were created by Him* (the Son of God) *and for Him: and He is before all things, and by Him all things consist: And He is the head of the body, the Church: Who is the beginning, the firstborn from the dead; that in all things He might have preeminence. For it pleased the Father, that in Him should all fullness dwell; And, having made peace through the blood of His Cross, by Him to reconcile all things unto Himself; by Him, whether they be things in earth or things in Heaven* (Col. 1:16-20).

And God said, *let there be light*: and there was light... And God called the light day, and the darkness he called night. And the evening and the morning were the first day. This was the **first "day" of the world**.

Discussion of the First Day of Creation

The first act of the **formative** creation of God was the creation of light. *And God said, let there be light: and there was light. And God saw the light that it was good: and God divided the light from the darkness. And God called the light day, and the darkness he called night. And the evening and the morning were the first day* (Gen. 1:3-5).

It may seem strange that light could appear and that day and night could follow one another from the first day of creation when the sun and other heavenly luminaries did not yet exist. This gave an excuse for the atheists of the eighteenth century (Voltaire, the encyclopedists and others) to mock the Holy Bible. These poor men did not suspect that their ignorant mockery would turn back against them.

Light, by its nature, is entirely independent of the sun (fire, electricity). Light, but not all of it, was concentrated in the heavenly luminaries only later, at the will of God.

Light is the result of the action of light waves, which is now produced primarily by the sun, but which can also be produced by other sources. If the primeval light could appear before the sun and could have been like, for example, the light of the northern lights, the result of the union of two opposing electric currents, then it is obvious that it (the northern light type of light) could have times when it began, then came to its greatest brilliance and then again began to lessen and then almost completely cease. In this manner, according to the Biblical expression, there could be days and nights before the sun appeared, and there could be evening and morning, which would serve specifically as a measure for the determining of these parts of time.

Some commentators point out that the ancient Hebrew words *erev* and *boker* — evening and morning — also mean "mixture" (confusion) and "order." St. John Chrysostom says, "(Moses) clearly called the end of the day and end of the night one day, in order to set forth a certain order and sequence in the visible (world), and so there would be no confusion."

One should always bear in mind that science has no limit to its knowledge. The more science learns, the more areas that are unknown open up before it. Therefore, science can never give its "final word." This has been proven many times already and is being proven even more so at the present time.

A number of years ago, science spoke its "final word." Science had proven what had only been a philosophical hypothesis in ancient thought, namely, that the so-called **prime basis of matter**, which consisted of the smallest **ultimate particle of matter**, could absolutely in no way be divided. Therefore, it was decided that the scientific name for this particle of matter, as the basis of matter, should be "atom," which in Greek means "indivisible."

However the newest scientific developments permit scientists to explore even this ultimate particle of matter, as it had seemed to be up to this point. In spite of its minute size, the atom turned out not to be a particle of matter but an entire "planetary system" in miniature. Inside every atom there is, as it were, its "heart" or "sun," the nucleus. The atomic "sun," the nucleus, is surrounded by "planets," electrons. The planets, electrons, whirl around their "sun" with incredible speed — 1,000 billion revolutions a second. Every atomic nucleus, "sun," is charged with electric energy positively. The atomic "planets," electrons, are charged negatively. Therefore the atomic nucleus attracts the electrons towards itself and holds them on their course of orbit according to the same laws, by which, the planets orbit around the sun in space. Moreover, in the world that surrounds us, there are as many varied forms of atomic "planetary systems" as there are forms of atoms (i.e., ninety-six), according to the table of elements of Mendelev.

In addition, contemporary electronic physics has discovered that the nucleus of atoms, in spite of their minute size, so minute that it is difficult to imagine, consists of bodies with parts. Nuclei of atoms are made up of so-called protons and neutrons, joined together in specific combinations and numbers. **Some unknown power joins them and holds them together!**

Thus the discovery by science of the composition of the atom becomes a discovery of the perfection in the creation of the world of a **wise Creator**. In addition, it completely changes our concept of matter. Such **matter** as the materialists understand it **does not exist**.

Contemporary science has determined that the **prime basis of matter is energy**, and the prime basis of energy is **the energy of light**. Now it becomes clear why at the beginning of the formation of matter, God created light.

In this way, the first lines of the Bible, for our generation, become the best testimony of the **divine inspiration of the Holy Bible**. How else could Moses have known that the creation of the world had to begin with light, **when this has become the attainment of science only in modern times?**

Thus the author of Genesis, Moses, by divine inspiration, **discovered the mystery of the composition of matter** which was unknown to anyone in those distant times. The discovery of atomic energy, "the life of the atom," in our days is merely a new proof of divine truth!

Wondrous are Thy works O Lord, in wisdom hast Thou made them all.

On the second "day" of the world God created the **firmament** — that unfathomable space which stretches above us and surrounds the earth, that is, the heaven visible to us.

Discussion of the Second Day of Creation

The second creative command formed the **firmament**. *And God said: let there be a firmament in the midst of the waters, and let it divide the waters from the waters. And God made the firmament, and divided the waters which were under the firmament from the waters which were above the firmament: and it was so. And God called the firmament heaven. And the evening and the morning were the second day* (Gen. 1:6-8). The firmament is the atmosphere, or the visible heaven (sky). The origin of the firmament, or of the visible heaven, can be imagined in this

The Heavens

way. The immeasurably vast mass of primeval liquid matter separated, at the command of God, into millions of separate spheres, which revolved on their axes and were carried about, each on its own orbit. **The space that appeared between these spheres became the firmament**; for in this space the movement of the newly created worlds was made firm by the Lord on definite and irrefutable laws of attraction, so that they neither collide nor interfere with each other in their movements. The water above the firmament is the liquid spheres which later hardened and, from the fourth day of creation, began to shine and twinkle over our heads; and the water under the firmament is our planet earth, which is stretched out beneath our feet. All this still bore the name of water, because on the second day of creation, it had not yet received a firm constitution and solid form.

It is worthwhile to note the point of one of the greatest teachers of the Church, St. John of Damascus, who lived in the VIII century. In the Irmos of the third ode of the fifth tone he says, ...*Who by Thy command hast fixed the earth upon **the void**, and hast **suspended** its weight by Thine irresistible might*. Thus, St. John of Damascus discovered a scientific truth many centuries before the time when it became understood by science.

On the third "day" of the world God gathered the water which was under the heaven into one plane, and the **dry land** appeared; and God called the dry land **earth** and the collection of waters **seas**; and he commanded the earth to bring forth **green plants, grass and trees**. The earth was covered with grass and every possible kind of plant and tree.

Discussion of the Third Day of Creation

Further, the earth receives a form such that life can appear on it, even though this was still lower life, plant life, to be specific. *And God said: let the waters under the heaven be gathered together unto one place, and let the dry land appear: and it was so...And God said, let the earth bring forth grass, the herb yielding seed, and the fruit tree yielding fruit after his kind, whose seed is in itself, upon the earth: and it was so...and God saw that it was good. And the evening and the morning were the third day* (Gen: 1:9-13). The separation of water from the dry land on the third day should not be understood to be as simple as the dividing of already prepared water, as it were, from the firmer parts of the earth. Water did not yet exist in the form and chemical composition that we know now. **First,** by the creative word of the Lord the formless and unordered matter of our planet was, on the third day of the world, in two forms. Water and dry land were created, and the latter immediately produced on its surface various bodies of water: rivers, lakes and seas. **Second,** our planet was clothed in a thin and transparent cover of atmospheric air, and **gases** appeared with their many combinations. **Third,** on the dry land itself, the subject of creative word was not only the surface of the earth with its mountains, valleys, and so forth, but also in its inner parts — various layers of earth, metals, minerals and so on. **Fourth,** by a special command of the Creator every possible kind of plant appeared on the earth. **Finally,** one must assume that on the third day of the world, the other dark and chaotic masses of heavenly bodies received their final form, in correspondence with their purpose, even though the author of Genesis speaks only about the earth. One should assume this on the basis that, on the second and fourth days, the Lord acted in the entire cosmos, and thus it could not be that the entire third day was devoted only to the earth, which is an insignificant speck in the entire make-up of the universe. One can imagine the creative work of the third day more clearly in this way. The earth was still a vast sea. Then God said, *Let the waters under the heaven be gathered together unto one place, and let the dry land appear: and it was so.* The condensing and gradual cooling matter in some places was lifted up, in other places, it sank down. The higher places stuck up out of the water, became the dry land, and the depressions and hollows were filled with the water that poured into them and became **the sea.** *And God called the dry land earth; and the gathering* *together of the waters he called seas: and God saw that it was good.* The earth still did not have that which was the purpose of its creation: there was still no life upon it, only barren, dead cliffs stared darkly upon the bodies of water. When the command for the water and dry land was fulfilled, and the necessary conditions for life were present, then, at the word of God, there was no delay in the appearance of its beginnings, in the form of plants. *And God said, let the earth bring forth grass, the herb yielding seed, and the fruit tree yielding fruit after his kind, whose seed is in itself, upon the earth: and it was so...and God saw that it was good. And the evening and the morning were the third day.*

The Earth

Certain scientists have found the remains of this plant life and have been stunned by its enormous size. What today would be a blade of our fern for example, in primal times was a huge tree. The threads of contemporary moss in primal times were several feet in perimeter. How could such a mighty plant life appear without the influence of the rays of the sun, which shone on the earth only after the fourth day? Scientific research here, as in many other instances, confirms the writings of Genesis as being completely undeniable, undistorted truth. Experiments were conducted with electric light for the development of plant life. One scientist (Famintsin) attained important results in this regard with the aid of strong light from a simple kerosene lantern. Thus, the given question, in light of scientific evidence, loses its force. A much more important objection in this matter should be considered, namely: in the same layers of earth in which only the first indications of organic life appeared, in which, according to Genesis, the earth brought forth only herbs and plant life, there are to be found, together with the plants, animal organisms: coral, soft-bodied and freshwater animals of the simplest forms. Even this objection is not insurmountable: the layers of the earth are not separated from each other by some kind of impenetrable wall. On the contrary, in the course of the millennia during which the earth has existed, every kind of movement and change has occurred in the positions of the layers, and for this reason they are mixed up and often one is found combined with another.

Although plant life could have developed with the primal light, still its development could not have taken place under such conditions with the direct purposefulness that is observed nowadays. While tremendous in size, it was poor in form and color. Evidently, it was in need of the correct, measured light of the present sun and stars.

O n the **fourth "day" of the world**, at the command of God, there shone forth above the earth the heavenly luminaries, **the sun, moon and stars**. From that time forth they have defined the passing of time in our present days, months and years.

Discussion of the Fourth Day of Creation

After the formation of the earth there follows the arrangement of the heavenly luminaries. *And God said, let there be lights in the firmament of the heaven to divide the day from the night ; and let them be for signs,*

The Sun, the Stars, and the Moon

and for seasons, and for days, and years: and let them be for lights in the firmament of the heaven to give light upon the earth: and it was so. And God made two great lights, the greater light to rule the day, the lesser light to rule the night: he made the stars also...and God saw that it was good. And the evening and the morning were the fourth day (Gen. 1:14-19).

The creative command: **let there be lights** is obviously different from the command of the Creator: **let there be light**, because in one place, the original creation is understood, while in the other, the creative formation of things already created. Here we must understand that this is not a new creation but rather the complete formation of the heavenly bodies.

How is one to imagine the origin of the heavenly bodies? In their internal and basic matter, the heavenly luminaries existed already before the fourth day; they were already the water above the firmament, from which innumerable spheric bodies were formed on the second day of creation. Now, on the fourth day, a number of these bodies were formed in such a way that the primal light was concentrated in them to an extreme degree and began to act powerfully. This brought about the bodies that shine, or the luminaries in the strict sense of the word, such as the sun and the stars. Some of the dark, spherical bodies remained dark, but had been made by the Creator in such a way that they reflect the light that shines on them from other bodies, these are planets which shine with borrowed or reflected light, such as the moon, Jupiter, Saturn, and the other planets.

On the **fifth "day"** of the world according to the Word of God, the water brought forth living creatures, that is, there appeared in the water **shellfish, insects, reptiles and fish**, and over the earth, in the firmament, **birds** began to fly.

Discussion of the Fifth Day of Creation

On the fifth day animals were created that live in the water and fly in the air. *And God said, let the waters bring forth abundantly the moving creature that hath life, and the fowl that might fly above the earth in the open firmament of heaven...and God saw that it was good. And God blessed them, saying, be fruitful, and multiply, and fill the waters in the seas, and let the fowl multiply in the earth. And the evening and the morning were the fifth day* (Gen. 1:20-23).

The creative command of God, of course, formed these creatures from the elements of the earth; but everywhere else, though even more so here, the formative power belongs to Him, and not to the natural elements. In the formation of animals, something new was introduced — a

The Animals of the Ocean

higher principle of life — animated, freely moving, and feeling creatures made their appearance.

In giving His blessing to multiply to the newly-created creatures, God, as it were, gave them the creative power by which they received their being, that is, He granted them the ability to reproduce from themselves new beings, each according to its kind.

A more detailed creative action of the fifth day could be imagined in the following way. The heavens were adorned with stars. On the earth gigantic plants were spread about, but still, upon the earth there were no living creatures which could enjoy the gifts of God. The necessary conditions did not yet exist as the atmosphere was full of harmful gases which could only aid the plant kingdom. The atmosphere contained so many extra additives, and especially carbon dioxide, that animal life was still impossible. The atmosphere had to be cleared of these harmful additives. The gigantic plants achieved this under the influence of the sun that shone forth on the fourth day. Carbon dioxide is one of the most necessary elements for plant life, and as the atmosphere was permeated with it, the newly-created plant life began to develop in a luxuriant and rapid manner, consuming the carbon dioxide and clearing the atmosphere of it. Enormous coal deposits are nothing other than atmospheric carbon dioxide that has been transformed by plant processes into a solid body. Thus the cleaning of the atmosphere was accomplished, and the conditions were suitable for the appearance of animal life. It did not take long for it to appear as the result of a new creative act.

And God said, let the waters bring forth abundantly the moving creature that hath life, and the fowl that might fly above the earth in the open firmament of heaven. As a result of this divine command, a new creative act took place, not just a formative one, as on the previous days, but a creative act in the full sense of the word, just like the first act of creating primal matter out of nothing.

Here there was created **"a moving creature"** (**"living soul"** Septuagint); something new was introduced, which had not yet existed in the primal matter. Indeed, the writer of Genesis for the second time, uses the verb *bara* — "to create out of nothing." *And God created great whales, and every living creature that moveth, which the water brought forth abundantly, after their kind, and every winged fowl after its kind.*

The most recent geological research explains and supplements this brief account by the writer of Genesis.

Digging into the depths of the layers of the earth, geologists reached a layer in which there first appeared the "living soul." This layer, consequently, is the cradle of animal life, and in it are found the simplest of the animal organisms.

The most ancient "living soul" known to geologists is the so-called Eo-zoon of Canada, which is found in the very lowest levels of the so-called Laurentian period. Afterwards, coral, infusoria and shellfish of various species appear. Higher in the earth's levels there appear the gigantic, monstrous reptiles and lizards. Of these, the best known are the ichthyosaurs, hileosaurs, plesiosaurs and pterodactyls. They are all astounding because of their enormous size.

Birds Created by God

The ichthyosaurus was up to forty feet long, in the form of a lizard, with the head of a dolphin, the teeth of a crocodile and a tail equipped with a leathery, fish-like fin. The hileosaurus was up to nine feet high and was a fearsome type of lizard. The plesiosaurus had the form of a gigantic turtle with a long neck of twenty feet, a tiny snakelike head and a stinger six feet long. The pterodactyl was a sort of flying dragon, with wings like a bat, long head, crocodile teeth and claws in general like a bat, but of enormous size. Some of these monsters are still to be found nowadays, but the present ones are tiny midgets in comparison with their ancestors. Perhaps this is a sign of the decline in the productive powers of the earth.

And God saw that it was good. And God blessed them, saying, Be fruitful, and multiply, and fill the waters in the seas, and let the fowl multiply in the earth. And the evening and the morning were the fifth day. (Gen. 1:22-23)

On the **sixth "day" of creation**, according to the Word of God, the earth brought forth a living soul, and there appeared on the earth **animals**, that is, cattle, reptiles and beasts. In conclusion, God created **man — man and woman** — according to His image and likeness, that is, spiritually similar to Him.

When He had finished the creation of the entire visible world with the creation of man, God saw that all He had made was very good.

Discussion of the Sixth Day of Creation

On the sixth and final day of creation, the animals that live on the earth and man were created. Just as the Lord addressed the water to bring forth fish and reptiles, so now for the bringing forth of the four-legged creatures He addressed the earth, in the same way as he addressed it for the bringing forth of plant life. One must understand it in this way: the Lord granted the earth life-producing power, and not, as certain naturalists think, that the earth, warmed by the rays of the sun brought forth the animals on its own. In all the vast realm of nature there is not the slightest hint that any one kind of animal could have come from another, for example that grass-eating animals turned into animals of prey. It is even more contrary to nature that the origin of animal life could have come from inorganic beginnings, from gases, minerals and the like. "When God said, 'let the earth bring forth,' " says St. Basil the Great, "this does not mean that the earth brings out what was already within her; but He Who gave the command gave the earth the power to bring it forth" (*Hexaemeron*).

In accordance with contemporary scientific research, one can conceive of the history of the sixth day of creation in the following account. The water and air were filled with life, but a third part of the earth still remained empty — the dry land, that part which was most convenient for the life of living creatures. Now the time came for populating it. *And God said: let the earth bring forth the living creature after his kind, cattle, and creeping thing, and beasts of the earth after his kind: and it was so. And God made the beasts of the earth after his kind, and cattle after their kind, and every thing that creepeth upon the earth after his kind: and God saw that it was good* (Gen. 1:24-25).

Scientific research, rising higher through the various layers of the earth (after the layer containing the monsters described above, along with fish and birds), comes across a new layer in which new organisms appear — the four-legged creatures. First there appeared on the earth species of enormous four-legged creatures that are no longer to be found: dinotheres, mastodons and mammoths (a kind of elephant with a huge, awkward form); then, the more developed animals, and finally, their present forms: lions, tigers, bears, horned cattle, etc.

On seeing this gradual appearance of various kinds, science involuntarily poses the question: how did all these species come to be? Are they unchanging forms that received their beginning in the creative-formative act or did they slowly appear, one from another, and all from one primal form?

As is well-known, in the last century Darwin's theory of evolution gained wide popularity. How does Darwin's theory apply to the Biblical history of creation?

Animals Created by God

The writer of Genesis says that the plants and animals were created "according to their kind," that is, not one plant or animal form, but many plants and animals. This does not mean that all the forms or variations within a species that exist now had to have their beginning in the original creative act. The Hebrew word *min*, which is translated with the meaning "kind," has a very wide meaning that is not contained in the scientific meaning of the word "species." It is broader than this in every way, not including all the present species and variants of animals and plants; at the same time it does not deny the possibility of a gradual development of these forms.

That changes can truly occur within a species is proved by indisputable facts. Many variations of plants, such as roses, carnations, and dahlias, as well as certain animals, such as some variations of chickens and pigeons which can be seen in zoos, developed not many centuries ago. Changes can also occur under the influence of climatic conditions, different soil, food, and the like. On this basis one can assume that the number of plant and animal forms in the primal world was not as great and diversified as at present.

The writer of Genesis, describing the creation in the strict sense (*bara*) of the first origins of animal-organic life, does not categorically deny the possibility of the development of other forms within a species. However, this does not give any basis for the acceptance of the theory of development in all its completeness: it clearly and definitely affirms that the animal and plant organisms were directly created " according to their kinds," that is, in various definite forms.

This theory does not have any firm basis in science either, and at the present time has suffered many serious objections. We will not cite all the scientific reasoning, but will point out at least one. The well-known American scientist Cressy Morrison (former president of the New York Academy of Sciences) says:

"The miracle of genes, a phenomenon which we know, but which was not known to Darwin, testifies to the creation of everything living.

"Genes are so infinitesimally small that if all the genes of all the people alive in the world today could be collected together, there would be less than a thimbleful. A thimble would not even be full! Nonetheless, these ultramicroscopic genes, and the chromosomes that accompany them, in every living cell of everything alive, are the absolute keys to all human, animal and vegetable characteristics. A thimble is a small place in which to put all the individual characteristics of five billion human beings. However, the facts are beyond question. Do these genes and cytoplasms, which may be collected in such a tiny space, contain the key to the psychology of every living creature?

"This is where evolution begins! It begins in the cell which holds and carries the genes. This fact, that several million atoms contained in the ultramicroscopic gene could be the absolute key that governs life on earth, proves that there was an intention to create everything that is alive, that someone foresaw them ahead of time, and that this foresight comes from a Creative Intelligence. No other hypothesis here can help solve the riddle of existence."

On the sixth day of creation the earth was already populated in all its parts. The world of living creatures was like a magnificent tree, whose roots consisted of the most simple organisms, and whose highest branches were the highest animals. But this tree was not complete, there was not yet a blossom which could complete and adorn; there was not yet man, the king of nature.

Now men too appeared. *And God said: let Us make man in Our image, after Our likeness: and let them have dominion over the fish of the sea, and over the fowl of the air, and over the cattle, and over all the*

The Creation of Adam and Eve

earth, and over every creeping thing that creepeth upon the earth. So God created man in His own image, in the image of God created He him; male and female created He them (Gen 1:26-27). Here for the third time a **creative act** (*bara*) occurred in the full sense, for man has in his nature something which had not been created in nature before, namely **spirit**, which distinguished him from all other beings.

Thus the history of the creation and formation of the world was finished. *And God saw every thing that He had made, and, behold, it was very good. And the evening and the morning were the sixth day... And on the seventh day God ended His work which He had made; and He rested on the seventh day from all His work which He had made. And God blessed the seventh day and sanctified it.*

In the period that follows after this, that is, in the **seventh "day" of the world**, which, as the Holy Fathers teach, is continuing even at the present time, God ceased to create. He blessed and hallowed this "day," and called it the **Sabbath**, that is, "rest"; and He commanded that men also rest on the seventh day from their regular work and dedicate it to the service of God and neighbor, that is, make this day free from worldly affairs — a holy day.

Upon completing creation, God left the world to live and develop according to the plan and laws established by Him, or, as it is generally said, according to the "laws of nature." At the same time, He never ceases to care for all creation, granting each creature what is necessary for life. God's care for the world is called "**Divine Providence**."

NOTE: The account of the creation of the world is to be found in Genesis, chaps. 1: 1-31; 2:1-3.

Adam Names the Animals

CHAPTER 3

How God Created the First People

God created man in a different way from the other creatures. Before His creation, God, in the Most-holy Trinity, confirmed His wish. He said: *Let Us make man in Our own image, after Our own likeness* (Gen 1:26).

God created man out of the dust of the earth, that is, from matter, from which all material things were created in the earthly world, and He breathed into his face **the spirit of life**; that is, He gave him a **spirit**, free, intelligent, alive, and immortal, according to His image and likeness, and man came into being with an immortal soul. By this "breath of God," or immortal soul, man is separated from all the other living creatures.

So we belong to two worlds: in body to the visible, material, earthly world, but in soul to the invisible, spiritual, heavenly world.

God gave the first man the name **Adam**, which means "taken from the earth." He then caused **Paradise**, a beautiful garden, to grow on the earth, and placed Adam to dwell there so that he would cultivate and keep it.

In Paradise all kinds of trees with the most beautiful fruit grew; among them there were two special trees: one was called the **tree of life**, the other the **tree of knowledge of good and evil**. Tasting of the fruits of the tree of life had the power to preserve man from illness and death. Concerning the tree of the knowledge of good and evil, God commanded man: *of every tree of the garden thou mayest freely eat, but of the tree of the knowledge of good and evil, thou shalt not eat of it: for in the day that thou eatest thereof thou shalt surely die* (Gen 2:16-17). Then, at the command of God, Adam gave names to all the beasts and birds of the air, but he did not find among them a companion and helper for himself. God then brought a deep sleep upon Adam; when he went to sleep, He took one of his ribs and closed the place with flesh. And from the rib taken from man, God created woman. Adam called her **Eve**, that is, the mother of men.

God blessed the first people in Paradise, and said to them: *Be fruitful and multiply, and fill the earth, and subdue it* (Gen. 1:28).

By having created woman from the rib of the first man, God showed us that all people come from one body and soul, that they should be one, and should love and care for one another.

NOTE: See Genesis, chaps. 1:27-29; 2:7-9; 2:15-25; 5:1-2.

CHAPTER 4

The Life of the First People in Paradise

The earthly Paradise, the splendid garden in which God settled the first people, Adam and Eve, was in the East between the rivers Tigris and Euphrates. The life of people in Paradise was full of joy and bliss. Their consciences were calm, their hearts pure, their minds brilliant. They did not fear illness or death and had no need of clothing. They were completely satisfied and without need of anything. Their food was the fruit of the trees of Paradise.

Among the animals there was no enmity; the powerful ones did not touch the weak ones, they lived together and fed on grass and plants. None of them feared man; they all loved and obeyed him.

But the highest blessedness of Adam and Eve was **in prayer**, a deeply spiritual prayer, in pure conversation with God. God appeared to them in Paradise. He was as a father to his children and granted them all that was necessary.

God created men, just as He created the angels, so that they would love God and one another and delight in the great joy of life, in the love of God. Therefore, as for the angels, He granted them complete freedom to love Him or not to love Him. Without freedom there can be no love. Love appears in the joyful fulfillment of the wishes of the one that you love.

But since men were less perfect than the angels, the Lord did not grant them to make a choice immediately and forever: to accept or reject this love, as He did with the angels.

God began to teach people love. For this purpose He gave men one small, easy commandment: **not to eat of the fruit of the tree of the knowledge of good and evil**. By fulfilling this commandment or wish of God, they could also express their love for Him. In time, passing from the simple to the more complex, they could be confirmed in love and be perfected in it. Adam and Eve obeyed God with love and joy, and in Paradise the will of God and the order of God was in everything.

NOTE: See Genesis, chaps. 2:10-14; 2:25.

Discussion About Man

When we say that man is made of soul and body, we express the fact that man does not consist of just dead material, matter, but also of a higher essence which gives life to this matter, or animates it. In actuality, man is made up of **three parts** consisting of **body, soul and spirit**. Apostle Paul says, *For the Word of God is quick* (alive), *and powerful, and sharper than any two-edged sword, piercing even to the dividing asunder of* **soul** *and* **spirit**, *and of the joints and marrow, and is a discerner of the thoughts and intents of the heart* (Heb. 4:12).

    1. BODY. The body of man was created by God *of the dust of the ground* (Gen. 2:7), and therefore belongs to the earth. *For dust thou art, and unto dust shalt thou return* (Gen. 3:19), it was said to the first man after his fall into sin. In his physical, bodily life, man is not different from any of the other living creatures or animals in satisfying the needs of the body. The needs of the body are various, but in general they all come down to the satisfaction of two basic instincts: 1) **the instinct of self-preservation** and 2) **the instinct of continuing the race**.

    Both of these instincts were placed by the Creator in the bodily nature of every living creature with a completely understandable and reasonable goal: that they not perish and be destroyed without a trace.

    For dealing with the external world, the body of man is equipped with five senses: **sight, hearing, smell, taste** and **touch**, without which man would be completely helpless in the world. This whole apparatus of the human body is extraordinarily complex and most wisely put together, but by itself would be merely a dead machine without motion if the soul did not bring it to life.

    2. SOUL. The soul was given by God as the life-giving principle in order to govern the body. In other words, the soul is the **life force** of man and of every living being; the scientists call it just this: vital life strength.

    The animals also have a soul, but it was brought forth from the earth together with the body. *And God said: let the waters bring forth abundantly the moving creature that hath life...great whales, and every living creature that moveth...cattle, and creeping thing, and beast of the earth...after his kind: and it was so* (Gen. 1:20-24).

    Only of man is it said that, after the creation of his body from the dust of the earth, the Lord *breathed into his nostrils the breath of life; and man became a living soul* (Gen. 2:7). This "breath of life" is the highest function in man, his spirit, by which he is immeasurably higher than all other living beings. Therefore, although the soul of man is in many ways similar to that of animals, still, in its higher part, it incomparably surpasses the souls of animals, thanks to its being joined with the spirit which is from God. The soul of man is the link between the body and spirit, being, as it were, a bridge from the body to the spirit.

    All the actions, or more precisely, "movements" of the soul, are so varied and complex, so interconnected, so changeable, and often so difficult to pinpoint, like lightning, that for convenience in distinguishing them, it is acceptable to divide them into three groups: **thoughts, feelings** and **desires**. These movements of the soul serve as the subject of the study of the science called psychology.

    1. The organ of the body which helps the soul perform mental activity, that is, **thought** and **intellectual work**, is the **brain**.

2. The central organ of **feeling** is generally considered to be the **heart**. It is the measure of what is pleasing and not pleasing to us. The heart is naturally considered the center of the life of man, a center in which all that enters the soul from outside is contained, and from which proceeds all that is manifested by the soul to the outside.

3. Man's **desires** are controlled by the **will**, which does not have a physical organ in our body, but for its fulfillment the members of our body are set apart, brought into action by the help of muscles and nerves.

The results of the activity of our mind and feeling, given birth by the heart, manifest one or another kind of influence on the will, and our body carries out one or another action or movement.

In this way, the soul and body are closely bound to one another. The body, with the help of the organs of external senses, relates one or another impression to the soul, and the soul, relying on this impression, in one way or another, governs the body and directs its activity. Because of this bond between body and soul this life is often called by a general term: "psychosomatic life." However, it is still necessary to distinguish between bodily life as being for the satisfaction of the needs of the body, and the life of the soul for the satisfaction of the needs of the soul.

What life of the body consists of has already been discussed. It is in satisfying two major instincts: the instinct of self-preservation and the instinct of preserving the species.

The life of the soul consists in satisfying the needs of the mind, feelings, and will; the soul **wishes** to acquire knowledge, and to experience one kind of feeling or another.

3. SPIRIT. But man's life is not at all exhausted by the satisfaction of only the needs of body and soul.

The body and soul are not the entire man, or rather do not form the complete man. Above the body and soul stands something yet higher, namely the spirit, which often shows itself as **judge** both of body and soul, and gives an opinion on everything from a special, lofty point of view. "The spirit," says Bishop Theophan, "as power proceeding from God, knows God, seeks God, and in Him alone it finds rest. By a certain spiritual, hidden sense, it is convinced of its proceeding from God, and feels its complete dependence on Him, and realizes that it is in every way obliged to please Him and live only for Him and by Him." This is exactly what Blessed Augustine also said, "Thou, O God, hast created us with longing for Thee, and our heart is not at ease until it comes to rest in Thee."

Spirit in man is shown in three forms: 1) fear of God, 2) conscience and 3) thirst for God.

1. Fear of God. This is, of course, not fear in our usual human understanding of the word. This is reverent trembling before the might of God, inextricably tied with unchanging faith in the truth of the existence of God, in the actuality of the existence of God as our Creator, Provider, Saviour, and giver of rewards. All peoples, no matter what level of development they may have had, all had faith in God. Even the ancient writer Cicero, two thousand years before our time, said: "There is not a single people that is so coarse and wild that it has no faith in God, even though it may not know His nature." "From the time," says the scientist Hettinger, "that America and Australia were discovered by Europeans and a multitude of new peoples entered into the history of the world, still his (Cicero's) words remain unshaken, and have become even more indubitable and more obvious than before. Thus, as many centuries as there are that history can count, so many proofs there are of this truth."

2. Conscience. The second way in which the spirit is made known in man is **conscience**. Conscience tells a man what is right and what is not right, what is pleasing to God and what is not pleasing, what he should and what he should not do. It not only tells, but also compels a man to fulfill what it has said, and rewards him with consolation when it is fulfilled or punishes him with pangs of conscience when it is not. Conscience is our internal judge, the guardian of the law of God. It was not in vain that people have called the conscience the "voice of God" in the soul of man.

3. Thirst for God. The third manifestation of the spirit in man is very aptly called **"thirst for God"** by Bishop Theophan the Recluse. It is inherent in the nature of our soul to seek God. Our spirit cannot be satisfied with anything created and earthly. No matter how many and how varied the earthly goods we might have, still we long for something more. This eternal human dissatisfaction, this constant insatiableness, this truly unquenchable thirst demonstrates that our spirit possesses a striving for something higher than all that surrounds it in earthly life, for something ideal, as it is often said. Since nothing earthly can quench this thirst in man, the spirit of man is restless, not finding any rest for itself until it finds complete satisfaction in God, with Whom the human spirit is always striving consciously or unconsciously, to have living communion.

Such are the manifestations of spirit in man, which must be the guiding principles in the life of every man: to live in communion with God and to live according to the will of God; to live according to these principles means to fulfill one's purpose on the earth and to inherit eternal life.

(From the article of Archimandrite Averky: *Dushevnost' i Dukhovnost*, Munich, 1949.)

CHAPTER 5

The Fall into Sin

The Devil was jealous of the blessedness in Paradise of the first people and he thought to deprive them of life in Paradise. For this purpose he entered into the serpent and hid in the branches of the tree of the knowledge of good and evil. When Eve passed by, the Devil whispered to her to eat of the fruit of the forbidden tree. With cunning, he asked Eve, *Yea, hath God said, 'Ye shall not eat of every tree of the garden'?*

Eve answered the serpent, *We may eat of the fruit of the trees of the garden: but of the fruit of the tree which is in the midst of the garden, God hath said, 'Ye shall not eat of it, neither shall ye touch it, lest ye die.'*

The Devil lied in order to seduce Eve. He said, *Ye shall not surely die: for God doth know that in the day ye eat thereof, then your eyes shall be opened, and ye shall be as gods, knowing good and evil.*

The tempting words of the Devil through the serpent acted upon Eve. She looked at the tree and saw that the tree was pleasant to the eyes, good for food, and gave knowledge; and she wanted to know good and evil. She took of the fruit from the forbidden tree and ate. Then she gave it to her husband, and he ate.

Man gave in to the temptation of the Devil and violated the commandment or will of God — **he sinned**, fell into sin. This is how man's fall into sin came about.

This first sin of Adam and Eve, or fall of man into sin, is called **ancestral** or **original sin**, for it is specifically this sin which is the beginning of all the other sins in man. The habit, or inclination to sin, passed on to all mankind.

NOTE: See Genesis, chap. 3:1-6.

CHAPTER 6

The Results of the Fall into Sin and the Promise of a Saviour

When the first people sinned, they became ashamed and afraid, as it happens with all people when they act foolishly. They immediately realized that they were naked. In order to cover their nakedness, they sewed for themselves clothes from the leaves of the fig tree, in the form of wide belts. Instead of receiving the perfection, equal to God's, that they had wanted, the opposite occurred: their minds were darkened, their consciences began to torment them, and they lost peace of mind. All this occurred because they **knew good and evil, contrary to the will of God, that is, by sin.**

Sin changed men so much that when they heard the voice of God in Paradise, in fear and shame they hid among the trees, immediately forgetting that no one can hide from God Who knows everything and is everywhere present. Thus, every sin separates men from God. God, in His compassion, began to call them to **repentance**, that is, for men to realize their sin, admit it before the Lord, and ask for forgiveness.

The Lord asked, "Adam, where art thou?"

Adam answered, "I heard Thy voice in the garden, and I was afraid, because I was naked, and I hid myself."

God again asked, "Who told thee that thou wast naked? Hast thou eaten of the tree, whereof I commanded thee that thou shouldest not eat?"

Adam said, "The woman that Thou gavest to be with me, she gave me of the tree, and I did eat." So Adam began to pass the blame onto Eve and even to God Himself, Who gave him the woman.

And the Lord said to Eve, "What is this that thou hast done?"

Eve in place of repentance answered, "The serpent beguiled me, and I did eat."

Then the Lord proclaimed the results of the sin committed by them.

To Eve God said, *I will greatly multiply thy sorrow and thy conception; in sorrow thou shalt bring forth children; and thy desire shall be to thy husband* (that is, you must be in obedience to him).

To Adam He said, [Because thou] *hast eaten of the tree, of which I commanded thee saying, Thou shalt not eat of it: cursed is the ground for thy sake...thorns also and thistles shall it bring forth to thee...in the sweat of thy face shalt thou eat bread* (that is, you will earn your food by heavy labor), *till thou return unto the ground* (that is, until you die);

for out of it wast thou taken: for dust thou art, and unto dust shalt thou return (Gen. 3:16-19).

To the Devil, who concealed himself in the serpent, and was most responsible for man's sin, He said, *Because thou hast done this, cursed art thou...* and He said that between him and man there would be a struggle, in which men will be the victors, specifically: **The seed of the woman shall crush thy head, and thou shalt strike at his heel** (Cf. Gen.

Adam and Eve Must Leave Paradise

3:15), that is, from woman there will come forth an **offspring** — **the Saviour of the world**, Who will be born of a virgin, will conquer the Devil and save man, but for this, He Himself must suffer.

This promise of God concerning the coming of the Saviour was received by men with faith and joy, because it gave them great consolation. In order that men would not forget this promise of God, God taught them to offer **sacrifices**. For this He commanded them to sacrifice a bull, a lamb or a goat, and to burn them with prayer for the forgiveness of sins and with faith in the future Saviour. Such a sacrifice was a prefiguration of the Saviour, Who had to suffer and pour out His blood for our sins, that is, by His all pure blood to wash our souls from sin and make them clean, holy and once more worthy of Paradise.

Here, in Paradise, the first offering for sin was offered; God made Adam and Eve coats of animal skins and clothed them. However, since people had become sinful, they could no longer live in Paradise, and the Lord expelled them. The Lord placed at the entrance to Paradise an angel-cherubim with a fiery sword in order to guard the way to the tree of life.

The ancestral sin of Adam and Eve, with all its consequences, was passed on through natural birth to all their offspring, to all mankind, to all of us. This is why we are born already sinful and are under all the consequences of sin: sorrow, illness, and death.

Thus, the consequences of the fall into sin turned out to be enormous and heavy. People were deprived of the blessed life of Paradise. The world, darkened by sin, was changed. The earth from that time began to produce a harvest only with much labor; in the fields, instead of good fruits, weeds began to grow; animals began to fear man, to become wild, and seek prey. Illness, suffering, and death appeared. Most importantly, people, through their sinfulness, lost the very close and direct communion with God. He no longer appeared to them visibly, as in Paradise — man's prayer became imperfect.

NOTE: See Genesis, chap. 3:7-24.

CHAPTER 7

Discussion of the Fall into Sin

When God created the first man, He saw that **he was very good**, that man was directed towards God in love. There were no conflicts in the first created man. Man was a complete **unity of spirit, soul and body**, one harmonious whole — the spirit of man was directed towards God, the soul was united or freely submitted to the spirit, and the body to the soul. There was unity of purpose, direction, and will. Man was holy, becoming like God.

The will of God is specifically this: that man **freely**, that is, **with love**, strive towards God, the source of eternal life and blessedness, and that in this way he remain continually in communion with God, in the blessedness of eternal life. Such were Adam and Eve. Therefore they had illuminated reason and **Adam knew every creature by name**. This means that for him the physical laws of the formation of the earth and the animal world were made manifest — those laws, which we are now only partially discovering. **By the fall into sin, men destroyed their internal harmony — the unity of spirit, soul and body** — they upset their nature. There was no more unity of purpose, direction, and will.

In vain some people wish to interpret the fall into sin as allegory, that is, that the fall into sin consisted of the physical love between Adam and Eve, forgetting that the Lord Himself commanded them, "be fruitful and multiply..." Moses clearly recounts that, "Eve first sinned alone, and not together with her husband." Metropolitan Philaret of Moscow writes "How could Moses have written that if he were writing only allegorically, which some people like to find here?"

The result of the fall into sin was that our fore-parents, by giving in to the temptation, ceased to regard the forbidden fruit as a matter of the commandment of God and began to see it in relationship to themselves, to their feelings, and heart, and understanding, departing from the unity of God's truth **into a multitude of private thoughts and private wishes, not concentrated in the will of God**, that is, **departing into lust**. Desire, having conceived sin, gives rise to active sin (James 1:14-15). Eve, tempted by the Devil, saw the forbidden tree not for what it was but what **she wanted**, in accordance with obvious forms of desire (I John 2:16; Gen. 3:6). What kinds of desire were found in the soul of Eve before the eating of the forbidden fruit? **And the woman saw that the tree was good for food**, that is, imagined a certain special, extraordinarily pleasant taste in the forbidden fruit — this is **lust of the flesh. And that it was pleasing to the eye**, that is, it seemed to the woman to be more beautiful than all the other fruit — this is **lust of the eyes,** or the passion to acquire. **It was desirable because it grants knowledge.** The woman wanted to know the loftier, divine knowledge which the tempter offered her — this is the **pride of life** or the love of glory.

The first sin is born **in sensuality,** with the striving for pleasant feelings, for physical comfort; **in the heart,** with the desire for pleasure without discernment; and **in the mind,** with the fantasy of arrogant, varied knowledge. Thus, **it penetrates all the powers of human nature.**

The disrupting of human nature also includes the fact that sin turned or tore the soul from the spirit, and the soul, as a result, began to be attracted to the body, to the flesh, and to depend on it. The body, losing its former lofty power of the soul and itself a creation from nothingness, began to have attraction to sensuality, to emptiness, to death. Therefore the result of sin is illness, destruction, and death. The mind of man was darkened, the will weakened, the feeling distorted, conflicts arose, and the human soul lost purposeful striving towards God.

In this manner, having stepped over the limits established by the commandment of God, man turned his soul away from God, the true fullness and universal focal point, and **became self-centered,** enclosed in the darkness of sensuality, in the coarseness of matter. The mind, will and activity of men turned away from God to material creation, from the heavenly to the earthly, from the unseen to the seen (cf. Gen. 3:6). Deceived by the wiles of the tempter, man by his own will *is compared to the mindless cattle, and is become like unto them* (Ps. 48:12).

The disruption of human nature by ancestral sin — the disruption of soul and spirit in man, which now has an attraction to the sensual, is clearly expressed in the words of the Apostle Paul, *For the good that I would do, I do not: but the evil which I would not, that I do. Now if I do that I would not, it is no more I that do it, but sin that dwelleth in me* (Rom. 7:19-20). Man constantly suffers from "pangs of conscience" when realizing his sinfulness, his criminality. In other words, it is impossible for man, by his own powers, without the interference or help of God, to restore his damaged and disrupted nature. Therefore, it was necessary for God Himself to come down and dwell upon the earth. The incarnation of the Son of God was necessary for the **restoration** of the fallen and corrupted nature of man, to save man from damnation and eternal death.

Why Did the Lord God Permit the First Man to Fall into Sin? And if He Permitted This, Why Did the Lord Not Simply ("Mechanically") Return Them After the Fall to the Former State of Life in Paradise?

Almighty God, without a doubt, could have prevented the fall of the first people, but He did not wish to stifle their **freedom**, because it is not in His nature to distort His own image in man. The image and likeness of God is expressed in the **free will of man**.

Prof. Nesmeloff explains this matter very well: "Because it is not clear and is even completely inconceivable for many people to understand why a mechanical salvation is impossible, we should examine this impossibility more closely. To save the first people by preserving the conditions in which they lived before the fall was impossible because their fall was such that they showed themselves to be not only mortal, but also to be criminal. This means that as long as they were aware of their crime, Paradise would in no way be possible for them because of their awareness of their own criminality. If it had happened that they forgot their crime, then by this same act they would only have confirmed their sinfulness, and the result would be that Paradise was impossible for them again because of their moral inability to approach that state in which their first life in Paradise took place. Consequently, the first people could not return themselves to the lost Paradise, **not because God did not wish it, but because their own moral condition did not permit and could not permit this.**

"The children of Adam and Eve were not guilty of their crime, and could not recognize themselves as criminal merely because their parents were criminals. There is no doubt that God, Who is likewise able to create man and to make an infant grow, could have brought forth the children of Adam from a state of sinlessness and placed them in the normal conditions of moral development. To achieve this, the following would be necessary:

a) The consent of God to the damnation of the first people;

b) The agreement of the first people to grant God rights over their children and to give up all hope of salvation forever; and,

c) The agreement of the children to leave their parents in a state of damnation.

"If we allow that the first two of these conditions would in some way be considered possible, nonetheless in no way would it be possible to realize the third necessary condition. For if the sons of Adam and Eve in fact did sin, then for them to let their father and mother perish for the crime that they committed would obviously only demonstrate that they were completely unworthy of Paradise and that they would have surely lost it themselves."

It would have been possible to destroy the men that sinned and create new ones, but would not the newly-created men, having a free will, have begun to sin? Man would then have been born in vain, and not even through a distant offspring would he have overcome the evil he had permitted to triumph over himself. But God was not willing to allow the man He had created to have been created in vain. For the omniscient God does not do anything in vain. The Lord God embraced the entire plan of the creation in His pre-eternal mind and there was included in His pre-eternal plan the incarnation of His Only-begotten Son for the salvation of fallen mankind.

In order not to violate the will of man, it was necessary that fallen mankind be restored **by compassion and by love**, so that man would wish voluntarily to return to God, and **not by force nor necessity**, for then men would not be worthy children of God. According to the pre-eternal mind of God, men must become like Him Himself, and sharers of eternal, blessed life with Him.

Thus, the all-wise, all-good and almighty Lord God did not count it unworthy of Himself to come down to the sinful earth, to take upon Himself our flesh, injured by sin, and to save us and return us to the paradisiacal blessedness of eternal life.

Concerning the Image and Likeness of God in Man

The Holy Church teaches that the **image of God** is to be understood as the **powers of the soul: mind, will, feeling**, which God granted to man; and **the likeness of God** is to be understood as the **ability** of man to direct the powers of his soul to becoming like God, **to be perfected in striving for truth and good**.

This can be more fully explained by the following:

The image of God is found in **the qualities and powers of the soul**. God is an invisible Spirit Who penetrates everything in the world, gives life to all, and at the same time He is a Being independent of the world. The **soul** of man, present in the entire body, and giving life to the body, even though it has a certain dependence on the body, still continues to exist after the death of the body. God is eternal; the soul of man is immortal. God is all-wise and all-knowing; the soul of man has the power to learn what is present, to remember the past and even at times to prophesy the future. God is all-good, that is, all-kind, all-merciful, and the soul of man has the power to love others and to sacrifice itself. God is almighty, the creator of all that is; the soul of man has the power and the ability to think, to make, to create, to build, etc. But, of course, there exists an immeasurable difference between God and the powers of the human soul. The powers of God are unlimited, and the powers of the human soul are very limited. God is a being that is absolutely free; the soul of man has only freedom of will. Therefore man can wish, but he can also not wish to be the likeness of God, for this depends on his own free desire, on his free will.

The likeness of God depends on the **direction of spiritual abilities**.
This requires that man work on himself spiritually. If a man strives for
truth and good, for the righteousness of God, then he becomes like God.
However, if a man loves only himself, lies, makes enemies, does evil,
cares only for earthly goods, thinks only about his body and does not
care for his soul, then such a person ceases to be in the likeness of God
and becomes in his life like a beast, and can finally become like an evil
spirit, a devil.

CHAPTER 8

Cain and Abel

After the expulsion of Adam and Eve from Paradise, they began to bear children, sons and daughters (cf. Gen. 5:4). They called their first son Cain and the second Abel. Cain was a worker of the soil and Abel shepherded flocks. Once, they brought offerings to God: Cain of the fruits of the earth, but Abel of the best beast of the flock.

Abel had a kind and meek nature; he brought his offering from a pure heart, with love and faith in the promised Saviour, with prayer for mercy and hope in the mercy of God; God accepted the sacrifice of Abel and its smoke rose into Heaven. Cain was cruel and evil. He offered his sacrifice only out of habit, without love and fear of God. The Lord did not accept his sacrifice, for the smoke from his sacrifice only spread along the earth.

Abel and His Brother Cain

After this, Cain became jealous of his brother. He called his brother out into the field and killed him. God spoke to Cain to make him repent, asking him, "Where is Abel, thy brother?"

Cain brazenly answered, "I know not; am I my brother's keeper?"

Then God said to him, "What hast thou done? The voice of thy brother's blood crieth unto Me from the ground. And now thou art cursed from the earth...a fugitive and a vagabond shalt thou be."

Cain, tormented by his conscience, ran with his wife from his parents into another land.

Human life is the gift of God; therefore, man does not have the right to deprive himself of it or to take another man's life. Taking the life of one's neighbor is called **murder**, and the taking of one's own life is called **suicide** which is the most terrible sin. Only in the case of the insane is the sin of suicide sometimes pardoned.

In place of the murdered Abel, God granted Adam and Eve a third son, the pious **Seth**, and then there were many other children. Adam and Eve lived for a long time on the earth. Adam lived 930 years. They endured many sufferings and anguish, and in their hearts they repented of their sin and firmly believed in the promised Saviour. This faith saved them and now they are numbered among the Holy Forefathers.

NOTE: See Genesis, chaps. 4:1-16, 25; 5:3-5.

CHAPTER 9

The Flood

The human race began to multiply very rapidly from the children of Adam and Eve. At that time people lived for a very long time, up to nine hundred years or more.

From Seth there came forth pious and good people, "sons of God," but from Cain, wicked and evil people, "sons of men." At first, the offspring of Seth lived separately from the offspring of Cain. They preserved faith in God and the coming Saviour. Later however, they began to take for themselves wives from the daughters of the offspring of Cain, and through them, began to adopt bad habits, to be corrupted, and to forget the true God.

After a considerable time, the wickedness of men was so great that, of all the people on earth, only one of the offspring of Seth remained faithful to God, the righteous **Noah** and his family.

Beholding the great corruption of mankind, the merciful Lord gave them 120 years for repentance and correction. But men not only did not correct themselves, they became even worse.

Then the Lord decided to cleanse the earth of the evil human race with water, but to preserve the righteous Noah and his family on the earth to continue the human race.

God said to Noah, "The end has come for all creatures, for the earth has been filled by them with evil works; and I shall obliterate them from the face of the earth. I shall bring upon the earth a flood of water to destroy all that is upon the earth" (Cf. Gen. 6:13-17). He commanded Noah to build an **ark**, a huge, rectangular vessel like a house, in which there would be room for his family and animals, and He gave him the precise measurements and directions for this. Noah accepted God's commandment with faith and began to build the ark.

When the ark was ready, Noah, at the command of God, entered into it with his wife, his three sons and their wives, and at God's direction, took with him all the animals and birds which could not live in the water: of the clean ones, that is, the ones which could be offered in sacrifice, seven pairs, and of the unclean ones, one pair, in order to preserve their kind upon the earth. He also took a reserve of food for them all for an entire year.

On that day when Noah entered into the ark, the waters of the flood gushed upon the earth, and *all the fountains of the great deep were broken up, and the windows of heaven were opened* (Gen. 7:11). There came about a mighty flood from the seas and oceans and from heaven rain poured down upon the earth for forty days and forty nights. The water rose over the earth higher than the highest mountains; it prevailed for 150 days and drowned all men and animals except the ones that were on the ark.

Noah and the Ark

After 150 days the water began slowly to recede. In the **seventh month** the ark came to rest on the mountains of Ararat (in present day Turkey). On the first day of the **tenth month** the tops of the mountains appeared. After **one year** came to an end, the water receded into its proper place.

Noah opened a window in the ark and released a raven, in order to learn whether or not the water had receded from the earth, but the raven flew out and returned to the protection of the ark.

Then Noah released a dove which, when it had flown away, could not find a place to live, because the water was still over the heights of the entire earth, and it returned to the ark. After seven days, Noah again released the dove from the ark. This time the dove returned in the evening and brought a fresh olive leaf in its beak. Noah understood that the water had receded from the earth and that plants had appeared upon it. After waiting another seven days, Noah again released the dove, and this time it did not return to him. He opened the roof of the ark and beheld that the earth had dried.

Then, at the command of God, Noah went forth from the ark with all his family, and released all the animals that were with him.

Noah erected an altar, a place for offering sacrifices, and he offered for his salvation a sacrifice of thanksgiving to God from all the clean animals and birds. God mercifully accepted the sacrifice of Noah,

The Dove Brings an Olive Branch

blessed him and his sons, and promised that there would never again be such a flood to destroy all life on earth for the sins of men, that is, there would never again be a **world-wide flood**. As a sign of this promise, the Lord showed a **rainbow** in the clouds, which from that time has served as a faithful reminder to men of this promise of God.

NOTE: See Genesis, chaps. 4:17-24; 5; 6:1-22; 7; 8; 9:1-17.

Discussion of the Flood

There is an objection to the story of the flood from those who do not believe. Some say that it would be impossible for the entire earth to be under water at the same time, as is recounted in the Bible. But, as the English scientist Arthur Hook points out: ''The scientific specialist Dr. John Murray determined that if the surface of the earth were changed into a flat, even surface, there is so much water in the oceans, which in certain places is up to six miles deep, that there is sufficient water to cover the entire earth with an even depth of two miles."

The flood may not even have covered the entire earth. One must recall the purpose for which God made the flood: *God saw that the wickedness of man was great in the earth, and that every imagination of the thoughts of his heart was only evil continually... So the Lord said, I will destroy man whom I have created from the face of the earth*

Mt. Ararat Where the Ark Rested

(Gen. 6:5,7). Consequently, the flood can be imagined as covering only that part of the earth populated by men, but how great an area this was at the time of the flood is entirely unknown to us. Moreover, the fact that the Bible speaks in several places of the flood extending *over the entire earth* need not disturb us. The Bible, and all religious literature which has as its purpose care for human souls, often calls an area of human habitation, or an isolated area of human habitation, or even just an isolated area of human civilization that has developed under the effect of Holy Scripture, "the earth," and even "the universe." Byzantium, which was nurtured on the Bible, called the Mediterranean basin "the universe"; and that is why she called her emperors "rulers of the universe," and why the Constantinopolitan Patriarch was given the title "ecumenical," or universal.

The widespread tradition of the flood testifies to its being an event that gripped all mankind, and that it was preserved in the memory of many branches of the human race. The same researcher, Arthur Hook, reports that the Chaldees, Phoenicians, Babylonians, Phrygians, Syrians, Persians, Greeks, and even the Armenians, all, to a greater or lesser degree, have mutually compatible accounts of the flood. The account of the Phrygians, for example, mentions Enoch as a prophet of the flood, and recounts that he wept and prayed over the fate of the hardened, unrepentant peoples of the antediluvian world. An ancient Phrygian coin was discovered with a wrought picture of the ark and the letters "N-O" on one side, which, undoubtedly refer to Noah. Further, we find that India and China have accounts of the flood, and that a **certain person with the seven members of his family** was saved from the flood. The Aztecs had a tradition about a man who made a vessel in order to save himself from a catastrophe that was about to occur.

In addition we should mention that on the basis of geological excavations, it is clear that there is in the earth a **thick layer of clay, of alluvial deposits**, which has no remains of organic animal life in it. This layer **is sharply distinguished**, and **sharply divides** the layers of the Paleolithic Age (Stone) from the later layers: **neolithic, bronze and iron ages**. The French scientist Mortilie called this layer Hiatus, that is, a break. It is assumed that this alluvial deposit came about from the depth of the sea with the action of a worldwide cataclysm; the land sank beneath the level of the ocean whose waters flooded the entire earth. Moses says of this, *and all the fountains of the great abyss were opened* (Gen. 7:11), and then he also speaks of rain. Furthermore, these alluvial deposits cover, in a thick layer, all Europe, North Africa and Western Asia to the highest peaks. The scientist Couvier called this sediment, this thick alluvial deposit, "Deluge."

For people who believe, these proofs, of course, are unnecessary, for they know that the Almighty Lord God, Who created Heaven and earth, could certainly flood the entire surface of the earth with the waters of a flood.

CHAPTER 10

The Life of Noah and His Children After the Flood

The sons of Noah who emerged with him from the ark were Shem, Ham and Japheth.

Noah began to work the earth and planted a vineyard. When he had made wine of the juice of the vine and had drunk it, he became intoxicated because he did not know as yet the strength of wine, and taking his clothes off, he lay naked in his tent. His son Ham, the father of Canaan, saw this. He acted without proper respect for his father and told his brothers about this. Shem and Japheth, however, took clothing, and came up to their father in such a way as not to see his nakedness and covered him. When Noah woke up and learned about the action of the youngest son, Ham, he condemned and cursed him in the person of his son Canaan, and said that his offspring would be in slavery to the offspring of his brothers. But Shem and Japheth he blessed and prophesied that the true faith would be preserved in the offspring of Shem, and the offspring of Japheth would spread across the earth and accept the true faith from the offspring of Shem.

Noah lived for 950 years. He was the last to live to such an advanced age. After him, the strength of the human race began to decline, and people could live for only 400 years. But even with this length of life, the population increased.

All that Noah foretold his sons was fulfilled precisely. The offspring of Shem are called the **Semites**, to whom there belong firstly the Hebrew people, with whom faith in the true God was preserved. The offspring of Japheth are called **Japhethites**, to whom there belong the peoples that populated Europe and Asia, who accepted faith in the true God from the Hebrews. The offspring of Ham are called **Hamites**. The Canaanite tribes which originally inhabited Palestine, and were later subjugated by the offspring of Shem and Japheth, belong to them.

NOTE: See Genesis, chaps. 9:18-39; 10.

CHAPTER 11

The Building of the Tower of Babel and the Scattering of Peoples

For a long time, the increasing offspring of Noah lived together in one land, not far from the Ararat mountains, and spoke one common language.

When the human race became numerous, evil deeds and conflicts between people began to multiply, and they saw that they would soon have to scatter across the entire earth. Before they separated, however, the offspring of Ham, together with others whom they attracted, decided to build a city and in the city a **tower** in the form of a **pillar**,

The Tower of Babel

reaching to Heaven, in order to be glorified, and not be in subjugation to the offspring of Shem and Japheth, as Noah had prophesied. They made bricks and set to work.

This proud project of the people was not pleasing to God. So that evil would not completely destroy them, since evil could be quickly spread due to a common language, the Lord changed the language of the builders so that they began to speak in different languages and could no longer understand one another. Then men were forced to abandon the work they had undertaken and scatter across the earth into various lands. The offspring of Japheth went to the west and settled in Europe. The offspring of Shem remained in Asia. The offspring of Ham went to Africa, but a part of them also remained in Asia.

The unfinished city was called **Babylon**, which means **confusion**. This whole land where this city was located was later to be called Babylonia, and also Chaldea.

Scattering across the earth, people began to forget their ancestry and began to make up separate, independent peoples and nations with their own customs and language.

The Lord saw that people learned more evil from one another than good, and for this reason He brought about the confusion of the languages and divided people into separate nations and gave each nation a separate goal and purpose in life.

NOTE: See Genesis, chap. 11.

CHAPTER 12

The Appearance of Idolatry

When people were scattered across the entire earth, they began to forget the invisible true God, the Creator of the world. The principal reason for this was that the sins which separate people from God clouded their reason.

There were fewer and fewer righteous men, and there was no one to teach men true faith in God. There appeared among men false faith, superstition. People saw about them much that was marvelous and

Krishna, a Pagan Hindu god

unintelligible, and in place of God they began to worship the sun, moon, stars, fire, water and various animals, to make images of them, to worship them, to offer sacrifice and build them temples or shrines. Such images of false gods are called **idols**, and the people who worship them are called **idolaters** or **pagans**. This is how idolatry began to appear on the earth.

Soon almost all men were pagans. Only in Asia, in the offspring of Shem was there a righteous man whose name was Abraham, who remained faithful to God.

CHAPTER 13

Abraham

Abraham lived in the land of Chaldea, not far from Babylon. He was a descendant of Shem and, with all his family, preserved true faith in God. He was wealthy, having an abundance of cattle, silver, gold, and many servants, but he had no children and grieved over this.

The Patriarch Abraham

God chose the righteous Abraham to preserve the true faith, through his offspring, for all mankind. In order to protect him and his offspring from the pagan people related to him, because the pagans among his relatives could more easily teach them idolatry, God appeared to Abraham and said, *Get thee out of thy country, and from thy kindred, and from thy father's house, unto a land that I will show thee: And I will make of thee a great nation, and I will bless thee, and make thy name great...**and in thee shall all families** (peoples) **of the earth be blessed*** (Gen 12:1-2). God promised Abraham that, in time, from his offspring

Chaldea, Abraham's Homeland, and Canaan, the Promised Land

there should be born the Saviour of the world, promised to the first men, Who should bless all peoples of the earth.

Abraham was seventy-five years old at that time. He obeyed the Lord, took his wife Sarah, his nephew Lot, all the possessions they had acquired, and all their servants, and moved into the land which the Lord showed him. This land was called **Canaan** and was very fertile. At that time the Canaanites lived there. They were one of the most wicked of all peoples. The Canaanites were the offspring of Canaan, the son of Ham. Here the Lord appeared to Abraham anew and said: *For all the*

The Oak of Mamre

land that thou seest, to thee will I give it, and to thy seed for ever (Gen. 13:15). Abraham built an altar and offered God a sacrifice of thanksgiving.

After this, the land of Canaan began to be called the **Promised Land**, since God promised to give it to Abraham and his offspring. Now it is called **Palestine**. This land is on the eastern shore of the Mediterranean Sea and the Jordan River flows down through its center.

When the flocks of Abraham and Lot began to grow plentiful, there was no longer enough room for them to remain together, and their shepherds began to argue with each other; then they decided to separate on friendly terms.

Abraham said to Lot *Let there be no strife, I pray thee, between me and thee...for we are brethren. Is not the whole land before thee? Separate thyself, I pray thee, from me...if thou depart to the right hand, then I will go the left* (Gen. 13:8-10).

Lot chose for himself the valley of the Jordan and settled in Sodom. Abraham remained in the land of Canaan and settled near Hebron, at the woods of Mamre. There, near the **oak of Mamre**, he set up his tent and built an altar to the Lord. This oak of Mamre is still alive in Palestine near the city of Hebron.

A short while after Lot had settled in Sodom, the neighboring King of Elam attacked Sodom, looted the city, took the people into captivity and seized their possessions. Among the captives was Lot. Abraham, when he learned of this, immediately gathered his servants together (318 men), called his neighbors to help, overtook the enemy, attacked him, and seized his loot.

When Abraham returned, he met solemnly with Melchizedek, who was a priest of the Most-high God and King of Salem. He offered bread and wine as a gift to Abraham and blessed him.

Nothing is known concerning Melchizedek, his background, and his death. The name **Melchizedek** means **king of righteousness**, and the word **Salem** means **peace**. Melchizedek was a prototype of Jesus Christ. Just as Melchizedek was at the same time priest and king, so Jesus Christ is High Priest and King. Just as neither the beginning nor the end of the life of Melchizedek is told, he, as it were, lives forever. So also Christ is eternal God, King and High Priest; we call Jesus Christ the High Priest forever according to the order of Melchizedek. And just as our Lord Jesus Christ gave us, in the form of bread and wine, His Body and Blood, that is, Holy Communion, so also Melchizedek, foreshadowing the Saviour, offered Abraham bread and wine and, since he

An Icon of Abraham Receiving the Three Strangers, Painted on a Piece of Wood from the Oak of Mamre

was older, blessed Abraham. Abraham accepted the blessing of Melchizedek with reverence and gave him the tenth part of his spoils.

NOTE: See Genesis, chaps. 12, 14, 15, 16, 17.

Melchizedek Blesses Abraham

CHAPTER 14

The Appearance of God to Abraham in the Form of Three Strangers

Once, on a hot day, Abraham sat under the shadow of the oak, at the entrance of his tent, and saw Three Strangers standing before him. Abraham loved to receive strangers. He immediately got up and ran to meet Them, bowed to the earth, and invited Them to rest at his home under the tree and to strengthen Themselves with food.

The strangers came to his abode. According to the custom of that time, Abraham washed Their feet, gave Them bread which had just been prepared by his wife Sarah, set forth oil, milk, and the best fatted calf, and called Them to eat.

And They said to him, "Where is Sarah, thy wife?"

He answered, "Behold, in the tent."

One of Them said, "I will certainly return to thee in a year; and, lo, Sarah thy wife shall have a son."

Sarah, who was standing out of sight in the entrance to the tent, heard these words. She laughed to herself and thought, "How can I have such a consolation, when I am already old?"

But the Stranger said, "Wherefore did Sarah laugh?...Is anything too hard for the Lord? At the time appointed I will return unto thee,... and Sarah shall bear a son."

Then Sarah was frightened and said, "I laughed not."

But He said to her, "Nay, but thou didst laugh."

Abraham then realized that before him were not simple strangers, but that God Himself was speaking with him.

At that time Abraham was ninety-nine years old and Sarah eighty-nine.

NOTE: See Genesis, chap. 18:1-16.

CHAPTER 15

The Destruction of Sodom and Gomorrah

When He departed from Abraham, God revealed to him that He was going to destroy the neighboring cities of Sodom and Gomorrah because they were the most wicked cities on the earth. The nephew of Abraham, the righteous Lot, was living in Sodom.

Abraham began to plead with the Lord that He be merciful to these cities if there were fifty righteous men in them.

The Lord said, "If I find fifty righteous men in Sodom, then I shall spare the whole city for their sake."

Abraham again asked, "Perhaps of the fifty righteous men five shall be lacking?"

The Lord said, "If I find there forty and five, I will not destroy it."

Then Abraham continued to speak with the Lord and beseech Him, continually lowering the number of righteous men, until he came to the number ten. He said, "Do not be angry, Master, but I will say once more: Perhaps ten (righteous men) shall be found there."

God said, "I shall not destroy it for ten's sake."

In these wretched cities the inhabitants were so evil and corrupt that there were not even ten righteous men to be found. These evil men even wanted to abuse the two angels that came to save the righteous Lot. They were prepared to break down the door, but the angels struck them with blindness and led Lot and his family, with his wife and two daughters, out of the city. They commanded them to run and not to look back, so as not to perish.

Then the Lord poured upon Sodom and Gomorrah a rain of sulphur and fire and destroyed these cities and all the people in them. The place was entirely laid waste, so that in the valley where they stood a salt lake was formed, which is now known by the name **Dead Sea**, in which no creature can live.

The wife of Lot, when she ran from the city, looked back at Sodom, and immediately was turned into a pillar of salt.

By looking back at Sodom, the wife of Lot showed that she regretted leaving the sinful city that was left behind. She looked back, hesitated, and immediately was turned into a pillar of salt. This is a strict lesson for us. When the Lord saves us from a sin, we must flee from it, not looking back at it, not hesitate nor regret giving it up.

NOTE: See Genesis, chaps. 18:16-33; 19:20.

CHAPTER 16

The Offering of Isaac as a Sacrifice

A year after the appearance of God to Abraham in the form of three strangers, the prophecy of God was fulfilled. Abraham and Sarah gave birth to a son whom they called Isaac. Abraham was then one hundred years old and Sarah ninety. They loved their only son very much.

Abraham Prepares to Sacrifice Isaac

When Isaac grew up, God wished to elevate the faith of Abraham and thus teach all men through him to love God and obey His will.

God appeared to Abraham and said, "Take now thy son, thine only son Isaac, whom thou lovest, and get thee into the land of Moriah, and offer him there for a burnt offering upon one of the mountains which I will tell thee of."

Abraham obeyed. He was very sorry for his only son, whom he loved more than his own self. He loved God more than everything, he had perfect faith in Him and knew that God never desires anything evil. He rose early in the morning, saddled a donkey and took his son Isaac and two servants with him. He also took wood and fire for the sacrifice and set out on his way.

On the third day of the journey they came to the mountain which the Lord showed him. Abraham left the servants and the donkey at the foot of the mountain, took the fire and knife, loaded the wood on Isaac, and went with him to the mountain.

Isaac As a Prototype of Christ the Saviour

When they both were climbing the mountain, Isaac asked Abraham, "My father, we have fire and wood, but where is the lamb for a burnt offering?"

Abraham answered, "My son, God will provide a lamb for Himself."

They both went further and came to the top of the mountain to the place indicated by the Lord. There Abraham built an altar, laid out the wood, bound his son Isaac and placed him on the altar on top of the wood. He lifted the knife in order to slay his son, but then the angel of the Lord called to him from Heaven and said, "Abraham, Abraham...lay not thy hand upon the lad, neither do thou anything unto him, for I know that thou fearest God, and for that reason thou hast not begrudged thine only son for Me." Not far away, Abraham saw a ram caught in a bush, and he offered it in place of Isaac.

For such faith, love, and obedience God blessed Abraham and promised him that he would have as many offspring as the stars in the heavens and the sand on the shore of the sea, and that in his offspring all the peoples of the earth would receive a blessing, that is, the Saviour of the world would come forth from his descendants.

The offering of Isaac in sacrifice was a prefiguration to men of the Saviour, Who, being the Son of God, would be offered by His Father as a sacrifice for the sins of all men by death on the Cross.

Isaac, appearing as a prefiguration of the Saviour over two thousand years before the Birth of Christ, foreshadowed, according to God's will, Jesus Christ. He, like Jesus Christ, went without complaint to the place of sacrifice. As Jesus Christ bore the Cross Himself, so Isaac himself carried the wood for the sacrifice.

The mountain on which Abraham offered Isaac in sacrifice received the name of Mount Moriah. Later, at God's command, King Solomon built the Temple of Jerusalem on this mountain.

NOTE: See Genesis, chaps. 21, 22.

Abraham's Journey with Isaac

CHAPTER 17

The Marriage of Isaac

Sarah, the wife of Abraham, died when she was 127. Abraham himself began to grow weak and decided to find a wife for his son Isaac, not a Canaanite, but a maiden of his own kindred. Isaac was then forty years old.

The Tomb of Abraham and Sarah

Abraham called his oldest servant, Eleazar, and said to him, "Swear by the Lord, the God of Heaven and earth, that thou shalt not take a wife unto my son from among the daughters of the Canaanites among whom I dwell, but thou shalt go unto my country, and to my kindred, and take a wife unto my son Isaac."

Eleazar gave the oath and immediately set out on his way. There was then the custom that the bridegroom gave the parents gifts for the bride; the more wealthy the bride, the more precious the gifts or dowry.

Eleazar took with him, as gifts, many expensive items and ten camels, and set out for Mesopotamia, to the city of Haran, where Nachor, Abraham's brother, was living.

Approaching the city, Eleazar stopped at a well. It was approaching evening, the time when the women usually came to draw water. Eleazar began to pray to God. He said, "O Lord God of my master Abraham, I pray Thee, send me good speed this day, and show kindness unto my master Abraham. Behold, I stand here by the well of water, and the daughters of the men of the city come out to draw water. And let it come to pass, that the maiden to whom I shall say, 'Let down thy pitcher, I pray thee that I may drink' and she shall say, 'Drink, and I will give thy camels drink also': let the same be she that thou hast appointed for Thy servant Isaac; and thereby shall I know that Thou hast showed kindness unto my master."

Eleazar had just finished the prayer when a beautiful maiden with a pitcher on her shoulders came to the well, drew water, and started back. Eleazar ran to her and said, "Let me, I pray thee, drink a little water of thy pitcher."

The maiden said, "Drink, my lord." And right away she lowered the pitcher from her shoulder, and gave him to drink. When Eleazar had drunk, the maiden said, "I will draw water for thy camels also, until they have done drinking." She straightway poured the water from her pitcher into the trough and ran again to the well to draw water, and drew water for all his camels. Eleazar watched her in silence with amazement.

When the camels stopped drinking, Eleazar took a golden ring and two bracelets for her arms, and gave them to her and asked her, "Whose daughter art thou? Tell me, I pray thee: is there room in thy father's house for us to lodge in?"

This maiden was named **Rebecca**. She answered, "I am the daughter of Bathuel, the son of Nahor. We have both straw and provender enough, and room to lodge in." Eleazar knelt down and gave thanks to God that He had heard his prayer.

Rebecca ran to the house and told all of this to her mother and all in the house. Rebecca had a brother, Laban. He immediately ran to the well and said to Eleazar, "Come in, thou blessed of the Lord: wherefore standest thou without? For I have prepared the house and room for the camels."

Eleazar entered the house. Laban unsaddled the camels, gave them straw and fodder. Right away they brought water to wash the feet of Eleazar and the men who were with him and offered them food.

Eleazar said, "I will not eat until I explain my business...I am Abraham's servant." Eleazar told in detail why he had come and how, at his prayer, the Lord granted a sign concerning Rebecca. When he had told everything, he asked, "Now, if ye will deal kindly and truly with my master, tell me; and if not, tell me."

Laban and Bathuel answered, "This is a doing of the Lord. We cannot contradict thee. Behold, Rebecca is before thee. Take her and go, and let her be thy master's son's wife, as the Lord hath spoken."

When Eleazar heard such words, he bowed down to the earth before the Lord with thanksgiving. Then he took the gold and silver items and clothing, and gave them to the bride, her brother, and mother.

On the next day, Eleazar asked that they let them go home. But the brother and mother of Rebecca began to persuade him to remain at least ten days. But Eleazar answered, "Hinder me not, for the Lord hath prospered my way."

Then the parents called Rebecca and asked her, "Wilt thou go with this man?"

Rebecca said, "I will go."

Then her parents blessed her and let her go. When Eleazar, with Rebecca and his men, approached the tents of Abraham on their camels, Isaac met them. Rebecca became the wife of Isaac. Love for Rebecca consoled Isaac in his mourning for the death of his mother, Sarah.

NOTE: See Genesis, chaps. 23, 24.

The marriage of Isaac is an example for all generations. How often young people go astray in this very important question in their life, upon entering into marriage. Some look for wealth, others for physical beauty, others for a good family, and so on.

Only rarely do they look for wisdom and a **meek and good heart**, that is, internal, spiritual beauty. The former qualities are temporary and pass away, but the latter, internal qualities are constant and do not depend on external circumstances.

An improper attitude towards marriage comes from the fact that people want to make their own happiness, without God, according to their own egotistical fancies.

Christian men and women who wish to enter into marriage must fervently pray that the Lord, the Seer of hearts, will Himself, according to His will, arrange their marriage and bless them with His Grace. Without God's blessing no one can find happiness, good order in married life, and a truly Christian family.

A good Christian family is a bulwark for good morals, the soil for the planting of good in mankind, the tool and means for the furthering of the holy Church of Christ and confirming it upon the earth.

The family is also the foundation of the nation, as Philaret, Metropolitan of Moscow, wrote, "In the family lie the seeds of everything that later sprouts and grows into the greater family which is called the nation."

CHAPTER 18

Esau and Jacob

Isaac had two sons; Esau and Jacob. Esau was a skilled hunter and often lived in the field. Jacob was meek and quiet, and lived in the tents together with his father and mother.

Isaac had greater love for Esau, who treated him with food from his hunt, but Rebecca had a greater love for Jacob. Esau, as the elder son, had the **birthright**, that is, seniority over Jacob in the blessing from his father.

Once Esau returned from the field tired and hungry. Jacob at that time was cooking himself lentil stew (proverbially called a mess of pottage). Esau said to him, "Feed me."

Jacob said, "Sell me this day thy birthright" since he wanted very much for the blessing that God gave to Abraham to refer to him and in this way to serve God zealously.

Esau answered, "Behold, I am dying of hunger; what do I care about this birthright?" By such an answer Esau showed his careless disregard for God's blessing.

Jacob said, "Swear to me."

Esau swore to it and sold his birthright to Jacob for a stew of lentils.

When Isaac grew old and blind, sensing that his life was approaching its end, he wished to bless Esau as his elder son. But thanks to the cleverness of Rebecca, he blessed Jacob instead of Esau. Isaac soon learned his mistake, but still confirmed his blessing on Jacob.

Esau hated his brother for this, and even wanted to murder him, so Jacob had to leave his own family.

At the suggestion of his parents, he set out for the homeland of his mother in Mesopotamia, to the land of Babylon, to her brother Laban, in order to live with him until the anger of Esau passed away. While there he married one of the daughters of Laban.

NOTE: See Genesis, chaps. 23; 24; 25; 27:1-9.

CHAPTER 19

Jacob's Vision of the Mystical Ladder

While on his way, Jacob stopped in a field to pass the night. He placed a stone under his head and went to sleep. He beheld in his sleep a ladder standing on the earth, with its top touching the heavens. The angels of God were ascending and descending on it, and at the top of the ladder stood the Lord Himself.

Jacob's Vision of the Ladder

The Lord said to Jacob, "I am the Lord God of Abraham and the God of Isaac. I will give the land whereon thou liest to thee, and to thy seed. Thy seed shall be as numerous as the dust of the earth, and in thy **seed** shall all the peoples of the earth be blessed. And, behold, I am with thee, and will keep thee in all places whither thou goest, and bring thee again into this land."

Here, by the term "seed" or "offspring," through which all peoples shall be blessed and granted happiness, is meant the **Saviour**. The **ladder**, then, which joins Heaven and earth, prefigured the **Mother of God**, through Whom the Son of God, being born of Her, came to earth for the salvation of man. The Mother of God, like that ladder, joined Heaven to earth.

On awakening Jacob said, "How awesome is this place! This is none other than the house of God, and this is the gate of Heaven." The stone on which he had slept, he set up as a monument and poured oil upon it as a sacrifice to God. He called this place, **Bethel**, which means "**house of God**." After this, with hope in God's help, he calmly continued his journey into Mesopotamia.

Jacob came into Haran to Laban, his uncle. Jacob told Laban about everything and remained to live and work for Laban. Laban asked Jacob what pay he wanted for his work. Jacob agreed to work for Laban seven years for his daughter, **Rachel**, in order to marry her, as he had fallen in love with her. But Laban cunningly gave Jacob not Rachel for a wife but his elder daughter, Leah, justifying himself by the local tradition that the younger daughter could not be married before the elder.

Then the deceived Jacob agreed to work another seven years for Rachel. After twenty years Jacob safely returned to his father in the land of Canaan with a large family and many possessions. Esau, who had not seen his brother for a long time, joyfully met Jacob on the way. The Lord, in special, mystical circumstances, tested the strength of Jacob and gave him a new name, **Israel**, which means "contender with God." Thus, Jacob became the founder of the people of Israel, that is, the **Hebrews**.

NOTE: See Genesis, chap. 28:10-22; chaps. 29-35.

CHAPTER 20

Joseph

Jacob had twelve sons: Reuben, Simeon, Levi, Judah, Issachar, Zebulon, Dan, Naphtali, Gad, Asher, Joseph and Benjamin. From them there later grew up the twelve tribes of the Hebrew people.

Of all his sons, Jacob loved Joseph most of all, for his meekness and obedience, and he sewed him a coat of many colors. But his brothers began to be jealous of Joseph and to hate him.

Once Joseph saw in a dream that he was with his brothers in the field and they were gathering sheaves. His sheaf stood up right in the middle, and the sheaves of his brothers surrounded his sheaf and

Joseph's Dream

bowed down to it. Another time, Joseph saw in a dream that the sun, the moon and eleven stars bowed down to him. When he related his dreams, his father said to him, "What is this dream which thou hast

Joseph is Sold by His Brothers

dreamed? Shall I and thy mother and thy brethren indeed come to bow down ourselves to thee to the earth?'' For this his brothers hated him even more.

Soon after this, his brothers were herding flocks far from home, and their father sent Joseph to visit them, and to learn whether or not his brothers were well and the cattle safe. As he approached them, his brothers recognized Joseph from a long way off and began to say, ''Behold, the dreamer cometh. Come now therefore, and let us slay him...and we shall see what will become of his dreams.'' Reuben, the oldest of the brothers, said, ''Shed no blood; but cast him into this pit.'' He himself thought how he might be able to save Joseph and return him to his father. The brothers obeyed. They took Joseph's coat of many colors off him and threw him into a deep pit, in which there was no water. At that time a merchant passed by them with merchandise for the land of Egypt. One of the brothers, Judah, advised to sell Joseph, and they sold him for twenty silver pieces. Then they took Joseph's coat, drenched it with the blood of a goat, took it to their father and said, ''We found this coat. Is it not Joseph's?'' Jacob recognized the coat. ''An evil beast hath devoured him!'' he cried with grief. Afterwards he mourned for his beloved son for a long time and could not find consolation.

Joseph was sold by his brothers on Judah's advice for twenty pieces of silver. He was a prefiguration of Christ, Who was sold by Judas for thirty pieces of silver.

NOTE: See Genesis, chap. 37; Exodus, chap. 1:1-4.

CHAPTER 21

Joseph in Egypt

The merchants brought Joseph to Egypt and sold him to a certain nobleman named Potiphar, or Pentrephorios. Living in Egypt among pagans, Joseph firmly kept his faith in the true God and feared in any way to sin before Him. He served his master faithfully. Potiphar loved him and made him the manager of his household, but the evil and conniving wife of Potiphar denounced Joseph before her husband. Potiphar believed his wife and put Joseph in prison.

Joseph Explains the Dreams

God saw the innocence of Joseph and helped him. In the same prison were the cup-bearer and the baker of Pharaoh, the Egyptian ruler. Once they saw dreams. The cup-bearer saw that he gathered grapes from three vineyards, pressed the juice out of them into a cup and gave it to Pharaoh. The baker saw that he was carrying three baskets of bread on his head and that birds came and ate them. Joseph explained these dreams. He said to the cup-bearer that in three days Pharaoh would forgive him and that he would again be the cup-bearer, but to the baker he said that in three days Pharaoh would order him to be hanged and that the birds would eat his body. All this was fulfilled as Joseph said.

Two years later Pharaoh had two dreams in the same night. He dreamed that he was standing on the bank of a river, and out of the river there first came seven fat and beautiful cows, and after them came seven thin cows. The thin cows ate the fat ones, but they did not get fatter. The other dream was that on a single stalk seven full ears were growing, but then seven dry and empty ears grew, and the empty ears swallowed the seven full ones. In the morning Pharaoh called in all the wise men of Egypt, but none of them could explain the dreams to him.

Then the cup-bearer remembered Joseph and told the King about him. They brought Joseph to Pharaoh, and he explained the dreams. "Both dreams," he said, "signify the same thing. In the land of Egypt there will be seven years of great plenty; after this there will come seven years of famine." At the same time, Joseph advised Pharaoh to prepare during the plentiful years enough grain to supply for the entire time of the famine.

Pharaoh understood that God Himself had revealed the meaning of the dreams to Joseph and made him his chief minister in the land of Egypt, first after himself, and entrusted to him the preparation of the grain.

NOTE: See Genesis, chap. 39-40; 41:1-46.

CHAPTER 22

Joseph's Meeting with His Brothers and the Moving of Jacob into Egypt with His Family

During the seven years of plenty, Joseph gathered in Egypt so much grain that it was sufficient not only for the years of hunger but also for sale to other lands. People began to come to Egypt from everywhere for grain because the famine was over the entire earth.

The sons of Jacob, from the land of Canaan, also came to Egypt for grain. They came to Joseph, bowed down to him to the earth, but did not recognize him. But Joseph recognized his brothers and involuntarily recollected his dreams from childhood. In order to learn whether or not his brothers had improved, he treated them severely and said to them, "Ye are spies. To see the nakedness of the land ye are come "

"Nay," his brothers answered, "but to buy food are thy servants come. We are twelve brethren, the sons of one man in the land of Canaan. We used to be twelve, but the youngest is this day with our father, and one is not."

"If ye speak the truth," said Joseph, "Then let one of you remain here, and the others take bread and bring the younger brother."

The brothers spoke among themselves, thinking that Joseph did not understand them, as they spoke through interpreters. "We are verily guilty concerning our brother, in that we saw his anguish of soul, when he besought us, and we would not hear. Therefore is this distress come upon us."

When Joseph heard what they were saying, he went out of the room and wept. Afterwards, he kept Simeon and let the rest of the brothers go.

After a year the brothers again came to Egypt for grain and brought with them their youngest brother Benjamin. Joseph, when he saw Benjamin with them, commanded to bring them to his house and to prepare a dinner for them. When he looked at Benjamin he was moved to tears of joy. So that his brothers would not notice his tears, he went into the next room and washed his face. After dinner, Joseph ordered the grain put into their sacks, but he ordered the silver cup from which he drank himself to be put into the sack of Benjamin. The next day he let them all go home.

The brothers had barely departed, when Joseph ordered his steward to overtake them and search them to see if they had not stolen his cup. The cup was found in Benjamin's sack. The brothers all returned to

Joseph, fell down before him to the ground and said, "God hath found out the iniquity of thy servants. Behold, we are thy servants."

"No," answered Joseph, "let the one who stole the cup remain as a slave, but you can return to your father."

Then Judah came forward and said to Joseph, "My lord! Our father is old and loveth this son more than all. I gave a pledge to bring him back safely. It is better that I should remain a slave with thee in place of him, but do thou let him go with his brethren to their father, for if he doth not return, our father shall die of grief."

Now Joseph saw that his brothers had learned their lesson, and no longer hid himself from them. He sent all his servants out of the room, began to weep and said to them, "I am Joseph your brother, whom ye sold into Egypt." The brothers were so astounded that they could not speak.

But Joseph continued, "Now therefore be not grieved, nor angry with yourselves, that ye sold me hither: for God did send me before you to preserve your lives. For these two years hath the famine been in the land, and yet there are five years more...Haste ye, and go up to my father, and say unto him..., come down unto me, and tarry not." After this he embraced and kissed Benjamin and all his brothers, and he wept as he embraced them.

When Jacob learned with tremendous joy that his son Joseph was alive, he moved with all his family to Egypt.

For seventeen years the aged Jacob-Israel lived in Egypt. When he began to approach death, he first blessed Joseph and his children, Manasses and Ephraim. Joseph brought his children to his father, so that the elder Manasses stood at Jacob's right hand and the younger Ephraim stood at his left. But Jacob **crossed** his hands so that his right hand was on the head of Ephraim and the left on the hand of Manasses. And he blessed them, Ephraim as the elder and Manasses as the younger.

This crossing of Jacob's hands for blessing was **a foreshadowing of the Cross of Christ**, and that people would receive the Lord's blessing not by seniority but according to their good works and worthiness.

Afterwards, when he had gathered all his sons about his bed, he gave each of them his blessing and prophesied of Judah that of his offspring there would come forth kings over the Hebrew people until the time when the Peacemaker, that is, Christ the Saviour, should come.

After this, he commanded his sons to bury him in the land of Canaan where his fathers were buried. Jacob-Israel died at the age of one hundred and forty years and was taken by his sons into the land of Canaan and buried there.

Fifty years after Jacob's death, Joseph also died. Before his death he said that God would lead the Hebrew people out of Egypt and return them to the land of Canaan. He commanded that his bones be taken to his native land. In Egypt the family of Jacob-Israel began to multiply rapidly and became the people which came to be known as the **Israelites** or the **Hebrews**. It was divided into twelve tribes according to the number of the twelve sons of Jacob.

The story of **Joseph**, who suffered from his brothers but who was later glorified and saved their lives, **was a foreshadowing of Christ the Saviour**. The Saviour also suffered at the hands of His own people, died on the Cross, then arose and was glorified and saved men from sin and eternal death.

NOTE: See Genesis, chaps. 41:47-57; 42-50.

Discussion: The Story of Joseph Written in the Language of Trees

Rationalists, men who recognize as the source of knowledge only reason, denying every experience and Divine Revelation, who do not believe in the historicity of the Biblical accounts, regard the story of Joseph as a legend. However, this account is not a legend but an actual happening which took place in the history of ancient Egypt. The author of these lines boldly confirms the historicity of this happening, as it turns out to have been recorded by nature itself and is written down in a most unexpected way. In the 1920's, in connection with work on this subject by many researchers in Russia, America, and Sweden, the author was occupied with research into the relation of the growth of trees and various natural influences, from rainfall, deposits, climate, fire, and pests. At that time the remains of trees that had been preserved in various paleontological and archeological collections were under investigation. Special attention was given to a collection of objects preserved from the times of ancient Egypt. Such items, in the Egyptian section of the Petersburg Hermitage, were in large quantity. They were all in excellent condition, which permitted the precise determination of what kind of wood was used for different items.

In this way it was determined that some of the items were made from trees which are still growing in Abyssinia and in the area of the upper lakes from which the Blue and White Nile find their source. These species were, of course, transported into Egypt. But there was a considerable number of items in the collection which had been made from different kinds of trees which still grow in the Nile valley. Of all these, the carpenters of ancient Egypt most frequently used two kinds: niletic acacia and sycamore. By studying the structure of the wood in these items, we were able to determine that there is a direct relationship between the width of the rings of the trees and the floods of the Nile.

Now, it is well known that the entire economy of Egypt depends on the size of these floods. When there is a generous flood, the entire population prospers, as the vegetation of the Nile valley in such years grows lushly and the fields give an abundant harvest. It turned out that in such years the trees, which grow along the banks of the Nile, have wide rings. In the years of small floods there are small harvests and hunger in the land, and the rings of the trees are narrow, as all growth suffers from the lack of moisture. When the relation between the harvests and the wide tree rings was determined, I came to the following conclusion: if the

Biblical account relates an occurrence that actually took place in Egypt, then the seven years of exceptional plenty and the seven years of poor harvests should have been recorded in the rings of the trees which grew at that time along the banks of the Nile.

I then asked the assistant of the curator of the Egyptian Section of the Hermitage (in those years, the curator was academician V. V. Struve), Mme. N. D. Flitner to show me which wooden items of the collection could belong to the times of the XIII-XVIII dynasties. Researchers of Biblical archeology place the history of the dwelling of the Hebrews in Egypt during this epoch. Mme. Flitner pointed out to me a group of such items. Among them there were a box for the preservation of perfumes, made of Niletic acacia; a sarcophagus of the queens, made of sycamore; and a number of other items. I made a diligent study of these items, beginning with the box for perfumes. It is a little box, about twelve cm. by seven cm. by eight cm. (I had precise measurements and photographs but they were lost when I fled from the USSR), and was made of one and the same piece of niletic acacia. The piece was cut up by the craftsmen into thin boards, from which, with tar, the box was glued together. The form of the layers of wood was visible on all the walls of the box, and this form was unique. On all the little boards there was clearly a difference between wide and very narrow bands. This series went: first a group of six exceptionally wide bands, and then immediately there followed a group of seven very narrow bands. The order of the bands of time can be determined without any difficulty by anyone who is familiar with the make-up of the so-called spring and fall wood patterns. As noted above, the width of the rings of trees on the banks of the Nile corresponds to its floods and, connected with this, to the harvest or lack of harvest. In this way, nature itself wrote down that at the time which corresponds to the epoch of the life of Joseph in Egypt, in that land there were several years in a row which had abundant harvests. In those years the trees formed extraordinarily thick rings. There turned out to be six such annual rings on the box that we examined. Before this the rings were not thin, so there was no noted difference with the Biblical account of the seven years of plenty. Regarding the following seven years of famine, the structure of the wood that we investigated testifies with undeniable precision.

Apart from this box, I also investigated the sarcophagus. Its state of preservation was somewhat worse than that of the box for perfumes, but still in the wood of the sycamore from whose trunk the sarcophagus was made, there could be seen the same kind of grouping of bands. This confirms with irrefutable clarity that at the basis of the Biblical account there lies an indubitable fact that is written in the pages of the great book of nature.

Concerning the discovery, I gave an account in a public lecture at a meeting in memory of D. N. Kaigorodov in February, 1928, and tried to publish it with the appendix of all the materials that had been attained by research. It was not possible to do this, as the censors in the USSR did not permit the printing of anything that could assist the strengthening of the authority of the books of Holy Scripture.

I wish to add another bit of information which refers to the history of ancient Egypt. In agreement with Biblical chronology, the sale of Joseph by his brothers into Egypt, and the consequent migration there of patriarch Jacob, took place eighteen centuries before the Birth of Christ. Certain historians set this date of the moving of Jacob precisely, namely 1825 B. C. It is worthy of note that under the pharaohs of the XII dynasty, particularly during Amenemhet III, who ruled in those years, the network of irrigation was considerably widened and perfected. The level of the water in the Nile under the pharaohs of the XII dynasty was marked on the cliffs near Semne at the second cataract. In the inscription found here, and which dates to the fourteenth year of the rule of Amenemhet (i.e., 1835 B. C.) there is marked the maximum level, which was seven meters above the level of the water now.

Clearly, special officers kept record of the height of the rising of the water in the Nile, since the government was fully aware of what a great significance the irrigation system had for the cultivation of the land, and this system depended on the amount of water in the Nile.

There was an especially great amount of work in the Fayum oasis during that period. Here were located the huge reservoirs which the Greeks called the Lake of Merides. The lake was joined by a canal with the irrigation ditches and this system made it possible to regulate the moisture of a very large area of the Fayum oasis.

The following should also be added. If it were possible to investigate the rich Egyptian collection of the British and Cairo museums, we, undoubtedly, would find a whole series of items witnessing to the veracity of the events which are narrated in the final chapters of the Book of Genesis. **Archpriest N. Smirnov** (from the newspaper *Nasha Strana*, Buenos Aires, 1960),

CHAPTER 23

The Story of Job the Long-suffering

In ancient times, east of Palestine, there lived a righteous man by the name of Job. He was a just and good man, who always strove to please God throughout his life. The Lord rewarded him for his piety with great wealth. He had many hundreds of large and thousands of small cattle. His large and close family of seven sons and three daughters comforted him.

But the Devil was jealous of Job. He began to vilify him before God, "Doth Job fear God for nothing?...But put forth Thine hand now, and touch all that he hath, and he will curse Thee to Thy face." Then God, in order to reveal to all how faithful Job was to Him and in order to teach people patience in their sufferings, permitted the Devil to take away all of Job's possessions. One day robbers came and drove away all his cattle, slew his servants, and a terrible tornado from the desert destroyed the house in which Job's children had gathered together, killing them all. Job not only did not complain against God, but he said, "God gave, and God hath taken away, blessed be the name of the Lord."

The Devil, put to shame, was not satisfied with this. Again he began to slander Job, "All a man hath will he give for his life. But put forth Thine hand now, and touch his bone and his flesh (that is, strike him down with disease), and he will curse Thee to Thy face." God permitted the Devil to deprive Job even of his health, and Job was stricken with the most terrible disease — leprosy. Then even his wife began to persuade him to complain against God. His friends, instead of consolation, only further grieved the innocent sufferer with their unjust suspicions. But Job remained firm, did not lose hope in the mercy of God and only begged the Lord to testify that he was suffering in innocence.

In his discourse with his friends, **Job prophesied about the Redeemer and of the future resurrection**: *I know that my Redeemer liveth and on the last day He shall raise from the dust this my corrupted skin, and in my flesh I shall see God. I shall see Him myself; mine eyes, and not the eyes of another, shall behold Him* (Job 19:25-27, Septuagint).

After this, God, having shown to all the example of devotion and long-suffering in His servant Job, appeared Himself and commanded his friends, who had regarded Job as a great sinner, to ask for prayers from him for themselves. God rewarded His faithful servant. Job regained his health. He had seven more sons and three daughters, gained back twice as much cattle as he had before, and lived another one hundred and forty years in honor, quietly, piously and happily.

The story of long-suffering Job teaches us that God sends misfortunes not just for sins, but that sometimes God sends misfortunes even to the righteous for an even greater confirmation in goodness, for the shaming of the Devil, and for the glorification of the righteousness of God. The history of the life of Job also reveals to us that earthly welfare does not always accompany a virtuous life for men and teaches us also to be sympathetic to those in misfortune. Job, by his innocent sufferings and patience, foreshadowed the Lord Jesus Christ. Therefore, in the days of the commemoration of the sufferings of Jesus Christ during Passion Week, this story in the Book of Job is read in church.

NOTE: See the Book of Job.

Bondage in Egypt

At first the Hebrews lived well in Egypt. But new pharaohs, as they mounted the throne of Egypt, began to forget Joseph and his services. They began to fear the increase of the Hebrew people and were afraid that the Hebrews would become more powerful than the Egyptians and rebel against them. The pharaohs began to burden them with forced labor. But the more they burdened them, the more they increased. Then one of the pharaohs gave the order to kill all the male infants that were born to the Hebrews.

At the time when the Hebrews still lived well, they had begun to forget God and to adopt pagan customs from the Egyptians. Now, when misfortunes came upon them, they remembered God and turned to Him with prayer for their salvation. The compassionate Lord heard them and sent them deliverance through the Prophet and leader **Moses**.

NOTE: See Exodus, chap. 1.

CHAPTER 24

Moses

Moses was born of a Hebrew who came from the tribe of Levi. His mother hid her son for three months from the Egyptians. When it was no longer possible to hide him, she took a reed basket, smeared it with tar, put the infant in it and placed the basket in the reeds at the bank of the river. The infant's sister, Miriam, watched over it from afar, to see what would happen.

The daughter of Pharaoh came to bathe with her servants at this place. Noticing the basket, she commanded that it be brought to her. When she saw the baby crying inside, she felt sorry for it. She said, "This is one of the Hebrews' children."

Miriam came up to her and asked, "Shall I go and call thee a nurse of the Hebrew women, that she may nurse the child for thee?"

The princess said, "Go."

Miriam went and brought her mother. The princess said to her, "Take this child away and nurse it for me, and I will give thee thy wages." She agreed joyfully.

When the infant grew up, his mother brought him to the princess. The princess took him with her, and he became like a son to her. She gave him the name **Moses**, which means "**taken up from the water.**"

Moses grew up in the royal palace and was taught all the wisdom of Egypt, but he knew that he was a Hebrew and loved his own people. Once Moses saw an Egyptian beating a Hebrew. He defended the Hebrew and killed the Egyptian. On another occasion Moses saw one Hebrew beating another Hebrew. Moses wanted to stop him, but he brazenly replied, "Intendest thou to kill me, as thou killedst the Egyptian?" Moses was frightened when he saw that people knew about what he had done. Then Moses fled from Egypt and Pharaoh into a different country, Arabia, the land of Midian. He settled in the home of the priest Jethro, married his daughter Zepphora, and shepherded his flock.

Once Moses went far away with the flocks, and climbed the mountain of Horeb. There he saw a bush which was burning but was not consumed; that is, it was enveloped in flames but did not burn up.

Moses decided to come closer and see why the bush did not burn up. Here he heard a voice from the midst of the bush, "Moses, Moses....Draw not nigh hither, put off thy shoes from off thy feet; for the place whereon thou standest is holy ground. I am the God of thy father, the God of Abraham, the God of Isaac, and the God of Jacob." Moses hid his face, for he was afraid to look at God.

Moses at the Burning Bush

The Lord said to him, "I have surely seen the affliction of My people which are in Egypt, and have heard their cry...and I am come down to deliver them out of the hand of the Egyptians, and to bring them up out of that land...unto the place of the Canaanites...I will send thee unto Pharoah, that thou mightest bring forth My people, the children of Israel, out of Egypt." At the same time, God granted Moses the power to work miracles. Since Moses was inflicted with a speech impediment, the Lord gave him his brother Aaron as a helper, who could speak publicly in his place.

The **bush** that did not burn up, that Moses saw through God's revelation to him, received the name "**burning bush**." It depicted the state of the chosen Hebrew people, which was persecuted but did not perish. It was also a foreshadowing of the **Mother of God**, Who was not burned by the fire of the divinity of the Son of God, when He came down through Her from Heaven to earth, and was born of Her.

NOTE: See Exodus, chaps. 2, 3, 4:1-28.

CHAPTER 25

Pascha (Passover) and the Exodus of the Hebrew People From Egypt

Moses returned to Egypt. At that time another pharaoh was ruling. After speaking with the elders of the Hebrew people, Moses and Aaron went to the Egyptian King and in God's name demanded of him that he let the Hebrews leave Egypt.

Pharaoh replied, "I do not know your God and will not let the Hebrew people go." He then commanded that the Hebrews be more severely burdened.

Then Moses, at God's command, brought down upon Egypt, one after another, ten plagues, so that Pharaoh would agree to release the Hebrew people from the land of Egypt. At the word of Moses, the water in the rivers, lakes and wells was turned into blood; hail and locusts destroyed all the plants; a three-day darkness covered the whole of Egypt. In spite of such misfortunes, Pharaoh still did not let the Hebrews go. Beginning with the second plague, every time he called Moses, he asked him to pray to the Lord to put an end to the misfortune and promised to let the Hebrews go. However, as soon as the plague passed, Pharaoh again hardened his heart and refused to let them go. Then the final, tenth and most frightful plague came down.

Before the tenth plague, the Lord commanded the Hebrews to choose for each family a **lamb** that was one year old, slaughter it, cook it and eat it with unleavened bread and bitter herbs, without breaking any of its bones. They were then to smear the blood of the lamb onto the lintel and doorposts of their houses. The Hebrews did as God commanded them.

On that night the angel of the Lord struck down all the first born (the first male offspring) in Egypt, from men to the cattle. He **passed over** only those houses on whose doors the mark with the blood had been made. Lamentation went up from every part of Egypt. Pharaoh summoned Moses and commanded him to leave Egypt with the Hebrew people as soon as possible.

Six hundred thousand men left with Moses, not counting women and children. Moses took with him the bones of Joseph, as Joseph himself had instructed in his last will. As soon as the Hebrews left Egypt, a pillar appeared before them in the form of a cloud in the daytime and fire at night. It guided them in their journey.

The day of the Hebrews' deliverance from bondage in Egypt forever remained in their memory. On this day the Lord established the main

The Old Testament Passover is a Prefiguration of the New Testament Pascha

feast of the Old Testament, which He called **Pascha**. The word **Pascha** means "passing by," "passover," or "deliverance from misfortune" — the angel of death passed over the Hebrew dwellings. Every year on the evening of this day the Hebrews slaughtered and prepared the Paschal lamb and ate it with unleavened bread. This feast lasted for seven days.

The Paschal lamb, by whose blood the first born of the Hebrews were delivered from death, foreshadowed the Saviour Himself, Jesus Christ, the Lamb of God, Who took upon Himself the sins of the world, Whose blood delivers all the faithful from eternal death.

The Old Testament Hebrew Pascha prefigured our New Testament Christian Pascha. In the Old Testament Pascha, death passed over the dwellings of the Hebrews. They were liberated from bondage in Egypt and given the Promised Land. Thus also in the Christian Pascha, **the Resurrection of Christ**, eternal death has **passed over** us. The Risen Christ, having freed us from the slavery of the Devil, has given us eternal life.

Christ died on the Cross on the day when the Paschal lambs were slain, and He rose immediately after the Hebrew Pascha. This is why the Church always celebrates the Resurrection of Christ after the Jewish Passover and calls the feast Pascha.

NOTE: See Exodus, chap. 4:29-31; chaps. 5-13.

CHAPTER 26

The Hebrews Pass Through the Red Sea and Other Miracles

The Hebrews, after their departure from Egypt, set out for the Red Sea. The Egyptians however, after burying their dead firstborn, began to regret having let the Hebrews go. Pharaoh, gathering all his army with chariots and mounted men, set out to pursue the Hebrews. He overtook them at the edge of the sea.

The Passing of the Israelites Through the Red Sea is a Foreshadowing of Holy Baptism

Upon seeing the terrible hosts of Pharaoh behind them, the Hebrews were terrified. Instead of supplicating God for help, they began to complain to Moses for bringing them out of Egypt. While offering them encouragement, Moses prayed in his heart to God and the Lord heard his prayer. The pillar of cloud stood behind the Hebrews and hid them from the Egyptians. The Lord said to Moses, "Take thy staff and stretch thy hand over the sea and divide it." Moses stretched his hand and staff over the sea. Then the Lord sent a strong east wind which blew all night, and the water drew back. The Hebrews went along the dry bottom as the water became like a wall on their right and left sides. When they heard movement in the Hebrew camp, the Egyptians chased the Hebrews into the depth of the sea and came as far across as the middle of the sea. At that time the Hebrews came out on the other side. Moses, again at God's command, stretched out his hand with his staff over the water. The water of the sea fell back into place and covered the entire army of Pharaoh and drowned the Egyptians.

Then the people of Israel, the Hebrews, with great joy sang a hymn of thanksgiving to the Lord God, their helper and protector.

Miriam the Prophetess, the sister of Aaron, took a tambourine in her hands, and all the women went out with their tambourines rejoicing. Miriam sang before them, "Sing unto the Lord, for He hath been greatly exalted; horse and rider hath He cast into the sea."

The Hebrews' passing through the Red Sea, whose waters separated and delivered the Hebrews from iniquity and bondage in Egypt, foreshadowed **Baptism** by which we are freed from the power of the Devil and slavery to sin.

At the time of the Hebrews' journey out of Egypt into the Promised Land, the Lord worked many other miracles as well. Once the Hebrews came to a place where the water was bitter. They could not drink it and complained against Moses. The Lord showed Moses a tree. As soon as they had placed the tree in the water, the water became sweet.

This tree which took the bitterness from the water was a foreshadowing of the **tree of the Cross of Christ**, which took away the bitterness of life — sin.

When the Hebrews had used up all the bread they had taken from Egypt, the Lord sent them bread from Heaven — manna. It looked like little white crumbs or pieces of hail and had the taste of bread with honey. This bread was called **manna**, because when the Hebrews saw it for the first time, they asked each other, *"man-na"* or "What is this?" Moses answered, "This is the bread which the Lord has given you for food." Manna covered the earth in the morning around the camp of the Hebrews, for the entire time of their journeying, on every day except the Sabbath.

When the Hebrews came to the place in the desert called Rephidim, where there was no water at all, they again began to complain against Moses. At God's command Moses struck a stone cliff with his staff and water flowed from it.

Manna in the desert and **water** from the stone cliff, which saved the Israelites from death, foreshadowed the true **food and drink** for us, which is the **Body and Blood of Christ**, which the Lord gives to us in Holy Communion, saving us from eternal death.

*The Food and Drink in the Desert is a Prefiguration of the Body and Blood
of Our Saviour*

In Rephidim, desert dwellers, the Amalekites, attacked them. Moses sent out Joshua, the son of Nun, with an army. Moses then went up to the nearest mountain with his brother Aaron and with Hur and began to pray, lifting both arms to Heaven, forming a cross.

Aaron noticed that when Moses held his hands up, the Hebrews prevailed over their enemies, but when he let them fall out of weariness, the Amalekites overcame the Hebrews. To ensure victory Aaron and Hur placed Moses on a stone and held his arms stretched out. Thus the Hebrews conquered the Amalekites.

Moses, when he was praying with his hands stretched forth, foreshadowed the victorious Cross of Christ, by whose power faithful Christians now conquer visible and invisible enemies.

In Rephidim Moses visited his father-in-law, Jethro, and brought him his wife and sons.

NOTE: Exodus, chaps. 14-18.

CHAPTER 27

God Gives the Law on Mt. Sinai

From the Red Sea the Hebrews continued to travel through the desert. They stopped at Mt. Sinai (Sinai and Horeb are the two peaks of one and the same mountain). Here Moses went up the mountain, where the Lord said to him, "Tell this to the sons of Israel, 'If you will hear My voice, you will be My people.' "

Moses Receives the Ten Commandments

When Moses came down from the mountain he told the people of God's will. The Hebrews replied, "We will be obedient and do everything the Lord said."

The Lord commanded Moses to prepare the people for the third day when God's Law would be made known. The Hebrews prepared themselves for the day by prayer and fasting.

On the third day, which was the fiftieth day from the Jewish Passover, that is, from the exodus of the people of Israel from Egypt, a thick cloud covered the top of Mt. Sinai. Lightning flashed, thunder resounded, and a loud blaring sound rang out. Smoke rose from the mountain, and the whole mountain violently shook. Amidst these awesome signs of His presence, the Lord delivered His laws in the form of Ten Commandments.

At God's command, Moses went up the mountain and stayed there forty days and forty nights without any food. God gave him two tablets or stone slabs, on which were written the Ten Commandments. In addition, the Lord gave Moses other church and civil laws. He also commanded him to build a tabernacle, a transportable temple of God.

After coming down from the mountain, Moses wrote down in books all these laws and everything that the Lord had revealed to him on Mt. Sinai. In this way we acquired the Sacred Scripture, or the Law of God.

The Ten Commandments, or precepts, which God gave His people,

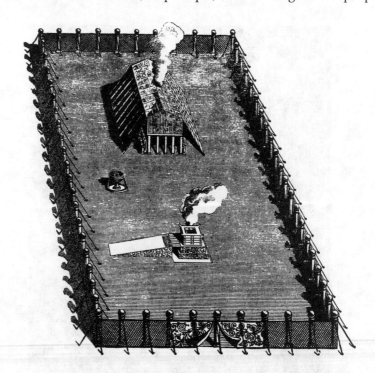

The Tabernacle

point out exactly what a man must do and what he must avoid if he wants to love God and his neighbor.

These are the commandments:

I. I am the Lord, thy God. Thou shalt have no other gods before me.

This commandment enjoins the love of God before everything else; apart from Him (God), worship will be rendered to no other divinity. Saints of God should also be honored, not as God is, but as people in whom God rejoices more than others, as our prayerful intercessors before Him.

II. Thou shalt not carve images, or fashion the likeness of anything in heaven above, or on earth below, or in the waters under the earth, to bow down and worship it.

Since everything on earth was created by God, then we should bow down to Him only and worship Him only. We must not make idols and bow down to them. When we venerate a holy icon, we must call to mind who is represented on it, and bow down to that person and not consider the icon itself as an object of worship.

III. Thou shalt not take the name of the Lord thy God in vain.

You must not utter the holy and great name of God idly, in empty chatter. Therefore, this commandment forbids swearing and uttering idle oaths.

IV. Remember to keep the Sabbath Day holy. There are six days for labor, for doing all the work you have to do. When the seventh day comes, it is a day of rest, consecrated to the Lord thy God.

Six days of the week a man must toil, labor and take care of everything he requires for his earthly life. The seventh day must be dedicated to God. That is, it must be kept separate for the Lord, to pray to Him, to read useful books for the glory of God, to help the poor and to do as many good things as possible for the Lord's sake. We must not be idle and by no means commit excesses. In the Old Testament, Saturday (the Sabbath) was thus celebrated. With us in the New Testament, in memory of the resurrection of Christ from the dead, Sunday is celebrated.

V. Honor thy father and thy mother. That is may be well with Thee, and that Thy days may be long upon the earth.

We must love and respect our parents, listen to their good advice, take care of them when they are ill, support them in their old age and when they need us. We must also be considerate of other relatives, old people, benefactors, teachers, spiritual fathers and superiors. In return for this God promises to prolong our earthly life and bless us.

VI. Thou shalt not kill.

Killing is understood to be not only the taking of one's own life or that of someone else, but also ordering or conspiring with others to commit murder. This commandment also forbids unrestrained anger and insulting one's neighbor by any abusive word. This commandment calls for a life of peace and harmony with one another, and also commands the gentle treatment of animals.

VII. Thou shalt not commit adultery.

By this commandment the Lord forbids a husband or wife to break mutual trust and love. God commands the single person to preserve purity of thoughts and desires. Gluttony, drunkenness and generally any excess or intemperance are also forbidden by this commandment.

VIII. Thou shalt not steal.

You should not take anything belonging to anyone else, openly or secretly, without asking. Do not cheat in business. In any transaction, calculate honestly. Do not conceal what you have found. Finish every task by the time you have promised and do it conscientiously.

IX. Thou shalt not bear false witness against thy neighbor.

This commandment forbids lying, slandering, speaking badly of people, judging them and also believing slanderers. This commandment enjoins that you keep your word honestly.

X. Thou shalt not covet thy neighbor's house, or set thy heart upon thy neighbor's wife, or servant or handmaid or ox or donkey or anything else that is his.

This commandment forbids the envy of another's property and enjoins that one be content with what one has. Unkind desires result from envy, and every unkind, wicked, evil thing results from unkind wishes.

Every person must know and fulfill the Law of God. He who keeps the commandments ensures for himself eternal salvation, as well as temporal well-being.

The feast of **Pentecost** (Old Testament) was observed in commemoration of the giving of the laws to Moses on Mt. Sinai.

NOTE: Exodus, chaps. 19, 20, 24, 32-34; and Deuteronomy, chap. 5.

CHAPTER 28

The Tabernacle

The Hebrew people made camp on Mt. Sinai for a whole year. At this time Moses, at God's command, constructed a tabernacle, or a transportable sanctuary, in the form of a tent. The tabernacle was constructed from expensive fabric and hung from poles. It had three sections: the **courtyard**, the **sanctuary** and the **Holy of Holies**.

Holy of Holies
Ark of the Covenant

The Sanctuary
Candlestick   Altar of incense   Table of showbread

The Courtyard
Water basin   Altar of sacrifice

The people came into the **courtyard** to pray. Here were placed the **altar**, on which sacrifices were made, and a copper **water basin**.

The priests came into the **sanctuary**, which had a table on which were **twenty loaves of bread**, a golden **seven-branch candlestick**, or lampstand, with seven lamps, and the **altar of incense**, that is, an altar on which the priests burned incense.

Into the **Holy of Holies**, which was separated from the sanctuary by a **curtain**, only the high priest could enter, and then only once a year. The **Ark of the Covenant** was placed in the Holy of Holies. The Ark of the Covenant was the name of a chest, made of wood and covered inside and out with gold, with a gold lid and with two golden images of the cherubim on it. The tablets with the Ten Commandments were kept in the Ark of the Covenant, as well as a chalice with manna, Aaron's rod, and later, the holy books. Along the two sides of the ark were two pairs of golden rings, into which gilded poles were inserted for carrying it.

When the tabernacle was ready, Moses consecrated it, together with all its fittings, with holy myrrh. While this was taking place, the glory of the Lord covered the tabernacle in the form of the cloud which accompanied the Hebrews on their journey. From this time on, the cloud was always over it.

For serving in the tabernacle, Moses, at God's command, appointed the tribe of Levi and ordained a high priest, priests, and Levites, assistants for the tabernacle.

Aaron, the brother of Moses, was made high priest. The priests were the four sons of Aaron; the other descendants of Levi were Levites. The high priest corresponded to our bishop, the priests to our priests and the Levites to our deacons and servers. God ordained that in the future the eldest of the line of Aaron would be high priest and the others of his descendants, priests.

The tabernacle represented the Church of Christ and also the **Mother of God**, Who, having contained God within Herself, was like the House of God.

NOTE: See Exodus, chaps. 25-34; Deuteronomy, chaps. 10,13,16; Leviticus, chaps. 1-7, 16, 23.

CHAPTER 29

The Forty-year Wandering of the Hebrew People
The Bronze Serpent

From Mt. Sinai the Israelites set out for the Promised Land, the land of Canaan. Along the way, time and again, they murmured in dissatisfaction and resentment against their journey. The Lord punished them for this, but on account of the prayers of Moses, pardoned them.

Even his own sister, Miriam, and Aaron reproached Moses for having married an Ethiopian and thus abusing his dignity as an envoy of God. Moses was the meekest of all the people and patiently bore their reproaches. The Lord punished Miriam with leprosy. Aaron, seeing that his sister had leprosy, said to Moses, "Because we have acted foolishly and sinned, do not deliver us into harm."

Then Moses ardently besought God to cure his sister, and the Lord healed her, but only after she had spent seven days in confinement outside the camp.

When the Israelites reached the border of the Promised Land, in the Paran desert, at God's command, Moses sent observers to survey the Promised Land. Twelve men were chosen, one from each tribe. Among those chosen were **Caleb**, from the tribe of Judah, and **Joshua**, from the tribe of Ephraim.

When the observers had traversed the whole country and surveyed it, they returned in forty days. They brought with them a branch of a grapevine they had cut off there with a bunch of grapes. The branch was so big that two men had to carry it on a pole. They also brought pomegranates and figs. All of them praised the fruitful earth. But ten of the twelve men who had been sent, all except Caleb and Joshua, stirred up the people, saying, "The nation that dwells upon it is powerful. They have very great and strong-walled towns. We will not go, for we shall not by any means be able to stand up against the nation, for it is much stronger than us. There we saw such giants before whom we were like grasshoppers."

Then the Israelites started to wail and murmur against Aaron and Moses, saying, "Why does the Lord bring us into this land, to perish by the sword? Our wives and our children shall be plunder for the enemy. Now then, it is better to return to Egypt."

Joshua, son of Nun, and Caleb persuaded the people not to go against the Lord's will, for the Lord Himself would help them to conquer the land which God had promised to their fathers. But the Israelites conspired to stone Moses, Aaron, Joshua and Caleb, appoint a new leader and turn back.

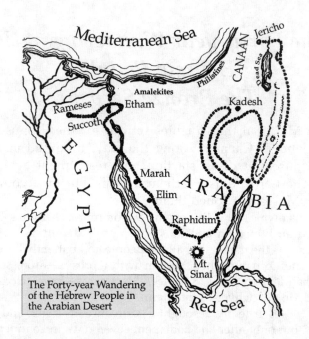

The Forty-year Wandering of the Hebrew People in the Arabian Desert

The Forty-Year Wanderings of the Israelites in the Desert

Then the glory of the Lord in the form of a cloud appeared in the tabernacle in front of all the people, and the Lord said unto Moses, "How long does this people provoke Me, and how long do they refuse to believe Me for all the signs which I have wrought among them? Say to them, 'As I live,' saith the Lord, 'surely as ye spoke into My ears so will I do to you. Your carcasses shall fall in this wilderness and all that murmured against Me shall not enter into the land for which I stretched out My hand to establish you upon it, except for Caleb and Joshua, the son of Nun. Tomorrow turn and get you into the wilderness by way of the Red Sea. And your little ones, whom ye said would become a prey shall inherit the land which you rejected. According to the number of the days during which you spied the land, forty days, you shall bear your sins for every day a year, unto forty years, that ye may know what it is to be abandoned by Me.' "

The ten spies, who by their unfavorable reports concerning the land had stirred up the people, were immediately stricken to death in front of the tabernacle. Having heard this condemnation of their sin, the Israelites did not wish to submit to the Lord's command and to go where they had been bidden. They said, "Behold, we that are here will go up to the place of which the Lord has spoken. We have sinned." This was as if to say, "We will now go and take the land. We repent of our sin. Why should we be punished for forty years?" Moses said to them, "Why do you transgress the word of the Lord? You shall not prosper." And he remained with the Ark of the Lord's Covenant in the encampment.

Against God's will, the Israelites dared to ascend the mountain, to the top where the Amalekites and the Canaanites were living. They were defeated and fled. So for forty years they wandered in the deserts of Sinai. Even during this time, however, the merciful Lord did not abandon them but visited them with many miracles.

Soon after being condemned to wander for forty years, a new revolt arose among the Israelites. Certain of them, whose leader was Korah, an elder of one of the tribes, were unhappy that the priesthood was a privilege only of the house of Aaron. Therefore the Lord punished them: the earth opened up and swallowed the rebels.

In order to end the arguments among the Israelites as to whom the

The Brass Serpent

priesthood belonged, Moses, at God's command, ordered that all the elders bring their staffs and place them for the night in the tabernacle. The next day everyone saw that the rod of Aaron had blossomed, shooting buds, flowering, and bearing almonds. Everyone then recognized Aaron as the high priest. At God's command, the rod of Aaron was placed in front of the Ark of the Covenant.

On another occasion, because of their murmuring against God, the Israelites were punished by a plague of poisonous snakes which bit the people and caused many to die. The Israelites repented and asked Moses to intercede for them before God. The Lord commanded Moses to make a bronze serpent and to place it on a pole. Whoever had been bitten, and with faith looked on the bronze serpent, remained alive.

This **bronze serpent** served as a **prefiguration of Christ the Saviour**. Christ was crucified on the Cross for all our sins. Now we, looking upon Him with faith, are healed of our sins and saved from eternal death.

During the forty-year wandering, all the adult Israelites who had come out of Egypt died, except for Joshua and Caleb. A new generation grew up which was destined to enter the Promised Land. Moses died in the last year of their wandering. Before his death, he appointed Joshua, son of Nun, as leader to replace him.

NOTE: See Numbers, chaps. 11-14, 16-17, 21:4-9 and Deuteronomy, chap. 1:19-46.

We Look to Christ for Forgiveness of Our Sins

CHAPTER 30

The Entry of the Israelites into the Promised Land

The Lord helped Joshua lead the Hebrew people into the Promised Land. When they entered this land, the Israelites had to cross the Jordan River. At God's command, Joshua told the priests to take the Ark of the Covenant into the river.

No sooner had they wet their feet in the water than the river parted. The water that flowed from the upper reaches of the river came to a stop

The Walls of Jericho Miraculously Fall

like a wall, and the lower part of the river flowed down to the sea and all the people crossed over the dry river bed.

After crossing the Jordan River, it was necessary to capture the city of Jericho, which had very high and strong walls. Joshua, by God's command, ordered the people, with the priests in front with the Ark of the Covenant, to walk around the city for seven days: once a day for six days, and on the seventh day, the ark was to be carried around seven times. After this, the walls of Jericho crumbled to their foundations at the sound of the priests' trumpets and the loud cries of all the people. In this way the Israelites took the city.

A great battle with the people of the land of Canaan took place by the city of Gabaon. The Israelites defeated their enemies and put them to flight while God rained stones from heaven on those who were fleeing, so that more perished from the stones than from the swords of the Israelites. The day was coming to an end, but the Israelites had not yet routed their enemies. Joshua then prayed to God and cried out aloud before the people, "Sun, stand still, and moon, do not move..." And the sun did stand still, and night did not come until the Israelites had defeated their enemies.

With God's help, in six years Joshua conquered the entire Promised Land and divided it by lot among the twelve tribes of Israel. The two sons of Joseph, Manasseh and Ephraim, received the portions of Levi and Joseph. The tribe of Levi served at the tabernacle and was supported by the tithes (ten percent of the income) collected from the people.

Before his death, Joshua commanded in his last testimony that the Israelites firmly preserve the faith in the true God and serve Him in purity and sincerity.

NOTE: See the Book of Joshua and Deuteronomy, chap. 27.

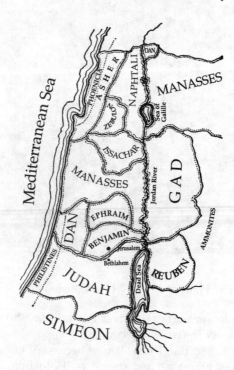

The Division of the Promised Land Among the Twelve Tribes

Discussion Of the Miracle Of Joshua

The account in the Holy Bible of Joshua stopping the sun's course is a favorite target for attacks and arguments on the part of atheists. However, new studies and discoveries of science, as well as archaeological investigations carried out in Mesopotamia confirm the indubitable historical veracity of all Biblical events.

A well known English scholar and archaeologist, **Arthur Hook,** touching on the question of Joshua's miracle, says, "We must first make it clear that there is no room for raising or stating the question of **whether God could perform such a miracle**; the question is rather, **did God perform it.**... If someone says to me that miracles are impossible, he invites me to accept a theory that He who created the universe did not have the power to later use a part of His own creation for His own ends; in other words, He who **created** the whole cannot **change** a part of it.

"In a careful study of the text, we discovered that there are several important thoughts that we can use as data from an astronomical point of view. This is as follows: for a man standing on the road leading to Mount Oronin, the sun was visible over Gabaon while the moon was over the valley of Aelon, at the same time a hail of great stones fell from heaven between **Mt. Oronin and Azeca**, and the day was lengthened by **almost** twenty-four hours.

"Let us now turn our attention to Joshua's words in his prayer. In it we find that his request was literally the following: "Sun, be silent over Gabaon." Here is used the Hebrew word *danam* which means, to be silent or inactive. Thus for example, in Psalm 30:12 (KJV), we read: *To the end that my glory may sing praise to thee, and **not be silent*** (danam). It is precisely this word that is used in the Hebrew original, in all three cases of the above quoted saying of Joshua, where we read: 'Stand,' 'stop,' or 'stood still.'

"Science has proved that light has vocal characteristics. In other words, it has a fast vibration or oscillation in the etheric waves, which itself produces light and gives rise to a special sound, although our ears do not have sufficient sensitivity to hear it. Many scholars are of the opinion that the action of the sun on the earth makes the latter revolve around its axis.

"So as to prolong the day according to Joshua's desire, the revolution of the earth around its axis — if this theory is taken as correct — would have had to be delayed to some extent. This occurrence could have taken place as a result of the neutralization or the reduction, to some degree, of the counteraction in the process of the influence of the sun on the earth.

"From this it is clear that Joshua's words are in exact accord with the findings of modern science: 'Sun, be still.'

"If therefore the influence of the sun was temporarily reduced, the earth would have had to revolve a little more slowly, and the day would have been longer. The great astronomer Newton has proved how easily the rotation of the earth could have been slowed down and be completely unnoticed by its inhabitants.''

Then A. Hook reports that one experienced scholar in Copenhagen told him that he had a theory concerning "huge stones" which fell from heaven and threw the Amorites into confusion. He assumed that by stones was meant a tail or a certain part of a comet which passes close to the earth. This scholar expressed his belief that if an investigation of the indicated place were to be undertaken, stones of meteoric origin would be found.

Very likely, we have here the explanation of the whole miraculous event. It is well known that heavenly bodies display characteristics of mutual magnetic attraction, and it is not groundless to assume that the approach of a big comet into the sphere of the influence of the earth could, to a significant extent, be a hindrance to the action of the sun on the earth.

Could we be talking about counter-attraction? "I think," said A. Hook, "that not one scholar would tell us that could not be. But in any

Joshua

case, it is wonderful that this rain of meteoric stones, which could perfectly well be the tail of some huge comet, had to coincide with the interruption in the process of the earth's turning on its axis."

"The scholar Manuel Velikovsky solidly maintains that the comet which approached the earth became the planet Venus. He testifies that the ancient Hindu documents and also the Egyptian written language, having known of the existence of planets and belonging to the fourth millennium B.C., do not mention Venus. On the other hand, Babylonian writings, dating to 1000 B.C., speak of the appearance of a new planet as 'a bright luminary, joined to other luminaries.' From this time on, in astronomical works, the planet Venus begins to figure.

"Astronomy demands facts for everything described in the Book of Joshua, and history confirms that this actually took place.

"Professor Totten in America very carefully investigated this subject from an astronomical point of view and published the results in a mathematical calculation. He shows that only once were the sun, moon and earth in positions similar to that described in the Book of Joshua. Working by his calculations which covered the period from our time to the time of Joshua, the professor finds that it is impossible not to come to the conclusion that one whole day, twenty-four hours, was added to world history.

"E. Mander, a scholar in the Royal Observatory in Greenwich, which is a marvelous center of astronomical science and research, also published a study on this subject. He determined the time of day when this miraculous occurrence took place, after determining the exact spot where Joshua was at that time.

"But this is still not all! We should turn our attention to the construction of the Biblical text: *So the sun stood still in the midst of heaven, and hasted not to go down about a whole day* (Joshua 10:13). The calculations of Prof. Totten establish that, although in world history exactly twenty-four hours somehow were added, yet in the time of Joshua it was only a matter of **23 hours 20 minutes**, as it is written in Scripture — *about a whole day.*

"Consequently, for the mentioned twenty-four hours required by astronomical calculations, there is a gap of forty minutes. Here we again have an example of the exactness of Holy Scripture. In the **Second Book of Kings, 20:8-11**, we read that at the request of King Ezekias, the Lord gave a sign through the Prophet Isaiah: 'the shadow on the sundial turned back ten degrees.' Ten degrees is exactly equal to forty minutes. These forty minutes, exactly to the minute, complete the twenty-four hours mysteriously added in the history of our planet, about which Prof. Totten spoke.

"Let us now look at what history says about Joshua's lengthening of a day," says the scholar A. Hook.

"There are three ancient eastern civilizations which have preserved their historical facts. These are the Greeks, Egyptians and Chinese. They all have legends about one unusually long day. The Greek Herodotus, who was called 'the father of history,' in 480 B.C. recounted that some

Egyptian priests showed him notes about the lengthening of one day by much more than twenty-four hours. In ancient Chinese records, it is directly asserted that an event happened in the reign of Emperor Io, and in Chinese genealogical lists it is pointed out that this emperor reigned in China in the time of Joshua.

"Lord Kingsbury, after making a special investigation of primitive Indians in America, found that the Mexicans, who achieved a high level of civilization a long time before America was discovered by Europeans, had a legend that 'the sun stood still' a whole day and this was in that year which they call 'seven rabbits.' The year of the seven rabbits exactly corresponds to that time when Joshua with the Israelites conquered Palestine.

"In this way we have independent proofs of the truth of the Biblical narrative not subject to any doubt, from the Greeks, Egyptians, Chinese and Mexicans. It is impossible not to accept the confirmation of such a host of witnesses as the absolutely last word.

"The scholar M. Velikovsky says that Finnish, Japanese, Peruvian and other legends corroborate this.

"However," A. Hook states, "one person told me after my lecture on this subject 'As far as this phenomenon is concerned, I must submit to the verdict of science, but I cannot admit that all this happened **only by the prayers of one man**.'

"Very likely this can also confuse others. Therefore I take the opportunity to note that this miracle sheds its wonderful light on the mystery of active prayer.

"God, of course, knew from the beginning that this event had to take place, but He also knew that Joshua had to pray. Joshua being in contact with God, as His worker (cf. II Cor. 6:1), was impelled to pray that his plans turn out to be in conformity with the designs of God. Prayer was a link between Joshua and the sublime occurrence which God had just intended to take place. If Joshua had not had any connection with God, he probably would have prepared his troops for a night attack and in that case, a lengthened day would have been disastrous for him.

"God's works are being accomplished around us and in any one of His innumerable means He can always adapt to any of our needs (Phil. cf. 4:19). God accomplishes this not by means of an alteration in His wise plans, but by inducing us, if we *are led by the Spirit of God* (Rom. 8:14), to adapt our deluded 'ego,' and alter our unreasonable actions to agree with the predetermined and divinely perfect intentions of the Creator. Then we receive the answer to our prayers. Experience has shown that people who have most completely surrendered themselves to God and with active preparedness have abandoned their own plans for the sake of God's plans always have their prayers answered, and these answers almost border on miracles." These are the words of the great scholar and archaeologist, Professor Arthur Hook.

(Compiled mainly from the book *The Trustworthiness of Biblical Miracles*, A. Hook and others).

CHAPTER 31

Judges

After the death of Joshua, the Israelites, surrounded by pagans, often forgot God and began to worship idols and indulge in vices. For this, God more than once deprived them of His help and turned them over to the power of the neighboring pagan people. This misfortune brought the Israelites to their senses and forced them to bring their minds back to God again. When they repented, the Lord sent them deliverers who liberated them from the enemy and ruled over them. These chosen ones of God were called judges. In all, the Israelites had fourteen judges.

Gideon

Amongst the judges Gideon is famous because, with few troops, but with God's help, he delivered the Israelites from the enemy Midianites, who oppressed the Israelites for seven years. The Israelites had to hide from them in gorges and fortifications. Such a misfortune forced the Israelites to convert and turn to God. Then the merciful Lord sent them a deliverer in the person of Gideon.

One day Gideon prepared to flee from the enemy and threshed the wheat in order to have bread for the road. At that time an angel of the Lord appeared to him and commanded him to gather his troops against the enemy. Gideon, fulfilling the command of God, began to gather his forces and collected thirty-two thousand soldiers. After this Gideon turned to the Lord with a request to give him a sign that the Lord would in fact use him to serve the Hebrew people. Gideon prayed thus, *If there is dew on the fleece alone, and it is dry on all the ground, then I shall know that Thou wilt deliver Israel by my hand* (Judges 6:37).

Gideon's prayer was heard. On the next day, having got up early, Gideon began to press the fleece and pressed out of it a whole cup of water, as it was covered with dew.

Then again Gideon turned to the Lord with a prayer: *Lord, let not Thine anger be hot against me, let me speak but this once: ...let it be dry only on the fleece and upon all the ground let there be dew* (Judges 6:37-40).

The Lord heard Gideon's second prayer and did so that night. Only the fleece was dry, and there was dew on all the ground.

Then the Lord said to Gideon, *The warriors that are with thee are too many. I will not give the Midianites into their hands, lest Israel vaunt themselves before Me, saying, 'My own hand hath saved me'* (Judges 7:2). Then the Lord commanded Gideon to let all those go home who were fearful. Twenty-two thousand returned, and ten thousand remained with Gideon.

The Lord again said to Gideon, "The people are yet too many," and He commanded Gideon to bring them to the water. At God's direction, Gideon separated those who drank the water by drawing it up with a cupped hand, from those who drank straight with the mouth as they bowed down to the water. There were 300 men who drank with a cupped hand. The Lord then said to Gideon, "By the 300 men that drank from the hand will I save you."

Gideon took with him the 300 soldiers, provisions, and trumpets and those that remained were sent home.

That night God led Gideon on a visit to the Midianite camp. The Midianites and the Amalekites had settled in the valley in numbers like grasshoppers; their camels were innumerable. There were as many as the sand by the seaside. Gideon, with his servant Phurah, made his way to the Midianite camp and heard one man tell another his dream, that a cake of barley bread tumbled into the Midianite camp, rolled up to a tent and hit it so that the tent fell, toppled over and crumbled.

To this the other soldier answered, "This is nothing else save the sword of Gideon; for into his hand hath God delivered Midian and all the host." And Gideon took heart.

Having returned to his camp, Gideon woke up his troops and gave each man a lamp within a pitcher and a trumpet. He divided them all into three companies and told them to surround the enemy camp and to do whatever his company did and to shout, "The sword of the Lord and of Gideon."

When everyone had taken his place, Gideon ordered his company to break the pitchers and with their lamps shining, to blow on their trumpets and cry, "The sword of the Lord and of Gideon." Both the other companies did this as well.

Such fear and terror came over the Midianites that in their great confusion and in the darkness they began to kill each other, and finally they turned in flight. Gideon completely routed them, and with a huge plunder returned home victorious.

After this victory the Israelites offered Gideon and his descendants royal power over them, but he refused it and said, *I will not rule over you neither shall my son rule over you: the Lord shall rule over you* (Judges 8:23).

Samson

The judge **Samson** was famous for his unusual and supernatural strength. Even from his birth, at the instruction of an angel of God, he was consecrated by his parents to God, and as a sign of this he could not

Samson Perishes

cut his hair. One day in a field a young lion attacked him. Samson grabbed the lion by the jaws and tore it to pieces, as if it were a baby goat. Many times, the Philistines, the enemies of the Israelites, attempted to seize him, but always unsuccessfully. Once he tore off new strong ropes with which he was bound. Another time, with an ass's jaw bone he massacred a thousand Philistines. A third time he carried away on his shoulders the gates of the Philistine city, Gaza, in which they wanted to hold him captive. Finally, a Philistine woman named Delilah, with whom he fell in love, having found out that his strength and power were contained in the long hair on his head, cut off his hair while he was asleep and handed him over to the Philistines. They took him, put out his eyes and imprisoned him in a dungeon. Having fettered him with two bronze chains, they forced him to work for them. In the meantime, the hair on Samson's head began to grow back, and at the same time his strength began to return, since his soul was cleansed by repentance for his delusions. One day the Philistines brought Samson out during a festival for general reviling in their pagan temple, and they made sport of him. Samson asked the boy who was leading him by the hand, to take him to the two columns on which the whole building rested, so that he could lean against them. Having prayed to God, he pushed against the columns with his hands and dislodged them from their place. The building collapsed. All the Philistines who were there were buried under the ruins of the building, and Samson himself with them.

Samuel

The Prophet **Samuel**, from the tribe of Levi, was the last judge of the Hebrew people.

For a long time Samuel's parents did not have any children. One day, Samuel's mother, Anna, during ardent prayer before the tabernacle, made a vow to God that if she were to bear a son she would consecrate him to the Lord. Anna's prayer was heard, and in a year she bore a son. Anna called him **Samuel**, which means **"obtained from God."**

When Samuel was a youth, his mother took him to the tabernacle and gave him over to the high priest Eli for the service of God. The high priest Eli was also at that time a judge of the Israelite people.

The high priest Eli had two sons, Hophri and Phineas, who were priests of the tabernacle, but they were depraved people. They celebrated the service to God without reverence and corrupted the people with their misbehavior. Eli saw Samuel's piety and appointed him to serve in the tabernacle.

Samuel always slept inside the tabernacle, not far from the place where Eli slept. Once Samuel heard a voice in a dream, which called to him, "Samuel, Samuel!"

Samuel immediately ran to Eli and said, "Here I am; you called me."

Eli replied, "I did not call you. Go back to sleep."

Samuel went and lay down, and again the voice called him, "Samuel, Samuel!" A second time Samuel went to Eli, but Eli again replied that he had not called him.

When this was repeated a third time, Eli understood that the Lord was calling the boy and said to him, "Go back to sleep. If the voice again calls you, say, 'Speak Lord, for Thy servant heareth.' "

Samuel went to sleep and again heard the voice calling him. Samuel replied as Eli had taught him. Then the Lord revealed to Samuel that the whole house of Eli would perish because Eli knew how impiously his sons acted, and he did not control them.

The next day Samuel passed on to Eli what the Lord had said to him. Eli obediently accepted the prediction. Soon Samuel's prediction was fulfilled.

The Philistines attacked the Israelite troops and killed them. Then Eli, at the request of the Israelite elders, sent the Ark of the Covenant to the camp with his sons, the priests Hophri and Phineas. But the ark did not help the Israelites. They again were massacred by the Philistines. Hophri and Phineas were killed, and the ark was captured. Thus the Lord showed the people that **holy things do not help those who do not respect the holy commandments of God.** When Eli found out that the ark was seized by the Philistines, he fell over backward from his seat and died.

The Ark of the Covenant, being greatly sacred to the Lord, did not long remain with the Philistines. God Himself convinced them by first smashing their idol Dagon, then sending the inhabitants of that town painful growths on the body. Finally, their fields were destroyed by mice. The frightened Philistines put the Ark of the Covenant in a new chariot, harnessed to it two young cows and let it go out of their land. The cows, without being driven, went by themselves to the Israelite land. The Israelites met the Ark of the Covenant with great joy.

After the high priest Eli, the Prophet **Samuel** was appointed judge of the Israelite people. Samuel governed the people not only as a judge but also as a prophet of God. He persuaded the Hebrew people to destroy all pagan idols, such as they had, to pray to God for forgiveness, and to fast. All the people repented and said, "We have sinned before the Lord." By Samuel's prayers the Lord saved the Hebrews from the Philistines. Samuel was strict and just and enjoyed great respect and love from everyone. He governed the people for forty years. In his old age he transferred his authority to his two sons, who accepted presents and judged unfairly. The impatient Hebrews began to ask Samuel to put a king over them, such as other nations had. Samuel tried to persuade the people to remain with their former form of government, but he was unsuccessful. Then Samuel prayed to the Lord, and the Lord said to him, "Listen to the voice of the people in everything that they say to you, for they did not reject you, but they rejected Me as a ruler over them." Then the Lord said that He warned the Israelites that a king would force all the people to serve him, would take the best land for himself, and they would have to give up everything to the king. The people did not heed Samuel's warning and said, "No, let a king rule over us, and we will be like other nations."

At God's command, Samuel anointed **Saul** as king, having poured on his head the consecrated oil, and then the Holy Spirit came down on Saul, and Saul received from above the power to rule the people.

Notes: See the Book of Judges and I Samuel, chaps. 1-10:1-16.

CHAPTER 32

The Story of Ruth

In the time of the judges, the neighboring pagan peoples were constant enemies of the Israelites. There were occasions though when several pagans from these people accepted faith in the true God, and then the Israelites considered them as their fellow-tribesmen. Such a person was the Moabite Ruth. This is her story.

Ruth

In Bethlehem, Judah, lived a man, whose name was Elimelech, with his wife Naomi. They had two sons, Mahlon and Chilian. During the famine Elimelech was obliged to move with his family to the land of Moab. There Elimelech soon died. His sons married the Moabites Orpah and Ruth, and after living with them not more than ten years, they both died. The widow Naomi remained with her daughters-in-law.

When Naomi heard that the Lord had sent a rich harvest to the Israelite land, she decided to return to her homeland. She and both her daughters-in-law went.

On the way Naomi began to urge them to return home, saying to them, "Go, return each of you to your mother's house. May the Lord grant you mercy for the way you dealt with the dead and with me," and she kissed them. The daughters-in-law sobbed and cried and did not want to leave her, but one of them, Orpah, with tears, obeyed Naomi and returned home.

But Ruth said, "Whither thou goest, I will go, and where thou lodgest, I will lodge; thy people shall be my people and thy God my God. Where thou diest, will I die and there will I be buried."

Naomi and Ruth, coming to the land of the Israelites, settled in the town of Bethlehem and lived on the wheat which Ruth picked up from the harvested fields. This was enough for sustenance, since it is written in the Law of God, *And when ye reap the harvest of your land, thou shalt not wholly reap the corners of thy field, neither shalt thou gather the gleanings of thy harvest; thou shalt leave them for the poor and the stranger* (Lev. 19:9-10).

The Lord God rewarded Ruth for her attachment and respectfulness towards her mother-in-law. The Israelites had a law: if one of them died, not leaving children, then the nearest relative had to marry the widow of the person who died, and the children from this marriage were considered the dead man's children. This law was called the Levinite Law.

At this time in Bethlehem there lived a rich man, Boaz, a relative of Ruth's dead husband. According to Levinite Law, Boaz married the poor Moabite Ruth. When a son was born to them, Obed, women said to Naomi, "Blessed be the Lord, Who hath not left thee this day without a kinsmen, that his name may be famous in Israel." Naomi rejoiced and was Obed's nurse.

In fact Obed's name was glorified in Israel, for he was the father of Jesse, the father of King David.

Note: See the Book of Ruth.

CHAPTER 33

Saul, First King of the Israelites

Saul was the son of a distinguished Jew by the name of Kish, from the tribe of Benjamin. He was tall, among the people he was a whole head higher, and no one of the Israelites was more handsome than he.

Soon after Saul was anointed, Samuel called the people together to elect a king. Lots were cast. The lot fell on Saul, and he was declared king. The people, admiring his height and beauty, cried out, "Long live the King!"

When Saul was made king, Samuel said to all the people: *If ye fear the Lord and serve Him and hearken to His voice and do not resist the mouth of the Lord, and ye and your king that reigns over you follow the Lord, it will be well with you. But if ye do not hearken to the voice of the Lord, and ye resist the mouth of the Lord, then shall the hand of the Lord be upon you and upon your king* (I Samuel 12:14,15).

Saul, in the first years of his reign, acted according to God's will, showing himself worthy of having been chosen. He gained for himself the people's love by many victories over the enemy. But when he stopped carrying out God's commands, having become presumptuous, the Spirit of God left him and Saul became gloomy and cruel.

Samuel grieved over Saul. The Lord said to him, "How long dost thou mourn for Saul? Go to Bethlehem, to Jesse, for I have seen among his sons a king for me." Samuel went to Bethlehem and at God's direction anointed David, the son of Jesse, from the tribe of Judah, to be king. The Spirit of God descended on David. David was the younger son of Jesse, blond, with beautiful eyes and a pleasant face. He was agile and brave, had a gentle and kind heart and was famed for his fine playing on the harp.

Saul was sick at heart and depressed from the action of an evil spirit. He was advised to divert himself with music, and he was told that in the town of Bethlehem at the house of Jesse was Jesse's son, David, who could play the harp well. David was summoned to the palace. When he came and played on the harp, Saul became better and more cheerful. Then the evil spirit left him.

Note: See I Samuel, chaps. 10:17-27, 11-16.

David's Victory Over Goliath

Once, during the reign of Saul, a battle took place between the Israelites and the Philistines. When the forces attacked each other a giant by the name of Goliath appeared from the Philistine camp. He shouted to the Israelites, *Why are ye come forth to set yourselves in battle array against us? Choose for yourselves a man, and let him come down to me. And if he will be able to fight against me and shall smite me, then we will be your servants, but if I should prevail and smite him, ye shall be our servants, and serve us* (I Sam. 17:8,9). For forty days, in the morning and the evening, this giant appeared and laughed at the Israelites, reviling the army of the living God. King Saul promised a huge reward to anyone who could defeat Goliath, but no one of the Israelites was of a mind to set himself against the giant.

At this time David came to the Israelites' camp to visit his older brothers and brought them food from their father. Having heard what Goliath said, David volunteered to fight with this giant and asked the King to give him permission.

But Saul said to him, "Thou art a mere youth, and he a man of war from his youth."

David replied, "Thy servant was tending the flock for his father, and when a lion came and a she-bear and took a sheep out of the flock, then I went forth after him and smote him and drew the spoil out of his mouth. And as he rose up against me, then I caught hold of his throat, and smote him and slew him. The Lord Who delivered me out of the paw of the lion and out of the paw of the bear, He will deliver me out of the hand of this uncircumcised Philistine."

Saul agreed and said, "Go, and the Lord be with thee."

David placed five smooth stones in his shepherd's bag, took a sling, and went out against Goliath. Goliath looked at David, who was very young, with contempt, and mockingly said, "Am I as a dog, that thou comest against me with a stick and stones?"

David replied, *Thou comest to me with sword and with spear and with shield, but I come to thee in the name of the Lord God of hosts, of the army of Israel which thou hast defied this day. And the Lord shall deliver thee this day into my hand...and all the earth shall know that there is a God in Israel* (I Sam. 17:45).

When Goliath began to approach, David ran to meet him, laid a stone in the sling and hurled it at the giant. The stone hit him right on the forehead, and Goliath fell senseless to the ground. David ran up to Goliath, took Goliath's own sword and with his own weapon cut off his head. When they saw this, the Philistines, terror-stricken, took to their heels and the Israelites chased them to the very gates of their cities and killed many. Saul made David the military leader. Then he gave his daughter to him in marriage.

When Saul and David returned victorious, the Israelite women came out to meet them singing and dancing, and they cried, "Saul has

King David

smitten his thousands, and David his ten thousands.'' This was unpleasant for King Saul. He began to envy David's glory and pondered on killing him. David withdrew to the desert and hid from Saul until his death.

    Note: See I Samuel, chaps. 16-31.

CHAPTER 34

King David

After the death of King Saul, David became the King of the Hebrew people. David, who was meek and pious, steadfastly believed in the true God and tried to do His will. He had endured much persecution from Saul and other enemies but did not become embittered, did not lift his hand against Saul, as he was the Lord's anointed, but placed all his hope in God, and the Lord delivered him from all his enemies.

But it came about that David fell into great sins. Then he repented to the depth of his soul for them. At night he washed his couch with tears, and afterwards improved himself and loved God more and more.

Thus once towards evening, King David went for a walk on the roof of his house and saw a very beautiful young lady. David wanted to have her as his wife. He found out that this lady was called Bathsheba and that she was the wife of Urias the Hittite (cf. II Sam. 11:2). At that time Urias was at war (the war then was with the Ammonites). David very much desired the death of Urias. The King could not get rid of this evil, sinful desire and ordered the military commander to place Urias in the front during the battle so that he would be killed. David's wish was fulfilled. Bathsheba, discovering that her husband was dead, wept for him.

When the time of mourning came to an end, King David sent for Bathsheba and took her into his house, and she became his wife. Thus King David accomplished a great evil, a two-fold sin, before the eyes of God. Soon Bathsheba bore a son, but David did not notice that he had committed a great sin in the eyes of God.

Then, at God's command, the Prophet Nathan went to King David and said, "There were two men in one city, one rich and the other poor. The rich man had very many flocks and herds, but the poor man had only one little ewe lamb, which he had purchased, and preserved and reared. It grew up with him and his children together, ate of his bread and drank of his cup, slept in his bosom and was to him as a daughter. Once a traveller came to the rich man, and he took not a lamb from his own flocks to slaughter for the traveller, but he took the poor man's lamb and slaughtered it for the guest."

King David became very angry with this person and said to Nathan, "As the Lord lives the man that did this thing shall surely die. And he shall restore the lamb seven-fold because he had no compassion."

Then Nathan said to David, "Thou art the man that has done this. Thus says the Lord God of Israel, 'I anointed thee to be king over Israel, and I rescued thee out of the hand of Saul. Why hast thou set at nought the word of the Lord? Thou hast taken the wife of Urias to be thy wife, and thou hast slain him with the sword of the children of Ammon. Now therefore the sword shall not depart from thy house for ever. I will raise up against thee evil out of thine own house.' "

Then David said to Nathan, "I have sinned against the Lord."

Nathan replied, "The Lord has taken away thy sin; thou shalt not die. Thy son that is born to thee shall surely die." With this the Prophet Nathan departed to his house.

David understood how evilly he had acted and deeply repented. With tears he prayed to God, and fasted and lay on the ground. On the seventh day the child died.

Great was David's sin, but his repentance was sincere and deep, and God forgave him. During the time of his repentance, King David wrote the **Psalm of repentance**, the 50th Psalm, which is a model of repentance and begins with these words, *Have mercy on me, O God, according to Thy great mercy; and according to the multitude of Thy compassions blot out my transgression. Wash me thoroughly from mine iniquity and cleanse me from my sin....*

For the great faith, meekness, and obedience of King David, the Lord blessed his reign and helped him in everything. He successfully waged wars with neighboring peoples.

David captured the city of Jerusalem and made it the capital of the Israelite kingdom. Instead of the dilapidated tabernacle of Moses, he placed in Jerusalem a new tabernacle and brought the Ark of the

The Ancient City of Jerusalem

Covenant to it with solemnity. David wanted to build a permanent temple, but the Lord said, *Thou shalt not build a house to my name because thou hast carried on great wars and hast shed blood abundantly. Thy son will build a house to My name, who will be king after thee* (I Chron. 22:6).

But at that time the Lord announced to David, **Thy kingdom will stand forever** (I Chron. 28:7). This meant that from his descendants would come the Saviour of the world, Christ, Who would reign forever. We know that Jesus Christ was often called the Son of David.

David wrote many sacred songs, or psalms, which he sang in prayer to God, playing on the harp or other musical instruments. In these hymns, David appealed to God, repented for his sins before God, celebrated the greatness of God, and foretold the coming of Christ and the suffering which Christ would undergo for us. Therefore, the holy Church calls Kind David a **psalmist** and **prophet**.

The Psalms of David are often read and sung in church at Divine Services. The sacred book in which all these psalms or songs are found is called the **Psalter**. The Psalter is the most frequently used book of the Old Testament. Many Christian prayers are composed with words from the psalms in this book.

David reigned for forty years and died a very old man. While still alive he appointed his son Solomon as his heir. The high priest Zadok and the Prophet Nathan anointed him King. Before his death David bequeathed to Solomon his wish that the Temple of God be built without fail.

Note: See II Samuel and I Chronicles.

CHAPTER 35

King Solomon

W hen Solomon ascended the throne, he brought a thousand offerings to God. One night after this God appeared to him in a dream and said, "Ask what you wish, and I shall give thee."

"Lord," replied Solomon, "thou hast made me King, and I am but a little child. Now give me wisdom and understanding, that I may govern this people."

Solomon's reply was pleasing to the Lord. And the Lord said: *Because you have not asked of Me long life, nor riches, nor victory over enemies, but have asked wisdom, in order to rule the people, I will give you wisdom so that there was none like you before, neither will be. And because you did not ask*

The Judgement of Solomon

for it, I will give you riches and glory. And if you will keep My commandments, I will also give you life (I Kings 3:5-9; II Chron. 1:7).

Solomon showed his wisdom above all in passing judgments. Soon after his accession, two women appeared before him for judgment. They lived in one house and each had a child. One night one of them crushed her child and laid it beside the other woman and took that woman's living child for herself. In the morning the women began to argue. "The living one is my son, and the dead one is thy son," each said. Thus they disputed before the King. Having heard them, Solomon decreed, "Fetch a sword."

A sword was brought to the King. Solomon said, "Divide the live child in two and give half of it to one, and half of it to the other."

At these words one of the women cried, "I pray thee, my Lord, give her the child, and in no wise slay it."

But the other said, "Let it be neither mine nor hers; divide it."

Then Solomon said, "Give the child to her that said, 'Give it to her, by no means slay it'; she is its mother."

The people heard about this and began to fear the King because everyone saw what wisdom God had given him.

Solomon expressed his wisdom both in ruling the people and in all other matters that concerned the king. His glory spread beyond the borders of the Israelite land to other neighboring peoples.

Fulfilling the wish of his father David, Solomon set about building the Temple of God in Jerusalem. A site for it was chosen on Mt. Moriah, which had been indicated to David and on which Abraham had brought Isaac to sacrifice. About 185,000 workers constructed the Temple in seven and a half years. It was built according to the model of Moses' tabernacle, and divided into the Holy of Holies, sanctuary and courtyard, but it was more spacious and more magnificent. The walls of the Temple were made of stone, on the outside they were covered with white marble and on the inside with gold. All the appurtenances of the Temple for religious services were made of gold.

When the Temple was ready, Solomon summoned all the elders and many of the people for its consecration. To the sound of trumpets and the singing of spiritual songs the Ark of the Covenant was brought in. The glory of the Lord, in the form of a cloud, filled the Temple so much that the priests could not continue the service. Then Solomon went up to his royal place, fell on his knees, and with uplifted hands prayed to God that in this place He would accept the prayers not only of the Israelites, but also of Gentiles. When he finished this prayer, fire came down from Heaven and consumed the sacrifices which had been prepared in the Temple.

Solomon's reign was peaceful and happy. People came from faraway lands to Jerusalem to see the King and hear his wisdom. The Queen of Sheba heard of Solomon's glory and came to put him to the test with riddles. After being convinced of his wisdom, she said: *Blessed be the Lord thy God, Who has taken pleasure in thee, to set thee upon the throne of Israel* (I Kings 10:9).

Before the end of his life, Solomon began to sin before God. He had many wives; there were pagans among them. For them, he built pagan temples and himself went there.

Then the Lord took away His blessing from Solomon, and riots and rebellions began against him among the Hebrew people. Solomon under-

Solomon's Temple

stood that this was God's punishment for his sins and began to repent. But his repentance was not so full from his heart as David's had been. Therefore, although the Lord forgave him and preserved his kingdom during his life, still He announced through a prophet that after the death of Solomon the Israelite kingdom would be split in two, and Solomon's son would inherit the smaller part.

Note: See I Kings, chaps. 3-11; I Chron., chaps. 22, 28, 29; II Chron., chaps. 1-9.

CHAPTER 36

The Division of the Israelite Kingdom Into Two: Judah and Israel

After Solomon's death, his son Rehoboam ruled. He spoke severely to the people. "My father made your yoke heavy, and I will add to your yoke. My father chastised you with whips, but I will chastise you with scorpions," (scorpions — whips at the end of which were clusters of threaded metallic nuts).

A large part of the Israelite kingdom then rose up against Rehoboam. Ten of the Israelite tribes separated from Rehoboam, chose for themselves Jeroboam, from the tribe of Ephraim, as King and made up a special kingdom which began to be called Israel. Two tribes, Judah and Benjamin, remained with Rehoboam and formed the Judean kingdom. The Israelites from this kingdom began to be called Jews.

In this way the Kingdom of Israel was divided into two: Judah and Israel. The city of Jerusalem remained the capital of the Judean kingdom, and the city of Samaria became the capital of Israel.

On great feasts the inhabitants of the Israelite kingdom went to worship God in the Temple in Jerusalem which did not please King Jeroboam. He was afraid that his subjects would become close friends with the Jews and would join the Judean kingdom. So that they would no longer go to Jerusalem, Jeroboam placed in two cities of his kingdom two golden calves and announced to the people, "There is no need for you to go to Jerusalem. Here are your gods which brought you out of Egypt." All the Israelite people began to worship these idols, instead of the true God, and after Jeroboam all the kings of the Israelite kingdom were godless, profane idolaters. They made the whole Israelite people impious.

In the Judean kingdom all the kings came from the line of David, but few of them were kind or pious. The people, imitating the impious kings, sinned much before God. To make the Hebrew people, both the Judeans and the Israelites, come to their senses, the Lord sent many **prophets**.

Note: See I Kings, chaps. 12-15; II Chron., chaps. 10-13.

CHAPTER 37

The Prophets

The prophets were people who, under the inspiration of the Holy Spirit, prophesied, that is, foretold what would be in the future, especially about the coming Saviour of the world. They announced the will of God, taught the people true faith and piety, and performed various signs and miracles.

They exposed the idolatry of the Hebrews and called them to repent. Some of them preached only orally, and others, in addition, left behind sacred books, written by them under the inspiration of the Holy Spirit.

The most famous of the prophets living in the Israelite kingdom were, Elijah, Elisha and Jonah, and of the prophets living in the Judean kingdom, Isaiah, Jeremiah, Micah, Ezekiel and Daniel.

The Prophet Elijah

The Prophet Elijah lived during the reign of the impious Israelite King Ahab, who worshipped the idol Baal and also forced the people to do so. Elijah came to Ahab and in the name of God announced to him, "Because of your godlessness, there will be neither dew nor rain during these years except by the word of my mouth."

So it came to pass. A terrible drought began. Even the grass died and there was a famine. Elijah, by God's will, settled in the desert by a stream where ravens brought him bread and meat, and he drank the water from the stream. When the stream dried up, God ordered the Prophet to go to the pagan town of Zarephath in Sidon to a poor widow and live with her. This widow, who lived with her son, had only one handful of flour and a little oil. Going to Zarephath, Elijah told her to bake bread for him and promised that the flour and oil would not diminish as long as the Lord did not send rain to the earth. The woman trusted the Prophet of God and did as he told her, her flour and oil did not diminish. Soon this widow's son fell ill and died. The Prophet Elijah for three days prayed to God for him and the boy came back to life.

The drought lasted for three and a half years. Elijah, at God's command, again came to Ahab and suggested to him that he gather the Israelite people on Mt. Carmel. When Ahab had assembled the people, Elijah said, "You are satisfied with being godless. Become acquainted with the true God. Come, let us offer sacrifice. You, to Baal, and I, to the Lord God, but let there be no fire put under it. Whoever sends down fire from Heaven to light the sacrifice, that will be the true God." All agreed.

The Prophet Elijah Fed by a Raven During the Drought

The priests of Baal were the first to bring sacrifice. They prepared an altar, put a calf on it and for a whole day hopped around and cried out around it, "Baal, Baal, hear us!" But there was no answer. Evening came. Then Elijah prepared an altar, dug a ditch around it, put firewood and the calf on the altar and told them to pour water on the sacrifice, so much so that the ditch was filled. Then Elijah turned to the Lord with prayer. Immediately fire from the Lord came down from Heaven, and burned not only the firewood and the sacrifice, but also obliterated the water which filled the ditch and the stones of which the altar was built. All the people fell on the ground in fear and cried out, "The Lord is the true God; the Lord is the true God!"

After this Elijah went up to the summit of the mountain and began to pray for rain. A wind blew from the mountain, revealing in the skies great clouds, and heavy rain began to fall.

Despite the miracles, Queen Jezebel, wife of Ahab, continued to per-

The Prophet Taken Up in a Fiery Chariot

secute Elijah for putting all the priests of Baal to death. Elijah hid in the desert since they sought to kill him. It seemed to him that he was the only believer in God and he lost heart. But the Lord reassured him, and appeared to him when Elijah spent the night in a cave on Mt. Horeb.

The voice of God said to him, "Elijah! Come and stand on the mountain in the sight of God." There blew a strong wind, which tore up the mountains and shattered the rocks, but the Lord was not in this wind. Then, there was an earthquake, but the Lord was also not in the earthquake. Then fire appeared, but the Lord was not in the fire. After all this there was the blowing of a calm wind, and in this was the Lord.

The Lord consoled Elijah and said that among the Israelites there were still 7,000 men who did not worship idols, and that after him He would raise up among them the Prophet Elisha, whom He commanded Elijah to anoint.

This appearance of the Lord showed Elijah that the Lord not only is a punishing and stern Judge, but a merciful Father. It also prefigured the coming to earth of Jesus Christ, Who would come not to judge and punish, but to forgive and save people.

Elijah, in accordance with God's direction, anointed Elisha as a prophet, who then became his disciple. Once when they were together, Elijah said to Elisha, "Ask what I shall do for thee before I am taken away from thee."

Elisha replied, "I pray thee, let a double portion of thy spirit be upon me."

Elijah said, "Thou hast asked a hard thing; nevertheless, if thou see me when I am taken from thee, then shall it be so unto thee; but if not, it shall not be so." They went on further. Suddenly there appeared a chariot of fire with horses of fire, and Elijah was taken up into Heaven in a whirlwind.

Elisha, seeing this, cried, "My father, my father, the chariot of Israel, and the horsemen thereof!"

These words of the Prophet Elisha meant that the holy Prophet Elijah, by his prayers, protected the kingdom of Israel from its enemies better than all the Israelite forces, the chariots and horses. At this time the mantle, that is, the outer garment of Elijah, fell at Elisha's feet. Elisha lifted this up and with it received the double gift of prophecy.

Note: See I Kings, chaps. 16-19; II Kings, chaps. 1, 2:1-15.

The Prophet Elisha

The holy Prophet Elisha was the son of a farmer named Shaphat (I Kings 19:19). God made the Prophet famous by many miracles.

After Elijah was taken up into Heaven Elisha had to cross the river Jordan. He struck the water with the mantle of Elijah. The water parted, and he crossed on the dry river bed.

When Elisha came to the city of Jericho, the inhabitants of the city said to him, "Our water is bad, and because of this the ground is barren." Elisha threw salt into the spring of water and the water became tasty and healthful.

Near the city of Bethel, Elisha saw children coming from the town who began to laugh at him and cry out, "Go away, thou baldhead, go away." He told them that for this disrespect to an elder they would be punished by God. At that moment two bears came out of the forest and tore to pieces forty-two of the children.

Once a poor widow came to Elisha. She was crying and said to him, "My husband is dead and left many debts. The creditor came to take my two sons to be servants."

"Tell me what hast thou in the house?" asked Elisha.

The woman replied, "Nothing, save a pot of oil."

Elisha said to her, "Go, borrow vessels for thyself from all thy neighbors, as many empty vessels as you can. And when thou art come in, thou shalt shut the door upon thee and upon thy sons, and thou shalt pour the oil into all those vessels."

The woman did this. The oil was poured until all the vessels were filled. She sold the oil, paid all the debts and there still remained enough money for her sons and her to live.

In the city of Shunem, a certain rich woman had a son. It came to pass that her son suddenly fell ill and died the same day. She went to Elisha and in despair fell at his feet. The Prophet came into the house where the child lay and for a long time prayed to God. The child came back to life.

The commander of the armies of the King of Syria, Naaman, was sick with leprosy. No one could cure him of this illness. Naaman's wife had a captive Jewish girl as a servant. Seeing the sufferings of her master she said, "O that my lord were before the Prophet of God in Samaria; then he would recover him from his leprosy."

Naaman went to the Prophet Elisha in the Israelite land. Elisha sent a servant to tell Naaman that he should wash seven times in the Jordan River. Naaman did as the Prophet ordered him and immediately became well. With rich gifts he returned to Elisha, but the Prophet took nothing from him.

When Naaman went home, Elisha's servant Gehazi caught up with him and took from him, in the name of the Prophet, silver and some clothes. Having hidden what he had received, Gehazi came to Elisha. "Whence comest thou, Gehazi?" Elisha asked him.

"Thy servant went no where," replied Gehazi.

Then the Prophet exposed his lie and said to him, "The leprosy of Naaman, besides his silver, shall cleave to thee." And Gehazi went out from Elisha, covered with leprosy.

Even after his death the Prophet Elisha performed a miracle. In the year after his death, a man was being carried past the cave in which Elisha was buried. But seeing their enemies, the men who were burying him hurriedly threw the dead man into the Prophet's cave. On falling, as soon as he touched Elisha's bones, he came to life and arose.

Note: See II Kings, chaps. 2-10; 13:1-21.

The Prophet Jonah

The Prophet Jonah lived after the Prophet Elisha. Once the Lord ordered him to go to the pagan city of Nineveh, the capital of the Assyrian empire, and to proclaim to the inhabitants of this city that the Lord would destroy them if they did not repent. But Jonah did not want to go and preach to the enemy of the Israelite people and did not obey the voice of God. He went on a ship which was heading for another country. But suddenly at sea a fierce storm arose. The ship was threatened with destruction, and everyone on it became frightened. The crew decided to cast lots to find out what had brought them such a calamity. The lots fell on Jonah. Jonah confessed his sin and said, "Yes, I have sinned in the

The Prophet Jonah and the Whale

face of the Lord! Cast me into the sea, and the sea shall be calm." When they threw him into the sea, the sea became quiet. By the will of God, **a huge fish** swallowed the Prophet, which in the Bible is called a huge whale. Jonah was in the belly of the whale for three days and three nights, praying to God for forgiveness. Here God revealed his wondrous power in a special way. He preserved him unharmed in the belly of the whale and forgave him.

In three days the whale threw up the Prophet, alive, onto the shore. After this Jonah went to Nineveh to fulfill God's will. A whole day he walked through the city and preached to everyone, saying, "In forty days, Nineveh shall be overthrown!" The inhabitants believed his words. They, together with the King, imposed a fast on themselves, began to pray and repent of their sins, and the Lord forgave them.

But Jonah murmured against such mercy of God and asked that God take his life. He probably thought that now he would be considered a false prophet.

This time the Lord brought Jonah to his senses. One night, in front of the tent that Jonah set up for himself near Nineveh, a big plant grew up and shaded him from the sun's intense heat. The next day though, a worm gnawed at this plant, and it dried up. Jonah very much grieved and felt sorry for the withered plant.

Then the Lord said to him, "Thou hadst pity on the plant, for which thou hast not suffered, neither didst thou cause it to grow. And shall not I spare Nineveh, the great city, in which dwell more than six score thousand persons that cannot discern between their right hand and their left hand; and also much cattle?"

The three-day stay of the Prophet Jonah in the belly of the whale and his miraculous salvation was a prefiguration of the three-day death and resurrection of Christ the Saviour.

Note: See Book of Jonah.

Discussion about Jonah's Three-day Stay in the Whale's Belly

"Superficial and unbelieving critics," says scholar Arthur Hook, "believe there are many obstacles to accepting that Jonah was in fact swallowed by a whale and that the Prophet spent three days and three nights in its belly and then was vomited out onto dry land.

"In the first place, not one person who believes in Christ can doubt what took place with the Prophet Jonah, for Christ Himself put the seal on this disputed subject when He said, *For as Jonah was three days and three nights in the whale's belly; so shall the Son of man be three days and three nights in the heart of the earth* (Matt. 12:40). Here Christ eliminates, at least as far as it concerned His disciples, the idea that the Book of the Prophet Jonah is an allegory, as critics like to assume. If it is said only in an allegorical sense that Jonah was in the whale's belly, then the conclusion follows that Christ's being in the heart of the earth in the course of three days and three nights also has only an allegorical significance. Here we have again an example of how the denial of the Old Testament paves the way for a denial of Christ Himself and His word"

To deny historicity to the Prophet Jonah is equivalent to a denial of all Scripture and this means repudiation of the faith. How can a person, after the innumerable failures of so-called 'scientific objections' be against the Bible? How many times have the refutations and sneers at the Bible by 'the wise men of this age' been turned back against them themselves. In fact, a simple acquaintance with the text of the original and some scientific knowledge give us the answer in many cases.

Everyone well knows that the text of the Bible was written in Hebrew. In Hebrew a whale is called *tannin*. In the Bible, however, the sea animal which swallowed Jonah is not called *tannin*, but *dag*, which means "big fish" or "monster of the deep."

For more than 1500 years the holy Church has testified to this by calling this creature which swallowed Jonah a "sea beast." For example, in the Irmos of the sixth ode of Friday's Canon of Matins, eighth tone, it is said, "Jonah, in the womb of a sea beast, stretches out his hands in the form of a Cross, thus clearly foreshadowing the saving Passion." In the sixth ode of the Canon of Matins for Tuesday, fifth tone, it is written, "As Thou hast saved the Prophet from the beast, O Lord, so, I pray, lead me up from the depths of the unconquered passions."

Science has pointed out to us that there exists a wide variety of types of whales. Thus, for example, there is a species of whales which have forty-four teeth in the lower jaw and reach 60-65 feet in length. However, they have a very small gullet, which may have given a basis for contending that Jonah could not be swallowed by a whale.

There is another form of whale, the "bottle-nosed" whale, which has a beak. Although it is a small whale, reaching up to thirty feet long, it has a rather large gullet and is fully capable of swallowing a man; but the Prophet could not have been swallowed by such a whale because it chews food and has teeth.

There are whales which do not have teeth, but are provided with "whalebones." Among such a type of whale there are whales which are called "fin-backs." These whales can be up to 88 feet long. The stomach of such a whale has from four to six chambers or compartments, each of which could easily contain a small group of people. This type of whale breathes air and has on its head a reserve air chamber which appears with the dilation of the nasal cavities. Before swallowing a very large object, the finback whale pushes it through to this chamber. If it happens that something too large is found in the head of this whale, then it will swim to the nearest land, lie in the shallow water and disgorge its burden.

The scholar Dr. Ranson **Garvey** testifies that his friend, in weight two-hundred pounds, crawled from the mouth of a dead whale into this air chamber. This scholar points out that a dog that fell from the side of a whale boat, after six days was found in the head of a whale, alive. From this account, it is evident that Jonah could remain in the 'womb,' that is, in the air chamber of such a whale, for three days and three nights and stay alive. The space in this chamber is equal to 686 cubic feet. Thus, from scientific data we can see that Jonah could have been swallowed by a whale.

Frank Bullen, the famous author of the work, *The Swimming of the Sperm Whale*, established that the sperm whale often, when it is dying, disgorges the contents of its stomach.

But the Biblical word *dag* refers to a "big fish." From this we can conclude that Jonah really was swallowed by a marine creature, by a huge fish. In that case we must consider the fish called "whale shark" or "bone shark."

This name, "whale shark," comes from the fact that it does not have teeth. The whale shark reaches seventy feet in length, and filters its food through huge plates in its mouth. This shark has a stomach large enough for a man to fit inside.

Concerning the fact that Jonah spent three days and three nights in the stomach of a big marine creature and stayed alive, we can first of all say, "With God everything is possible." It is interesting to recall the story in *Reader's Digest* about a sailor swallowed by a whale-shark. In 48 hours the shark was killed. When the whale-shark was opened up, imagine the surprise of all those who had gathered when they found a sailor alive, though in an unconscious state, after having been swallowed by this creature. In addition, the sailor had no after-effects of his stay in the stomach of the whale-shark except a loss of hair and a few blisters on his skin. He related that only fear gave him no peace while living in the whale's stomach. When he had come to consciousness and understood where he was, he again immediately lost consciousness.

"Recently," writes Fr. I.S., "in the Hawaiian islands Japanese fishermen killed a big white shark. In its stomach they found a full skeleton of a man. It turned out that this was a soldier, entered in the list of deserters, in the clothes of the style of the North American army."

Thus we see that Jonah could have been swallowed by a big fish even without violating the natural laws of nature. All nonsense and contradiction disappear. Surely and invariably the Word of God can never be found to be in contradiction with scientific truth. This was also established by the father of Russian science, **Lomonosov**.

It is necessary for us believers to say that it is quite obvious that the events which happened to the Prophet Jonah were undoubtedly the work of the power of God, Who, as Creator of the very laws of nature, has a free will to control them, when He finds it necessary, according to His all-powerful providential action.

The scholar and genius **Pascal** said, "The last step of reason consists in admitting the existence of many things which are outside the limits of our knowledge, and if reason does not accept this knowledge, it is absolutely weak." **Robert Mayer** said, "If superficial minds show off by denying the existence of something higher in the super-material and super-sensually perceived world, this pitiful denial by a few minds cannot be blamed on science."

(Compiled from the book *The Truth Of Biblical Miracles*, A. Hook and *Prophet Jonah And the Small Gullet Of the Whale* by Archpriest Paul Kalinovitch.)

CHAPTER 38

The Downfall of the Israelite Kingdom

God patiently, with long suffering, called on the Israelite people through many of His prophets, to turn from evil and come to believe in Him. But neither the kings nor the people listened to them.

Finally, when the people's evil deeds had reached the ultimate limits, the Lord withdrew from the Israelite kingdom and it perished. The Assyrian King Shalmaneser conquered and destroyed the Israelite kingdom. He sent a large part of the Israelite people to his own country. In their place he settled pagans from his own kingdom. These pagans assimilated with the Israelites who remained and formed a people who came to be called Samaritans, from the name Samaria, which was the main city of the destroyed Israelite kingdom.

The Samaritans spoke an impure Hebrew language. They accepted faith in the true God, but not completely, because they did not abandon their former pagan customs and they honored only one of the prophets, Moses. The Jews despised the Samaritans and would not sit with them at the table and even tried not to speak to them. The Israelite kingdom existed for 257 years.

Note: See II Kings, chap. 17.

The Judean Kingdom

After the collapse of the Israelite kingdom, the Judean kingdom existed for still another 100 years, since among the Judean kings there were a few pious ones. In addition, the people remembered God more than in the Israelite kingdom. The prophets sent by God to the Judean kingdom exposed the evil deeds of the Jews and foretold much about the coming of the Saviour to earth. The Prophet Micah foretold that the Saviour would be born in the city of Bethlehem (Micah 5:2). The Prophet Joel foretold the descent of the Holy Spirit on the apostles and all those who believed in the Saviour.

The Prophet Isaiah

Especially famous among the Jewish prophets was the Prophet **Isaiah**. Isaiah was a descendant of King David and a relative of the kings of the Jews. The Lord made him a prophet through an extraordinary vision. Isaiah saw the Lord sitting on a high throne. Around Him stood six-winged Seraphim, and they called out, "Holy, holy, holy is the Lord of hosts! The whole earth is full of His glory!" One of the Seraphim took with tongs a burning coal from the heavenly altar, touched Isaiah's lips and said, "Behold, thy sins are purged." After this the Lord ordered him to go and expose the unbelief and vices of the Jews.

The Prophet Isaiah foretold that the Judean kingdom would be destroyed by enemies, the Jews would be taken into captivity and then again would return to their homeland.

The Prophet Isaiah

With particular clarity Isaiah foretold that the Saviour, Christ, would come from the house of David, that the Saviour would be born from a virgin and would not be a simple man, but also God. *Behold, a virgin shall conceive, and bear a son, and shall call His name Immanuel* (Is. 7:14) which means, "God is with us."

He foretold that the Saviour would suffer and die for our sins. *But He was wounded for our transgressions, He was bruised for our iniquities: the chastisement of our peace was upon Him; and with His stripes we are healed...He was oppressed, and He was afflicted, yet He opened not His mouth: He is brought as a lamb to the slaughter, and as a sheep before her shearers is dumb, so He openeth not His mouth* (Is. 53:5, 7).

Isaiah also prophesied that the Saviour would be crucified with **evildoers**, and would be buried not with them, but in the tomb of a rich man. Through faith in Christ the Saviour, people would save themselves from eternal damnation. For the clarity of his predictions about Christ the Saviour, the Prophet Isaiah is called "**the Old Testament Evangelist.**"

At that time Isaiah was ardently exposing the wrongdoing of the Jewish King, Manasseh. The impious King placed altars to pagan idols in Solomon's Temple. However, at the end of Manasseh's life, after being taken captive and put in prison, he repented and asked God's forgiveness. Under the influence of their impious King, the Jewish people began to completely forget the true God. The Jews even stopped celebrating the Passover and other feasts established by Moses.

The holy Prophet Isaiah endured a martyr's death. For exposing the wrongdoing of King Manasseh, he was sawed in two.

Note: See II Kings, chaps. 16 and 18-23; II Chronicles, chaps. 28-35; Book of Isaiah and other prophets.

The Fall of the Judean Kingdom The Prophet Jeremiah

For a long time the Lord endured the sins of the Jewish people and awaited their repentance, but the people did not reform themselves. Through the Prophet Jeremiah God clearly foretold that for their evil deeds, the Jewish people would be subjugated and led into captivity by the Babylonians and that the Jews would be in captivity for **seventy years**.

At first, the Babylonian King **Nebuchadnezzar** (Jer. 37:1) subjugated the Jewish King, but he preserved Jerusalem and did not destroy all the Jewish kingdom.

The Prophet Jeremiah persuaded the Jews to submit to Babylon. He pointed out that the Babylonians had been sent against the Jews by God as a punishment for the sins of the kings and the people, and for their apostasy from the faith. He told them that the only way to rid themselves of the disaster was to repent, reform, and pray to God.

But neither the King nor the people listened to the Prophet and instead they started a revolt. Then the Babylonian King **Nebuchadnezzar** took Jerusalem, plundered it, set it on fire, and destroyed Solomon's Temple to the foundation. At that time the Ark of the Covenant was hidden in a cave by the Prophet Jeremiah.

All the Jewish people were taken into captivity (in 589 B.C.). Only the poorest Jews were left on their land to cultivate the vineyards and fields. The Prophet Jeremiah remained in Jerusalem. He grieved over the ungodliness of his people amidst the ruins of the city and continued to teach virtue to those inhabitants who stayed.

Note: See II Kings, chaps. 24-25; Book of the Prophet Jeremiah; II Chronicles, chap. 36:5-21.

The Babylonian Captivity

The Jews had a hard life in the Babylonian captivity, but the Lord did not abandon His chosen people in exile. So as to arouse repentance in the Jews and comfort them, the Lord sent to them His prophets during the captivity. The Prophet Ezekiel and the Prophet Daniel were particularly remarkable during this period.

The Prophet Ezekiel

Ezekiel was a contemporary of the Prophet Jeremiah. While in the Babylonian captivity, even before the final destruction of the Judean kingdom, he was called by God to be a prophet.

The Prophet Ezekiel was made famous by his prophecies about the **resurrection of the dead**, which simultaneously symbolically represented the restoration to freedom of the Jewish people.

The Prophet had a vision from the Lord. He saw a field strewn with men's bones.

God asked him, "Son of man, will these bones live?"

Ezekiel replied, "O Lord God, Thou knowest this."

The Lord said, "Prophesy upon these bones, and thou shalt say to them, 'Ye dry bones, hear the word of the Lord.' "

The Word of the Lord was as follows: *Thus saith the Lord to these bones; Behold I will bring upon you the breath of life and I will lay sinews upon you, and bring up flesh upon you, and will spread skin upon you, and will put My Spirit into you, and ye shall live; and ye shall know that I am the Lord* (Ezek. 37:3-6).

When Ezekiel prophesied, at God's command there was a noise and movement and the bones began to come together, each bone to its appointed bone. Ezekiel saw there were sinews on them, and flesh appeared, and skin covered them on top, but there was no spirit in them.

And the Lord said: Prophesy to the wind; prophesy, son of man, and say to the wind, 'Thus saith the Lord: Come from the four winds, and breathe upon these dead men, and let them live' (Ezek. 37:9).

The words, "**from the four winds**," mean that from four ends of the world (north, south, east and west) dead souls, wherever they might be, must gather in the field covered with spiritless bodies and come to life.

Ezekiel uttered the prophecy as the Lord commanded him, and the Spirit entered them and they came to life and stood on their feet.

The Lord said, *These bones are the whole house of Israel....Therefore prophesy and say, 'Thus saith the Lord: Behold I will open your tombs, and will bring you into the land of Israel. And ye shall know that I am the Lord, when I have opened your graves, that I may bring up My people from their graves. And I will put My Spirit within you, and ye shall live, and I will place you upon your own land; and ye shall know that I am the Lord'* (Ezek. 37:11-14).

This **great prophecy**, besides pointing to the restoration of the Is-raelite people, was given to us by God as a **graphic portrayal of the general resurrection of the dead** at the second coming of the Saviour, when, according to the all-powerful Word of God, all the bodies of dead people will unite with their spirits and come to life.

Note: See II Kings, chap. 25:27-30; II Chron., chap. 36:10-23; Ezekiel, chap. 37:1-14.

The Prophet Daniel

The Prophet Daniel was descended from the royal family. While still a young boy, he was taken prisoner to a Babylonian prison. In prison, by the will of King Nebuchadnezzar, Daniel was chosen with several other imprisoned youths of the children of Israel to serve in the King's palace. The King ordered that they be brought up in the palace, taught in various fields of knowledge and in the language of the Chaldeans. The King appointed them a daily provision of food from his own table. Among those chosen besides Daniel were **Ananias, Azarias, and Misael.**

Daniel and his three friends firmly kept faith in the true God. They did not wish to eat the King's meat in order to avoid being defiled by anything forbidden by the Law of Moses. They begged the prince of eunuchs to give them only bread and vegetables. The prince would not agree for fear they would lose weight, and the King would decapitate him. But Daniel asked him to do as they asked for ten days. When ten days had passed, Daniel and his friends not only did not lose weight, but they appeared fatter, more healthy and fairer than all the other children. After this they were not required to eat the King's food. For such strict observance of the Law, for their fasting and piety, God rewarded these young boys with great ability and success in their studies. In tests, they proved to be more intelligent and better than the others, and they were given positions in the King's palace. To Daniel, God gave the gift of interpreting dreams, as He had once to Joseph.

The rise of the Hebrew youths benefited the Jews in captivity. The piety of the youths served to defend the Jews from oppression and to better their life in captivity. Furthermore, through them the pagans were able to come to a knowledge of the true God and to glorify Him.

One day Nebuchadnezzar had an unusual dream, but when he awoke in the morning, he could not remember it. This dream greatly distressed the King. He convened all his wise men and magicians and

The Prophet Daniel

ordered them to recall this dream and explain it. But they were not able to do it and said, *There is not a man upon the earth that can recall the dream for the king* (Dan. 2:10). Nebuchadnezzar was infuriated and wanted to destroy all the wise men of Babylon.

Then Daniel asked the King to give him some time, and he would explain the dream. Going home, Daniel fervently implored God to reveal to him this mystery. In a vision at night, God revealed to him the dream of Nebuchadnezzar and its meaning.

Daniel went to the King and said, *O king, thy thoughts came into thy mind upon thy bed, what should come to pass hereafter ...Thou, O king, sawest and behold a great image. This great image, whose brightness was excellent, stood before thee; and the form thereof was terrible. This image's head was of fine gold, his breast and his arms of silver, his belly and his thighs of brass, his legs of iron, his feet part of iron and part of clay* (Dan. 2:29, 31-33). Then from a

The Prophet Daniel Explains the Dream

mountain, by itself, a stone was cut out without hands, and it smote the image upon his feet that were of iron and clay, and broke them in pieces. Then the whole image fell apart and turned into dust, and the stone became a great mountain and filled the whole earth. This, O King, is thy dream!

"This dream," continued Daniel, "means the following. Thou art a king of kings, for the God of Heaven hath given thee a kingdom, power, and strength, and glory, and He hath made thee ruler over all. Thou art this head of gold. After thee shall arise another kingdom inferior to thee, and another third kingdom of brass which shall bear rule over all the earth. The fourth kingdom shall be as strong as iron: forasmuch as iron breaketh in pieces and all these shall it break in pieces and bruise. But at the same time that the kingdom shall be divided, the kingdom shall be partly strong and partly broken. In the days of these last kings shall the God of Heaven set up an eternal kingdom which shall not be left to other people, but it shall break in pieces and consume all these kingdoms, and it shall stand for ever. Thus the great God hath made known to the King what shall come to pass hereafter."

Hearing this, King Nebuchadnezzar stood up and bowed down to the earth before Daniel, and said, *Of a truth it is, that your God is a God of gods, and a Lord of kings!* (Dan. 2:47).

He honored Daniel greatly by giving him great gifts, seating him in the gate of the King, and making him ruler over the whole province of Babylon and chief of the governors, over all the wise men of Babylon. His three friends Ananian, Azarias, and Misael were set over the affairs of the province of Babylon.

The prophecy of Daniel was precisely fulfilled. After the **Babylonian kingdom**, there followed three great kingdoms: the **Median-Persian**, the **Macedonian** or **Greek**, and the **Roman**, each of which reigned over the Jewish people. Jesus Christ, the Saviour of the world, appeared on earth during the Roman empire, and established His universal, eternal kingdom, the holy Church.

The **mountain**, from which was carved the stone, represents the Holy Virgin Mary, and the **stone**, Christ and His eternal kingdom.

Note: See the Book of Daniel, chapters 1-2.

Friends of the Prophet Daniel — Ananias, Azarias, and Misael—the Furnace of Babylon

Shortly after, the friends of the Prophet Daniel, Ananias, Azarias, and Misael (Shadrach, Meshach and Abednego KJV), underwent a great trial of their faith. King Nebuchadnezzar set up in the plain of Dura, in the province of Babylon, a great image of gold. For its dedication all the important and distinguished people of the Babylonian kingdom were gathered. It was declared to all the people that when they heard the sound of the trumpet and musical instruments, they must fall down and worship the golden image. Whosoever did not comply with the order of the King would be thrown into a burning fiery furnace. Upon the sound of the trumpet, all fell to the ground. Only three — Ananias, Azarias, and Misael — failed to worship the image.

The King was enraged, and commanded that the furnace be heated seven times hotter than usual, and to bind them and cast them into the burning fiery furnace. The flames were so fierce that the soldiers who threw them in the furnace fell dead. But Ananias, Azarias, and Misael remained unharmed, because the Lord sent His angel to guard them in the midst of the flames. They sang, glorifying the Lord.

The Three Youths in the Furnace

Nebuchadnezzar sat on a high throne near the furnace. When he heard the singing, he was astonished, then dumbfounded. He rose up in haste and said to his counselors, "But I see four men loose, walking in the midst of the fire, and they are not burnt, and the form of the fourth is like the Son of God." Then he came near to the furnace and said, "Shadrach, Meshach and Abednego, ye servants of the most high God, come out and come here."

When they came, it was seen that the fire had had no power over them, even their coats and hair were not singed, nor did they smell of fire. Nebuchadnezzar, seeing this said, "Blessed be your God, Who sent His angel and delivered his servants that trusted in Him."

The King forbade anyone, on penalty of death, to speak anything amiss against the God of Israel.

Note: See the Book of Daniel, chap. 3.

CHAPTER 39

The Fall of the Babylonian Kingdom

After the death of Nebuchadnezzar, the kingdom of Babylon began to fall apart. The successors of Nebuchadnezzar changed frequently. Finally, after seven years, **Belshazzar** (whom the Prophet Daniel calls the son of Nebuchadnezzar) came to the throne and ruled about seventeen years. In the seventeenth year of his reign, when the Medes and the Persians threatened to attack him, Belshazzar carelessly feasted in Babylon, not thinking of the danger.

One day during a feast, King Belshazzar, for the profanation of the true God and in praise of his idols, commanded that the vessels be brought which Nebuchadnezzar had taken out of the Temple in Jerusalem; he and all those with him drank wine in them. Such blasphemy resulted in the judgment of God. A hand appeared in the air which wrote some sort of words on the wall.

Belshazzar began to tremble from fear, and he cried aloud to bring in the astrologers, the Chaldeans, and the soothsayers. The wise men of Babylon came, but none of them was able to read the handwriting on the wall.

Now the Queen came into the banquet house and said to Belshazzar, "Let not thy thoughts trouble thee, O King. There is a man in thy kingdom, in whom is the Spirit of the Holy God — it is Daniel. He will explain the meaning of the words." At that time Daniel was far away from the King's court.

When Daniel was brought in, the King said to him, "If thou canst read the writing, and make known to me the interpretation thereof, thou shalt be clothed with scarlet, and have a chain of gold about thy neck and shalt be the third ruler in the kingdom."

Daniel refused the rewards. He reminded the King of how God persuaded the proud Nebuchadnezzar. "And thou his son, O Belshazzar, hast not humbled thine heart, though thou knowest all this; but hast lifted up thyself against the Lord of Heaven, and hast drunk wine in the vessels of His House; and thou hast praised the idols; and the God in Whose hand thy breath is, and Whose are all thy ways, hast thou not glorified. For this reason God sent a hand which wrote these letters. This is what is written:

MENE, TEKEL, PERES

"**MENE** means God hath **numbered** thy kingdom and determined its end;

"**TEKEL** means thou art **weighed** in the balance, and art found to be wanting;

The Prophet Daniel Interprets the Writing on the Wall

"**PERES** means thy kingdom is **divided** and given to the Medes and Persians."

The King immediately rewarded Daniel as he had promised.

That same night the Median and Persian armies, under the leadership of the Persian King Cyrus, invaded the city and took possession of it. Belshazzar was slain and the Babylonian kingdom fell. In its place arose the kingdom of the Medes and the Persians — the **silver** in the vision of Nebuchadnezzar, as the Prophet Daniel had explained to him. The Persian King Cyrus made Darius, the Median, King over Babylon.

Note: See the Book of Daniel, chap. 5.

CHAPTER 40

The Median-Persian Empire Prophet Daniel in the Lion's Den

K ing Darius came to love Daniel and made him one of the three main rulers in his kingdom; the King thought to set him over the whole realm. Other important persons envied Daniel and decided to kill him. They knew that three times a day Daniel prayed to God, opening the window toward Jerusalem. Therefore, they came to the King and asked him to establish a royal statute that within thirty days, whosoever shall ask a petition of any god or man, save the King, should be cast into a den of lions. The King agreed. But the Prophet Daniel, as before, did not cease to pray to God every day and beg His mercy. His enemies reported this to the King. Then Darius understood that he had been deceived, but he was unable to change his order, and he was compelled to permit Daniel to be thrown to the lions.

The next day, early in the morning, the King hurried to the lions' den and cried, *Daniel, servant of the living God! Is thy God, whom you serve continually, able to deliver thee from the lions?* (Dan. 6:20).

Daniel answered him from the den. *O king! My God hath sent His angel, and hath shut the lions' mouths, forasmuch as before Him innocency was found in me; and also before thee O king, have I done no hurt* (Dan. 6:21-22).

The King then commanded that they should take Daniel up out of the den, and they cast his accusers into the den of lions. Before they had even come to the bottom of the den, the lions seized them and broke all their bones in pieces.

Then King Darius wrote a decree. *I make a decree, that in every dominion of my kingdom men tremble and fear before the God of Daniel: for He is the living God, and steadfast forever, and His kingdom that which shall not be destroyed, and His dominion shall be even unto the end* (Dan. 6:26).

The Prophet Daniel prospered in the reign of Darius, and in the reign of Cyrus the Persian. He made many predictions which were later fulfilled.

Daniel predicted the birth of Christ the Saviour precisely in **seventy weeks** of years, that is, in 490 years. He predicted also that Christ would be put to death, and after Him would follow the destruction of the Temple and city and the cessation of the Old Testament sacrifices (Dan. 9: 23-27).

Note: See the Book of Daniel.

CHAPTER 41

The Return of the Jews from Captivity in Babylon and the Construction of the Second Temple

The Jews were in captivity in Babylon seventy years. The Persian King Cyrus, in the first year of his reign over Babylon, allowed the Jews to return from captivity to their fatherland and to build a Temple to the Lord in Jerusalem. Forty-two thousand Jews returned to their homeland. The Jews who remained in Babylon helped them with gold, silver and other necessities, and beyond that with rich donations to the Temple. The King returned the sacred vessels which were taken from the Temple of Solomon by Nebuchadnezzar.

Having returned to Jerusalem, the Jews first of all resumed sacrifices to the Lord God, and then, the next year, they laid the foundations for the new Temple. The Samaritans, having found out about it, expressed a desire to take part in the building of the Temple, but the Jews, in order to keep the services to God pure, refused them. After nineteen years the Temple was finished. The new Temple was not as rich and splendid as the Temple of Solomon. The old folk, remembering the splendor of the former Temple, wept over the fact that this second Temple was poorer and smaller than before.

But the Prophet **Haggai**, whom the Lord sent to the Jews, comforted them. He predicted that the glory of this latter Temple would be greater than that of the former because to this Temple would come the Desire of all nations, Christ the Saviour of the World (cf. Haggai 2:6-9).

The Prophet **Zechariah** foretold the triumphant entry of the Saviour into Jerusalem upon a colt, the foal of a donkey (cf. Zech. 9:9).

The Prophet **Malachi** prophesied that the advent of the Messiah was near and that before Him would be sent a Forerunner, that is a precursor like the Prophet Elijah, to prepare people to receive the Saviour (cf. Mal. 3:1, 4:5). Malachi was the last prophet of the Jews. After him for more than four hundred years, words of the prophets were not heard among the Hebrew people, until the appearance of the Forerunner of Christ, John the Baptist.

CHAPTER 42

The Greek Empire
The Translation of the Books of the Old Testament into the Greek Language

For a long time, about two hundred years, the Median-Persian empire continued. The Jews, upon returning from captivity in Babylon, remained under the power of the Persian King.

Then the Persian kingdom was conquered by the Greek King Alexander the Great, King of Macedonia, who was also sovereign over Egypt and Syria. Alexander the Great, the most powerful king of his time, respected the holy Temple of Jerusalem and throughout his life he was especially protective of the Hebrew people.

After his death the kingdom disintegrated, and it fell to four of his military chiefs. One of these, Ptolemy, having become King of Egypt, subjugated the Hebrews and brought many thousands of Jews to Egypt.

Under his son, **King Ptolemy II Philadelphus**, who was kindly disposed to the Jews, a magnificent work was done. By his command **the books of the Old Testament were translated from the Hebrew language into Greek**. The translation was made by seventy interpreters, that is, scholars. Greek was the most commonly used language of that time. This translation was of enormous benefit for it enabled even the pagans to read the Holy Scriptures in a language known to them. In this way the empire of the Greek King served to spread the truth about God among the heathens.

For about a hundred years the Jews were under the power of the Greek kings reigning in Egypt. However, the Greek kings reigning in Syria did not treat the Hebrews and the faith in the true God in the manner that the Egyptian kings did. While living under the power of Syrian kings, the Jews endured much sorrow. The Syrian kings began to persecute them for the true faith and to force them into idolatry. An especially brutal oppressor was the King Antiochus Epiphanes.

Martyrs for the Faith, the Maccabees

King Antiochus Epiphanes wanted all of his subjects to speak the same language, Greek, and to worship only Greek gods, that is, idols. Many of the Jews obeyed the King, but there were others who were ready to die rather than to forsake the true faith.

The Maccabean Martyrs

The royal rulers tried to force the elder Eleazar to eat food forbidden by the law of Moses — pork. When he refused, they tried to persuade him to bring his own meat, such as was lawful for him to use, and to pretend that he ate the flesh taken of the sacrifice commanded by the King. To this he answered, "It is not becoming at my age to be a hypocrite; if young people find out that Eleazar, being fourscore and ten years old, has now gone to a strange religion, then they may be tempted to desert the faith." Then they turned him over to the torturers, and Eleazar died courageously for the faith.

Once the woman Solomonia and her seven sons were brought before the king himself. The King compelled them to eat pork, but they boldly replied, "We are ready to die, rather than to transgress the laws of our fathers." Then the King handed them over to brutal torture. They cut out their tongues, cut off their fingers and toes, pulled the skin off their heads, and burned them alive in hot frying pans. Thus six of the brothers were martyred. The King tenderly tried to convince the youngest not to oppose him. He assured him with oaths that he would reward him, and finally turned to his mother to counsel her son to save his life. But she bowed herself toward him and said, "O my son, fear not this tormentor, but being worthy of thy brethren, accept death, that I may receive thee again in the future eternal life." The King then turned the youngest son over to death by torture harsher than all the rest. Last of all, after the sons the mother died. This family of martyrs is known as the **Maccabean martyrs**.

In defense of the true faith and their homeland there arose a priest Mattathias with his five sons. Many zealots of the Law of God soon gathered around them. One of the sons of Mattathias was especially distinguished for bravery, Judas Maccabeus (named for the **Maccabean martyrs**). Judas Maccabeus won many victories over the Syrians with only a small group of soldiers. But once, he was surrounded by a large army of Syrians (22,000 troops), and he had only 800 men. Judas died the death of a hero. He would not consent to flee from his enemy and thereby darken his glory.

His brother Simon finally defeated the Syrian army, and having rid the city of Jerusalem of them, purified the Temple, and freed his people from the power of the Greek kings. In gratitude for this, the Jews established that from that time until the advent of the Saviour, the eldest of the family of Simon would be the chief priest and ruler of the people.

Note: See the Books of the Maccabees.

Translator's note: In the King James Version, these books are found in the apocrypha of the Old Testament. KJV does not include the story of Simon.

CHAPTER 43

The Roman Empire
The Universal Expectation of the Messiah

Having been freed from the empire of the Greek kings, the Jews did not have long to make use of their freedom. The Romans, having conquered the whole known world, also subjugated the Jews (64 B.C.). They placed over Palestine the procurator Antipater from the tribe of Esau, an Idumean (or Edomite). He very cleverly secured the confidence of the Romans, but was soon poisoned.

After him, his son Herod, called Herod the Great, was appointed governor of Galilee. He was a suspicious, brutal and cunning man. He also, like his father, skillfully gained the confidence of the Roman authorities and was declared King of the Jews. In order to find favor among the Jews, King Herod restored the Jerusalem Temple. Having received the title of King, he was still subordinate to **Caesar**, the Roman Emperor. From the time that the Jews came under Roman power, they were always subject to a **Roman ruler**, a deputy of the Roman Emperor. The Jews were allowed to keep their **Sanhedrin**, their council of high priests and elders of the people; but the power of the Sanhedrin was strictly limited. The Sanhedrin, for example, could not impose the death penalty without the permission of the Roman ruler, to whom belonged the highest authority in Israel.

The worldwide control of the Roman empire shook paganism to its foundations. Rome was the capital of the world and there gathered the scholars, writers, merchants and other representatives of all the nations. Each one brought with him his own pagan faith. These people, seeing the endless variety of pagan idol-deities, became convinced that all these pagan gods were devised by the people themselves.

Many of the pagans began to lose faith and hope in the future. In order to seek blissful oblivion, they began to indulge in every sort of amusement. Some, falling into despondency, ended their lives by suicide.

But the best of them, observing that the world was headed toward destruction, nevertheless maintained the hope that from somewhere would come a **Saviour**, if not from among the people, then from above. The Jews, dispersed throughout all the world after their captivity in Babylon and other later captivities, spread the news about the imminent coming of the Saviour of the world. Therefore, the gaze of the best people in the pagan world began to turn to the east, to Palestine.

Among the Romans and other pagan people there arose the general belief that in the East there would soon appear a powerful king who would subjugate the entire world.

In Palestine itself, among the Jews, the expectation of the Messiah was especially intense. Everyone felt that the time was coming for the fulfillment of the prophecies and the salvation of Israel.

The prophecies of the Prophet Daniel about the date of the appearance of Christ were especially precise. He foretold that after a period of seventy weeks of years came to an end, a fourth great kingdom would arise during which the Saviour would arrive. This was the exact specification of the time of the advent of Christ.

Upon the appearance of every prominent preacher, everyone involuntarily asked if he were the Christ. Even the semi-pagan Samaritans hoped that soon would come Christ the Saviour, Who would resolve all the quarrelsome questions between them and the Jews concerning the faith. Unfortunately, not only the pagans, but also the Jews themselves mistakenly imagined what Christ would be like. They did not picture Him as the Prophet Isaiah and other prophets represented Him, as one that would bear our sins, suffer for us and, though innocent, be condemned to death. The Jews had no idea that Christ the Saviour would come to earth for the purpose of teaching people, through His example, word, deeds, and suffering, to love God and each other. They desired to see Christ not like this, but rather with worldly power and glory. Therefore, they thought that Christ would come in worldly glory and would be the earthly king over the Jewish people. He would free the Jews from the power of Rome and would subjugate the whole world, and the Jews would reign over all the peoples of the earth.

Only a few devout and righteous people awaited Christ with humility, faith and love. They expected the true Saviour of the world, Who would come to deliver people from enslavement to sin and the power of the Devil. He would **"trample on the head of the serpent,"** as **God** said to the first people in Paradise, to save people from eternal death and to open the gates to the Kingdom of Heaven for eternal blessed life with God.

When the time came, God gave the promised Saviour of the world, His Only-begotten Son, Jesus Christ. The Son of God dwelt in the Holy Virgin Mary, and by the action of the Holy Spirit, received from her a human body and soul; that is, He was born from the Most-holy Virgin Mary and became **God Incarnate**.

The birth of Jesus Christ occurred in the days when Herod the Great, the Edomite, reigned over the Jews, in the time of the Roman Emperor Augustus.

Palestine

The land of Palestine, upon whose soil our Saviour lived, is comprised of a comparatively small strip of land, about 150 miles long and 80 miles wide, situated along the eastern coast of the Mediterranean Sea.

In the north of Palestine, on the slopes of Mt. Lebanon, lies **Galilee**. Picturesque hills, green pastures, and innumerable gardens make Galilee the most beautiful part of Palestine. Its chief adornment is the **Sea of Galilee**, which is also known as the Lake of Gennesaret or Tiberias. It is more than twelve miles in length, and a little more than five miles in width. At the time of the Saviour, the shores of this sea were covered with lush vegetation. Palm trees were growing there, along with vineyards, fig trees, almond trees, and flowering oleander. Beautiful cities, Capernaum, Tiberias, Chorazin, and Bethsaida,

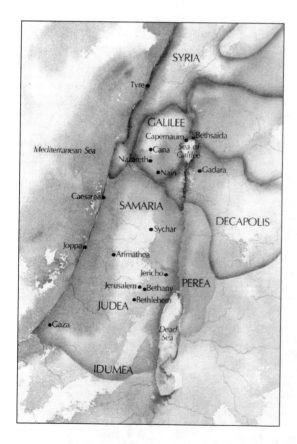

Palestine at the Time of the Saviour

situated on the banks of this sea, were not large, but densely populated. The inhabitants led simple and industrious lives. They cultivated every plot of land, and engaged in commerce and various trades, the chief of which was fishing.

To the south of Galilee lies **Samaria**. The inhabitants of Samaria, the Samaritans, were in constant conflict with the Jews. They even built themselves a separate temple on Mount Gerizim in order to avoid going to Jerusalem.

The largest part of Palestine, to the south of Samaria, is called **Judea**. The western part of it is level plain, interrupted by small streams flowing into the Mediterranean Sea. This plain gradually rises toward the east and is bordered by the Judean hills; from ancient times it was famous for its fertility. The slopes of the Judean hills are dressed in green, covered with whole groves of olive trees; more distant and higher mountains become rockier and more dismal. Among these hills is the great city of **Jerusalem**, the capital of Judea and of all Palestine.

The largest river in Palestine is the **Jordan**. The Jordan begins in the mountains of Lebanon in the form of sparkling mountain streams. Downstream in the valley these streams form a single river which spills into and forms the Sea of Galilee. From this sea, the Jordan flows out in the form of a fast wide river with low, green banks; at that time this was called the Valley of the Jordan. Approaching Judea, the banks of the Jordan become higher and drier, composed of bare rocks, devoid of any vegetation. Only the backwaters along the Jordan are thickly covered with reeds. There crocodiles swim, and wild beasts hide. This was the Jordan desert in which John the Baptist lived and preached. At the end of its course, the Jordan flows into a most wild and uninhabited country and empties into the Dead Sea.

Now we call the land of Palestine the **Holy Land**, since it was sanctified by the life of the Saviour.

The Jordan River

THE NEW
TESTAMENT

CHAPTER 1

The Nativity of the Holy Virgin Mary

When the time drew near for the birth of the Saviour of the world, there lived in the Galilean city of Nazareth a descendant of King David, **Joachim**, with his wife **Anna**. They were both pious people and were known not for their royal ancestry, but for their humility and charity.

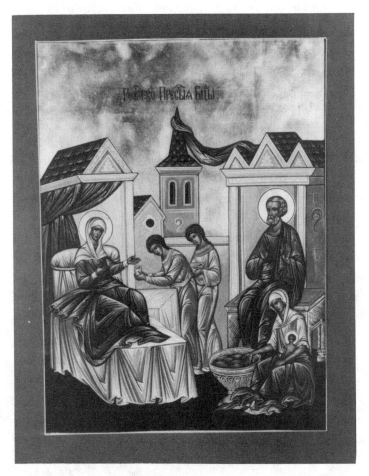

The Nativity of the Virgin Mary

Their entire lives were permeated with love for God and people. They lived to a ripe old age but never had children and this grieved them very much. In spite of their old age, they did not cease to petition

God to send them children. They made a vow, that if a child were born to them, they would consecrate it to the service of God. At that time, every Jew hoped that his posterity would take part in the kingdom of the Messiah, that is, Christ the Saviour. Therefore, every childless Jew was held in contempt by the others, for this was considered a great punishment by God for one's sins. This was especially trying to Joachim, as a descendant of King David, because from his seed Christ was to be born.

For their patience, great faith, love for God and for each other, God sent Joachim and Anna great joy. Toward the end of their lives a daughter was born to them. According to the command of an angel of God, She was given the name **Mary**. The birth of Mary brought joy not only to Her parents, but to all people, because She was foreordained by God to be the **Mother of the Son of God, the Saviour of the world**. The Nativity of the Holy Virgin Mary is celebrated by the Holy Orthodox Church as one of its major holidays on **the 8th of September** (September 21 n.s.).

Troparion of the Feast

Thy Nativity, O Theotokos Virgin, hath proclaimed joy to all the world; for from Thee hath dawned the Sun of Righteousness, Christ our God, annulling the curse, and bestowing the blessing, abolishing death and granting us life eternal.

Nazareth

CHAPTER 2

The Entry into the Temple of the Most-holy Virgin Mary

When the Virgin Mary reached the age of three years, Her pious parents prepared to fulfill their promise. They called together their relatives, invited friends the same age as their daughter, dressed Her in Her finest clothes, and accompanied by the people singing hymns, they brought Her to the Temple in Jerusalem, to be consecrated to God. Her friends, and Mary Herself, walked with burning candles in their hands. Led by the chief priest, the priests, while singing hymns, came out of the Temple to meet them.

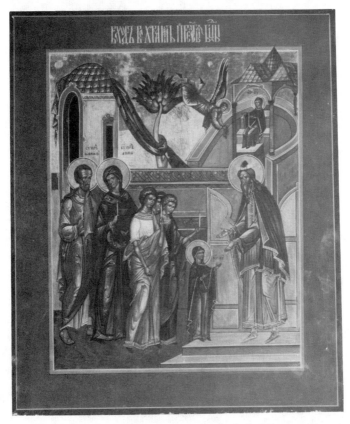

The Entry into the Temple of the Most-holy Virgin Mary

Joachim and Anna, with reverent prayers, set Mary on the first step of the flight of stairs leading to the Temple. This staircase had fifteen high steps, according to the number of the psalms which the priests chanted upon entering the Temple.

Saints Joachim and Anna

There, three-year-old Mary Herself climbed the high steps without any assistance. At the top the chief priest met and blessed Her, as he always did with all who came to be consecrated to God. Then, by the inspiration of the Holy Spirit, he led Her into the Holy of Holies. This was the most sacred place in the Temple. No one had the right to enter there except him, and he only once a year. The Holy Spirit enlightened the chief priest with the knowledge that Mary, the chosen young girl, was worthy to enter the most sacred place. She was destined by God to become the Mother of the Son of God, Who would open the way for all people into the Kingdom of Heaven.

Fulfilling their promise, Joachim and Anna returned home, and Mary remained to live at the Temple. There She, with other girls, studied the Law of God and handiwork. She prayed a great deal, read the Holy Scriptures, and strictly observed the fasts. Mary lived at the

Temple of God about eleven years and grew deeply devout, in everything was submissive to God, and was extraordinarily meek and industrious.

The Most-holy Mary decided to consecrate Her entire life to the one God alone. For this She vowed that She would never marry; that is, She would remain a virgin forever. The Holy Spirit and holy angels protected the godly young girl.

The Entry into the Temple of the Most-holy Virgin Mary is celebrated in the Holy Orthodox Church on the **21st of November** (December 4 n.s.). This day is considered a great holyday, which in the hymns of the Church is called the **harbinger of God's good-will toward man**. Starting with this holyday we begin to sing "**Christ is born...**" during Matins.

Troparion of the Feast

Today is the prelude of God's good-will and the heralding of the salvation of mankind. The Virgin is presented openly, and She proclaimeth Christ unto all. Then, with a great voice let us cry aloud: Rejoice, O Thou fulfillment of the Creator's dispensation.

The Holy Virgin Mary with Joseph

When the Virgin Mary reached fourteen years of age, it was necessary by law for Her to leave the Temple. She either had to go back to Her parents or marry. Joachim and Anna had already reposed by that time. The priests wanted to give her in marriage, but Mary explained to them Her vow to God — to remain forever virgin. Then the priests, guided by God, betrothed Her to a distant relative, the 80-year-old Joseph, so that he would take care of Her and keep Her virginity.

Joseph lived in the city of Nazareth. He was also descended from the royal family of David. However, he was not a rich man, but a carpenter.

The Holy Virgin Mary in the home of Joseph led a humble and solitary life, as before in the Temple. In Her free time She read the books of the Holy Scripture and prayed to God.

Note: Here is presented a short summary of the Birth of the Mother of God and Her childhood as described in **Holy Tradition**, piously preserved in the Holy Orthodox Church. (About **Holy Tradition**, see Part IV *On Christian Faith and Life*, in the section "About supernatural revelation by God — about Holy Tradition and Holy Scriptures.")

CHAPTER 3

The Announcement of the Angel About the Birth of the Forerunner

God, through the Prophet Malachi, foretold that before the advent in the world of Christ the Saviour Himself, there would appear **the Forerunner**, that is, the Predecessor of the Saviour. The Forerunner would be a great prophet; he would proclaim to the people the imminent appearance of Christ, preparing them to meet Christ the Saviour.

For the birth of the Forerunner, God chose relatives of the Holy Virgin Mary, the priest **Zacharias** and his wife **Elizabeth**. Already old, they had no children. They fervently prayed to God to deliver them from such unhappiness.

One day Zacharias was serving in the Temple in Jerusalem. When he entered the sanctuary for the censing, there appeared to him an angel of the Lord, standing on the right side of the table on which the incense was burning. Zacharias was confused; terror overcame him. The angel said to him, "Fear not, Zacharias, for your prayer is heard; and thy wife Elizabeth shall bear thee a son, and thou shalt call his name John. And thou shalt have joy and gladness...For he shall be great in the sight of the Lord...and he shall be filled with the Holy Spirit even from his mother's womb. And many of the children of Israel shall he turn to the Lord their God." He would come first; that is, he would be the Forerunner before the Lord the Saviour. "And he shall go before Him

The Announcement of the Birth of Saint John the Baptist

in the spirit and power of Elijah...to make ready a people prepared for the Lord." Zacharias, overwhelmed with joy, could not believe immediately, and said, "How shall I know this? For I am an old man and my wife well stricken in years." The angel, answering, said, "I am Gabriel, that stand in the presence of God; and am sent to speak unto thee...behold, thou shalt be dumb, and not able to speak, until the day that these things shall be performed, because thou believest not my words."

In the meantime, the praying people awaited Zacharias and were amazed that he delayed so long in the sanctuary of the Temple. Coming out he was unable to speak with the people, explaining with signs. Then everyone understood that he had experienced a vision in the sanctuary. At the end of his services for the day in the Temple, Zacharias went home.

When Elizabeth found out about the great favor God was bestowing on them, she hid her joy from people with humility, and thanked God.

Note: This sacred event is described in the Holy Gospels by the Apostle and Evangelist Luke (Luke 1:5-25).

The Birthplace of St. John the Baptist

CHAPTER 4

The Annunciation to the Holy Virgin Mary

Six months after the appearance of the angel to Zacharias, the Archangel Gabriel was sent by God to the city of Nazareth to the Holy Virgin Mary with the glorious news that the Lord had chosen Her to be the mother of the Saviour of the world.

The Archangel appeared in the home of the righteous Joseph while Mary was reading the Holy Scriptures. He came to Her and said,

The Annunciation

"Rejoice, who art full of grace (that is, filled with the grace of God — the gift of the Holy Spirit) the Lord is with Thee: blessed art Thou among women."

Mary was troubled by the words of the angel and thought: what manner of salutation could this be?

The Archangel said to Her, "Fear not, Mary; for Thou hast found favor with God. And, behold, Thou shalt conceive in Thy womb, and bring forth a Son, and shalt call His name **Jesus**. He shall be great, and shall be called the Son of the Highest, and He shall reign for ever."

Mary in bewilderment asked the Archangel, "How shall this be, seeing I know not a man?"

The angel answered Her that all this would be accomplished by the power of Almighty God. "The Holy Spirit shall come over Thee, and the power of the Highest shall overshadow Thee; therefore also that Holy One which shall be born of Thee shall be called the Son of God. And behold, Thy cousin Elizabeth, she hath also conceived a son in her old age; and this is the sixth month with her, who was called barren. For with God nothing shall be impossible."

Then Mary with humility said, "Behold the handmaid of the Lord; be it unto Me according to thy word."

And the Archangel Gabriel departed from Her.

The Annunciation of the Holy Virgin is celebrated by the Holy Orthodox Church on the **25th of March** (7th of April, n.s.). The Feast of the Annunciation is one of the greatest feasts. The word annunciation, in Russian and Greek means "good news" or "joyful tidings," news that the emancipation of man from sin and eternal death has begun.

Troparion of the Feast

Today is the fountainhead of our salvation, and the manifestation of the mystery which was from eternity. The Son of God becometh the Virgin's Son, and Gabriel proclaimeth the good tidings of grace; wherefore, we also cry to the Theotokos with him: Rejoice, Thou who art full of grace! The Lord is with Thee.

Note: See the Gospel of Luke 1: 26-38.

CHAPTER 5

The Visit of the Most-holy Virgin Mary to the Righteous Elizabeth

The Most-holy Virgin Mary, having found out from the angel that Her cousin Elizabeth, wife of the priest Zacharias, would soon give birth to a son, hurried to visit her.

Entering the home, She greeted Elizabeth. Upon hearing this greeting, Elizabeth was filled with the Holy Spirit, and she realized that Mary was honored to be the Mother of God. Speaking with a loud voice she said, "Blessed art Thou among women, and blessed is the fruit of Thy womb. And whence is this to me, that the Mother of my Lord should come to me?"

The Meeting with St. Elizabeth

The Most-holy Virgin Mary in answer to the words of Elizabeth, praised God and said, "My soul doth magnify the Lord, and My spirit hath rejoiced in God my Saviour, for He hath regarded the low estate of His handmaiden, for behold, from henceforth all generations shall call Me blessed. For He that is mighty hath done to me great things; and holy is His name. And His mercy is on them that fear Him from generation to generation." For about three months the Virgin Mary stayed with Elizabeth, and then returned home to Nazareth.

God also informed the righteous aged Joseph of the imminent birth of the Saviour by the Holy Virgin Mary. An angel of God, appearing to him in a dream, revealed that Mary would bring forth a Son by the action of the Holy Spirit, as the Lord God had said through the Prophet Isaiah (cf. 7:14). "And thou shalt call his name Jesus for he shall save his people from their sins," said the angel to Joseph.

Note: See the Gospels of Luke, 1:39-56 and Matthew, 1:18-25.

CHAPTER 6

The Nativity of St. John the Baptist

S oon after the visit to them by the Mother of God, a son was born to the righteous Zacharias and Elizabeth. Neighboring relatives of Elizabeth rejoiced with her over God's mercy. On the eighth day, according to Jewish law, a name had to be given to the infant. The gathering of friends and relatives

The Nativity of St. John the Baptist

wanted to call him Zacharias after the name of his father. But Elizabeth said, "Not so; but he shall be called John."

They said, "There is none of thy kindred that is called by this name," and they made signs to his father, how he would have him called.

Zacharias asked for a writing tablet and wrote, "His name is John." And they all marvelled. His speech returned immediately, and he began praising God, and prophesied by the inspiration of the Holy Spirit, that soon would come the Saviour, and that John would be His Forerunner, to prepare people to receive the Saviour.

Fear came on all who heard about this miraculous event, and they marvelled, saying about John, "What manner of child shall this be?"

The Lord guarded the child, and he grew and waxed strong in spirit, and was in the desert till the day of his showing unto Israel.

Sts. Zacharias and Elizabeth the Parents of St. John

The birth of the Holy and Chief Prophet and Forerunner of Christ
John is celebrated on the 24th of June (July 7, n.s.).

Note: See the Gospel of Luke, 1:57-80.

Bethlehem

CHAPTER 7

The Nativity of Christ the Saviour

The Nativity of Christ the Saviour

The Chapel of the Nativity in Bethlehem Where Christ Was Born

A t the time of the reign in Judea of Herod, who was under the power of Rome, the Roman Emperor Caesar Augustus sent out a decree that all the world should be taxed. Every Jew had to register in his own city, where his ancestors lived.

The Upper Church of the Nativity in Bethlehem

Joseph and the Virgin Mary were descended from the house and lineage of David, and therefore went out of Nazareth into the city of David, **Bethlehem**. Arriving in Bethlehem, they were not able to find room in the inn, and stayed outside the city, in a cave, where shepherds drove their cattle in bad weather. In this cave that night the Holy Virgin

A Greek Orthodox Church in the Shepherds' Field

Mary brought forth Her Child — the Son of God, Christ, the Saviour of the world. She wrapped the Divine Child in swaddling clothes and laid Him in a manger, where they put feed for the cattle.

The shepherds in Bethlehem were the first to find out about the birth of the Saviour. On this night they were watching their flocks in the field. Suddenly an angel of the Lord came upon them, and the glory of the Lord shown round about them. The shepherds were sore afraid.

The angel said to them, "Fear not. I bring you good tidings of great joy, which shall be to all people. For unto you is born this day in the city of David (Bethlehem) a Saviour, which is Christ the Lord. And this shall be a sign unto you. You shall find the Babe wrapped in swaddling clothes, lying in a manger."

Suddenly there was with the angel a multitude of the heavenly host praising God, and saying, "**Glory to God in the highest, and on earth peace, good will among men.**"

When the angels were gone away from them, the shepherds said one to another, "Let us now go even unto Bethlehem, and see this thing which is come to pass, which the Lord hath made known to us."

They came with haste, and found Mary and Joseph, and the Babe lying in a manger. They worshipped the Child and told how they had seen and listened to the angel. Mary kept all these things in her heart.

Then the shepherds returned to their flocks, glorifying and praising God for all the things that they had heard and seen.

Eight days after the birth of the Saviour, His Mother with Joseph, according to the law, gave Him the name **Jesus**, which had been given by God through the angel.

Note: See the Gospel of Luke, 2:1-21.

Adoration of the Magi

While Joseph and the Holy Mother of God and the Child Jesus were still in Bethlehem, **Magi** (wise men) from distant countries in the East (Persia or Babylonia) came to Jerusalem.

The Magi were scholarly people who observed and studied the stars. At that time people believed that upon the birth of a great person there would appear in the heavens a new star. Many pagans, taught by the Jews in dispersion, knew of the coming into the world of the Messiah the Great King of Israel, Who was to subdue the whole world. Therefore they waited, knowing that when He was born, there would appear a new star in the heavens. The wise men were pious people, and the Lord, by His mercy, gave them such a sign — in heaven there appeared a new, extraordinary star. Having seen this star, the wise men immediately understood that the awaited King had been born. They prepared for the journey and went to the capital of the Jewish kingdom, Jerusalem, to find out where this King was born and to worship Him.

In Jerusalem, the wise men began to ask, "Where is He that is born King of the Jews? For we have seen His star in the east, and are come to worship Him."

When King Herod heard this he was troubled. He was in everything a cruel and suspicious man. Because of one of his suspicions he sent his own children to execution. Now he was especially terrified, afraid that they would seize his power and hand over his royal throne to the newborn King. And all the people of Jerusalem were agitated, upon hearing such news.

Herod gathered all the chief priests and scribes of the people, men learned in the books of the Holy Scripture, and demanded of them where Christ should be born.

They answered, "In Bethlehem of Judea: for thus it is written by the Prophet Micah."

Then Herod, when he had secretly called the wise men, inquired of them diligently what time the star appeared. He sent them to Bethlehem, and said, "Go and search diligently for the young Child; and when ye have found Him; bring me word again, that I may come and worship Him also." In so doing Herod thought to kill the new born King.

When they had heard the King, the wise men departed; and lo, the star which they saw in the east went before them, till it came and stood over where the young Child was.

At that time the holy elder Joseph and the Most-holy Virgin Mary with the Child lived in the city, in the house where they moved from the cave, as the people after the census had begun to disperse.

The wise men came into the house and saw the young child Jesus with His mother. They fell down, and worshipped Him, and presented Him gifts: **gold, frankincense** (incense), and **myrrh** (expensive fragrant oil).

By their gifts, the wise men signified that the newborn child Jesus is King, and God, and man. Gold they brought to Him as King (as a tribute, or tax); incense, as God (as incense is used during worship services); and myrrh, as a man who must die (because the deceased were then anointed and rubbed with perfumed oil).

Afterward the Wise Men wanted to return to Jerusalem to Herod, but they were warned by God in a dream that they should not return to Herod. Then they departed into their own country another way.

Tradition preserves the names of the wise men, who then became Christians: **Melchior, Gasper and Balthasar.** Their memory is celebrated by the Church on the day of the Nativity of Christ.

The Nativity of our Lord Jesus Christ is celebrated in the Orthodox Church on the **25th of December** (January 7 n.s.). For this great feast we prepare ourselves by keeping the fast, which is called the **Nativity Fast** (or Advent).

Note: See the Gospel of Matthew, 2:1-12.

Troparion of the Feast

Thy, Nativity O Christ our God, hath shined upon the world the light of knowledge; for thereby, they that worshipped the stars were taught by a star to worship Thee, the Sun of righteousness, and to know Thee, the Dayspring from on high. O Lord, glory to Thee.

"Those who worshipped the stars" were the wise men who studied the sky and worshipped the stars.

Kontakion of the Feast

Today the Virgin giveth birth to Him Who is transcendent in essence; and the earth offereth a cave to Him Who is unapproachable. Angels with shepherds give glory; with a star the Magi do journey; for our sake a young Child is born, Who is pre-eternal God.

CHAPTER 8

The Meeting of the Lord

According to the law of Moses, all Hebrew parents must bring their first born son on the fortieth day after birth to the Temple to be consecrated to God. It was the custom to bring a sacrifice in thanksgiving to God. The law was established in remembrance of the exodus of the Hebrews from Egypt — freedom from slavery, when the first-born Hebrews were spared from death.

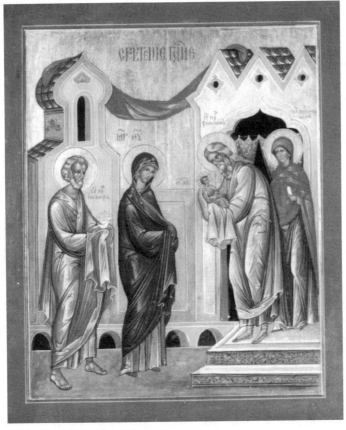

The Meeting of the Lord

In fulfillment of this law, the Mother of God with Joseph brought the infant Jesus to the Temple in Jerusalem, and for their sacrifice brought two fledgling doves.

At this time in Jerusalem, there lived an old man by the name of **Simeon**. He was a righteous, pious man, and he awaited the coming of the Messiah. It was foretold to him by the Holy Spirit that he would not die until he had seen Christ the Lord. Simeon waited for the fulfillment of the promise of God for a long time. According to tradition he lived about 300 years. Then, one day, by the inspiration of the Holy Spirit, he went to the Temple. When Mary with Joseph brought the infant Jesus, Simeon met the Child, took Him in his arms and glorifying God said, **"Now lettest Thou Thy servant depart in peace, O Master, according to Thy word, for mine eyes have seen Thy salvation, which Thou hast prepared before the face of all peoples, a light of revelation for the Gentiles, and the glory of Thy people Israel.**

Simeon called the new-born Lord, **"a light to enlighten the Gentiles,"** that is, all the tribes and nations, and **"the glory of Thy people"** that is, **"Israel."** There are two Israels, the Old Testament and the New Testament one. In the Old Testament it was the chosen Hebrew people or Israelites, and in the New Testament — it is the whole Orthodox Christian world.

Joseph and the Mother of God marvelled at the words of Simeon. Simeon blessed them, and turning to the Mother of God, he prophesied to Her about the Child, "Behold, this Child is set for the fall and rising again of many in Israel; yea, a sword shall pass through Thy own soul, also." That meant that She Herself would endure profound grief over Her Son, when He would suffer.

There was in the Temple the pious widow **Anna**, a prophetess, eighty-four years a widow, who served God with fasting and prayers night and day. She recognized the Saviour and coming in that instant, glorified the Lord and spoke of Him to all those in Jerusalem who awaited the coming to earth of Christ the Saviour.

When they had performed all things according to the Law of the Lord, the Mother of God with the Child and Joseph returned home.

This event, in which Saints Simeon and Anna **met in the Temple** the **infant Christ**, presented by the Mother of God and Joseph, and glorified Him, is called the Feast of the **Meeting of the Lord**, and is celebrated in the Holy Orthodox Church as one of the great feast days on the **2nd of February** (February 15th n.s.).

The righteous Simeon is called the God-receiver, that is, he who received in his hands God the Saviour.

Note: See the Gospel of Luke, 2:22-39.

Troparion of the Feast

Rejoice, Thou Who art full of grace, O Virgin Theotokos, for from Thee hath risen the Sun of Righteousness, Christ our God, enlightening those in darkness. Rejoice, thou also, O righteous Elder, as thou receivest in thine arms the Redeemer of our souls, Who also granteth unto us the Resurrection.

CHAPTER 9

The Flight into Egypt and the Slaying of the Innocents

The Return to Nazareth

When all was fulfilled according to the Law concerning Jesus in the Temple in Jerusalem, and the wise men were already on the road to their home, an angel of the Lord appeared to Joseph in a dream and said, "Arise, and take the young Child and His Mother, and flee into Egypt, and lie thou there until I bring thee word, for Herod will seek the young Child to destroy Him."

Joseph immediately arose, saddled his donkey, quickly gathered the necessary things, took the young Child and His Mother and the

The Slaying of the Innocent Children

same night went into Egypt. According to tradition, James, son of Joseph, accompanied them on this journey.

In the meantime, Herod impatiently awaited the return of the wise men. When the wise men did not return from Bethlehem, he concluded that the wise men, not finding a newborn king, were ashamed to return to Jerusalem. For the time being, Herod was tranquil.

But after forty days the news spread throughout Jerusalem that Mary had presented in the Temple Her newborn Son, and that the aged Simeon had come to the Temple to meet this Child and had prophesied that He was the Christ. Then Herod realized that the wise men had figured out his evil intent and had purposely avoided returning to him. He was exceedingly angry.

Not knowing how to find the Christ Child, King Herod gave the disastrous order to kill all the children that were in Bethlehem and its surroundings from two years old and under. He hoped that among these children would be killed the Christ. Thus he calculated according to the time when he had diligently questioned the wise men. The soldiers sent by Herod killed 14,000 children. Everywhere were heard the howls and screams of the mothers, whose crying for their children, innocent children, killed by the order of the brutal King would not be comforted. They were the first martyrs to spill their blood for Christ.

Soon after this Herod was punished for his cruelty. He came down with a terrible illness. His body rotted alive and was eaten by worms, and he died in terrible torment.

After the death of Herod, an angel of the Lord appeared to Joseph in Egypt and said, "Arise, and take the young Child and His mother and go into the land of Israel; for they are dead which sought the young Child's life." Joseph did as he was told and took his family into the land of Israel. But when he heard that Archelaus reigned in Judea in the place of Herod his father and that he was just as cruel, Joseph was afraid to go there. Being warned of God in a dream, Joseph turned aside into the parts of Galilee, into his native city Nazareth. There Joseph dwelt with the child Jesus and His Mother.

The child Jesus grew and became strong in spirit, filled with wisdom; and the grace of God was upon Him. From the earliest years of His childhood, Jesus Christ exhibited unusual intelligence and remarkable sanctity in all His actions.

Note: See the Gospels of Matthew, 2:13-23 and Luke, 2:40.

CHAPTER 10

The Saviour in the Temple as a Youth

Joseph and the Most-holy Virgin Mary went to Jerusalem, to the Temple of God, to celebrate the Passover every year. When Jesus reached the age of twelve years, they took Him with them.

At the end of the feast Joseph and Mary went home. The boy Jesus remained in Jerusalem. Joseph and the Mother of God did not notice it, for they thought that He was coming with relatives and friends. After a whole day on the road, toward evening, they started to look for Jesus among their relatives and acquaintances, but they did not find Him. In great anxiety they returned to Jerusalem, looking for Him. After three days they found Jesus in the Temple and were amazed. He sat among the scholars, listened to them with attention, questioned them and

The Lord Teaching in the Temple as a Youth

The Temple at the Time of the Saviour

Himself answered their questions. His unusual intelligence and answers left them wonderstruck.

His All-holy Mother went to Him and said, "My Son! Why have You thus dealt with us? Behold, Thy father and I have sought Thee sorrowing."

He said unto them, "How is it that you sought Me? Did ye not know that I must be about My Father's business?"

By these words the boy Jesus Christ showed that He was supposed to be in the Temple of God and that He was not simply a man, but the Son of God, Who came to earth for a great work, which God the Father had commissioned Him to do. They did not then understand His words, but the Holy Virgin Mary kept all His sayings in Her heart.

Jesus Christ went with Joseph and His Mother to Nazareth and was subject to them. He helped Joseph in his trade, learning carpentry, ceaselessly increasing in wisdom and stature, and in favor with God and man.

Note: See the Gospel of Luke, 2:41-52.

CHAPTER 11

The Preaching of St John the Baptist

John, son of the righteous Zacharias and Elizabeth, lived from his youth in the wilderness and there spent his time in fasting and prayer. His clothing was made of camel's hair and about his loins was a leather girdle, and his food was locusts (a wild plant, not insects) and wild honey.

When John reached thirty years of age, the Lord directed him to go to the valley of the Jordan River and proclaim to all the people that the Saviour of the world would soon appear, and that all should prepare to meet Him with repentance and baptism.

John went to the region of the Jordan and started to preach, **"Repent, for the Kingdom of Heaven is at hand,"** that is, the time was drawing near when the long awaited Saviour would appear, Who would summon everyone to His kingdom.

For a long time God had not sent a prophet to the Hebrew people. From the time of the last prophet, Malachi, there had passed four hundred years. Therefore, when they heard of the appearance of the Prophet John, and about his marvelous life and teaching, people came from all directions to hear him. Whoever believed his words and repented of their sins, John **baptized** in the river Jordan that is, he immersed each one in the water while placing his hands on the head of the baptized. Therefore John the Forerunner was called the **Baptist**. In the process John required of everyone that the repentance be sincere and that the correction in oneself be accompanied by good works.

The baptism of John meant that as the body is washed and cleansed by water, thus the soul of a person who repents and believes in the Saviour is cleansed by Christ of all his sins when he is baptized into the Church.

Among those who came to John were some people who considered themselves righteous and who did not wish to repent, and indeed were vicious and evil, as for example were the Pharisees and Sadducees — leaders of the Hebrew people. The **Pharisees** were proud of their descent from Abraham, praised themselves for fulfilling the Law, and considered themselves worthy to enter the Kingdom of Christ the Messiah. The **Sadducees** did not believe in the resurrection of the dead and in the future life. To these people John said, "Who warned you to flee from the wrath to come?" That is, who told you that you by your own power could escape the anger of God and eternal punishment in the future life? "Bring forth fruits worthy for repentance. And think not to say within yourselves: we have Abraham as our father; for I say unto

St. John the Baptist

you, that God is able of these stones to raise up children unto Abraham. Remember, every tree which bringeth not forth good fruit is hewn down, and cast into the fire."

Hearing these words, the people asked him, "What shall we do then?"

John answered, "He that has two coats, let him impart to him that has none; and he that has food, let him do likewise," that is, first of all, do good.

Then publicans, or tax collectors, came and asked, "Master, what shall we do?" The publicans collected taxes for the Romans. The Jews hated the power of the Romans. Besides that, several of the publicans collected more than was proper and oppressed the people. The Jews despised all the publicans and considered them unworthy to enter the approaching Kingdom of Christ. John said to them, "Exact no more than that which is appointed you."

The soldiers also asked of him, "What shall we do?" It often happened that the soldiers, dissatisfied with their wages, took property that belonged to other people, treated poor people badly, and accused other people for their own profit. John said to them, "Do violence to no man, neither accuse any falsely; and be content with your wages."

Many then wondered if John was Christ the Saviour, but John explained that he was not the Christ. **"I baptize you with water,"** he said, **"but after me One mightier than I is coming,"** that is, soon after me will come He for whom you wait — Christ, **"the latchet of Whose shoes I am not worthy to unloose"**; that is, I am unworthy to even be His servant, to take off His shoes for Him. **"He shall baptize you with the Holy Spirit and with fire"**; that is, the baptism which He will give will burn up your sins like fire, and give you the gifts of the Holy Spirit.

The holy Prophet John preached to many others, teaching the people who came to him.

Note: See the Gospels of Matthew 3:1-12; Mark 1:1-18; Luke 3:1-18; John 1:15-28.

CHAPTER 12

The Baptism of the Lord Jesus Christ

During the time that John the Forerunner preached on the banks of the Jordan River and baptized people, Jesus Christ reached thirty years of age. He also went from Nazareth to the Jordan River to John, to receive baptism from him.

The Baptism of the Lord

John did not consider himself worthy to baptize Jesus Christ and began to shrink back from Him saying, "I have need to be baptized of Thee, and comest Thou to me?"

But Jesus, answering, said to Him, "Suffer it to be so now," that is, do not hold back from me now, "for thus it becometh us to fulfill all righteousness," — to fulfill everything in the Law of God and to set an example for people. Then John obeyed and baptized Jesus Christ.

Upon completion of the baptism, when Jesus Christ came out of the water, suddenly the heavens were opened over Him; and John saw the Spirit of God descending like a dove and lighting upon Him, and heard the voice of God the Father from Heaven saying, "**This is My beloved Son, in Whom I am well pleased.**"

Then John was finally convinced that Jesus was the expected Messiah, Son of God, Saviour of the world.

The Baptism of our Lord Jesus Christ is celebrated in the Holy Orthodox Church as one of the great feasts, on **January 6th** (January 19 n.s.). The celebration of the Baptism of the Lord is also called **Theophany**, or the Manifestation of God, because at the time of baptism God revealed Himself to people as the Holy Trinity in this way: **God the Father** spoke from Heaven, the incarnate **Son of God** was baptized, and the **Holy Spirit** descended in the form of a dove. Also, at the time of baptism, for the first time people could see that in the person of Jesus Christ there appeared not only man, but also **God**.

The day before the feast is an established fast day. The same strict fast is observed and the same types of services are celebrated as on the Eve of Christ's Nativity (Christmas). Because the Saviour by His own baptism sanctified the water, on this feast there is a blessing of water. On the day before, water is blessed in church, and on the feast itself under the open sky, in rivers, lakes, pools and wells. This Blessing of the Waters is often called "**The Procession to the Jordan.**"

Note: See the Gospels of Matthew, 3:13-17; Mark, 1:9-11; Luke 3:21-22; John 1:32-34.

Troparion of the Feast

When Thou wast baptized in the Jordan, O Lord, the worship of the Trinity was made manifest; for the voice of the Father bare witness to Thee, calling Thee His beloved Son. And the Spirit in the form of a dove confirmed the certainty of the word. O Christ our God Who hast appeared and hast enlightened the world, glory be to Thee!

CHAPTER 13

The Lord Jesus Christ in the Wilderness and His Temptation by the Devil

After His baptism, the Lord Jesus Christ went into the wilderness in order to prepare in solitude, by fasting and prayer, for the accomplishing of His great work for which He had come to earth. For forty days and forty nights He was in the wilderness with the beasts, not eating any food.

Then the Devil came to Christ and tried to seduce Him into sin

The Mountain of Temptation

with cunning questions and delusions, as he does to every man.

The Devil said to Jesus Christ, as if to say, in vain do You torment Yourself with hunger, "If Thou be the Son of God, command that these stones be made bread."

The Saviour said to him in answer, **It is written (in the Bible), man shall not live by bread alone, but by every word that proceedeth out of the mouth of God** (Deut. 8:3).

Then the Devil led Jesus Christ to Jerusalem, set Him on a pinnacle of the Temple and said, "If You are the Son of God, cast Yourself down (for You there is no danger), because in the Scripture it is written: *He shall give His angels charge over Thee, and on their hands shall they bear Thee up, lest at any time Thou dash Thy foot against a stone* (Ps. 90:11,12).

But Jesus said to him, **It is written again, Thou shalt not tempt the Lord thy God**, that is, where it is not necessary, do not demand and do not expect miracles (Deut. 6:16).

After that, the Devil took Him upon a high mountain and there in the twinkling of an eye, showed Him all the kingdoms of the world and the glory of them, and said, "All these things I will give Thee, because power over them has been handed over to me, and I can give it to whomever I will. All these things I will give Thee, if Thou will fall down and worship me."

Jesus Christ said to him, **Get thee hence, Satan: for it is written, Thou shalt worship the Lord thy God, and Him only shalt thou serve** (Deut. 6:13).

Then the Devil in disgrace left Jesus Christ for the time being, and immediately angels came and ministered unto Him.

Thus, the Saviour conquered temptation from the Devil, and demonstrated in so doing that He came to free people from the power of the Devil, without any concessions to evil.

Following the example of the fast of Christ, the Holy Orthodox Church established a forty day fast which is called **Great Lent** and begins seven weeks before Pascha (Easter) — the bright Resurrection of Christ, and also established other fasts. The fast enables a person to cleanse himself of evil, of sinful inclinations, to help him fix his thoughts on God and to be closer to Him.

Note: See the Gospels of Matthew 4:1-11; Mark 1:12-13; Luke 4:1-13.

CHAPTER 14

The Lord Jesus Christ Appears to the People. His First Disciples

Returning from the wilderness Jesus Christ again went to the shore of the Jordan where John was baptizing. Seeing Jesus, John said to the people, "Behold the Lamb of God, that taketh upon Himself the sins of the world," that is, Jesus Christ, the true Lamb of God, Who for as many as a thousand years had been prefigured in sacrificial offerings. Like the innocent lambs and calves, slaughtered for burnt offerings, He meekly will take upon Himself suffering and death and will shed His blood, for the sins of the whole world, in order to save people from eternal death.

The Holy Spirit as He Appeared at the Baptism of the Lord

And John witnessed saying, "I saw the Spirit descending from Heaven like a dove, and He abode upon Him. And I saw and bore record that this is the Son of God."

Again the next day John, looking upon Jesus as He walked, said to two of his disciples standing with him, "Behold the Lamb of God!"

The two disciples heard John speak and they followed Jesus. One of them was **Andrew**, who because he was the first to follow Christ is called the "**First-called.**" The other was **John the Theologian**. Then Andrew brought his brother Simon to Jesus Christ. The Saviour, perceiving in him strong faith, said, "Thou art Simon the son of Jonah. Thou shalt be called Cephas (**Peter**)," which is by interpretation, a stone. The following day the Saviour called **Philip**, and Philip brought to Him **Nathaniel**.

After this Jesus Christ went to the cities and towns of the Hebrew land to preach the **Gospel** to the people, the joyful blessed news that He is the promised Messiah, come to earth to save people from the power of the Devil, sin, and eternal death, and to give to people **eternal salvation — the Kingdom of God**.

Jesus Christ often set forth the teaching about the Kingdom of God in **parables**, that is, in images, comparisons or examples from our daily life, in order to more graphically and more fully set forth His teaching. Both the visible and invisible world were created by God. There exists a marvelous unity and affinity between the two worlds. Therefore, the visible world speaks to us about the laws of the invisible, heavenly world. **Our entire earthly life**, with all life of the visible world, is a **great parable of God about the laws of the future life** in the Kingdom of Heaven.

In order to convince people that He is the promised Messiah and Son of God, Jesus Christ performed many **miracles**, that is, unusual deeds which a person of ordinary powers could not do and which could be accomplished only by the special power of God. Many of the Jews believed in Jesus Christ and multitudes followed after Him, listening to His divine teaching. Others, especially rulers of the Hebrew people, Pharisees, Sadducees, elders and priests, wishing to exercise power and rule over the people, having evil hearts, did not wish to accept His teachings of truth and to believe that He is the Saviour, and they became the enemies of Christ.

Notes: See the Gospels of John 1:29-51; Luke 4:14-15, 32-37; Matthew 4:17; Mark 1:22; Matthew 5, 6 and 7; 13:34-35; Mark 4:3-34; Matt. 11:4-6; 5:23-25; 21:45-46; 26:3-4.

CHAPTER 15

The First Miracle of Jesus Christ

Soon after the first disciples were called by the Saviour, in the city of Cana, not far from Nazareth, there was a wedding. To this wedding were invited Jesus Christ with His Most-pure Mother and the disciples. When it came time for the wedding banquet there was insufficient wine. The Mother of God noticed it and said to Jesus Christ, "They have no wine."

But Jesus answered, "My hour is not yet come."

From this answer the Holy Virgin understood that the time had not yet come for Him to reveal His divine power, but She knew of the love of Her Son for the people and was sure that He certainly would help the needy, and therefore She said to the servants, "Whatsoever He saith unto you, do it."

In the house there were six large waterpots of stone in which was poured water for purification, after the manner of the Jews. Jesus Christ ordered to fill the waterpots with water. When they filled them to the brim, He said to the servants, "Draw out now, and bear to the governor of the feast."

The servants drew and bare it to the governor. The ruler of the feast tried it and saw it was the very best wine. Then he called the bridegroom and said, "Every man at the beginning doth set forth good wine, then that which is worse, but thou hast kept the good wine until now." The governor said this because he did not know from whence came the wine. Only the servants which drew the water knew.

Thus the Saviour began His miracles and revealed His glory, and His disciples believed in Him.

The first miracle of Jesus Christ was accomplished on the request of His Mother. From this we can see that **Her prayers for us have great power.**

Note: See the Gospel of John, 2:1-12.

CHAPTER 16

The Merchants are Banished from the Temple

The Jews' Passover was at hand. Jesus Christ went up to Jerusalem. Upon entering the Temple, He found great disorder. There they sold sheep, bullocks and doves; money changers were sitting at their tables. The lowing of the cattle, the bleating of the sheep, the talking of the people, the quarrels about the prices, the jingle of the coins — all this gave the Temple the semblance of a bazaar rather than the house of God.

Jesus Christ made a whip of small ropes and drove all the traders with their cattle out of the Temple. He overthrew the tables of the money changers and poured out their money. He said to them that sold doves,

The Lord Banishes the Traders from the Temple

"Take these things away; make not My Father's house a house of merchandise." No one dared to disobey Jesus.

Having seen this, the chief Jews of the Temple came in a fury. They approached the Saviour and said, "What sign showest Thou unto us, seeing that Thou doest these things?"

Jesus Christ answered them, "Destroy this temple, and in three days I will raise it up." But He spoke of the temple of His body and by these words predicted that when they killed Him, He would rise in three days.

When therefore He was risen from the dead, His disciples remembered that He had said this unto them, and they believed the word of Jesus.

During Jesus Christ's stay in Jerusalem during the feast of Passover, many people, seeing the miracles which He performed, believed in Him.

Note: See the Gospel of John, 2:13-25.

CHAPTER 17

The Conversation of Jesus Christ with Nicodemus

Among the people struck by the miracles of Jesus Christ and believing in Him, was a Pharisee, **Nicodemus**, one of the rulers of the Jews. He came to Jesus by night, unknown to all, so that the Pharisees and rulers of the Jews, who disliked Jesus Christ, would not find out about this.

Nicodemus wanted to find out if Jesus Christ really was the expected Saviour of the world, and whom He would bring into His Kingdom, that is, what must a man do to enter His Kingdom. He said to the Saviour, "Rabbi, we know that Thou art a teacher come from God, for no man can do these miracles that Thou doest, except God be with Him."

The Saviour, speaking with Nicodemus said, "Verily I say unto Thee, except a man be born again, he cannot see the Kingdom of God." Nicodemus was very astonished to think a man could be born again. But the Saviour spoke to him not about the usual physical birth, but about **spiritual** birth, that is, that a man must be completely changed in soul, perfectly **good and merciful,** and that such a change in a man may be accomplished only by the power of God.

The Saviour said to Nicodemus, "Verily, verily I say unto thee, except a man be born of water (by Baptism) and of the Spirit (Who descends upon a man during Baptism), he cannot enter into the Kingdom of God." The Lord explained to Nicodemus that man, born only of earthly parents, remains sinful, meaning, unworthy of the Kingdom of Heaven. Having been born of the Holy Spirit, a man becomes cleansed from sin, holy. How this change in the soul of a man is accomplished, this work of God, is not understood by people.

Therefore the Saviour said to Nicodemus that He came to earth to suffer and to die for people, not to a royal throne does He come but to a **cross**. As Moses raised a serpent in the wilderness (that is, suspended on a pole a bronze serpent, to save from death the Jews who had been bitten by venomous snakes), thus the Son of Man must be suspended (that is, thus Christ, the Son of Man, must be hung on a wooden cross), so that all who believe in Him shall not perish, but have everlasting life. God so loved the world, that He gave His Only-begotten Son (through suffering and death) for the salvation of people, and sent Him into the world not to judge people, but to save them.

Nicodemus from this time became a secret disciple of Jesus Christ.

Note: See the Gospel of John 3:1-21.

CHAPTER 18

The Conversation of Jesus Christ with the Woman of Samaria

Returning from Judea into Galilee, Jesus Christ with His disciples went through Samaria, past a city called **Sychar** (in ancient times called Shechem). Before the city on the southern side was a well, dug, according to tradition, by the patriarch Jacob.

Jesus Christ, wearied with His journey, sat on the well to rest. It was about noontime, and His disciples went into the city to buy food.

The Lord Speaks with the Samaritan Woman

At that time there came to the well a woman of Samaria to draw water.

Jesus Christ said to her, "Give me water to drink!"

The words of the Saviour greatly surprised the Samaritan woman. She said, "How is it that Thou, being a Jew, askest drink of me, who am a woman of Samaria? For the Jews have no dealings with the Samaritans."

Jesus said to her, "If thou knewest the gift of God, (that is, the great mercy of God, which God has sent to you in this meeting), and Who it is that saith to thee, 'Give me water to drink,' thou wouldest have asked of Him, and He would have given thee living water."

The Saviour called His divine teaching the living water. As water saves the man dying of thirst, thus His divine teaching saves man from eternal death and leads him to blessed eternal life. But the Samaritan woman thought that He spoke about ordinary well water, which by them was called "living" water.

The woman with astonishment asked Him, "Sir, Thou hast nothing to draw with and the well is deep. From whence then hast Thou that living water? Art Thou greater than our father Jacob, who gave us the well, and drank thereof himself, and his children, and his cattle?"

Jesus Christ said to her in answer, "Whosoever drinketh of this water shall thirst again; but whosoever drinketh of the water that I shall give him shall never thirst; but the water that I shall give him shall be in him a well of water springing up into everlasting life."

But the Samaritan woman did not understand these words of the Saviour and said, "Sir, give me this water, that I thirst not, neither come here to draw."

Jesus Christ, wishing the Samaritan woman to understand what He had said to her, first told her to call her husband. He said, "Go, call thy husband and come here."

The woman said, "I have no husband."

Then Jesus Christ said to her, "Thou hast well said, 'I have no husband,' for thou hast had five husbands; and he whom thou now hast is not thy husband. In that Thou saidst the truth."

The Samaritan woman, struck by the omniscience of the Saviour, Who revealed everything about her sinful life, now understood that it was not an ordinary man speaking. She immediately asked Him to resolve the ancient question between the Samaritans and the Jews: which faith was more correct and which service was more pleasing to God. "Sir, I perceive that Thou art a prophet. Our fathers worshipped in this mountain (by this she meant Mount Gerizim upon which were visible the ruins of the demolished Samaritan Temple); and ye say, that in Jerusalem is the place where men ought to worship."

Jesus Christ said to her, **"Woman, believe Me, the hour cometh, when ye shall neither in this mountain, nor yet at Jerusalem, worship the Father. Ye worship ye know not what: we know what we worship; for salvation is of the Jews."** Until that time only the Jews had the true faith, their services alone were done correctly and were pleasing to God. **"But the hour cometh, and now is, when the true worshippers shall** worship the Father in spirit and in truth: for the Father seeketh such to worship Him. God is a Spirit (unseen, bodiless): and they that worship Him must worship Him in spirit and in truth." That is, the true and God-pleasing service occurs when people worship the Heavenly Father not only with their bodies and not only by outward signs and words, but with all their being — with all their soul — when they truly believe in God, love and honor Him, and by their good works and mercy to others fulfill the will of God.

Having heard this new teaching, the Samaritan woman said to Jesus Christ, "I know that the **Messiah** cometh, Who is called **Christ**; when He is come, He will tell us all things."

Then Jesus Christ said to her, "The Messiah — **I am the One, Who is speaking to you.**"

Upon this scene came His disciples, and marvelled that He talked with the Samaritan woman. Yet no man asked the Saviour about what He had spoken with her.

The woman then left her waterpot and hurried into the city. There she started to tell the people, "Come, see a Man, Who told me all things that I ever did. Is not this the Christ?" Then they went out of the city, and came to the well where Christ was.

Meanwhile the disciples besought him saying, "Rabbi, eat." But the Saviour said to them, "I have food to eat of which you do not know." So the disciples said to one another, "Has anyone brought Him food?" Jesus said to them, "My food is to do the will of Him who sent Me and to accomplish His work. Do you not say, 'There are yet four months, then comes the harvest?' I tell you, lift up your eyes and see how the fields (and the Lord showed them Samaritans — inhabitants of the city who at that time came to Him) are already white for harvest (how these people want to see the Saviour Christ, how they were inclined to listen to Him and receive Him). He who reaps receives wages, and gathers fruit for eternal life, so that sower and reaper may rejoice together. For here the saying holds true, 'One sows and another reaps.' I sent you to reap that for which you did not labor; others have labored, and you have entered into their labor."

The Samaritans who came from the city, of whom many believed in Him because of the words of the woman, asked the Saviour to remain with them. He went to them and stayed there two days, and taught them.

After this more Samaritans believed in Him. They said to the woman, "It is no longer because of your words that we believe, for we have heard for ourselves, and we know that He is **truly the Saviour of the world, the Christ.**"

By tradition, it is known that the Samaritan woman who spoke with Christ at Jacob's well, spent the remainder of her life preaching the Gospel of Christ. For preaching faith in Christ she suffered in the year 66 (she was thrown by tormentors into a well). The Holy Church celebrates her memory on **March 20**th (April 2 n.s.) Her name is the **holy Martyr Photina** (Svetlana in Russian).

Note: See the Gospel of John, 4:1-42.

Jesus Heals a Nobleman's Son

When Jesus Christ came to Galilee, the Galileans welcomed Him with faith, having seen the miracles that He had done in Jerusalem at Passover. Jesus Christ came again into Cana in Galilee, where He had changed the water into wine. There came to Him a nobleman from Capernaum, who served at the royal palace, who begged the Saviour to come down and heal his son, for he was at the point of death.

Jesus Christ said to him, "Go, your son will live." The nobleman believed the word that Jesus spoke to him and went home to Capernaum. As he was going down, his servants met him and told him that his son was alive.

So he asked them the hour when he began to revive. The servants said to him, "Yesterday at the seventh hour the fever left him."

The father knew that that was the hour when Jesus had said to him, "Your son will live." The nobleman and all his household believed in Jesus Christ.

From Cana, Jesus Christ went around the cities and towns of Galilee, in order to preach His teaching everywhere. Preaching, He healed sickness and every kind of infirmity among the people. Word of Him spread throughout the land, and from everywhere the sick, the possessed, lunatics, and paralytics came to Him, and He healed them. He refused help to no one, and all found consolation in Him.

By the example of His life, the Saviour taught that everyone who wishes to be in the Kingdom of God, must be kind, must do good to all and help everyone, as far as each one's strength allows.

Note: See the Gospel of John 4:43-54.

CHAPTER 19

The Healing of the Paralytic at the Pool of Bethesda

From Galilee Jesus Christ again went up to Jerusalem for the feast of Passover.

Not far from the Temple, by the sheep gate through which they drove the sheep for sacrifices, was a pool with five porticoes, or galleries. This pool with the galleries was called **Bethesda**, which means **house of mercy**. In the galleries beside the pool lay many sick, blind, lame and withered. They were all waiting for the moving of the water, for an angel of the Lord went down at a certain season into the pool, and stirred the

The Healing of the Paralytic

water. Whoever stepped in first after the stirring of the water was healed of whatever disease he had.

Jesus Christ visited this house of mercy. There He saw a man who had an infirmity thirty-eight years. Jesus Christ said to him, "Do you want to be healed?"

The sick man answered, "Sir, I have no man to put me into the pool when the water is stirred, and while I am going another steps down before me."

The Ruins of the Bethesda Pool As It Appears Today

Jesus Christ said to him, "Rise, take up your bed and walk."

At once the man was healed, and he took up his bed and walked. That day was the Sabbath. So the Jews said to the man who was cured, "It is the Sabbath, it is not lawful for you to carry your bed."

But he answered them, "The Man Who healed me said to me, 'Take up your bed and walk.' "

They asked him, "Do you know Who this Man is?"

The man was not able to answer them for he did not know Who Jesus Christ was, because Christ, after healing him, had withdrawn into the crowd.

Afterward, Jesus found him in the Temple and said to him, "See, you are well! Sin no more, so that nothing worse befall you."

The man went away and told the Jews that it was Jesus Christ Who had healed him.

The elders of the Jews began to persecute Jesus Christ and to seek a chance to kill Him, because He did this on the Sabbath. They taught that on the Sabbath it was a sin to do any work, even good deeds.

Jesus said to them, "My Father is working still, and I am working. Truly, truly, I say to you, the Son can do nothing of His own accord, but only what He (the Son) sees the Father doing; for whatever He (God the Father) does, the Son does likewise. For as the Father raises the dead and gives them life, so also the Son gives life to whom He will. He who does not honor the Son does not honor the Father Who sent Him. Search the Scriptures because you think that in them you have eternal life; it is they that bear witness of Me."

This was why the Jews sought all the more to kill Him, because He not only broke the Sabbath but also called God His Father, making Himself equal with God.

Note: See the Gospel of John, 5:1-16.

Healing of the Man with a Withered Hand

It came to pass also on another Sabbath that Jesus entered the synagogue (the house of meeting and prayer). There was a man there with a withered hand. The Pharisees, wishing to find some charge to make against the Saviour, watched closely to see whether or not He would heal the sick man on the Sabbath.

The Saviour, knowing their thoughts, said to the man, "Rise up, and stand forth in the midst."

Then turning to the Pharisees, He said, "I will ask you one thing. Is it lawful on the Sabbath days to do good, or to do evil, to save life, or to destroy it?"

They remained silent.

And looking round about them all, He said, "What man of you, if he has one sheep and it falls into a pit on the Sabbath, will not lay hold of it and lift it out? Of how much more value is a man than a sheep! So it is lawful to do good on the Sabbath."

Then the Saviour turned to the man and said, "Stretch out your hand."

The man extended his withered hand, and it was restored, whole like the other.

The Pharisees were filled with madness and went out of the synagogue, and took counsel among themselves, how to destroy Jesus.

Jesus with his disciples withdrew from there, and many followed Him, and He, preaching, healed all the sick.

Note: See the Gospels of Matthew 12:9-14; Mark 3:1-6; and Luke 6:6-11.

CHAPTER 20

The Lord Chooses Twelve Apostles

Gradually the number of disciples of Jesus Christ increased. One day, while in Galilee, Jesus Christ went out into a mountain to pray and continued all night in prayer to God. When it was day, He called His disciples to Him, and of them He chose twelve, whom He named **apostles**, that is, messengers, as He sent them to preach His teaching.

The names of the twelve apostles are as follows:

1. **Simon**, whom the Saviour called **Peter**,

2. **Andrew**, brother of Simon Peter, known as the "**First-called**,"

3. **James**, the son of Zebedee,

4. **John**, the son of Zebedee, brother of James, called the **Theologian**. These two brothers, James and John, the Saviour called "**sons of thunder**," because of their fiery zeal.

5. **Philip**,

6. **Nathaniel**, son of Tolmai, and therefore called **Bartholomew**,

7. **Thomas**, also called **Didymus**, which means "**the twin**,"

8. **Matthew**, also known as **Levi**, a former tax collector,

9. **James**, son of Alphaeus, also known as Cleopas, called "the less, or younger or smaller," in contrast to James the son of Zebedee,

10. **Simon**, named the **Canaanite**, otherwise known as the **Zealot**,

11. **Judas**, son of James, who also bore another name, **Lebbaeus**, called **Thaddeus**,

12. **Judas Iscariot** (from the city of Karioth), who later betrayed Jesus Christ.

To the apostles the Lord gave power to heal the sick, to cast out unclean spirits, and to resurrect the dead.

In addition to these twelve chief apostles, Jesus Christ also chose another **seventy apostles**: Mark, Luke, Cleopas and others. He also sent them out to preach.

When the seventy apostles returned from preaching, they said with joy to Jesus Christ, *Lord, even the devils are subject unto us through Thy name* (Luke 10:17).

He said to them, *Do not rejoice that the spirits are subject unto you; but rather rejoice because your names are written in heaven* (Luke 10:20). That is, do not rejoice over the miracles which are given to you for your preaching, but rejoice over the fact that you will receive blessings and eternal life with God in the Kingdom of Heaven.

Besides the disciples, there constantly accompanied Jesus Christ some women who had been healed by Him, **Mary Magdalene** (from the

The Twelve Apostles

city of Magdala), out of whom Jesus cast seven devils; **Joanna**, the wife of Chuza, Herod's steward; **Susanna**, and many others.

Note: See the Gospels of Matthew 10:2-14; Mark 3:13-19; Luke 6:12-16; 8, 1-3.

CHAPTER 21

The Sermon on the Mount

After choosing the apostles, Jesus Christ came down with them from the mountain heights to a level place. There, numerous disciples waited for Him and a multitude of people gathered from every corner of Israel and neighboring places. They came to listen to Him and to be healed of their sickness. They all sought to touch the Saviour, because from Him flowed power, and He healed everyone.

Seeing the multitudes before Him, Jesus Christ, surrounded by His disciples, went up into a mountain and sat, to teach the people.

At first the Lord indicated what His disciples, that is, all Christians, must be like. How they must fulfill the law of God in order to receive blessed (that is, joyful and blissful in the highest degree), eternal life in the Kingdom of Heaven. For this He gave **nine commandments of blessedness**, or **Beatitudes**. Then the Lord gave teachings on the providence of God, on not judging others, on the power of prayer, on charity and on many others. This sermon of Jesus Christ is called the **Sermon on the Mount**.

Thus, during a clear spring day, in a gentle, refreshing breeze from the Sea of Galilee, on the slope of a mountain covered with greenery and flowers, the Saviour gave to the people the New Testament law of love.

In the Old Testament, the Lord gave the Law in the uninhabited wilderness on Mt. Sinai. Then a menacing, dark cloud covered the summit of the mountain; thunder rumbled, lightning flashed and the sound of trumpets blared. No one dared to approach the mountain except Moses, to whom the Lord handed the ten commandments of the Law.

Now the Lord was open to the crowded throng of people. All were trying to draw closer to Him and to touch Him, even though it be only the hem of His robe, to receive from Him beneficial strength. No one went away from Him without being comforted.

The Old Testament law is the law of strict righteousness, and the New Testament law of Christ is the law of divine love and grace, which gives to people the strength to fulfill God's law. Jesus Christ Himself said, *I am not come to destroy* (the law), *but to fulfill* (Matt. 5:17).

The Beatitudes — Commandments of Blessedness

Jesus Christ, our Lord and Saviour, as a loving Father, shows us the way by which people may enter the Kingdom of Heaven, the Kingdom of God. To all who fulfill His laws, Christ, as King of Heaven and earth, promises **eternal blessedness** (great joy, the highest happiness) in the future, eternal life. Therefore such people He calls **blessed**.

1. Blessed are the poor in spirit (humble), **for theirs is** (i.e., is given to them) **the Kingdom of Heaven.**

Poor in spirit refers to those people who feel and acknowledge their sins and spiritual unworthiness. They keep in mind that without God's help, by themselves, they are not able to do good, and therefore they do not accept praise for anything, nor are they proud, either before God or before people. These people are humble.

2. Blessed are those who mourn (over their sins), **for they shall be comforted.**

Those who **mourn** — people who grieve and shed tears over their sins and spiritual unworthiness. God forgives their sins. He gives them comfort even here on earth, and in Heaven, eternal joy.

3. Blessed are the meek, for they shall inherit the earth.

The **meek** — people who patiently endure all misfortune without becoming bitter, without grumbling at God, and humbly bear all unpleasantness and offenses from people, not growing angry at anyone. They will receive possession of the heavenly dwelling place, that is the renewed land in the Kingdom of Heaven.

4. Blessed are those who hunger and thirst for righteousness, for they shall be filled.

Those who **hunger and thirst after righteousness** are people who fervently seek righteousness as sincerely as they strive after food. They pray that God will supply water with which to cleanse them of their sins and help them live righteously (they wish to set themselves right with God). The desire of these people will be fulfilled, they will be satisfied, they will be justified.

5. Blessed are the merciful, for they shall obtain mercy.

The **merciful** — people having good hearts, who are charitable and compassionate toward all, as much as they are able. Such people will be pardoned by God. To them will be revealed special mercy by God.

6. Blessed are the pure in heart, for they shall see God.

The **pure in heart** — people who not only avoid bad deeds, but who strive to keep their souls pure, to guard them against evil thoughts and desires. They are close to God (their souls always sense Him), and in the future life, in the Kingdom of Heaven, they will be with God eternally. They will see Him.

7. Blessed are the peacemakers, for they shall be called the sons of God.

The **peacemakers** — people who dislike any kind of quarrel. They themselves try to live with everyone peacefully and amicably and to reconcile one to another. They become like the Son of God, Who came to earth to reconcile sinful mankind with the righteous God. Such people will be called sons or children of God, and will be especially close to God.

8. Blessed are those who are persecuted for righteousness' sake, for theirs is the Kingdom of Heaven.

Those **persecuted for righteousness' sake** — people who love to live righteously, according to the law of God, who suffer and endure for this righteousness all kinds of persecution, deprivation, and hardship, but do not change because of them. For this they will receive the Kingdom of Heaven.

9. Blessed are you when men revile you and persecute you and utter all kinds of evil against you falsely on My account. Rejoice and be glad, for your reward is great in Heaven.

Here the Lord says that if they defame you (scoff at you, attack you, disgrace you), oppress you and falsely speak evil of you (slander or unjustly accuse you), and you endure all this because of your faith in Me, then do not grieve, but rejoice and be glad, because the greatest reward awaits you in Heaven, that is, the highest degree of eternal blessedness.

The Providence of God

Jesus Christ taught that God provides and cares for all creation, but especially provides for people. The Lord cares for us more and better than the most good and intelligent father for his children. He gives help in everything that is necessary for our lives and for that which is truly useful for us.

"Take no thought for your life, what you shall eat, or what you shall drink, nor yet for your body, what ye shall put on," said the Saviour. "Behold the birds of the air, for they sow not, neither do they reap, nor gather into barns; yet your heavenly Father feeds them. Are you not of more value that they? Consider the lilies of the field, how they grow. They neither toil nor spin. Yet I tell you, even Solomon in all his glory was not arrayed like one of these. But if God so clothes the grass of the field, which today is alive and tomorrow is thrown in the oven, will He not much more clothe you, O men of little faith? Your heavenly Father knows that you need them all. But **seek first the Kingdom of God and His righteousness, and all these things shall be yours as well.**"

On Not Judging One's Neighbors

Jesus Christ did not give an order to judge other people. He said, "Judge not that you be not judged. For with the judgement you pronounce you will be judged (if you are lenient toward the actions of other people, then God will be merciful in His judgement of you). And the measure you give will be the measure you get. Why do you see the **speck** that is in your brother's eye, but do not notice the **beam** that is in your own eye? (This means: why do you love to notice in others insignificant sins and shortcommings, when in yourself you do not wish to see large sins and vices?) Or how can you say to your brother, 'Let me take the speck out of your eye,' when there is the log in your own eye? You hypocrite! First take the log out of your own eye (try first of all to correct yourself), and then you will see clearly to take the speck out of your brother's eye (then you will be able to correct a sin in another without insulting or humiliating him)."

On Forgiving One's Neighbor

"Forgive, and you will be forgiven," said Jesus Christ. "For if you forgive them their trespasses, your heavenly Father also will forgive you, but if you do not forgive men their trespasses, neither will your Father forgive your trespasses."

On Love for One's Neighbor

Jesus Christ commanded us to love not only our neighbors, but all people, even those who offend us and are malicious towards us, that is, our enemies. He said, "You have heard that it was said (by your teachers — the scribes and the Pharisees), 'You shall love your neighbor and hate your enemy.' But I say to you, Love your enemies and bless those who abuse you and persecute you, that you may be sons of your Father Who is in Heaven. For He makes His sun rise on the evil and the good, and sends rain on the just and on the unjust."

For if you love only those who love you, or do good only to those who do good to you and help only those from whom you hope to receive something, for what is God to reward you? Do not even the sinners do the same? Do not even the Gentiles do the same?

Therefore, be merciful even as your Father is merciful, be perfect, as your heavenly Father is perfect.

How to Treat One's Neighbors

As to how we must treat our neighbors always, under all circumstances, Jesus Christ gave us the rule, "**As you wish that men would do to you** (and we, of course, wish that all people would love us, treat us well and forgive us) **do so to them likewise**." Do not do to others that which you would not like to have done to you.

The Power of Prayer

If we sincerely pray to God and ask His help, then God will do everything that will serve for our true well-being. Jesus Christ said concerning this, "Ask, and it will be given you; seek, and you shall find; knock, and it will be opened to you. Is there among you such a man who when his son asks him for bread, would give him a stone? And when he asks for fish, would give him a serpent? If you then, who are evil, know how to give good gifts to your children, how much more will the heavenly Father give good to those who ask Him!"

About Alms

Every good work we do we must do not to gain praise from people, not to show off before others, not for rewards from people, but for the love of God and neighbor. Jesus Christ said, "Beware of practicing your piety before men in order to be seen by them; for then you will have no reward from your Father Who is in Heaven. Thus, when you give alms, sound no trumpet before you (do not broadcast it, as the hypocrites do in the synagogues and in the streets, that they may be praised by men. Truly, I say to you, they have their reward. But when you give alms, do not let your left hand know what your right hand is doing. Do not pride yourself on the good that you have done, forget about it, so that your alms may be in secret; and your Father Who sees in secret all that you do for the sake of your soul, will reward you openly" — if not immediately, then at His last judgement.

The Necessity of Good Works

So that people would know that to enter the Kingdom of God it is not sufficient to simply have good feelings and wishes, but it is also necessary to have good works, Jesus Christ said, "Not everyone who says to me, 'Lord, Lord,' shall enter the Kingdom of Heaven, but he who does the will of My Father Who is in Heaven." That is, it is not enough to be only believing and devout, but it is also necessary to do whatever good deed the Lord expects of us.

When Jesus Christ finished His sayings, the crowds were astonished at His teaching, for He taught them as one Who had authority, and not as the scribes and Pharisees. When He came down from the mountain great crowds followed Him, and by His great mercy, He performed great miracles.

Note: See the Gospels of Matthew, chaps. 5, 6 and 7; and Luke 6:12-41.

CHAPTER 22

The Power of Faith and Prayer for Others — The Healing of the Paralytic in Capernaum

The Lord Jesus Christ taught us to pray not only for ourselves, but also for others, for our neighbors; for by His love the Lord imparts mercy to those for whom others are praying.

While in the city of Capernaum, Jesus Christ taught in one home. The inhabitants of the city, as soon as they heard that he was at the house, gathered together in such great numbers that there was no longer room for them, not even near the door. Among the number of listeners were Pharisees and teachers of the law who had come from every village of Galilee and Judea and even from Jerusalem.

The Lord Heals the Paralytic

While preaching the Saviour performed many miracles and healed the sick.

At that time, four men came, bringing to Him a paralytic on a bed, and they sought to bring him in the house to the Saviour, but they found no way to make their way in because of the crowd of people.

Then they went up on the roof, made an opening and let down the cot on which the paralytic lay, straight to the feet of the Saviour. When Jesus Christ saw the faith of the people who brought the sick man, He said to the paralytic, "My son, your sins are forgiven."

The Pharisees and the scribes began to question in their hearts, "Who is this that speaks blasphemies? Who can forgive sins but God alone?"

Jesus Christ, knowing their thoughts, said to them, "Which is easier to say, 'Your sins are forgiven you,' or to say 'Rise and walk?' But that you may know that the Son of man hath power on earth to forgive sins, I say to you "Rise, take up your bed and go home." And immediately he rose before them, and took up that on which he lay, and went home, glorifying God for receiving mercy.

Thus, the Lord healed the sick man by the faith and prayers of his friends. When the crowds saw it, amazement seized them all, and they glorified God, and were filled with awe, saying, "We have seen strange things today; we never saw anything like this!"

Note: See the Gospels of Matthew 9:1-8; Mark 2:1-12; Luke 5:17-26.

Raising the Widow's Son at Nain

One day Jesus Christ went from Capernaum to the city of Nain. Many of His disciples and a great crowd went with Him. As He drew near to the gate of the city, a man who had died was being carried out, the only son of his mother, a widow. The unhappy woman walked and cried bitterly, and a large crowd from the city was with her. When the Lord saw her, He had compassion on the deep grief of the poor mother, and said to her, "Do not weep."

He came and touched the bier on which the dead one lay (among the Jews, the dead were wrapped in shrouds and carried on biers, or stretchers, to the cemetery for burial). The bearers stood still. Then Jesus said to the dead man, "Young man, I say to you arise!"

The dead man sat up and began to speak, and Jesus Christ gave the resurrected youth to his mother.

Seeing this miracle, fear seized them all. They glorified God, saying, "A great prophet has risen among us! God has visited His people."

Note: See the Gospel of Luke 7:11-17.

CHAPTER 23

Parables
The Parable of the Sower

Jesus Christ, while in Capernaum, went to the shore of the Sea of Galilee. Many people gathered around Him. He got into a small boat and sat there. The people stood on the beach, and from the boat, He began to teach them in parables.

Jesus Christ said, "A sower went out to sow. And as he sowed, some seeds fell along the path, and were trodden under foot, and the birds came and devoured them. Other seeds fell on rocky ground, where they had not much soil; immediately they sprang up, since they had no depth of soil, but soon they were scorched, and since they had no roots they withered away. Other seeds fell among thorns, and the thorns grew up and choked them. Other seeds fell on good rich soil, and grew and yielded abundant fruit."

Then, when the disciples asked Jesus Christ, "What does this parable mean?" He explained to them:

Seed — the Word of God (the Gospels).

Sower — the one who spreads the Word of God.

The Sower and the Seeds

Soil — the heart of man.

The ground along the path where the seed fell indicates careless and profligate people, in the hearts of whom the Word of God does not have access. The Devil without trouble steals it and carries it away from them, so that they do not believe and are not saved.

Rocky ground signifies people who are inconstant and faint-hearted. They willingly hear the Word of God, but it does not take hold in their souls, and they fall away from the faith at the first temptation, grief, or persecution over the Word of God. **Thorns** signify people for whom everyday cares, wealth, and various vices stifle in the heart the Word of God.

Good rich soil signifies people with good hearts. They pay attention to the Word of God, treasure it in their hearts, and patiently try to fulfil everything that it teaches. Their fruit is good deeds, for which they are awarded the Kingdom of Heaven.

Note: See the Gospels of Matthew 13:1-23; Mark 4:1-20; Luke 8:4-15.

The Parable of the Mustard Seed

Jesus Christ taught that the Kingdom of God, the Kingdom of Heaven, began and was founded on that which He established on earth, that is, the Church of Christ, which began small and then spread over all the earth. He said, "The Kingdom of Heaven is like a grain of mustard seed, which a man took and sowed in his field. This seed is indeed the least of all seeds; but when it is grown it is the greatest among plants and becomes a tree, so that the birds of the air come and lodge in its branches." The Saviour spoke many other parables, teaching the people.

Note: See the Gospels of Matthew 13: 31-32; Mark 4: 30-32; Luke 13: 18-19.

The Parable of the Leaven

Explaining the teaching of the Kingdom of God, the Lord Jesus Christ said, "With what shall I compare the Kingdom of God? The Kingdom of God is like leaven which a woman took and hid in three measures of meal, till it was all leavened."

Short and simple is this parable, but a deep double meaning is contained in it: the **general historical** process of the salvation of people, and the **individual** process of the salvation of each person.

The historical process — After the world-wide flood, three races of people descended from the sons of Noah, Shem, Ham and Japheth: the Semites, the Hamites, and Japhetites. They were the three measures of meal in which Christ puts His heavenly leaven — the Holy Spirit — Who is put in all races of mankind, without limitation or exclusion.

As the woman, with the help of the leaven, turned the meal from its usual state into bread, thus Christ, with the help of the Holy Spirit, turns usual, natural people into sons of God, to the immortal life of the Kingdom of Heaven.

The process of the leavening began on the day of the descent of the Holy Spirit on the apostles and continues to our day, and will continue to the end of the age — **until all are leavened**.

The individual process — The Saviour, through baptism in the name of the Holy Trinity, gives heavenly leaven—gifts of the Holy Spirit, heavenly strength, to the soul of each person, that is, to the main powers of a person's soul: intelligence, feeling (heart), and will (**three measures**). All three powers of the soul of a person grow harmoniously and rise toward Heaven, being filled with the light of intelligence, the warmth of love, and the glory of good works, turning individuals into sons and daughters of God, heirs of the Kingdom of Heaven.

The Lord used a woman in His example because a woman, as a wife and mother, lovingly prepares the homemade bread for the children and the household, whereas a male-baker prepares bread for sale, distributing the income for gain. (According to Bishop Nikolai Velimirovich.)

Note: See the Gospels of Matthew: 13:33; Luke 13:20-21.

The Parable of the Wheat and the Weeds

Jesus Christ taught that in His Kingdom on earth, in the Church of Christ, until the last day of the world there would be sinners.

The Lord said, "The Kingdom of Heaven may be compared to a man who sowed good seed in his field; but while men were sleeping, his enemy came and sowed weeds among the wheat, and went away.

"So when the plants came up and bore grain, then the weeds appeared also. And the servants of the householder came and said to him, 'Sir, did you not sow good seed in your field? How then has it weeds?'

"He said to them, 'An enemy has done this.'

"The servants said to him, 'Then do you want us to go and gather them?'

"But he said, 'No, lest in gathering the weeds you root up the wheat along with them. Let both grow together until the harvest; and at harvest time I will tell the reapers, gather the weeds first and bind them in bundles to be burned, but gather the wheat into my barn.' "

The disciples, when they were left alone with the Lord, asked Him to explain this parable.

Jesus Christ said:

"The **Sower** of the good seed is the Son of man, the Lord Jesus Christ Himself. The **field** is the world. The **good seed** means the sons of the Kingdom, good, devout people who accept the teachings of Christ. The **weeds** are the sons of the Evil One, wicked, evil people. The **enemy** who sowed the weeds is the Devil. The **harvest** is the end of the world, and the **reapers** are angels.

"Just as the weeds are gathered and burned with fire, so will it be at the close of the age. The Son of man will send His angels, and they will gather out of His kingdom all causes of sin and all evildoers, and throw them into the furnace of fire; there men will weep and gnash their teeth.

Then the righteous will shine like the sun in the kingdom of their Father," in the kingdom of eternal blessed life.

How often, at the sight of the disgraceful behavior of immoral, evil people, we ask, "Lord, why do You not punish these evil people now? Why do You allow them to use all the good things of the world? Why do they burden and oppress the good?"

To all these questions this parable gives the answer: **let them grow together one with the other until the harvest, until the day of the Last Judgement.** Such is the will of God. Because the Lord in giving man His image and likeness gives free will. Evil crops up in the world because of the work of the Devil, who constantly and cunningly sows evil in the world — who spreads among people unbelief and every kind of lawlessness. To expose all sin might harm tender souls if they saw it.

In the free choice of good and the rejection of evil, man exalts God, glorifies God, and improves himself; and by enduring suffering from evil, he receives from God the highest reward in the Kingdom of Heaven.

In this manner God, without any coercion, gives people of good will the possibility of receiving eternal, blessed life in the Kingdom of Heaven, and people of evil intent — eternal torment in Hell.

Note: See the Gospel of Matthew 13:24-30, 36-43.

About the Coming of the Kingdom of God on Earth

One day the Pharisees asked Jesus Christ, "When will the Kingdom of God come?"

The Saviour answered, "The Kingdom of God is not coming with signs to be observed; nor will they say, 'Lo, here it is!' or 'There!' for behold, **the Kingdom of God is within you.**"

This means that the Kingdom of God does not have boundaries, it is everywhere unlimited. Therefore, to look for the Kingdom of God, we do not have to go somewhere far away, overseas, to distant lands. For this it is not required of us to climb up to the clouds or descend into the depths. One must seek the Kingdom of Heaven in the place where we live, that is, where we are placed by the providence of God, because the Kingdom of God develops and ripens **within man, in the heart of a person**. The Kingdom of God is "**righteousness, peace, and joy of the Holy Spirit**," when the conscience and will of a man enter into complete harmony, joined into one with the intelligence and the will of God. Then everything contrary to the will of God becomes loathsome to a man. The visible realization of the Kingdom of God on earth is the Holy Church of Christ. In it everything is arrayed according to the Law of God.

Note: See the Gospel of Luke 17:20-21.

CHAPTER 24

The Stilling of the Storm

One day Jesus Christ and His disciples sailed in a boat across the Sea of Galilee. Other boats were with them. During the voyage Jesus was asleep in the stern. A great storm of wind arose. The waves beat into the boat, so that the boat was already filling with water, but still Jesus Christ slept. The disciples, terrified, woke the Lord and said to Him, "Lord! Save us, we are perishing!" Jesus Christ awoke and rebuked the wind and said to the sea, "Peace! Be still!"

The Sea of Galilee

Immediately the wind ceased, and there was a great calm.

Then, turning to the disciples, He said, "Why are you afraid? Have you no faith?"

All who were there were filled with awe and said to one another, "Who is this that even the wind and sea obey Him?"

Note: See the Gospels of Matthew 8:23-27; Mark 4:35-41; and Luke 8:22-25.

CHAPTER 25

Raising of the Daughter of Jairus

There was a Hebrew elder, a ruler of the synagogue, by the name of Jairus, and at his house his twelve-year-old only daughter lay near death.

Jairus came to Jesus Christ, fell at His feet and besought Him, saying, "My little daughter is at the point of death. Come and lay Your hands on her, so that she may be made well and live."

Seeing the faith of Jairus, Jesus Christ went with him. On the way, they met a man sent from Jairus's house, who said to him, "Your daughter is dead; do not trouble the Teacher any more."

But Jesus, on hearing this, said to Jairus, "Do not fear, only believe, and she will be saved." When they came to the house, they saw a great tumult. Everyone was weeping and wailing.

The Lord said to them, "Do not weep; for the girl is not dead but sleeping." They did not understand His words and started laughing at Him, knowing that she was dead. But Jesus Christ sent the crowd outside the house, and taking with Him only the girl's parents and three disciples, Peter, James, and John, entered the room where the dead girl lay. He took her by the hand and said, "**Talitha cumi**," which means, "Little girl, I say unto thee, arise."

And her spirit returned. The girl got up at once and walked. Her overjoyed parents were greatly amazed. Jesus Christ directed them to give her something to eat, and strictly charged them to tell no one what had happened. But the news of this event spread through all that land.

Note: See the Gospels of Matthew 9:18-26; Mark 5:21-43; Luke 8:41-56.

CHAPTER 26

The Beheading of St John the Baptist

The preaching of John the Baptist was of short duration. Having prepared people to receive the Saviour, he ended his life with a martyr's death. Soon after the baptism of the Lord, John was put in prison by the Galilean King Herod. This Galilean King, Herod Antipas, was the son of Herod the Great, who slaughtered the fourteen thousand Bethlehem infants.

John upbraided King Herod, because he had married his brother Philip's wife, Herodias, even though his brother was still alive. Herodias became embittered against John for this and wanted Herod to kill him. But Herod would not agree to this because he considered John to be a great prophet and feared the people. However, to appease her, he put him in prison. Herodias was not satisfied with this, especially as Herod himself listened with pleasure to the admonitions of John and often acted on his words.

About a year passed after the Forerunner's imprisonment, and Herod, celebrating his birthday, gave a banquet for his courtiers and officers, and a thousand leading men of Galilee. Salome, the daughter of Herodias and stepdaughter of Herod, also came to this banquet. She danced for Herod, which pleased him and his guests.

Herod said to her, "Ask me for whatever you wish," and he swore he would give her even half of his kingdom.

She went and asked her mother, "What shall I ask for?"

Herodias answered, "The head of John the Baptist."

Salome with haste returned to Herod and said, "I want you to give me at once the head of John the Baptist on a platter."

Herod was exceedingly sorry, but because of his oaths and his guests he did not want to break his word to her, and he sent a soldier to the prison to cut off the head of John. The soldier fulfilled the order of the king, brought the head of John the Baptist on a platter and gave it to Salome, and Salome gave it to her mother Herodias.

When his disciples heard of the death of John the Baptist, they came and took his body, and laid it in a tomb.

NOTE: See the Gospels of St Mathew 14:1-12; St Mark 6: 14-29; and St. Luke 9, 7-9.

The day of the martyrdom of St. John the Baptist is commemorated by the Holy Orthodox Church on the **29th of August** (11 September n.s.) and is called the **Beheading of John the Baptist**. A strict fast is prescribed on this day in order to remind us of the strict life of St. John the Baptist for which he was blessed by God, and to avoid the excesses of

The Beheading of St. John the Baptist

Herod which led to such a terrible sin. The Holy Church teaches that St. John the Forerunner is the greatest of all saints after the Mother of God.

CHAPTER 27

The Miraculous Feeding of the People with Five Loaves

Soon after the death of John the Baptist, Jesus Christ with His disciples withdrew by boat to another shore of the sea. The people ran after them on foot along the shore. When the boat landed a great throng of people had gathered. Jesus Christ, seeing the crowd of people, had compassion on them because they were like sheep without a shepherd. He began to teach them many things and spoke to them of the Kingdom of God, and healed their sick. The people so zealously listened to Him that they did not notice that the day was drawing to a close.

The disciples came to Jesus Christ and said, "This is an isolated place, and the hour is now late; send them away, to go into the country and villages round about and buy themselves something to eat."

But the Lord answered the disciples, "They need not go away; you give them something to eat."

The Apostle Philip said to Him, "Two hundred denarii worth of bread is not sufficient for them, that everyone of them may take a little."

Jesus said, "How many loaves have you? Go and see."

When they had found out, the Apostle Andrew said, "There is a boy here who has five barley loaves, and two small fish, but what are they among so many?"

The Lord said, "Bring them here to me," and directed the disciples to seat the people in groups of hundreds and fifties. Then Jesus Christ took the five loaves and the two fish and looked up to Heaven, blessed them, broke them and gave the loaves to the disciples, and the disciples gave them to the crowds.

They all ate and were satisfied. When they were filled, Jesus Christ said to His disciples, "Gather up the fragments that remain, that nothing be lost."

The disciples took up what was left over and filled twelve full baskets, and those who ate were about five thousand men, not counting the women and children.

In another instance, the Lord fed four thousand men, also not counting women and children, with seven loaves and a few fish.

Note: See the Gospels of Matthew 14:14-21; Mark 6:32-44; Luke 9:10-17; John 6:1-15.

CHAPTER 28

Jesus Christ Walking on the Water

After the miraculous feeding of the people with five loaves of bread, Jesus Christ commanded His disciples to get into the boat and go to the other side of the Sea of Galilee to Bethsaida.

The Lord Saves St. Peter

He dismissed the crowd and then went into the hills to pray.

Night fell. The boat with the disciples was already out on the sea, beaten by the waves because a strong wind was blowing.

Before dawn, Jesus Christ, knowing the distress of the disciples, came to them, walking on the sea. But when they saw Him walking on the sea, they thought it was a ghost and cried out in fear. Jesus Christ immediately spoke to them and said, "Take heart, it is I; have no fear."

Then the Apostle Peter answered Him, "Lord, if it is you, let me come to you on the water."

The Lord said, "Come."

So Peter got out of the boat and walked on the water and came toward Jesus. But when he saw the wind and the big waves, he was afraid, from fear his faith vanished, and beginning to sink, he cried out, "Lord! Save me!"

Jesus Christ immediately reached out His hand and caught him, saying to him, "O man of little faith, why did you doubt?" And when they got into the boat, the wind ceased.

The disciples worshipped Jesus Christ and said, "**Truly you are the Son of God.**"

Note: See the Gospels of Matthew 14:22-36; Mark 6:45-56; John 6:16-21.

CHAPTER 29

The Healing of the Daughter of the Canaanite Woman

One day Jesus Christ went to the region of Tyre and Sidon. There came to Him a Canaanite woman, of pagan faith, and she began to cry out loudly, "Have mercy on me, O Lord, Son of David! My daughter is severely possessed by a demon."

Wishing to show His disciples the strength of the faith of this woman, Jesus Christ did not answer her a word.

Then the disciples began to beg Him saying, "Send her away, for she is crying after us."

But Jesus answered, "I am sent only to the lost sheep of the house of Israel."

But she came and knelt before Him saying, "Lord! Help me."

Jesus Christ said to her, "Let the children first be fed, for it is not right to take the children's bread and throw it to the dogs." He said this because the Jews considered themselves the children of Abraham, children of God and sons of the Kingdom of Heaven, and they looked upon the Gentiles as dogs. Therefore, the Saviour was intentionally addressing the Jews in this instance and equating a dog to this woman, wishing to show the Jews all the incorrectness and injustice of their attitude toward the pagans. Among the pagans He found strong faith, such as did not exist among the Jews. He called them "the lost sheep of the house of Israel." Moreover, by these words the Saviour showed the woman that He must live and do His work first of all among the Jews, as they believed in the true God. Most importantly, the Saviour saw the believing heart of this woman and rejoiced that in her there was an example to show all people what faith must be.

The woman humbly answered to this, "Yes, Lord; yet even the dogs under the table eat the children's crumbs." With these words the Canaanite woman demonstrated not only her great humility and consciousness that a pagan person could not be as close to God as those in the true faith, but conveyed by this her great faith that the merciful God extends mercy to all people.

Then Jesus Christ said to her, "O woman, great is your faith! Be it done for you as you desire." And her daughter was healed instantly. Returning home, the woman found her daughter restored to health, peacefully lying in bed.

Note: See the Gospels of Matthew 15:21-28; Mark 7:24-30.

CHAPTER 30

The Confession of Peter.
The First Prediction of the Lord about
His Forthcoming Suffering, Death and
Resurrection

Then Jesus went on with His disciples to the villages of Caesarea Philippi, and on the way He asked His disciples,
"Who do men say that I am?" They answered, "Some say
John the Baptist, others say Elijah, and others Jeremiah or one of
the prophets who has risen."

"But Who do you say that I am?" asked Jesus Christ.

The Apostle Peter answered for them all, "**You are the Christ, the
Son of the living God**."

The Saviour praised Peter for such faith and said to him, "You are
Peter (a rock, according to his faith); and on this rock (on such faith: that I
am the Son of God) I will build My Church, and the powers of Satan
shall not prevail against it. And to you Peter, I will give the keys to the
Kingdom of Heaven (such power is given to My Church), that whatever
you bind on earth shall be bound in Heaven; and whatever you loose on
earth shall be loosed in Heaven." (This means: for whomever among the
believers belonging to the Church, you do not forgive their sins, they
shall not be forgiven by God; and for whomever you forgive sins, they
shall be forgiven by God.) This is the same authority that the Saviour
gave to all His other apostles (cf. John 20:22-23). He spoke firstly to Peter
because the Apostle Peter was the first of them all to confess before Him
his faith — that He is the **Christ, Son of God**.

From this time Jesus Christ began to reveal to His disciples that for
the salvation of people He would have to suffer much from the elders,
chief priests and scribes, and would be killed, and on the third day rise
again.

Peter took Him and began to rebuke Him, "God forbid, Lord! This
shall never happen to You." By these words of Peter, it is evident that he
had the Jewish understanding of the Messiah and still did not understand the teaching about the salvation of people through the suffering of
Christ; in him the earthly feelings still prevailed over the spiritual. The
question of Peter was like the temptation of the Devil, who also offered
to the Lord earthly power instead of spiritual power, the kingdom of this
age instead of the Kingdom of Heaven. Therefore Jesus Christ answered
him, "Get behind Me, Satan! You are a hindrance to Me; for you are not
on the side of God, but of men." Then, He called to the multitude with

His disciples and said to them, "If any man would come after Me, let him deny himself (let him not think of his own convenience), take up his cross (sorrows, suffering and labor sent to him by God), and follow Me. For whoever would save his life will lose it; and whoever loses his life for My sake and the Gospel's will save it. For **what does it profit a man if he,** seeking to accumulate earthly blessings personally for himself, **gains for himself even the whole world and forfeits his soul,**" making it unworthy of the Kingdom of God, of eternal life?

Note: See the Gospels of Matthew 16:13-28, Mark 8:27-38 and 9:1; Luke 9:18-27.

CHAPTER 31

The Transfiguration of the Lord

In order to strengthen the faith of His disciples, when they would see His suffering, Jesus Christ took three disciples, Peter, James and John, and led them up on a high mountain to pray. According to ancient Church Tradition it was the beautiful **Mount Tabor**, covered with luxurious growth from the foot to the summit.

Mount Tabor

As the Saviour was praying, the disciples slept from fatigue. When they woke up, they saw Jesus Christ transfigured before them. His face shone like the sun and His garments became white as snow and glistened as light. There appeared with Him, in heavenly glory, two prophets,

The Transfiguration of the Lord

Moses and Elijah, and they were talking with Jesus about the suffering and death which He would have to endure in Jerusalem. Extraordinary joy filled the hearts of the disciples during this time. Peter exclaimed, "Lord, it is well that we are here. If you wish, I will make three booths here, one for You and one for Moses and one for Elijah," not knowing what He was saying. Suddenly a bright cloud overshadowed them, and they heard the voice of God the Father saying, **"This is My beloved Son, in Whom I am well pleased. Listen to Him!"**

When the disciples heard this, they fell on their faces. Jesus Christ came to them, touched them and said, "Rise, and have no fear." When the disciples lifted up their eyes, they saw Jesus Christ as He usually appeared.

As they were coming down the mountain, Jesus Christ commanded them to tell no one about the vision until He was raised from the dead.

Note: See the Gospels of Matthew 17:1-13; Mark 9:2-13; Luke 9:28-36.

The Holy Orthodox Church celebrates the glorious **Transfiguration of our Lord Jesus Christ**, on **August 6** (August 19 n.s.). This day is one of the major feast days. By His Transfiguration, the Saviour showed us how people will become in the future life, in the Kingdom of Heaven, if they follow God's Law, and how the entire earthly world will be transfigured. The Lord also reminds us that we can be transfigured even now if we lead a truly Christian life.

On the Feast of Transfiguration, after the Liturgy, fruit is brought to the church to be blessed for eating: grapes and, in general, fruit from orchards such as apples, pears and plums, in order to ask the Lord's blessing on the fruits of the harvest.

Troparion of the Feast

Thou wast transfigured on the mountain, O Christ our God, showing to Thy disciples Thy glory as each one could endure; shine forth Thou on us, who are sinners all, Thy light ever-unending through the prayers of the Theotokos. O Light-giver, glory to Thee.

Kontakion of the Feast

On the mount Thou was transfigured, and Thy disciples, as much as they could bear, beheld Thy glory, O Christ our God; so that when they would see Thee crucified, they would know Thy passion to be willing, and would preach to the world that Thou, in truth, are the Effulgence of the Father.

The Most Important Teaching of Jesus Christ: Love for God and Neighbor

More than once did people ask Jesus Christ which was His most important teaching, in order to inherit eternal life in the Kingdom of God. Some asked because they wanted to know, and others, to find a reason to accuse Him.

Thus one day a Jewish lawyer (a man who studied the Law of God), wishing to put Jesus Christ to the test, asked Him, "Teacher, which is the great commandment in the law?"

Jesus Christ said to him, **"You shall love the Lord your God with all your heart, and with all your soul, and with all your mind and with all your strength. This is the great and first commandment. And a second is like it. You shall love your neighbor as yourself. On these two commandments rest all the law and the prophets."**

This means everything that the Law of God teaches, about which the prophets spoke, is contained entirely in these two major laws. That is, all the commandments of the law and its teachings speak to us about love. If we had within ourselves such love, then all the remaining laws could be abolished, for they are all subdivisions of the law about love. Thus, for example, if we loved our neighbor, then we would not be able to offend him, or cheat him, much less kill him, or envy him and, in general, we would not wish him any kind of evil. On the contrary, we would pity him, care for him and be ready to sacrifice everything for him. Therefore Jesus Christ said, *There are no other commandments greater than these* (Mark 12:31).

The lawyer said to Him, "You are right, Teacher! You have truly said that to love God with all one's being and to love one's neighbor as oneself, is much more than all the whole burnt offerings and sacrifices."

When Jesus Christ saw that he answered wisely, He said to him, "You are not far from the kingdom of God."

Note: See the Gospels of Matthew 22:35-40; Mark 12:28-34; Luke 10:25-28.

CHAPTER 32

The Parable of the Good Samaritan

One Jew, a lawyer, desiring to justify himself, since the Jews considered "their neighbors" to be only Jews, and all others were to be held in contempt, asked Jesus Christ, "And who is my neighbor?"

In order to teach people to consider every other person as their neighbor, no matter who he might be, of whatever nationality or descent or belief; and also that we must be compassionate and merciful to all people, doing what we can to help those in need and misfortune, Jesus Christ answered him with a parable.

"A man (a Jew) was going down from Jerusalem to Jericho, and he fell among robbers, who stripped him and beat him, and departed,

The Good Samaritan

leaving him half-dead. Now by chance a priest was going down that road, and when he saw him he passed by on the other side. So likewise a Levite (a Jewish church official), when he came to the place and saw him, passed by on the other side.

"But a Samaritan, as he journeyed, came to where he was. (The Jews despised the Samaritans so much that they would not sit at the same table with them, and even tried to avoid speaking to them.) When the Samaritan saw him covered with wounds, he had compassion on him. He went to him, and bound up his wounds, pouring on them oil and wine. Then he set him on his own beast and brought him to an inn, and took care of him. And the next day he took out two denarii (a denarius was a Roman silver coin) and gave them to the innkeeper saying, 'Take care of him; and whatever more you spend, I will repay you when I come back.' "

Then Jesus Christ asked the lawyer, "Which of these three do you think was a neighbor to the man who fell among the robbers?"

The lawyer replied, "The one who showed mercy on him (that is, the Samaritan)."

And Jesus Christ said to him, "Go and do likewise."

Note: See the Gospel of Luke 10:29-37.

The parable of the **Good Samaritan**, besides its direct and clear concept of **love for every neighbor**, also has an allegorical, profound and mystical meaning according to the teachings of the Holy Fathers.

The man, going from Jerusalem to Jericho, is none other than our forefather, Adam, and in his person, all humanity. Not remaining steadfast in the good, and losing the blessedness of Paradise, Adam and Eve were compelled to leave the "Heavenly Jerusalem" (Paradise) and wander in the world, where they immediately encountered calamities and every possible adversity. The **robbers** are the diabolic powers which envied the innocent condition of man and enticed him onto the road of sin, depriving our fore-parents of faithfulness to the commandments of God (of life in Paradise). The **wounds** are the sores of sin weakening us. **The priest and Levite** represent the Law, given to us through Moses and the clergy in the person of Aaron, that by themselves cannot save man. The image of the **Good Samaritan** refers to Jesus Christ Himself, Who for the healing of our infirmities, under the appearance of oil and wine gave to us the New Testament law and grace. The **inn** — the Church of God in which is found everything necessary for our healing, and the **innkeeper** — the pastors and teachers in the Church to whom God entrusts the care of the flock. The **morning departure of the Samaritan** — the Resurrection and Ascension of Christ, and the **two denarii** given to the innkeeper — Divine Revelation, kept by means of Scripture and Holy Tradition. Finally, **the promise of the Samaritan to stop at the inn on his return-trip to settle the debt** is an indication of the second coming of Jesus Christ to earth, when He *shall reward every man according to his works* (Matt. 16:27).

CHAPTER 33

Jesus Christ with Martha and Mary

Preaching to the people, Jesus Christ arrived in **Bethany**. This town is situated not far from Jerusalem, beyond the Mount of Olives. Here He was received in the home of a woman by the name of **Martha**, who had a brother **Lazarus** and a sister **Mary**.

In the home of Lazarus Jesus Christ gave the instruction that **care for the salvation of the soul is more important than all other work**. The occasion which served to illustrate this teaching was given to Him by the sisters of Lazarus. Both of them greeted Him with the same joy, but they expressed their joy differently. Mary sat at the feet of Jesus and listened to His teaching. Martha in the meantime strenuously busied herself with elaborate refreshments for Him.

The Lord Visiting with Martha and Mary

Whether it was because it seemed to Martha that she could not manage to serve everyone all by herself, or whether it seemed to her that her sister did not receive Jesus Christ as she ought, Martha went to the

The Site Where Martha and Mary Once Lived

Saviour and said, "Lord, do You not care that my sister has left me to serve alone? Tell her then to help me."

But the Lord answered her, "**Martha, Martha you are anxious and troubled about many things**" (Martha's energy was directed to superfluous things, to worldly, transitory things that one can manage to do without); "**but only one thing is needful**" (attention to the Word of God and fulfillment of His will). "**Mary has chosen the good portion, which shall not be taken away from her.**"

It happened on one occasion when Jesus Christ talked with the people that one woman could not contain the joy in her soul from His words, and loudly exclaimed from the crowd, "**Blessed** (fortunate in the highest degree) **is the Mother who bore You and nursed You!**"

But the Saviour said, "**Yea rather, blessed are those who hear the Word of God and keep it,**" that is, those who live by the commandments of God. This was not said to imply that the Mother of God did not keep the Law of God, but to emphasize the fact that even greater than Her physical care for the Saviour was Her obedience to God's word.

Note: See the Gospel of Luke 10:38-42 and 11:27-28.

CHAPTER 34

The Saviour Accuses the Pharisees of Sin — Blasphemy Against the Holy Spirit. Glorification by Christ of the Mother of God

The enemies of Christ, the Pharisees, took counsel among themselves as to how to kill Jesus Christ. But the Saviour, aware of this, moved away from there. A large crowd of people followed after Him, and He, in His tenderheartedness, healed all their sick.

When the Saviour and His disciples entered one house, so many people came together that they could not even eat. Then a blind and dumb demoniac was brought to the Saviour. The Lord healed him so that the dumb man spoke and saw. All the people were amazed and said, "Can this be the Son of David?" But when the Pharisees heard it they said bitterly, "It is only by Beelzebub, the prince of demons (the Devil, Satan), that this man casts out demons."

Then Jesus Christ said, "How can Satan cast out Satan? If a kingdom is divided against itself, that kingdom cannot stand. And if a house is divided against itself, that house will not be able to stand. No one can enter a strong man's house and plunder his goods, unless he first binds the strong man; then, indeed, he may plunder his house. And if Satan has risen up against himself and is divided, he cannot stand, but is coming to an end. But if it is by the finger of God that I cast out demons, then the Kingdom of God has come upon you.

"Therefore, truly I say to you, every sin and blasphemy will be forgiven men, but the blasphemy against the Spirit will not be forgiven either in this age or in the age to come."

The mercy of God is without end and if a person knows his sin and repents, then there is no sin which can overcome the great mercy of God. Sins and blasphemies, from error or delusion, occur often and are easily washed away by repentance.

However, whoever knowingly and persistently rejects the most saving mercy of God, which is a blessing of the Holy Spirit, and consciously calls the deeds of the omnipotent God the works of the Devil, has no means of repentance, and without repentance there is not and can never be salvation.

The Holy Church thus determines that blasphemy against the Holy Spirit is conscious, hardened opposition to the truth. The Holy Spirit constitutes all truth (John 16:13, 14:26, 15:26), He is the Spirit of Truth (John 14:17) — thus the Lord Himself calls Him.

While He was still speaking, the Saviour's Mother and brothers came and stood outside but they could not reach Him due to the crowd. (By "brothers" at that time, in Hebrew and in general, in the eastern custom was meant all close relatives.)

The Pharisees took advantage of this instance to interrupt His teaching and to provoke distrust in the people about His divine parentage, and said, "Your mother and your brothers are outside, wishing to speak to You."

Then Jesus Christ wanted to remind the people once again that He was the Son of the Holy Virgin Mary only physically, but that at the same time He was, from eternity, the Son of God and had come to earth to save the sinful race of man, to fulfill the will of His Heavenly Father. Therefore, He Himself, as well as His Most-pure Mother and all the faithful, are obliged firstly to do the will of the Heavenly Father. **Thus it is necessary to put this lofty, eternal, spiritual obligation higher than temporal, earthly ones.**

The Lord knew that His Mother kept in Her heart all His words. **She herself attentively served and fulfilled His divine teaching; setting Her as an example to all** He said, "Who are My Mother and My brothers?" And stretching out His hand toward His disciples, He said, "Here are My Mother and My brothers! For whoever does the will of My Father in Heaven (as My Mother fulfills it), is My brother, and sister and mother."

Thus the Lord held on high the dignity of His Most-pure Mother, Who was blessed not only in that She bore God Incarnate, but even more so in that She became the first **to perfectly fulfill His divine will**.

He, as the Son of God, knew that His Mother now came to Him not to interfere with His preaching the Gospel about the Kingdom of God, but to suffer with Him. In truth, the cruel internal pain pierced Her heart. Because of love for Her divine Son She agonized to witness His suffering. But submission to the will of God, love for sinners, for whose redemption from eternal death Her Son and God offered himself as a sacrifice of propitiation, prompted Her to accept without a murmur everything that was predestined by the plan of the Holy Trinity from the foundation of the world.

Jesus Christ, as the Son of Man, was pained over the grief of His Mother, and as God, gave Her the strength to endure this terrible ordeal. The Mother suffered over Her beloved Son, surrounded by desecration and dishonor, but, as the Mother of God Incarnate, She wished to be considered worthy of bearing this supernatural suffering, and in everything relying on Him, She awaited this hour with steadfastness.

Note: See the Gospels of Matthew 12:22-37, 46-50; Mark 3:20-35; Luke 11:14-23; 8:19-21.

The Most-holy Mother of God accomplished the supreme spiritual feat on earth, the spiritual feat of perfect humility, which is love. She either spoke the word of God or remained quiet. "During the life of Her Son, She was in the shadows," writes the author of *Humility in Christ*, "and in His Ascension She remained inconspicuous. However, having now our only Intercessor in the Most Holy Mother of God, we know that Her life was better than that of any other person whoever lived on earth." After Her Dormition, She was exalted by God not only higher than all the saints who were ever pleasing to God, but higher than all the hosts of Heaven, "**more honorable than the Cherubim and beyond compare more glorious than the Seraphim.**"

Thus in the person of the Most Holy Mother of God are realized the immutable words of the Lord: *Seek first the Kingdom of God, and His righteousness, and all these things shall be added unto you* (Matt. 6:33; Luke 12:31).

Who Is Meant in the Gospels by "Brothers" of the Lord Jesus Christ?

"Brothers and sisters" of the Lord, as used in the Gospels, has a meaning completely different than what is meant by brothers and sisters of the Lord in contemporary terms. According to the custom of Eastern peoples of that time, as is now kept in the life of the Arabic people living in Palestine and Asia Minor, "**brothers**" meant not only the relation of brother, but also cousins, second cousins and, **in general, all close relatives**.

There could not have been any actual brothers of the Lord, as the Mother of God bore only one Son, the Lord Jesus Christ, and is called by the Holy Church Ever-virgin because She was so until the birth of Christ, and in giving birth and after the birth of Christ remained the same, as She vowed to God never to enter into marriage. St. Joseph was not a real husband to Her, **he was only betrothed**, the custodian of Her virginity. This means that brothers and sisters of the Lord in the flesh could only have been first and second cousins, and then only by maternal lineage, in the lineage of His Most-pure Mother. Blood relatives by paternal lineage did not exist for the Saviour, for He had no father in the flesh.

In the Gospel account no clarification is given for the "brothers of Christ," although several of them are even mentioned by name: James, Joses, Simon and Judas (cf. Matt. 13:54-56). Much has been written about the "brothers of Christ," many judgements made and theories proposed, but they all contain contradictions or are lacking in fact.

If these "brothers" of Christ appear in the literal sense, that is, they were actual relatives **by flesh**, then they could have been **second cousins**. The Apostle Matthew speaks of their mother as being Mary, the mother of James and Joses, the wife of Cleophas, who appears to have been a cousin of the Most-holy Mary. The Apostle John also calls her a *sister of His Mother* (John 19:25).

These "brothers" of the Lord could have been pseudo "stepbrothers" by the surrogate father Joseph, Her betrothed. They could

St. Joseph

have been sons of St. Joseph by his first marriage, from his real marriage which occurred before his engagement to the Holy Virgin Mary. There is nothing amazing about this, as for example, according to the Gospel of Mark the genealogy of Jesus Christ is given through the lineage of Joseph, the betrothed, according to Jewish law. The words of the Jews spoken about the Saviour also indicate this possibility. *Where did this Man get this wisdom and these mighty works? Is not this the carpenter's son? Is not His Mother called Mary? And are not all His brothers James and Joseph and Simon and Judas? And are not all His sisters with us? Where then did this Man get all these things* (Matt 13:54-56). An indication supporting this position is given by the Apostle John. *So His brothers said to Him, 'Leave here and go to Judea, that your disciples may see the works You are doing'* (John 7:3). It is also known that the opinion that the "brothers" of the Lord were children of Joseph by his first marriage is from the most **ancient tradition**.

This ancient tradition would not have had any opposition if the Apostle Matthew had not mentioned that the mother of James and Joseph was Mary, whom the Apostle John names Mary of Cleophas, sister of His Mother (Matt.27:56; John 19:25); therefore several scholars came to the conclusion that "brothers" of the Lord were His second cousins by blood.

But, as the Holy Orthodox Church does not repudiate the ancient tradition cited above, we consider it necessary to speak about it.

In the *Lives of the Saints* on December 26, it says that **St. Joseph the Betrothed** was the son of Jacob. Jacob was the son of Matthan. But Jacob was married, according to the **levirate law**, to the wife of his brother Heli who died childless. The levirate law prescribes that if a man dies childless, his brother should take his wife and *raise up seed unto his brother* (Deut. 25:5-6). By this law, Joseph was the son of Heli, although according to the flesh he was the son of Jacob. That is why the holy Evangelist Luke, in presenting the lineage of Christ, called Heli the father of Joseph, speaking of Christ thus: *And Jesus Himself began to be about thirty years of age, being **as it was supposed** the son of Joseph, who was the son of Heli, who was the son of Mathat,...*(Luke 3:23).

Church tradition indicates that St. Joseph had a wife and children. Thus, Nikiphoros, the ancient Greek historian, following St. Hippolytus, says that St. Joseph was married to Salome. "But do not think, he adds, that this is the Salome that was the Salome that was in Bethlehem and was called the grandmother of the Lord. The former was a relative of Elizabeth and the Most-holy Mother of God and the latter was a daughter of Haggai, the brother of Zacharias, the father of John the Forerunner. Haggai and Zacharias were sons of the priest Barachus. With Salome, daughter of Haggai as a wife, St. Joseph had his four sons, Jacob, Simon, Jude and Joseph, and two daughters, Esther and Thamar, or as some say, Martha. The Synaxarion for the Sunday of the Myrrhbearers adds still a third daughter by the name of Salome, who married Zebedee. But George Kedrin, in speaking of the two daughters of Joseph, says that one of them was Maria, who was given in marriage to Cleophas, the brother of Joseph, already after the return of Joseph from Egypt. But it seems that this Mary is the same person as Martha and Thamar (in the Georgian lists of saints, among the holy Myrrhbearing Women St. Thamar is listed under the name of Tamara). No matter what kind of daughter she was, and how many daughters Joseph had, in any case, Joseph undoubtedly was married and had sons and daughters. Upon the death of his wife Salome, Joseph lived a widower for the rest of the time, passing his days in chastity.

The Holy Gospels bear witness to his holy and immaculate life with the following short but laudatory words, **Her husband Joseph, being a just man** (Matt. 1:19). And what could be a greater witness? He was so just that his sanctity exceeded that of the other righteous forefathers and patriarchs. For who could be worthy to be betrothed to and the surrogate husband of the Most-pure Virgin Mother of God? And to whom was given the honor to become the stepfather of Christ? Truly he was worthy of such an honor and of such an appointment on account of his perfectly virtuous life. When he was already an old man, eighty years old, the Holy Virgin Mary became betrothed to him, and She was given to him for the protection of Her virginity. So he served Her with reverence and awe, as the Mother of God, and as his and all the world's Lady and Sovereign, being assured of this by the angel who appeared to him in a dream. He also served the God-child born of Her, earning a living for them by the work of his hands. St. Joseph died at the age of a hundred and ten years.

CHAPTER 35

Healing of the Man Born Blind

It happened on one feast day in Jerusalem, that after the Saviour finished His sermon and was leaving the Temple, He saw on the street a **man blind from birth**.

The Jews thought that every misfortune befalling a man was punishment for his sins. If the misfortune befell a child, then they considered that to be punishment for the sins of his parents. Therefore His disciples asked Him, "Master, who sinned, this man or his parents, that he was born blind?"

Jesus Christ answered, "**Neither this man sinned, nor his parents: but that the works of God should be manifest in him.**"

When He had thus spoken, He spat on the ground, and made mud of the spittle, and He anointed the eyes of the blind man with the clay. Then the Saviour said to the blind man, "Go, wash in the pool of Siloam" (as one water spring in the city was called. The word Siloam means "sent").

In order to heal the man blind from birth, the Saviour could have simply given the word and the blind man would have begun to see. Therefore, if He now anointed the eyes of the blind man, He did it not because a healing power was contained in the clay, but so that by touching his eyes He would awaken in him faith and show the onlookers that the blind man received the words of the Saviour with faith.

The man blind from birth therefore went to the pool of Siloam, washed, and began to see, and he returned seeing. The neighbors and they who before had seen that he was blind were amazed and said, "Is this not the blind man who sat and begged?"

Some said, "It is he." Others said, "He only resembles him."

He himself said, "I am he who was blind."

Then they said to him, "How were your eyes opened?"

The healed man answered, "A man named Jesus made clay, anointed my eyes, and said to me, 'Go to the pool of Siloam and wash.' I went and washed and I received sight."

Then they said to him, "Where is He?" The healed man answered, "I know not."

They brought to the Pharisees the man who had formerly been blind. Now it was a Sabbath day when Christ healed him. The Pharisees also asked him how he had received his sight. And the healed man said to them, "He put clay on my eyes, and I washed, and I see."

Some of the Pharisees said, "This man is not from God, for He does not keep the Sabbath." But others said, "How can a man who is a sinner do such wonders?"

There was a division among them. So they again said to the blind man, "What do you say about Him, since He has opened your eyes?"

The healed man said, "He is a Prophet."

The Pharisees did not believe that he had been blind and had received his sight. They called the parents of the man who had received his sight, and asked them, "Is this your son, who you say was born blind? How then does he now see?"

His parents answered, "We know that this is our son, and that he was born blind. But how he now sees, we do not know, nor do we know who opened his eyes. Ask him, he is of age; he will speak for himself."

His parents said this because they feared the Pharisees, for the Jews had already agreed that if any one should confess Jesus of Nazareth to be Christ the Messiah, the Saviour of the world, he was to be put out of the synagogue, that is, to be considered apostate from their faith and law. Therefore his parents, out of fear of the Pharisees, said, "He is of age, ask him."

So for the second time they called the man who had been blind, and said to him, "Give God the praise; we know that this Man is a sinner." That is, "For your healing thank God, not that Man; He is a sinner."

The healed man said to them, "Whether he is a sinner or not, I know not; one thing I know that whereas I was blind, now I see." The Pharisees began to ask him again, "What did He do to you. How did He open your eyes?" The healed one answered them, "I have told you already, and you would not listen. Why do you want to hear it again? Do you too want to become His disciples?"

The Pharisees became angry, reviled him and said, "You are His disciple, but we are disciples of Moses. We know that God has spoken to Moses, but as for this Man, we do not know where He comes from."

The healed man answered, "Why this is a marvel! You do not know where He comes from, and yet He opened my eyes. We know that God does not listen to sinners, but if anyone is a worshipper of God and does His will, God listens to him. Never since the world began has it been heard that anyone opened the eyes of a man born blind. If this Man were not from God, He could do nothing."

These simple and wise words with which no one could take issue, angered the Pharisees. They said to him, "You were altogether born in sins, and you would teach us?" And they cast him out.

Jesus Christ heard that they had cast him out, and having found him He said, "Do you believe in the Son of man?"

The healed man answered, "And Who is He, Sir, that I may believe in Him?"

Jesus said to him, "You have seen Him, and it is He who speaks to you."

Then the healed one with great joy said, "Lord, I believe," and he worshipped Him.

Note: See the Gospel of John 9:1-38.

CHAPTER 36

The Parable of the Rich Fool

Jesus Christ taught, "Take heed, and **beware of covetousness** (that is, beware of the love of accumulating wealth, beware of the attachment to riches), **for a man's life does not consist in the abundance of his possessions**."

So that people could understand this better, the Lord told them a parable about a rich fool.

The land of a rich man brought forth plentifully, and he thought to himself, "What shall I do, for I have nowhere to store my crops?" And he said, "I will do this. I will pull down my barns and build larger ones; and there I will store all my grain and my goods. And I will say to my soul, 'Soul, you have ample goods laid up for many years; take your ease, eat, drink, be merry.' "

But God said to him, "Fool! This night your soul is required of you, and the things you have prepared, whose will they be?"

After the parable, the Lord said, "So is he who lays up treasure for himself, and is not rich toward God." This is what happens with everyone who gathers wealth only for himself, for his subsistence and pleasure, and not for God, or not for good works pleasing to God — not to assist neighbors or to relieve their suffering. Death will come to the man, and his earthly riches will not transport his soul to that brilliant future life.

"Therefore I tell you," said the Saviour, "do not be anxious about your life, what you shall eat, nor about your body, what you shall put on. For life is more than food, and the body more than clothing. Your Heavenly Father knows you have need of them. **Instead, seek first His Kingdom and His righteousness, and all these things shall be yours as well**." First of all take care of the salvation of your soul by fulfilling the commandments of God. Show mercy to your neighbor, deal righteously with your soul, that you may be worthy of the Kingdom of God. Then everything else, everything that is necessary for your physical existence, for life on earth, the Lord will provide for you.

Note: See the Gospel of Luke 12:15-31.

The Gift of Prayer to the Disciples

One day Jesus Christ was praying, and when He had ceased, one of His disciples said to Him, "Lord, teach us to pray, as John taught his disciples."

Jesus Christ said to them, "When you pray, say: **Our Father Who art in the heavens, Hallowed be Thy name; Thy Kingdom come; Thy will be done on earth as it is in heaven. Give us this day our daily bread and forgive us our debts, as we forgive our debtors; and lead us not into temptation, but deliver us from the evil one. For Thine is the Kingdom and the power and the glory forever. Amen."**

Note: See the Gospels of Luke 11:1-4; Matthew 6:9-13.

On Forgiving Offenses. The Parable of the Merciful King and the Unmerciful Creditor

During one conversation with Jesus Christ, the Apostle Peter came to Him and asked, "Lord! How often shall my brother (my neighbor) sin against me (that is, if he in some way offends me), and I forgive him? As many as seven times?"

Jesus Christ said to him, "I do not say to you seven times, but **seventy times seven**," that is, forgive without counting the times.

To explain this better, Jesus Christ told a parable. "One man owed the king **ten thousand talents** (about ten thousand dollars). As he could not pay, the King ordered him to be sold, with his wife and children and all that he had, and payment to be made. So the servant fell on his knees, imploring him, 'Lord, have patience with me, and I will pay you everything.' And out of pity for him the lord of that servant released him and forgave him the debt. But that same servant, as he went out, came upon one of his fellow servants who owed him a **hundred denarii**, (about twenty dollars). Seizing him by the throat, he said, 'Pay what you owe.' So his fellow servant fell down and besought him, 'Have patience with me, and I will pay you.' He refused and went and put him in prison till he should pay the debt. When his fellow servants saw what had taken place, they were greatly distressed, and they went and reported to their lord all that had taken place. Then his lord summoned him and said to him, 'You wicked servant! I forgave you all that debt because you besought me; and should not you have had mercy on your fellow servant, as I had mercy on you?' And in anger his lord delivered him to the jailers, till he should pay all his debt."

After the parable, Jesus Christ said, "So also My Heavenly Father will do to every one of you, if you do not forgive your brother from your heart."

In this parable the king represents God. The man who owed a huge sum to the king represents us. The debt is our sins. By the fellow servants are meant those people who in some way are guilty before us (our debtors).

From this parable, it is evident that everyone who is evil to his neighbor for some sort of fault of theirs, and does not want to forgive them, does not deserve the mercy of God.

Note: See the Gospels of Matthew 18:21-35 and Luke 17:3-4.

The Healing of Ten Lepers

At the entrance of one village, Jesus Christ met ten lepers. Nine of them were Jews and one a Samaritan. Their common grief united them. The lepers were forbidden to come close to people because their disease was infectious. Therefore they stood at a distance and lifted up their voices and said, "Jesus, Master, have mercy on us."

Jesus Christ said, "Go and show yourselves to the priests."

The priests inspected those who recovered from leprosy and testified to their right to live in cities and towns. The lepers went to the priests; and as they walked on the road, they were cleansed of the leprosy, that is, they were restored to health. One of them, seeing that he was healed, returned to Jesus Christ, with a loud voice glorified God, and falling at the feet of Christ, thanked Him. It was the Samaritan. The Jews had left without giving thanks.

Then Jesus Christ said, "Were not ten cleansed? Where are the nine? Was no one found to return and give praise to God, except this foreigner?"

Then, turning to the thankful Samaritan, he said, "Rise and go your way; your faith has made you well." From this it is clear that we must always be thankful to God for His mercy which He extends to us.

Note: See the Gospel of Luke 7:11-19.

The Parable of the Rich Man and Lazarus

Concerning people who love wealth and do not help the needy, Jesus Christ told this parable.

"There was a rich man, who was clothed in purple (garments made from expensive red material) and linen (fine white garments), and who feasted sumptuously every day. At his gate lay a poor man named Lazarus, who was covered with sores. He desired to be fed with what fell from the rich man's table; moreover the dogs came and licked his sores.

The poor man died and was carried by the angels to Abraham's bosom (the place of blessedness of the righteous, Paradise). The rich man also died and was buried. And in Hades, being in torment, he lifted up his eyes, and saw Abraham far off and Lazarus in his bosom, and he called out, "Father Abraham, have mercy upon me, and send Lazarus to dip the end of his finger in water and cool my tongue, for I am in anguish in this flame."

But Abraham said to him, "Son, remember that you in your lifetime received good things, but Lazarus in like manner evil things; but now he is comforted here, and you are in anguish. And besides all this, between us and you a great chasm has been fixed, in order that those who would pass from here to you may not be able, and none may cross from there to us."

And then the formerly rich man said to Abraham, "Then I beg you, father, to send him to my father's house, for I have five brothers, so that he may warn them, lest they also come into this place of torment."

The Rich Man and Lazarus

But Abraham said, "They have Moses and the prophets (their Holy Scripture); let them hear them."

And he said, "No, Father Abraham; but if some one goes to them from the dead, they will repent."

Then Abraham said to him, "If they do not hear Moses and the prophets, neither will they be convinced if someone should rise from the dead."

In this parable, the Lord clearly indicates that if a rich man wastes his wealth only on his pleasure, and does not help the needy, does not think about his soul and its eternal fate, then he will be judged and will not receive blessedness in the future life. At the same time, he who patiently, humbly, **without grumbling**, **endures suffering**, will receive eternal, blessed life in the Kingdom of Heaven.

Note: See the Gospel of Luke 16:19-31.

The Parable of the Pharisee and the Publican

Warning all of us not to become proud, boastful, considering ourselves righteous and better than others, but rather to be humble, and

The Publican and the Pharisee

seeing our sins, to grieve over them, judging no one, because only a humble man is raised in spirit to God, Jesus Christ told the following parable.

Two men went up into the Temple to pray. One was a Pharisee and the other a publican (tax collector).

The Pharisee stood up front and prayed thus, "God, I thank Thee that I am not like other men, extortioners, unjust, adulterers, or even like this tax collector. I fast twice a week, and I give one tenth of all that I receive to the priests."

But the publican, standing far off, would not even lift up his eyes to Heaven, and beat his breast, saying, "**God be merciful to me a sinner!**"

Jesus Christ said, "I tell you, this man went down to his house justified rather than the other; for every one who exalts himself will be humbled, but he who humbles himself will be exalted."

Note: See the Gospel of Luke 18:9-14.

Blessing the Children

Many brought their children to Jesus Christ that He might touch them, lay His hands on them and bless them. The disciples of Christ rebuked them, thinking it was not worth having the children disturb the Master.

But when Jesus Christ saw it, He was indignant, called the disciples to Him and said, "Let the children come to me and do not hinder them, for to such belongs the Kingdom of Heaven. Truly I say to you, whoever does not receive the Kingdom of God like a child, shall not enter it."

Taking the children in His arms, Jesus Christ laid His hands on them and blessed them.

From this we are given to understand, that innocence, guilelessness, simplicity and goodness of soul, which are traits mainly of children, lead men into the Kingdom of Heaven.

Note: See the Gospels of Matthew 19:13-15; Mark 10:13-16; Luke 18:15-17.

The Lord Blesses the Children

CHAPTER 37

The Parable of the Prodigal Son

Tax collectors and sinners came to Jesus Christ to listen to Him. The proud Pharisees and scribes, teachers of the Jewish people, murmured about Jesus Christ for this and said, "He receives sinners and eats with them."

But Jesus Christ told several parables which showed that God joyfully and lovingly receives every repentant sinner. Here is one of them.

There was a man who had two sons. The youngest said to his father, "Father, give me the share of the property that falls to me." The father granted the request and divided his property between them. Not many days later, the youngest son gathered all he had and journeyed into a far country, and there he squandered his property in loose living. When he had spent everything, a great famine arose in that country, and he began to be in want. So he went and joined himself to one of the citizens of that country, who sent him into his fields to feed swine. He would gladly have eaten the food that the swine ate, but no one gave him anything.

When he came to himself, he remembered his father, was filled with remorse over his deed, and thought, "How many of my father's hired servants have bread enough and to spare, but I perish here with hunger! I will arise and go to my father, and I will say to him, 'Father, I have sinned against Heaven and before you; I am no longer worthy to be called your son; treat me as one of your hired servants.'"

Thus he did. He got up and went to his father. But while he was yet at a distance, his father saw him and had compassion on him and ran and embraced him and kissed him.

The son said to him, "Father! I have sinned against Heaven and before you, I am no longer worthy to be called your son."

But the father said to his servants, "Bring quickly the best robe and put it on him, and put a ring on his hand and shoes on his feet, and bring the fatted calf and kill it, and let us eat and make merry, for this my son was dead and is alive again; he was lost and is found." And they began to make merry.

Now his elder son was in the field, and he came and drew near to the house and heard music and dancing. He called one of the servants and asked what this meant.

The servant said to him, "Your brother has come, and your father has killed the fatted calf because he received him safe and sound." But the elder son was angry and refused to go in. His father came out and entreated him.

But he answered his father, "Lo, these many years I have served you, and I never disobeyed your command. Yet you never gave me a kid

The Prodigal Son

that I might make merry with my friends. But when this son of yours came, who has devoured your living wantonly, you killed the fatted calf for him!"

The father said to him, "Son, you are always with me, and all that is mine is yours. It was fitting to make merry and be glad, for this your brother was dead and is alive; he was lost and is found."

In this parable, the father represents God, and the prodigal son, the repentant sinner. Resembling the prodigal son is every person who in his soul turns away from God and pursues his self-willed, sinful life. By his sins he destroys his soul and all the gifts — life, health, strength, capabilities — which were bestowed on him by God. When the sinner, coming to himself, brings to God sincere repentance, with humility and hope in His mercy, then the Lord, as a compassionate Father, rejoices with His angels over the return of the sinner, forgives him all his sins, as if they never were and returns to him all His mercy and gifts.

By the story about the elder son, the Saviour teaches that all faithful Christians must with all their souls desire salvation for everyone, to rejoice over the return of the sinner, not envying the love that God gives them and not considering themselves more worthy of God's mercy than the one who returns to God from his former immoral life.

Note: See the Gospel of Luke 15:11-32.

Predictions of Jesus Christ About the End of the World and About His Second Coming

Jesus Christ made predictions about what is in store in the future for our entire world and all the people. He taught that the end of the world is coming, and that the earthly existence of the human race will cease. Then He will come to earth a second time and will resurrect all people, at which time the bodies of all people will again become joined to their souls and they will come back to life. Then Jesus Christ will pronounce judgement over people, rendering to each according to his works. "Marvel not at this: for the hour is coming, in which all that are in the graves shall hear the voice of the Son of God. And they that hear shall live, and shall come forth from their graves — they that have done good, unto the resurrection of life; and they that have done evil, unto the resurrection of damnation."

The disciples asked, "Tell us when this will be, and what will be the sign of Your (second) coming and of the close of the age?" In answer Jesus Christ forewarned them that before His coming in glory on earth, there would occur a time of suffering for people, such as has never occurred before from the beginning of the world. There will be various misfortunes: famines, floods, earthquakes and wars. Lawlessness will increase, faith will grow weak, most people's love will grow cold. Many false prophets and teachers will appear, who will seduce people and corrupt them with their ruinous, destructive teaching. But first, the Gospel of Christ will be preached to all the corners of the earth, in witness to all people.

Before the end of the world there will be great, terrifying signs in the heavens. The sea will roar and be agitated. Loss of heart and perplexity will possess people, so that they will grow faint from fear and the expectation of disasters coming to the world. Immediately after the tribulation of those days the sun will be darkened, and the moon will not give its light, and the stars will fall from heaven, and the powers of the heavens will be shaken. Then will appear the sign of Jesus Christ (His cross) in the heavens. Then all the tribes of the earth will mourn from fear of the judgement of God, and they will see Jesus Christ coming on the clouds of heaven with power and great glory. As lightning flashes in the heavens from the east to the west and is immediately visible from everywhere, so, visible to all will the Son of God suddenly come.

About the day and the hour of His coming to earth Jesus Christ did not tell His disciples. "Of that day or that hour no one knows but only the Father," He said, and He taught to watch and always be ready to meet the Lord.

Note: See the Gospels of John 5:24-29; Matthew 24:3-44; Mark 13:3-37; Luke 17:20-37 and 21:7-36.

Parable of the Ten Virgins

In order that people would always be ready to meet the Lord, the judgement of God, which means to be ready for death, since death is the beginning of the judgement of God over men, Jesus Christ told the parable of the ten virgins. In this parable, the Lord likens us to virgins who had gathered for a marriage. According to Eastern wedding customs, the groom went for his bride, who awaited him in the home of her father. Her friends, virgins, had to meet the groom with burning lanterns in late evening, and accompany him to the fiancee.

Then the Kingdom of Heaven shall be compared to ten virgins, said the Saviour, who took their lamps and went to meet the bridegroom. Five of them were foolish, and five were wise. For when the foolish took their lamps, they took no oil with them; but the wise took flasks of oil

The Ten Virgins

with their lamps. As the bridegroom was delayed, they all slumbered and slept. But at midnight there was a cry, "Behold, the bridegroom! Come out to meet him." Then all those virgins rose and trimmed their lamps. And the foolish said to the wise, "Give us some of your oil, for our lamps are going out." But the wise replied, "Perhaps there will not be enough for us and for you; go rather to the dealers and buy for your-selves." And while they went to buy, the bridegroom came, and those who were ready went in with him to the marriage feast, and the door was shut.

Afterward the other virgins came also, saying, "Lord, lord, open to us."

But he replied, "Truly, I say to you, I do not know you." After fin-ishing this parable, the Saviour said, "Watch therefore, always be pre-pared, for you know neither the day nor the hour in which comes the **Son of man**."

The "**foolish virgins**" correspond to those careless people, who know that they will have to appear at the judgement of God, but who do not prepare themselves for it while they are alive on earth, while death has not overtaken them. They do not repent of their sins and do not do good deeds. The "**oil in the lamps**" means good deeds, especially works of mercy. The "**sleep of the virgins**" represents the death of people.

Our Judge ("**The Bridegroom**"), Jesus Christ, will come to earth and all the dead will awaken from the sleep of death, that is, they will be res-urrected. As death finds one, prepared or unprepared for the judgement of God, so he will appear before the judgement of God. Then careless people will not be able to look for help from anywhere, and they will hear from Christ the bitter words, "I do not know you; depart from Me."

Note: See the Gospel of Matthew 25:1-13.

The Parable of the Talents

Jesus Christ told yet another parable reproving our laziness and negligence.

The Son of man is like a man who, going on a journey into a far country, called his servants and entrusted to them his property. To one he gave five talents, to another two talents, to another one talent, to each according to his ability. Then he went away.

He who had received the five talents went at once and traded with them; and he made five talents more. So too, he who had the two talents made two talents more. But he who had received the one talent did not want to work, and he went and dug in the ground and hid his master's money.

After a long time, the master of those servants came and settled ac-counts with them. He who had received the five talents came forward, bringing five talents more saying, "Master, you delivered to me five tal-ents; here I have made five talents more."

His master said to him, "Well done, good and faithful servant; you have been faithful over a little. I will set you over much; enter into the joy of your master."

And he also who had the two talents came forward, saying, "Master, you gave me two talents. Here I have made two more talents."

His master said to him, "Well done, good and faithful servant. You have been faithful over a little, I will set you over much. Enter into the joy of your master."

He also who had received one talent came forward, saying, "Master, I knew you to be a hard man, reaping where you did not sow, and gathering where you did not winnow. So I was afraid, and I went and hid your talent in the ground. Here you have what is yours."

But his master answered him, "You wicked and slothful servant! You knew that I reap where I have not sowed, and gather where I have not winnowed. Then you ought to have invested my money with the bankers, and at my coming I should have received what was my own with interest. So take the talent from him, and give it to him who has the ten talents. For every one who has will be given more, and he will have abundance; but from him who has not, even what he has will be taken away. Cast the worthless servant into the outer darkness where men will weep and gnash their teeth."

Having told this parable, Jesus Christ exclaimed, "He who has ears to hear, let him hear!"

This parable means that all people receive various gifts from God, such as life, health, strength, spiritual capacity, learning, gifts of the Holy Spirit, the good things of life, and so on, in order to use these gifts in the service of God and neighbor. All these are gifts of God and are understood in the parable under the name of talents. God knows how much each person needs, according to his ability, and therefore some people receive more, others less. He who uses the gifts of God must give an account to God at His second coming. He who uses them to the advantage of himself and others will receive praise from the Lord and eternal heavenly joy, but lazy and careless people will be condemned by the Lord to eternal suffering.

Note: See the Gospels of Matthew 25:14-30; Luke 19:11-28.

The Last Judgement

Concerning His fearful last judgement over all people at the time of His second coming, Jesus Christ taught the following.

When the Son of man comes in His glory, and all the angels with Him, then He will sit as King on the throne of His glory. Before Him will be gathered all the nations, and He will separate them one from another, the faithful and good from the godless and evil, as a shepherd separates the sheep from the goats. He will place the sheep, the righteous, at His right hand, but the goats or sinners at the left.

Then the King will say to those at his right hand, "Come, O blessed of My Father, inherit the kingdom prepared for you from the creation of the world. For I was hungry, and you gave Me food. I was thirsty and you gave Me drink. I was a stranger and you welcomed Me. I was naked and you clothed Me. I was sick and you visited Me. I was in prison, and you came to Me."

The Last Judgement

Then the righteous will answer Him, "Lord! When did we see Thee hungry and feed Thee, or thirsty and gave Thee drink? And when did we see Thee a stranger and welcome Thee, or naked and clothe Thee? And when did we see Thee sick or in prison and visit Thee?"

The King will answer them, "Truly I say to you: as you did it to one of the least of these My brethren (for needy people), you did it to Me."

Then He will say to those at His left hand, "Depart from Me, you cursed, into the eternal fire prepared for the Devil and his angels. For I was hungry and you gave Me no food. I was thirsty and you gave Me no drink. I was a stranger and you did not welcome Me; naked, and you did not clothe Me; sick, and in prison, and you did not visit Me."

Then they also will answer, "Lord, when did we see Thee hungry, or thirsty, or a stranger, or naked, or sick, or in prison and did not minister to Thee?"

But the King will answer them, "Truly I say to you: as you did not do it for one of the least of these, you did not do it for Me." And they will go away into eternal punishment, but the righteous into eternal life.

Great and terrifying will be that day for all of us. Therefore this judgement is called **terrible**, for our deeds, words, and our most secret thoughts and desires will be revealed to all. Then there will be no one to help us, for the **judgement of God is just**, and each will be judged according to his deeds.

Note: See the Gospel of Matthew 25:31-46.

CHAPTER 38

The Raising of Lazarus

The Jewish feast of the Passover drew near, and with it occurred the last days of the life of Jesus Christ on earth. The malice of the Pharisees and Jewish leaders reached its peak. Their hearts hardened from envy, love of power, and other vices, and they did not want to accept the simple and compassionate teachings of Christ. They awaited a convenient occasion to seize the Saviour and put Him to death and now the time for them had arrived. The power of darkness set in, and the Lord was being betrayed into the hands of men.

At this time in the village of Bethany, Lazarus, the brother of Martha and Mary, was ill. The Lord loved Lazarus and his sisters and often visited this blessed family.

When Lazarus fell ill, Jesus Christ was not in Judea. The sisters sent to Him, saying, "Lord! The one whom You love is ill."

But when Jesus Christ heard it He said, "This illness is not unto death; it is for the glory of God, so that the Son of God may be glorified by means of it."

The Saviour stayed two days longer in the place where He was. Then He said to the disciples, "Let us go into Judea again. Our friend Lazarus has fallen asleep, but I go to awaken him." Jesus Christ spoke to them about the death of Lazarus, and the disciples thought that He was talking about usual sleep, and since sleep at a time of illness is a good sign of recovery, they said, "Lord, if he has fallen asleep, he will recover."

Then Jesus Christ told them plainly, "Lazarus is dead, and for your sake I am glad I was not there, so that you may believe. But let us go to him."

When Jesus came to Bethany, Lazarus had already been in the tomb four days. Many of the Jews from Jerusalem had come to Martha and Mary to console them.

Martha first heard that Jesus was coming and hurried to meet Him. Mary, in deep grief, sat in the house. When Martha met the Saviour, she said, "Lord, if You had been here, my brother would not have died. And even now I know that whatever You ask from God, God will give You."

Jesus Christ said to her, "Your brother will rise again."

Martha said to Him, "I know that He will rise again in the resurrection at the last day (that is, in the general resurrection at the end of the world)."

The Raising of Lazarus

Then Jesus said to her, "I am the resurrection and the life; he who believes in Me, though he die, yet shall he live. And whoever lives and believes in Me shall never die. Do you believe this?"

Martha said to Him, "Yes, Lord; I believe that You are the Christ, the Son of God, Who is to come into the world." When she had said this, she quickly went home and quietly said to her sister Mary, "The Teacher is here and is calling for you."

Mary, as soon as she heard this joyful news, rose quickly and went to Jesus Christ. When the Jews who were with her in the house consoling her saw Mary rise quickly and go out, they followed her, supposing that she was going to the tomb to weep there. The Saviour had not yet come to the village, but was still in the place where Martha had met Him.

Mary, when she came where Jesus was, fell at His feet, saying to Him, "Lord, if You had been here, my brother would not have died."

When Jesus Christ saw her weeping, and the Jews who came with her also weeping, He was deeply troubled in spirit and said, "Where have you laid him?"

They said to Him, "Lord, come and see." Jesus Christ wept.

When they came to the tomb of Lazarus, it was a cave and the entrance was blocked up with a stone. Christ said, "Take away the stone."

Martha said to Him, "Lord! By this time there will be an odor, for he has been dead four days."

Jesus said to her, "Did I not tell you that if you would believe you would see the glory of God?" So they took away the stone.

Then Jesus lifted His eyes to Heaven and said to God His Father, "Father, I thank Thee that Thou hast heard Me. I know that Thou hearest Me always, but I have said this on account of the people standing by, that they may believe that Thou didst send Me."

When He had said this, He cried with a loud voice, "Lazarus, come forth." The dead man came out, His hands and feet bound with ban-

Lazarus' Tomb Today

dages, and his face wrapped with a cloth, as the Jews dressed the dead.

Jesus said to them, "Unbind him, and let him go." Then many of the Jews, who had been there and seen this miracle, believed in Jesus Christ. But some of them went to the Pharisees and told them what Jesus had done. The enemies of Christ, the chief priests and the Pharisees, were

The Entrance to the Tomb

troubled, and fearing that all the people would believe in Jesus Christ, gathered a council and decided to kill Jesus Christ. Word of this great miracle began to spread all over Jerusalem. Many Jews went to the home of Lazarus to see him, and having seen, believed in Jesus Christ. Then the chief priests and scribes plotted to kill Lazarus. But Lazarus, after his resurrection by the Saviour, lived a long time and was later a bishop on the island of Cyprus.

Note: See the Gospel of John 11:1-57 and 12:9-11.

This great miracle of the Saviour, the raising of Lazarus, is commemorated by the Holy Orthodox Church on the Saturday of the sixth week of the Great Fast (the eve of Palm Sunday).

CHAPTER 39

The Triumphal Entry into Jerusalem

Soon after the raising of Lazarus, six days before the Jewish Passover, Jesus Christ made a triumphal entry into Jerusalem, to show that He was the true Christ the King and was going to death voluntarily.

When they drew near to Jerusalem, coming to the village of Bethpage, at the Mount of Olives, Jesus Christ sent two of His disciples, saying to them, "Go into the village opposite you, and immediately you will find a donkey tied, and a colt with her, on which no one has ever sat. Untie it and bring it to me. If any one says anything to you, you shall say, 'The Lord needs it.' "

The disciples went away and found it as He had told them. They brought the donkey and the colt and put their garments on the colt, and Jesus sat on it.

In the meantime, in Jerusalem they learned that Jesus, the One Who raised Lazarus from the dead after four days, was coming to Jerusalem. Crowds of people, gathered from everywhere for the feast of the Passover, went to meet Him. Many took off their outer garments and spread them on the road before Him. Others cut palm branches, carried them in their hands and spread them on the road. And all the people, those who went before and those who followed, cried out with joy, **"Hosanna** (Salvation) **to the Son of David! Blessed is He Who comes in the name of the Lord."** That is, worthy of praise is the One Who comes in the name of the Lord, sent from God. **"King of Israel! Hosanna in the highest!"**

When He drew near to Jerusalem the Saviour looked upon it with sorrow. He knew that the people would reject Him, their Saviour, and that Jerusalem would be destroyed. Jesus Christ wept over it and said, "Would that even today you knew the things that would give you salvation! But now they are hid from your eyes." That is, you stubbornly close your eyes to all of God's favor bestowed on you. "For the days shall come upon you, when your enemies will cast up a bank about you and surround you, and hem you in on every side, and dash you to the ground, you and your children with you, and they will not leave one stone upon another because you did not know (did not want to acknowledge) the time of your visitation (the time when the Lord visited you)."

When Jesus Christ entered Jerusalem, all the city was stirred, saying, "Who is this?"

The Entry into Jerusalem

The crowds answered, "This is the prophet Jesus from Nazareth of Galilee," and told them about how He had called Lazarus forth from the tomb and raised him from the dead.

Jesus entered the Temple and again, as in the first year of His teaching, drove out all who sold and bought in the Temple, saying to them "It is written, 'My house shall be called a house of prayer,' but you have made it a den of robbers."

The blind and the lame came to Him in the Temple, and He healed them. The people, seeing the wonderful things Jesus Christ did, began to praise Him even more. Even little children who were in the Temple cried out, "**Hosanna to the Son of David.**"

The chief priests and the scribes were indignant and they said to Him, "Do you hear what they are saying?"

Jesus Christ said to them, "Yes, have you never read, *Out of the mouths of babes and sucklings hast Thou perfected praise?* (Ps. 8:3). Jesus Christ taught daily in the Temple, and when evening came He went out of the city. The chief priests and the scribes and the principal men of the people sought an opportunity to destroy Him, but they could not, for all the people were very anxious to hear Him.

Note: See the Gospels of Matthew 21:1-17; Mark 11:1-19, Luke 19:29-48; John 12:12-19.

The triumphant Entry of the Lord into Jerusalem is celebrated by the Holy Orthodox Church on the last Sunday before the bright feast of Pascha. This is one of the great feasts, and it is also called **Palm Sunday**, because on this feast during the All-night Vigil service, or at Matins, blessed branches of palms, pussy willows or other early spring growth are distributed to the faithful. In ancient times the king was met with green branches, when he was returning in triumph after victory over his enemies. And we, holding in our hands the branches of the first blossoms of spring glorify the Saviour, as the Victor over death, because He raised the dead, and on this very day entered Jerusalem to die for our sins and to rise again, thereby saving us from eternal death and eternal torment. The branches serve for us then as a **symbol of the victory** of Christ **over death** and should remind us of the future resurrection of all of us from death.

Troparion of the Feast

In confirming the common Resurrection, O Christ God, Thou didst raise up Lazarus from the dead before Thy passion. Wherefore, we also, like the children bearing the symbols of victory, cry to Thee, the vanquisher of death: Hosanna in the highest; blessed is He that cometh in the name of the Lord.

CHAPTER 40

The Parable of the Wicked Tenants

Speaking in the Temple, the Lord Jesus Christ, turning to the high priests, scribes, and elders of the people, told them this parable.

There was a Landowner, Who planted a vineyard and set a hedge around it, and dug a wine press in it, built a tower and let it out to tenants, and went into another country.

When the season of fruit drew near, He sent his servants to the ten-

A Model of the Temple at the Time of the Savior

ants to get His fruit; and the tenants took His servants and beat one, killed another, and stoned another. Again He sent other servants, more than the first, and they did the same.

Afterward, He sent His only Son to them, saying "They will respect my Son."

But when the tenants saw the Son, they said to themselves, "This is the Heir. Come, let us kill Him and have His inheritance." And they took Him and cast Him out of the vineyard, and killed Him."

Having told the parable, the Saviour asked them, "When, therefore, the Owner of the vineyard comes, what will He do to those tenants?"

They said to Him, "He will put those wretches to a miserable death, and let out the vineyard to other tenants who will give Him the fruits in their season."

The Lord Jesus Christ emphasized their answer, saying, "Therefore I tell you, the Kingdom of God will be taken away from you and given to a nation which will produce the fruits of it."

Then the chief priests and Pharisees with the elders understood that the Saviour was speaking about them. In a rage they tried to arrest Him, but they feared the multitude because they considered Him to be a prophet.

The explanation of this parable is thus: The **Householder** is God. :he **tenants** are the Jewish people, chosen by God to preserve the true faith. The **hedges** around the vineyard are the commandments of God, given through Moses. The **wine press**, where the juice of the grapes flows, is the sacrifice in the Old Testament covenant prefiguring the death on the cross of Jesus Christ; the **tower** is the Temple in Jerusalem. The **overseers** are the chief priests, scribes, and elders of the Jewish people. The **servants** of the Householder are the holy prophets. The **Son of the Householder** is the Son of God, our Lord Jesus Christ. Standing at the head of the Jewish people, the chief priests, scribes, and elders had received the power to prepare the people to accept the Saviour, but they used this power only for their own benefit. God sent prophets to them, but they persecuted and killed them. Thus they turned out to be murderers of prophets, and then murderers of the apostles. Their Saviour they rejected, and leading Him out from their city, they crucified Him. Therefore the Kingdom of God was taken away from them and given to another people, the Church of Christ, opened to all peoples.

The Question Concerning Tribute to Caesar

The Lord Jesus Christ continued to teach in the Temple, and the Jewish elders took counsel among themselves about how to entangle Him in His speech, in order to accuse Him in front of the people, or before the Roman authorities.

Having thought up a crafty question, they sent several Pharisees to the Saviour from among their young apprentices and Herodians, or recognized lawyers of Roman authorities. Pretending respect, they began flatteringly to say to Him, "Teacher, we know that You are true and teach the way of God truthfully, and favor no man; for you do not regard the position of men. Tell us then, **is it lawful to pay taxes to Caesar, or not?**"

The enemies of Christ who thought up this tricky question reasoned thus: if Jesus Christ answers that it is appropriate to pay the tribute, then he calls upon Himself indignation among the people, as the Jews recognized only God as their king. They considered it to be unlawful and against God's will to be subject to a foreign king, moreover a heathen, and only by coercion did they render tribute to Ceasar. If Jesus Christ answered that it was not necessary to pay tribute to Caesar, then in that case He would immediately be guilty before the Roman authority, as one who stirred up the people against the Roman powers, as against Caesar.

But Jesus Christ, knowing their malice, said to them, "Why do you tempt Me, you hypocrites? (Hypocrites — people who affectedly, for some advantage, try to present themselves before others as pious and virtuous) Show me the money for the tax."

They brought Him a denarius, a Roman coin.

The Saviour asked, "Whose likeness and inscription is on it?"

They said, "Caesar's."

Then Jesus Christ said to them, "**Render therefore to Caesar the things that are Caesar's and to God the things that are God's.**" This means, give back to Caesar that which you receive from him, pay tribute to him for that which you use from him (money, armies, etc.), submit to him in everything that is not against God's commandments, paying taxes is a sign of submission, a legal obligation and necessity. But at the same time, steadfastly fulfill everything that God requires from us in His commandments and lovingly serve Him, for to God you owe your existence, your very life.

The answer of the Saviour amazed them all by the wisdom and unusual simplicity, so that the questioners fell silent and in shame went away.

The Question Concerning the Resurrection

After this, having beforehand composed their argument, some Sadducees, those who say that there is no resurrection, came to the Saviour. They thought they could catch Him with a question and said, "Teacher, Moses said, 'If a man dies, having no children, his brother must marry his widow, and raise up children for his brother.' Now, there were seven brothers among us. The first married and died, and having no children, left his wife to his brother. So too the second and third, down to the seventh. After them all, the woman died. In the resurrection therefore, to which of the seven will she be wife? For they all had her."

But Jesus Christ answered them, "You are wrong, because you know neither the Scriptures nor the power of God. For in the resurrection they neither marry nor are given in marriage, but are like angels in Heaven. And as for the resurrection of the dead, have you not read what was said to you by God, '**I am the God of Abraham, of Isaac, and of Jacob** He is not the God of the dead but of the living.' "

In that time, Abraham, Isaac, and Jacob were no longer living on earth; it followed that if God still nevertheless called Himself their God, that meant they were alive for Him, or He would be calling Himself God of the nonexistent.

Again, when the crowd heard it, they were astonished at the answer of Jesus Christ. Some of the scribes answered, "Teacher! You have spoken well."

About the Divinity of Christ the Messiah

The Pharisees, standing at that time at some distance, now gathered together and came closer to Jesus Christ, but they did not dare to ask Him any question. Then Jesus Christ Himself, turning to the gathered Pharisees, asked them a question, saying, "**What do you think of the Christ? Whose Son is He?**"

The Pharisees immediately answered, "David's."

The word "son" in Hebrew meant not only son in the proper sense, but also line of descent. Therefore, the expression, "Son of David," meant in the lineage of David.

Jesus Christ again asked, "How is it then that David, inspired by the Spirit, calls Him Lord, saying, '**The Lord said to my Lord**: Sit at My right hand, till I put Thy enemies under Thy feet?' If David thus called Him Lord, how is He his Son?"

No one was able to answer Him a word. The Pharisees, not understanding the Scriptures in spirit and truth, did not understand that Christ, as God-man, was of the lineage of David only by His human

The Priests and Pharisees Plot Against the Lord

nature; but by His divine nature He always existed, for He is, as **Son of God, existing from eternity.**

From that day, no one dared to ask Him any more questions. Thus was the scholarly pride of man disgraced before the divine wisdom of the Saviour. Multitudes of people listened to the Lord with rejoicing.

Then Jesus Christ turned to His disciples and the crowds, and in a formidable speech before them all He clearly exposed the hypocrisy of the Pharisees and the scribes and predicted woe to them.

Jesus Christ with grief said, "Woe to you, scribes and Pharisees, hypocrites! You shut the Kingdom of Heaven against men, for you neither enter yourselves, nor allow those who would enter to go in.

"Woe to you, scribes and Pharisees, hypocrites! You tithe mint and dill and cumin (things of little worth), and have neglected the weightier matters of the law: justice and mercy and faith. These you ought to have done, without neglecting the others. You blind guides, straining at a gnat and swallowing a camel!" This means that they painstakingly care for trivial things, and important matters they leave unattended.

"You outwardly seem to the people to be righteous, but inwardly you are full of hypocrisy and lawlessness..."

This was the last admonition of the Lord, the last attempt to save them from terrible judgement. But on their faces there was no repentance, but rather there was repressed anger toward the Saviour.

Note: See the Gospels of Matthew 21:33-46, 22:15-46; and 23; Mark 12:1-40; Luke 20:9-47.

The Widow's Coin

At the entrance to the Temple of Jerusalem there was placed a treasury, that is, a collection box, in which worshippers put their free-will offerings for the Temple.

Jesus Christ sat down opposite the treasury and watched the multitude putting their offering into the treasury. Many rich people put in large sums.

A poor widow came and put in two copper coins, which make a penny, the smallest denomination of money. Such a gift might seem to people scarcely worthy of notice. But the Lord who sees into men's hearts, pointed out to His disciples precisely this humble gift of the poor woman. The Lord valued her gift for its internal worth. Having called His disciples to Him, He said to them, "Truly I say to you, this poor widow has put in **more than all** those who are contributing to the treasury. For they all contributed out of their abundance; but she out of her poverty has put in everything she had, her whole living." She contributed her last coin, and by so doing consecrated to God everything that she had.

Note: See the Gospels of Mark 12:41-44; Luke 21:1-4.

CHAPTER 41

The Betrayal by Judas

On the fourth day after His triumphant entrance into Jerusalem, Jesus Christ said to His disciples, "You know that after two days the Passover is coming, and the Son of man will be delivered up to be crucified."

On this day, which in our reckoning was **Wednesday**, the chief priests, scribes, and elders of the people gathered in the palace of the high priest, who was called Caiaphas, and took counsel together, in order to arrest Jesus Christ by stealth and kill Him, but not during the feast, as there were many people gathered. They did not want a tumult among the people.

One of the twelve, who was called Judas Iscariot, was very greedy for money and the teachings of Christ had not corrected his spirit. He went to the chief priests and said, "What will you give me if I deliver Him to you?" They were glad and promised him thirty pieces of silver.

From that moment, Judas sought an opportunity to betray Jesus Christ, though not in front of the people.

Note: See the Gospels of Matt. 26:1-5 and 14-16; Mark 14: 1-2 and 10-11; Luke 22:1-6.

CHAPTER 42

The Mystical (Last) Supper

On the fifth day after the Lord's entrance into Jerusalem, which according to our reckoning is Thursday (on Friday evening, the first day of unleavened bread, they sacrificed the Passover lamb), the disciples came to Jesus saying, "Where will you have us prepare the Passover for you to eat?"

The Last Supper

Jesus Christ said to them, "Go into the city, and a man carrying a jar of water will meet you. Follow him, and wherever he enters say to the householder, 'The Teacher says where is My guest room, where I am to eat the Passover with My disciples?' And he will show you a large upper room furnished and ready. There prepare for us."

He sent two of His disciples, Peter and John. They went and found it as He had told them, and they prepared the Passover.

That evening, Jesus Christ, knowing that He would be betrayed that night, came with His twelve apostles to the prepared upper room. When they were seated at the table, Jesus Christ said, "I have earnestly desired to eat this Passover with you before I suffer; for I tell you I shall not eat it again until it is fulfilled in the Kingdom of God." Then He rose, laid aside His garments, and girded Himself with a towel. He poured water into a basin and began to wash the disciples' feet, and to wipe them with the towel with which He was girded.

When He had washed their feet and taken His garments and resumed His place, He said to them, "Do you know what I have done to you? You call Me Teacher and Lord, and you are right, for so I am. If I then, your Lord and Teacher, have washed your feet, you also ought to wash one another's feet. For I have given you an example, that you also should do as I have done to you."

The Washing of the Disciples' Feet

By this example the Lord demonstrated not only His love for His disciples, but also taught them humility, that is, not to consider it beneath oneself to serve someone, even though he may be of lesser status.

After eating the Old Testament Jewish Passover, Jesus Christ established on this evening the sacrament of Holy Communion. Therefore the occasion is called in the Orthodox Church the "Mystical Supper."

Jesus Christ took bread, blessed it, broke it in pieces, and giving it to the disciples said, "**Take, eat; this is My Body, which is broken for you,** for the remission of sins"; for you It is handed over to suffering and death for the forgiveness of sins. He took a cup of wine, and when He had given thanks to God the Father for all His mercy to the race of mankind, He gave it to the disciples, saying "**Drink of it, all of you; for this is My Blood of the New Covenant, Which is poured out for you, for the remission of sins.**"

These words indicate that under the appearance of bread and wine the Saviour taught His disciples that it was His own Body and own Blood, which on the next day He gave up to suffering and death for our sins. How the bread and wine become the Body and Blood of the Lord is a mystery, incomprehensible even to the angels, and is therefore called a **mystery**.

After giving the Eucharist to the apostles, the Lord gave the commandment to always perform this sacrament. He said, *Do this in remembrance of Me* (I Cor. 11:25). This sacrament is performed by us now and will continue to be performed until the end of the age, in the divine service called the **Liturgy**.

During the sacramental Last Supper, the Saviour revealed to the apostles that one of them would betray Him. They were very sorrowful and bewildered. Looking at one another, in fear they began to ask after one another, "Is it I, Lord?" Judas said, "Is it I, Master?" The Saviour quietly said to him, "You have said it," but no one heard it. John was reclining next to the Saviour. Peter beckoned to him and said, "Tell us who it is of whom He speaks." John, lying close to the breast of the Saviour, quietly said, "Lord, who is it?" Jesus Christ quietly answered, "It is he to whom I shall give this morsel, when I have dipped it." So when He had dipped the morsel in a dish with salt, He gave it to Judas, son of Simon Iscariot, and said to him, "What you are going to do, do quickly."

Now no one at the table knew why He said this to him. Some thought that, because Judas had the money bag, Jesus was telling him "Buy what we need for the feast"; or, that he should give something to the poor. So, after receiving the morsel, he immediately went out, and it was night.

Jesus Christ continued to talk with His disciples and said, "Little children, yet a little while I am with you. A new commandment I give to you, that you love one another, even as I have loved you. By this all men will know that you are My disciples, if you have love for one another. Greater love has no man than this, that he give his life for his friends. You are My friends, if you fulfill that which I have commanded you."

During this conversation, Jesus Christ foretold to the disciples that they all would be offended because of Him that night; all would scatter, leaving Him alone. The Apostle Peter declared, "Though they all be offended because of You, I will never be offended."

Then the Saviour said to him, "Truly I say to you, this very night, before the cock crows, you will deny Me three times and will say that you do not know Me."

But Peter more vehemently began to assure Him, saying, "If I must die with You, I will not deny You." So said all the disciples. Nevertheless, the words of the Saviour saddened them. Comforting them, the Lord said, "Let not your heart be troubled. Believe in God (the Father) and believe in Me (the Son of God)."

The Saviour promised His disciples that He would send from His Father another Comforter and Teacher, instead of Himself, that is, the **Holy Spirit**. He said, "I will pray to the Father, and He will give you another Comforter, the Spirit of truth, Whom the world cannot receive, because it neither sees Him nor knows Him. You know Him, for He abides with you and will be in you." That means that the Holy Spirit will be with all true believers in Jesus Christ, in the Church of Christ. *Yet a little while, and the world will see Me no more, but you will see Me; because I live* (I am life; and death cannot conquer Me), *you will live also. The Comforter, the Holy Spirit, whom the Father will send in My name, He will teach you all things, and bring to your remembrance all that I have said to you. The Holy Spirit — even the Spirit of truth,* **Who proceeds from the Father,** *He will bear witness of Me. You also are witnesses, because you have been with Me from the beginning* (John 15:26-27).

Jesus Christ also predicted to His disciples that they would have to suffer much evil and persecution from people because they (the disciples) believe in Him. "In the world you have tribulation; but be of good cheer," said the Saviour, "I have overcome the world" (conquered evil in the world).

Jesus Christ concluded His conversation with a prayer for His disciples and for all who believe in Him, that the Heavenly Father may keep them in steadfast faith, in love, and that they may be **in unity** among themselves.

When the Lord finished the supper, during the conversation, He stood with His eleven disciples and when they had sung a hymn, He went forth across the Kidron valley to the Mount of Olives, into the garden of Gethsemane.

Note: See the Gospels of Matthew 26:17-35; Mark 14:12-31; Luke 22:7-39; John 13, 14, 15, 16, 17, and 18:1.

CHAPTER 43

The Prayer of Jesus Christ in the Garden of Gethsemane and His Being Taken Captive

Entering the garden of Gethsemane, Jesus Christ said to His disciples, "Sit here while I go yonder and pray."

Taking with Him Peter, James, and John, He went deep into the garden, and He began to be sorrowful and troubled. Then He said to them, "My soul is very sorrowful, even to death; remain here and watch with Me." And going a little farther, he fell on His face and prayed, "My

The Lord Prays in the Garden at Gethsemane

Father, if it be possible, let this cup pass from Me; nevertheless, not as I will but as Thou wilt."

Having prayed thus, Jesus Christ returned to the three disciples and found them sleeping. He said to them, "So you could not watch with me one hour? Watch and pray that you may not enter into temptation." Again, for the second time, He went away and prayed. And again He

Judas Betrays the Lord in the Garden

came and found them sleeping, for their eyes were heavy, and they did not know what to answer Him.

So, leaving them again, He went away and prayed for the third time, saying the same words. And there appeared to Him an angel from Heaven, strengthening Him. And being in agony He prayed more earnestly, and His sweat became like great drops of blood falling from His brow to the ground.

And when He rose from prayer, He came to the disciples and said, "Are you still sleeping and taking your rest? It is enough; the hour has come; the Son of man is betrayed into the hands of sinners. Rise, let us be going. See, My betrayer is at hand."

While He was still speaking, Judas, the betrayer, came with a great crowd with lanterns and torches and weapons. It was a band of soldiers and some officers, sent by the chief priests and Pharisees to seize Jesus Christ. Judas spoke with them, "The One I shall kiss is the man; seize Him."

He came up to Jesus at once and said, "Hail, Master!" And he

The Garden of Gethsamane Today

kissed Him.

Jesus Christ said to Him, "Friend, why are you here? Would you betray the Son of man with a kiss?" These words of the Saviour were for Judas the last appeal to repentance.

Then Jesus Christ, knowing all that was to befall Him, came forward to the throng and said to them, "Whom do you seek?"

From the crowd they answered, "Jesus of Nazareth."

The Saviour answered, "It is I."

From these words the soldiers and officers drew back and fell to the ground. When they had recovered from fear and rose, in confusion they tried to seize the disciples of Christ.

The Saviour again said, "Whom do you seek?"

They said, "Jesus of Nazareth."

"I told you that I am He," answered the Saviour. "So, if you seek Me, let those men go."

So the band of soldiers and the officers seized and bound Jesus Christ. The apostles wanted to defend their Teacher. Peter, having a sword, drew it and struck the high priest's servant, and cut off his right ear.

But Jesus Christ said to Peter, "Put your sword into its sheath, for all who take the sword shall perish by the sword. Do you think that I cannot appeal to My Father, and He will at once send me more than twelve legions of angels? How then should the Scriptures be fulfilled, that it must be so? Shall I not drink the cup (of suffering) which the Father has given Me (for the salvation of people)?"

Having said this, Jesus Christ touched the ear of Malchus, healed him, and voluntarily gave Himself into the hands of His enemies.

In the crowd of hired soldiers, there were also chief priests and captains of the Temple and elders of the Jews. Jesus Christ, turning to them, said, "Have you come out as against a robber, with swords and clubs? When I was with you day after day in the Temple, you did not lay hands on Me. But this is your hour and that of the power of darkness."

The soldiers who had seized the Saviour, led Him to the high priest. Then the apostles forsook the Saviour, and in fear fled. Only two of them, John and Peter, followed Him at a distance.

Note: See the Gospels of Matthew 26:36-56; Mark 14:32-52; Luke 22:40-53; John 18:1-12.

CHAPTER 44

The Sanhedrin's Judgement of Jesus Christ

First the soldiers led the bound Jesus Christ to the old high priest Annas, who at that time was not serving in the Temple and lived in retirement. This chief priest interrogated Jesus Christ about His teaching and His disciples, in order to find some fault in Him.

The Saviour answered him, "I have spoken openly to the world. I have always taught in synagogues and in the Temple, where all the Jews

An Ancient Fresco Depicting the Trial of the Lord before the High Priest

come together. I have said nothing secretly. Why do you ask Me? Ask those who have heard Me, what I said to them. They know what I said."

One of the officers of the high priest, standing by, struck Jesus on the cheek and said, "Is that how You answer the high priest?" The Lord, turning to him, said to this, "If I have spoken wrongly, bear witness to the wrong; but if I have spoken rightly, why do you strike Me?"

After questioning by the high priest Annas, the bound Jesus Christ was sent through the courtyard to Annas' son-in-law, the high priest Caiaphas.

The Lord is Led Away

Caiaphas was the high priest that year. He had advised the Sanhedrin to kill Jesus Christ, saying, "You know nothing at all; you do not understand that it is expedient for you that one man should die for the people, and that the whole nation should not perish."

The holy Apostle John, pointing out the **importance of this sacred rank of high priest**, explains that in spite of his criminal design, the high priest Caiaphas involuntarily prophesied about the Saviour, that He would have to suffer for the redemption of the people. Therefore the Apostle John said, *He did not say this of his own accord, but being high priest that year, he prophesied that Jesus should die for the nation.* And here he adds, *and not for the nation only* (for the Jews, because Caiaphas spoke only about the Hebrew nation), *but to gather into one the children of God* (the Gentiles), who are scattered abroad (John 11:49-52).

At the house of the high priest Caiaphas that night, there gathered many members of the Sanhedrin. The Sanhedrin, as the highest court of law, usually had to convene in the Temple by day. Elders and Jewish scribes also came. All of them had agreed in advance to condemn Jesus Christ to death. But to do this it was necessary to find some sort of guilt punishable by death. And since no one could find any sort of guilt in Him, they hired false witnesses to make untrue accusations against Jesus Christ. Many such false witnesses came forward. But they were not able to say anything that could condemn Jesus Christ. At last two such false witnesses came forward and said, "We heard Him say, I will destroy this Temple that is made with hands, and in three days I will build another, not made with hands." But such testimony was not enough to condemn Him to death. To all these false witnesses, Jesus Christ made no answer.

The high priest Caiaphas stood up and said, "Have You no answer to make? What is it that these men testify against You?" Jesus Christ was silent.

Caiaphas said to Him, "I adjure You by the living God, tell us if You are Christ, the Son of God."

To this question Jesus Christ gave answer and said, "I am, but I tell you hereafter you will see the Son of man sitting at the right hand of Power, and coming on the clouds of heaven."

Then the high priest tore his robes, as a sign of indignation and horror, and said, "Why do we still need witnesses? You have now heard His blasphemy (that He, being a man, calls Himself the Son of God). What is your decision?" They all answered in one voice, "He deserves death."

After this they gave Jesus Christ into custody. Some began to spit on Him. The men who were holding Him mocked Him and beat Him. Others, covering His face, struck Him and with laughter asked, "Prophesy to us, You Christ, who is it that struck You?" All these insults Jesus Christ endured without murmuring.

Note: See the Gospels of Matthew 26:57-68; 27:1; Mark 14:53-65, 15:1; Luke 22:54, 63-71; John 18:12-14, 19-24.

CHAPTER 45

The Apostle Peter's Denial

When they led Jesus Christ to the high priest's house, the Apostle John, who was known to the high priest, entered the court, but Peter remained outside at the door. Then John spoke to the maid who kept the door and brought Peter in.

The maid, seeing Peter, said to him, "Are you not also one of the disciples of this man (Jesus Christ)?"

Peter answered, "No."

The night was cold. The officers kindled a fire in the middle of the courtyard and sat, warming themselves. Peter also warmed himself with them. Soon another maid, seeing him as he sat in the light warming himself, said to the guards, "This man also was with Jesus of Nazareth."

But Peter again denied it saying "Woman, I do not know him."

After an interval of about an hour still another insisted to Peter, "Certainly, you also were with Him; for your accent betrays you. You are a Galilean." One of the servants of the high priest, a kinsman of the man, Malchus, whose ear Peter had cut off, asked, "Did I not see you in the garden with Him?"

Peter began to invoke a curse on himself and swear, "I do not know this man of Whom you speak." While he was still speaking, the cock crowed, and reminded Peter of the words of the Lord, how He had said to him, "Before the cock crows today, you will deny Me three times." The Lord, being among the guards in the court, turned and looked at Peter. The gaze of the Lord penetrated the heart of Peter. Shame and repentance seized him, and he went out from the court and wept bitterly over his grievous sin.

From that moment on Peter never forgot his fall. St. Clement, a disciple of Peter, tells how Peter throughout all his remaining days, at the midnight crowing of the cock, fell on his knees and in a flood of tears, repented of his denial, although the Lord Himself, immediately after His resurrection, forgave him. The ancient traditional teaching is still preserved, that the eyes of the Apostle Peter were red from frequent and bitter weeping.

Note: See the Gospel of Matthew 26:69-75; Mark 14:66-72; Luke 22:55-62; John 18:15-18, 25-27.

The Death of Judas

Friday morning came. Immediately the chief priests with the elders and scribes convened their council. They brought Jesus Christ and again condemned Him to death for calling Himself Christ, the Son of God.

When Judas, His betrayer, found out that He was condemned to death, he understood all the horror of his act. Perhaps he did not expect such a sentence, or supposed that Christ would not permit it, or would deliver Himself from His enemies in some miraculous way. Judas understood to what his love of money had led. Tormenting guilt seized his soul. He went to the chief priests and elders and brought back the thirty pieces of silver, saying, "I have sinned in betraying innocent blood."

They said to him, "What is that to us? See to it yourself" (that is, you yourself must answer for your deed).

But Judas did not want to humbly repent in prayer and tears before the merciful God. Cold despair and depression overcame his soul. Throwing down the pieces of silver in the Temple before the chief priests, he departed, and he went and hanged himself. The chief priests, taking the pieces of silver said, "It is not lawful to put them into the treasury, since they are blood money." So they took counsel, and bought with it the potter's field, to bury strangers in. Therefore that field (a cemetery) has been called in Hebrew *Akaldema*, which means, "field of blood."

Then was fulfilled what had been spoken by the Prophet Jeremiah, saying, "And they took thirty pieces of silver, the price of Him on Whom a price had been set by the sons of Israel, and they gave them for the potter's field."

Note: See the Gospel of Matthew 27:3-10.

CHAPTER 46

The Trial of Jesus Christ Before Pilate

The chief priests and Jewish elders, having condemned Jesus Christ to death, themselves were not able to carry out their sentence without confirmation from the ruler of the region, the Roman governor in Judea. At this time the Roman governor in Judea was **Pontius Pilate**.

On the occasion of the feast of Passover, Pilate was in Jerusalem and was living not far from the Temple in the **Praetorium**, the house of the main court, the praetor. In front of the praetor was built an open platform, which was called **Lithostrotos**, and in Hebrew and Aramaic, **Gabbatha**.

Early in the morning, on Friday, the chief priests and elders of the Jews led the bound Jesus Christ to trial before Pilate, so that he could confirm the death sentence handed over to Jesus. But they themselves did not enter the praetorium in order not to defile themselves before Passover by being in the house of a gentile.

Pilate came out to them on the Lithostrotos, or "the Pavement," and seeing the members of the Sanhedrin, asked, "What accusation do you bring against this man?"

They answered, "If this man were not an evildoer, we would not have handed Him over to you."

Pilate said to them, "Take Him yourselves and judge Him by your own laws."

They said to him, "It is not lawful for us to put any man to death," and they began to accuse the Saviour, saying, "We found this man perverting our nation, and forbidding us to give tribute to Caesar, and saying that He Himself is Christ the King."

Pilate asked Jesus Christ, "Are you the King of the Jews?"

Jesus Christ answered, "You have said so" (which means, "Yes, I am King").

When the chief priests and the elders accused the Saviour, He answered nothing. Pilate again asked Him, "Have you no answer to make? See how many charges they bring against You."

But Jesus made no further answer, so that Pilate wondered in amazement. Pilate entered the praetorium again and called Jesus, asking Him, "Are You the King of the Jews?"

Jesus Christ answered, "Do you say this of your own accord, or did others say it to you about me?"

"Am I a Jew?" answered Pilate. "Your own nation and the chief priests have handed You over to me. What have You done?"

The Lord before Pilate

Jesus Christ answered, "My kingdom is not of this world. If My kingdom were of this world, My servants would fight, that I might not be handed over to the Jews, but My kingdom is not from here."

"So You are a king?" asked Pilate.

Jesus Christ answered, "You say that I am a king. For this I was born, and for this I have come into the world, to bear witness to the truth. Every one who is of the truth hears My voice."

From these words Pilate recognized that before him stood a preacher of the truth, a teacher of the people, and not an agitator against the power of Rome.

Pilate said to Him, "What is truth?" And not waiting for an answer, he went out again to the Jews on the Lithostrotos and told them, "I find no crime in this man."

The chief priests and elders were agitated, saying, "He stirs up the people, teaching throughout all Judea, from Galilee even to here."

Pilate, having heard mention Galilee, asked, "Is He in fact a Galilean?" When he learned that He belonged to Herod's jurisdiction, he sent Him to the court of the Galilean King, Herod, who by chance was himself in Jerusalem at that time. Pilate was glad to rid himself of this unpleasant case.

Note: See the Gospels of Matthew 27:2,11-14; Mark 15:1-5; Luke 23:1-7; John 18:28-38.

Jesus Christ Before King Herod

The Galilean King, Herod Antipas, who had put John the Baptist to death, had heard a great deal about Jesus Christ and had desired to see Him for a long time. When they brought Jesus Christ to Him, he was very glad, for he was hoping to see some miracle done by Him. Herod questioned Him at some length, but the Lord made no answer. The chief priests and the sentries stood by, vehemently accusing Him.

Then Herod with his soldiers, having treated Him with contempt and mocked Him, arrayed Him in a gorgeous robe as a sign of His innocence, and sent Him back to Pilate.

From that very day Pilate and Herod became friends with each other, for before this they had been at enmity with each other.

Note: See the Gospel of Luke 23:8-12.

The Lord is Judged Before Herod

CHAPTER 47

Pilate's Last Judgment over Jesus Christ

When they again brought the Lord Jesus Christ to Pilate, there had already gathered a large crowd of people, chiefs and elders. Pilate then called together the chief priests, rulers, and the people, saying to them, "You brought me this man as One Who was perverting the people; and after examining Him before you, I did not find this man guilty of any of your charges against Him. I sent Him to Herod, and Herod also found nothing done by Him to deserve death. I will therefore chastise and release Him."

The Jews had the custom at the feast of Passover of releasing to the crowd any one prisoner whom they wanted. Pilate, using this occasion, said to the people, "You have the custom that at Passover I should release to you one prisoner. Do you want me to release for you the King of the Jews?" Pilate was sure that the people would ask for Jesus, because he perceived that it was out of envy and malice that the chief priests had delivered Him up.

While he was sitting on the judgment seat, his wife sent word to him, "Have nothing to do with that righteous man, for I have suffered much over Him today in a dream."

In the meantime the chief priests and the elders stirred up the crowd to have Pilate release to them Barabbas. Barabbas was a notorious criminal, who had been thrown into prison with his companions for an insurrection started in the city and for murder.

Then the people, persuaded by the elders, began to shout, "Release to us Barabbas!"

Pilate, desiring to release Jesus, addressed them once more, "Which of the two do you want me to release to you: Barabbas or Jesus, called Christ?"

They all shouted, "Not Him, but Barabbas!"

Then Pilate asked them, "Then what shall I do with Jesus, Who is called Christ?"

They shouted, "Let Him be crucified!"

Pilate again said to them, "Why, what evil has He done? I have found no crime deserving death; I will therefore chastise Him and release Him."

But they shouted all the more, "Crucify Him! Let Him be crucified!"

Then Pilate, thinking he could arouse compassion from the people for Christ, ordered the soldiers to scourge Him. The soldiers led Jesus Christ to the courtyard, stripped Him and cruelly beat Him. Then they arrayed Him in a purple robe (a short purple robe without sleeves, fastened on the right shoulder), placed a plaited crown of thorns on His

The Lord Is Beaten and Mocked

head, and put in His right hand a reed instead of the royal scepter. They began to mock Him. They knelt down in homage before Him, and said, "Hail, King of the Jews!" They spat on Him and, taking the reed, struck Him on His head and face.

After this Pilate led Him to the Jews and said, "Behold I bring Him out to you that you may know that I find no crime in Him." So Jesus Christ came out wearing the crown of thorns and the purple robe. Pilate said to them "Here is the Man!" With these words, Pilate meant to say, "Look at how He is tortured and disgraced," thinking that the Jews would take pity on Him. But not such were the enemies of Christ. When the chief priests and officers saw Jesus Christ, they cried out, "Crucify Him! Crucify Him!"

Pilate said to them, "Take Him yourselves and crucify Him, for I find no crime in Him."

The Jews answered him, "We have a law, and by that law He ought to die, because He has made Himself the Son of God."

When Pilate heard these words, he was even more frightened. He entered the praetorium again and said to Jesus, "Where are You from?"

The Gate Where Pilate Brought the Lord to the People and Said, "Behold the Man."

But the Saviour gave him no answer.

Pilate therefore said to Him, "You will not speak to me? Do you not know that I have power to release You and power to crucify You?"

Then Jesus Christ answered, "You would have no power over Me unless it had been given you from above; therefore he who delivered Me to you has the greater sin." After this Pilate more vigorously sought to release Jesus Christ.

But the Jews cried out, "If you release this man, you are not Caesar's friend; everyone who makes himself a king sets himself against Caesar." When Pilate heard these words, he decided it was better to condemn an innocent man to death than to risk the danger of royal disgrace before the Emperor.

Then Pilate brought Jesus Christ out and sat down on the judgment seat at a place called the Pavement and said to the Jews, "Here is your King!"

But they cried out, "Away with Him, away with Him, crucify Him!"

The Lord Is Crowned With Thorns

Pilate said to them, "Shall I crucify your King?"

The chief priests answered, "We have no king but Caesar."

Pilate, seeing that he was gaining nothing, but rather that a riot was beginning, took water and washed his hands before the crowd, saying, "I am innocent of this man's blood; see to it yourselves" (let the blame fall on you).

All the people answered, "His blood be on us and on our children!" Thus the Jews invoked upon themselves and their descendants responsibility for the death of the Lord Jesus Christ, unless they repent.

Then Pilate released Barabbas for them, and delivered Jesus Christ to them to be crucified.

Note: See the Gospels of Matthew, 27:15-26; Mark 15:6-15; Luke 23:13-25; John 18:39-40 and 19:1-16.

The Road to Golgotha

Since Jesus Christ was condemned to be crucified, He was then handed over to the soldiers. Again they beat, insulted and mocked Him. After they had made fun of Him, they took off the purple robe and dressed Him in His own clothing. The condemned person had to carry his own cross to the place of crucifixion; therefore the soldiers laid the cross on the shoulders of the Saviour and led Him to the place intended for crucifixion. The place was a hill which was called Golgotha, or the place of the skull. Golgotha was situated west of Jerusalem not far from the city gate called the Judgment Gate.

A great multitude of people followed Him. The road was hilly. Ex-

The Lord Is Led to Golgotha

hausted by beating and lashing, worn out by spiritual suffering, Jesus Christ could hardly walk, several times falling from the weight of the cross. When they went out of the city gate where the road began to go uphill, Jesus Christ was unable to continue carrying the cross. The soldiers came upon a man who was compassionately watching Christ. It was **Simon, a Cyrenian**, returning from work in the country. The soldiers seized him and compelled him to carry the cross of Christ.

Among the people who followed Christ were many women who wept and lamented for Him. Jesus Christ, turning to them, said, "Daughters of Jerusalem, do not weep for Me, but weep for yourselves and for your children. For behold the days are coming when they will say, Blessed are the women who never had children. Then they will begin to say to the mountains: fall on us, and to the hills: cover us."

Thus the Lord predicted the terrifying misfortune which would befall Jerusalem and the Jewish people soon after His earthly life.

Note: See the Gospel of Matthew 27:27-32; Mark 15:16-21; Luke 23:26-32; John 19:16-17.

The Shrine At Golgotha Where the Cross Stood

CHAPTER 48

The Crucifixion and Death of Jesus Christ

Hanging on a cross was the most disgraceful, agonizing, and cruel form of death penalty. In those times such a death penalty was imposed only on the most hardened criminals: thieves, murderers, instigators of rebellion, and felons. The torture of a crucified man is impossible to describe. Besides unbearable pain in every part of the body, the crucified underwent the ordeal of terrible thirst and spiritual suffering until dead. Death was so slow that many suffered on the cross for several days. Even the executioners, habitually brutal people, could not keep their composure while looking at the suffering of a crucified man. They prepared a beverage by which they tried to quench his unbearable thirst; or by adding various substances they tried to temporarily dull consciousness and alleviate the suffering. By Jewish law, a crucified man was considered cursed. The chiefs of the Jews wanted to disgrace Jesus Christ forever by condemning Him to such a death.

When they brought Jesus Christ to Golgotha, the soldiers offered Him sour wine to drink, mingled with bitter substances to lessen the suffering. The Lord, when He tasted it, did not wish to drink it. He did not want to lessen the suffering. This suffering He took upon Himself voluntarily for the sins of all people; therefore he wanted to bear it consciously to the end.

When all was ready, the soldiers crucified Jesus Christ. It was about midday, by Jewish reckoning the sixth hour of the day. When they crucified Him, He prayed for His tormentors, saying, "Father, forgive them; for they know not what they do."

They crucified two robbers with Jesus Christ, one on His right and one on His left. Thus the scripture of the Prophet Isaiah was fulfilled which says, *He was reckoned with transgressors* (Is. 53:12).

According to the order of Pilate, a title plate was attached to the cross over the head of Jesus Christ, indicating His guilt. On it was written in Hebrew, Greek and Latin, **"Jesus of Nazareth, King of the Jews,"** and many read it. Thus the sign did not please the enemies of Christ. Therefore the chief priest went to Pilate and said, "Do not write, King of the Jews, but write that He says, I am King of the Jews."

Pilate answered, "What I have written I have written."

The Crucifixion

In the meantime, the soldiers who had crucified Jesus Christ took His garments and began to divide them among themselves. The outer garment they divided in four parts, one for each soldier. The tunic (the inside garment) was seamless, woven from top to bottom. So they said to one another, "Let us not tear it, but cast lots for it to see whose it shall be." And having cast lots the soldiers, sitting, guarded the place of execution. This fulfilled the ancient prophecy of King David, *They parted my garments among them, and for my clothing they cast lots* (Ps. 21:19).

His enemies did not cease to insult Jesus Christ even on the cross. Those who passed by derided Him, wagging their heads and saying, "Aha! You Who would destroy the Temple and build it in three days, save Yourself, and come down from the cross."

So also the chief priests, with the scribes and the elders, mocked Him, saying, "He saved others; He cannot save Himself. If He is the King of Israel, let Him come down now from the cross, so that we can see, and then we will believe in Him. He trusts in God; let God deliver Him now if He desires Him; for He said, 'I am the Son of God.'"

Following their example the pagan soldiers, who sat near the crosses and kept watch over the crucified, taunted Him, saying, "If you are King of the Jews, save Yourself!"

Even one of the crucified thieves, who was to the left of the Saviour, railed at Him saying, "If you are the Christ, save Yourself and us!"

But the other thief, on the right, rebuked Him saying, "Do you not fear God since you are under the same sentence of condemnation (the same torture and death)? We are indeed justly condemned; so we receive the due reward of our deeds; but this Man has done nothing wrong." Having said this, he turned to Jesus Christ with the prayer, **"Remember me Lord, when You come into Your kingdom."**

The merciful Saviour accepted the sincere repentance of this sinner, indicating such wonderful faith in Him, and answered the wise thief, **"Truly I say to you, today you will be with Me in Paradise."**

Standing by the cross of Jesus were His mother, the Apostle John, Mary Magdalene, and several other women who revered Him. It is impossible to describe the grief of His mother, seeing the unbearable suffering of Her Son. When Jesus Christ saw His mother, and the disciple whom He loved standing near, He said to His mother, **"Woman, behold, your son!"** Then He said to John, **"Behold your Mother!"** And from that hour the disciple took Her to his own home and cared for Her until the end of Her life.

Meanwhile, during the suffering of the Saviour on Golgotha, there occurred a great sign. From the hour that the Saviour was crucified, from the sixth hour (by our calculation about 12 o'clock noon), the sun darkened, and there was darkness over the whole land until the ninth hour (by our calculation three o'clock in the afternoon), until the Saviour died.

This remarkable, worldwide darkness was noticed by pagan historians, the Roman astronomer Flegontus and Junius Africanus. A noted philosopher from Asia, Dionysius the Areopagite, in Egypt in the city of Heliopolis at the time, observed the sudden darkness and said, "Either the Creator is suffering or the world is coming to an end." Later Dionysius the Areopagite converted to Christianity and became the first bishop of Athens.

About the ninth hour Jesus Christ cried out with a loud voice, "**Eloi, Eloi, lama sabachthani?**" which means, "My God, my God, why hast Thou forsaken Me?" These were the beginning words from the 21st psalm of King David in which David clearly foretold the suffering on the cross of the Saviour. By these words the Lord for the last time reminded people that He is the true Christ, Saviour of the world.

Some of the bystanders hearing it said, "Behold, He is calling Elijah." Others said, "Let us see whether Elijah will come to save Him."

The Lord Jesus Christ, knowing that all was now finished, pronounced, "**I thirst.**" Then one of the soldiers at once ran and took a sponge, filled it with vinegar, put it on a stick and raised it to the parched lips of the Saviour. When He had received the vinegar, the Saviour said, "**It is finished.**" That is, the promise of God was fulfilled, the salvation of the human race was accomplished.

Then He, crying with a loud voice, said, "**Father, into Thy hands I commit My spirit.**" And He bowed His head, and gave up His spirit.

In the same hour, the veil of the Temple, covering the Holy of Holies, was torn in two, from the top edge to the bottom, and the earth shook, and the rocks were split. The tombs were opened, and many bodies of the saints who had reposed were raised. Coming out of the tombs after His resurrection, they went to Jerusalem and appeared to many.

When the centurion (chief of the soldiers) and the soldiers who were with him keeping watch over the Saviour saw the earthquake and what took place they were filled with awe and said, "**Truly this was the Son of God.**" All the multitudes who had assembled to see the sight in fear began returning home beating their breasts.

Friday evening came. At that hour it was necessary to partake of the Passover meal. The Jews did not want to leave the bodies on the cross on the Sabbath because it was the Passover Sabbath, considered a feast day. Therefore they asked Pilate permission to break the legs of the crucified so that they would die more quickly and might be removed from the crosses and taken away. Pilate gave permission. So the soldiers came and broke the legs of the first, and of the other who had been crucified with him. When they came to Jesus Christ they saw that He was already dead and therefore they did not break His legs. One of the soldiers, in order to leave no doubt that He was dead, pierced His side with a spear, and immediately blood and water came out.

Note: See the Gospels of Matthew 27:33-56; Mark 15:22-41; Luke 23:33-49; John 19:18-37.

CHAPTER 49

The Taking Down from the Cross and Burial of the Saviour

When evening had come, soon after everything had been done, a respected member of the council, a rich man named **Joseph of Arimathea**, went to Pilate. Joseph was a secret disciple of Jesus Christ, secret from fear of the Jews. He was a good, righteous man, not participating in the council's condemnation. He asked Pilate for permission to take down the body of Christ from the cross and bury it.

St. Joseph of Arimathea Asks Pilate for the Body of the Lord

Pilate wondered if He were already dead, and summoning the centurion, he asked him whether He was already dead. When he learned from the centurion that it was so, he granted Joseph the body for burial.

Joseph, having bought a shroud (a linen cloth for burial), went to Golgotha. Another secret disciple of Jesus Christ and a member of the Sanhedrin, Nicodemus, went also. He brought with him expensive fragrant oil for burial, which was composed of myrrh and aloes.

They took down the body of the Saviour from the cross, anointed Him with the spices, wrapped Him in the funeral shroud and laid Him in the new tomb, in the garden next to Golgotha. This tomb was a cave which Joseph of Arimathea had hewn in the rock for his own burial, and in which no one

The Lord Is Taken from the Cross

had ever yet been laid. There they laid the body of Christ, since this tomb was close to Golgotha and they had little time because of the Jewish day of preparation for Passover. They rolled a large stone before the door of the tomb and departed.

Mary Magdalene, Mary the mother of James the Younger and of Joses, and other women were there and saw where the body of Christ was laid. Returning home, they bought expensive myrrh to anoint the body of Christ as soon as the first day of the great feast was over. On the first day they rested according to the commandment.

The enemies of Christ did not rest, in spite of their great feast. On the next day, on Saturday, the chief priest and the Pharisees, breaking the peace of the Sabbath, gathered before Pilate and said, "Sir, we remember how that imposter (as they dared to call Jesus Christ), while

The Place Where Our Lord's Body Was Anointed for Burial

He was still alive, said, 'After three days I will rise again.' Therefore, order the sepulcher to be made secure until the third day, lest His disciples go and steal Him away and tell the people, 'He has risen from the dead,' making the last fraud worse than the first."

Pilate said to them, "You have a guard of soldiers; go make the tomb as secure as you can." So the chief priests and Pharisees went to the tomb of Jesus Christ and carefully inspected the cave, made it secure by sealing the stone, and set a guard at the tomb.

While the body of the Saviour lay in the tomb, He descended spiritually into Hades, the temporary dwelling place of souls before the Resurrection of Christ, to the souls of people who had died before His suffering and death. All the souls of righteous people, who awaited the coming of the Saviour, He liberated from Hades.

The Lord's Tomb

Notes: See the Gospels of Mathew 27:57-66; Mark 15:42-47; Luke 23:50-56; John 19:38-42.

The Passion of Christ is commemorated by the Holy Orthodox Church the week preceding **Pascha**. This week is called **Passion Week**. This entire week Christians should spend in fasting and prayer.

On **Great Wednesday** of Passion Week the betrayal of Jesus Christ by Judas Iscariot is commemorated.

On **Great Thursday** evening during the evening service, which is Matins for Great Friday, the twelve passages of the Gospel relating to the suffering of Jesus Christ are read.

On **Great Friday during Vespers**, which is served at two or three o'clock in the afternoon, the burial **shroud**, the holy image of the Saviour lying in the tomb, is carried from the altar and placed in the middle of the church. This is done in memory of the removal of the body of Christ from the cross and His burial.

On **Great Saturday during Matins**, while all the bells are rung and while the hymn "Holy God, Holy Mighty, Holy Immortal, have mercy on us" is sung, the shroud is taken in procession in memory of the descent of Jesus Christ into Hades, when His body remained in the tomb, and his victory over hell and death.

We prepare ourselves for Passion Week and the holiday of Pascha by fasting. This fast continues for forty days and is called the **Great Fast**.

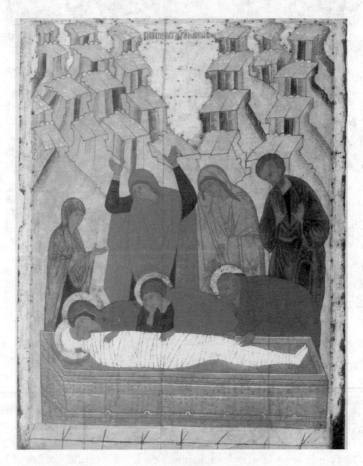

The Lord Is Placed in the Tomb

In addition to these weeks, the Holy Orthodox Church fasts every **Wednesday** and **Friday**, except during certain weeks in the year; on Wednesday in memory of the betrayal of Jesus Christ by Judas, and on Friday in memory of the suffering of Jesus Christ. We express faith in the power of the suffering on the Cross for us by Jesus Christ, by making the sign of the Cross when we pray.

CHAPTER 50

The Resurrection of the Lord Jesus Christ

After the Sabbath, during the night on the third day after His suffering and death, **the Lord Jesus Christ resurrected by the power of His divinity.** His body was transformed. He left the tomb unseen by the guards, **without** rolling away the stone or breaking the seal placed by the Sanhedrin. From that moment on the guards unknowingly guarded an empty sepulcher. Suddenly there occurred a great earthquake. An angel of the Lord descended from Heaven. He proceeded to roll back the stone from the entrance to the tomb of the Lord, and sat upon it. His appearance was like lightning and his raiment white as snow. The soldiers standing guard at the tomb were terrified and became like dead men. Regaining consciousness after the fright, they dispersed.

On this day, the first day of the week, at dawn when the Sabbath rest had just ended, Mary Magdalene, Mary the mother of James, Joanna, Salome, and other women, having taken the fragrant myrrh which they had prepared, went to the tomb of Jesus Christ to anoint His body, not having had time to do this during the burial. The Church calls these women the holy Myrrhbearers. They still did not know that a guard had been placed at the tomb of the Lord and that the entrance to the cave had been sealed. Therefore they did not expect to meet anyone there and said among themselves, "Who will roll away the stone from the door of the tomb?" The stone was very large and Mary Magdalene, walking ahead of the other myrrhbearing women, arrived at the tomb first. The sun had not yet risen, and it was dark. Seeing that the stone was rolled away from the tomb, Mary hastened to Peter and John and said, "They have taken the Lord from the tomb and we know not where they have laid Him." Hearing these words, Peter and John immediately ran to the tomb with Mary Magdalene following after them.

At this time the other women, who had been walking with Mary Magdalene, arrived at the tomb, and also saw that the stone was rolled away. They suddenly saw a shining angel sitting on the stone. Turning to them the angel said. "Fear not, for I know that you seek Jesus, Who was crucified. He is not here, for He is risen as He said when He was with you. Come, see the place where the Lord lay. Go quickly and tell His disciples that He is risen from the dead."

The Resurrection of Christ

They entered into the tomb and did not find the body of the Lord Jesus Christ. They saw, however, an angel in white garments seated on

The Angel Announces that the Lord Is Risen

the right side of the place where the Lord had lain, and they were struck with fear.

The angel said to them, "Be not afraid. You seek Jesus of Nazareth, Who was crucified. He is risen; He is not here. Behold the place where they laid Him. Go your way, tell His disciples and Peter (who by his denial fell from the number of the disciples), that He is going before you to Galilee. There you will see Him, as He told you."

While the women stood in perplexity, behold, two angels stood by them in dazzling apparel. Since they were frightened the women bowed their faces to the ground in fear.

The angels said to them, "Why do you seek the living among the dead? He is not here. **He is risen.** Remember how He told you while He was still in Galilee, that the Son of man must be delivered into the hands of sinful men, and be crucified, and on the third day rise?"

Then the women remembered the words of the Lord. They went out and fled from the tomb, for they were overcome by fear and trembling. Then in awe and with great joy they ran to tell His disciples. On the road they said nothing to anyone, since they were afraid. When they reached the disciples, the women told them everything that they had seen and heard. However, these words seemed to the disciples like an idle story, and they did not believe them.

In the meantime Peter and John ran to the tomb. John outran Peter and reached the tomb first, but did not enter the tomb. Stooping to look in, he saw the linen cloths lying there. Then Simon Peter came and went into the tomb. He saw the linen cloths lying, and the covering which had been on Christ's head, not lying with the linen clothes but rolled up in a place by itself. Then John, who had reached the tomb first, also went in, and he saw all this and believed in the resurrection of Christ. Peter marveled over the incident. Then the disciples went back to their homes.

When Peter and John left, Mary Magdalene, who had followed after them, stayed at the tomb. She stood weeping outside the tomb, and as she wept she stooped to look into the tomb, and saw two angels in white, sitting one at the head and one at the feet of where the body of the Saviour had lain. The angels said to her, "Woman, why are you weeping?"

Mary Magdalene said to them, "Because they have taken away my Lord, and I do not know where they have laid Him." Saying this, she turned around and saw Jesus Christ standing, but from her extreme grief and tears, and from her conviction that the dead do not rise, she did not know that it was Jesus.

Jesus Christ said to her, "Woman, why are you weeping? Whom do you seek?"

Supposing Him to be the gardener, Mary Magdalene said to Him, "Sir, if you have carried Him away, tell me where you have laid Him, and I will take Him away."

Then Jesus Christ said to her, "**Mary!**"

The familiar voice brought her out of her grief to her senses, and she realized that before her stood the Lord Jesus Christ Himself. She exclaimed, **"Teacher!"** and with indescribable joy cast herself at the feet of the Saviour. In her joy she did not fully grasp the majesty of this moment.

Jesus Christ, showing her the holy and great mystery of His resurrection, said, "Do not touch Me, for I have not yet ascended to the Father; but go to my brethren (the disciples) and say to them: I am ascending to My Father and your Father, to My God and your God."

Then Mary Magdalene hurried to His disciples and related the news that she had seen the risen Lord and what things He had said to her. **This was the first appearance of Christ after His resurrection.**

On the way, Mary Magdalene met Mary, mother of James, also returning from the tomb of the Lord. When they went to tell the disciples, suddenly Jesus Christ Himself met them and said, "Rejoice!"

They ran, took hold of His feet, and worshipped Him. Then Jesus Christ said to them, "Do not be afraid. Go and tell My brethren to go to Galilee, and there they will see Me." **Thus the risen Christ appeared a second time.**

The Lord Appears to Mary Magdalene

Mary Magdalene with Mary, the mother of James, went to the eleven disciples and all the others who were grieving and weeping, and announced their great joy. However, hearing from them that Jesus Christ was alive and that they had seen Him, still they did not believe.

After this, Jesus Christ appeared separately to Peter and convinced him of His resurrection. **This was His third appearance.** Only then did many people cease to doubt the reality of the resurrection of Christ, although there remained unbelievers among them.

The Holy Church confesses from ancient times that before the other appearances, **Jesus Christ gladdened His Most-holy Mother**, announcing His resurrection to Her through an angel. Concerning this the Holy Church sings:

The Angel cried unto Her Who is full of grace: O pure Virgin, rejoice! and again I say, rejoice! for Thy Son is risen from the grave on the third day, and hath raised the dead, O ye people, be joyful!

Shine, shine, O New Jerusalem, for the glory of the Lord is risen upon thee; dance now and be glad, O Sion, and do Thou exalt, O pure Theotokos, in the arising of Him Whom Thou didst bear.

Meanwhile, the soldiers guarding the tomb of the Lord, who had dispersed in fear, went to Jerusalem. Several of them went to the chief priests and told them all that had taken place at the tomb of Jesus Christ. When they had assembled with the elders they took counsel. Due to their stubbornness, the enemies of Jesus Christ did not want to confirm His resurrection and made up their minds to conceal this event from the people. They bribed the soldiers, giving them money, and said, "Tell the people, 'His disciples came by night and stole Him away while we were asleep.' If Pilate hears about it, we will quiet him and keep you out of trouble." So the soldiers took the money and did as they were directed; and this story has been spread among the Jews, so that many of them believe it to this day.

The deception and falsehood of this story is evident to everyone. If the soldiers had been asleep, then they would not have seen what had happened, and if they had seen what had happened, it means they were not asleep and could have detained the thief. The guard was supposed to keep watch and guard. No one could really believe that the guard, composed of several people, could have slept. If all the soldiers had fallen asleep, then they would have been subjected to strict punishment. Why were none of them punished, but left alone and even rewarded? How were the terrified disciples, locked in their houses out of fear, able to decide, without having weapons against armed troops, to undertake such a daring venture? Furthermore, why would they do it, since they themselves had lost faith in the Saviour? Besides, how could they have rolled away the large stone without waking anyone? All this is quite impossible. On the contrary, the disciples themselves thought that someone had stolen the body of the Saviour, and only after seeing the empty tomb, they understood that after a theft it would not have been left so. Finally, why did the leaders of the Jews not search for the body of Christ and not punish the disciples? Thus the enemies of Christ tried to cover an act of God with a coarse fabrication of lies and deceit, but they turned out to be powerless against the truth.

Note: See the Gospels of Matthew 28:1-15; Mark 16:1-11; Luke 24:1-12, John 20:1-18. See also I Corinthians, 15:3-5.

CHAPTER 51

The Appearance of the Risen Jesus Christ to Two Disciples on the Road to Emmaus

Toward evening of that very day in which Jesus Christ resurrected and appeared to Mary Magdalene, Mary, mother of James, and Peter, two disciples of Christ from the Seventy, Cleopas and Luke, were going from Jerusalem to a village named **Emmaus**. Emmaus was situated about seven miles from Jerusalem.

On the road they were talking with each other about all the things that had recently happened in Jerusalem, about the suffering and death of the Saviour. While they were talking about all that had happened, Jesus Christ Himself drew near and went with them, but their eyes were kept from recognizing Him. Jesus Christ said to them, "What is this conversation you are holding with each other as you walk, and why are you so sad?"

Cleopas answered Him, "Are you the only visitor to Jerusalem, who does not know the things that have happened there in these days?"

Jesus Christ said to him, "What things?"

They said to Him, "Concerning Jesus of Nazareth, Who was a prophet mighty in deed and word before God and all the people, and how our chief priests and rulers delivered Him up to be condemned to death, and crucified Him. We had hoped that He was the One to redeem Israel. Yes, and besides all this, it is now the third day since this happened. Moreover, some women of our company amazed us. They were at the tomb early in the morning and did not find His body, and they came back saying that they had even seen a vision of angels, who said that He was alive. Some of those who were with us went to the tomb, and found it just as the women had said; but Him they did not see."

Then Jesus Christ said to them, "O foolish men, and slow of heart to believe all that the prophets have spoken! Was it not necessary that the Christ should suffer these things and enter into His glory?" And beginning with Moses and all the prophets, He interpreted to them in all the Scriptures the things concerning Himself. The disciples were amazed as everything became clear to them. As they drew near to Emmaus, Jesus Christ appeared to be going further. But they constrained Him, saying, "Stay with us, for it is toward evening, and the day is now far spent." So Jesus Christ went in to stay with them. When He was at table with them, He took the bread and blessed, and broke it, and gave it to them. Then their eyes were opened, and they recognized Him, but He vanished out of their sight. **This was the fourth appearance of the resurrected Christ.** Cleopas and Luke in great joy said to each other, "Did not our hearts burn with joy within us while He talked to us on the road, while He explained to us the Scriptures?" They rose that same hour, and despite the late time of day, returned to Jerusalem, where they found ten disciples gathered together, all except the Apostle Thomas, and those who were with them. All of them joyfully met Cleopas and Luke and said, "The Lord has risen indeed and has appeared to Simon!" Then Cleopas and Luke told what had happened on the road to Emmaus, how the Lord Himself had walked with them and talked, and how they recognized Him in the breaking of bread.

Note: See the Gospels of Mark 16:12-13; Luke 24:13-35.

The Lord Appears to Sts. Luke and Cleopas

CHAPTER 52

The Appearance of the Lord to All the Apostles and Other Disciples, Except the Apostle Thomas

As the apostles were talking with the disciples of Christ just returned from Emmaus, Cleopas and Luke, the door of the house in which they were gathered being locked from fear of the Jews, suddenly Jesus Christ Himself stood among them and said to them, "**Peace be unto you.**"

They were startled and frightened and supposed that they saw a spirit. Jesus Christ said to them, "Why are you troubled, and why do doubts arise in your hearts? See My hands and My feet, that it is I Myself. Touch Me and see; for a spirit has not flesh and bones as you see that I have."

Saying this, He showed them His hands and feet, and rib. The disciples were overjoyed seeing the Lord. Due to their great joy they still did not believe, but only marvelled. To strengthen their faith, Jesus Christ said to them, "Have you anything here to eat?"

The disciples gave Him a piece of broiled fish and some honeycomb. Jesus Christ took it and ate before them. Then He said to them, "These are the words which I spoke to you, while I was still with you, that everything written about Me in the law of Moses and the prophets and the psalms must be fulfilled."

Then He opened their minds to comprehend the Scriptures. Finishing His conversation with His disciples Jesus Christ for the second time said, "**Peace be with you. As the Father has sent Me, even so I send you.**" And when He had said this, He breathed on them and said to them, "**Receive the Holy Spirit. If you forgive sins, they are forgiven by God. If you retain sins, they are retained.**"

This was the fifth appearance of the Lord Jesus Christ, on the first day of His glorious resurrection, giving all His disciples great, inexpressible joy. Only Thomas, one of the twelve disciples, called *the Twin*, was not with them when Jesus came. When the other disciples told him that they had seen the risen Lord, Thomas said to them, "Unless I see in His hands the print of the nails, and place my finger in the mark of the nails, and place my hand in His side, I will not believe."

Note: See the Gospels of Mark 16:14; Luke 24:36-45; John 20:19-25.

CHAPTER 53

The Appearance of the Lord to the Apostle Thomas and the Other Apostles

Eight days later, His disciples were again in the house and Thomas was with them. The doors were shut, as they were the first time. Jesus Christ came and stood among them and said, "**Peace be unto you!**"

The Lord Appears to Saint Thomas and to the Other Apostles

THE NEW TESTAMENT 373

Then, turning to Thomas, He said to him, "Put your finger here, and see My hands; and put out your hand, and place it in My side. Do not be faithless but believing."

Then Thomas exclaimed, **"My Lord and My God!"**

Jesus Christ said to him, **"Have you believed because you have seen Me? Blessed are those who have not seen and yet believe."**

Note: See the Gospel of John 20:26-29.

The Appearance of Jesus Christ to the Apostles beside the Sea of Tiberias and Reinstatement of Peter, Who Had Denied Christ, to Apostleship

According to the instruction of Jesus Christ, His disciples went to Galilee. There they took up their usual business. One day Peter, Thomas, Nathaniel (Bartholemew), the sons of Zebedee, James and John, and two other of His disciples fished all night in the Sea of Tiberias (Sea of Galilee) and caught nothing. Just as day was breaking, Jesus Christ stood on the beach, yet the disciples did not know it was He.

Jesus Christ said to them, "Children, have you any fish?"

They answered, "No."

Jesus Christ said to them, "Cast the net on the right side of the boat, and you will find some." The disciples cast the net on the right side of the boat and now they were not able to haul it in, due to the quantity of fish.

Then John said to Peter, **"It is the Lord!"**

When Peter heard that it was the Lord, he put on his clothes, for he was stripped for work, sprang into the sea, and swam to shore, to Jesus Christ. But the other disciples came in the boat dragging the net full of fish, for they were not far from the land. When they reached land, they saw a charcoal fire there with fish lying on it, and bread.

Jesus Christ said to the disciples, "Bring some of the fish that you have just caught." Peter went and hauled the net ashore, full of large fish, a hundred and fifty-three of them; and although there were so many, the net was not torn. Jesus Christ said to them, "Come and eat." Now none of the disciples dared ask Him, "Who are you?" They knew it was the Lord. Jesus Christ took the bread and gave it to them, and also the fish.

When they had finished eating, Jesus Christ showed Peter that He would forgive him his denial and elevate him again into the company of His chosen Apostles. Peter, by his denial, had sinned more than the other disciples. Therefore the Lord asked him, "Simon, son of Jonah, do you love Me more than the other disciples do?"

Peter said to Him, "Yes, Lord. You know that I love You."

Jesus Christ said to him, "Feed My lambs."

A second time Jesus Christ said to Peter, "Simon, son of Jonah, do you love Me?"

Peter again answered, "Yes, Lord. You know that I love You."

Jesus Christ said to him, "Feed My sheep."

Finally, Jesus Christ said to him the third time, "Simon, son of Jonah, do you love Me?"

Peter was grieved because the Lord said to him the third time, "Do you love Me?" And he said to Him, "Lord, You know everything; You know that I love You."

The Lord Appears to the Disciples at the Sea of Tiberias

Jesus Christ said to him, "Feed My sheep."

Thus the Lord helped Peter make amends three times for denying Him three times, and witness to his love for Him. After each of his answers Jesus Christ returned him, in the presence of the other apostles, to the apostolic calling and made him a pastor to His sheep.

After this Jesus Christ said to Peter, "Truly, truly, I say to you, when you were young, you girded yourself and walked where you would; but when you are old, **you will stretch out your hands** and another will gird you and carry you where you do not wish to go." This the Saviour said to show Peter by what death He was to glorify God. He would accept a martyr's end for Christ (crucifixion). After this Jesus Christ said to him, "Follow me."

Peter turned and saw John following them. When Peter saw him, he asked "Lord! What about this man?"

Jesus Christ said to him, "If it is my will that he remain until I come, what is that to you? Follow Me." The saying spread abroad among the brethren that this disciple was not to die, although Jesus Christ did not say that.

Note: See the Gospel of John, chap. 21.

The Appearance of Jesus Christ to the Apostles and More Than Five Hundred Disciples

Now, as Jesus Christ had directed them, the eleven apostles went to the mountain in Galilee. There more than five hundred disciples came to them. Then Jesus Christ appeared before them all. Seeing Him they worshipped Him, but some doubted.

Jesus Christ came and said to them, "All authority in Heaven and on earth has been given to me. Go therefore and make disciples of all nations, **baptizing them in the name of the Father and of the Son and of the Holy Spirit**, teaching them to observe all that I have commanded you; and lo, I am with you always, to the end of the age. Amen."

Then Jesus Christ appeared separately to James.

Thus, in the course of forty days after His resurrection, Jesus Christ appeared to His disciples, giving much conclusive evidence of His resurrection, and He talked with them about the Kingdom of God.

Notes: See the Gospels of Matthew 28:16-20; Mark 16:15-16 (not in English versions); I Corinthians 15:6-8; and the Acts of the Apostles 1:3.

CHRIST IS RISEN!

The great event, the **Glorious Resurrection of Christ**, is celebrated by the Holy Orthodox Church as the greatest of all feastdays. It is the Feast of Feasts, and celebration of celebrations. This Feast is called **Pascha** (Greek for ''Passover''), that is, the day on which is **accomplished our passage (passover) from death to life and from earth to Heaven**. The celebration of the Resurrection of Christ continues for a whole week, and services held in the church are celebrated more festively than on all other days. On the first day of the Feast Matins begins at midnight. Before the beginning of Matins, the celebrants, vested in

The Lord Appears to the Twelve Apostles and More Than Five Hundred Disciples

brilliant robes, together with the faithful, accompanied by the ringing of bells, carrying burning candles, the cross and icons, proceed around the church, emulating the myrrhbearing women who proceeded to the tomb of the Saviour in the early morning. During the procession everyone sings, "**Thy Resurrection, O Christ Savior, the angels hymn in the heavens; vouchsafe also us on earth with pure hearts to glorify Thee.**" The first exclamation of Matins is made before the closed doors of the church while the festal hymn "Christ is Risen..." is repeated many times; and then while singing the hymn they enter the church. The services continue all night with open Royal Doors, signifying that now, by the Resurrection of Christ, the gates of the Kingdom of Heaven are opened for all. On every day of this great feast we greet one another with the brotherly kiss and the words, "**Christ is Risen!**" and answer with the words, "**Truly He is Risen!**" We greet each other in this way and exchange colored eggs, which symbolize the new, blessed life revealed from the tomb of the Saviour. Bells ring all week. From the first day of Holy Pascha until vespers of the Feast of the Holy Trinity, one is not permitted to kneel in church or make prostrations.

On the first Tuesday after Bright Week, the Holy Church, extending the gladness of the Resurrection of Christ to those who died in the hope of the general resurrection, especially commemorates the dead, and therefore this day is called "**Paschal Soul Day.**" On this day the Liturgy is celebrated with commemoration of the dead. On this day it is customary to visit the graves of one's close relatives. This custom differs in some aspects among local churches.

Besides this, the day of the Resurrection of Christ is celebrated by us on every **Sunday** of the year.

Troparion for the Feast of Pascha

Christ is risen from the dead, trampling down death by death, and on those in the tombs bestowing life.

Kontakion for the Feast of Pascha

Though Thou didst descend into the grave, O Immortal One, yet didst Thou destroy the power of hades. And didst rise as victor, O Christ our God, calling to the myrrh-bearing women: Rejoice! And giving peace unto Thine Apostles, Thou Who dost grant resurrection to the fallen.

CHAPTER 54

The Ascension of the Lord

When the day of the Jewish Pentecost drew near, the disciples of Christ returned from Galilee to Jerusalem.

On the fortieth day after the resurrection of Jesus Christ they were all together in one house. Jesus Christ appeared to them and spoke with them saying, "Thus it is written, that the Christ should suffer and on the third day rise from the dead, and that repentance and forgiveness of sins should be preached in His name to all nations, beginning from Jerusalem. You are witnesses of these things. Go into all the world and preach the Gospel to all creation. He who believes and is baptized will be saved, but he who does not believe will be condemned. And these signs will accompany those who believe: in My name they will cast out demons; they will speak in new tongues; they will pick up serpents, and if they drink any deadly thing, it will not hurt them; they will lay their hands on the sick, and they will recover."

Then the Saviour said to the disciples that soon the Holy Spirit would come upon them, and until that time He charged them not to depart from Jerusalem. He said, "I send the promise of My Father upon you; but stay in the city, until you are clothed with power from on high; for John baptized with water, but before many days you shall be baptized with the Holy Spirit."

Conversing with the disciples, the Saviour led them out of the city as far as Bethany, to the Mount of Olives. The disciples, overjoyed with the words of the Saviour, surrounded Him and started to ask, "Lord, will You at this time restore the kingdom to Israel?"

The Saviour said to them, "It is not for you to know the times or seasons which the Father has fixed by His own authority. But you shall receive power when the Holy Spirit has come upon you; and you shall be My witnesses in Jerusalem and in all Judea and Samaria and to the end of the earth."

When He had said this, Jesus Christ lifted up His hands and blessed His disciples. While He blessed them, He parted from them and He was lifted up to Heaven, and soon a cloud took Him out of their sight.

Thus our Lord and Saviour Jesus Christ ascended in His physical body to Heaven and sat down at the right Hand of God the Father. His human soul and body took on the indivisible glory with His divinity. In His divinity, He always is and will be in Heaven and everywhere.

The disciples worshipped the ascended Lord and for a long time continued to stand and gaze into Heaven after Him. Then two angels in white robes appeared before them and said, "Men of Galilee, why do

The Ascension of the Lord

you stand looking into Heaven? This Jesus, Who was taken up from you into Heaven, will come to earth in the same way (that is, in the flesh), as you saw Him go into heaven.''

After this the disciples of Jesus Christ returned to Jerusalem with great joy and stayed there together, awaiting the descent of the Holy Spirit. All of them, together in soul, spent the time in prayer and were continually in the Temple of God, praising and thanking God. With them were several women and Mary, the Most-holy Mother of the Lord Jesus Christ, with their relatives.

In those days the apostles, prayerfully, by casting lots, chose from among the other disciples of Christ the twelfth apostle, **Matthias**, to take the place of Judas the betrayer, who perished.

Ascended to Heaven, Jesus Christ, according to His own promise, invisibly always comes to earth among those who believe in Him and will come again to earth in a visible form to judge the living and the dead, who will then rise from the dead. After this will begin the life of the next age, another, eternal life which for true believers and pious people will be completely blessed, but for disbelievers and sinners will be a time of great torment.

Notes: See the Gospels of Mark 16:15-19 and Luke 24:46-53; Acts of the Apostles 1, 2:4-26.

The Ascension of our Lord Jesus Christ is celebrated by the Holy Orthodox Church as one of the Great Feasts, on the fortieth day after Pascha.

Troparion of the Feast

Thou didst ascend into glory, O Christ our God, having gladdened Thy disciples with the promise of the Holy Spirit; and they were assured by the blessing that Thou art the Son of God, the Redeemer of the world.

The Mount of Olives

CHAPTER 55

The Descent of the Holy Spirit on the Apostles

The tenth day after the Ascension of Jesus Christ was the fiftieth day after the Resurrection of Christ. It was the Jews' great feast of Pentecost, which commemorated the giving of the Law on Mt. Sinai.

All the apostles, the Mother of God, and the other disciples of Christ and other of the faithful, were all together in one room in Jerusalem. It was the third hour of the day by the Hebrew reckoning of hours, according to our system — nine o'clock in the morning. Suddenly a sound came from Heaven, like the rush of a mighty wind, and it filled all the house where they were sitting. There descended on them tongues that looked like fire, which rested on each one of them. They were all filled with the Holy Spirit and began to speak in other languages, previously unknown to them. Thus the Holy Spirit, according to the promise of the Saviour, descended on the apostles in the form of **tongues of fire**, as a sign that He gave the apostles the ability and zeal to preach the teachings of Christ to all peoples. He descended in the form of **fire** as a sign of the power to cleanse sins, to sanctify and warm souls.

On the occasion of the feast of Pentecost, there were in Jerusalem many Jews who had come from various nations. Hearing the noise, a great multitude of people came together around the house where the disciples of Christ were. They were all bewildered and asked each other, "Are not all these who are speaking Galileans? How is it that we hear, each of us in his own native language? How are they able to tell in our languages the mighty works of God?" In disbelief they said, "They are filled with new wine."

Then the Apostle Peter, standing with the eleven, said that they were not drunk, but that the Holy Spirit had descended upon them, that it had been prophesied by the Prophet Joel, and that Jesus Christ, Whom the Jews had crucified, had risen from the dead, ascended into Heaven and poured out on them the Holy Spirit. Finishing this sermon about Jesus Christ, the Apostle Peter said, "Let all the house of Israel therefore know assuredly that God has made Him both Lord and Christ, this Jesus, Whom you crucified."

The sermon of Peter so moved those who heard it that many more believed in Jesus Christ. They asked Peter and the rest of the apostles, "Brethren, what shall we do?"

The Descent of the Holy Spirit on the Apostles

Peter said to them, "Repent, and be baptized, every one of you in the name of Jesus Christ for the forgiveness of your sins; then you shall also receive the gift of the Holy Spirit."

So those who believed in Christ readily accepted baptism, and there were added that day about three thousand souls. Thus began the building of the Kingdom of God on earth, the holy Church of Christ.

From the day of the descent of the Holy Spirit the Christian faith quickly began to spread with the help of God, and the number of believers in the Lord Jesus Christ multiplied. Instructed by the Holy Spirit, the apostles preached boldly to all about Jesus Christ, the Son of God, about His suffering for us and resurrection from the dead. The Lord helped them with many great miracles which were performed by the apostles in the name of the Lord Jesus Christ. At first the apostles preached to the Jews, and then dispersed to various countries to preach to all people. To perform the sacraments and to preach Christianity the apostles established, by the laying on of hands, **bishops, presbyters** and **deacons**.

This grace of the Holy Spirit, which was clearly conferred on the apostles in the form of tongues of fire, is now conferred in our Holy Orthodox Church invisibly in its sacraments, through the **successors to the apostles**, the pastors of the Church, its **bishops and priests**.

Note: See the Acts of the Apostles 2:14-23.

The Descent of the Holy Spirit on the Apostles in celebrated by the Holy Orthodox Church as one of the greatest feastdays on the fiftieth day after Pascha, because the Holy Spirit descended on the Apostles on the fiftieth day after the resurrection of Jesus Christ. It is therefore called **Pentecost**, or **Holy Trinity Day**, for from this day the action of the Holy Trinity was revealed to the world, and people learned to venerate and glorify the three Persons of the one God, the **Father and Son and Holy Spirit**.

On this feastday it is customary to decorate the church and its hall with greenery, and to hold flowers during the Liturgy, thus expressing our joy and thanksgiving to God for His Holy and Life-giving Spirit, which renews people, and gives them birth through baptism into a new life. The flowers and greenery signify life.

The day following Holy Trinity Day is called Spirit Day and is devoted to glorification of the Holy Spirit.

Troparion of Pentecost

Blessed art Thou, Christ our God, Who hast shown forth the fishermen as supremely wise, by sending down upon them the Holy Spirit, and through them, didst draw the world into Thy net. O Lover of mankind, glory be to Thee.

CHAPTER 56

The Life of the First Christians

Soon after the descent of the Holy Spirit, the Apostles Peter and John went into the Temple for prayer at the ninth hour, or in our terms, three o'clock in the afternoon, the hour of the death of our Lord Jesus Christ. At the gate of the Temple which was called Beautiful, there sat a beggar, lame from birth. He stretched out his hand to the apostles and asked for alms.

The Apostle Peter said to him, "I have no silver and gold, but I give you what I have. In the name of Jesus Christ of Nazareth, stand up and walk." He took him by the right hand and raised him up.

Immediately the feet and ankles of the lame man were made strong. He started to walk and entered the Temple with the apostles. All the people were filled with wonder at this great miracle, and ran to the portico called Solomon's, where the apostles were. Here the Apostle Peter delivered a second sermon about the risen Lord. Many of those who heard his word believed, and the number of the men came to about five thousand.

The many great miracles performed by the Lord through the apostles and the abundant gifts of the Holy Spirit, which moved through them, excited in the believers reverential fear and at the same time, joy and happiness. They tried in everything to fulfill the commandments of Christ and to live holy and pure lives. The believers gathered in the Temple every day and listened to the preaching of the apostles, and on the **day of the Resurrection**, the first day of the week — Sunday, they gathered in homes for the breaking of bread, for the sacrament of Holy Communion. All of them were united in great love, so that it was as if they had one heart and one soul. Many sold their possessions and asked the apostles to distribute the money received to the poor. All of the believers gave thanks to God. For their love and good deeds they gained the respect and love of the surrounding people, and the number of believers increased daily.

With time, all the believers in the Lord Jesus Christ began to be called **Christians**, and the teaching and life by faith in Christ — **Christianity**.

Note: See Acts of the Apostles 2:42-47; 3; 4; 11:26.

CHAPTER 57

Persecution of the Christians by the Jews — The First Martyr St. Stephen

The glory and victory of Christianity and its rapid spread gave rise to fear and envy among the Jewish leaders. They began to pursue the Christians, to arouse the simple Jewish people against them, and to accuse them to the Roman authorities. The Jews seized Christians, threw them into prisons and killed them.

The first one to suffer at the hands of the Jews in Jerusalem was St. Stephen, one of the first deacons. He is called the first martyr, since he was the first to be tortured for Christ.

For preaching about the Saviour, the Jews cast him outside the city and began to stone him to death. He prayed, saying, "Lord Jesus, receive my spirit," and then with the words, "Lord, do not hold this sin against them," he died.

By killing St. Stephen and many other of the faithful, the Jews were still not able to weaken faith in Christ. On the contrary, by doing this they greatly kindled its spread among the inhabitants of Jerusalem. Because of the persecution, Christians dispersed into Judea, Samaria and other countries, and everywhere they went they preached about the Lord Saviour and His teaching. No power in the world could stop the victorious spread of Christianity, for faith in Christ is the true faith. The teaching of Christ is divine teaching, and life according to the faith and teaching of Christ is true holy life, the Kingdom of God. The Heavenly Father strengthened the faithful, the Saviour was with them, and they were comforted by the Holy Spirit, the Comforter.

Note: See Acts of the Apostles 6; 7; 8:1-2,4.

The Conversion of Saul

When they stoned St. Stephen the first martyr, one Jewish youth by the name of Saul, who guarded the clothing of the people while stoning St. Stephen, approved of this murder. Saul was against Christians, and took part in persecuting them. He entered Christians' homes, seized them and delivered them to prison, thus tormenting the Church of Christ. Not satisfied with persecuting Christians in the land of the Jews, he asked permission of the high priest to go to the Syrian city of Damascus to search for Christians there and to take them bound to Jerusalem to be judged and martyred.

As Saul was going to Damascus and drew near the city, he was suddenly overcome by a light from Heaven. He fell to the ground and heard a voice saying to him, "Saul, Saul, why do you persecute Me?"

Saul asked, "Who are you, Lord?"

The Lord said, "I am Jesus, Whom you are persecuting. It is difficult for you to kick against the spur."

Saul in fear and trepidation said, "Lord! What are You ordering me to do?"

The Lord said to him, "Rise and enter the city to which you are going; there you will be told what you are to do."

The men who were travelling with him stood speechless, hearing the voice but seeing no one. Saul arose from the ground. When his eyes were opened, he could see nothing. So they led him by the hand and

The Stoning of St. Stephen

brought him into Damascus. He spent three days in prayer, and neither ate nor drank.

Now there was at that time a disciple at Damascus, one of the seventy apostles of the Lord, named Ananias. The voice of the Lord ordered him to go to the house where Saul was and lay his hands on him to restore his sight. The Apostle Ananias went to Saul, and when he laid his hands on him something like scales fell from the eyes of Saul, and

Saint Paul

immediately he regained his sight. Then he arose, and was baptized by Ananias. The baptism of Saul took place in the year 37 A.D.

Saul took the name **Paul** and became an outcast by preaching faith in Christ. Then the Lord Jesus Christ again appeared to Paul and ordered him to go to the pagans and to preach the Christian faith.

The Apostle Paul ended his life as a martyr. For his great apostolic labors, like the Apostle Peter, he is called by the Church **foremost among the apostles**.

Note: See Acts of the Apostles 8:1-3; 9:1-30; and 22:17-21.

CHAPTER 58

The Dormition of the Mother of God

The Most-holy Mother of God, after the Ascension of Jesus Christ, continued to live on earth several years. One Christian historian says ten years, and another, twenty-two years. Apostle John the Theologian, according to the instructions of Jesus Christ, took Her into his home and cared for Her with great love as Her own son, until the end of Her life. The Most-holy Mother of God became a mother to all twelve of the apostles in general. They prayed with Her with great joy and were comforted to listen to Her instructive conversations about the Saviour. When the Christian faith had spread to other lands, many Christians came from distant countries to see and hear Her.

Living in Jerusalem, the Mother of God loved to visit those places the Saviour had frequented, where he had suffered, died, rose from the dead, and ascended to Heaven. She prayed at these places, weeping, remembering the suffering of the Saviour, and rejoicing at the places of His Resurrection and Ascension. She often prayed that Christ would soon take Her to Himself in Heaven.

One day, when the Most-holy Mary was praying thus on the Mount of Olives, the Archangel Gabriel appeared to Her with a branch from a date palm in Paradise, and told Her the joyful news that in three days She would finish Her earthly life, and the Lord would take Her to Himself. The Most-holy Mother of God silently rejoiced over this news. She told Her adopted son, John, and began to prepare for Her end. At that time the other apostles were not in Jerusalem, as they had dispersed to other countries to preach about the Saviour. The Mother of God wanted to bid farewell to them, and so the Lord, in a miraculous manner gathered all the apostles to Her, except Thomas, transporting them by His omnipotent power.

Grief befell them over losing the Mother of the Lord and their own spiritual Mother, when they learned why God had gathered them. But the Mother of God comforted them, promising not to leave them and all Christians after Her death, and promising also to pray for them. Then She blessed them all.

At the hour of Her death, an extraordinary light shone in the room where the Mother of God lay. The Lord Jesus Christ Himself, surrounded by angels, appeared and received Her pure soul.

The apostles buried the pure body of the Mother of God according to Her wishes, in the Garden of Gethsemane, where the body of Her parents and the righteous Joseph were buried. At the funeral, many miracles were performed. From touching the deathbed of the Mother of God, the blind regained their sight, demons were driven away, and all sorts of illnesses were cured. Crowds of people followed Her most pure body. Jewish priests and leaders tried to break up this holy procession, but the Lord invisibly protected it. One of the Jewish priests, by the name of

The Dormition of the Mother of God

Athonius, ran up and seized the bier on which was laid the body of the Mother of God, in order to overturn it. But an invisible angel chopped off both his hands. Athonius, struck by such a wondrous miracle, repented and the Apostle Peter healed him.

Three days after the burial of the Mother of God, the absent Apostle
Thomas arrived in Jerusalem. He was greatly saddened that he had not
been able to say farewell to the Mother of God, and with all his heart de-

The Tomb of the Mother of God

sired to venerate Her most pure remains. The apostles felt so sorry for
him that they decided to go and roll away the stone from the tomb, to
give him the possibility to venerate for the last time the body of the
Mother of God. But when they opened the tomb, Her most holy body
was nowhere to be found, but only one piece of burial shroud was there.
The amazed apostles returned to the house together and prayed to God
to reveal to them what had become of the body of the Mother of God. In

the evening, at the end of dinner during prayer, they heard angelic singing. Looking up the apostles saw in the air the Mother of God, surrounded by angels, in the radiance of heavenly glory. The Mother of God said to the apostles, "Rejoice! I am with you always, and will pray for you before God."

The apostles exclaimed to Her in joy, "Most-holy Mother of God, help us!"

Thus the Lord Jesus Christ glorified His Most-holy Mother. He resurrected Her and took Her most holy body to Himself and set Her higher than all His angels.

Note: A full description of the Dormition of the Mother of God is found in Church Tradition, preserved by the Holy Orthodox Church.

The Dormition of our Most-holy Lady Mother of God is celebrated by the Holy Orthodox Church, as one of its major feasts, on the **15th of August** (28th of August n.s.). Preceding this feast there is a two-week fast, beginning from the 1st of August. This feast is called the **Dormition** ("falling asleep") because the Mother of God died quietly, as if falling asleep, and more importantly because of the short sojourn of Her body in the grave. After three days She was resurrected by the Lord and ascended into Heaven.

Troparion of the Feast

In giving birth Thou didst preserve Thy virginity; in Thy dormition Thou didst not forsake the world, O Theotokos. Thou wast translated unto life, since Thou art the Mother of Life; and by Thine intercessions dost Thou deliver our souls from death.

The Church of the Mother of God's Tomb

CHAPTER 59

The Apostolic Council in Jerusalem

When Christianity had spread throughout the known world, and multitudes of pagans began to accept the Christian faith, some Christians were troubled. Christians of Jewish background held that Christians from pagan religions had to strictly observe the rituals of the Law of Moses. As a prerequisite, it should be necessary to turn them first to the Jewish faith, as otherwise, they could not be saved. This led to heated disagreements among the Christians.

No single apostle was able to resolve such an important question alone. It was determined by the holy apostles, together with the presbyters or priests, in harmony with the commandments of Christ (cf. Matt. 18:17), to convene the first **Apostolic Council** in Jerusalem in the year 51 A.D.

After long discussions the issue was settled by the words of the Apostle Peter. He arose and said that the Lord, having elected him in the early days to preach to the gentiles, did not make any distinction between Jews and gentiles but to all gave the Holy Spirit, and therefore Christians converted from pagan religions did not have to keep the rituals of the law of Moses. "We believe," the Apostle finished his speech, **"that we shall be saved through the grace of the Lord Jesus Christ."**

The speech of the Apostle Peter created a deep impression and was then strengthened still more after the Apostles Paul and Barnabas related what signs and wonders God had done through them among the Gentiles.

After this, the Apostle **James**, the "brother of the Lord" arose to address those present at the council. To him, as bishop of the Jerusalem Church and president of the council (first among equals), belonged the last word. His opinions were furthermore important because he himself was a strict adherent of the Law and received for this not only from Christians, but also from Jews themselves, the epithet **"righteous."** Honor was accorded him by his position in the Church, first bishop of Jerusalem, placed there by the Lord Himself. St. James led a strict ascetic life, and he wore a gold name plate which was worn only by the chief priests. He spent whole hours alone in the Temple, praying for his people. In Jerusalem he was honored and respected by the people.

St. James approved the opinion of the Apostle Peter. He showed that it was in agreement with prophecy (Amos 9:11-12), and consequently, with divine providence. He proposed, "we should not trouble those of the gentiles, who turn to God, with keeping the rituals of the

Law of Moses; but they must refrain from idol worship, from fornication, and from things strangled and blood. They should not do to others what they do not want done to themselves."

This proposal of the Apostle James was accepted by the apostles, presbyters and the whole Council, unanimously, as a resolution of the Council. It was made known to all Christians in a Council decree, which began with the words, **"It has seemed good to the Holy Spirit and to us...."**

Thus the Apostolic Council showed Christians that the decree of the Council, in agreement with the word of the Lord (John 16:13;14:16) is established by the Holy Spirit. This letter of the Apostolic Council brought great joy and comfort to the Christians.

Note: See Acts of the Apostles 15:1-35.

The Preaching Labors of the Apostles

In a short time the apostles of Christ, by their preaching, which was inspired in them by the Holy Spirit, won multitudes of pagans to Christ, simple and unsophisticated people as well as scholars and even kings. The apostles suffered much difficulty in their holy work, enduring much grief and need. All the apostles, with the exception of John the Theologian, met a martyr's end. The Apostle John the Theologian died in exile at a great old age. The number of Christians grew from year to year, even after the deaths of the apostles, and the Christian faith spread to all the ends of the earth.

The apostles preached verbally for the most part. But in order that the teaching of Christ be better preserved, several of them, under the inspiration of the Holy Spirit, wrote it down in books. Therefore these books are called the **Holy Scriptures**, as were the books of the prophets before Christ.

Two of the twelve apostles, **Matthew** and **John**, and two of the seventy apostles, **Mark** and **Luke**, each wrote a book about the life on earth of Christ the Saviour and His teaching. These four books are called the **Gospels** ("good news") because in them are preserved the teachings of Christ, which the Saviour Himself called the Gospel. The apostles writing them are called the Gospel writers, or **Evangelists**.

The Evangelist Luke wrote another book, **the Acts of the Apostles** or, the deeds and labors of the apostles. This book records how the apostles spread the Christian faith in the first years.

Others of the apostles: **James**, son of Alphaeus, **Peter**, as well as **John** the Theologian and **Jude** (Judas) the brother of James, wrote seven general epistles, letters to Christians all over the world, and taught in these letters how to believe and live according to the teachings of Christ. One of the letters is by the Apostle James, two by Peter, three by John and one by Jude.

The Apostle **Paul** wrote fourteen epistles to distant churches and people.

The Cave Where Saint John the Theologian Wrote the Book of Revelation

The Apostle John the Theologian, in addition to the Gospel and three epistles, wrote still another book, the **Apocalypse**, or **Revelation**. In this book is found the future destiny of the Christian Church and of the whole world.

Of course, the apostles did not write everything that they taught and had heard from the Saviour in the books. The Evangelist John the Theologian himself wrote, "But there are also many other things which Jesus did; were every one of them to be written, I suppose that the world itself could not contain the books that would be written."

The teachings and rules which the apostles conveyed to the Christians by their words and example firmly preserved Christianity. These teachings, given to them orally and only later written down by the saints, are called **apostolic tradition**, or **Holy Tradition**.

Together with the apostles and after them, **apostolic men**, or disciples of the apostles, preached the Gospel. These pastors, teachers and fathers of the Church of Christ spread and strengthened the Church of Christ by their speaking, writing, and by their holy lives.

CHAPTER 60

A Short Summary of the Preaching and Lives of the Holy Apostles

The holy **foremost-of-the-Apostles, Peter** (Simon), preached first in Judea and then in Antioch, in Bithynia, in Asia, in Cilicia, also throughout Italy and in Rome itself. In Rome he was crucified head down, by order of the Emperor Nero. The Apostle Peter and the Apostle Paul, as the apostles who labored more than all the others in preaching the Christian faith, are called the **holy foremost-of-the-Apostles** by the Holy Church.

The holy **foremost-of-the-Apostles, Paul** (Saul) preached in many countries beginning in Jerusalem and ending in Rome, the capital of the world. In Rome he was beheaded by Emperor Nero.

The **holy Apostle Andrew the First-Called**, preached within the boundaries of what later became Russia. He erected a cross on a Kievan hill and predicted the future enlightenment of Russia by the Christian faith. He preached on the shores of the Black Sea and in other countries. In Byzantium he ordained, by the laying on of hands, the bishop Stachys, one of the seventy disciples. In the city of Patras in Achaea (Greece), pagans crucified him on a cross formed in the shape of the letter X, which therefore came to be known as the **Cross of St. Andrew.**

The **holy Apostle James, the son of Zebedee**, preached in Jerusalem and was the first of the apostles to suffer for Christ. On orders from the Judaean King Herod Agrippa, he was beheaded in Jerusalem.

The **holy Apostle and Evangelist John the Theologian,** after torture in Rome, was sent in exile to the Isle of Patmos. St. John lived longer than all the other apostles and died peacefully in Asia, in the city of Ephesus. According to tradition, the apostle, by his own desire, was buried alive by his disciples. When soon after burial, Christians came to open his grave, the body of St. John was not to be found.

The **holy Apostle Philip** preached in Asian countries with the Apostle Bartholomew and his sister Miriam. In Phrygia, a province of Asia Minor, in the city of Hierpolis, he met a martyr's death. He was crucified head down.

The **holy Apostle Bartholomew** (Nathaniel) at first preached together with the Apostle Philip in Syria and Asia, after which he went to India and translated the Gospel of Matthew into the Indian language. Later he preached in Armenia where he suffered a martyr's death in the city of Albanopolis.

The **holy Apostle Thomas,** called Didymus ("the twin"), preached in many Asiatic countries, going to India, where he met a martyr's end for Christ. He was pierced with spears and then beheaded with a sword.

The **holy Apostle and Evangelist Matthew** preached for a long time in Judea and then in all parts of Ethiopia (later Abyssinia, Nubia, Kordofan, Darfun; and now present-day Ethiopia and the Sudan). He was killed by the sword in one of the cities of ancient Ethiopia.

The **holy Apostle James, the son of Alphaeus,** preached in Syria, Egypt and in other countries. In one of these he was crucified on a cross, suffering a martyr's death for Christ.

The **holy Apostle Judas, the brother of James,** also called Thaddeus or Lebbaeus, preached in Judah, Galilee, Samaria and Idumea, in Arabia, Syria and Mesopotamia. In Persia he was hung on a wooden cross and shot with arrows.

The **holy Apostle Simon the Zealot,** a Canaanite, preached in Mauritania in Africa. He was also in England, formerly called Britannia. For preaching faith in Christ, he was crucified on a cross, according to one source, in Georgia, on the order of the Georgian King Aderhi, and according to another source, in Persia.

The **holy Apostle Matthias** was chosen from the seventy, to take the place of the fallen Judas. He preached in Judea and in outer Ethiopia. Returning to Judea, he suffered for Christ, being first stoned and then beheaded.

The **holy Apostle and Evangelist Mark** was from among the seventy apostles and labored with the Apostle Peter. He also preached on the shores of the Adriatic sea. He received a martyr's end in Alexandria by being dragged behind a chariot along the stones in the city streets.

The **holy Apostle and Evangelist Luke** was from among the seventy apostles and labored with the Apostle Paul. He later preached in Egypt, and ended his spiritual feat with a martyr's death by hanging.

The **holy Apostle James the Righteous,** one of the seventy, was the first bishop of Jerusalem, as established by the Lord Himself. He is called the "Brother of the Lord." According to tradition he was the son of Joseph the Betrothed, by his first marriage. St. James was thrown from the roof of the Jerusalem Temple by the Jews, and then killed by a blow on the head. This was about 62 A.D.

The holy Apostle James was the first to formulate the order of the Divine Liturgy which was the foundation for liturgies by St. Basil the Great and St. John Chrysostom which we celebrate now. The Liturgy of St. James is now celebrated in Jerusalem and elsewhere on his feast day.

CHAPTER 61

The Worldwide Persecution of Christians. The Destruction of Jerusalem

During the course of the first three centuries, Christians endured almost constant persecution, first from the unbelieving Jews, and then from pagans.

The Jews who did not accept the Saviour promised by God, the Lord Jesus Christ, but rather condemned Him to death with crazed shouts of "Let His blood be upon us and on our children," and who also killed many Christians, were finally punished for all their lawlessness. Jerusalem and the Temple of God were destroyed to their foundations by the Roman soldiers, when the Jews arose in revolt. This happened in 70 A.D., as the Lord had **prophesied**. The place where the first Temple of God had stood was ploughed under, so that **not a stone was left upon a stone**.

The Jewish people were scattered all over the world. More than a million Jews were annihilated. Tens of thousands of them were sold into slavery. In their place, inhabitants of other nations settled in Palestine, and again built up the ruined cities, among which was the city of Jerusalem. The Christian faith began to flourish among the pagans.

The spread of the Christian faith among the pagans provoked persecution of the Christians by pagan Roman emperors. Adherents of the pagan faith convinced the Emperor that Christians were enemies of the state, enemies of the Emperor and of all mankind. Persecution of the Christians was so cruel that it is difficult to describe. The Christians underwent the most terrifying tortures imaginable.

The first cruel persecution began in the year 64 after the birth of Christ, under the Emperor Nero. Nero burned the city of Rome for his amusement, and then laid the whole blame on the Christians. By his command the Christians were tracked down and seized, given up to be torn to pieces in the circus by wild animals. They dressed them in animal skins and set dogs on them, crucified them on crosses, poured tar over them and burned them instead of torches at night to light Nero's garden. The Apostles Peter and Paul suffered during this persecution in Rome. In 67 A.D., Paul was beheaded by the sword and Peter was crucified on a cross; but by his own special request, he was crucified head down, because he did not consider himself worthy to die the same death as the Lord Jesus Christ.

The most terrible was the last persecution of Christians under the Emperor Diocletian. This persecution lasted from 303 A.D. to 313 A.D. At that time a hundred thousand Christians were killed with the greatest variety of torments. During this persecution, the Holy Scriptures were seized and burned.

At the time of the persecution Lactantius, a noted Christian writer and teacher of philosophy in Nicomedia, wrote, "If I had a hundred mouths and a breast of iron, still I would not be able to enumerate all the

The Persecution of Christians

various kinds of torments endured by the believers."

They tortured in one place from ten to one hundred men in a day. Many of the exhausted and mutilated were revived by medical care so that they could be tortured again. They tortured Christians without regarding sex or age. "I myself was an eyewitness of it," wrote the historian **Eusebius**. "The iron implements became blunt and broken, and the executioners themselves were wearied and had to take turns to relieve each other."

But the suffering and spiritual feats of the martyrs strengthened and spread the Christian faith among other people. Many pagans, seeing the faith and feats of the Christian martyrs and the miracles springing from them were themselves convinced of the truth of the Christian faith, and accepted Christianity. The more they persecuted and tortured the Christians, the more the Christian faith was strengthened.

CHAPTER 62

The End of Persecution. The Elevation of the Cross of the Lord

The persecution of the Christians ceased only in the beginning of the fourth century, under the Roman Emperor **Constantine the Great**.

The Emperor Constantine himself was conquered by the power and the glory of the sign of the Cross of Christ. One day, on the eve of a decisive battle, he and all his soldiers saw a cross of light in the sky with the inscription, "By this sign you will conquer" (in Greek, NIKA). The following night the Lord Jesus Christ Himself appeared with the Cross in His hand and told him that by this sign he would conquer the enemy and directed that each soldier's shield be monogrammed with the holy Cross. Constantine fulfilled the command of God and conquered the enemy. He placed his empire under the protection of the saving sign of Christ. He took Christianity under his protection and proclaimed faith in Christ to be the state religion. He outlawed punishment by crucifixion and issued laws favoring the Church of Christ. For his merit and zeal in propagating the Christian faith, Constantine the Great with his mother Helen, received the title **Holy Rulers, Equal-of-the-Apostles**.

Equal-of-the-Apostles Emperor Constantine desired to build God's churches on the Christian holy places in Palestine, the places of the birth, suffering and resurrection of the Lord Jesus Christ and others, and to find the Cross on which the Saviour was crucified. His mother, the Equal-of-the Apostles St. Helen, took upon herself the task of fulfilling the Emperor's wishes with great joy.

In 326 A.D. Empress Helen journeyed to Jerusalem. She devoted much labor to finding the Cross of Christ, since the enemies of Christ had hidden the Cross, burying it in the ground. Finally, she was directed to an elderly Jew by the name of Judas, who knew where the Cross of the Lord was. After much questioning and conversation, they induced him to reveal its location. It seems that the holy Cross had been thrown into a cave and heaped over with debris and dirt, and above it had been built a pagan temple. Empress Helen ordered the building to be torn down and the cave unearthed.

When they uncovered the cave, they found three crosses in it and apart from them lay a sign with the inscription, "Jesus of Nazareth, King of the Jews." It was necessary to find out which of the three crosses was the Cross of the Saviour. The Patriarch of Jerusalem, Macarius, and Empress Helen firmly hoped and believed that God would show them the Cross of the Saviour.

On the advice of the Patriarch, they brought the crosses one at a time to a very sick woman. From two of the crosses nothing happened, but when they brought the third cross she immediately became well. It happened, that at this moment a dead man was carried by on the way to his burial. They brought the crosses one at a time to the dead man, and when they brought the third cross, the dead man revived. By this means they found the Cross of the Lord, through which the Lord worked miracles and showed the **life-giving power** of His Cross.

The Empress Helen, the Patriarch Macarius and all the people with them thankfully venerated the Cross of Christ and kissed it with great joy. Christians, finding out about this great event, gathered in a crowd of innumerable people at the place where the Cross of the Lord had been found. Everyone wanted to approach the holy life-giving Cross, but because of the size of the crowd, that was impossible. So all began to ask at least to be able to see it. Then the Patriarch stood on a high place, and in order to make it visible to all, **he lifted it up** several times. The crowd,

St. Constantine and His Mother St. Helen

seeing the Cross of the Saviour, bowed and exclaimed, "Lord have mercy!"

The holy Equal-of-the-Apostles Emperor Constantine and Empress Helen built a vast and splendid church in honor of the **Resurrection of Christ.** They also built churches on the Mount of Olives, in Bethlehem, and in Hebron at the Oak of Mamre.

The Elevation of the Cross

The Empress Helen sent a portion of the Cross of the Lord to her son, Emperor Constantine, and another portion she left in Jerusalem. This precious remnant of the Cross of Christ is still kept at the present day in the Church of the Resurrection of Christ at the Holy Sepulcher.

After finding the Life-giving Cross of the Lord, Judas, who had shown the location of the Cross, became a Christian. Later, for his virtuous life, he was ordained a bishop, with the name **Cyriacus**, and was raised to the position of Patriarch of Jerusalem. He suffered for Christ

The Cave Where the Cross Was Found in the Church of the Holy Sepulcher

under Julian the Apostate. The memory of St. Cyriacus the holy martyr is celebrated **October 28th** (November 10th n.s.).

In remembrance of the finding of the Cross of Christ and Its elevation, the Holy Orthodox Church established the feast of the **Exaltation of the Honorable and Life-giving Cross of the Lord**. This feast is one of the great feastdays and is celebrated on **September 14th** (September 27th n.s.).

During the All-night vigil service, at Matins, the Cross is carried out for veneration. While singing the great doxology, the priest, dressed in full vestments and carrying on his head the Holy Cross decorated with flowers, during the singing of "**Holy God...**" carries it from the altar to the middle of the church and places it on an analogion. During the thrice-repeated singing of the festal hymn, " **Save O Lord, Thy people...**," the priest censes the Holy Cross. Then during the singing of, "**Before Thy Cross we bow down, O Master, and Thy holy Resurrection we glorify**," everyone venerates and kisses the Holy Cross. Decorating the Holy Cross with greenery and flowers signifies the conviction that through It, through the suffering and death of the Saviour on It, eternal life is given to us. On this feastday, strict fasting is observed to deepen reverence for the memory of the Saviour's suffering by crucifixion, and to cleanse us from sin.

A Piece of the True Cross Enshrined on Mount Athos

CHAPTER 63

New Enemies of Christianity

In spite of the decisive victory of Christianity over the pagans, they still attempted to advance against Christianity again, during the reign of Emperor **Julian the Apostate**.

Julian was the son of the brother of Constantine the Great. When he became Emperor, although first brought up as a Christian, he began to worship idols and declared himself a pagan and vigorously oppressed Christianity. Inaugurating persecution of the Christians, Julian decided to rebuild the Temple in Jerusalem for the Jews, and he funded the project. But the Lord defended the holy faith. Christians, as well as pagan writers, record an earthquake and balls of fire that sprang out from under the earth and put a stop to Julian's attempt to reestablish the Jerusalem Temple. Even those stones which had been preserved underground from the former Temple were cast up, so that in the full sense of the phrase not one stone remained on another stone.

Thus, the pagan **Ammianus Marcellinus**, a contemporary of Emperor Julian and his advisor, wrote, "terrible balls of flame, which were often expelled from the foundation, made that place inaccessible, burning repeatedly those who worked there; in this manner this enterprise was halted spontaneously, driving away persistent workmen," (Bk 23, chap. 1).

A contemporary and schoolmate of Julian, **St. Gregory the Theologian**, in a speech against Julian, said that at this time in heaven there appeared a blazing cross and the clothing of onlookers was imprinted with crosses. Many foreign observers, as the historians write, gathered to look at the spectacle of the struggle with the mysterious, spontaneous fire.

The enemies of Christianity had to confess their powerlessness, but they did not repent of their evil. In a battle with the Persians, an enemy's arrow struck Julian. Dying, he mournfully cried out, **"You have conquered me, Galilean!"** as he called the Lord Jesus Christ.

After the death of Julian the Apostate, all the following Roman Emperors took care to affirm Christianity throughout the empire.

In the seventh century there began new suffering for the Christians in the East. In 614 A.D. the Persian King **Chosroes** seized Jerusalem, and turned over ninety thousand Christians to the Jews for punishment. Patriarch Zacharias and many other Christians were led off to captivity. They burned the Church of the Resurrection, stole the treasures of the church and carried the **Cross of Christ** into Persia. Fourteen years later, in 628 A.D., the Greek Emperor Heraclius conquered the Persians, returned all the captive Christians, led by the Patriarch Zacharias, and the Holy Cross was returned with honor to Jerusalem.

Rejoicing and thanking God, the Emperor Heraclius wanted to bring the Cross to Jerusalem in person. But at Golgotha an invisible power blocked the Cross, and the Emperor was powerless to carry on. Then the Patriarch Zacharias showed the Emperor that the Son of God, the Heavenly King, carried the Cross to Golgotha in humility and disgrace. The Emperor humbly listened to the Patriarch, took off his royal robes and, barefooted, carried the Holy Cross into the church on Golgotha, where the Patriarch again elevated the Holy Cross above the people.

Soon after this great event the false prophet **Mohammed** appeared in Arabia. Suffering from childhood with epilepsy, a nervous disorder, and hallucinations (falsely taken as visions), he himself believed in his calling to found a new religion, and at age forty he began his preaching. In the year 632, with his followers he conquered Mecca, his birthplace in Arabia, and established his religion. Then his followers, by the power of arms, subjugated Egypt, Syria, Palestine and even Jerusalem. Gradually, Islam (the teachings of Mohammed) spread more and more, and the Greek empire grew weaker and weaker. Finally in the middle of the 15th century (1454 A.D.), under the Emperor Constantine XI (Constantine Drageses Palaeologus), the Turks conquered Constantinople.

A Moslem Mosque in Jerusalem Where the Temple Once Stood

CHAPTER 64

The Ecumenical Councils

Among Christians there sometimes appear people who incorrectly expound on Christian teachings and who want their incorrect teaching to be binding on the whole Church.

The Church calls such false teaching **heresy**, and the false teachers, **heretics**. When general persecution of the Christians ceased, heresies especially started to trouble the life of the Church. The Devil, unable to defeat the Church from without, now began to attack it from within.

The Seven Ecumenical Councils

Following the example of the Apostles, **councils** of bishops, pastors, and teachers of the Church from the whole known world were convened for the struggle against the heretics and for the instruction of all Christians in the correct **Orthodox** faith

When it was necessary to resolve the question whether Christians converted from pagan religions should fulfill the ceremonies of the laws of Moses the Holy Fathers gathered at the **Apostolic Council of 51 A.D.** in Jerusalem (see Acts 15: 1-35). So also the fathers of the Church, **the bishops** to whom the **apostles transferred their power**, received by laying on of hands, gathered at the Councils when some sort of teaching contrary to Christian faith arose.

These general conferences of the entire Christian world, called **Ecumenical Councils**, maintained the truth of Christ by the guidance of the Holy Spirit and participation of the whole Christian Church. There have been seven Ecumenical Councils.

At the **First** and **Second** Ecumenical Councils the **Symbol of Faith** or **Creed**, was composed. The Creed is a short statement of all the tenets of the Orthodox Christian faith. Every Orthodox Christian is obliged to know it. We sing it at the Divine Liturgy and recite it during our morning prayers.

The **Seventh** Ecumenical Council defended and affirmed the veneration of holy icons.

The Triumph of Orthodoxy at the Seventh Ecumenical Council

CHAPTER 65

The Fall of the Roman Church. The Enlightenment of the Slavs

Not long after the period of the Ecumenical Councils, the Western part of the Church fell away from the Ecumenical Orthodox Church and formed what eventually has become known as the Roman Catholic Church.

This is how it happened. After the Apostles installed their successors to guide the Church, the bishops, who, had an equal degree of priesthood, had different powers. Bishops of the smaller cities were

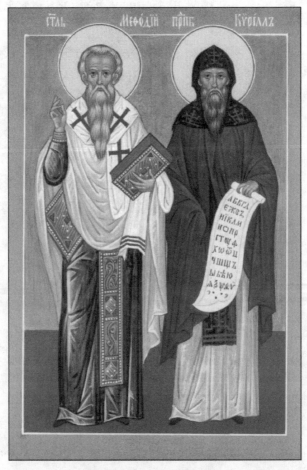

Sts. Cyril and Methodius

subordinate to the bishops of the larger cities, who were called **metropolitans**. The metropolitans in turn were subordinate to the bishops in the capital cities, who were called **patriarchs**. The highest power in the Church belonged to councils, to which even the patriarchs were subordinate.

In ancient times there were five patriarchs, the patriarchs of **Rome, Constantinople, Alexandria, Antioch and Jerusalem**. The Patriarch of Rome came to be known as a pope. For a long time other bishops were also thus named. The word "pope" means father.

All five patriarchs had equal rights and did not claim authority outside their own patriarchate. None of them was higher or lower than another, and only in honor did the Roman patriarch come first, because of the prominent position of Rome as the capital of the empire. Over the course of time however the Roman pope, expanding his realm, began to strengthen in power and sought to subordinate all the other patriarchs to himself, so that the pope might become the sole head of the Christian Church. Such a claim by the Roman pope was recognized to be uncanonical. This, along with the change in the Creed, was the chief cause of the separation of the Western church from Orthodoxy.

Subsequently the Protestant confessions separated from the Roman Catholic church. At about the time of the fall of the Roman Church, the Ecumenical Orthodox Church was enlarged by the entrance of the Slavic people, who were converted to Christianity.

The first missionaries to the Slavs were the brothers, Sts. **Cyril** and **Methodius**, who selflessly labored to spread the Christian faith among the Slavs. They composed the Slavonic alphabet and translated the Holy Scriptures and service books into the Slavic language.

After their death, Christianity became firmly established among the Bulgarians and Serbians, and later all the Russian people were baptized into the Christian faith.

The Baptism of Russia

The land of Russia became a Christian country almost a thousand years after the appearance of our Saviour in the world. Before that time, people in the Russian land worshipped idols and were pagans. The main idols were the sun god and the god of thunder and lightning, Perun. Besides these there were many lesser gods, to protect the household, the courtyard, water, woods, etc. In the lives of these pagans there were many superstitious, false beliefs, savage customs, even human sacrifice to idols.

According to tradition, the **holy Apostle Andrew the First-called** preached the Gospel in **Scythia**, in the land which later became Russia. Having climbed the Kievan mountains, he placed a wooden cross there and prophesied that in this land the true faith of Christ would shine.

The holy Apostle Andrew missionized the future land of Russia from the south to the north, from the Kievan mountains to Novgorod,

The Baptism of Russia

and was even on the island of Valaam. The latest historical evidence testifies to this. Local, northern Russian tradition shows that the Apostle Andrew the First-called, enlightener of the Scythians and the Slavs, came from Kiev to Novgorod. From there he traveled along the Volga River to Lake Ladoga and then to Valaam where he blessed the mountain with a **stone cross**. He destroyed the temples of Veles and Perun, and converted to the Christian faith the priests of the idols and the pagan inhabitants of the island, laying at Valaam the foundation for confession of faith in Christ. Several of his disciples who had accompanied him remained as pastors for the newly gathered flock of Christ.

In the ancient manuscript **"Opoved,"** kept in the library of the Valaam monastery, mention of this is made: "St. Andrew of Jerusalem came to Goliad, Kosoch, Roden, Scythe, Scythia, and Slavonia via contiguous meadows (steppes), reached Smolensk, and the home guard at Scothe of the Great Slaviansky. Leaving Ladoga, he went by boat over the stormy, turbulent lake to Valaam, placing stone crosses and blessing everywhere with the sign of the Cross. His disciples Silus, Phirsus, Elisha, Lukoslav, Joseph, and Cosmas set missions everywhere and all the rulers came from Slovensk and Smolensk. Many pagan priests were baptized, and the temples of Perun and Veles were destroyed and obliterated."

Another ancient document, **"Vseletnik"** (All the Years) of the Kievan Metropolitan Hilarion, 1051 A.D., affirms the travels of St. Andrew the Apostle on Valaam.

In the "Vseletnik" it is written, "November 30th. St. Andrew the All-praised, First-called Apostle and Standard-bearer of the Church we extol, for of old he came to Kiev, Smolensk, Novgorod, Dpyzino and Valaam."

Evidence supports that which the oral and written tradition of Valaam affirms, that the Orthodox Christian faith was established on Valaam by St. Andrew the Apostle. Whether Christianity continued on Valaam without interruption until the time of the founding of a monastery is impossible to determine positively.

Evidence from the ancient manuscript **"Opoved,"** suggests that on Valaam, after the Apostle Andrew, there existed a continual governmental organization with its *vetche* (popular assembly in ancient Russia), as in Novgorod. Valaam was known in foreign lands, and in times of danger people sought safety there. A stone cross of St. Andrew the Apostle was kept there until the time of St. Sergius of Valaam, which indicated the existence of Christianity. Before the founding of a monastery on it, Valaam belonged to the Slavs, and probably existed in civic unity with Novgorod. On Valaam, traces of the Orthodox Christian faith remained until the time of St. Sergius, although paganism continued along side Christianity.

The first of the Russian princes to be baptized, according to tradition, were the Kievan princes Ashold and Dir in 867 A.D. Almost a hundred years after them, the wise Russian princess **Olga**, noticing the chaste lives of Kievan Christians, was influenced by the truth of their faith and accepted holy baptism in 957 A.D. She traveled to Constantinople with a large retinue and was baptized by the Patriarch himself, and took the name Helena. Returning home, she tried to persuade her son Svyatoslav to convert to Christianity, but he, being by nature a rigorous military man, did not consent.

God provided Christian enlightenment to the Russian land through Prince **Vladimir**, grandson of Olga. At first, Vladimir was a zealous pagan and led an unchaste life. In his presence two Christians,

Theodore and John (father and son), were sacrificed to idols, becoming the first martyrs of Russia. Vladimir soon sensed the total emptiness of paganism and began to think about another, better faith.

When it became known that a Russian prince was seeking another faith, representatives of various religions began to come to him: Mohammedans, Jews, German Catholics and Greek Orthodox. The Greek Orthodox representative made the deepest impression on Vladimir. In concluding his conversation he showed Vladimir a picture of the Last Judgement.

Vladimir said, "It would be good to be with the righteous, that are on the right side."

"Be baptized, and you will be with them," answered the representative.

Prince Vladimir consulted with his boyars, members of the Russian aristocratic order, who advised him to send ten wise envoys to the various countries to discover which faith was the best.

The envoys visited the countries from which the representatives had come. Returning to Kiev, they told the prince everything they had seen, and they praised the Greek Orthodox faith. They said that there was nowhere a faith better than the Greeks' nor such people as they. "When we stood during the service in the Greek Church, we were not sure whether we were on earth or in heaven," they said. And then it came to be that having tasted sweetness they no longer wanted the bitter. Having found the Greek Orthodox faith, they no longer wanted to worship their idols.

The boyars remarked to Vladimir about this, "If the Greek Orthodox faith was not better than the others, then your grandmother, Princess Olga, would not have converted to it — she, the wisest of people."

Then Prince Vladimir finally decided to accept the Orthodox faith. But as a pagan, he considered it would be humiliating to ask the Greeks about it. So, about a year later, he sent a military expedition against Greece and took the city of Korsun. The city of Korsun, or Cherson, was located in the Crimea, at that time part of the Greek empire. He then demanded of the Greek Emperors Basil and Constantine, co-rulers at the time, that they hand over to him their sister Anna. The Emperors answered that they could not give their sister to a pagan. Then Vladimir explained to them his desire to convert to the Christian faith and asked them to send Princess Anna and also a priest to baptize him. The Emperors immediately sent a priest to Korsun, accompanied by the Princess Anna. It happened at that time that Vladimir's eyes began to fail, so badly that he became blind. Princess Anna advised Vladimir to be baptized immediately. Vladimir took the advice of the princess and was baptized, taking the name Basil. No sooner had he been baptized and emerged from the font than the scales fell from his eyes, and he was able to see. Vladimir recovered physically and spiritually, and in joy exclaimed, "Now I have found the true God!"

Prince Vladimir married Princess Anna and returned to Kiev. With him came a contingent from Greece, consisting of a metropolitan, six bishops, many priests, and everything they needed for the services of

Sts. Vladimir and Olga

the Church. This was in the year 988 A.D.

First Vladimir suggested to his twelve sons that they be baptized, and they were. After them, many boyars were baptized. Finally, Vladimir ordered all the inhabitants of Kiev to come on a designated day to the Dnieper River, and there in the presence of the prince, the spiritual mystery of Holy Baptism was performed. Prince Vladimir joyously directed his gaze to Heaven, prayed to God that the Lord Who had made Heaven and earth would bless the Russian people, grant them to know Him, the true God, and would strengthen the true faith in the Russian people. On this great day, Heaven and earth rejoiced.

Having converted to Christianity, Vladimir changed in every way. From a coarse and savage pagan, he became a pious and merciful Christian. He ordered all the poor people to come to his royal court and receive there everything they needed, food, clothing, and even money. Furthermore, carts were loaded with bread, meat, fish, vegetables, honey and kvass and sent around to the cities and villages for all the sick and needy who were unable to come.

The people loved their **Grand Prince** and nicknamed him "Beautiful Sun," and as to the sun, the people turned to him and with him walked toward God.

The Holy Church numbers Grand Prince Vladimir and Princess Olga among its saints. Prince Vladimir received the title of **Equal-of-the-Apostles** for his apostolic zeal.

With the help of God, Orthodox Christianity soon spread from Kiev and flourished throughout the Russian land. The Russian people embraced the Orthodox faith with all their soul and were spiritually enlightened by it. All the arts, schools, monasteries, literature, the whole of Russian culture, spiritual as well as secular, was inspired by Orthodoxy. The light of Christ shone over the country, and it became known forever as Holy Russia, and the people, " The Russian Orthodox people."

Sources Used in the Translation of Part III

Dvornik, Francis. *The Idea of Apostolicity in Byzantium and the Legend of the Apostle Andrew*. Cambridge, Mass. Harvard University Press, 1958. S.U.: D.F. 552.8 D8 V.4

Toney, Charles Ca. "The Name 'Iscariot'," *Harvard Theological Review*, Vol. 36, 1943, pp. 51-62.

Throckmorton, B.H. Jr., *Gospel Parallels, a Synopsis of the First Three Gospels* (RSV), N.Y. Thomas Nelson and Sons, c 1949. Second edition revised.

Ioseliani, P. *A Short History of the Georgian Church*, translated from the Russian by the Rev. S.C. Malan, 2nd edition. Jordanville, N.Y. Holy Trinity Monastery, 1983.

Aharoni, Yohanan and Michael Avi-Yonah. *The Macmillan Bible Atlas*, Rev. ed., N.Y. Macmillan, c. 1977.

Columbia Heppincott Gazatteer of the World, Morningside Hts, N.Y. Columbia University Press, 1966.

PART IV

CHRISTIAN FAITH AND LIFE

CHAPTER 1

The Purpose of Man

God created us in His own likeness and image. He gave us **intelligence, free will and an immortal soul**, so that knowing God and becoming like Him, we would all become better, **perfect ourselves**, and inherit eternal blessed life with God. Therefore the existence of man on earth has **deep meaning, great purpose and a high goal.**

In the universe created by God, there is not, nor can there be, anything unplanned. If a man lives without faith in God, not abiding by the commandments of God, not for future eternal life, then the existence of such a man on earth becomes senseless. For people living without God, life seems incomprehensible and accidental, and such people are often worse than beasts.

For each man, in order to fulfill his purpose on earth and to receive eternal salvation, it is necessary, in the first place, **to know the true God and to rightly believe in Him,** that is, to have the true faith. Secondly, one must **live according to this faith;** that is, to love God and people and to do good works.

The Apostle Paul says that *without faith it is impossible to please God* (Heb. 11:6), and the Apostle James adds that faith without good works means without love, and such faith is ineffective and dead faith.

Thus, for our salvation, it is necessary to have the correct faith, and a life in keeping with that faith, the doing of good works.

True teaching about the necessity to rightly believe in God and how to live with people, is contained in the Orthodox Christian Faith, which is founded on **Divine revelation**. Divine revelation is the name given to all that God Himself reveals to people about Himself and about true faith in Him. God conveys His revelation to people by two means: **natural revelation and supernatural revelation.**

Natural Revelation

Natural revelation is called Divine revelation when God reveals Himself through normal, natural means to each person, through our visible **world** (nature) and through our **conscience**, that is, the voice of God in us. It tells us what is good and what is bad. God also reveals Himself through life, through the history of all mankind. If a nation loses faith in God, then misfortune and unhappiness overtake it. If it does not repent, then it perishes and vanishes from the earth. Let us remember the Flood, the destruction of Sodom and Gomorrah, the Hebrew nation dispersed to all corners of the earth, and so on.

The entire world which surrounds us is a great book of Divine revelation, testifying to the omnipotence and wisdom of God the Creator. People who study this world are, with very rare exceptions, believers. In order to study something, it is necessary to have faith that everything fulfills a given concept and exists according to a definite plan.

"Even the most simple machine is not able to come into existence by chance. Even if we see a systematically arranged group of stones, we immediately conclude from the form of their arrangement, that a human being put them there. A chance arrangement is always without form, irregular. Long ago Cicero, an ancient scholar and orator, who lived before the birth of Christ, said that even if one threw alphabet blocks a million times, a line of poetry would not result from them. The universe which surrounds us is much more complicated than the most intricate machine, and it contains much more thought than the most profound poem" (from a discussion by Archbishop Nathaniel).

The Apostle Paul was a well-educated person for his time. He says *every house is built by some man; but He that built all things is God* (Heb 3:4).

The great scientist **Newton**, who discovered the laws of movement of the heavenly bodies, thereby disclosing a great mystery of creation, was a religious man and studied theology. Each time he pronounced the name of God, he reverently stood up and took off his hat.

The renowned **Pascal**, a mathematical genius and one of the creators of modern physics, was not only a believer but one of the greatest **religious** thinkers in Europe. Pascal said, "The contradictions which most of all might seem to separate me from religious knowledge, on the contrary, lead me to it."

Louis Pasteur, the founder of contemporary bacteriology, and a thinker more profound than others in penetrating the mystery of organic life, exclaimed, "The more I occupy myself with the study of nature, the more I stand in reverent amazement before the works of the Creator."

The famous biologist **Linnaeus** concluded his book about plants with these words, "Truly God exists, great, eternal, without Whom nothing is able to exist."

The astronomer **Kepler** confessed, "O, great is our Lord and great is His omnipotence, and His wisdom is without boundary. And you, my soul, sing praise to your Lord for all your life."

Even **Darwin**, the scholar who was afterwards exploited by half-learned men to refute belief in God, was a very religious man all his life. For many years he was the lay leader of his parish. He never thought that his findings contradicted belief in God. After Darwin set forth his teaching about the evolutionary development of life on earth, he was asked, "In the chain of evolution, where was the first link?"

Darwin answered, "It was riveted to the throne of the Most High."

The geologist Lyell wrote, "With every geological finding we discover enlightening demonstrations of the foresight, power and wisdom of the creative intelligence of God."

The historian Muller declared, "Only with the recognition of God and by thorough study of the New Testament did I begin to understand the meaning of history."

It is possible to cite an unlimited number of scholarly witnesses to belief in God, but we think for the present it is enough to relate one more eloquent argument. The scientist Dennert conducted a survey about belief in God with 432 naturalists. Fifty-six of them did not respond, 349 indicated belief in God, and only eighteen declared that they either did not believe, or were indifferent to faith. The result of this survey of scholars concurs with results of other similar investigations.

"Only half-knowledge brings people to godlessness. No one is able to deny the existence of God, except those for whom it is profitable to do so," says the English scholar **Bacon.**

The young holy Great-martyr **Barbara**, seeing the majesty and beauty of God's world, came to a knowledge of the true God. Thus God reveals Himself through the visible world to each person who is intelligent and of good will.

Belief in God is the fundamental essence of a person's soul. The soul is given to man from God. It is a spark in man and a reflection of God in man. Originating in God, having a kindred being in Him, the soul by itself, according to its own will, turns to God, seeks Him. *My soul thirsts for God, for the living God* (Ps. 42:2). As when eyes turn to the light and are constructed in such a way that they are able to see, thus the soul of man rushes to God, has the need of intimacy with Him, and only in God finds peace and joy. A flower stretches toward the sun, from which it receives warmth and light, without which it is not able to live and grow. As with the flower, the constant, irrepressible inclination of man to God comes from the fact that only in God is our soul able to find all that it needs for a righteous and healthy life.

Therefore, people in all times have believed in some deity and offered their prayers to it, although they often have erred by believing in God incorrectly. They never lost faith in a deity, always keeping some form of religion.

General belief in a Supreme Being was known even in the time of Aristotle, the great Greek scholar, philosopher, and naturalist, born in the year 384 B.C. Scholars confirm that all peoples who have inhabited the earth, without exception, have had their own religion, faith, prayers, temples, and offerings. "Ethnography, the science which studies the existence of all people inhabiting the earth, does not know of a people without religion," says the German geographer and traveller Ratzel.

If there exist pockets of atheistic persuasion, they are rare exceptions, unhealthy deviations from the norm. As the existence of the blind, deaf, and dumb does not disprove the fact that mankind possesses the gifts of sight, hearing, and speech; as the existence of idiots does not deny that man is a reasonable being, so the existence of atheists does not disprove the fact of the existence of religion in every society.

However, natural revelation alone is not enough, for sin obscures the intelligence, will, and conscience of a man. Proof of this is revealed in every possible pagan religion, in which truth is mixed with the falsities of human fabrications.

Therefore, the Lord supplements natural revelation with supernatural revelation. (Compiled from Frank's book *Religion and Science*, and *Does God Exist?* by G. Shorets and others.)

CHAPTER 2

Supernatural Divine Revelation. Holy Tradition and Holy Scripture

God's revelations about Himself to certain people are most often effected by unusual means, or in a supernatural manner. God reveals Himself directly through Himself or through His angels. Such revelation is called supernatural divine revelation.

As not all people are able to receive revelation from God Himself, due to their impurity through sin and weakness of soul and body, the Lord chooses special righteous people who are able to receive this revelation.

Among the first people who declared the revelations of God were Adam, Noah, Moses, and other prophets and righteous people. They accepted everything from God and preached the beginnings of Divine revelation.

In fulfillment of Divine revelation, God Himself came to earth incarnate in the Son of God, our Lord Jesus Christ, and spread the revelation to the whole earth through His Apostles and disciples.

This Divine revelation and its dissemination among people is preserved in the true, holy Orthodox Church in two ways: by means of **Holy Tradition** and **Holy Scripture**.

The primary means of dissemination of Divine revelation is Holy Tradition. From the beginning of the world until Moses there were no holy books. Teaching about belief in God was handed down by tradition, that is, by word of mouth and example, from one to another, from ancestor to descendant. Jesus Christ Himself conveyed His Divine teaching and precepts to His disciples by word of mouth, by preaching, and by the example of His life, not by books (scriptures). By preaching and example, the Apostles first spread the faith and maintained the Christian Church.

Holy Tradition always precedes Holy Scriptures. This is obvious because books are not useful for all people, but tradition is accessible to all without exception.

Eventually, so that God's revelation might be kept in complete faithfulness, by the inspiration of the Lord, several holy people wrote the most important aspects of tradition in books. The Holy Spirit helped them invisibly, so that everything in these written books would be correct and true. All these books, written by the Spirit of God through people sanctified by God, prophets, apostles, and others, are called Holy Scripture, or the Bible.

The word "Bible" comes from Greek and means "book." This name shows that holy books, as coming from God Himself, surpass all other books.

The books of the Holy Scripture, written by various people at different times, are divided into two parts, the books of the Old Testament, and those of the New Testament.

The books of the Old Testament were written prior to the birth of Christ. The books of the New Testament were written after the birth of Christ. All of these holy books are known by the Biblical word "testament," because the word means testimony, and the Divine teaching contained in them is the testimony of God to mankind. The word "Testament" further suggests the agreement or a covenant of God with people.

The contents of the Old Testament deal mainly with God's promise to give mankind a Saviour and to prepare them to accept Him. This was accomplished by gradual revelation through holy commandments, prophesies, prefigurations, prayers and divine services.

The main theme of the New Testament is the fulfillment of God's promise to send a Saviour, His Only-begotten Son, our Lord Jesus Christ, Who gave mankind the New Testament, the new covenant.

The Old Testament books, if each one is counted separately, number thirty-eight. Sometimes several books are combined into one, and in this form, they number twenty-two books, according to the number of letters in the Hebrew alphabet.

The Old Testament books are divided into four sections, the law, history, wisdom literature, and the prophets.

I. The books of the **law,** which constitute the main foundation of the Old Testament, are as follows:

1. **Genesis**
2. **Exodus**
3. **Leviticus**
4. **Numbers**
5. **Deuteronomy**

These five books were written by the Prophet Moses. They describe the creation of the world and man, the fall into sin, God's promise of a Saviour of the world, and the life of people in the first times. The majority of their contents is an account of the law given by God through Moses. Jesus Christ Himself calls them the laws of Moses (cf. Luke 24:44).

II. The books of **history,** which primarily contain the history of the religion and life of the Hebrew people, preserving faith in the true God, are the following:

6. **Joshua**
7. **Judges,** and as a supplement, the book of **Ruth**.
8. **First and Second Kings,** as two parts of the same book.
9. **Third and Fourth Kings**
10. **First and Second Chronicles** (additional)
11. **First and Second Books of Ezra and Nehemiah**

12. **Esther**

III. The **books of wisdom**, which are composed mainly of teachings about faith and spiritual life, are the following:

13. **Job**

14. The **Psalter**, composed of 150 psalms or sacred songs, written under the inspiration of the Holy Spirit. A majority of the psalms were written by King David. The Psalter is used for almost every Orthodox service of worship.

15. **Proverbs** of Solomon

16. **Ecclesiastes** (Church teachings)

17. **Song of Solomon**

IV. The **books of the Prophets**, which contain prophecies or predictions about the future, and their visions of the Saviour, Jesus Christ, are the following:

18. **Isaiah**

19. **Jeremiah**

20. **Ezekiel**

21. **Daniel**

22. **Books of the Twelve Prophets**, also known as the lesser Prophets: Hosea, Joel, Amos, Obadiah, Jonah, Micah, Nahum, Zephaniah, Habakkuk, Haggai, Zechariah, Malachi.

These are the **canonical** books of the Old Testament, meaning that they are undoubtedly true, judging by their origin and by their content. The word "canonica" comes from Greek and means "model, true, correct."

Besides the canonical books, a part of the Old Testament is composed of **non-canonical** books, sometimes called the Apocrypha among non-Orthodox. These are the books which the Jews lost and which are not in the contemporary Hebrew text of the Old Testament. They are found in the Greek translations of the Old Testament, made by the 70 translators of the Septuagint three centuries before the birth of Christ (271 B.C.). These books have been included in the Bible from ancient times and are considered by the Church to be sacred Scripture. The translation of the Septuagint is accorded special respect in the Orthodox Church. The Slavonic translation of the Bible was made from it.

To the non-canonical books of the Old Testament belong:

1. **Tobit**

2. **Judith**

3. **The Wisdom of Solomon**

4. **Ecclesiasticus**, or the **Wisdom of Sirach**

5. **Baruch**

6. Three books of **Maccabees**

7. **The Second and Third book of Esdras**

8. The additions to the (Book of Esther,) **II Chronicles (The Prayer of Manasseh) and Daniel (**The Song of the Three Youths, **Susanna** and **Bel and the Dragon)**

There are twenty-seven sacred books of the **New Testament**, and all of them are canonical. In content, they, like the Old Testament, may be subdivided into four groups, the law, history, the epistles, and prophecy.

I. Books of the **Law** which serve as the foundation of the New Testament are:

1. **The Gospel of Matthew**
2. **The Gospel of Mark**
3. **The Gospel of Luke**
4. **The Gospel of John**

The word "gospel," or in Greek, *evangelion*, means "good news." It is the good news about the arrival in the world of the Saviour of the world, our Lord Jesus Christ, promised by God. The Gospels relate the account of His life on earth, death on the Cross, resurrection from the dead, and ascension into heaven. They also set forth His Divine teachings and miracles. The Gospels were written by holy apostles, disciples of Jesus Christ.

II. Books of **History**.

5. The **Acts of the Apostles**, written by the Evangelist Luke, tells of the descent of the Holy Spirit on the Apostles and about the spread of the Christian Church through them.

III. The **Epistles**.

6-12. Seven general epistles to the churches, or, letters to all Christians: one of the Apostle James, two of the Apostle Peter, three of the Apostle and Evangelist John, and one of the Apostle Jude.

13-26. Fourteen epistles of the Apostle Paul: one to the Romans, two to the Corinthians, one to the Galatians, one to the Ephesians, one to the Philippians, one to the Colossians, two to the Thessalonians, two to Timothy, the bishop of Ephesus, one to Titus, the bishop of Crete, one to Philemon, and one to the Hebrews.

IV. Books of **Prophecy**.

27. The **Apocalypse**, or **Revelation** to John, written by the holy Apostle and Evangelist John, contains a vision of the future destiny of the Church of Christ and of the whole world.

The sacred books of the New Testament were first written in Greek, which at that time was in common usage. Only the Gospel of Matthew and the Epistle of St. Paul to the Hebrews were first written in Hebrew. The Gospel of Matthew, however, was translated into Greek in the first century, most likely by the Apostle Matthew himself.

The books of both the New Testament and the Old Testament appeared by God's revelation, were written by the inspiration of the Holy Spirit, and are therefore called divinely inspired. Apostle Paul says, *All Scripture is given by inspiration of God, and is profitable for doctrine, for reproof, for correction, and for instruction in righteousness* (II Tim. 3:16).

The loftiness and purity of Christian teaching in these writings, prophecies, and miracles convince one of the divine origin of Holy Scripture. With special signs, the divine inspiration of sacred books is revealed in the mighty acts of the word of God toward mankind. Wherever the Apostles preached, the hearts of people submitted to the teaching of Christ. The Jews and pagans of the world armed themselves with every evil power known to man against the Christians. Christian martyrs died by the thousands, yet the word of God grew and became firmly established. There are examples in which people started to study the Bible with the hope of disproving the teachings contained therein, and in the end became sincerely reverent and deeply believing people. Each one of us, attentively reading Holy Scripture, can experience in himself the Lord's almighty power, and be convinced that it is the revelation of God Himself.

All Divine revelation is preserved in the **Holy Church**. The books of Holy Scripture, and Holy Tradition — that is, that which was not originally written down in these books, but handed down by word of mouth and only afterwards written down by saints in the early centuries of Christianity (4th and 5th centuries) and consequently have profound antiquity and authenticity — all this is preserved in the **Holy Church**. The Church was founded by the Saviour Himself, our Lord Jesus Christ, and established as the custodian of His Divine revelation. God the Holy Spirit invisibly guards Her.

The Holy Orthodox Church, after the death of the Apostles, was guided by **Holy Scripture** and **Holy Tradition**. We read there the words of the prophets and Apostles as if we ourselves lived with them and listened to them.

In special cases, for the accusation of heretics or to resolve various misunderstandings, **on the order of the Saviour Himself** (Matt. 18:17) and by the **example of the Apostles** (Apostolic Council in 51 A.D., Acts 15:1-35), **councils** assembled. Some of these were **Ecumenical**, at which were gathered from the entire known world as many pastors and teachers of the Church as was possible. Other councils were **local**, where just pastors and teachers of a particular region assembled.

The decision of an **Ecumenical Council** is the **highest earthly authority of the Holy Church of Christ**, guided by the Holy Spirit, as it was stated in the decision of the first Apostolic Council, "**For it seemed good to the Holy Spirit and to us...**" (Acts 15:28).

There were seven Ecumenical Councils. At the first and second councils the Orthodox Creed was formulated.

CHAPTER 3

Short Summaries of the Ecumenical Councils

There have been seven Ecumenical Councils in the true Orthodox Christian Church: 1. **Nicea**; 2. **Constantinople**; 3. **Ephesus**; 4. **Chalcedon**; 5. the **second at Constantinople**; 6. the **third at Constantinople**; 7. the **second at Nicea**.

The First Ecumenical Council

The First Ecumenical Council was convened in **325 A.D.**, in the city of **Nicea**, under the Emperor Constantine I. This Council was called because of the false doctrine of the Alexandrian priest **Arius**, who rejected the Divine nature and pre-eternal birth of the second person of the Holy Trinity, namely the Divine Son of God the Father, and taught that the Son of God is only the highest creation.

318 bishops participated in this Council, among whom were St. Nicholas the Wonderworker, St. James, bishop of Nisibis, St. Spiridon of Tremithus, and St. Athanasius, who was at that time a deacon.

The Council condemned and repudiated the heresy of Arius and affirmed the immutable truth, **the dogma that the Son of God is true God, born of God the Father before all ages, and is eternal, as is God the Father; He was begotten, and not made, and is of one essence with God the Father**. In order that all Orthodox Christians may know exactly the true teaching of the faith, it was clearly and concisely summarized in the first of seven sections of the Creed, or Symbol of Faith.

At this Council, it was resolved to celebrate Pascha on the first Sunday after the first full moon following the spring equinox, after the Jewish Passover. It also determined that priests should be married, and it established many other rules or canons.

The Second Ecumenical Council

The Second Ecumenical Council was convened in the year 381, in the city of Constantinople, under the Emperor Theodosius I. This Council was convoked against the false teaching of the Arian bishop of Constantinople, Macedonius, who rejected the deity of the third Person of the Holy Trinity, the Holy Spirit. He taught that the Holy Spirit is not God, and called Him a creature, or a created power, and therefore subservient to God the Father and God the Son, like an angel.

There were 150 bishops present at the Council, among whom were Gregory the Theologian, who presided over the Council, Gregory of Nyssa, Meletius of Antioch, Amphilochius of Iconium and Cyril of Jerusalem.

At the Council, the Macedonian heresy was condemned and repudiated. The Council affirmed as **a dogma the equality and the single essence of God the Holy Spirit with God the Father and God the Son**.

The Council also supplemented the Nicene Creed, or "Symbol of Faith," with five Articles in which is set forth its teaching about the Holy Spirit, about the Church, about the Mysteries, about the resurrection of the dead, and the life in the world to come. Thus they composed the **Nicene-Constantinopolitan** Creed, which serves as a guide to the Church for all time.

The Third Ecumenical Council

The Third Ecumenical Council was convened in the year 431 A.D., in the city of Ephesus, under Emperor Theodosius II. The Council was called because of the false doctrine of Nestorius, Archbishop of Constantinople, who profanely taught that the Most-holy Virgin Mary simply gave birth to the man Christ, with whom then God united morally and dwelled in Him, as in a temple, as previously He had dwelled in Moses and other prophets. Therefore, Nestorius called the Lord Jesus Christ, God-bearing, and not God incarnate; and the Holy Virgin was called the Christ-bearer (Christotokos) and not the God-bearer (Theotokos).

The 200 bishops present at the Council condemned and repudiated the heresy of Nestorius and decreed that one should recognize that **united in Jesus Christ at the time of the incarnation were two natures, divine and human, and that one should confess Jesus Christ as true God and true Man, and the Holy Virgin Mary as the God-bearer (Theotokos)**.

The Council also affirmed the **Nicene-Constantinopolitan Creed**, and strictly prohibited making any changes or additions to it.

The Fourth Ecumenical Council

The Fourth Ecumenical Council was convened in 451 A.D., in the city of Chalcedon, under Emperor Marcian. The Council met to challenge the false doctrine of an archimandrite of a Constantinople monastery, Eutychius, who rejected the human nature of the Lord Jesus Christ. Refuting one heresy and defending the divinity of Jesus Christ, he himself fell into an extreme, and taught that in the Lord Jesus Christ human nature was completely absorbed in the Divine, and therefore it followed that one need only recognize the Divine nature. This false doctrine is called **Monophysitism,** and followers of it are called **Monophysites**.

The Council of 650 bishops condemned and repudiated the false doctrine of Eutychius and defined the true teaching of the Church, namely that our Lord Jesus Christ is perfect God, and **as God He is eternally born from God. As man, He was born of the Holy Virgin and in every way is like us, except in sin**. Through the incarnation, birth from the Holy Virgin, divinity and humanity are united in Him as a single Person, infused and immutable, thus reputing Eutychius; indivisible and inseparable, reputing Nestorius.

The Fifth Ecumenical Council

The Fifth Ecumenical Council was convened in 553 A.D., in the city of Constantinople, under the famous Emperor, Justinian I. It was called to quell a controversy between Nestorians and Eutychians. The major points of contention were the well-known works of the Antiochian school of the Syrian church, entitled "The Three Chapters." Theodore of Mopsuestia, Theodoret of Cyrus, and Ibas of Edessa, clearly expressed the Nestorian error, although at the Fourth Ecumenical Council, nothing had been mentioned of their works.

Nestorians, in argument with Eutychians (Monophysites), referred to these works, and Eutychians found in them an excuse to reject the Fourth Ecumenical Council and to slander the universal Orthodox Church, charging that it was deviating toward Nestorianism.

The Council was attended by 165 bishops, who condemned all three works and Theodore of Mopsuestia himself, as not having repented. Concerning the other two, censure was limited only to their Nestorian works. They themselves were pardoned. They renounced their false opinions and died in peace with the Church. The Council reiterated its censure of the heresies of Nestorius and Eutychius.

The Sixth Ecumenical Council

The Sixth Ecumenical Council was convened in the year 680 A.D., in the city of Constantinople, under the Emperor Constantine IV, and was composed of 170 bishops.

The council was convoked against the false doctrine of heretics, **Monothelites, who, although they recognized in Jesus Christ two natures, God and man, ascribed to Him only a Divine will**.

After the Fifth Ecumenical Council, agitation provoked by the Monothelites continued and threatened the Greek Emperor with great danger. Emperor Heraclius, wishing reconciliation, decided to incline Orthodoxy to concession to the Monothelites, and by the power of his office, ordered recognition that in Jesus Christ is one will and two energies.

Among the defenders and advocates of the true teachings of the Church, were St. Sophronius, Patriarch of Jerusalem, and a monk from

Constantinople, St. Maximus the Confessor, who for his firmness in the faith had suffered having his tongue cut out and his hand chopped off.

The Sixth Ecumenical Council condemned and repudiated the heresy of Monothelitism, and formulated the recognition that in Jesus Christ are two natures, Divine and human, and in these two natures there are **two wills**, but that **the human will in Christ is not against, but rather is submissive to His Divine will**.

It is worthy of attention that at this Council excommunication was pronounced against a number of other heretics, and also against the Roman Pope Honorius, as one who acknowledged the teaching of one will. The formulation of the Council was signed by a Roman delegation, consisting of Presbyters Theodore and Gregory, and Deacon John. This clearly shows that the highest power in Christendom belongs to the Ecumenical Council, and not to the Pope of Rome.

After eleven years, the Council again opened a meeting in the imperial palace, called Cupola Hall (in Greek, *Trullos*), in order to resolve questions of primary importance pertaining to the Church hierarchy. In this regard, it supplemented the Fifth and Sixth Ecumenical Councils, and therefore is called the Fifth-Sixth (Quintsext) Synod.

This Council established canons by which the Church must be guided, namely, 85 canons of the holy Apostles, canons of the six Ecumenical and seven local councils, and canons of thirteen Fathers of the Church. These canons afterward were supplemented by canons of the Seventh Ecumenical Council and another two local councils, and comprise the so-called "Nomocanon," in English, "The Rudder," which is the foundation of Orthodox Church government.

Here several innovations of the Roman Church were condemned as not being in agreement with the spiritual decisions of the Ecumenical Church, namely, the requirement that priests and deacons be celibate, a strict fast on Saturdays of the Great Fast, and the representation of Christ in the form of a lamb, or in any way other than He appeared on the earth.

The Seventh Ecumenical Council

The Seventh Ecumenical Council was convened in 787 A.D., in the city of Nicea, under the Empress Irene, widow of the Emperor Leo IV, and was composed of 367 fathers.

The Council was convened against the iconoclastic heresy, which had been raging for sixty years before the Council, under the Greek Emperor Leo III, who, wishing to convert the Mohammedans to Christianity, considered it necessary to do away with the veneration of icons. This heresy continued under his son, Constantine V Copronymus, and his grandson, Leo IV.

The Council condemned and repudiated the **iconoclastic heresy** and determined **to provide** and **to put in the holy churches, together with the likeness of the honored and Life-giving Cross of the Lord, holy icons, to honor and render homage to them, elevating the soul**

and heart to the Lord God, the Mother of God and the Saints, who are represented in these icons. After the Seventh Ecumenical Council, persecution of the holy icons arose anew under the Emperors Leo V, of Armenian origin, Michael II, and Theophilus, and for twenty-five years disturbed the Church.

Veneration of the holy icons was finally restored and affirmed by the **local synod of Constantinople in 843 A.D., under the Empress Theodora**.

At this council, in thanksgiving to the Lord God for having given the Church victory over the iconoclasts and all heretics, the celebration of the **Triumph of Orthodoxy** was established on the first Sunday of Great Lent, which is celebrated by the Orthodox Church throughout the world.

Note: The Roman Catholic Church, in addition to these seven Councils, recognizes more than 20 "ecumenical" councils. Incorrectly included in this number were councils in the Western Church, held after the separation of the Western Church. Protestants, in spite of the example of the Apostles and acknowledgment of the entire Christian Church, do not recognize a single one of the Ecumenical Councils.

CHAPTER 4

The Christian Faith

The Symbol of Faith or Creed

The Creed is a concise summary of all the truths of the Christian Faith, composed and affirmed in the First and Second Ecumenical Councils. Whoever does not accept these truths is not an Orthodox Christian.

The entire Symbol of Faith is as follows:

I believe in one God, the Father Almighty, Maker of Heaven and earth, and of all things visible and invisible.

And in one Lord Jesus Christ, the Son of God, the Only-begotten, begotten of the Father before all ages; Light of Light: true God of true God; begotten, not made; of one essence with the Father; by Whom all things were made;

Who for us men, and for our salvation, came down from the Heavens, and was incarnate of the Holy Spirit and the Virgin Mary, and became man;

And was crucified for us under Pontius Pilate, and suffered, and was buried.

And rose again on the third day according to the Scriptures.

And ascended into the Heavens, and sitteth at the right hand of the Father;

And shall come again, with glory, to judge both the living and the dead; Whose kingdom shall have no end.

And in the Holy Spirit, the Lord, the Giver of Life; Who proceedeth from the Father; Who with the Father and the Son together is worshipped and glorified; Who spake by the Prophets.

In one, Holy, Catholic, and Apostolic Church.

I confess one Baptism for the remission of sins.

I look for the resurrection of the dead.

And the life of the age to come.

Amen.

The First Article of the Creed

1. I believe in one God, the Father Almighty, Maker of Heaven and earth, and of all things visible and invisible.

To believe in God means to be steadfastly sure that God exists, that He cares for us, and to wholeheartedly accept His Divine revelation; that is, everything that He revealed about Himself, and about the salvation of people by the incarnate Son of God, our Lord Jesus Christ.

But in order that our faith be alive and active, it is necessary to confess it. To confess faith means to openly express internal faith in God by words and good works, and that neither danger, persecution, suffering, nor even death are able to force us to renounce our faith in the true God. Only by such a firm confession will we be able to save our souls. *For man believeth unto righteousness and with the mouth confession is made unto salvation* (Rom. 10:10), says Apostle Paul.

The holy martyrs serve as examples of steadfast and courageous confession of faith. They had such faith in God and were so animated by love for the Lord Jesus Christ that for His name's sake they renounced all earthly gain, underwent persecution and such martyric sufferings that could be contrived only by the most evil imagination of man.

The words of the Symbol of Faith, "**In one God**," indicate the uniqueness of the true God. God is one, and there is no other beside Him (Ex. 44:6, Ex. 20:2-3, Deut. 6:4; John 17:3; I Cor. 8:4-6). This reminder is given in order to repudiate pagan teachings about many gods.

God is the highest Being, above all that is mundane or supernatural. To know the being of God is impossible. It is higher than the knowledge not only of men, but even of the angels. From the revelation of God, from the clear testimonies of the Holy Scriptures, we are able to get an understanding of the existence and the basic nature of God. **God is Spirit** (John 4:24); **living** (Jer. 10:10; I Thess. 1:9); **self-existent**, that is, dependent on no one, and having received life from Himself — **He is** (Ex. 3:14; I John 2:13); **everlasting** (Ps. 90:2; Ex. 40:28); **unchanging** (James 1:17; Mala. 3:6; Ps. 102:27); **omnipresent** (Ps. 139:7-12; Acts 17:27); **omniscient** (I John 3:29, Heb. 4:13); **omnipotent** (Gen. 17:1; Luke 1:37; Ps. 32:9); **all good** (Matt. 19:17, Ps. 24:8); **wise** (Ps. 104:24; Rom. 14:26; I Tim. 1:17); **righteous** (Ps. 7:12; Ps. 10:7; II Rom. 6:11); **self-sufficient** (Acts 17:25); **all blessed** (I Tim. 6:15).

The assertion that God is Spirit does not contradict those places in the Holy Scriptures in which bodily members are ascribed to God. These expressions are used symbolically in the spiritual writings when they speak of the nature of God. For instance, eyes or ears indicate the omniscience of God, and so forth.

God is one, but not solitary. God is one in essence, but triple in Persons, Father, Son, and Holy Spirit, the Most-holy Trinity, consubstantial and indivisible. **One in three Persons**, each Person eternally loving the others. *God is love* (I John 4:16).

The inter-relationship between the Persons of the Holy Trinity is such that God the Father is not born from and does not proceed from the other persons. The Son of God was born from God the Father before all ages, and the Holy Spirit always proceeds from God the Father. All three Persons of the Holy Trinity in being and nature are completely equal within God Himself. As God the Father is true God, so God the Son is true God, and God the Holy Spirit is true God, but all three Persons are a single Deity — One God.

How one God exists in three Persons is a mystery, incomprehensible to our intelligence, but we believe this according to the testimony of Divine revelation. The mystery of the Holy Trinity was revealed to us by the Lord Jesus Christ Himself, when he sent the Apostles to preach. He said, *Go therefore and teach all nations, baptizing them in the name of the Father and of the Son and of the Holy Spirit* (Matt. 28:19). The Apostle and Evangelist John also clearly testifies both to the trinitarian Persons of God and to the single essence of the Persons. *There are Three Witnesses in Heaven* (about the Divinity of the Son of God); *Father, the Word, and the Holy Spirit; and these Three are one* (I John 5:7).

Apostle Paul, addressing the Corinthian Christians, says, *The grace of our Lord Jesus Christ and the love of God the Father and the communion of the Holy Spirit be with you all* (II Cor. 13:14).

For clarification of this great mystery we point out the world which, as a revelation of the creation of God, speaks to us of the incomprehensible mystery of the trinitarian essence of the Creator. The imprint of this mystery lies deep in the nature of every created entity. **The trinitarian unity**, as an underlying idea, is intrinsic to all the works of the Creator, glorifying the Trinity. For example, the speech of all persons in the world has three persons: I; you; he, she, or it. Time is expressed as past, present and future. The states of matter are liquid, solid and gas. All the various colors in the world are make up of the three primary colors, red, blue and yellow. Man conducts himself by means of thought, word and deed. Deeds, in their turn, have a beginning, a middle, and an end. Even man is a trinitarian unity of body, mind and soul. The salvation of our souls is made up of three Christian virtues, faith, hope and love.

We are able to understand the mystery of the **Holy Trinity** in part only with the heart, by love found in the Holy Orthodox Church of Christ, that is, by living in love.

We call God Almighty because He, as King of Heaven, governs all and maintains everything by His strength and power.

Furthermore, we call God Maker of heaven and earth because everything that exists, both in the visible, physical world and in the invisible, spiritual world, that is, the entire universe, was created by God in Three Persons. God the Father created with the Word, His Only-begotten Son, and with the cooperation of the Holy Spirit.

To the **invisible** or spiritual world belong **angels** — spirits — bodiless, immortal beings, endowed with reason, will and power. Also to the spiritual world belongs the **soul** of each person.

The word "angel" is a Greek word which means "messenger," because God sends angels to announce His will to people. Each Christian has his own Guardian Angel, who invisibly helps him in matters of salvation, and guards him from the wicked activity of the evil one. The evil one is called the Devil (slanderer), and Satan (one who is against God). The evil spirits were also created good and free. However, they became proud, fell from God, and became deceitful and evil. Since that time, they have envied everything good and lead men into sin in order to destroy them. Because of sin, all people die physically. They would die a more terrible second, spiritual death, when the soul surrenders to sin and perishes in estrangement from God, if people were not saved from this eternal destruction by the incarnate Son of God.

In the following six articles of the Symbol of Faith, beginning with the second Article and ending with the seventh, are set forth teachings about the Second Person of the Holy Trinity, the Son of God, our Lord and Saviour Jesus Christ.

The Second Article of the Creed

2. (I believe) ...**and in one Lord Jesus Christ, the Son of God, the Only-begotten, begotten of the Father before all ages. Light of Light, true God of true God, begotten, not made, of one essence with the Father, by Whom all things were made**.

In the second article of the Creed, we speak of our Lord Jesus Christ, Son of God, and confess that we know that He is the Second Person of the Holy Trinity, that He is of the Essence of God, and was so before His birth on earth.

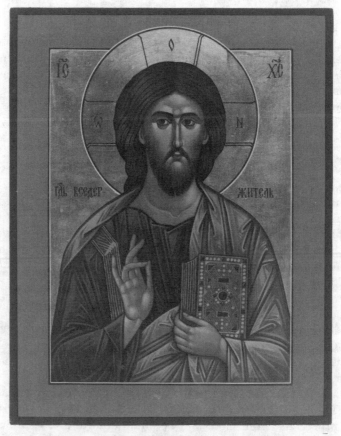

The Lord Jesus Christ All-powerful

The Lord Jesus Christ is the **only-begotten Son of God**. He is the only Son of God the Father, begotten of the essence of the Father, as light from light. From true God the Father is begotten true God the Son, and is begotten before all ages, before the beginning of time. So the Son is eternally with God the Father, and also the Holy Spirit, of one essence with the Father. Jesus Christ Himself said, *I and My Father are one* (John 10:30). The words of Jesus Christ, *My Father is greater than I* (John 14:28) pertain to His manhood.

If angels and saints sometimes are called sons of God, that means that they are sons of God only by grace, by the mercy of God, through faith in the Lord Jesus Christ.

To the word "**begotten**," in the Symbol of Faith, are added the words "not made." These words were added to refute the false heresy of Arius, who held that the Son of God was not begotten, but made.

The words "**by Whom all things were made**," means **by Whom**, by the Son of God, **all things were made**. Everything existing in the visible world and the invisible, was made by and through the Son, *and without Him was not anything made that was made* (John 1:3).

The Son of God, with His incarnation on earth, received the name Jesus Christ. This name indicates His human nature. The name **Jesus** is the Greek rendering of the Hebrew name, Joshua, and means Saviour. This name was twice stated by God through angels before the birth of Christ, because the eternal Son of God descended to earth and was incarnate for the salvation of men.

The name, **Christ**, is a Greek word and means the **Anointed One**. It corresponds to the Hebrew, "Messiah." In the Old Testament, anointment was used to set apart prophets, high priests, and kings who, at the assumption of their office, were anointed by oils and thus received the gifts of the Holy Spirit necessary for worthy fulfillment of their duties.

The Son of God was called the Anointed One, Christ, in accordance with His physical nature, because He had all the gifts of the Holy Spirit, prophetic knowledge, sanctity of a high priest and the power of a king.

Note: When the articles of the Creed, beginning with the second and ending with the seventh, are read separately, it is necessary to prefix each of them with "I believe." Example: "I believe in One Lord Jesus Christ, the Son of God ..."

Discussion of the Pre-eternal Birth of the Son of God

We live in **time**, and temporal things change. When the world reaches the end of its temporal existence, at the second coming of the Saviour, then it will change and become **eternal**. There will be "new heavens and a new earth" (Isaiah 65:17; 66:22; II Peter 3:13; Rev. 21:1).

Living in temporal conditions, it is difficult for us to imagine eternity. However, to some degree at least, we are able to imagine it by means of science or philosophy.

Thus eternity is **unchangeable**. It is **outside time. God, the Holy Trinity, is eternal and unchanging**. Therefore, never was the Father without the Son, or without the Holy Spirit.

The holy Fathers and Teachers of the Church explain that the Father was always with the Son, Who was born from Him, for without the Son He would not be called the Father. If God the Father ever existed without having a son, and would have made Himself a father, not having been a father before, that would mean that God was subject to change, from not having begotten to having begotten. But such an idea is worse that all blasphemy, for God is **eternal** and **unchanging**. Thus the statement in the Symbol of Faith, "begotten of the Father before all ages," means before the existence of our time, eternally.

St. John of Damascus explains, "When we say that He (the Son of God) was begotten before all ages, we show that His birth is not in time, and is without beginning. For not from nothingness was the Son of God brought into being. This aureole of glory, the image of the hypostasis of the Father, living wisdom and strength, hypostatic Word, essential, perfect, and living likeness of the invisible Father, was always **with the Father and in the Father, and was born of Him eternally and without beginning**."

The concept of "begetting" as being completely independent from the process of being begotten exists only in the material world, with material time and limitation. The spirit is not bound or subordinate to laws of matter. Similarly, the natural material begetting is in no way applicable to the spiritual begetting. Therefore, the Ecumenical Councils, conveying the main point of the Divine begetting of the Son from the Father, affirmed the words of the Symbol of Faith, "Light of Light, true God of true God, begotten, not made, of one essence with the Father..." The Son of God, in accordance with His essential perfect union with God the Father, is **always, eternally** begotten, like "Light of Light," without passion, not by the law of the created, material world. We are not able to completely comprehend this while we live within the intellectual (rational) framework of the material world. Therefore, the trinitarian nature of God is called the "Mystery of the Holy Trinity."

A comparison for clarification of the mystery of the Holy Trinity is given by the Fathers of the Church. John of Damascus says, "As fire and the light proceeding from it exist together, not fire first and then the light proceeding from it, and as light being begotten from the fire always abides in it and is not at all separated from it, thus the Son is begotten of the Father, no way separated from Him."

In another comparison, we are able to see that sunbeams, which are found on earth performing their life-giving activity, are never separated or broken away from the sun. By these comparisons, the words of the Gospels become understandable: *No man hath seen God at any time; the only begotten Son, Which is in the bosom of the Father, He hath declared Him* (John 1:18)

St. John the Evangelist calls the Only-begotten Son of God, Jesus Christ, the Word. *In the beginning was the Word, and the Word was with*

God, and the Word was God (John 1:1). The designation of the second Person of the Holy Trinity as the Son of God was revealed from on high to the Apostle John (Rev. 19:11, 13), though in part it was known in the Old Testament in a hidden way (Ps. 32:6; 18:15).

The Fathers of the Church explain, "As the mind giving birth to a word, begets without pain, does not divide, is not exhausted, and does not undergo some sort of bodily existence, thus the Divine begetting is passionless, inexplicable, incomprehensible, without division."

"As the word," says Archbishop Innocent, "is an exact expression of an idea, not separating itself from it and not merging with it, thus the Word was to God, a true and exact likeness of His existence, indivisible, without confusion, and always existing with Him. The Word of God was not a phenomenon or an affinity by the power of God, but is God Himself, the second Person of the Holy Trinity."

The Third Article of the Creed

3. Who for us men, and for our salvation, came down from the Heavens, and was incarnate of the Holy Spirit and the Virgin Mary, and became man.

The third article of the Symbol of Faith is the statement of how the Son of God descended from Heaven to earth, took upon Himself a body, human in every way but without sin, and was **incarnate.** He took on not only the body, but the soul of a man and became perfectly human without ceasing to be God at the same time. He became God incarnate.

The Son of God descended from Heaven and became a man (God incarnate) in order to save people from the power of the Devil, sin and eternal death. *Sin is the transgression of the law* (I John 3:4). That is, sin is an offense against the Law of God. Sin arises in people by the action of the Devil, who tempted Eve in Paradise, and through her, Adam, and persuaded them to break the commandment of God.

The fall into sin of the first people, Adam and Eve, broke down the nature of mankind. Sin in people clouded their intelligence and will. To the body it brought sickness and death. People began to suffer and to die. By their own power, people were not able to conquer sin in themselves and in their descendants, or to correct their intelligence, soul and heart, and to destroy death. This can be accomplished only by God, the Creator of all.

The merciful Lord gave a promise to people that the Saviour of the world would come to earth to deliver people from the power of the Devil and eternal death.

When the time of salvation came, the Son of God came to dwell within the pure Virgin Mary and, through the descent of the Holy Spirit upon Her, received from Her the nature of man and was born in a supernatural way "of the Holy Spirit and the Virgin Mary."

The Most-holy Virgin Mary was a descendant of the family of King David. She was the daughter of the righteous Joachim and Anna. The

Most-holy Mary is called a **Virgin** because She, out of love for God, promised to never marry. She is called **Ever-virgin** because She always remained a virgin, before the birth of the Saviour, at the time of the birth, and after the birth.

The holy Orthodox Church calls the Virgin Mary the God-Bearer (Theotokos), and holds Her more sacred than all created beings, not only people, but angels. "More honorable than the Cherubim, and beyond compare more glorious than the Seraphim" we declare of Her because She is the Mother of God Himself. Thus, according to the inspiration of the Holy Spirit, the righteous Elizabeth addressed Her, *and whence is this to me, that the Mother of My Lord should come to me?* (Luke 1:43)

Through His prophets, the Lord God showed many signs of the coming of the Saviour into the world. For example:

The Prophet **Isaiah** predicted that the Saviour would be born of a Virgin (Isaiah 7:14) and with remarkable clarity foretold His suffering (Isaiah 5:7-8; 9; 10; 11; 12; 53).

The Prophet **Micah** prophesied that the Saviour would be born in Bethlehem (Micah 5:2; Matt. 2:4-6).

The Prophet **Malachi** predicted that the Saviour would come to the newly built temple in Jerusalem, and that before Him would be sent the Forerunner, like the prophet Elias (Mal. 3:1-15).

The Prophet **Zechariah** predicted the triumphal entry of the Saviour into Jerusalem on a "colt, the foal of an ass" (Zech. 9:9).

King **David** in the twenty-first psalm described the Saviour's suffering on the cross with such accuracy that it seems as if he had seen the crucifixion himself.

The Prophet **Daniel**, 490 years **before Christ**, prophesied the date of the appearance of the Saviour, predicted His crucifixion, and after it, the destruction of the Temple in Jerusalem and the cessation of Old Testament sacrifices (Daniel 9).

When the Son of God, Jesus Christ, came to earth, many righteous people recognized Him as the Saviour of the world. The **wise men** of the East recognized Him by the star which shone in the East before the birth of Christ. The **shepherds** in Bethlehem recognized Him from the angels' proclamation. **Simeon** and **Anna** recognized Him by a revelation from the Holy Spirit when he was brought to the Temple. **John the Baptist** recognized Him in the Jordan River, at the time of baptism, when the Holy Spirit descended upon Him in the form of a dove, and the voice of the Father testified, *This is My beloved Son, in Whom I am well pleased* (Matt. 3:17). **Many people** recognized Him by the superiority of His teaching and especially by the miracles that He did.

For our salvation Jesus Christ accomplished His **teachings**, His **life**, His **death**, and His **resurrection**. His teachings are for our salvation when we accept them with all our heart, and behave in accordance with them, when we emulate in our own lives the life of the Saviour. As the false word of the Devil, accepted by the first people, became in people the seeds of sin and death, so the true word of Christ, sincerely accepted by Christians, becomes in them the seeds of holy and immortal life.

Discussion of the Incarnation of the Son of God

St. Sylvester (IV century), in conversation with the Jews about the faith, said, "God, Who brings everything into being, when He created man and saw his inclination to every evil, did not despise the perishing work of His hand, but rather deigned that His Son, existing inseparably from Him (for God is everywhere), should come to us on earth. Thus He descended and was born of the Holy Virgin and became subject to the law, *to redeem them that were under the law* (Gal. 4:4-5).

"That He was born of a Virgin was predicted by the Prophet Isaiah with these words, *Behold, a virgin shall conceive, and bear a son, and shall call His name Immanuel* (Is. 7:14). This name, as you know, designates the advent of God to people, and in translation from Hebrew means **God with us**. Thus, the Prophet, a long time before, predicted that God would be born from a virgin.

"For God, nothing is impossible; but regarding the Devil, it is necessary to conquer by that which was first conquered. Those first conquered were men, men not born by the usual order of nature, not from the seed of man, but from clay, furthermore, from soil clean and pure as the **Virgin**, for it had never offended God. It had not been defiled by either the blood of a murdered brother or killed animals. Therefore it was not infected with decaying bodies, nor was it defiled by any unclean or indecent acts.

"From such soil flesh was created for our ancestors, which was brought to life by the breath of God.

"But if the all-evil Devil conquered such a man, then it is necessary that the Devil be conquered by such a man. Such a man is our Lord Jesus Christ, born not by the usual laws of nature, but from the pure and holy womb of the Virgin, as Adam came from the soil uninfected by sin. As Adam was brought to life by the Spirit of God, so this One (Jesus Christ) was incarnated by the action of the Holy Spirit, Who descended upon the Most-holy Virgin. He became perfect God and perfect man, in every way except sin, having two natures, Divine and human, but one Person. In His human nature He suffered for us, but His Divinity remained without suffering."

For clarification of this explanation, St. Sylvester gives an example. "When a tree, illuminated by the rays of the sun, is cut down by a hatchet, then along with this felled tree, the rays of the sun are not also cut down. Likewise, when the human nature of Christ, united with God, endures suffering, then this suffering does not touch the Divinity."

During the course of the first century of Christianity, Jewish scribes, known as the Massoretes, preservers of tradition, removed all the manuscripts of the sacred books from all the synagogues throughout the world, and replaced them with their own transcriptions, which were rewritten with strict precision and with repeated verifications from letter to letter by the massoretic scribes themselves.

The degree of invariability and immutability of the massoretic texts is astounding. However, all this uniformity amounts to absolutely nothing. Only standardization of the texts was achieved. But those mistakes which already existed at the moment of the massoretic revision were not corrected. On the contrary, some distortions were purposely introduced by the Massoretes to obscure the clarity of the prophecies which foretold Christ the Saviour.

Of these distortions we will point out first of all the famous alteration by the Massoretes of Isaiah 7:14: *Behold, a virgin shall conceive and bear a son....* Knowing that this passage was a favorite of Christians, and testifies best of all to the most-blameless birth of our Lord, the Massoretes, while carrying out their reform, inserted the word *al'ma* ("young woman") in place of the word *vetula* ("virgin") in all the Hebrew texts throughout the world. At the time, the ancient Christian apologists reasonably objected to the interpretation of the Jewish scribes, "And what kind of a sign, about which the prophet speaks here, would the birth of a son to a young woman have been, since this is shown to be an everyday occurrence?"

In a manuscript of the Prophet Isaiah written before the birth of Christ, which was discovered not too many years ago, the word "virgin" is used in Isaiah 7:14, and not "young woman."

Therefore, it is clear why the Church prefers the Septuagint and Peshitta translations for the authoritative text of the Old Testament, and principally the first, for the Septuagint text was produced under the inspiration of the Holy Spirit by the concerted effort of the Old Testament Church.

Septuagint: The first and most exact translation of the Holy Scriptures was the translation of all the books of the Old Testament from Hebrew into Greek, done "according to the Seventy" (actually seventy-two) translators, or as they are called, interpreters, in the third century before the birth of Christ, about the year 270 B.C.

The Egyptian King Ptolemy Philadelphus, wishing to have in his library the sacred books of Hebrew law, ordered his librarian, Demetrius Phalereus, to acquire those books and to translate them into the language of the most common usage — Greek.

On the order of the King, an embassy with rich gifts for the temple was dispatched to the high priest Eleazar in Jerusalem, with the request to deliver to Alexandria all extant Hebrew sacred books and to send able people to make a translation of them.

The inspired high priest Eleazar fulfilled the request of the Egyptian King with extraordinary seriousness. In order that this great undertaking receive the participation of the entire Old Testament Church, a fast was established for all of the God-chosen nation, and prayer was intensified by all. The twelve tribes of Israel were summoned and the order given to choose six men to be translators from each tribe, in order that they could labor together to translate the Holy Scriptures into the Greek language. The chosen translators, having arrived at the city of the King of Egypt, lovingly undertook their holy labor, and with good progress finished it in a short time. Thus, under the influence of the Holy Spirit, this translation appeared, the fruit of a concerted, heroic effort of the entire Old Testament Church. This translation was in general use at the time of the earthly life of our Lord, Jesus Christ, and was used by the Apostles of Christ, the Fathers of the Church, and all the leaders of the Church.

Peshitta: In the first and second centuries there appeared a translation of the Holy Scriptures in the Syriac language known as the Peshitta, meaning simple or faithful. For the Orthodox Church, these two translations (the "Septuagint" and the "Peshitta") are the two translations in general use. But for the Roman Catholic Church, there is still another translation done by St. Jerome, known as the Vulgate. It appears undoubtedly more authoritative than the contemporary Hebrew original. (Compiled from the books [in Russian] *Discussions on the Holy Scriptures*, by Bishop Nathaniel, and *Summary of Study of the Old Testament of the Bible*, by Archbishop Vitaly, and other sources.)

It is extremely instructive that in close study the facts of the Gospel narrative, which at first glance seem questionable or hardly probable or plausible, always turn out to testify in favor of the Gospels, once again confirming the accuracy of the events reported in them.

Several decades ago, independent critics considered completely implausible the story in the Gospel of Luke in which Joseph, with the Holy Virgin betrothed to him, *went up from Galilee, out of the city of Nazareth, into Judaea, unto the city of David, which is called Bethlehem; because he was of the house and lineage of David:* (Luke 2:4). They went in order to fulfill the command for a census, a project carried out when Cyrenius Quirinin was governor of Syria (cf. Luke 2:2). In this undertaking, according to the account of St. Luke, it was necessary to go to register not at the place of residence, but to the place of family origin. Critics considered this to be an impossible task, first because the alarm and disorder created throughout the country if everyone at the same time left his habitual place of residence in order to go to the city from which his ancestors came would be daunting. Secondly, the story contradicts the well-established facts which were recorded concerning the Roman Census. It is well known that the Romans required registration at the place of habitual residence.

At a superficial glance these objections appear to undermine the reliability of the narration of St. Luke and seem formidable. However, every objection fades in the light of the indisputably established facts. Recently a document was discovered relating to the years 103-104 A.D. and the administration of the governor of Egypt, Gaius Vibius Maximus. In this document he is directed to report the census, exactly according to the order which is stated in the Gospel of St. Luke: **in view of the census, each person must go to that place where his family originated**. If this is so, then the objection to the account of St. Luke, that it is in contradiction to the usual Roman procedure, fails. From the statement of Vibius Maximus we learn that the Romans accommodated themselves to the customs and manners of the subjugated country. The narration of the census procedure in St. Luke is shown to be an irreproachable and exact account. (From the preface to *Four Gospels* published in *Truth* Paris, 1943.)

Discussion of the Miracles of God

Materialists categorically reject the possibility of miracles of God in the world. They maintain that miracles contradict the laws of nature. Miracles, they say, are incompatible with the scientific truth of strict conformity of all natural phenomenon. Is that so? We will attempt to answer.

Prof. S.L. Frank says, "The mechanical engineer Galileo teaches that all bodies, irrespective of their specific weight, fall to earth with the same speed and acceleration. Is the generally known fact that a bit of fluff falls to the ground much more slowly than an iron weight a contradiction to this law? Or that in water, wood does not fall at all? Is this law broken by the fact that an airplane does not fall, but is capable of rising higher and flies over the earth? Obviously not.

"For the law of Galileo, like all the laws of nature, contains a silent reservation: 'subject to various other conditions,' or 'if all outside influences are held constant.' "

Stated abstractly, the establishment of the attraction between the earth and a body of matter by its gravitational pull is not broken in the least. Only the concrete total sum appears altered or becomes complicated from the interference of new outside variables, as yet unaccounted for in the original law. In the first case — the power of the resistance of the air or water; in the second — the power of the motor, forcing the propeller to rotate and cut into the air. In the same manner, those events which are called miraculous can also be attributed to the effect of supplementary variables, not another variable of nature, but a supernatural power.

If Christ, as it is said in the Gospels, walked on water as on dry land, then this fact no more breaks the law of gravity than the fact of the flight of an airplane over the earth, or the flotation of a body lighter than water. In the latter instances, the action of the law of gravity is not broken, but is **overcome** by the power of the motor, or the resistance of the water. In the first instance, the law is utterly overcome by the power of God Incarnate, Christ.

If a man recovers from fatal illness after fervent prayers to God (his own or someone else's), then this miracle also hardly breaks medicine's established natural course of the illness, any more than successful surgical intervention of a doctor breaks it. In the latter case, the illness ends through mechanical alteration of circumstances conditional to it, and in the former, through influence on these conditions by the supreme power of God.

"If a man," says Archpriest Gerasim Shorets, "due to his free will, has the ability to influence nature, then is it possible that God does not have this ability? He, the Creator of the laws of nature?

"It is possible to make interesting observations about people who negate miracles," he continues. "Many of them who mock Biblical miracles, and regard believers in their veracity as backward men, themselves believe in commonplace and absurd things. They believe in ill-fated meetings, in the number thirteen, in a hare running across a road, like fools.

"Many of them, who with pride point to science to demonstrate the impossibility of miracles, themselves believe in what should really be classified as miracles, but which are twenty times less worthy of faith or confidence than the Biblical miracles attested to by many respectable people, a large part of whom would joyfully lay down their lives in affirmation of the truth.

"Those who deny miracles themselves believe only in those miracles which happened, according to their explanation, millions of years ago, and which were observed by no one.

"They do not believe in the creation of the world by God, but they do believe in its arbitrary origin, or that an embryo of organic life fell to earth from an unknown planet.

"They do not believe that Christ is able to resurrect a man, that is, bring back to life a previously living organism, but they believe that in former times, organic life sprang from lifeless matter.

"They do not believe that God, Creator of fire and people, could make three children fireproof, but they believe that embryonic organisms were sustained over the course of millions of years in the midst of the scorching heat of the world's haze and melted granite..."

No, serious scientific truth raises no objections to the miracles to which materialists refer. The objections are based only on their assumptions, hypotheses, and natural-philosophical theory, or their own materialistic faith.

Thus, while supposedly refuting the miracles of God on the basis of science, the scoffers reveal themselves as being ignorant regarding the questions of science, insufficiently educated in philosophy, or conscious opponents of belief in God.

(Compiled from a pamphlet: *Religion and Science* by Prof. S. Frank; and a pamphlet *Did Jesus Christ Live?* by Archpriest Shorets; and others.)

The Fourth Article of the Creed

4. And was crucified for us under Pontius Pilate, and suffered, and was buried.

In the fourth article of the Creed, it is stated that the Lord Jesus Christ was crucified on the cross for us during the reign of Pontius Pilate, the Roman governor over Judea; He was crucified for our sins and for our salvation, because He Himself was without sin. At that time, He **really suffered, died,** and was **buried**.

Of course the Saviour suffered not as God, Who cannot suffer, but as man. He suffered not for His sin, of which He had none, but for the sins of the whole human race. After His death, His body was buried in the tomb of Joseph of Arimathea. But from the time of the burial until His Resurrection, He descended in soul into hades and liberated all those who believed in Him, beginning with Adam and Eve.

Hades is the name of the place of estrangement from God, devoid of light or bliss. There Satan reigns. In regard to the soul the word "hades" signifies a condition of great affliction and torment.

The Lord Jesus Christ, as perfect man and Son of God, because He by one word is able to annihilate all enemies, voluntarily offered Himself as a sacrifice for the sins of people through crucifixion on a cross. Execution by hanging on a cross was the most infamous, cruel, and terrible form of capital punishment. It was the symbol of every human evil, and the most striking display of the power of the Devil. This terrible execution, devised by men according to the suggestion of the Devil, subjected people to hate, malice, embitterment and death. The Saviour, having endured disgraceful execution on the Cross, died, but rose from the dead. Through the Cross, life shone forth! Christ destroyed the main support of the Devil, and turned the Cross into an instrument of eternal victory over evil and death. The Lord sanctified the Cross with His pure blood and by His sacrificial heroic feat of love. The most terrible criminal, if he be repentant, is not rejected by the Saviour. From this moment, neither suffering nor death are able to deprive us of eternal bliss if we are with Christ the Saviour. On the contrary, the way of the Cross has become the path to eternal glory in the Kingdom of God.

The words in the Creed "suffered and was buried" were directed against some heretics who falsely taught that the Lord did not suffer torment on the Cross, but that His suffering only appeared to be suffering and death.

The words "under Pontius Pilate" point out the true historical event of the suffering of Christ, which occurred at this specific time. During the hours of Christ's suffering on the Cross, *there was darkness over all the earth* (Luke 23:44), states the Evangelist. Early historical writings of the Roman astronomer Phlegontus, Thaddeus, and Julius Africanus note this darkness.

One of these exclaimed, "One of the gods has died!" A well-known philosopher from Athens, Dionysius the Areopagite, was at that time in the city of Heliopolis, in Egypt. Observing the sudden darkness, he said,"...either the Creator is suffering, or the world is coming to an end." Afterwards, after the preaching of the Apostle Paul, Dionysius accepted Christianity and became the first bishop of Athens.

Glory to Thy long-suffering, O Lord!
Before Thy Cross we bow down, O Master, and Thy holy
Resurrection we glorify.

The Resurrection of Christ is discussed in the following, fifth article of the Creed

Discussion of the Cross of Christ

Christ revealed the name of God. The name is **Love**.

From his first deep breath, man began to sense God's everlasting love toward him. Here, too, originated the divine tragedy between God and His first-created, intelligent creature. This creature was not able to comprehend the complete perfection of the love that was offered. Man had to experience the agony of severed relations with God, and having tasted of and learned the horror of this estrangement, was then able to experience His love once again.

Adam had no fear. It is true that perfect love casts out fear. However, as attested to by the Fathers of the Church, fear always precedes love. This fear does not consist of apprehension of violence, but is born from a feeling of the loftiness of God. By fear, man measures the distance between himself and God.

Even when considering the lives of the saints, we experience fear, breathing the air of the mountain heights, in which we ourselves could not survive.

The approach of God tramples down fear by His presence and gives us bliss. However, having fear at the depth of our existence, we treat the love of God with reverence.

It was necessary for man during his life to learn what he was in comparison with his Creator. Having broken off from God and having gone away from Him, he glances back, and from afar sees and feels his omnipotent Creator.

How did Adam tear himself away from God? Everything that Adam did conformed to the love of God for him. His life was fervent love, but this was not by his own merit. Everything he did was done by the grace of his Creator, as a result of His love.

We, born in sin and not having this love, but having to acquire it, which is the goal of our life, are not able to understand the condition of Adam. Everything that we do by our own will for our own sake is sin, and only in subduing our own will, sacrificing ourselves out of love for another, do we join the Light, do we find interior orderliness according to God.

Adam was entirely of God. Everything in him was light. Only in one respect did he not reach perfection: in him was the possibility to eat the fruit of knowledge of good and evil. In this he should have constrained his will out of obedience and love; through this he fell away from God and sank into darkness.

Without sacrifice, there is no love. All the love of Adam towards God was dependent, if one may say, only upon his rejection of the fruit. Adam did not feel the slightest compulsion, because true love does not tolerate constraint.

Having tasted the fruit, Adam at once extinguished the light in himself and was filled with darkness. There was nothing for him to love. The darkness manifested itself in him by the sensation of nakedness. He hid from the Father. He lost God, and God lost His friend. For in order to love Adam as in former times, since Adam was now refusing love, it was necessary to create him again. Man was left to himself. In the bitter experience of separation from Love, he had to know the full depth of this misery, that when the Light was again revealed to him, he would voluntarily prefer this Light to the light he had chosen, thanks to the knowledge of good and evil. Again, he would voluntarily return to the world of Love from his own world which he created over the course of a thousand-year period of isolation from the Truth, from a world of his own, created by himself, with delights, with his own buildings, with his own ideals.

Suffused with darkness and the ability to understand good and evil, man acquired the capability of killing people like himself. But developing within himself this quality, man ceased to be content with murder alone. This became nothing to him. He began to kill his brother with torment. But even this appeared to be nothing. He began to kill his brother with taunting. But even this was not enough.

Then he invented something that, while not killing, put his brother in a helpless position, so that by his own helplessness he provoked the laughter of passersby, in order that his brother might die from humiliation and terrible pangs of pain.

At this point in the development of the quality of evil, God clearly revealed to people Who He is, the Creator of everything visible and invisible. If He were a vengeful Deity, He probably would have had to destroy the whole human race because that creature so maliciously laughed at the idea of his Creator. But Love acted completely to the contrary.

Our Heavenly Father gave His Only-begotten Son, that He should hang on the evil tree of hate and extreme bitterness created by man. The Son, having been crucified and having satisfied as far as was necessary the malice of His enemies, died. After three days, the Father resurrected the Son and engraved this new event on the hearts of people.

From this point in history, notions of people in the world and their understanding underwent a full revolution. The Cross, formerly only an instrument of terrible torture and cruel execution, became the single eternal support of man. The way, truth and life begins with the Cross, without which it is impossible to be saved.

There followed a new history of man, in which it is impossible for anyone to excuse himself through ignorance or lack of understanding. God was crucified on the cross. There need be no blindness!

If the world before Christ was a savage world, and inhabitants were dwelling in the jungle of their ignorance, then after Christ the world without the Cross becomes a world of apostates and damned people to whom will be said in time: *get thee hence from Me, into the fire which has been prepared for the devil and his angels* (Matt. 25:41). Those who follow Christ are openly called friends of the Lord.

I call you not servants, says the Saviour, *for the servant knoweth not what his lord doeth: but I have called you friends; for all things that I have heard of My Father, I have made known unto you. Ye are My friends, if ye do whatsoever I command you* (John 15:15,14).

God's love to us is beyond measure, radiating from the Cross of Christ! Great and unbounded is the Cross of Christ. It is impossible to comprehend the width and length of it, the depth and the height. But as far as possible, let us at least try to understand.

"How **wide** is the Cross of Christ?" asks one bishop, and answers, "It is as wide as the world, just as Christ died for the whole world, as it is written: *He is the propitiation for our sins: and not for ours only, but also for the sins of the whole world* (I John 2:2).

That is how wide the Cross is.

How **long** is the Cross of Christ? It is long enough to last throughout all ages, as long as there remains on earth but one sinner who might be saved; until there disappear sorrow, suffering and everything that is against the Lord in God's world.

That is how long the Cross is.

How **high** is the Cross of Christ? It is as high as Heaven, as the Throne of the Lord. Indeed, it is as high as the highest Heaven; for when Christ was crucified on the Cross, Heaven descended to earth, and earth ascended to Heaven.

That is how high the Cross is.

How **deep** is the Cross of Christ? That is a great mystery, which is not given to us to understand and about which we can only reverently conjecture. If the height of the Cross extends to Heaven, then by its depth it reaches down to hell, to the most inveterate sinner in the deepest depths into which he might fall — as Christ descended into hell and *preached unto the spirits in prison* (I Peter 3:19).

That, we dare to hope, is how deep the Cross of the Lord is.

The Cross of Christ is the beginning and ending of our salvation (Cf. John 3:16-17, 36).

Without the Cross we are not Christians, we are not members of the Church of Christ, we are not sons of God. For the Cross we were born, with the Cross we live, and with the Cross we die (Matt. 10:38; 16:24; 28:19. Luke 14:27; Mark 10:21; 16:6).

The Cross of Christ is a piece of armor, or a garment which we put on (Matt. 20:22-23; Mark 10:38-39; Luke 12:50) at the time of our earthly toils and labors in order that by it we be distinguished from all heterodox or unbelievers (Rev. 7:3; Ezekiel 9:4).

The Cross of Christ is laudation for Christians and formidable punishment for those who loathe and shun it, for those who fall away from the Church of Christ because of it, and for the enemies of God (Gal 6:14; I Cor 1:18; Heb. 13:13; 6:6; Philip. 3:18).

The Cross of Christ is a spiritual sword by which visible and invisible enemies are vanquished.

The Cross of Christ is a divine weapon to drive away every enemy and adversary (I Cor. 1:18: Luke 1:71-74; Matt. 22:44).

Finally, the Cross of Christ will be an awful sign on the day of Tribulation and Last Judgement of God for all adversaries of the name of Christ, antichrists (Matt. 24:30).

(Compiled from *Humility in Christ*, P. Ivanovna; the Journal *Eternal*, and *Lessons and Examples in Christian Faith* by the V. Rev. Gregory Diachenko.)

Discussion Of Two Providential Acts of God, Phenomena For Us In Our Sinful World

In our day the rational world is increasingly indifferent to the Christian faith. Unbelief, godlessness, and atheism are becoming firmly established everywhere.

But for the edification of the faithful, to strengthen us who vacillate in the face of the convictions of atheists, we will describe two historical events which are striking even to the materialistic world.

The first of them occurred on the day of the suffering of our Saviour on the cross, and the other in our time.

I. When the Saviour suffered on the cross all nature trembled, the light of the sun was hidden, and *darkness was on all the earth*, as the Evangelist relates. This extraordinary event had been predicted many centuries before by the Prophet Amos: *The end is come upon my people of Israel: I will not again pass by them any more* (Amos 8:2). *And it shall come to pass in that day, saith the Lord God, that I will cause the sun to go down at noon, and I will darken the earth in the clear day* (Amos 8:9)...*and I will make it as the mourning of an only Son...* (Amos 8:10).

The eclipse of the sun at the time of the crucifixion of Jesus Christ, in spite of the singularity of the event against all the laws of nature, as, for instance, there was a full moon — the moon did not stand between the earth and the sun — is an historical fact, fully described in pagan accounts:

1. The Roman historian and astronomer **Phlegontus** reports that the eclipse was so severe that it was possible to see stars in the sky.

2. The eclipse is reported by the scholar **Julius Africanus** and the Greek historian **Thaddeus**.

3. A noted philosopher from Athens, **Dionysius the Areopagite,** who was at that time in the Egyptian city of Heliopolis, observing the sudden darkness, said "Either the Creator is suffering or the world is coming to an end."

II. The second event is the miraculous appearance of the Holy Fire on Great Saturday in the Tomb of the Saviour in Jerusalem. The appearance of the Holy Fire has occurred annually for centuries, and continues to do so in our times. The exact date of the first appearance of the Holy Fire is difficult to determine. Historians of the Church refer to the writings of the Holy Fathers St. Gregory of Nyssa and St. John the Damascene, who both mention its occurrence. The Crusaders spoke about the Holy Fire, and pilgrims have consistently verified its presence throughout the centuries down to the present day.

The reception of the Holy Fire belongs exclusively to the Orthodox Patriarch. Heterodox (non-Orthodox) representatives have tried to receive it, without success. The Catholics ostentatiously withdrew from participation in this triumph of grace, despite the observation of the Roman Pope Urban II at the Council of the Cross at Clermont. He witnessed the Holy Fire in the Tomb of the Saviour, and concluded with the words, "Whose heart, no matter how petrified, would not be softened by such a phenomenon?"

The following account serves to show that the appearance of the Holy Fire in the Tomb of the Saviour occurs under the strict and thorough surveillance of the civil authorities. All flames in the church are extinguished the day before, on Good Friday, under police control. The premises of the Tomb of the Saviour are thoroughly inspected by the civil authorities, and then upon leaving the Tomb is sealed by them. The Patriarch unvests and stands clad only in a cassock. He is examined from head to toe to see if there is not some sort of incendiary device on him. Only after this is the seal removed from the entrance to the Tomb of the Saviour and the Patriarch enters it to receive the Holy Fire. After some time, and after fervent prayer, the Patriarch receives the Holy Fire, lights a bundle of candles (thirty-three in all, one for each year of the earthly life of the Saviour), passes them to those present in the church, and the whole church lights up in a sea of fire. The Holy Fire, during the course of ten to fifteen minutes, does not scorch.

Peoples of many nations, Greeks, Russians, Armenians, Arabs, Englishmen, Americans, Frenchmen, Turks, Jews, and others, gather to observe this glorious event.

The appearance of the Holy Fire is the greatest visible manifestation of the Paradise of God in our sinful world, serving for the enlightenment and salvation of us sinners.

On the Holy Fire at the Tomb of the Lord

In our time of spiritual barrenness, people's lives are limited to earthly preoccupations; great interest and curiosity attend every novelty. Man is totally disinterested in spiritual matters, or in the manifestation of God's benevolence to our sinful world.

Thus, very few are aware of the miraculous appearance of the **Holy Fire**, which has appeared over the centuries from year to year on Great Saturday in the Tomb of the Lord in Jerusalem, in the place of the burial and glorious resurrection of our Lord, Jesus Christ.

As a reminder of this extraordinary miraculous appearance we bring true evidence, revealed in the letter of a Russian pilgrim and eyewitness of the appearance of the Holy Fire two years in succession, Maria Pavlovna Chreshchatetskaya. This letter was written to Fr. Nicholas Samoukov, a hieromonk at Holy Trinity Monastery in Jordanville, New York, in answer to questions given her about it.

Furke, France
April 30, 1958

"Esteemed and dear in the Lord Fr. Nicholas, Christ is risen!...if the Lord wills, I will go to Novo Diveyevo, and then will not delay to come to Jordanville, and personally tell you everything that interests you. Until then I will attempt to answer all your questions.

"My companion was the nun, Maria Torskaya.

"We travelled from the Mount of Olives monastery to the Holy Sepulchre by bus. The weather was beautiful. The crowds were beyond measure, in the thousands. The mood of the people was enthusiastic. Of the nationalities present there were Greeks, Russians, Armenians, Arabs, English, Americans, French, Turks, and even Hebrews, who illegally got on the Arab side. Greeks and Arabs prevailed, I think. In the church the people behaved themselves outrageously from our point of view, with shouting and leaping and in general, making a lot of noise. But from their point of view, if they do not carry on this way (it is the way they pray), then the Holy Fire will not descend.

"I have already said that the people were beyond number, not only in the church, but around the church. When the Patriarch appears before the Tomb enclosure all the people quiet down, and there is complete silence until the appearance of the Holy Fire.

"First there is a procession around the church with many banners, three times around, with the Patriarch in full vestments. Then it stops in front of the Tomb enclosure. They take all the robes and the miter from the Patriarch. He remains in only a cassock, and the Turkish authorities examine him from head to foot to see if there is any incendiary device on him. This process takes until about 1:00 P.M.

The Miracle of the Holy Fire at Jerusalem

"I think that the Patriarch waited for the fire for not more than five to seven minutes.

"Last year another Russian pilgrim and I, coming from America, clearly saw (we were very lucky to have a good vantage point) a thin zigzag of light like lightning flash from above and strike downwards; and momentarily there appeared the fire in the Tomb of the Saviour, where it spread on cotton wads which were lit from the fire.

"The Patriarch lit a bundle of candles (thirty-three in the bundle) and passed them immediately through a special window-like opening made in the wall, and in a twinkling, from one to another, the fire spread throughout the enormous church, below and above. At this moment, the whole church reverberated from the wildly enthusiastic cries of the rejoicing crowds.

"For fifteen minutes or so, the Holy Fire does not scorch. I personally put all the diseased places of my body in the flame and did not feel it at all. A monk from the Mt. of Olives monastery, Fr. Savva, washed himself in it, immersed his whole face in it though he has a moustache and a beard, and not one hair caught fire, not even singed.

"In such a throng of people and with such a sea of fire, if it had been our usual fire, there would have been an inevitable conflagration. But from year to year, the same event happens, and there is never the slightest hint of fire.

"Women not only entered the altar, but even passed through the Royal Doors, but at this time the Grace was so powerful that it cleansed and protected everything.

"After receiving the Holy Fire, attendants carry the Patriarch, as he does not have the strength to walk. Evidently from the great exertion, he is left covered with beads of perspiration and totally drained of strength. Furthermore, they say that in their ecstasy, the people could tear off all his clothes. As I said before, last year I had a very good vantage point, above, next to the Tomb enclosure itself, so I was able to see things that others could not. This year, with the nun Torskaya, I entered the altar, and here I saw clearly how they carried the Patriarch straight into the vestry, since it was right next to me.

"There can be no doubt that this is unusual fire.

"Probably you have heard about the wondrous occurrence in the 1800's when the heterodox did not wish to allow Orthodox Christians into the church or the Patriarch into the Tomb enclosure. They themselves wanted to take possession of the holy flame. They closed the church and posted guards so that no one could enter the church. The Patriarch stood with the people on the outside, praying and lamenting.

"At the moment when the heterodox awaited the fire in the Tomb of the Saviour, and while the Orthodox Christians stood outside, there was a loud bang, the stone column cracked, and from it came the blessed flame which they all caught instantly.

"A Turk, an employee of the government, shouted "All-powerful is the Christian God, and I am a Christian!" The Turks killed him.

"From that time not one of the heterodox has attempted to encroach upon the holy flame again.

"Thus the column stands, cracked and blackened from the fire, in edification to all. Everyone who passes by kisses it.

"Perhaps in my haste my writing is not completely clear, but when I come, I will personally finish telling you about it.

"With love in Christ,
"Maria Chreshchatetskaya"

"The Holy Fire of Great Saturday," from a letter by Schema-monk Nicodemus

The Russian schemamonk, Fr. Nicodemus of Mount Athos, visiting Jerusalem in 1958, describes wonderfully in a letter the unusual triumph which he observed at the time of the reception of the holy flame.

"On Great Saturday, about 12:00 noon, I, sinful Schemamonk Nicodemus, had the good fortune to follow the Patriarch from the altar of the Church of the Resurrection of Christ in the procession of the Cross, going around the Tomb enclosure three times, and thus I was able to see that which is rarely observed at the life-giving Tomb.

The Sealed Door at the Lord's Tomb Before the Patriarch Enters

"After the third time around, the Patriarch (Greek Orthodox of Jerusalem) stopped before the locked and sealed door to the Tomb of the Saviour. I stood at the right side of a candlestick before the Tomb enclosure, a few steps away from the Patriarch.

"The Patriarch disrobed to his cassock. They took from him his miter, sakkos, and omophorion.

Police and state officials searched the Patriarch. Then they tore the tape from the seal off the door of the Tomb enclosure and permitted the

Patriarch to go inside the chapel. Along with the Greek Orthodox Patriarch, they admitted the Armenian Patriarch. The Armenian Patriarch did not take part in the procession of the Cross, but stood with his people on the left side of the tomb enclosure.

"Several others were permitted inside the chapel. Clergymen, upon a signal from the Patriarch, extinguished the Holy Fire from the previous year on the berth of the life-bearing Tomb and picked up everything in order to prepare for the reception of the Holy Fire.

"When the Arab police, who were to carry out both the Patriarch and the Holy Fire, entered the chapel, the door was closed after them.

"As is known to everyone, the chapel has two compartments, the altar of the Angel, and the life-bearing Tomb of the Saviour itself, the grotto or cave.

"Only the Greek Orthodox Patriarch enters the inner grotto of the Tomb. The others, with the police and the Armenian Patriarch, stand in the adjoining chapel of the Angel and wait silently.

"The door of the chapel is closed. Everyone is quiet, and silence reigns throughout the whole church of the Resurrection of Christ. All the devout await the Holy Fire in silence.

"It is necessary to explain about the preparation of the Tomb of the Saviour. On the evening of Great Friday, the flames in the whole church and in the chapel are extinguished under the control of the police.

"In the middle of the berth of the life-giving Tomb is placed a lamp on a pedestal, filled with oil and with a floating wick set, but unlit.

"Around the edge of the berth a ribbon is placed, and all over the berth they unpack pieces of cotton wadding. Thus prepared under the surveillance of the police, the Tomb enclosure is locked and sealed. The locked Tomb of the Saviour remains undisturbed until Great Saturday, when the Patriarch enters the cave of the Tomb of the Saviour to receive the Holy Fire.

"Then on Great Saturday, they admit the Patriarch into the cave of the life-giving Tomb, and the door is shut behind them. There is absolute silence...

"In the cave itself, it is dark. The Patriarch, alone there, silently prays to the Saviour... sometimes for ten minutes, sometimes more. At the time of my visit, fifteen minutes passed. Then suddenly in the darkness, on the berth of the life-giving Tomb, beads of bright blue began to spill about, multiplying, and turning into dark blue fire. From them, the prepared balls of cotton caught fire, then the ribbon, and the lamp. Everything became enveloped in the flame from the Holy Fire...

"The Patriarch quickly ignited his two bundles of candles. Upon entering the chapel of the Angel, he gave a light to the Armenian pilgrims through the oval window.

"During the appearance of the Holy Fire an uproar of joy and rapture like a clap of thunder resounds from the vast expanse of the church of the Resurrection of Christ.

"Then, to put out the fire on the berth of the Tomb of the Saviour (it does not burn here), they take away the burning lamp and the cotton wads with the ribbon.

"Two Arab policemen carry the Patriarch from the Tomb enclosure on their shoulders, with the support of assisting clergymen, and quickly carry him into the altar of the church of the Resurrection of Christ.

"One priest with the burning lamp goes before the Patriarch. All this is so fast that not many in the chapel are able to light their candles. Nor was I able to. Instead, I endeavored to join the throng of people following the Patriarch as he entered the altar, where I lit my bundle of candles with the Holy Fire from the hand of the Patriarch himself.

Schemamonk Nicodemus, Mt. Athos

Note: The church of the Resurrection of Christ is commonly known in English literature as the Church of the Holy Sepulchre.

The Lifebearing Tomb of the Lord

(An excerpt from a letter from the Greek archimandrite, Fr. Kiriakos, curator of the Tomb of the Saviour in Jerusalem, about the appearance of the Holy Fire.)

"...and regarding the Holy Fire, neither I nor anyone else has the right to be with the blessed Patriarch inside the cave of the Tomb of the Saviour at this time, except the Armenian bishop and those admitted only as far as the chapel of the Angel.

"The Patriarch of Jerusalem alone enters the inner grotto, in which is found the lifegiving Tomb.

"Several centuries ago, the Armenians tried to dispute the right of the Orthodox to receive the holy fire in the grotto of the Tomb. Then the Orthodox were denied access to the church of the Resurrection of Christ, and they were forced to stand in the courtyard. After the lapse of some time, while the Patriarch and the people prayed in the court of the cathedral, the Fire erupted from a column which was near the entrance. The Armenians received nothing.

"From this time we have never again been driven away from the Lifebearing Tomb. The column, to this day, stands cracked and charred."

Archimandrite Kiriakos, curator of the Lifebearing Tomb of the Saviour, Jerusalem, October 2, 1960.

The Fifth Article of the Creed

5. And He arose again on the third day according to the Scriptures.

The fifth article of the Creed speaks about the Resurrection of Jesus Christ on the third day after His death.

Since in the writings of the prophets of the Old Testament there were clear predictions about the suffering, death, burial of the Saviour, and His Resurrection, it is stated "according to the Scriptures." The words, "according to the Scriptures," pertain not only to the fifth, but also to the fourth article of the Creed.

Jesus Christ died on Great Friday about three o'clock in the afternoon and rose after midnight of the following Saturday, on the first day of the week, called from that time the Christian Sabbath, the day of the Resurrection of Christ. But in those days, a part of a day belonged to the whole day, so it is said that He was in the tomb three days.

The circumstances of Jesus Christ from the time of His death until the Resurrection are expressed in the Orthodox Christian Church by the following words," In the grave bodily, but in hades with Thy soul as God; in paradise with the thief, and on the throne with the Father and the Spirit wast thou Who fillest all things, O Christ the Inexpressible."

We know that in the Old and New Testaments several people rose from the dead, but there the dead were raised by someone else, and the resurrected rose in their former earthly corruptible bodies, and therefore, had to die again. Jesus Christ rose from the dead by **Himself**, by the power of His own Divinity; He rose and was changed in His body, which became immortal and eternal. He came forth from the tomb, not disturbing the Sanhedrin's seal, not rolling away the stone, and invisible to the guards.

The Lord revealed His Resurrection to people first through an angel, who rolled the stone away from the entrance to the tomb. The Resurrection was witnessed by soldiers guarding the tomb, who dispersed in fright. Then the angel announced the Resurrection of Jesus Christ to the Myrrhbearing women. Finally, Jesus Christ Himself, over the course of forty days, repeatedly appeared to His disciples, with many tangible demonstrations of His Resurrection. He allowed the disciples to touch His wounds from the nails and the lance, He ate before them, and spoke with them about the mysteries of the Kingdom of God.

On the day of the Resurrection of Christ we sing: "Christ is risen from the dead, trampling down death by death, and on those in the tomb bestowing life."

By death, the Lord conquered death, and to all in the graves, that is, all the dead, He gave life. Now the Lord abides in this new, resurrected body forever. Also in the new body of the resurrection lives the Mother of God, Whom the Lord resurrected after Her death. All people will receive a new, changed body at the second coming of the Saviour, when there will be a general resurrection, which the eleventh article of the Creed speaks about.

Thus is fulfilled the prophecy spoken through the Prophet Hosea: *I will ransom them from the power of the grave; I will redeem them from death:* (Hosea 13:14). *O death, where is thy sting? O grave, where is thy victory?* (I Cor. 15:55).

Discussion of the Resurrection of Christ

The Resurrection of Christ is the greatest event in the history of the world, and therefore Christians replaced the Old Testament Sabbath with this commemoration. The feast of the Resurrection of Christ is the "one king and lord of sabbaths, the feast of feasts, and the triumph of triumphs." The triumph of the Resurrection is the meaning and foundation of our Christian faith, *And if Christ be not risen, then is our*

preaching in vain, and your faith is also vain (I Cor. 15:14), says the
Apostle of Christ.

If there had been no Resurrection of Christ, then not only would
there be no Christianity, but even the faith in God, in the power of good
and truth, would have been undermined. The meaning of life would
have been lost. If the dead Christ had not been resurrected, then not
only would there be no salvation for anyone through Him, for to whom
can death and helplessness show help, but there would have been the
greatest triumph of evil in history. The days of Golgotha, and in
general, the entire earthly life of the Lord Jesus Christ, would have
been the most wicked mockery of evil over good, of the Devil over the
entire world of light and idealism. No more powerful or inevitable
motive for dark despair could exist, for if this Righteous One were
shown to be powerless, if such a Great Personality vanished into the
abyss of nonexistence, then what are we to expect for ourselves, and
what are we preparing ourselves for? There would be no righteous life
for mankind. Life would be only "an empty and stupid joke"
(Lermontov), or, in the apt words of the great Christian author,
Dostoevsky, life would be "devilish vaudeville," mere play-acting.

But Christ is risen, and the *father of lies, a murderer from the
beginning* — the devil (John 8:44) is rendered profane and powerless.
Life is victorious, death and evil are brought to emptiness and
pettiness, Christ is risen, and in full brilliance His majestic, regal
Divinity begins to shine.

"It is astonishing that serious people can believe in such
foolishness, and this in the twentieth century ... the age of science and
experimentation... Reason does not permit belief in the Resurrection of
Jesus Christ," says the non-believer.

"The historic fact of the Resurrection of Christ, as well as all His
teachings, has undergone criticism from many scholarly people and
rationalists. Several of them have devoted their entire lives to proving
that the Gospel narrative about the Resurrection is a fraud, a mistake,
or a delusion. From the earliest times a malicious fable has appeared
stating *that His disciples came by night and stole Him away, while we slept*
(Matt. 28:13). Though they first spoke fearfully about the earthquake at
the tomb, the rolling away of the stone, and the appearance of the angel
as lightning, the guards, bribed by the Jewish priests, then spread the
lie that Christ was stolen from the tomb. The absurdity of this
fabrication is immediately apparent to anyone.

It is completely inadmissible that the guard, composed of several
men, could have fallen asleep. Where was their the military discipline?
It was in fact a Roman guard, and the Roman army, by its iron
discipline and courage, was one of the best armies in the world. If the
soldiers slept, then they would not have been able to see, and if they
saw, it means they did not sleep. In that case, they would not have
given the Apostles the opportunity to perform the "theft"; on the
contrary, they would have arrested the thieves and would have
presented the dead body together with the thieves to the authorities.

But if there had been a theft, is it possible that the executioners of Christ would have left the "thieves" at large to preach His Resurrection? By the power of their authority, they would have forced the Apostles to produce the stolen body for them, in order to expose their lies and deception, and to suppress their preaching about Christ at its inception. Yes indeed, if the disciples had stolen the body of the Saviour, then it would have been necessary to bring them into court immediately, to convict them with the evidence of guilt, and thereby prevent their teaching. But the murderers of Christ did not do it, because they did not believe the soldiers would be able to support their own slander in court.

It is not possible that the enemies of Christ failed to verify the testimony of the soldiers. They, of course, did not fail to thoroughly, albeit secretly, verify the words of the soldiers, **the first witnesses of the miracle of the Resurrection**. Undoubtedly, they personally, although not in the full body of the Sanhedrin, went to the tomb of Christ and saw that it was empty. After analysis, they were unable not to acknowledge that Christ really rose from the dead. But why were they so shamefully silent about it? Why did they not as a body confess their grave sin and in this way guard their people against a threatening disaster?

For these corrupt people earthly goods were closer and more dear than the blessings of Heaven. They did not trust repentance as a means to gain forgiveness. At the same time, they understood very well that their repentance for slaying the Messiah would entail for them swift, unmerciful stoning by those people whom they drew into participation in this evil deed. In fear for their lives they kept quiet. Thus **they proved to be powerless in a confrontation with truth**. They were forced to confine themselves to issuing a mere order to the Apostles *not to speak at all or teach in the name of Jesus* (Acts 4:18). Prohibiting preaching about Jesus Christ, they avoided the question of where was the body of Jesus. *For we cannot but speak the things which we have seen and heard* (Acts 4:20), said the Apostles, who continued to conquer the world with their preaching about the Resurrection of Christ.

Furthermore, could the Apostles, who were peaceful, timid people, who remained at home under lock and key *for fear of the Jews* (John 20:19), and who were unarmed,... could they decide on such an insolent, daring, and purposeless undertaking as the theft of a body from under the nose of the guards? How would they be able to do battle with such formidable Roman guards? Besides, the details do not resemble a theft.

The idea of theft was first thought of by the Apostles themselves when they, after the announcement from Mary Magdalene, dispersed in fear and thought that the theft of the body was a new outrage of the enemy against Him. Going into the grotto of the tomb, the Apostles saw that the grave, although it was empty, did not appear to have been robbed. For if thieves had taken the body of Jesus Christ, they would have taken Him in the shroud. But the linen lay rolled up and the sudarium, a long, narrow linen napkin wound about the head, was not lying with the linen *but folded together in a place by itself* (John 20:7).

Therefore, this absurd Jewish fabrication was discarded long ago. In its place, skeptics advance a hypothesis of lethargic sleep and pleurisy with effusion to explain the water which flowed from the side. According to this theory, Jesus Christ fell into a deep faint and perhaps lethargy, and therefore was taken for dead. He was taken down from the cross and buried. Due to the approaching holy day of Passover they had to hurry with the burial, and in their haste, neither friends nor enemies had the chance to examine Him and ascertain that He was really dead. The action of the aromatics and the influence of the cold air of the cave brought Him back to consciousness. He got up, and although still weak, attempted to get out of the tomb. His cries and pounding frightened the guards, and they ran away. Availing himself of the flight of the guards, the gardener, or one of the disciples, rolled away the stone and liberated Him from the grave. His appearance in a white shroud gave Him the appearance of an angel, the herald of the Resurrection. Jesus Christ spent forty days in the company of the disciples, and then, from his pleurisy, really died.

The story is totally improbable and does not stand up under the slightest criticism. The Gospels say that from the pierced side of the Lord issued blood and water. From a medical point of view, this appearance showed paralysis of the heart, certain death. But even if Jesus Christ had remained alive, then due to a lack of breath from the tightly tied shroud, saturated with aromatics, that life would have ceased under the adverse conditions in the tomb. Weak and exhausted, He would hardly have been in a condition to move the stone and produce cries and pounding loud enough to terrify the guards. The Gospels speak in sufficient detail about conversations with Jesus Christ, about the joy with which He filled the hearts of His disciples, about the walk with His disciples on the long road, and so on. Does all this resemble someone just regaining consciousness from a faint or mortally ill lethargy? In fact, such a person would be a pitiful and exhausted sick man. In the opinion of specialists, He would not have been able to take two steps with perforated feet, nor take hold of anything with His hands. Even such opponents of Christ as Strauss (David Frederick Strauss, 1808-1847, German theologian and philosopher, famous for "demythologizing" the Bible) correctly noted that this half dead man would surely have been a disappointment to His followers. For Him to inspire such mighty faith that it spread throughout the world, subjugated a powerful empire to Him, awakened in all of those who saw Him the enthusiasm for martyrdom — is psychologically inconceivable and impossible. The Apostles remained persuaded of the Resurrection of Christ for their entire lives. If the Resurrection was imaginary, then sooner or later the real death of Jesus Christ would have followed, and that would have ended all the activities and accounts of the Apostles. Quite to the contrary, they began to preach with a certainty which they had never demonstrated during the earthly life of Christ.

The more common theory in our day is the apparition theory, that Christ did not actually rise from the dead, but that the disciples reported that they saw the Lord living and speaking with them. The disciples were so taken with the identity of Jesus Christ and hence become so intimately linked with the idea of His approaching Kingdom that they could not be reconciled with the fact of His death. Under the strain of anticipation they allowed themselves such massive hallucinations that they, giving way to self-deception, gave the accounts recorded in the Gospels.

It is true that in history and in present day reality hallucinations, however occur, both with individuals and with crowds, although the latter case is very rare. Hallucinations, however, are found among people who wish to see and hear something, who are mentally prepared for it. Their cerebral condition is ready to perceive that which they intensely await. But let us return to the Gospel story. In order to be deceived, to see something which did not exist, it would have been necessary to wait for the Resurrection, to believe that His Resurrection was near and would come to pass. Who among the Apostles had such faith? When Mary Magdalene and the other women went to the tomb, they thought, *Who shall roll us away the stone...?* (Mark 16:3) When Mary Magdalene saw that the tomb was empty, the idea of the Resurrection did not occur to her. Even when she saw the Lord she did not recognize Him. Why? She believed that dead people do not arise. The Apostles reacted in a similar manner when the news was brought to them *He is not here, but He is risen* (Luke 24:6). *Their words seemed to them as idle tales, and they believed them not* (Luke 24:11). Thomas not only did not believe when he saw, but for him it was even necessary to feel. *Reach hither thy finger, and behold My hands...* (John 20:27). It was the most sober, most convincing verification of the fact.

Jesus appeared to the Myrrhbearing women, to Peter, Luke and Cleopas (Luke 24:18), to the ten disciples, to the eleven, even to five hundred believers, and finally, to the Apostle Paul... **How could all of them be deceived? Is it possible that among this group there was not one single person with a sober, clear mind, with healthy senses and critical faculties?** As professionals affirm, hallucinations are more often visual or auditory sensations. Rarely do they occur in combination with others, and extremely seldom do hallucinations occur in the realm of sensation by touch. Where all three senses are involved together in a hallucination appearing to at least the ten and then eleven men, and even to the five hundred, and where broiled fish and honeycomb are eaten by it and disappear, as is stated in the Gospel (Luke 24:42),... such a hallucination has never been known in history, and never will be.

Thus the Apostles indeed saw the Resurrected One: the Resurrection is an indubitable historical fact. Skeptics are not able to undermine the Gospel story; they only refute each other, and some of them openly acknowledge their helplessness in struggling against

Christ. The German scholar DeWette (Wilhelm Martin Lebrecht DeWette, 1780-1849, German Protestant theologian and Biblical scholar), who over the course of ten years led the skeptics, on his deathbed confessed that "the event of the Resurrection, although the means by which it happened is completely obscured by impenetrable darkness, nevertheless appears to be as indisputable as the death of Caesar."

Discussing the trustworthiness of the miracles of the Resurrection and the Ascension, physicist Balfour Stewart said, "Was the well-known power of nature preserved according to the immutable laws in these cases, or was it somehow overcome by a higher force? Undoubtedly it was overcome during the Resurrection as during the Ascension. We are obliged to analyze the evidence of these great events, which is accomplished in a most credible manner. History, in narrating these events, has borne this test so well that every suggestion that this did not really happen leads to the greatest moral and spiritual confusion."

Why did not Jesus Christ appear among the Jews after the Resurrection? St. John Chrysostom explains that the appearance of the risen Lord would have been useless for the Jews, and that if there had been the slightest possibility that by it they could be converted, then without doubt the Lord would not have denied the Jews. But after He resurrected Lazarus, they were completely antagonistic. The Jews started to seek opportunities to kill not only Jesus Christ but Lazarus as well. If Christ had appeared to the Jews after the Resurrection, in one way or another they would have decided to kill God again.

Thus, Christ is risen from the dead. The most convincing evidence of the fact of the Resurrection of Christ is that mighty change which it produced in the Apostles, and through them, in the whole universe. On it rests all the culture of the last two thousand years. Could the fantasy of thirteen dreamers support it? They changed all history. Without the Resurrection of Christ we would not have Christianity or Christian culture. World history would have taken a completely different direction. Without the living power of the Christian faith, the ancient world would have decomposed and perished. It is impossible to believe that imagination alone could have produced such greatness and so much good.

By this demonstration all opposition to the miracle of the Resurrection of our Lord Jesus Christ falls away. Even the briefest critical analysis of the objections elucidates their total groundlessness. But malicious criticism does not weaken. "The Devil fights with God, and the field of battle is in the hearts of people," writes Dostoevsky.

In our time, new but lame arguments are advanced: God does not exist; Christ as a historical figure never existed, and therefore there was no Resurrection; the Gospels are pure mythology, fiction not supported by actual historical events. They are a compilation of ancient pagan myths about legendary gods. These "critics" have to realize that in the various myths, only gods such as Osiris and Dionysius died and rose again, but never God Incarnate. That Jesus Christ was **God Incarnate** is indisputable by evidence from the Gospels. Along with the Gospels we have the testimony of pagans, opponents of Christianity. For example, Pliny the Younger, the Roman consul and governor of Bithynia and Pontica in Asia Minor, in his letter to Emperor Trajan (about 112 A.D.) wrote, "They (Christians) gather and sing hymns to Christ, as God. They do not swear, do not tell lies, do not steal, do not commit adultery." Pliny did not write, "they sing to their God, to Christ," but he wrote, "to Christ, as God." Therefore he knew that Christ for the Christians was not only **God, but man**.

A contemporary of Pliny, Tacitus, one of the most accurate historians, reports, about 115 A.D., "Christ, during the reign of Tiberius, under Procurator Pontius Pilate, was sentenced to death."

Many pieces of evidence about Jesus Christ as a historical figure are in the Hebrew Talmud. It is true that these references are written with malice and hatred, calling the Saviour "apostate," "Nazarene," etc. Very little is said in the Talmud about the miracles of the Nazarene.

Especially striking is evidence of the former persecutor of Christians, Saul, later the first among the Apostles, Paul. The authenticity of his testimony is beyond dispute. This is understood by the most furious enemies of Christianity. "The strength of Paul's testimony," says one of our prominent authors and thinkers, "is such that even if there were none other, we would still know with greater exactitude than about many other historical figures, not only that Christ did exist, but how He lived, what He said and did, how He died, and how He rose from the dead."

The truth of the Resurrection of Christ the Saviour consists of the fact that it was the Resurrection of **God Incarnate**. He resurrected the human body, and by this transformed the human being into a spiritual, divine body for eternal life with God. In this lies the victory of the Saviour over death **for all generations**.

"The bodily Resurrection of the Saviour from the dead is an historical, true fact," says one of our well-known Orthodox missionaries, and he enumerates this in the following points:

1. Christ predicted His Resurrection (Mt. 16:21; 20:19; Mark 9:9).

2. After the Resurrection He testified about the event (Luke 24:46).

3. He appeared in visible form:

a. On the morning of the Resurrection to Mary Magdalene (Mark 16:9).

b. To the women going away from the tomb (Matt. 28:9).

c. To Peter near Jerusalem (Luke 24:34; I Cor 15:5).

d. To two disciples on the road to Emmaus (Luke 24:13).

e. On the evening of the Resurrection, to the Apostles, except Thomas (John 20:19).

f. A week later in the evening to all the Apostles (John 20:26).

g. After several days at the Sea of Tiberias to seven disciples (John 21:1-3).

h. Not long after, on the mountain near Galilee, to eleven Apostles (Matt. 28:17).

i. To five hundred of the faithful (I Cor. 15:6).

j. To his brother "according to the flesh," James, and all the Apostles (I Cor. 15:7).

k. At the time of the Ascension on the Mount of Olives, to all the Apostles (Luke 24:50).

l. To the Apostle Paul (I Cor. 9:1; 15:8).

m. To the first archdeacon, Stephen (Acts 7:55).

n. Until the Ascension, over the course of forty days, explaining the Kingdom of God (Acts 1:3).

4. He ate and drank with the disciples (Luke 24:42).

5. He showed His hands and feet with the wounds, which He received from being nailed to the cross (Luke 24:40).

6. He gave admonitions (Matt. 28:18; Mark 16:15; Luke 24:17; John 21:15; 20:21; Acts 1:7).

7. He travelled with the Apostles (Luke 21:15).

8. The Myrrhbearing women and the eleven disciples worshipped Him (Matt. 28:9, 17).

9. Angels proclaimed the Resurrection of Christ (Matt. 28:6; Mark 16:6; Luke 24:6).

10. The event was reported by Roman soldiers keeping watch at the tomb (Matt. 28:11).

11. The Apostles identified themselves as witnesses of the Resurrection of Christ (Acts 2:32; 10:39), and they relied on this actual historical fact for the foundation of all their preaching (Acts 2:22; 3:26; 4:10; 10:39). At the same time, it is especially significant that the Apostles do not give an account of the precise moment of the Resurrection of Christ. They only say *that...which we have heard, which we have seen with our eyes...and our hands have handled... declare we unto you...* (I John 1:1-3). The exact moment of the Resurrection of Christ no one was able to witness. Even the soldiers, keeping watch at the tomb, did not observe the exact moment of the Resurrection. The risen Christ was invisible to them. In fact, the Apostles were not able to witness it, as they had hid and locked themselves in their houses *for fear of the Jews* (John 2:19). That is why not one of the four Gospels contains a description of the exact moment of the Resurrection, although there are detailed accounts of all events preceding the Resurrection and detailed accounts after the Resurrection.

We know that if the Resurrection of Christ were fiction, then no matter how much of a genius the author is, he would not omit the center and theme of his composition. He would, without fail, touch upon the moment of the Resurrection in his account, because man's innate curiosity demands it.

But the Apostles did not do this. This constitutes the highest proof of the authenticity of their witness. For they were not writers, but guileless and simple men, influenced by the Holy Spirit, **actual**

witnesses of the true event of the Resurrection of Christ and the whole Gospel story.

The Apostles themselves said, *And if Christ be not risen, then is our preaching in vain, and your faith is also in vain. But now is Christ risen from the dead, and become the first-fruits of them that slept* (I Cor. 15:14,20). He is the first to partake of our future resurrection.

Only then did the Apostles and the first Christians go to death, **when they had made certain of the actual Resurrection of the Saviour, of His victory over hell and death**. Only in this case were they able, as the poet said, "To go to execution singing hymns and looking into the jaws of unfed beasts with unflinching gaze." Thus, the miracle of the Resurrection is accomplished in deed. **Christ is risen indeed!**

Compiled chiefly from an article by Archpriest Gerasim Shorets, *Christ is Risen*, from his brochure, *Did Christ Live?* Additions from a book by D.M. Merezhkovsky, *Jesus the Unknown*; an article by Archpriest I. Chernavin, *Did Christ Rise from the Dead?*; and other sources.

The Sixth Article of the Creed

6. And ascended into the Heavens, and sitteth at the right hand of the Father.

In the sixth article of the Creed, it is stated that Jesus Christ ascended into Heaven with His pure body, and sits at the right hand of God the Father.

The Ascension of the Lord occurred forty days after His Resurrection. The Lord Jesus Christ ascended to Heaven in body and soul, and in His Divinity He always abides with the Father.

"Sitteth at the right hand of the Father" means on the right side, in the place of honor and glory. These words mean that the human body and soul of Christ was received with the glory that Christ has by His Divinity.

By His Ascension, our Lord Jesus Christ united earth and Heaven and glorified our human nature, raising it to the throne of God. He showed us that our fatherland is in Heaven, in the Kingdom of God, which is now open to all who truly believe in Him.

To him that overcometh will I grant to sit with Me in My throne, even as I also overcame, and am set down with My Father in His throne (Rev. 3:21).

The Seventh Article of the Creed

7. And He shall come again, with glory, to judge both the living and the dead, Whose kingdom shall have no end.

In the seventh article of the Creed it is stated that Jesus Christ will come to earth again to judge all people, living and dead, who will all rise at that time, and that after the terrible Last Judgment the Kingdom of Christ will begin, of which there will be no end.

The second coming of the Saviour is clearly discussed in Holy Scripture. For example, when Jesus Christ ascended into Heaven, angels appeared and said to the Apostles, "This Jesus, Who is taken up from you into Heaven, will come again to earth in the same form, in the body of a man, as you saw Him going up to Heaven."

The second coming of Christ will not be at all like the first. The first time He came in the humble form of a man to suffer for us and by this to save us from sin. He was born in a stable for cattle, lived, not having a place to lay His head, and died between criminals on the cross. In the second coming He will appear suddenly as a King, with majesty. *For as the lightning cometh out of the east, and shineth even unto the west, so shall also the coming of the Son of man be* (Matt.24:27). The second coming of Christ the Saviour will be extraordinary: *The sun shall be darkened, and the moon shall not give her light, and the stars shall fall from heaven, and the powers of the heavens shall be shaken; and then shall appear the sign of the Son of man, (a cross) in heaven; and then shall all the tribes of the earth mourn, and they shall see the Son of man coming in the clouds of heaven with power and great glory* (Matt. 24:29-30), ...*and all the holy angels with Him, then shall He sit upon the throne of His glory: And before Him shall be gathered all nations* (Matt. 25:31-46), and He will judge all people, all of us, the righteous and the sinful.

This judgment is called **terrible**, because the conscience of every man will be revealed before all. Not only the good and evil deeds will be disclosed, but also the manner in which each man conducted his earthly life; every spoken word, secret wish, and thought will be laid bare.

According to this judgment, the righteous will enter into eternal life, and the sinners into eternal torment — for doing evil deeds and failing to repent of them, or to make amends through good deeds and a righteous life.

For the hour is coming, says the Lord Himself, *in which all that are in the graves shall hear His voice, and shall come forth; they that have done good, unto the resurrection of life; and they that have done evil, unto the resurrection of damnation* (John 5:28-29).

The exact hour of the second coming of the Lord to earth is known to no man. It is a secret which, by the word of the Lord Himself, no one knows, not even the angels of God, only the Heavenly Father alone. Therefore, we must always be ready to appear before the judgment of God.

Although the exact time is not known to us, God's word reveals several signs of the approach of the coming of the Lord. Before this time the Gospels will be preached to all people. The Jews will return in great numbers to Christ.

At the same time there will be more corruption, lack of faith, less love toward one's neighbor, and increased wickedness and calamity among people. False prophets will appear. Discord and war will grow stronger among the people; famine and starvation, epidemics and earthquakes will occur in various places. Finally, when evil reaches its highest manifestation on earth, Antichrist will appear.

Antichrist, the antagonist of Christ, will appear before the end of the world, and will seek to exterminate Christian faith on the earth with all his power. But with the coming of Christ, the dominion of the Antichrist will end in terrible ruin, as will he, since he is a disciple of the Devil himself.

After all these things have come to pass the eternal Kingdom of Christ will begin.

The Eighth Article of the Creed

8. And in the Holy Spirit, the Lord, the Giver of Life, Who proceedeth from the Father, Who with the Father and the Son together is worshipped and glorified, Who spake by the Prophets.

The eighth Article of the Creed speaks about the third Person of the Holy Trinity, the **Holy Spirit**. The Holy Spirit is also true God, as is the Father and the Son. This we confess, calling Him **Lord**.

The Holy Spirit is also called the **Giver of Life** because He, together with God the Father and God the Son, **gives life to all**, especially **spiritual life**. It follows that He is likewise the Creator of the world, equal to the Father and the Son. It is said about the creation of the world: *And the Spirit of God moved upon the face of the waters* (Gen. 1:2). Jesus Christ Himself said about the blessed regeneration by the Spirit, *...Except a man be born of water and of the Spirit, he cannot enter into the Kingdom of God* (John 3:5).

Thus the Holy Spirit is true God, the third Person of the Triune God. To Him we must render the same worship and glory as to the Father and the Son.

The words, "Who proceedeth from the Father," define the personal hypostatic nature of the Holy Spirit, by which He is distinguished from God the Father, and from the Son, begotten of the Father. His nature is such that the **Holy Spirit continually proceeds from the Father**. Jesus Christ Himself spoke on this point to His disciples: *But when the Comforter is come, Whom I will send unto you from the Father, even the Spirit of truth, Which proceedeth from the Father, He shall testify of Me* (John 15:26).

The words, "Who spake by the Prophets," means who spoke through the prophets. The prophets predicted the future and wrote Holy Scriptures under the inspiration of the Holy Spirit, and therefore their books are called divinely inspired. The words, "spake by the Prophets," are stated so that no one need doubt that the Holy Scriptures were written under the inspiration of the Holy Spirit, not by the authors themselves, as ordinary books are written. They therefore contain the highest God-given truth, the Word of God, or Divine revelation.

The fact that the Holy Spirit spoke through the Apostles is not mentioned in the Symbol of Faith because at the time of its composition no one doubted it.

The Holy Spirit now conveys His gifts to true Christians through the Church of Christ, in prayer and the Holy Mysteries. In the Holy Mysteries the Holy Spirit enlightens the faithful with the light of Christ's teaching, warms their hearts by love for God and neighbor, and purifies them of every stain of sin.

Jesus Christ called the Holy Spirit, *Spirit of Truth* (John 14:17; 15:26; 16:13) and warned us, *All manner of sin and blasphemy shall be forgiven unto men; but the blasphemy against the Holy Spirit shall not be forgiven unto men* (Matt. 12:31).

"Blasphemy against the Holy Spirit" is conscious and hardened opposition to the truth, *because the Spirit is truth* (I John 5:6). Conscious and hardened resistance to the truth leads man away from humility and repentance, and **without repentance there can be no forgiveness**. That is why the sin of blasphemy against the Spirit cannot be forgiven, since one who does not acknowledge his sin does not seek to have it forgiven.

The Holy Spirit was revealed to people in visible form at the Baptism of the Lord in the form of a **dove**, and on the day of Pentecost when He descended to the Apostles in the form of **tongues of fire**. He appeared also as a cloud of light in the Old Testament and at the Transfiguration of Christ.

The Ninth Article of the Creed

9. In one Holy, Catholic and Apostolic Church.

The ninth article of the Creed speaks about the Church of Christ, which Jesus Christ founded on earth for the sanctification of sinful people and for their reconciliation with God.

The Church is called a union of all Orthodox Christians, living and dead, *for He is not a God of the dead, but of the living: for all live unto Him* (Luke 20:38), united among themselves in **faith** and Christian **love**, by its hierarchy and by its sacraments.

Each individual Orthodox Christian is a member or a part of the Church. When we say that we believe **in one Holy, Catholic, and Apostolic Church**, the Church is understood to include all people who confess one and the same Orthodox Faith. It does not only mean the building where we go to pray to God and which is also called the church of God. Jesus Christ entrusted the visible construction and government of the Church to the Apostles, and then to their successors, the bishops, and through them He invisibly rules the Church. The Lord Jesus Christ alone is the true Head of the Church, and no other head of the Christian Church exists or ever will. Jesus Christ is Head, and the **Church is the spiritual body of Christ** (Eph. 1:22-23; 5:23).

The holy Apostle Paul says, *For as the body is one, and hath many members, and all the members of that one body, being many, are one body: so also is Christ. For by one Spirit are we all baptized into one body, whether we be Jews or Gentiles, whether we be bond or free; and have been all made to*

The Church on the Earth and in Heaven

drink into one Spirit (I Cor. 12:12-13). Thus, *ye are the body of Christ, and members in particular* (I Cor. 12:27). *He* (Jesus Christ) *gave some, apostles; and some, prophets; and some, evangelists; and some, pastors and teachers; for the perfecting of the saints, for the work of the ministry, for the edifying of the body of Christ* (the Church) (Eph. 4:11-12).

Jesus Christ said that His Church is invincible and will endure forever. *I will build My Church, and the gates of hell shall not prevail against it* (Matt. 16:18). *I am with you always, even unto the end of the world. Amen* (Matt. 28:20).

The truth of God, His teaching, is preserved in the one Church of Christ, ...*the Church of the living God, the pillar and ground of the truth* (I Tim. 3:15). Jesus Christ said, *But the Comforter, which is the Holy Spirit, Whom the Father will send in My Name, He shall teach you all things, and bring all things to your remembrance, whatsoever I have said unto you* (John 14:26) that the Holy Spirit *may abide with you forever* (John 14:16).

He who obeys the Church, obeys Christ Himself, and he who does not obey, but rejects her, rejects also the Lord Himself. If one *does not obey the Church, let him be to you like as a heathen man, and a publican,* said the Lord Himself (Matt. 18:17).

The Church of Christ is **one**, because it is one spiritual body, has one head, Christ, and is inspired by one Spirit (cf. Eph. 4:4-6). It has one goal, the sanctification of people, and everywhere the same teachings of God, and the same sacraments. Therefore, the Church cannot fall into ruin or become divided. Heretics may fall from Her or become separated from Her; they then cease to be members of the Church. The Church by their action does not cease to be united. The Church obliges all of us *to keep the unity of the Spirit in the bond of peace* (Eph. 4:5).

The existence of geographical divisions of the Orthodox Church, such as Jerusalem, Constantinople, Antioch, Alexandria, Russia and others, does not violate the unity of the Church of Christ at all. For they all are revealed to be members of one body, One Universal Church of Christ. **They all confess the same faith, and have prayers and sacraments in common.**

The Church of Christ is **Holy**, because it is sanctified by the Lord Jesus Christ Himself, through His suffering, with His divine teachings and with the Holy Sacraments established by Him, in which the Grace of the Holy Spirit is given to the faithful. *Christ also loved the Church, and gave Himself for it; that He might sanctify it ...* (Eph. 5:25-26).

The sanctity of the Church is not violated by Christians when they sin because they can always cleanse themselves through the Mystery of Repentance. If someone remains unrepentant, then he visibly or invisibly withdraws from the Church.

The Church of Christ is **Catholic**. Catholicity is the unity of all believing Orthodox Christians, united in truth by the love of Christ and the grace of the Holy Spirit. The Catholic Church is bound neither by natural boundaries nor time nor by people, and it consists of all true believers everywhere. Therefore it is also called **universal**.

The One, Holy, Catholic, and Apostolic Church of Christ is furthermore called **Apostolic**, because the Lord spread it and strengthened it through the holy Apostles. The word Apostolic is essential because the Church uninterruptedly and without change has preserved the Apostolic **teaching** and the **succession** of the gift of the Holy Spirit through holy ordination.

The **highest visible authority** in the Church belongs to the **Ecumenical Council**. Primacy in the Ecumenical Church is composed of the patriarchs, then of lesser prelates — metropolitans, archbishops and bishops. Local councils, if their decisions are in agreement with the spirit of Orthodoxy as revealed in the past, also have authority.

The One, Holy, Catholic, and Apostolic Church is furthermore called **Orthodox** (from the Greek, *ortho*, correct, straight, true, and *doxa*, glory, worship, in the sense also of dogma, piety, teaching), because, under the guidance of the Holy Spirit, It unchanging, correctly and gloriously keeps the teachings of Jesus Christ — so that we may **glorify God in a way that pleases Him**.

The Tenth Article of the Creed

10. I confess one Baptism for the remission of sins.

The tenth article of the Creed speaks about the Mystery of Baptism and about the remaining Mysteries.

Jesus Christ, sending His disciples out to preach, said, *Go ye therefore, and teach all nations, baptizing them in the name of the Father and of the Son, and of the Holy Spirit,* and added, **Teaching them to observe all things whatsoever I have commanded you** (Matt. 28:19-20). By this the Lord clearly stated that other mysteries had been established by Him.

By **sacraments**, or mysteries, are meant those holy acts through which the Holy Spirit mysteriously and invisibly confers Grace (the saving power of God) upon man.

The holy Orthodox Church has **seven Mysteries: Baptism, Chrismation, Confession, Holy Communion, Marriage, Ordination, and Holy Unction**.

The Symbol of Faith mentions only Baptism because that Mystery is the door into the Church of Christ. Only those who have been baptized can avail themselves of the other sacraments.

Moreover, at the time of the composition of the Creed, there were quarrels and doubts. For example, some thought that heretics who returned to the Church should be baptized a second time. The Ecumenical Council said that Baptism could be performed only one time for any given person. Therefore it is said — "I confess **one** Baptism." It is understood that this **one Baptism** must be performed in the true Church for it to be valid. This is true of all the Mysteries.

The Mystery of Baptism

The Mystery of Baptism is the sacred act in which the believer in Christ, through threefold bodily immersion in water, while calling upon the name of the Holy Trinity — **the Father and the Son and the Holy Spirit** — is **washed** of all sin committed by him prior to Baptism and given the grace to fight against the inclination to sin which has become habitual in man since the sin of Adam and Eve. The believer is

reborn by the grace of the Holy Spirit into new spiritual life and **becomes a member of the Church**.

The Mystery of Baptism was established by our Lord Jesus Christ Himself. He sanctified Baptism by His own example, being baptized by St. John the Baptist. Then, after His Resurrection, He gave the Apostles the commandment: *Go ye therefore, and teach all nations, baptizing them in the name of the Father, and of the Son, and of the Holy Spirit* (Matt. 28:19).

...go ye therefore, and teach all nations, baptizing them in the name of the Father, and of the Son, and of the Holy Spirit. (Mt. 28, 19).

...the servant of God (name) is baptized in the name of the Father, amen, and of the Son, amen, and of the Holy Spirit, amen.

Baptism is necessary for anyone who wishes to be a member of the Church of Christ. "Except a man be born **of water and of the Spirit**, he cannot enter into the Kingdom of God," said the Lord Himself (John 3:5). To receive Baptism it is necessary to have faith and repentance.

The Orthodox Church baptizes infants on the faith of their parents and godparents. Present at the Baptism are godparents, to whom the faith of the baptized child is entrusted before the Church. When the child grows older, the godparents are obliged to teach him the faith and to endeavor to help the baptized become a true Christian. This is the sacred responsibility of the godparents, and they sin grievously if they neglect their duty. That the gifts of the Spirit are given on the faith of others, we are given proof of in the Gospels, concerning the healing of the cripple: *When Jesus saw their faith, he said unto the sick of the palsy, Son, thy sins be forgiven thee* (Mark 2:5).

Sectarians contend that babies should not be baptized and criticize the Orthodox for performing the sacrament for infants. The foundation for the baptism of infants is that Baptism has replaced the Old Testament circumcision, which was done when an infant was eight days old. Christian Baptism is called *circumcision made without hands* (Col. 2:11-12). The Apostles baptized whole families in which without doubt there were children. Babies as well as adults are participants in the sinful inclination inherited from Adam and have need to be cleansed and strengthened against it.

The Lord Himself said, *Suffer (let) the little children to come unto Me, and forbid them not: for of such is the Kingdom of God* (Luke 18:16).

Thus, Baptism is spiritual birth, and as a person is born once, so also the Sacrament of Baptism is done once, *One Lord, one faith, one baptism* (Eph. 4:5).

The Mystery of Chrismation

The holy apostles Peter and John laid their hands on the baptized and they received the Holy Spirit. (Acts 8, 14-17).

The priest anoints the baptized with holy Chrism pronouncing the words, "the seal of the gift of the Holy Spirit. Amen"

Chrismation is the Mystery which bestows the gifts of the Holy Spirit on the believer in order to strengthen him in the Christian spiritual life.

Jesus Christ spoke about the gifts of Grace of the Holy Spirit when He said, *He that believeth on Me, as the Scripture hath said, out of his belly shall flow rivers of living water. But this spake He of the Spirit, which they that believe on Him should receive: For the Holy Spirit was not yet given; because that Jesus was not yet glorified* (John 7:38-39).

The Apostle Paul says, *Now He which establisheth us with you in Christ, and hath anointed us is God; Who hath also sealed us, and given the earnest* (i.e., pledge or token) *of the Spirit in our hearts* (II Cor. 1:21-22).

The gifts of Grace of the Holy Spirit are necessary for every believer in Christ. There are furthermore extraordinary gifts of the Holy Spirit which are conveyed only to certain people, such as prophets, apostles and kings.

The first Apostles accomplished the Mystery of Chrismation through the laying on of hands (Acts 8:14-17; 19:2-6). Then at the end of the first century, the Mystery of Chrismation came to be performed by anointment with holy oil, after the example of the Old Testament Church, as the Apostles themselves were not always able to perform the Mystery through the laying on of hands.

Holy Chrism is special oil that is prepared in a prescribed manner from fragrant substances and is then consecrated.

The first chrism was sanctified by the Apostles themselves and their successors, the bishops. Only bishops may consecrate this chrism. By anointing with the chrism sanctified by the bishops, priests are able to perform the Mystery of Chrismation.

During the performance of the Mystery with the holy chrism, they anoint the following parts of the body with the sign of the Cross, the forehead, eyes, ears, mouth, chest, hands and feet, while pronouncing the words, "The seal of the gift of the Holy Spirit. Amen."

The Mystery of Confession

Confession is the Mystery in which the believer admits his sins before God in the presence of a priest and receives through the priest forgiveness of sins as if from the Lord Jesus Christ Himself.

Jesus Christ gave to the **Apostles**, and through them to all **priests**, the power to forgive **sins**. *Receive ye the Holy Spirit: whosoever sins ye remit, they are remitted unto them; and whosoever sins ye retain, they are retained* (John 20:22-23).

Even John the Baptist, preparing people to receive the Saviour, preached *the Baptism of repentance for the remission of sins ... And were all baptized of him in the river of Jordan, confessing their sins* (Mark 1:4-5).

Having received this power from the Lord, the Apostles performed the Mystery of Confession: *And many that believed came, and confessed, and showed their deeds* (Acts 19:18).

...Receive ye the Holy Spirit: whosesoever sins ye remit they are remitted unto them, and whosesoever sins ye retain they are retained (Jn. 20, 22-23).

The priest, in the name of the Lord Jesus Christ and through the authority given him, absolves the sins of those who repent.

Forgiveness of sins (absolution) by means of confession requires peace with all one's neighbors, sincere contrition for sins committed, confession, firm determination to correct one's life, faith in the Lord Jesus Christ and hope in His mercy.

In certain cases an "epitimia" (a Greek word meaning "prohibition" or "restriction") is laid on the repenting believer, consisting of some pious act or some deprivation directed at overcoming a sinful habit.

The Mystery of Holy Communion

Holy Communion is the Mystery in which the faithful Orthodox Christian receives, in the form of bread and wine, the Body and Blood of the Lord Jesus Christ, and through this Mystery is united with Christ and becomes a participant in eternal life.

The Mystery of Holy Communion was established by our Lord Jesus Christ Himself at the time of the Mystical Supper, on the evening before His suffering and death. He Himself celebrated the Mystery first. "Jesus took bread, and gave thanks (to God the Father for all His mercy toward mankind), and brake it, and gave it to His disciples, saying, 'Take, eat; this is My body.'

The institution by the Lord Jesus Christ of the Mystery of Holy Communion

The faithful are given Communion in church.

"And He took the cup, and gave thanks, and gave it to them, saying, 'Drink ye all of it; For this is My blood of the New Testament, which is shed for many for the remission of sins' " (Matt. 26:26-28; Mark 14:22-24; Luke 22:19-24; I Cor. 11:23-25).

Then, after establishing the Mystery of Holy Communion, Jesus Christ commanded the disciples to perform it at all times: "This do in remembrance of Me."

In instructing the people, Jesus Christ said, *Except ye eat the flesh of the Son of man, and drink His blood, ye have no life in you. Whosoever eateth My flesh and drinketh My blood, hath eternal life; and I will raise him up at the last day. For My Flesh is meat indeed, and My blood is drink indeed. He that eateth My flesh and drinketh My blood, abideth in Me, and I in him* (John 6:53-56).

In obedience to the commandments of Christ, the Mystery of Holy Communion is continually celebrated in the Church of Christ and will be continued until the end of the age, during the service known as the Divine Liturgy, when the bread and wine, by the power and the action of the Holy Spirit, is changed into the true body and true blood of Christ.

The bread used for Holy Communion is a single loaf, as all the believers in Christ constitute His **one** body, the head of which is Christ Himself. *For we being many are one bread, and one body: for we are all partakers of that one bread*, said the Apostle Paul (I Cor. 10:17).

The first Christians received Holy Communion every Sunday. The Church commands us to receive Holy Communion at least once during every fast, and as often as possible.

Preparation for receiving the Mystery of Holy Communion consists of fasting, prayer, reconciliation with all, and then, **Confession**, that is, cleansing of the conscience in the Mystery of Confession.

The Mystery of Holy Communion, in Greek, is called the Eucharist, which means "thanksgiving."

The Mystery of Marriage

Marriage is the Mystery during which public vows are made before the priest and the Church by the groom and the bride to be faithful to each other. Their conjugal union is blessed as an image of the spiritual union of Christ with the Church. The Grace of God is requested and given for their mutual assistance, unanimity, and for the blessed procreation and Christian upbringing of children.

Marriage was established by God in Paradise. At the time of the creation of Adam and Eve, *God blessed them, and God said unto them, Be fruitful, and multiply, and fill the earth, and subdue it* (Gen. 1:28).

Jesus Christ sanctified Marriage by His own presence at the wedding in Cana of Galilee and confirmed it as a divine institution by saying, *Have ye not read, that he which made them at the beginning made them male and female* (Gen. 1:27). And said, *For this cause shall a man leave father and mother and shall cleave to his wife: and the twain shall be one flesh* (Gen. 2:24). *Wherefore they are no more twain, but one flesh. What therefore God hath joined together, let not man put asunder* (Matt. 19:4-6).

The Apostle Paul compares the union of marriage with the union of Christ and the Church (cf. Ephes. 5:22-32).

The union of Jesus Christ with the Church is founded upon the love of Christ for the Church, and on the complete devotion of the Church to the will of Christ. Hence the husband is obliged to love his wife selflessly, and the wife is obliged to voluntarily, lovingly obey her husband.

Husbands, says the Apostle Paul, *love your wives, even as Christ also loved the church, and gave Himself for it... he that loveth his wife loveth himself* (Eph. 5:25,48). *Wives, submit yourselves unto your own husbands, as unto the Lord, for the husband is the head of the wife, even as Christ is the head of the church: and He is the Saviour of the body* (Eph. 5:22-23). Therefore each spouse, husband or wife, is obliged to preserve mutual love and respect, mutual sacrifice and fidelity. Like all Sacraments, Marriage is given to man in order to help him save his soul. If the husband and wife do not live in a Christian manner the Sacrament of

...A man shall leave father and mother and shall cleave to his wife, and they twain shall be one flesh...(Mt. 19: 4-6).

The priest blesses the couple thrice with the words, "O Lord our God, crown them with glory and honor!"

Marriage will not save them. Good Christian family life is the source of personal and public good. The family is the foundation of the Church of Christ.

The Mystery of Marriage is not obligatory for all, but individuals who willingly remain unmarried are obliged to lead clean, pure and virgin lives, which, by the teaching of the Word of God, is higher than married life and is one of the greatest spiritual feats (Matt. 19:11-12; I Cor. 7:8,9,26,32,35,37,40).

The Mystery of Ordination

Ordination is the Mystery in which a duly appointed man, through the laying on of hands by the bishop, receives the Grace of the Holy Spirit, strengthening him for divine service in the Church of Christ as bishop, presbyter (priest), or deacon. This Mystery is

The descent of the Holy
Spirit on the Apostles.

The bishop lays his hands on
the candidate to be ordained
and calls down upon him the
Grace of the All-holy Spirit

performed only for people selected and consecrated to become clergy. The degrees of the clergy are three: deacon, priest, and bishop.

A man ordained **deacon** receives Grace to assist during the performance of Mysteries. A man ordained **priest** receives Grace to celebrate the Mysteries. A man ordained **bishop** receives Grace not only to celebrate the Mysteries, but also to ordain others to celebrate the Mysteries.

The Mystery of Ordination is divinely established. The Apostle Paul testified that the Lord Jesus Christ Himself *gave some, apostles; and some, prophets; and some, evangelists; and some, **pastors** and **teachers**; for the perfecting of the saints, for the work of the ministry, for the edifying of the body of Christ.*

The Apostles, performing this Mystery under the guidance of the Holy Spirit, raised up deacons, presbyters, and bishops, through the laying on of hands.

The selection and ordination of the first deacons by the Apostles is described in the book of Acts: *Whom they set before the apostles: and when they had prayed, they laid hands on them* (Acts 6:6).

With regard to the ordination of presbyters it is written, *And when they had ordained them elders in every church, and had prayed with fasting, they commended them to the Lord, on Whom they believed* (Acts 14:23).

In the epistles of the Apostle Paul to the bishops Timothy and Titus it is said, *Wherefore I put thee* (Bishop Timothy) *in remembrance that thou stir up the gift of God, which is in thee by the putting on of my hands* (II Tim 1:6). *For this cause left I thee in Crete, that thou shouldest set in order the things that are wanting, and ordain presbyters in every city, as I had appointed thee* (Titus 1:5). Appealing to Timothy, the Apostle Paul says, *Lay hands suddenly on no man, neither be partaker of other men's sins: keep thyself pure* (I Tim 5:22). *Against a presbyter receive not an accusation, but before two or three witnesses* (I Tim 5:19).

The Mystery of Holy Unction

Holy Unction is the Mystery for the sick in which by anointing with Holy Oil, the Grace of God is invoked for physical and spiritual healing.

St. James writes in his epistle about the Mystery of Holy Unction.

The Mystery of Holy Unction.

From these letters we see that the Apostles reserved to the bishops the power to ordain presbyters through the laying on of hands, and to have jurisdiction over presbyters, deacons, and servers.

The Mystery of Holy Unction is still called in Russian *soborovaniye*, "the gathering," because several clergymen are called to perform it, although if necessary, it can be done by one priest.

The Mystery comes from the Apostles. Having received from the Lord Jesus Christ power in the time of preaching to heal all the sick and infirm, *they anointed with oil many that were sick, and healed them* (Mark 6:13).

Especially detailed is the account of this Mystery by the Apostle James. *Is any sick among you? Let him call for the presbyters of the church; and let them pray over him, anointing him with oil in the name of the Lord. And the prayer of faith shall save the sick, and the Lord shall raise him up; and if he have committed sins, they shall be forgiven him* (James 5:14-15).

The Apostles did not preach anything of their own but taught only that which was commanded them by the Lord and that which was inspired by the Holy Spirit. The Apostle Paul says, *But I certify you brethren, that the Gospel which was preached of me is not after man. For I neither received it of man, neither was I taught it, but by the revelation of Jesus Christ* (Gal 1:11-12).

Holy Unction is not given to infants because infants cannot knowingly commit sins.

The Eleventh Article of the Creed

11. I look for the resurrection of the dead.

The eleventh article of the Creed speaks about the general resurrection of the dead, which will come at the end of the world.

The resurrection of the dead that we look for will occur at the same time as the second and glorious coming of our Lord Jesus Christ. At that time all the bodies of the dead will be united with their souls, and they will come to life.

Faith in the resurrection of the dead was expressed as early as **Abraham**, at the time of the sacrifice of his son Isaac (cf. Heb. 11:17); by **Job** in the midst of his extreme suffering, *For I know that my Redeemer liveth, and that He shall stand at the latter day upon the earth: And though after my skin has been thus destroyed, yet in my flesh shall I see God* (Job 19:25-26); the Prophet **Isaiah**, *Thy dead men shall live, together with my dead body shall they arise. Awake and sing, ye that dwell in the dust; for thy dew is as the dew of herbs, and the earth shall cast out the dead* (Isaiah 26:19).

The Prophet Ezekiel contemplated the resurrection of the dead in a vision of a field strewn with dry bones. By the will of the Holy Spirit the bones came together, bone to bone, became covered with flesh, and the breath of the Spirit came into them (Ezekiel 37).

Jesus Christ speaks about the resurrection of the dead more than once, *Verily, verily, I say unto you, the hour is coming and now is, when the dead shall hear the voice of the Son of God: and they that hear shall live* (John 5:25). *Marvel not at this: for the hour is coming, in the which all that are in the graves shall hear His voice, and shall come forth; they that have done good, unto the resurrection of life; and they that have done evil, unto the resurrection of damnation* (John 5:28-29). *Whosoever eateth My flesh and drinketh My blood hath eternal life: and I will raise him up at the last day* (John 6:54).

In answering the questions of the unbelieving Sadducees about the resurrection of the dead, Jesus Christ said, *Ye do err, not knowing the Scriptures, nor the power of God. For in the resurrection they neither marry, nor are given in marriage, but are as the angels of God in Heaven. But as touching the resurrection of the dead, have ye not read that which was spoken unto you by God, saying, I am the God of Abraham, and the God of Isaac, and the God of Jacob? God is not the God of the dead, but of the living* (Matt. 22:29-32).

The Apostle Paul says, *But now is Christ risen from the dead, and become the firstfruits of them that slept. For since by man came death, by Man came also the resurrection of the dead. For as in Adam all die, even so in Christ shall all be made alive* (I Cor. 15:20-22).

At the moment of the general resurrection the bodies of dead people shall be changed. In essence, the bodies will be the same as we now have, but in quality they will excel our present bodies. They will be spiritual, incorruptible and immortal. Changed also will be the bodies of those people who are alive at the time of the second coming of the Saviour. The Apostle Paul says: **It is sown a natural body; it is raised a spiritual body** ... *we shall not all sleep, but we shall all be changed. In a moment, in the twinkling of an eye, at the last trump: for the trumpet shall sound, and the dead shall be raised incorruptible, and we shall be changed* (I Cor. 15:44, 51-52).

Corresponding to the change in man himself, all the visible world will change. From the corruptible it will turn into the incorruptible.

The souls of people who died before the general resurrection exist under differing conditions. The souls of the righteous will experience a foretaste of eternal blessedness, and the souls of sinners a foretaste of eternal torment. The state of the souls of the dead is determined at the particular judgment, which takes place after the death of each person. This is clearly evident from the teaching of the Lord Jesus Christ about the rich man and Lazarus (cf. Luke 16:19-31). The Apostle Paul also points this out when he says, *Having a desire to depart, and to be with Christ; which is far better* (Philip. 1:23,24).

Death has great significance in the life of every man. It is the demarcation point by which the time of preparation is ended and the time of reward is begun. But as this particular judgment is not final, the souls of sinful people who died with faith in Christ and repentance are able to receive relief from suffering beyond the grave and even be completely delivered from it by the prayers of the Church, augmented by works of charity done for them by the living, and especially by commemorating them in the bloodless sacrifice of the Body and Blood of Christ. For this purpose the Orthodox Church established commemoration of the dead, which has been performed regularly since Apostolic times. Commemoration of the dead comprises one of the main parts of the Divine Liturgy. This is evident from the first Christian Liturgy of the Apostle James.

The Apostle John says, *If any man see his brother sin a sin which is not unto death, he shall ask, and He (God) shall give him life* (I John 5:16).

The Apostle Paul in his epistle to Bishop Timothy writes, *I exhort therefore, that, first of all, supplications, prayers, intercessions, and giving of thanks, be made for all men, for kings, and for all that are in authority; that we may lead a quiet and peaceable life in all godliness and honesty. For this is good and acceptable in the sight of God our Saviour; Who will have all men to be saved, and to come unto the knowledge of the truth* (I Tim. 2:1-4).

The Apostle James says, *Confess your faults one to another and pray one for another, that ye may be healed. The effectual fervent prayer of a righteous man availeth much* (James 5:16).

If we should pray for the living, then we should also pray for the dead, because to God there are no dead. To God all are living. The Lord Jesus Christ Himself said, *For He is not a God of the dead, but of the living: for all live unto Him* (Luke 20:38).

The Apostle Paul wrote to the Christians, *For whether we live, we live unto the Lord; and whether we die, we die unto the Lord: whether we live therefore, or die, we are the Lord's* (Rom. 14:8).

Even in the Old Testament it was the custom to pray for the dead. Thus, for example, the Prophet Baruch prayed for the dead saying, *Lord Almighty, God of Israel! Hear the prayer of the dead of Israel and of their sons who sinned before Thee... Do not bring to remembrance the unrighteousness of our fathers* (Baruch 3:4-5). Judas Maccabaeus prayed and brought offerings for dead soldiers (II Macc. 12:39-45). Thus, teachings about prayer for the dead are founded upon Holy Scriptures as well as Holy Tradition.

Discussion of the General Resurrection of the Dead

The truth of the general resurrection of the dead is clearly and definitively revealed in the Holy Scriptures. It also flows from the fundamental powers of our immortal souls, and from our understanding of an Eternal, Omnipresent and All-righteous God.

As early as the Old Testament, the righteous had faith in the general resurrection of the dead on the basis of Divine Revelation (Job 19:25-26; Isaiah 26:19; Ezekiel 37; Daniel 12:2; Macc. 7:9 and others).

In general, all of the righteous people in the Old testament considered themselves strangers and pilgrims on this earth and sought the Heavenly Fatherland (Heb. 11:13-20).

Through the Prophet Hosea the Lord said, *I will ransom them from the power of the grave; I will redeem them from death: O death, Where is thy sting? O Hades, where is thy victory? repentance shall be hid from Mine eyes* (Hosea 13:14).

In the New Testament, the Lord Jesus Christ preaches about the resurrection of the dead clearly and definitely: *Verily, verily, I say unto you, the hour is coming, and now is, when the dead shall hear the voice of the Son of God: and they that hear shall live... they that have done good, unto the resurrection of life; and they that have done evil, unto the resurrection of damnation* (John 5:25,29).

The Saviour affirms the teaching of the resurrection by the Mystery of Holy Communion. *Whosoever eateth My flesh, and drinketh My blood, hath eternal life; and I will raise him up at the last day* (John 6:54).

When the Saviour speaks about the purpose of His advent on earth, He points out eternal life specifically. *For God so loved the world, that He gave His only begotten Son, that whosoever believeth in Him should not perish, but have everlasting life* (John 3:15-16).

During His stay on earth the Saviour raised the dead, and He Himself rose from the dead, becoming, according to the words of the Apostle Paul, *the firstfruits of them that slept* (I Cor. 15:20).

The Apostle placed the truth of the resurrection of the dead above all doubt and contended that it is intimately connected with the resurrection of Christ and with all the teaching in the Gospels. *Now if Christ be preached that He rose from the dead, how say some among you that there is no resurrection of the dead? But if there be no resurrection of the dead, then is Christ not risen: And if Christ be not risen, then is our preaching in vain, and your faith is also in vain... If in this life only we have hope in Christ, we are of all men most miserable. But now is Christ risen from the dead, and become the firstfruits of them that slept* (I Cor. 15:12-20).

Besides that, the Apostle Paul points out the natural phenomenon in nature which convinces us of the truth of the resurrection. *But some man will say, How are the dead raised up? And with what body do they come? Thou fool, that which thou sowest is not quickened except it die: and that which thou sowest, thou sowest not that body that shall be, but bare grain; it may of chance be wheat, or of some other grain: But God giveth it a body as it hath pleased Him, and to every seed his own body... So also is the resurrection of the dead. It is sown in corruption; it is raised in incorruption: It is sown in dishonour; it is raised in glory: it is sown in weakness; it is raised in power: It is sown a natural body; it is raised a spiritual body* (I Cor. 15:35-44).

The Lord Himself said, *Except a corn of wheat fall into the ground and die, it abideth alone; but if it die, it bringeth forth much fruit* (John 12:24). Nature itself shows us this marvelous, authentic phenomenon. A kernel, thrown on the ground decomposes, decays, rots — and then what? Is that all that occurs? No, not at all! From it begins growth. It grows into ears with new grains, despite the fact that it appeared to be reduced to dust. Is not this marvel worthy of our attention? Is it not obvious that this witnesses to the fact that **the Omniscient Creator through death lays the beginning of life, and out of ruin creates new being**?

Thus, **the mystery of the resurrection of the dead is always before our eyes**. It is evident to us in nature, and strengthens our faith, and denounces our skepticism.

But, in spite of this, the question may occur in our soul, "How can the dead be raised, when the body of the dead turns into dust and is destroyed?" If Almighty God gave us existence once from a handful of earth, then obviously He can take the handful of earth a second time and reanimate it. If God brought forth the whole world from chaos; if He created it from nothing, then is it possible that He is unable to form our bodies anew from a handful of earth, and give us the same bodies as before, only in a renewed form?

Figuratively, the Lord already showed the Prophet the mystery of our resurrection from the dead. He was shown a vision of a field strewn with the dry bones of men. From these bones, by the word of God uttered by the Son of man, the figures of men were formed and, perhaps by the same capability as existed at the primeval creation of man, the Spirit reanimated them. By the word of the Lord, as dictated to the Prophet, first movement occurred in the bones, bone became joined to bone, each according to its place; then the bones became bound with tendons, clothed with flesh, and covered with skin. Finally, upon the second sound of the voice of God, pronounced by the Son of man, the spirit of life came forth in them. They all began to live, stood on their feet, and they constituted a great multitude of people (Ezek. 37:1-10). Will not the future resurrection of the dead follow likewise? **Wonderful indeed are the works of God! Marvelous is the holy faith that we profess!**

Thus, by the righteous determination of God, our frail body, like a seed, is condemned to die at first. It decays to dust, and then rises again. The place where the dead are interred is in essence a cornfield, in which our bodies are sown by the hand of death, like seeds. The earth, our mother, is a stronghold, where in the midst of decay, our immortality is kept. *It is sown a natural body; it is raised a spiritual body* (I Cor. 15:44).

God did not condemn us to death in order to obliterate His creation, but in order to recreate it, to make it capable of future imperishable life.

It remains for us people to reverently submit to the wise judgment of God, to accept with faith Divine Revelation about our fate, and to look with Christian hope for the resurrection of the dead and the life of the age to come. (Taken from the book *Lessons and Examples of Christian Faith,* and other books by Archpriest Gregory Diachenko.)

The Twelfth Article of the Creed

12. And (look for) the life of the age to come. Amen.

The twelfth article of the Creed mentions the life of the future age; that is, the eternal life which will begin after the general resurrection of the dead, the renewal of the whole world, and Christ's judgment over all.

For righteous people, eternal life will be so joyful and blessed that in our present state we are not even able to describe it. The Apostle Paul says, *Eye hath not seen, nor ear heard, neither have entered into the heart of man, the things which God hath prepared for them that love Him* (I Cor. 2:9).

This understanding of the blessedness of the righteous arises from visions of God in light and glory, and from union with Him. In Paradise, the souls of the righteous will be united with bodies which will be illumined with the light of God as the body of the Lord Jesus Christ was at the time of His Transfiguration on Mount Tabor.

The Apostle Paul writes, *It is sown in dishonour; it is raised in glory* (I Cor. 15:43).

The Lord Jesus Christ Himself said, *Then shall the righteous shine forth as the sun in the kingdom of their Father* (Matt. 13:43).

The states of the righteous will be in various degrees of blessedness, corresponding to the virtue of each. The Apostle Paul said, *There is one glory of the sun, and another of the moon, and another glory of the stars: for one star differeth from another star in glory. So also is the resurrection of the dead* (I Cor. 15:41-42).

For unbelievers and unrepentant sinners life in the future age will be one of eternal torment. The Lord says to them, *Depart from Me ye cursed, into everlasting fire, prepared for the Devil and his angels ... and these shall go away into everlasting punishment* (Matt. 25:41,46).

This torment of sinners will proceed from their estrangement from God, from the clear realization of their sins, from severe pangs of conscience, from having to stay among evil spirits where the eternal, unquenchable fire burns.

What is this unquenchable fire? The Word of God does not define it, but uses the term to portray the inexplicable, inexpressible torment of hell.

Thus punishment of sinners will not be because God wants them destroyed, but they themselves *perish because they did not accept the love of truth for their salvation* (II Thess. 2:10).

The Creed is concluded with the word "Amen," which means "truly" or "so be it." By saying this word after the Creed, we attest to the fact that all that is stated therein we acknowledge to be undoubtedly and invariably true.

CHAPTER 5

Christian Life

Genuine good Christian life may be led only by those who have faith in Christ and who strive to live by this faith; that is, those who by their good works fulfill the will of God. Good works are an expression of our love, and love is the foundation of all Christian life. *God is love; and he that dwelleth in love dwelleth in God, and God in him* (John 4:16). *For God so loved the world, that He gave His only begotten Son, that whosoever believeth in Him should not perish, but have everlasting life* (John 3:16). Thus God by this act revealed His love to mankind.

Love which is not accompanied by good works is not true love, but is merely lip service. That is why the Word of God says, *Faith without works is dead* (James 2:20). The Lord Jesus Christ Himself said, *Not every one that saith unto Me, Lord, Lord, shall enter into the Kingdom of Heaven* (Matt. 7:21). *For we are his workmanship, created in Christ Jesus unto good works, which God hath before ordained that we should walk in them* (Eph. 2:10).

Furthermore we have received from God special means for discerning good deeds from evil. The means are the **internal** law of God, or conscience, and the **external** law of God, or the His commandments of God.

The word **conscience** denotes the internal, spiritual strength of a man, or the manifestation of the soul of a man. The conscience, as the internal law of God ("voice of God"), is present in every person.

The conscience is the internal voice which tells us what is good and what is evil, what is proper and what is improper, what is righteous and what is not. The voice of the conscience obligates us to do good and to shun evil. For every thing good the conscience rewards us with internal peace and calm. For everything wrong, incorrect, improper, or evil, the conscience judges and punishes so that a person acting against the conscience feels himself in moral discord, tormented by pangs of conscience.

But the conscience, as the spiritual strength of a man, requires development and improvement along with the other spiritual faculties of a man, namely, with his mind, heart, and will. The mind, heart, and will of man have become darkened from the time of Adam and Eve. From that time the voice of conscience has been shown to be weak and insufficient as a manifestation of spiritual strength. If man does not develop spiritual strength in himself, then the internal voice of conscience in man falls asleep by degrees and dies, as in a "man without conscience."

From this it is clear that the internal law of conscience alone is not enough for man. Even in Paradise God revealed His will to the first people. It follows that in order to exist in an innocent, righteous state, it is necessary for a man to have the external law from God. Even more so is it needed as a result of the fall from Grace.

In order that man would always remain in "fear of his conscience," the Lord God gave us the **external law**, the commandments of God.

This law was given in its simplest form in Old Testament times, when Moses received the Law on Mount Sinai. The most important Ten Commandments were written on two stone tablets. These commandments were made more profound and lofty in the Saviour's Sermon on the Mount, in His nine points known as the Beatitudes. But the Lord also confirmed that the Old Testament Ten Commandments were to be known and fulfilled.

The Saviour said, *Think not that I am come to destroy the Law, or the prophets: I am not come to destroy but to fulfill* (Matt. 5:17).

When a young man asked, *Good Master, what good thing shall I do, that I may have eternal life?* — the Lord answered right away, *If thou wilt enter into life, keep the commandments* (Matt. 19:16-17).

However, the Lord taught that these commandments, according to His interpretation, must be kept to a high degree of perfection. Thus, the Lord Jesus Christ suggests that believers should not only shun transgression of the Law, but should not even think about it or desire it, thus requiring from them a more clean heart.

Mount Sinai

CHAPTER 6

The Ten Commandments of God's Law

I. I am the Lord thy God. Thou shalt have no other gods beside Me.

II. Thou shalt not make unto thee any graven image, nor any likeness of anything that is in Heaven above, nor that is in the earth beneath, nor that is in the waters under the earth: thou shalt not bow down to them, nor serve them.

III. Thou shalt not take the Name of the Lord thy God in vain.

IV. Remember the Sabbath day, to keep it holy; Six days shalt thou labor, and do all thy work: but the seventh day is the Sabbath of the Lord thy God.

V. Honor thy father and thy mother that it may be well with thee and that thy days may be long on the earth.

VI. Thou shalt not kill.

VII. Thou shalt not commit adultery.

VIII. Thou shalt not steal.

IX. Thou shalt not bear false witness against thy neighbor.

X. Thou shalt not covet thy neighbor's wife; thou shall not covet thy neighbor's house, nor his land, nor his manservant, nor his maidservant, nor his ox, nor his ass, nor any of his cattle, nor anything that is thy neighbor's.

The Ten Commandments of the Law were arranged on two tablets because they legislate two aspects of love: **love for God and love for neighbor**.

Indicating these two aspects of love, the Lord Jesus Christ in answering the question, *Which is the greatest commandment in the Law?* said, *Thou shalt love the Lord thy God with all thy heart, and with all thy soul, and with all thy mind. This is the first and great commandment. And the second is like unto it, Thou shalt love thy neighbor as thyself. On these two commandments hang all the Law and the prophets* (Matt. 22:37-40).

To love God is our first and most important obligation, because He is our Creator, Provider, and Saviour. *For in Him we live, and move, and have our being* (Acts 17:28).

Then follows the obligation to **love our neighbor**, which serves as an expression of our love for God. Whoever does not love his neighbor does not love God. The Apostle John the Theologian explains, *If a man say, I love God, and hateth his brother, he is a liar: for he that loveth not his brother whom he hath seen, how can he love God whom he hath not seen?* (I John 4:20).

By loving God and neighbor we discover true love for ourself, because true love for ourself consists in fulfilling our obligations towards God and neighbor. It is expressed in care for one's soul, in cleansing oneself of sin, in subordinating the body to the spirit, in limiting our personal necessities. We must guard our health and care for the development of our spiritual strength and capacities in order to manifest our love to God and neighbor.

By this concept, love of ourself is shown not to be a detriment to our neighbor. On the contrary, we owe love to ourselves in order to bring sacrificial love to our neighbor. *Greater love hath no man than this, that a man lay down his life for his friends* (his neighbors) (John 15:13). Love toward ourself and love toward our neighbor must be offered as a sacrifice of love to God. The Lord Jesus Christ speaks about this thus: *He that loveth father or mother more than Me is not worthy of Me; and he that loveth son or daughter more than Me is not worthy of Me. And he that taketh not his cross* (i.e., who, from all his superfluous burdens of life, refuses the suffering and trials which the Lord sends, but instead goes the easy path of wickedness) *and followeth after Me, is not worthy of Me* (Matt. 10:37-38).

If a man first of all loves God, then naturally he cannot fail to love father and mother and children and all his neighbors; and this love is sanctified by Divine Grace. If a man loves anyone of these without loving God, then such love may even be criminal, as, for example, when a man for the happiness of a beloved friend might deprive others of their happiness, treat them unjustly, cruelly, etc.

Thus, although all the commandments and the Law of God are contained in two commandments of love, in order to more clearly show us our obligations to God and neighbor, they are further broken down into the Ten Commandments. Our obligations to God are described in the first four commandments, and our obligations to our neighbor — in the last six commandments.

The First Commandment of the Law of God

1. I am the Lord thy God. Thou shalt have no other gods beside Me.

The first commandment of the Lord God asserts His existence and admonishes us to honor Him, the One true God. We must not render divine homage to anyone but Him. That is, we must study what is written by God and about Him, or theology.

Theology is the highest branch of knowledge. It is our first and most important obligation. All scholarly human knowledge loses its true meaning, its underlying idea and purpose, if it is not illumined by the light of theology. Instead of good, such knowledge leads to a life of much evil.

In order to acquire knowledge of the true God, we must:

1. Read and thoroughly study the Holy Scriptures, which convey to us true and most perfect knowledge of God.

2. Read the works of the Holy Fathers and teachers of the Church, which is necessary in order to understand the Holy Scriptures rightly and to guard oneself from incorrect interpretations and thinking.

3. Frequently attend church, because in the church services are contained lessons about God and His works.

4. Listen to the sermons of the priest and read books of religious and moral content.

5. Study the works of God — nature, as well as the story of the race of man, which reveal to us God's marvelous plan.

This commandment imposes on us definite obligations of worship. We must:

1. **Believe in God**, that is, have the most sincere and firm conviction of His existence.

2. **Walk before the Lord**, that is, always be conscious of God and do everything as before the eyes of God (behave carefully), and always remember that God sees not only our deeds but also our thoughts.

3. **Place our hope in God, love God, and obey God**. Always be ready to do what He commands and not grumble when He does not do for us as we ourselves would like. In fact, only God knows when and what to give to us, and what is profitable and what is harmful to us.

The highest form of love of God is **respect**, or **fear of God** — fear to become estranged from God because of our sins.

4. **Do homage to God, glorify and give thanks to the Lord God**, our Creator, Provider and Saviour, remembering all His gifts and mercy to us.

5. **Fearlessly confess God** before all. Acknowledge that He is our God, and do not abandon the faith even though this confession might bring suffering and even death.

Sins against the first commandment are:

1. **Atheism** — when people completely reject the existence of God. Such people the Prophet David calls fools. *The fool hath said in his heart, There is no God* (Ps.13:1).

2. **Polytheism** — when instead of the One true God, people acknowledge many imaginary gods.

3. **Unbelief** — when people, while acknowledging the existence of God, do not believe in His Divine Providence and Revelation. This unbelief often comes from incorrect education and upbringing, from pride and conceit, from enthusiasm for evil examples, from careless regard for the guidance of the Church, and from a sinful life.

4. **Heresy** — when people imagine or invent teachings contrary to God's truth, or stubbornly and intentionally distort the truth of God.

5. **Schism** — self-willed deviation from the union of Divine worship, from union with the Orthodox Church.

6. **Apostasy** — when people disavow the true faith, fearing such things as persecution and mockery; or from enthusiasm for false teachings.

7. **Despair** — when people, forgetting the endless mercy of God, do not hope to receive from God help and salvation. Horrible examples of despair occur in cases of suicide.

8. **Sorcery** (witchery) — when people, abandoning faith in the power of God, turn to various occult and evil powers.

9. **Superstition** — when people believe in some ordinary thing or occurrence, attributing supernatural powers to it.

10. **Laziness** in prayer and in all pious deeds.

11. **Love for creatures, including people, more than for God**.

12. **Flattery** — when people care more about pleasing other people than pleasing God.

13. **Self-sufficiency** — when people hope more in themselves or in other people than in the mercy and help of God.

The commandment of God does not contradict our obligation to venerate angels and saints of God and to pray to them. We honor them not as God Himself, but as faithful servants of God, who are obedient and who lead God-pleasing lives. The angels and saints of God are close to God and are able to intercede on our behalf. We must ask their help and defense in firm trust that the Lord, for their sake, quickly hears our sinful prayers. The Word of God says, *Pray for one another, that ye may be healed. The effectual fervent prayer of a righteous man availeth much* (James 5:16). *For He is not a God of the dead, but of the living: for all live unto Him* (Luke 20:38).

The Second Commandment of the Law of God

2. Thou shalt not make unto thee any graven image, or any likeness of anything that is in heaven above, or that is in the earth beneath, or that is in the waters under the earth: thou shalt not bow down thyself to them, nor serve them.

The second commandment of the Lord God prohibits idolatry, that is, forbids making any idols for worship, or rendering homage to likenesses of anything that we see in heaven (sun, moon, stars), or that is found on earth (plants, animals, people), or found in the waters (fish). The Lord forbids worshipping and serving these idols instead of the true God, as pagans do.

In forbidding worship of idols, one must never be confused about the Orthodox veneration of holy icons and relics. Protestants and various sectarians criticize us for "worshipping them." But in venerating holy icons we do not consider them gods or idols. They are only likenesses, representations of God, or of the angels or of the saints. The word **icon** comes from the Greek and means **likeness**. In venerating icons and praying before icons, we do not pray to the material icons (the paint, wood or metal), but to the saint who is represented thereon.

Everyone knows how much easier it is to turn one's thoughts to the Saviour when he sees His Most-pure Image or His Cross, than when he sees only empty walls, or a bookcase.

Holy icons are given to us for venerating the memory of the acts of God and His saints and for devoted elevation of our thoughts to God and His saints. Veneration of icons warms our hearts with love for our Creator and Saviour. Holy icons are similar to the Holy Scriptures, except that they are written with faces and objects instead of letters.

Even in the Old Testament icons were used. At the same time that Moses received the commandment forbidding idols, he received from God instructions to place in the Tabernacle, the mobile Hebrew temple, holy gold icons of Cherubim on the lid of the Ark of the Covenant. The Lord said to Moses, *Make them in the two ends of the mercy seat... and there I will meet with thee, and I will commune with thee from above the mercy seat from between the two Cherubim which are upon the Ark of the testimony, of all things which I will give thee in commandment unto the children of Israel* (Exod. 25:18,22). The Lord also ordered Moses to make likenesses of cherubim on the veil separating the Sanctuary from the Holy of Holies; and on the interior side of the veil covering, a fine cloth of ancient times, thought to have been made of linen, fine wool, cotton or silk, which covered not only the top but the sides of the Tabernacle (cf. Exod. 26:1-37).

In Solomon's Temple there were sculptured and embroidered icons of Cherubim on all the walls and on the Temple veil (cf. I Kings 6:27-29; II Chron. 3:7-14). The Cherubim on the Ark of the Covenant were consecrated (cf. II Chron. 3:10). When the Temple was ready, *the glory of the Lord* (in the form of a cloud) *filled the temple* (I Kings 8:11). The likenesses of the Cherubim were pleasing to the Lord, and the people, looking at them, prayed and worshipped.

There were no icons of the Lord God in the Tabernacle or in the Temple of Solomon, because He had not yet revealed Himself in the flesh as God incarnate. There were no likenesses of the Old Testament righteous men, because the people had not yet been redeemed and justified (Rom. 3:9,25; Matt. 11:11).

The Lord Jesus Christ sent a miraculous icon of His Face to King Abgar of Edessa. It was known as the **Icon-Not-Made-By-Hands**. Praying before the Icon-Not-Made-By-Hands of Christ, Abgar was healed of an incurable illness. The Evangelist Luke was a physician and an artist. He painted and left for posterity icons of the Mother of God. Several of them are found in Russia and in Greece.

Many holy icons have been glorified by miracles.

Likenesses of animals or even of the Devil do not defile a holy icon if they are necessary to depict an event necessary for visual instruction. As is known, mention of them in writing does not defile the Holy Scriptures.

Nor does veneration of holy relics contradict the second commandment. In the holy relics we honor the Grace of God, which acts through the remains of the saints.

For Christians, idolatry in the form handed down to us from pagans is impossible. However, instead of uncivilized idolatry, there exist among us much more subtle forms of idolatry, such idolatry as worship of sinful passions like greed, gluttony, pride, vanity, lust and so on.

Covetousness (greed) is the desire to acquire wealth. The Apostle Paul says that *covetousness... is idolatry* (Col. 3:5). For the rich man love of gain is an idol which he serves and worships more than God.

Gluttony consists of love of dainty dishes and drunkenness. The Apostle Paul says about people who put the feeling of satisfaction for food and drink as the highest thing in life, that their *god is their belly* (Philip. 3:19).

Pride and Vanity. The proud and vain man has an excessively high opinion of his worth, his intelligence, beauty, and wealth. The vain man considers only himself. He considers his ideas and wishes higher than the will of God. He regards the opinions and advice of other people with contempt and derision, but his own ideas he does not reject, no matter how false they may be. The greedy and vain person makes an idol of himself, both for himself and for others.

By prohibiting these lesser idols, the second commandment inspires the following virtues in their place: **unacquisitiveness, generosity, self-denial, fasting, and humility**.

The Third Commandment of the Law of God

3. Thou shalt not take the Name of the Lord thy God in vain.

The third commandment forbids us to pronounce the name of God in vain, without due reverence. One uses the name of God in vain when one pronounces it in empty conversation, in jest and in sport.

Forbidding the use of God's name thoughtlessly or disrespectfully, this commandment forbids the sins which come from thoughtlessness and irreverence in regard to God. Among such sins are:

Swearing — thoughtless, habitual oaths in casual conversation;

Blasphemy — audacious words against God;

Sacrilege — when people scoff or jest at sacred things;

Breaking promises given to God;

Perjury (oath breaking);

Making false oaths by the name of God.

The name of God must be pronounced with awe and reverence, in prayer, in studies about God, and in lawful vows and oaths.

Reverent, lawful vows are not forbidden by this commandment. God Himself used an oath about which the Apostle Paul reminisces in his epistle to the Hebrews: *For men verily swear by the greater: and an oath for confirmation is to them an end of all strife. Wherein God, willing more abundantly to show unto the heirs of promise the immutability of His counsel, confirmed it by an oath* (Heb. 6:16-17).

The Fourth Commandment of the Law of God

4. Remember the Sabbath day, to keep it holy. Six days shalt thou labor, and do all thy work, but the seventh day is the Sabbath of the Lord thy God.

The fourth commandment of the Lord God directs that six days be spent in labor and devoted to duties such as one's vocation, but that the seventh day be devoted to the service of God, for holy work and acts pleasing to God.

Holy works and acts pleasing to God are understood to be: work for the salvation of one's soul, prayer both in church and at home, study of the commandments of God, enlightenment of the mind and heart by wholesome learning, reading of the Holy Scriptures and other spiritually helpful books, pious conversation, helping the poor, visiting the sick and prisoners, comforting the grieving, and other good deeds.

In the Old Testament, the Sabbath (which in Hebrew means rest, peace) is celebrated on the seventh day of the week, Saturday, in remembrance of God's creation of the world (on the seventh day God rested from acts of creation). In the New Testament, at the time of the Apostles, it began to be celebrated on the first day of the week, Sunday, in remembrance of the resurrection of Christ.

In the category of the seventh day it is necessary to include not only the day of the Resurrection, but also other feast days and fasts established by the Church. In the Old Testament the Sabbath also included other feasts: Passover, Pentecost, the Feast of Tabernacles, etc.

The most important Christian feast day is called "The Feast of Feasts" and "The Triumph of Triumphs," the **Bright Resurrection of Christ**, called **Holy Pascha** (Easter), which occurs on the first Sunday after the spring full moon, after the Jewish Passover, in the period between the 22nd of March (April 4th new style) and the 25th of April (May 8th, new style).

Then follow the twelve great feasts established to honor our Lord Jesus Christ and His Mother, the Holy Virgin Mary:

1. The Nativity of the Theotokos September 8 (21, n.s.).

2. The Entry into the Temple of the Theotokos, November 21 (December 4, n.s.).

3. The Annunciation of the Most-holy Virgin Mary, March 25 (April 7, n.s.).

4. The Nativity of Christ, December 25 (January 7, n.s.).

5. The Entry of the Lord, February 2 (15, n.s.).

6. The Theophany (or Epiphany), January 6 (19, n.s.).

7. The Transfiguration of our Lord Jesus Christ, August 6 (19, n.s.).

8. The Entrance of the Lord into Jerusalem (Palm Sunday), the last Sunday before **Pascha**.

9. The Ascension of our Lord Jesus Christ, on the fortieth day after **Pascha**.

10. Pentecost, or Trinity Sunday, on the fiftieth day after **Pascha**.

11. The Elevation of the Precious and Life-giving Cross, September 14 (27, n.s.).

12. The Dormition of the Mother of God, August 15 (28, n.s.).

Of the remaining feast days, some of the most important are:

The Circumcision of our Lord Jesus Christ, January 1 (14, n.s.).

The Protection of the Mother of God, October 1 (14, n.s.).

The Kazan Icon of the Mother of God, October 22 (November 4, n.s.).

The Nativity of St. John the Baptist, June 24 (July 7, n.s.).

The Beheading of St. John the Baptist, August 29 (September 11, n.s.).

The feast of the Apostles, St. Peter and St. Paul, June 29 (July 12, n.s.).

The Apostle John the Theologian, May 8 (May 21 n.s.) and September 26 (October 9, n.s.).

The feasts of St. Nicholas the Wonderworker, May 9 (May 22, n.s.) and December 6 (19, n.s.).

Fasts established by the Church are:

1. **The Great Fast**, before Pascha.

The Fast lasts for **seven weeks**: six weeks are the fast itself and the seventh week is Holy Week — in remembrance of the suffering of Christ the Saviour.

2. **Nativity Fast**, before the feast day of Nativity, the birth of Christ.

It begins on the 14th of November (27, n.s.), the day after commemorating the Apostle Philip and is therefore sometimes called the fast of St. Philip. The fast lasts for forty days.

3. **Dormition Fast**, before the feast day of the Dormition of the Mother of God.

It lasts for **two weeks**, from the 1st of August (August 14, n.s.) until August 14 (27, n.s.).

4. **The Apostles'** or **Peter's Fast**, before the feast day of the Apostles Peter and Paul.

It begins one week after Trinity Sunday (Pentecost) and continues until the 29th of June (July 12, n.s.). Its length is determined by whether Pascha is early or late. The longest it can be is six weeks, and the shortest is a week and one day.

One day fasts:

1. **Nativity Eve** — the day before the Birth of Christ, 24th of December (January 6, n.s.). An especially strict fast during the Nativity Fast. Customarily, one does not eat until the appearance of the first star, and then only strict lenten food, no meat, fish or dairy products.

2. **The Eve of the Theophany** — the day before the Baptism of the Lord, the 6th of January (January 19, n.s.).

3. The day of the **Beheading of St. John the Baptist**, 29th of August (September 11, n.s.).

4. The day of the **Elevation of the Cross of the Lord**, in commemoration of the finding of the Cross of the Lord, 14th of September (September 27, n.s.).

5. **Wednesdays** and **Fridays** of every week. Wednesday — in remembrance of the betrayal of the Saviour by Judas. Friday — in remembrance of Christ's suffering and death on the cross.

There is no fasting on Wednesdays and Fridays in the following weeks: in Bright Week, the week of Pascha; in the interval between Christmas and Theophany; in the week of the Holy Trinity (from Pentecost until the beginning of Peter's fast), in the week of the Publican and the Pharisee (before the Great Fast); and in Cheese-fare week immediately preceding the Great Fast, when dairy products, but not meat, are allowed.

At the time of the fasts it is especially necessary to resolve to cleanse oneself of all bad habits and passions such as anger, envy, lust and enmity. One must refrain from a dissipating, carefree life, from games, from shows and spectacles, from dancing. One must not read books which give rise to impure thoughts and desires in the soul. One must not eat meat or dairy products, since according to the experience of the Saints these foods strengthen our passions and make it more difficult to pray, but only permitted fasting foods such as vegetables, and when permitted, fish, and only making use of these foods in moderation. During a fast of many days one should have confession and receive Holy Communion.

Those who break the fourth commandment are those who are lazy on the first six days, doing no work, as well as those who work on a holy day.

No less guilty are those who may cease worldly pursuits and work, but who spend the time in amusements and games, who indulge in pleasure and drunkenness, not thinking about serving God. Especially sinful is indulging in distractions the evening before a feast day, when we should be at the Vigil, and in the morning, after the Liturgy. For Orthodox Christians a feast day begins in the evening when the All-night Vigil is served. To devote this time to dancing, movies, or other diversions instead of prayer, is to make a mockery of the feast day.

The Fifth Commandment of the Law of God

5. Honor thy father and thy mother that it may be well with thee and that thy days may be long on the earth.

The fifth commandment of the Lord God orders us to honor our parents and for this promises a happy and long life. To honor parents means to love them, to be respectful toward them, to refrain from offending them by either word or act, to obey them, to help them in labor, to care for them when they are in need, especially when they are sick and old, and also to pray for them to God both during this life and when they die. Disrespect toward a parent is a great sin. In the Old Testament, anyone who slandered his father or his mother was punished by death (Mark 7:10; Exod. 21:17).

We must also give equal honor to those persons who have authority over us as parents to us. Among such people are **pastors** and **spiritual fathers**, laboring for our salvation, instructing us in the faith and praying for us; **government officials,** who work for our domestic tranquility and defend us against oppression and plundering; **teachers** and **benefactors**, who try to teach us and provide everything that is good and useful to us; and in general, our elders, having much experience in life and who therefore can give us good advice. It is a sin not to respect our elders, especially those in old age. It is a sin to regard their experience with distrust, indifference, and sometimes to refer to their remarks and instruction with derision, to consider them "backward" people, and to consider that their view is outmoded, has served its time. Even in the Old Testament the Lord said through Moses, *Thou shalt rise up before the hoary head, and honor the face of the old man, and fear thy God* (Lev. 19:32).

But if it happens that parents or superiors require of one something that goes against our faith and the Law of God, then one must say to them, as the Apostles said to the leaders of the Jews: *Whether it be right in the sight of God to hearken unto you more than unto God, judge ye* (Acts 4:19). Then one must suffer for the faith and the Law of God no matter what happens.

The Sixth Commandment of the Law of God

6. Thou shalt not kill.

The sixth commandment of the Lord God forbids murder, taking the lives of other people, or taking one's own life (suicide).

Life is the greatest gift of God. Therefore, to deprive oneself or someone else of life is a most terrible, grave, and enormous sin. Suicide is the most terrible of all sins committed against the sixth commandment, because in suicide, besides the sin of killing, there is also the grave sin of despair, grumbling against God, and insolent uprising against the

Providence of God. Furthermore, suicide precludes the possibility of repentance.

A person is guilty of murder even if he kills another person accidentally, without thinking. Such a murder is a grievous sin, because in this case the murderer is guilty due to his carelessness.

A person is guilty of murder even when he does not commit the murder himself, but promotes the murder or allows someone else to do it. For example:

1. A judge, condemning the accused to death when his innocence is known.

2. Anyone who does not save a neighbor from death, when he is fully capable of doing it.

3. Anyone who helps another commit murder by his decree, advice, collaboration, or rationalization; or who condones and justifies a death and by that gives opportunity for more killing.

4. Anyone who by hard labor or cruel punishment exhausts victims into a weakened state and thus hastens their death.

5. Anyone who through self-indulgence in various vices curtails one's own life.

Other sins against the sixth commandment are: wishing that someone were dead, not rendering help to the indigent and sick, not living with other people in peace and concord, but on the contrary, maintaining hatred, envy, and malice towards others, instigating quarrels, brawls, and distress among others. Sin against the sixth commandment is doing anything which injures the weak, children in particular. The Gospel of Christ says, *Whosoever hateth his brother is a murderer* (I John 3:15).

Besides physical killing, there is yet a more terrible and accountable murder: spiritual killing. Among the sins of spiritual murder is **seduction**. That is, when one leads astray or seduces his neighbor into unbelief or into a life of vice, and by this renders the soul of his neighbor liable to spiritual death.

The Saviour said, *But whosoever shall offend one of these little ones which believe in Me, it were better for him that a millstone were hanged about his neck, and that he were drowned in the depth of the sea... woe to that man by whom the offense cometh!* (Matt. 18:6-7).

In order to avoid sin against the sixth commandment, Christians must help the poor, serve the sick, comfort the sorrowful, lighten the conditions of the unfortunate, with everyone be kind and loving, reconcile themselves with anyone who has grown angry, forgive offenses, do good to enemies, and refrain from harmful examples, either by word or deed, especially before children.

It is impossible to equate criminal murder with the killing that occurs in battle. War is a great social evil, but at the same time war is an enormous catastrophe permitted by the Lord for a lesson and correction of people, just as He permits epidemics, starvation, fires, and other misfortunes. Therefore, killing in a war is not viewed by the Church as a particular sin of man. Furthermore, every soldier should be ready, according to the commandment of Christ, to "lay down his life for his friends," for the defense of his faith and his homeland.

Among the military there are many saints glorified by miracles.

However, even in war it is possible to be guilty of murder, when, for example, a soldier kills someone who has surrendered, or when a soldier allows brutality, etc.

Capital punishment of a criminal applies also to social ills and is a great evil. But it is allowed in exceptional cases when according to justice, it appears that it alone can stop a multitude of murders and crimes. But in terms of justice, the administrators carrying out the execution answer before God. Capital punishment of hardened criminals is often the only means by which they will be brought to repentance. Note that without the will of God, not a hair would fall from anyone's head.

The Seventh Commandment of the Law of God

7. Thou shalt not commit adultery.

The seventh commandment forbids adultery, that is, unfaithfulness to one's spouse and all unlawful lust.

God forbids a husband and a wife to break the bonds of mutual faith and love. Of the unmarried, God requires pure thoughts and desires, to be chaste in word and deed, in thought and desire.

In order to do this it is necessary to avoid everything that could give rise to unclean feelings in the heart: obscenity, immodest and shameless songs and dances, suggestive plays, movies, and pictures, immoral books, drunkenness, etc.

God's word commands us to maintain our bodies in purity, because our body *is a member of the body of Christ and a temple of the Holy Spirit.* Fornicators, and all who indulge in lustful acts or imagination sin against their own bodies, they weaken the health of their body, inflict illness upon it and impair its spiritual capability, especially imagination and memory.

The Eighth Commandment of the Law of God

8. Thou shalt not steal.
There are many forms of stealing:
1. **Theft,** to steal someone else's property.
2. **Robbery,** taking someone else's property by force.
3. **Sacrilege,** to misuse that which belongs to the Church.
4. **Extortion,** or **bribery,** to unlawfully accept gifts from people for goods or services which are supposed to be rendered free of charge.
5. **Parasitism,** to accept renumeration or payment for services which are supposed to be rendered and then fail to do the work.
6. **Usury,** to charge an exorbitant rate of interest on a loan.

7. **Fraud**, to appropriate someone else's property by cunning. For example, to avoid paying debts, to embezzle funds without regard for the proprietor's things or money, to cheat in measuring or deceive in weighing for a sale; to hold back the wages of a hired worker; to take a sum of money for some needy person, and then keep it for something else, and so on. Also, children deceive when they are lazy students, while at the same time their parents and society pay for their education, and teachers expend labor on their behalf.

Forbidding every form of taking property of a neighbor, this commandment instructs us to be **unmercenary**, **honest**, **industrious**, **merciful** and **truthful**. In order to avoid sin against this commandment, one must love one's neighbor as much as oneself, and not do anything to him that he would not like to have done to himself.

The highest virtue inspired by the eighth commandment is complete poverty, renunciation of all property. But God does not obligate everyone to this virtue. He proposes it only to those who wish to attain high moral perfection. *If thou wilt be perfect, go and sell what thou hast, and give to the poor, and thou shalt have treasure in heaven* (Matt. 19:21).

Many spiritual heroes have followed the advice of this Gospel passage: St. Anthony the Great, St. Paul of Thebes, St. Nicholas the Wonderworker, and many others.

The Ninth Commandment of the Law of God

9. Thou shalt not bear false witness.

The ninth commandment of the Lord God forbids us to speak falsehoods about our neighbor, and in general forbids all lies. For example:

1. Perjury in court.
2. False complaints.
3. Gossip, slander, and defamation, which are diabolical acts since the word "devil" means libeler, slanderer, defamer.

Repugnant to Christians are even those little white lies which are not intended to cause harm to a neighbor. Lying is not becoming to the calling of a Christian and not in harmony with love and consideration for one's neighbor. The Apostle Paul says, *Wherefore putting away lying, speak every man truth with his neighbor: for we are members one of another* (Eph. 4:25).

It is never appropriate to blame or judge others, if we have not been specifically required to do so because of the responsibility of our position or duty. *Judge not that ye be not judged*, says the Saviour.

It is necessary to keep in mind that **judging, reproach, and mockery will not reform a neighbor; only love, tolerance, and good harmony** will. It is also necessary to always bear in mind that each of us has many weaknesses and faults.

One must always keep a restraint on his tongue. One must speak only the truth and curb oneself from disparaging remarks and idle chatter. Speech is a gift of God. Jesus Christ said, *But I say unto you, that every idle word that men shall speak, they shall give account thereof in the day of judgment. For by thy words thou shalt be justified, and by thy words thou shalt be condemned* (Matt. 12: 36-37).

The Tenth Commandment of the Law of God

10. Thou shalt not covet thy neighbor's wife, thou shalt not covet thy neighbor's house, nor his land, nor his manservant, nor his ox, nor his ass, nor anything that is thy neighbor's.

The tenth commandment of the Lord God forbids not only doing something bad to someone near us, but also forbids even bad desires and thoughts in connection with them.

The sin against this commandment is called **envy**. A person who is envious, who entertains the idea of wanting something that belongs to someone else, can pass from the desire to the evil deed.

But beyond this, envy in itself can defile the soul, rendering it impure before God, as it is stated in the Word of God, *The thoughts of the wicked are an abomination to the Lord* (Prov. 15:26, Wis. of Sol. 2:25).

One of the main tasks of true Christianity is to cleanse one's soul of all impurity, in accordance with the admonition of the Apostle, *Let us cleanse ourselves from all filthiness of the flesh and spirit, perfecting holiness in the fear of God* (II Cor. 7:1).

In order to avoid sin against the tenth commandment, it is necessary to maintain a pure heart, free of any earthly attachment, free of all wicked thoughts and desires, and to be satisfied with that which one has, to thank God for it, never to desire anything that is anyone else's, but to rejoice for others in what they have.

CHAPTER 7

The Nine Beatitudes

The Beatitudes, or the commandments of blessedness, given us by the Saviour, do not in anyway annul the commandments of the Law. On the contrary, these commandments complement each other.

The Ten Commandments of the Law are restricted to prohibiting those acts which would be sinful. The Beatitudes explain to us how we may attain Christian perfection or grace.

The Ten Commandments were given in Old Testament times to restrain wild, primitive people from evil. The Beatitudes are given to Christians to show them what disposition to have in order to draw closer and closer to God, to acquire holiness, and together with that, blessedness, which is the highest degree of happiness.

Holiness, arising from proximity to God, is the loftiest blessedness, the greatest happiness that anyone could possibly desire.

The Old Testament Law is a strict code of righteousness, but the New Testament law of Christ is the law of Divine love and grace, the only means by which people are given the strength to live in full observance of the Law of God and to approach perfection.

Jesus Christ, calling us to the eternal Kingdom of God, shows us the way to it through fulfillment of His commandments. For their fulfillment He, the King of Heaven and earth, promises **eternal blessedness** in the future eternal life.

Our Saviour teaches:

1. Blessed are the poor in spirit, for theirs is the Kingdom of Heaven.

2. Blessed are they that mourn, for they shall be comforted.

3. Blessed are the meek, for they shall inherit the earth.

4. Blessed are they that do hunger and thirst after righteousness, for they shall be filled.

5. Blessed are the merciful, for they shall obtain mercy.

6. Blessed are the pure in heart, for they shall see God.

7. Blessed are the peacemakers, for they shall be called the children of God.

8. Blessed are they which are persecuted for righteousness' sake, for theirs is the Kingdom of Heaven.

9. Blessed are you when men shall revile you, and persecute you, and shall say all manner of evil against you falsely, for My sake. Rejoice, and be exceeding glad; for great is your reward in Heaven.

In each of these teachings of the Lord, one should observe the commandments on the one hand and promises of reward on the other.

For the fulfillment of the commandments of the Beatitudes it is necessary to have contact with God through **prayer**, both internal and external. One must struggle against sinful inclinations through **fasting,** abstinence, and so on.

The First Beatitude

1. Blessed are the poor in spirit, for theirs is the Kingdom of Heaven.

Blessed — joyful in the highest degree and pleasing to God; **poor in spirit** — humble, those who are conscious of their imperfections and unworthiness before God, and never think that they are better or more holy than others.

Spiritual lowliness is the conviction that our entire life and all our spiritual and physical blessings, such as life, health, strength, spiritual capability, knowledge, riches, and every good thing of life, all this is the gift of our Creator God. Without help from Heaven, it is impossible to acquire either material well-being or spiritual riches. All this is the gift of God.

Spiritual lowliness is called **humility. Humility** is the foundation of all Christian virtue, because it is the opposite of pride, and pride introduced all evil into the world. Due to pride the first among the angles became the Devil; the first people sinned, their descendants quarrelled and went to war among themselves from pride. *The first sin was pride* (Ecclus. 10:15).

Without humility it is impossible to return to God. Nor are any of the other Christian virtues possible. Humility permits us to know ourselves, to correctly assess our worth and deficiencies. It acts beneficially in the fulfillment of our obligations to our neighbor, arouses and strengthens in us faith in God, hope and love for Him. It attracts the mercy of God to us and also disposes people to us.

The Word of God says, *A sacrifice unto God is a broken spirit; a heart that is broken and humbled God will not despise* (Ps. 50:17). *Surely he scorneth the scorners: but he giveth grace unto the lowly* (Prov. 3:34). *Learn of me,* instructs the Saviour, *for I am meek and lowly in heart: and ye shall find rest unto your souls* (Matt. 11:29).

Physical misery or privation can result in the acquisition of much spiritual humility if this privation or need is accepted with good will, without a murmur. But physical privation does not always result in spiritual humility, it can lead to bitterness.

Even the wealthy can be spiritually humble if they understand that visible, material wealth is decadent and transitory, fleeting, and that it is no substitute for spiritual riches. They must understand the word of the Lord, *For what is a man profited, if he shall gain the whole world, and lose his own soul?* (Matt. 16:26).

But Christian humility must be strictly distinguished from self-seeking self-abasement, such as fawning and flattery, which discredit human dignity.

It is necessary to strictly reject so-called "noble self-love" or "defense against affronts to one's honor," which reflect prejudices, pernicious superstitions which were inherited from **Roman paganism** hostile to Christianity. The true Christian must decisively renounce these superstitions which resulted in the anti-Christian and shameful custom of the duel and revenge.

In reward for meekness of spirit, humility, the Lord Jesus Christ promises the Kingdom of Heaven, a life of eternal blessedness. Participation in the Kingdom of God for the humble begins here and now — by means of faith and hope in God; but the ultimate reward in all of its fullness will be seen in the future life.

The Mount Where the Beatitudes Were Given

The Second Beatitude

2. Blessed are they that mourn, for they shall be comforted.

The weeping about which the second beatitude speaks is first of all true tribulation of heart, and repentant tears for our sins, over our guilt before the merciful God (for example, the tears of the Apostle Peter after his renunciation).

For godly sorrow worketh repentance to salvation not to be repented of: but the sorrow of the world worketh death, said the Apostle Paul (II Cor. 7:10).

Tribulation and tears coming from misfortunes which befall us can be spiritually beneficial. For example, the death of one of our close ones can result in beneficial tears, if the sorrow is permeated by faith and hope, patience and devotion to the will of God. Jesus Christ Himself wept over the death of Lazarus.

Even more so can tears and tribulation lead to blessedness when they are shed over the suffering of our unfortunate neighbor, if these sincere tears are accompanied by Christian deeds of love and mercy.

Worldly grief is grief without hope in God. It proceeds not from acknowledgment of one's sins before God, but rather from disappointment in ambition, aspiration to power, desire for gain. Such sadness, characterized by despondency and despair, leads to spiritual death, which can also result in physical death, by suicide or simply weakness due to lack of will to live. An example of such grief is that of Judas Iscariot, the betrayer of Christ the Saviour.

As a reward for mourning the Lord promises that they that mourn will be comforted. They will receive forgiveness of sins, and through this, internal peace. The mourners will receive eternal joy, eternal blessedness.

The Third Beatitude

3. Blessed are the meek, for they shall inherit the earth.

Meekness is peaceful, fully developed Christian love, free from all malice. It is manifested in the spirit of a man who never becomes angry, and never permits himself to grumble against God or people.

Meek people do not become irritated and they do not vex or aggravate other people. Christian meekness expresses itself mainly in patient endurance of insults inflicted by others and is the opposite of anger, malice, self-exaltation and vengeance.

A meek person always regrets the hardness of heart of the offending party. He desires his correction, prays to God for forgiveness of his deeds, remembering the precept of the Apostle: *If it be possible, as much as lieth in you, live peaceably with all men. Dearly beloved, avenge not yourselves, but rather give place unto wrath: for it is written, Vengeance is mine; I will repay, saith the Lord* (Romans 12:18-19).

The best example of meekness given to us is that of our Lord Jesus Christ praying on the cross for His enemies. He taught us to not take vengeance on our enemies but to do good to them. *Take my yoke upon you and learn of me; for I am meek and lowly in heart: and ye shall find rest unto your souls* (Matt. 11:29). Meekness tames even the hardest hearts. We can be convinced of this by observing the lives of people, and we find confirmation of it throughout the history of Christian persecutions.

A Christian may become angry only with himself, at his own fall into sin, and at the tempter — the Devil.

The Lord promises the meek that they will inherit the earth. This promise indicates that meek people in the present life will be preserved on earth by the power of God, in spite of all the intrigues of men and the most cruel persecution. But in the future life, they will be heirs of the heavenly homeland, the **new earth** (II Peter 3:13) with its eternal blessings.

The Fourth Beatitude

4. Blessed are they that do hunger and thirst after righteousness, for they shall be filled.

Those who hunger and thirst for righteousness are those people who deeply acknowledge their sinfulness, their guilt before God, and have a burning desire for righteousness. They try to serve God by a righteous life according to the commandments of Christ, which requires from Christians the most holy righteousness in all their relations with their neighbors.

The expression "hunger and thirst" indicates that our yearning for righteousness must be very strong, as strong as our desire to appease our appetite and thirst. King David beautifully expressed such yearning, *As the hart panteth after the fountains of water, so panteth my soul after thee, O God. My soul thirsted for God, the mighty the living* (Ps. 4:1-2).

God promised that those who hunger and thirst for righteousness will be **filled**. By this is meant spiritual satisfaction, comprised of internal spiritual peace, a calm conscience, justification, and forgiveness. Such satisfaction in the present, earthly life occurs only in part. The Lord reveals the mysteries of His kingdom to those who hunger and thirst after righteousness, more than to others. Their hearts in this world are delighted with knowledge revealed in the divine truths of the Gospel, in Orthodox teachings.

Full satiety, full satisfaction of the holy yearnings of the human soul, and from this highest joy and blessedness, will be granted them in the future, blessed life with God. As the psalmist King David says, *I shall be filled when Thy glory is made manifest to me* (Ps. 16:16).

The Fifth Beatitude

5. Blessed are the merciful, for they shall obtain mercy.

The merciful are those who have compassion on others, who with all their hearts pity those who have fallen into misfortune or unhappiness, and who try to help them with good works.

Works of mercy are both physical and spiritual.

Bodily works of mercy:
1. Feeding the hungry.
2. Giving drink to the thirsty.
3. Clothing the naked.
4. Visiting those in prison.
5. Visiting the sick and helping them recover or preparing them for a Christian death.
6. Inviting strangers and foreigners and travellers into one's home and giving them rest.
7. Burying the dead.

Spiritual works of mercy:
1. By word and example *to convert the sinner from the error of his way* (James 5:20).
2. Teaching the ignorant truth and goodness.
3. Dispensing good and timely advice to neighbors who are in distress or danger.
4. Comforting the grieving.
5. Refraining from returning evil for evil.
6. Forgiving offenses with all one's heart.
7. Praying to God for everyone.

To the merciful, God promises in return that they will **receive mercy**. In the future judgment of Christ they will be shown the special mercy for the righteous. They will be delivered from eternal punishment for their sins to the degree to which they showed mercy to others on earth (See Matt: 25:31-46).

The Sixth Beatitude

6. Blessed are the pure in heart, for they shall see God.

The pure in heart are those people who not only do not sin openly, but who do not conceal unclean thoughts, desires and feelings in their hearts. The hearts of such people are free from attachment and infatuation with physical, earthly things. In general they are free from sinful passions caused by self-centeredness, egotism and pride. People with pure hearts unceasingly think about God.

In order to acquire a pure heart, it is necessary to observe the fasts proclaimed by the Church, and to guard oneself against gluttony, drunkenness, depraved spectacles and amusements, improper teachings and indecent books.

Purity of heart is far superior to simple sincerity. Sincerity requires only that a person be candid and single hearted in relation to his neighbor. But purity of heart requires complete suppression of depraved thoughts and constant remembrance of God and His holy commandments.

To the pure in heart God promises that they will see God. Here on earth they will see Him through Grace, mysteriously, with the spiritual eyes of their hearts. They can see God in His revelations, images and likenesses. In the future, eternal life, they will see God *as He is* (I John 3:2). Furthermore, since contemplation of God is a source of the highest blessing, the promise to see God is a promise of the highest degree of blessedness.

The Seventh Beatitude

7. Blessed are the peacemakers, for they shall be called the children of God.

Peacemakers are people living with everyone in peace and harmony and fostering peace among people. When other people are at enmity among themselves they try to reconcile them, or at least pray to God for their reconciliation.

Peacemakers remember the words of the Saviour, *Peace I leave with you, My peace I give unto you* (John 14:27). *If it be possible, as much as lieth in you, live peaceably with all men,* said the Apostle Paul (Romans 12:18).

To the peacemakers the Lord promises that they will be called sons of God. They will be the closest to God, heirs of God, joint-heirs with Christ. The peacemakers by their spiritual feat resemble the Only-begotten Son of God, Jesus Christ, Who came to earth to reconcile sinful people with Divine judgment and establish peace among people in place of the animosity reigning among them. Therefore to the peacemakers is promised the epithet, "sons of God," and inexpressible blessedness.

The Eighth Beatitude

8. Blessed are they which are persecuted for righteousness' sake, for theirs is the Kingdom of Heaven.

For righteousness' sake, is meant to live righteously according to the commandments of God, and resolutely fulfilling Christian obligations. **Persecuted** — for their righteous and pious life, they suffer oppression, persecution, privation and adversity at the hands of the unrighteous enemies of truth and goodness, but nothing can cause them to waver from the truth.

Persecution is inevitable for Christians living according to the Gospel's righteousness, because evil people detest righteousness, as truth exposes their evil deeds, and always persecute people who stand up for the truth. The Only-begotten Son of God, Jesus Christ, was Himself crucified by haters of God's truth. For all His followers He predicted: *If they have persecuted Me, they will also persecute you* (John 15:20). *All that will live godly in Christ Jesus shall suffer persecution*, says the Apostle Paul (II Tim. 3:12).

In order to endure persecution patiently for righteousness' sake, a person must have love for the truth, be steadfast and firm in virtuous living, have courage and patience, and faith and hope in the help and protection of God.

To those persecuted for righteousness' sake, for their struggles in confessing the truth, the Lord promises the Kingdom of Heaven, spiritual triumph, joy and blessedness in the heavenly dwellings of the future eternal life (see Luke 22: 28-30).

The Ninth Beatitude

9. Blessed are ye when men shall revile you, and persecute you, and shall say all manner of evil against you falsely, for my sake. Rejoice, and be exceeding glad, for great is your reward in Heaven.

In the last, the ninth commandment, our Lord Jesus Christ calls especially blessed those who for the sake of Christ and for the true Orthodox faith in Him, patiently bear disgrace, persecution, malice, defamation, mockery, privation and even death. Such a spiritual feat is known as **martyrdom**. There is no higher spiritual feat than martyrdom.

The courage of Christian martyrs must be distinguished from fanaticism, which is irrational zeal not according to reason. Christian courage must also be distinguished from the lack of feeling brought on by despair or pretended indifference, with which some criminals because of their incorrigible hardness and pride, serve out their sentences and go to execution.

Christian courage is based on the highest of Christian virtues, on faith in God, on hope in God, on love for God and neighbor, on complete obedience and unshaken faith in the Lord God.

The highest form of martyrdom was suffered by Jesus Christ Himself, and in like manner, the Apostles and an innumerable multitude of Christians, who with joy went to martyrdom for the name of Christ.

Wherefore seeing we also are compassed about with so great a cloud of witnesses, let us lay aside every weight and the sin which doth so easily beset us, and let us run with patience the race that is set before us, and looking unto Jesus the Author and Finisher of our faith, Who for the joy that was set before Him endured the cross, despising the shame, and is set down at the right hand of the throne of God. For consider Him that endured such contradiction of sinners against Himself, lest ye be wearied and faint in your minds (Heb. 12:1-3).

For the spiritual feat of martyrdom, the Lord promises a reward in Heaven. But here on earth the Lord glorifies many martyrs for their firm confession of faith with incorruptible bodies and miracles.

If ye be reproached for the name of Christ, happy are ye; for the spirit of glory and of God resteth upon you: on their part He is evil spoken of, but on your part He is glorified. But let none of you suffer as a murderer, or as a thief, or as an evildoer, or as a busybody in other men's matters. Yet if any man suffer as a Christian, let him not be ashamed; but let him glorify God on this behalf (I Pet. 4:14-16).

Numberless **Christians martyrs rejoiced during unspeakable torture**, accounts of which are preserved in factual accounts of lives of the Saints. Note: In Roman courts, special scribes were obligated to write protocols (official records) of judicial procedures and legal decisions. Such protocols of interrogations, made in Roman courts during the legal process of Christian martyrs, after the period of persecutions were carefully preserved by the Church. The protocols came to be trustworthy accounts of the feats of martyrdom of the Christians.

Discussion on the Meaning of Evil

The concept of evil in the world imposes a grave burden of doubt in the hearts of many faithful people. It seems inconceivable that God would permit evil. In fact, God in His Omnipotence could easily eliminate evil. How could a merciful God allow the evil deed of a single offender doom thousands, sometimes millions, or even half of humanity to poverty, grief or disaster? What then is the meaning of evil? With God nothing is without reason. In order to answer this question, it is necessary to recall what evil is.

By the term evil we do not mean suffering, need and deprivation, but sin and moral guilt. God does not desire evil. Almighty God cannot approve of evil. More than that, God forbids evil. God punishes evil. **Evil or sin is in contradiction to the will of God**.

Sin began, as we know, when the highest angel, created by God, insolently rejected obedience to the blessed will of God and became the Devil. **Evil is caused by the Devil**. He inspires or influences the occurrence of sin in man.

It is not the body which is the source of sin as many believe. The body becomes an instrument of sin or of good not of itself but through the will of a person. True faith in Christ elucidates the following two causes of sin in the world:

1. The first cause lies in the free will of man. Our free will is the mark of our likeness to God. This gift of God elevates mankind to the highest of all earthly creatures. By freely choosing good and rejecting evil man exalts God, glorifies Him and perfects himself.

In the book of the Wisdom of Sirach (Ecclesiasticus 15:14), it says, *He (God) in the beginning made man and left him in the hand of his own free will.*

By this God gives to people of good will the possibility to attain Heaven, and to people of evil will, the other world. However it happens, the result is only by means of a person's free will.

Saint Cyril of Jerusalem says, "If nature were fused together and it were not possible to do good by free will, then for whom would God prepare the inexplicable crown? Sheep are gentle, but they will never be crowned for their gentleness, because their gentleness comes not from their own free will but their very nature."

Saint Basil the Great says, "Why is not sinlessness incorporated into our nature, so that it would be impossible to sin, even if we wanted to? You do not recognize good and faithful servants when you keep them restricted, but only when you see that they voluntarily fulfill their responsibilities before you. Virtue comes on the condition of free will, not of necessity; and free will depends on the condition that we be free. Therefore, whoever reproaches the Creator for not creating us sinless prefers the irrational, immovable nature, not having any yearnings, to the nature gifted with judgment and independence." In other words, he prefers robots to intelligent creatures.

Thus, the internal cause for the origin of evil, or sin, consists of the free will of man.

2. The second basis for the existence of evil consists in the fact that God directs evil to good. But God does not tolerate evil for the sake of good. For God, it is not necessary to pay such a high price.

God does not wish for evil under any circumstances. But when evil penetrated into the world through the fault of sinful people, then God, in His plan for the world, compelled even evil to serve good. For example, the sons of Jacob sold his brother Joseph into slavery. They committed an evil deed, but God turned the evil into good. Joseph rose in Egypt and acquired the capacity to save from starvation the family from which the Messiah would come. When Joseph saw his brothers several years later, he said to them, "You intended evil against me, but God turned it into good!"

In the days of the Apostles, the Jews persecuted Christians in Palestine. The Christians had to flee from Judea, the land sanctified by the life and blood of the Saviour. But everywhere they went they sowed the words of the Gospel. The sins of the persecutors were directed into spreading Christianity.

The pagan emperors of Rome persecuted the young Christian Church. Tens of thousands of martyrs shed their blood for Christ. The blood of the martyrs became seeds for millions of new Christians. The fury of the persecutors, their sins of hatred and murder were directed by God in this instance into the building up of the Church. They thought and accomplished evil. God turned all of their deeds to the good. The entire history of mankind, right up to the events of our day, testifies to the truth of these words. The greatest downfall of man concurred with the greatest religious triumph, the turning of men to God.

We need only have patience and wait, *one day is with the Lord as a thousand years, and a thousand years as one day* (II Peter 3:8).

But this intertwining of evil into the plan for the management of the world did not appear to be some sort of belated addition for the correction of creation. The intertwining of evil was provided for in the act of the eternal will of God, in which was determined the creation of the world. For God is the eternal today! His foresight extends to eternity. It functions always and without interruption. (Extracted from a brochure by L. Lusin, "Who is Right?" with additions.)

Conclusion

Our lives must always be guided by the knowledge we acquire of the true faith and Christian piety. In order to make use of our piety and knowledge of the faith, it is necessary for each Christian to have the virtue of discernment, Christian good sense. In addressing the Christians, the Apostle Peter said, *Giving all diligence, add to your faith virtue; and to virtue knowledge* (II Peter 1:5). For whatever is done without discerning knowledge may turn out to be unwise. Even good can bring harm instead of benefit.

The teachings of the Orthodox Church which we have learned concerning faith and Christian life must be manifest in deeds, and not hypocritically, but sincerely fulfilling everything we know from this teaching. *If ye know these things, happy are ye if ye do them* (John 13:17).

If we become aware that we sin, that we do not fulfill the teaching as we must, then we must force ourselves quickly to the most sincere repentance. We must firmly resolve to shun the sin henceforth, making reparation for it by opposing it with good works.

When it seems to us that we are doing well in fulfilling one commandment or another, we must never become complacent or proud of this. With the deepest humility and thanksgiving we must acknowledge that we have hardly fulfilled our **obligation**. As Christ the Saviour said, *When ye shall have done all those things which are commanded you, say, We are unprofitable servants: we have done that which was our duty to do* (Luke 17:10).

CHAPTER 8

Contemporary Teaching and Faith in God

Science acknowledged long ago that the domain of analysis is almost in no way comparable to the domain of the unsearchable. More than that, the more that science discovers by scientific analysis, the broader are the fields that have yet to be investigated. "Every new discovery expands the realm of the unknown by arithmetic proportions" (A.C. Morrison). Science will never complete its work as long as the world stands.

Spokesmen of scientific analysis acknowledge that their knowledge of the world must be complemented by another source. That source is **religion**.

A great scientist of our time, Max Planck, who was awarded the Nobel Prize for physics in 1918, says , "Religion and science are not mutually exclusive as was believed earlier and has been feared by many of our contemporaries; on the contrary, they are in complete accord and complement each other."

Prof. M.M. Novikov, Rector of the University of Moscow, who was awarded a gold doctoral diploma in 1965 from the University of Heidelberg, and who in 1957 was an active member of the New York Academy of Science, in his article "The Path of a Naturalist to Religion," writes, "One of the most striking facts in the history of science is that physics, the rigorous base of natural science, became the way of the ideal. It led to the conclusion that physical appearance is determined by divine, spiritual strength. This view was also expressed by three prominent scholars.

"The theory of relativity of Albert Einstein is well known in general social circles. But not every one is aware that it led the scientist to the formulation of 'Cosmic religion.' This religion, as does every other religion, acknowledges the existence of the supreme Spirit, the creator of earthly harmony.

"The quantum theory of Max Planck had great significance for the development of natural science. On an occasion that interests us, this author writes, 'The only primary data for the natural scientist is gathered by sensual perception and conclusions are drawn from its measurement.' From here, guided by the method of inductive reasoning, he attempts to come as close as possible to God and His natural order as the highest but forever unattainable goal. It follows that if both religion and natural science require faith in God for their validity, **then for the first (religion) God stands at the beginning, and for the second (science), at the conclusion of all intellectual activity. For religion, God supplies the foundation; for science, He is the crown of any elaboration on world-outlook.** Man depends on natural science for knowledge, but on religion, for civilized behavior. But the basis of our knowledge is nothing more than our sensual perception of the solid, primary particle.

"The assumption of the existence of some regular world order is prerequisite to formulation of fruitful scientific hypotheses. But formulating scientific hypotheses is not a suitable method for directing our behavior. For, with the display of our will, we are not able to wait for the time when all our knowledge is found perfect, and we acquire omniscience. In fact, life frequently requires us to make quick decisions."

Later Planck shows that if we attribute to God goodness and love in addition to omnipotence and omniscience, then proximity to Him supplies the seeking man with consolation in the sensation of happiness in high measure. "Against this presentation, from the point of view of natural science, it is impossible to advance the slightest objection."

A great sensation was caused by the work of August Heisenberg, Nobel Prize winner in 1932. He formulated the principle of indeterminacy (the uncertainty principle), which states that it is impossible to determine the existence of elementary particles except within certain limits — elementary particles being the smallest undecomposable units of matter. Furthermore, it is impossible to know simultaneously the exact position of the particle and the velocity of its movement. We maintain that electrons exist, but we are unable to distinguish them, one from another. Thus our previous understanding of matter becomes superfluous. The world, according to Heisenberg, consists of something, the essence of which is unknown. That "something" appears in the form of a particle, then in the form of a wave. If one seeks a name, then that "something" must be designated by the word energy, and that in quotation marks. Thus, so-called laws of natural science are not precisely regular, but are static in character (i.e., the activity of energy defying calculation).

To this consideration it is appropriate to add that the understanding of an indeterminate "something" is also applicable to vital phenomena. But in this case it takes a completely different character. Mathematical equations which describe elementary physical processes are not applicable to life processes. Life is composed of an autonomous, self-acting field, as Drish affirmed.

The noted professor I. A. Ilyin says, "In the present state of knowledge it is eminently well understood that the 'scientific' picture of the world is changing all the time. Everything is becoming more complicated, deepening, absorbed in detail, and never appearing as part of a full, clear whole... In the present state of knowledge it is known that science will never be in a condition to explain its last prerequisite or to define its fundamental understanding. For example, a scientist will never be able to establish exactly what an 'atom' is, or an 'electron,' a 'vitamin,' 'energy,' or 'psychological function.' He knows that all his 'definitions,' 'explanations' and 'theories' are only vague attempts to approximate the vivid mysteries of the material and spiritual world. Concerning the productivity of science there can be no dispute; all contemporary technology and medicine testify to it. But as to what seems to be the theoretical truth of these demonstrations, there science swims on a problematic, conjectural sea of mystery."

One of the most noted American scholars, president of the New York Academy of Science, A. Cressy Morrison, argues for the existence of God in his brilliant "Seven Reasons Why I Believe in God."

"We are still only in the dawn of scientific knowledge," says Morrison. "The closer we come to daybreak, the more brightly shines our morning, the more clearly the creation of the omniscient Creator is illumined before us. Now in the spirit of scientific humility, in the spirit of faith based on knowledge, we are all the more confirmed in our conviction of the existence of God.

"I personally number seven circumstances which determine my belief in God. They are:

"**First**: Absolutely distinct mathematical laws demonstrate the universality of the creation by a Supreme Intelligence.

"Suppose you take ten pennies and mark them from one to ten. Put them in a bag and give them a good shake. Now try to draw them out in sequence from one to ten putting each coin back in your sack after each draw. Your chance of drawing number one is one in ten. Your chance of drawing one and two in succession would be one in one hundred. Your chance of drawing one, two and three in succession would be one in a thousand. Your chance of drawing from number one to number ten in succession would reach the unbelievable figure of one chance in ten billion.

"By these same mathematical arguments they say that for origin and development of life on earth, such an incredible number of interrelated and interdependent events would have been required that without intelligent direction, simply by chance, there is no way it could possibly have arisen. The velocity of the rotation of the earth is a thousand miles an hour. If the earth rotated with the speed of one hundred miles an hour, then our days and nights would be ten times as long as now. The hot sun of summer would then burn up our vegetation each long day, and every sprout would freeze in such a night.

"The sun has a surface temperature of 12,000 degrees Fahrenheit, and our earth is just far enough away so that this 'eternal fire' warms us just enough and not too much. If the temperature on earth had changed so much as fifty degrees on the average for a single year, all vegetation would be dead and man with it, roasted or frozen.

"The earth is tilted at an angle of twenty-three degrees. This gives us our seasons of the year. If it had not been tilted, the water vapor from the ocean would move north and south, piling up continents of ice. If the moon, instead of being at its present distance, were removed from us only by 50,000 miles, our high tides and low tides would be so enormous that twice a day all the lowlands of all the continents would be submerged by a rush of water so enormous that even the mountains would soon be eroded away. Had the crust of the earth been ten feet thicker, there would be no oxygen and all life would be doomed to destruction. If the oceans were comparatively deeper, the carbon dioxide would absorb all the oxygen, and all life would again perish. If the atmosphere enveloping our earthly sphere were a little thinner, some of the meteors which are now burned in the outer atmosphere by the millions every day would strike all parts of the earth, and would set fire to every burnable object.

"These and innumerable other examples attest to the fact that **for life to arise spontaneously on earth there is not one chance in a whole multitude of millions.**

"**Second**: The wealth of source material from which life draws strength for fulfillment of its mission, in itself testifies to the presence of a self-sufficient and omnipotent Intelligence.

"What life is, no man has yet fathomed. It has no weight or dimensions. Life has force. A germinating kernel can demolish a rock. Life conquers water, dry land and air, possesses their elements, cramming them together, dissolving them, transforming their combinations.

"Life is a sculptor and shapes all living things, an artist that designs the leaf of every tree, that colors the flowers. Life is a musician and has taught each bird to sing its love songs, the insects to call each other in the music of their multitudinous sounds. Life is a chemist that gives taste to our fruits and perfume to the rose. Life's chemistry changes water and carbonic acid into wood and sugar but in doing so, releases oxygen that animals may have the breath of life.

"Here before us is a drop of protoplasm, an almost invisible drop, transparent, jellylike, capable of motion, drawing energy from the sun. This single cell, this transparent, mist-like droplet, holds within itself the germ of all life, and has the power to distribute this life to every living thing, great and small. The powers of this droplet of protoplasm are greater than the powers of our existence, greater than all the animals or people, for all life came from it and without it no living thing would have been or could be. It is not nature that created life. Rocks split by fire and fresh water seas would not have been sufficient to meet the requirements for the origin of life.

"Who puts life into the speck of protoplasm?

"**Third**: The intelligence of animals is indisputable evidence of the wisdom of the Creator, who instilled instincts in His creatures, without which they would be completely helpless.

"The young salmon spends years at sea, then it returns to its native river and travels up the side of the river into which flows the tributary in which it was born. What brings them back with such precision? If a salmon going up a river is transferred to another tributary, it will at once realize it is not in the right tributary and will fight its way down to the mainstream and then turn up against the current to finish his destiny.

"Another great mystery is hidden in the behavior of the eel. These amazing creatures migrate at maturity from all ponds and rivers everywhere — those from Europe across thousands of miles of ocean — and go to the ocean depths south of Bermuda. There they breed and die. The little ones, with no apparent means of knowing anything to prevent their being lost in the ocean depths, go the way of their fathers, to the same streams, ponds and seas from which they first began their journey to the Bermuda islands. No American eel has ever been caught in European waters, and no European eel has ever been caught in American waters. Nature has also delayed the maturity of the European eel by a year or more to make up for its much greater journey. What is the source of this sense of direction and will power?

"A wasp, having overcome a grasshopper, stings it in exactly the right place. From this blow the grasshopper 'dies.' It loses consciousness but continues to live, as a form of preserved meat. After this, the wasp lays her eggs exactly in the right place that when they hatch, her children can eat without killing the insect on which they feed. Dead meat would be poison for them. Having completed her work, the wasp mother flies away and dies. She never sees her young. Is it not beyond doubt that the wasp must have done all this right the first time and every time, for otherwise there would be no wasps. This mysterious knowledge cannot be explained by the fact that wasps teach one another. It is deposited in their flesh and blood.

"**Fourth**: Man functions with more than animal instinct. He has reason. There has never been an animal which has had the capacity to count to ten. It is not able to comprehend the meaning of ten numerals. Instinct is like a single note on a flute, beautiful but limited; whereas the human brain contains all the notes of all the instruments in the orchestra. It is worth mentioning one point: thanks to our intelligence, we are able to understand what we are, we have self-awareness, and this capability is provided only by the spark of Universal Intelligence implanted in us.

"**Fifth**: The miracle of genes — the existence of which was unknown to Darwin — testifies to the fact that for all life there was manifested care.

"The genes are so infinitesimal that if all of them which are responsible for all human beings on earth today could be collected and put in one place, they would all be able to fit in a thimble. And the thimble still would not be full! These ultramicroscopic genes are the absolute keys to all human, animal and vegetable characteristics. A thimble is a small place in which to put all the individual characteristics of four billion human beings. However, the facts are beyond question. If this is so, does it follow that the gene contains in itself the key to the psychology of each separate being, containing all of this in such a tiny space?

"Here is the beginning of evolution! It begins at the cell, the entity which holds and carries the genes. The fact that a few million atoms contained in ultramicroscopic genes can be the absolute key governing life on earth, is evidence proving the manifest care for all life that someone provided for them beforehand, and that this providence proceeds from a Creative Intelligence. No other hypothesis in this case is able to help solve this riddle of existence.

"**Sixth**: How strange is the system of checks and balances in nature. We are compelled to acknowledge that only the most perfect intelligence is able to envisage all the correlations arising from such a complicated system of checks and balances.

"Many years ago in Australia, several species of cactus were planted for use as a hedge. The cactus had no insect enemies in Australia and soon began a prodigious growth. People began to seek the means to fight against it. The march of the cactus persisted until it had covered an area as great as England, crowded the inhabitants out of towns and villages and destroyed their farms, making cultivation impossible. No device the people discovered could stop its spread. The entomologists scoured the world and finally found an insect which lived exclusively on cactus, would eat nothing else, would breed freely, and which had no enemies in Australia. As soon as this insect conquered the cactus, the cactus pest retreated, and with it all but a protective residue of the insects, enough to hold the cactus in check forever.

The checks and balances have been provided, and have been persistently effective. Why indeed did not the insects which multiplied so incredibly quickly overcome all life? Because the insects have no lungs like man possesses, but breathe through tubes. When insects grow large, the tubes cannot grow in ratio to the increasing size of the body of the insect. Because of the mechanism of their structure and their method of breathing, there could never be an insect of great size. If this physical check had not been provided, man could not exist. Imagine a bumblebee as big as a lion.

"**Seventh**: The fact that man is capable of grasping the idea of the existence of God, is in itself sufficient evidence.

The conception of God arises from that mysterious capability of mankind which we call imagination. Only because of this power and only by means of its help, man, and no other living creature on earth, is able to find confirmation through abstract things. The expanse of knowledge which is opened by this capacity is perfectly immense. Indeed, thanks to precisely the imagination of man, the possibility of spiritual reality arises. Man is able to define, with obvious purpose, the great truth that Heaven exists everywhere and in everything, the truth that God lives everywhere and in all, and that He lives in our hearts.

"Thus, from science as well as from imagination, we find confirmation of the words of the psalmist, *The heavens declare the glory of God; and the firmament showeth his handiwork* (Ps. 19:1)."

The famous surgeon and professor in the universities of Cologne, Bonn and Berlin, August Bier (1861-1949) says, "If it ever happened that science and religion fell into disagreement, harmony would be restored through discovery of more precise basic data."

We will conclude our discussion by coming back to the words of the scholar, A.C. Morrison, "Man recognizes the necessity of moral principles; in them exists the feeling of debt, and from this, faith in God is born. The richness of religious experience finds the soul of man and lifts him, step by step, until he feels the Divine presence. The instinctive cry of man, 'My God,' is natural, and the crudest prayer lifts one closer to his Creator.

"Respect, sacrifice, strength of character, moral foundations, ingenuity are not born from negativism or atheism, the amazing self-deception which replaces God with man. Without faith, culture disappears, order becomes disorder, and evil prevails.

"Let us then hold fast to our belief in the Creator, in Divine love and in the brotherhood of man, lifting ourselves closer to Him by doing His will as we know it and firmly believing we are, as His creation, worthy of His care."

To the words of A. Cressy Morrison we add the words of the psychiatrist and Orthodox theologian I. M. Andreev, "True knowledge is incompatible with pride. Humility is a necessary condition for the capacity of grasping the Truth. Only humble scholars, as well as humble religious thinkers, bearing in mind the words of the Saviour, *Without me ye can do nothing*, and *I am the way, the truth, and the life* (John 15:5; John 14:6), are able to travel the right path, by the right method, toward the comprehension of the Truth. *For God resisteth the proud, but giveth grace unto the humble* (James 4:6)."

PART V

THE DIVINE SERVICES OF THE ORTHODOX CHURCH

CHAPTER 1

The Concept of Serving God, Divine Services

The worship of God or the pleasing of God through good thoughts, words, and deeds, i.e., the fulfillment of God's will, is called, in general, divine service.

Divine service began on the earth with the very creation of the first human beings in **Paradise.** The divine services of the first human beings in Paradise consisted of freely glorifying God, His wisdom, goodness, omnipotence, and the other divine perfections which are manifest in the creation of the world and in His providence concerning it.

After their fall into sin mankind had an even greater obligation to pray to God, beseeching Him for salvation. In addition to prayer to the Lord as divine service, mankind established the practice of **sacrificial offerings.** Sacrifice expresses the thought that all which we possess is not ours but is God's. The combination of prayer with sacrificial offerings serves to remind humanity that God receives its prayers because of the sacrifice which was later offered for all mankind by the Saviour of the world, the Son of God come to earth.

Originally divine services occurred freely in open places. There were neither holy temples nor ordained priests. People offered sacrifices to God wherever they desired and prayed with words of prayer suggested to them by their own feelings and attitudes.

At the command of God, in the time of the Prophet Moses, the **Tabernacle** was constructed (the first Old Testament Temple to the One True God). **Consecrated persons** were selected, the high priest, other priests, and Levites. Specific **sacrifices** for various situations were instituted, and **feasts** were ordained such as Passover, Pentecost, the New Year and the Day of Purification.

When the Lord Jesus Christ came to earth, He taught us to worship the Heavenly Father in every place. Nevertheless, He often visited the Old Testament Temple in Jerusalem as a place with the special grace-filled presence of God. He was concerned for the order of the Temple and preached in it. His holy Apostles regarded it in the same way until the time of the open persecutions, which were instigated against Christians on the part of the Jews.

In the Apostolic period, as the Acts of the Apostles describe, there were special places for the gathering of the faithful and for the accomplishment of the Mystery of Communion. These places were called churches and there divine services were celebrated by bishops, priests, and deacons, who were consecrated to this duty by the laying on of hands in the Mystery of Ordination.

The order of Christian divine service was established by the successors of the Apostles under the guidance of the Holy Spirit and following the apostolic command given to them, *Let all things be done decently and in order* (I Cor. 14:40). This ordained order of divine services is strictly preserved in our holy **Orthodox Church of Christ.**

Orthodox ecclesiastical divine service means the office or service to God composed of readings and chanting of prayers, the reading of the Word of God, and the performance of sacred ritual, accomplished according to a definite order, as headed by clergy (a bishop or priest).

Ecclesiastical divine service is distinguished from private prayer in that it is served **by clergy,** lawfully ordained to this service through the Mystery of Ordination, and is performed primarily in church.

Orthodox public worship has as its purpose the edification of the faithful by setting forth the true doctrines of Christ through **readings and chanting**, and to dispose them towards prayer and repentance. The services represent the most important events from sacred history accomplished for our salvation both before the birth of Christ and after. They inspire the faithful to give thanks to God for all the benefits received from Him, they intensify the supplications for further mercies upon us from Him, and help us to acquire peace in our souls.

The most important aspect is that through divine services the **Orthodox Christian enters into a mystical union with God** through the Mysteries celebrated in divine worship, especially the Mystery of Holy Communion, and thus receives from God the powers of Divine Grace with which to live a righteous life.

CHAPTER 2

The Church Building and Its Arrangement

In the Old Testament the Lord Himself gave mankind directions through the Prophet Moses as to how the Temple should be set up for divine worship. New Testament churches were constructed on the basis of the Old Testament Temple.

The Altar

Just as the Old Testament Temple (initially a tent) was separated into three portions, the **Holy of Holies**, the **Sanctuary** and the **Courts**, so an Orthodox church is distinguished by three sections, the **Altar** (or Sanctuary), the **Nave** (Middle Portion) and the **Narthex** (Vestibule).

As the Holy of Holies signified then, so now the **Altar** represents the Kingdom of Heaven. No one could enter the Holy of Holies except the High Priest once a year, and only with the blood of a purification sacrifice. The Kingdom of Heaven, after the fall of man into sin, was closed to us. The High Priest was a prototype of Christ, and his action told the people that a time would come when Christ, through the shedding of His blood and suffering on the Cross and Resurrection, would open the Kingdom of Heaven to all. Therefore, when Christ died on the Cross the veil of the temple which closed off the Holy of Holies was

The Main Church at Holy Trinity Monastery

torn in two, and from this moment Christ opened the gates of the Kingdom of Heaven to all those who with faith would come unto Him.

The Sanctuary of the Temple corresponds in our Orthodox churches to the **Nave** or **middle part of the building**. No one had the right to enter the Old Testament sanctuary except the priest, but all believing Christians may stand within our churches because the Kingdom of God is closed to none.

The Courts of the Old Testament Temple in which all the people could be found have their counterpart in an Orthodox Church in the **Narthex** which now, however, has no essential significance. Earlier, the catechumens who were preparing to become Christians, but were still not ready for the Mystery of Baptism, stood there. Today those who have sinned grievously or those who have apostatized from the Church are temporarily sent to stand in the narthex for correction.

An Orthodox Church is built with the altar at the eastern end, directed towards the light from whence the sun rises. The Lord Jesus Christ is for us the "Dayspring," for from Him has dawned upon us the eternal Divine Light. In the Church prayers we call Jesus Christ the "Sun of Righteousness" and "Dayspring from on high."

Every church consecrated to God bears the name of one or another sacred event or Saint, in memory of that occasion or person. Examples include churches dedicated to the Trinity, the Transfiguration, the Ascension, the Annunciation, the Protection of the Mother of God, the Archangel Michael, St. Nicholas, etc. If there are several altars in the church then each of them is dedicated to the memory of a different event or saint. All altars, save the main one, are called side altars.

A church in its external appearance is distinguished from other buildings. Most are designed in the form of the **Cross** to signify that it is a place sacred to Him Who was crucified for us and that the Cross of the Lord Jesus Christ delivered us from the tyranny of the Devil. A church may be built in the form of an elongated **ship** to symbolize the image of the ark of Noah that brings us through the sea of life to the calm haven of the Kingdom of Heaven. Sometimes a church is built in the form of a **circle** to remind us that the Church of Christ is eternal, without beginning or end. A church can even be built in the form of an **octagon**, like a **star**, suggesting that the Church is like a guiding star which shines into this world.

A church building is usually capped by a **dome** which is an image of Heaven. The dome comes to a point upon which is a **cross**, to the glory of the head of the Church, Jesus Christ. Often a church is topped by several cupolas. **Two** cupolas symbolize the two natures of Jesus Christ, human and divine; **three** — the three Persons of the Holy Trinity; **five** — Jesus Christ and the four Evangelists; **seven** — the seven Mysteries and the seven Ecumenical Councils; **nine** — the nine ranks of angels; **thirteen** — Jesus Christ and the twelve Apostles; and sometimes there are even more cupolas.

Over the entrance of the building, or at times next to it, a **bell-tower** or belfry is built to hold the bells.

The patterns of ringing the bells are used to call the faithful to prayer, to the divine services, and also to mark the most important moments of the services being conducted in the church. The ringing of one bell is called an "**annunciation**," that is, the announcement of the good, joyous news of a divine service; the ringing of all the bells to express Christian joy on the occasion of a solemn feast is called a "**festive peal**." The tolling of bells on a grievous occasion is called a "**knell**." The sound of bells reminds us of the higher, heavenly world.

The most important part of the church is the **Altar** or **Sanctuary**. The Sanctuary is the holiest place in the entire church and is where the **Altar Table** or "Throne" upon which the Mystery of Holy Communion served by the priest is located. The Sanctuary is built upon a raised portion that is usually higher than the other portions of the church so that all that is done there will be audible and visible during the service. The very word "Altar" means an elevated place of sacrifice.

The **Altar Table** is the term for the special, sacred, usually cube-shaped table found in the center of the Sanctuary and adorned with two vestments: the **lower** which is of white linen, and the **upper** which is of a more expensive material, usually of brocade. The very Lord Himself, as King and Master of the Church, is present there mysteriously and invisibly. Only ordained clergy may touch the Altar Table or venerate it. Upon the Altar Table one finds the Antimins, the Gospel, the Cross, the Tabernacle and the Communion Set.

The **Antimins** is a silk cloth consecrated by a bishop upon which Jesus Christ is depicted being placed in the tomb. Into the other side a fragment of the relics of a saint must be sewn, since in the first centuries of Christianity the Divine Liturgy was always celebrated upon the graves of the martyrs. One is not allowed to celebrate the Liturgy without an Antimins. The word is from the Greek and means "instead of an altar table."

In order to protect the Antimins it is folded into another silk cloth called the **Iliton**. It is to remind us of the cloth which was wrapped around the head of the Saviour in the tomb. On top of the Antimins rests the **sponge** for collecting the particles of the Holy Gifts during the liturgy.

The **Gospel** is the Word of God, the teachings of our Lord Jesus Christ. The **Cross** is the sword of God by which the Lord conquers the Devil and death. The **Tabernacle** is the ark in which the Holy Gifts are kept for communing the ill. Usually it is in the form of a model of the church building. The **Communion Set** is a small tabernacle which contains the utensils for bringing Holy Communion to those who are ill.

Behind the Altar Table stands the **Candelabrum**, a stand for seven lamps, and behind it is the **Altar Cross**. The place behind the Altar at the very farthest eastern end of the church is called the **High Place**. Usually it is raised. When in his own cathedral, the bishop sits here during certain portions of the services.

To the left of the Altar Table in the northern part of the sanctuary stands another smaller table similarly vested on all sides like the Altar

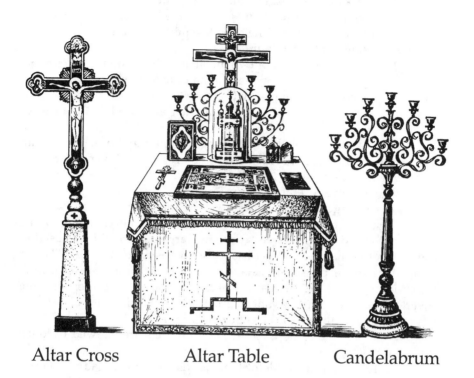

Altar Cross Altar Table Candelabrum

Communion Set

Tabernacle Cross Antimins Altar Gospel

Table. It is here that the Gifts are prepared before the Liturgy. This table is the **Table of Oblation**. Upon the Table of Oblation are kept the **sacred vessels** and all that pertains to them. They include:

1. The holy **Chalice** or cup into which, before the Liturgy, wine is poured with water, which is transformed later during the Liturgy into the Blood of Christ.

2. The **Diskos** which is a small round plate on a stand. The bread is placed upon it for consecration at the Divine Liturgy, for transformation into the Body of Christ. The diskos symbolizes simultaneously the manger and tomb of the Saviour.

3. The **Star** is composed of two metal arcs fixed about the center so that they can be closed and opened into a cruciform shape. It is placed on the diskos so that the cover will not disturb the cut out portions of prosphora. The star symbolizes the star that appeared at the birth of Christ.

4. The **Spear** is a blade resembling a miniature spear for cutting out the Lamb and other portions from the prosphora. It symbolizes the spear which wounded Christ upon the Cross.

5. The **Spoon** is used to administer Holy Communion.

6. The **Sponge** or **cloth** is used to clean and wipe the vessels.

The small covers which are used to cover the chalice and the diskos are called the **Coverlets**, while the large covers which is used to cover both the chalice and the diskos together is called the **Aer**. The aer symbolizes the expanse of the heavens in which the star appeared, which led the Magi to the manger of the Saviour. It, together with the coverlets, represents the swaddling clothes in which Jesus Christ was wrapped after birth and also His burial shroud.

No one but the bishops, priest, and deacons are allowed to touch these holy things.

Also found on the Table of Oblation is the **Cup** or ladle which is used in the beginning of Proskomedia to pour the mixture of wine and water into the holy chalice. Before Communion, hot water is added to the contents of the chalice.

Located in the sanctuary is the **censer** which is used for censing during the divine services. Censing was instituted in the Old Testament Church by God Himself. We offer the incense as an offering to God and use it to sanctify objects.

Censing before the Holy Altar and the icons expresses our respect and reverence for them. When the laity praying in church are censed this expresses the desire that their prayer would be heart-felt and truly reverent and might ascend to Heaven like the smoke of incense and that the Grace of God might envelop them even as the smoke of incense envelops them in the church. While being censed, the faithful should respond with a bow.

The **dikiri** and **trikiri**, which are used by a bishop to bless the people, and the altar fans are kept in the sanctuary also.

Dikiri refers to the candlestick that holds two candles, which remind us of the two natures of Christ, the divine and the human.

Trikiri refers to the candlestick that holds three candles, which remind us of our faith in the Holy Trinity.

The **altar-fans** refer to the metal circles with long, wooden handles on which are represented the Seraphim. The deacons hold the fans over the Holy Gifts during the consecration, and over the Gospel book in procession. Earlier they were made of ostrich feathers and were used to

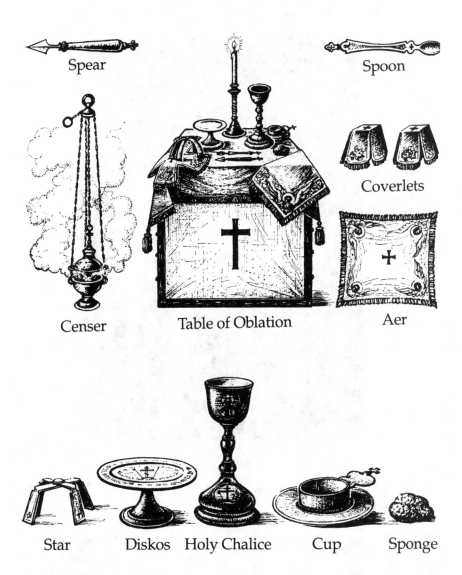

Spear

Spoon

Censer

Table of Oblation

Coverlets

Aer

Star   Diskos   Holy Chalice   Cup   Sponge

keep insects away from the Holy Gifts. Today the waving of these fans is symbolic and represents the presence of the heavenly hosts during the celebration of the Liturgy.

To the side of the sanctuary area is found the **Vestry**. The vestments, sacred robes used during the divine services, are kept here, as well as the ecclesiastical vessels and books.

The altar is separated from the middle portion of the church

The Iconostasis

building by a special kind of wall upon which are hung icons and is thus called the **Iconostasis**.

The iconostasis has three doors or gates. The middle and largest is found in the very center of the screen and is called the **Royal Gates** because through them passes the very Lord Himself, Jesus Christ, the King of Glory, Who comes in the Holy Gifts invisibly. No one is allowed to pass through the Royal Gates other than the clergy. A curtain is hung across the Royal Gates, on the inside, which is drawn and withdrawn during the course of the divine services. Icons of the **Annunciation of the Theotokos** and the **Four Evangelists, Sts. Matthew, Mark, Luke, and John,** are usually on the Royal Gates. An icon of the Mystical Supper is placed above the Royal Gates, since the faithful stand before them when partaking of Communion.

To the right of the Royal Gates there is always an icon of the **Saviour**, and on the left, one of the **Mother of God**.

The **southern door** is located to the right of the icon of the Saviour, while the **northern door** is to the left of the Theotokos icon. Generally, the **Archangels Michael and Gabriel** are depicted on these two side doors, though sometimes icons of the first deacons Sts. Philip and Stephen, or the high priest Aaron and the Prophet Moses are placed here. These side doors are also called the "deacon's doors," since the deacons pass through them frequently.

On the far ends next to the doors are placed the icons of especially revered saints. The first icon to the right of the Saviour icon is almost always the **icon of the church**, that is, the representation of the feast or Saint to whom the church building is dedicated.

On the highest point above the iconostasis is placed the **Cross** with an image upon it of our crucified Lord, Jesus Christ.

If the iconostasis is built with more than one row of icons, then usually on the second row are placed the icons of the twelve Great Feasts; on the third row— the Apostles; on the fourth row — the Prophets; and on the top— the Cross.

Icons are also placed on the walls of the church, either in special large frames or shrines, or on analogions, high, slanted stands, for veneration.

The **raised platform**, upon which stand the altar and the iconostasis, extends forward for several feet into the middle portion of the church. This elevation in front of the iconostasis is called the **solea**.

The middle of the solea, directly in front of the Royal Gates is called the **ambo** or place of ascending. From the ambo the deacon intones the litanies and reads the Gospels. From here, as well, the priest delivers sermons, and the faithful partake of Holy Communion.

At the end of the solea near the side walls of the church are found the **cliros**, or choirs for the readers and chanters. Above the cliros are hung the **banners**, icons made of either cloth embroidery or metalwork fastened to long poles. They are carried in processions as ecclesiastical flags.

Usually on the side of the nave is a small **table for the reposed**, on which is an image of the Crucifixion, before which are placed candles. A Pannykhida (memorial service) is served at this table.

Candlestands are placed in front of the iconostasis or behind the analogions, upon which the faithful place candles during the service. A **chandelier** or **polycandelabrum** hangs from the central dome in the middle of the church. This large metal chandelier holds either a large number of candles or lights which are lit during the most festive moments of the services.

CHAPTER 3

The Clergy and Their Sacred Vestments

Following the example of the Old Testament Church, in which there were a high priest, priests, and Levites, the holy Apostles also instituted in the New Testament Christian Church the **priesthood: bishops, priests**, and **deacons**.

They are all called members of the **clergy** because by means of the Mystery of the priesthood they receive the Grace of the Holy Spirit for sacred service in the Church of Christ: enabling them to celebrate the divine services; teach the laity the Christian faith and holy life; and direct ecclesiastical affairs.

The **bishops** comprise the highest rank in the Church, and therefore receive the highest degree of Grace. Bishops are also called **hierarchs**, or leaders of the priests. They may celebrate all the **Mysteries** and all ecclesiastical services. Bishops have the right not only to serve the usual Liturgy, but they alone may consecrate others into the priesthood, as well as consecrate Holy Chrism and the Antimins.

In their degree of priesthood they are **equal**, though the senior and most deserving of the bishops are termed **archbishops**, while the bishops whose sees are centered in major cities are termed **metropolitans**, after the Greek word for a large city, "metropolis." The bishops of the ancient major cities of the Roman Empire, Jerusalem, Constantinople, Rome, Alexandria and Antioch, and of the capitals of some Orthodox countries such as Belgrade and Moscow, are called **patriarchs**.

From 1721 to 1917 the Russian Orthodox Church was governed by the Most Holy Synod. In 1917 an All-Russian Council was summoned and restored the rule of the Church to the "Most Holy Patriarch of Moscow and All Russia."

A bishop sometimes is given another bishop, called a **vicar bishop**, to assist him in his duties.

Priests comprise the second rank of the sacred ministry under the bishop. Priests may serve, with an episcopal blessing, all the Mysteries and ecclesiastical services, with the exception of the Mystery of Ordination and the sanctification of Holy Chrism or an Antimins. The congregation of Christians subject to the supervision of the priest is termed his **parish**. The more worthy and distinguished priests are granted the title of **archpriest**; the first among these priests is called a **protopresbyter**.

If a priest is also a tonsured **monk** he is known as a **hieromonk**. Hieromonks appointed to direct monasteries, or those honored independently of any appointment, are usually given the title of **igumen** or abbot. Those of a higher rank are called **archimandrites**, and bishops are chosen from this rank.

Deacons form the third and lowest rank of the sacred ministry; in

Greek "deacon" means a "server." Deacons assist a bishop or priest during the serving of the Divine Liturgy or other Mysteries and services, but they may not serve alone. The participation of a deacon in the divine services is not obligatory, and therefore many churches conduct services without them.

Some deacons, particularly in cathedral churches, are deemed worthy of the title of **protodeacon**. Monks who have received the rank of deacon are called **hierodeacons**, and the senior of them is called an **archdeacon**.

The **subdeacons** are also ordained and help in the altar. They primarily take part in episcopal services. They vest the serving bishop in his sacred vestments, hold the trikiri and dikiri, and hand them to the bishop to bless those present. They also may assist in changing the altar covers.

In addition to the three orders of sacred ministry, other lower orders of service in the Church include the **readers** or **"psaltis"** (Greek), and the **sacristans** or **"ecclesiarchs."** They belong to the ranks of church servers who are not ordained to their duties through the Mystery of Ordination, but only by a short series of prayers with an episcopal blessing.

Readers have the duty to read and chant both on the cliros during divine services, and at homes when services are conducted by a priest.

The **sacristan** is obliged to call the faithful to the divine services with bell-ringing, to light the lamps and candles in the church, to ready and to hand the censer to the serving priest, and to assist the readers in the readings and chantings.

Those who conduct services must be dressed in special, sacred robes or **vestments**. These are made of brocade or some similarly suitable material and adorned with crosses or other symbolic signs.

The vestments of the diaconate are the **sticharion**, the **orarion** and the **cuffs**.

The **sticharion** is a long garment, open down the length of the sides for a deacon, but entirely unslitted for servers, in the form of a cross with an opening for one's head and with wide sleeves. The deacon's sticharion may also be worn by subdeacons. The right to wear a sticharion may also be granted to readers and servers. The sticharion signifies purity of soul, necessary for a person of ecclesiastical rank.

The **orarion** is a long, wide band of the same material as the sticharion with fringe on the ends. It is worn over the left shoulder on top of the sticharion. For simple deacons it is worn as shown, for protodeacons it is wound once around the body. The orarion signifies the Grace of God which the deacon received in the Mystery of Ordination.

The **cuffs** or manacles are of the same material as the sticharion, and are worn around the wrists and laced with cords. They remind those conducting the services that they celebrate the Mysteries or

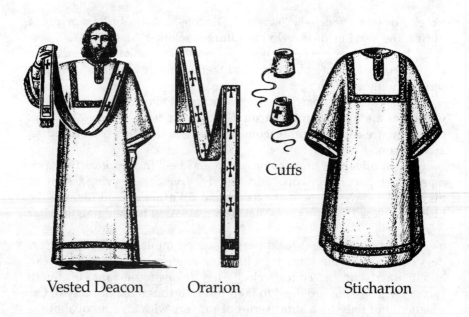

Cuffs

Vested Deacon   Orarion   Sticharion

partake of the Mysteries of the Christian faith not by their own powers, but by the power and Grace of God. They also remind us of the bonds that tied the hands of the Saviour during His passion.

The vestments of a priest include the **under-vestment** or sticharion, the **epitrachelion** (stole), the **belt**, the **cuffs**, and the **phelonion**.

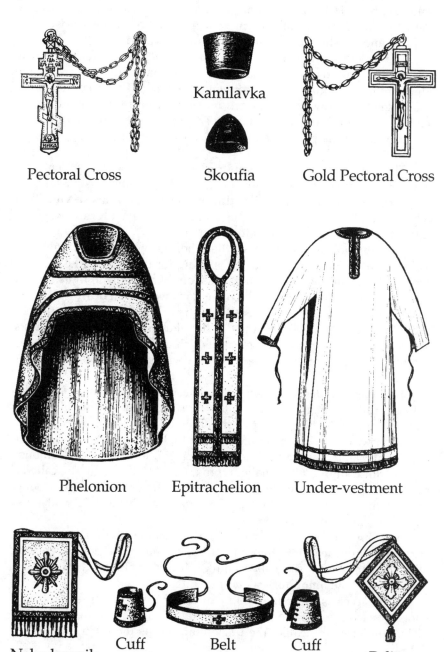

Pectoral Cross   Kamilavka   Gold Pectoral Cross

Skoufia

Phelonion   Epitrachelion   Under-vestment

Nabedrennik   Cuff   Belt   Cuff   Palitsa

The **under-vestment** is just a simpler form of sticharion, differing from the sticharion in that the sleeves are narrow with laces at the wrist, and it is usually made of a fine, white material. The white color reminds the priest that he must always be of pure soul and lead a blameless life. It also recalls the tunic which the Lord Jesus Christ wore on earth and in which He accomplished our salvation.

The **stole** or **epitrachelion** is similar to the deacon's orarion, only it is worn around the neck and comes down in front so that the two inner edges are fastened together for convenience. It signifies the double portion of grace bestowed on a priest, in comparison to that of a deacon, for the celebration of the Mysteries. The priest may not conduct any service without his epitrachelion, just as a deacon must have his orarion.

The **belt** is worn over the epitrachelion and under-vestment and signifies readiness to serve the Lord. It also symbolizes the divine power that strengthens the priest during the course of his serving. The belt also recalls the towel which the Saviour was given for the washing of the disciples' feet at the Mystical Supper.

The **phelonion** is worn over the other garments. It is a long and wide cape without sleeves with an opening for the head at the top and cut away in front to give the hands freedom of movement. In its form it resembles the purple mantle which the Lord was given during His passion. The ribbons sewn on it recall the streams of blood which flowed over His garments. In addition to this the phelonion reminds the priests of the garment of righteousness with which they must be vested as servants of Christ. A priest wears a **pectoral cross** around his neck, over the phelonion.

For long and dedicated service a priest is given an award called a **nabedrennik** or thigh shield, which is a stiffened, rectangular cloth hung on the right hip from the shoulder by a strap fastened at two upper corners, and which signifies a spiritual sword. Other awards are the **skoufia** and **kamilavka** (head coverings), and another diamond-shaped cloth, similar to the nabedrennik, worn on the right hip, called a **palitsa** (in which case the former is worn on the left). It also represents the spiritual sword, the Word of God with which the celebrant must battle disbelief and irreverence.

The **bishop** is vested with all the vestments of a priest, the **sticharion, epitrachelion, belt** and **cuffs**, but the phelonion is replaced with the **saccos** and the nabedrennik with the **palitsa**. In addition, a bishop wears the **omophorion** and the **miter**.

The **saccos** is the outer vestment of a bishop which resembles a shorter deacon's sticharion so that the sticharion and epitrachelion are visible underneath. It, like the phelonion, recalls the purple mantle of the Saviour.

The **palitsa** is hung by a strap from the upper corner over the right hip on top of the sakkos. For exceptional service the right to wear the palitsa is granted by the ruling bishop to worthy archpriests. For archimandrites, as well as for a bishop, the palitsa is an indispensable appurtenance to their vestments.

Around the shoulders, over the saccos, a bishop wears the **omophorion**. This is a long, wide fabric usually adorned with crosses. It is wrapped around the shoulders of the bishop so that one end falls

Cross

Miter

Panagia

Trikiri

Dikiri

Cuffs

Altar-fans

Staff

Palitsa

Saccos
with the Great Omophorion,
under the Saccos is an Epitrachelion
and an Under-vestment

Bishops mantle

Orlets

Small omophorion

in front and the other behind. Omophorion is a Greek word meaning "that which goes over the shoulders" and is exclusively an episcopal vestment. As with the priest and his epitrachelion, the bishop may not conduct any service without his omophorion. It reminds the bishop that he must be concerned for the salvation of the fallen like the good shepherd who, when he has found the lost sheep, carries it home on his shoulder.

At all times, as part of his normal attire and for services, the bishop wears a **panagia** around his neck in addition to a cross. The panagia, which means "all-holy" in Greek, is a small, round icon of the Saviour or the Theotokos, sometimes adorned with precious stones.

When serving, the bishop wears a **miter** on his head, adorned with small icons and precious stones. According to some, it signifies the crown of thorns which was placed on the head of the Saviour, and to others it represents the Gospel of Christ to which the bishop always remains subject. Archimandrites wear the miter as well, and in exceptional cases a ruling bishop can grant the right to wear one to the more worthy archpriests in place of the kamilavka.

During the divine services the bishops use a **staff** as a sign of ultimate pastoral authority. A staff is also granted to archimandrites and abbots as heads of monasteries.

During the service an "**orlets**," a circular rug with the image of an eagle flying over a city, is put under the bishop's feet. This symbolizes that the bishop should soar from the earthly to the heavenly like an eagle, and as an eagle can see clearly over distances, so must a bishop oversee all parts of his diocese.

The street clothing of a bishop, priest or deacon includes a black **cassock** and a **riassa**. Over the riassa the bishop wears a panagia and a cross, while a priest only wears a cross.

CHAPTER 4

The Order of Divine Services

T he order of divine services are divided into three cycles:
daily, **weekly**, and **yearly**.

The Daily Cycle of Divine Services

The **daily cycle of divine services** consists of those which are cele-
brated by the holy Orthodox Church during the course of one day.
There are nine daily services: **Vespers, Compline, Midnight Office,
Matins, First Hour, Third Hour, Sixth Hour**, and **Ninth Hour**, and the
Divine Liturgy.

Following the example of Moses, who in describing the creation of
the world by God, began the "day" with evening, the Orthodox Church
day begins with the evening service, Vespers.

Vespers is the service celebrated towards the end of the day, in
which we express our gratitude to God for the day which has passed.

Compline is the service composed of the reading of a series of
prayers, in which we ask the Lord God for the forgiveness of sins and
that He grant us, upon retiring, repose of body and soul and preserve
us from the wiles of the Devil during our sleep.

The Midnight Office is appointed to be read at midnight in remembrance of the prayer of the Saviour during the night in the Garden
of Gethsemane. This service summons the faithful to be ready at all
times for the day of the Dread Judgement, which will come unexpect-
edly like "a bridegroom in the night," as the parable of the ten virgins
reminds us.

Matins is celebrated in the morning prior to the rising of the sun.
In this service we give thanks to God for the night which has passed,
and we ask of Him mercy for the approaching day.

The First Hour corresponds to the first three hours of our day, 6 to
9 A.M. In Old and New Testament times an "hour" meant a "watch"
that lasted for three of our hours, and each service of the daily cycle
corresponds to one of these three-hour divisions. This First Hour sanctifies the already breaking day with prayer.

The Third Hour covers the time from 9 A.M. to 12 P.M. and recalls
the descent of the Holy Spirit upon the Apostles.

The Sixth Hour corresponds to the period from 12 to 3 P.M. and
reminds us of the Passion and Crucifixion of our Lord Jesus Christ.

The Ninth Hour represents the hours from 3 to 6 P.M. and reminds us of the death on the Cross of our Lord Jesus Christ.

The Ninth Hour represents the hours from 3 to 6 P.M. and reminds us of the death on the Cross of our Lord Jesus Christ.

The Divine Liturgy is the main divine service. During the course of its celebration the entire earthly life of the Saviour is called to mind, and the **Mystery of Holy Communion** is celebrated as instituted by the Saviour Himself in the Mystical Supper. It must be celebrated in the morning before the midday meal.

In ancient times monastics and hermits conducted all of these services separately, at the time appointed for each. Later, to accommodate the faithful, they were combined into three groups: **evening, morning** and **daytime**.

The **evening** services consist of Ninth Hour, Vespers and Compline.

The **morning** services consist of Midnight Office, Matins and First Hour.

The **daytime** services are Third and Sixth Hours, and the Divine Liturgy.

On the eve of major feasts and Sundays a service is conducted in the evening, uniting Vespers, Matins and First Hour. Such a service is termed an **All-night Vigil** because among early Christians and in some monasteries today the service is continued through the course of the entire night.

A Schematic Outline of the Daily Cycle of Services

Evening
1. Ninth Hour — three o'clock in the afternoon
2. Vespers — six o'clock in the afternoon
3. Compline — nine o'clock in the evening

Morning
1. Midnight Office — twelve midnight
2. Matins — three o'clock in the morning
3. First Hour — six o'clock in the morning

Daytime
1. Third Hour — nine o'clock in the morning
2. Sixth Hour — twelve noon
3. Divine Liturgy

The Weekly Cycle of Divine Services

The Weekly or Seven-day Cycle of Divine Services is the term for the order of services which extends for the duration of the seven weekdays. Each day of the week is dedicated to one or another important event or an exceptionally revered saint.

On **Sunday**, the Church remembers and glorifies the **Resurrection of Christ**.

On **Monday**, the first day after the Resurrection, the bodiless hosts are celebrated, the **angels** which were created before the human race, and which are the closest servants of God.

On **Tuesday**, **St. John the Baptist** is glorified as the greatest of the prophets and righteous of the Old Testament.

On **Wednesday**, the betrayal of the Lord by Judas is remembered, and in connection with this the services are centered around the **Cross of the Lord**. This day is a fast day.

On **Thursday the Holy Apostles** and **St. Nicholas the Wonder-worker** are glorified.

On **Friday** the Passion and death of the Saviour on the Cross is remembered, and the services honor the **Cross of the Lord**. This day is kept as a fast day also.

On **Saturday**, the Sabbath or **Day of Rest**, the **Mother of God** is glorified (who is also glorified on every other day), along with the **forefathers**, **prophets**, **apostles**, **martyrs**, **monastics**, **righteous** and **all the saints** who have attained peace in the Lord. Also, all those who have **reposed** in the true faith and in the hope of resurrection and life eternal are remembered.

The Annual Cycle of Divine Services

The Annual Cycle of Divine Services is the term for the order of services conducted during the course of the entire calendar year.

Each day of the year is dedicated to the memory of one or more saints and to special sacred events, either in the form of feast days or fasts.

Of all the feasts of the year the greatest is the **feast of the Bright Resurrection of Christ, Pascha**, the feast of feasts. Pascha occurs no earlier than the twenty-second of March (the fourth of April, new style) and no later than the twenty-fifth of April (the eighth of May, new style), on the first Sunday after the equinoxal new moon and always after the Jewish celebration of Passover.

In addition, throughout the year **twelve great feasts** are held in honor of our Lord Jesus Christ and the Theotokos. Also, there are feasts in honor of the **great saints** and in honor of the bodiless hosts of heaven, the **angels**. Thus the festivals of the year are distinguished, by their content, into those of the **Lord**, the **Theotokos**, and the **saints**.

With regard to their date, the celebration of the feasts is divided into those which are **immovable**, those which occur every year on the same calendar date of the months, and those which are **movable**, those which occur on the same day of the week, but may fall on various dates of a month due to their relationship to the celebration of Pascha.

In the solemnity of their celebration the church services of the feasts are distinguished according to various degrees. The great feasts are always celebrated with an **All-night Vigil**, other lesser feasts sometimes have a Vigil, according to custom. The solemnity and joy of other days in the church year is determined by guidelines indicated in the rubrics.

The church year begins on the first of September, according to the Julian (Old Style) calendar, and the entire yearly cycle of divine services is constructed around its relationship to Pascha.

A more detailed account of the feasts and fasts is to be found in the section on "Faith and the Christian Life," under the explanation of the fourth commandment of the Law of God, and in the sacred history of the New Testament.

CHAPTER 5

Divine Service Books

The first place among the books used in the divine services is occupied by the **Gospel**, the **Epistle** and the **Psalter**. These books are taken from the **Sacred Scriptures**, the Bible, and therefore are termed the "divine service" books.

After these come the following books: the **Clergy Service Books**, the **Horologion (Book of Hours)**, the **Book of Needs**, the **Octoechos**, the **Monthly Menaion**, the **General Menaion**, the **Festal Menaion**, the **Lenten Triodion**, the **Pentecostarion**, the **Typicon (or Book of Rubrics)**, the **Irmologion**, and the **Canonik**. These books were composed in accordance with the Holy Scriptures and Holy Tradition by the fathers and teachers of the Orthodox Church and are called the church service books.

The **Gospel** is the Word of God. It consists of the first four books of the New Testament written by the Evangelists Matthew, Mark, Luke and John. The Gospels contain an account of the earthly life of our Lord Jesus Christ: His teaching, miracles, passion and death on the Cross, His glorious Resurrection and His Ascension into Heaven. For the services, the Gospel is specially divided into the usual chapters and verses, but also into special sections. At the end of the volume one finds a series of tables which indicate when the various sections are to be read during the church year.

The **Epistle** is the term which refers to the book which contains the following books of the New Testament: the Acts of the Apostles, the catholic (general) epistles and the epistles of the Apostle Paul, thus excluding only the book of Revelation. The Epistle, like the Gospel, is divided, in addition to chapters and verses, into sections with tables at the back of the book indicating when and how to read them.

The **Psalter** is the book of the Prophet and King David. It is so termed because the majority of the psalms in it were written by the holy Prophet David. In these psalms the holy Prophet opens his soul to God with all the grief of repentance for sins committed, and joy and glorification of the infinite perfection of God. He expresses his gratitude for all the mercies of His care and seeks help amid all the obstacles that confront him. For this reason the Psalter is used more than any other service book during the course of the services.

The Psalter is divided, for use during services, into twenty sections called "kathismas" (derived from the Greek word "to sit", as it is customary to sit while they are being read). Each of these is divided into three portions called "Glories," since "Glory to the Father, and to the Son, and to the Holy Spirit..." is read between each part.

In addition to the simple Psalter there is also a "service" Psalter which contains three additions: a) the Horologion, b) the troparia and kontakia taken from all the other service books, and c) the entire prayer rule which should be said by those intending to partake of the Mystery of Holy Communion.

The **Clergy Service Book** is for the use of priests and deacons. It contains the order of Vespers, Matins and the Liturgy, with emphasis on the parts said by those serving. At the end of the book are found the dismissals, prokeimena, megalynaria, and a menologion, or list of saints commemorated daily by the Church.

The **Pontifical Service Book** is distinguished by the fact that it also contains the order of consecrating an Antimins and the services for tonsuring readers, and ordaining subdeacons, deacons and priests.

The **Horologion** is the book which serves as the basic guide for readers and chanters on cliros. The Horologion contains the unchanging parts of all the daily services, except the Liturgy.

The **Book of Needs** is the book which includes the order of services for the various Mysteries with the exception of the Mysteries of Holy Communion and Ordination. Other services included are the Order of Burial of the Reposed, the Order of Blessing of Water, the Prayers for the Birth of a Child, the Naming of a Child and his "Churching," as well as blessings for other occasions.

The **Octoechos**, or Book of the Eight Tones, contains all the hymns in the form of verses, troparia, kontakia, canons, etc., which are divided into eight groups of melodies, or "tones." Each tone in turn contains the hymnody for an entire week, so that the complete Octoechos is repeated every eight weeks throughout most of the year. The arrangement of ecclesiastical chanting into tones was entirely the work of the famous hymnographer of the Byzantine Church, St. John of Damascus (eighth century). The text of the Octoechos is ascribed to him, although one should note that many parts of it are the work of St. Metrophanes, bishop of Smyrna, St. Joseph the Hymnographer, and others over the centuries.

The **Monthly Menaion** contains the prayers and hymns in honor of the saints of each day of the year and the solemn festival services for the feasts of the Lord and the Theotokos which fall on fixed calendar dates. Following the number of twelve months, it is divided into twelve volumes.

The **General Menaion** contains the hymnography common to an entire category of saints, for example, in honor of prophets, or apostles, or martyrs, or monastics. It is used in cases when a special service to a particular saint is not available.

The **Festal Menaion** contains all the services for the immovable great feasts, as extracted from the Monthly Menaion.

The **Lenten Triodion** contains all the special parts of the services for the course of the Great Fast prior to Pascha and the Sunday services in the weeks preceding it, beginning with the Sunday of the Publican and the Pharisee. This service book derives its name from the Greek word "triod," which means tri-hymned, and refers to the fact that for each day of the Fast the canons chanted do not comprise the usual nine odes, based on nine great hymns from the Old and New Testament, but only three.

The **Pentecostarion** includes the hymnography used from the feast of Holy Pascha through the Sunday of All Saints, the first Sunday after Pentecost.

The **Typikon** or Book of Rubrics contains a detailed account of which days and times different services ought to be conducted and in which specific order they should be read or chanted, as contained in the Service Book of the Clergy, the Horologion, the Octoechos and the other divine service books.

The **Irmologion** contains the initial hymns or "irmosi" from each of the nine odes of the various canons as chanted at Matins since these are not always printed in full in the various service books.

The Ectenias (Litanies)

During the course of the divine services we often hear a series of prayerful supplications which are intoned slowly by either a deacon or the priest in the name of all those praying. After each petition the choir sings, "Lord, have mercy" or "Grant this, O Lord." These are called ectenias (litanies), which are Greek words meaning "entreaty" or "ardent supplication".

These are five of the most frequently used litanies:

1) The **Great Litany** or **Litany of Peace** which begins with the words **"In peace, let us pray to the Lord."** It contains many different petitions for prosperity and salvation of various groups, and after each one the choir chants "Lord, have mercy."

2) The **Small Litany** is a shortened form of the Great Litany. It begins with the words **"Again and again** in peace let us pray to the Lord."** It contains three petitions.

3) The **Augmented Litany** begins with the words **"Have mercy upon us, O God, according to Thy great mercy, we pray Thee, hearken and have mercy."** After each petition the choir responds with **"Lord, have mercy"** thrice. Therefore the litany is termed **"augmented,"** since it is an intensified supplication.

4) The **Litany of Fervent Supplication** begins with the words **"Let us complete our morning (or evening) prayer unto the Lord."** After each of the petitions of this litany, except for the first two, the choir responds with **"Grant this, O Lord."**

5) The **Litany for the Reposed** is composed of entreaties to the Lord that He might grant rest in the Heavenly Kingdom to the souls of the departed by forgiving them all their sins.

Each of these litanies concludes with an exclamation by the priest that glorifies the Most-holy Trinity.

CHAPTER 6

Reflections on the Major Services, the Various Liturgies and Their Basic Rubrics

The All-night Vigil

The **All-night Vigil** is the divine service which is served on the evening prior to the days of specially celebrated feasts. It consists of the combination of Vespers, Matins and First Hour, during which both services are conducted with greater solemnity and with more illumination of the church than on other days.

This service is given the name "**All-night**," because in ancient times, it began in the later evening and it continued through the entire night until dawn.

Later, in condescension to the weakness of the faithful, this service was begun earlier, and certain contractions were made in the readings and chanting, and therefore it now does not last so long as it did. However, the former term "**All-night**" is preserved.

Vespers

Vespers recalls and represents events of the Old Testament: the creation of the world, the fall into sin of the first human beings, their expulsion from Paradise, their repentance and prayer for salvation, the hope of mankind in accordance with the promise of God for a Saviour and finally, the fulfillment of that promise.

The Vespers of an All-night Vigil begins with the opening of the Royal Gates. The priest and deacon silently cense the Altar Table and the entire sanctuary so that clouds of incense fill the depths of the sanctuary. This silent censing represents the beginning of the creation of the world. *In the beginning God created heaven and earth.* And the earth was without form and void, and the Spirit of God hovered over the original material earth, breathing upon it a life-creating power, but the creating word of God had not yet begun to resound.

Then the priest stands before the Altar and intones the first exclamation to the glory of the Creator and Founder of the world, the Most-holy Trinity, "**Glory to the Holy, Consubstantial, Life-creating, and Indivisible Trinity, always, now and ever, and unto the ages of ages.**"

Then he four times summons the faithful, **"O come, let us worship God our King. O come let us worship and fall down before Christ, our King and our God. O come let us worship and fall down before Christ Himself, our King and our God. O come let us worship and fall down before Him."** For *All things were made by Him; and without him was not anything made that was made* (John 1:3).

In response to this summons, the choir solemnly chants the 103rd Psalm, which describes the **creation of the world** and glorifies the wisdom of God: *Bless the Lord, O my soul. Blessed art Thou, O Lord, O Lord my God, Thou hast been magnified exceedingly... In wisdom hast Thou made them all... Wondrous are Thy works, O Lord... Glory to Thee, O Lord, Who hast made them all.*

During the chanting of this psalm the priest goes forth from the sanctuary and completes the censing of the entire church and the faithful therein, while a deacon precedes him bearing a lit candle in his hand.

This sacred action not only reminds those praying of the creation of the world, but primarily of the blessed life in Paradise of the first human beings, when the Lord God Himself walked among them. The open Royal Gates signify that at that time the gates of Paradise were open for all people.

Then man was deceived by the Devil and transgressed against the will of God and fell into sin. Because of their fall, mankind was deprived of blessed life in Paradise. They were driven out of Paradise and the gates were closed to them. To symbolize this expulsion, following the censing of the church and the conclusion of the chanting of the psalm, the Royal Gates are closed.

Then the deacon comes out from the sanctuary and stands before the closed Royal Gates, as Adam did before the sealed entrance into Paradise, and intones the **Great Litany:**

In peace let us pray to the Lord. Let us pray to the Lord when we have been reconciled with all our neighbors, so that we feel no anger or hostility towards them. **For the peace from above, and for the salvation of our souls, let us pray to the Lord.** Let us pray that the Lord send down upon us "from on high" the peace of Heaven and that He save our souls.

After the Great Litany and the exclamation of the priest, certain selected verses are usually sung from the first three psalms of the Psalter: **Blessed is the man that hath not walked in the counsel of the ungodly**, that is, he who has not lived or acted on the advice of those who are irreverent and impious. **For the Lord knoweth the way of the righteous, and the way of the ungodly shall perish.** For the Lord knows the life of the righteous and the life of the impious leads to ruin. The deacon then intones the **Little Litany, "Again and again, in peace let us pray to the Lord..."** After this litany the choir chants the verses of certain psalms that express the longing of man for salvation and Paradise: *Lord, I have cried unto Thee, hearken unto me. Hearken unto me, O Lord... Attend to the voice of my supplication, when I cry unto Thee... Let my* *prayer be set forth as incense before Thee, the lifting up of my hands as an evening sacrifice. Hearken unto me, O Lord.* During the chanting of these verses the deacon censes the church once more.

This entire period of the divine service, beginning with the opening of the Royal Gates, through the petitions of the Great Ectenia and the chanting of the psalms, represents the miserable state of mankind to which it was subjected by the fall of our forefathers into sin. With the fall all the deprivations, pains and sufferings we experience came into our lives. We cry out to God, "Lord, have mercy" and request peace and salvation for our souls. We feel contrition that we heeded the ungodly counsel of the Devil. We ask God for the forgiveness of our sins and deliverance from troubles, and we place all our hope in the mercy of God. The censing by the deacon at this time signifies the sacrifices of the Old Testament and our own prayers as well, which we offer to God.

Alternating with the chanting of the Old Testament verses of these psalms of "Lord, I have cried" are New testament hymns composed in honor of the saint or feast of the day.

The last verse is called the **Theotokion**, or **Dogmatikon**, since it is sung in honor of the Mother of God, and in it is set forth the dogma on the incarnation of the Son of God from the Virgin Mary. On the twelve great feasts, instead of the Theotokion a special verse is chanted in honor of the feast.

During the chanting of the Theotokion the Royal Gates are opened, and the **Vespers Entry** is made; a candle bearer comes through the north door of the Sanctuary, followed by the deacon with the censer and finally the priest. The priest stops on the ambo facing the Royal Gates and after blessing the entry with the sign of the Cross, and the deacon's intoning of the words **"Wisdom, let us attend!"** the priest reenters the Altar together with the deacon through the Royal Gates and goes to stand next to the High Place behind the Holy Table.

At this time the choir chants a hymn to the Son of God, our Lord Jesus Christ: **"O Gentle Light of the holy glory of the immortal, heavenly, holy blessed Father, O Jesus Christ: having come to the setting of the sun, having beheld the evening light, we praise the Father, the Son, and the Holy Spirit: God. Meet it is for Thee at all times to be hymned with reverent voices, O Son of God, Giver of Life. Wherefore, the world doth glorify Thee."**

In this hymn the Son of God is called the Gentle Light that comes from the Heavenly Father, because He came to this earth not in the fullness of divine glory but in the gentle radiance of this glory. This hymn also says that only with reverent voices, and not our sinful mouths, can He be exalted worthily and the necessary glorification be accomplished.

The entry during Vespers reminds the faithful how the Old Testament righteous, in harmony with the promise of God that was manifest in prototypes and prophecies, expected the coming of the Saviour, and how He appeared in the world for the salvation of the human race.

The censer with incense used at the entry signifies that our prayers, by the intercession of our Lord the Saviour, are offered to God like incense. It also signifies the presence of the Holy Spirit in the church.

The blessing with the sign of the Cross shows that by means of the Cross of the Lord the doors into Paradise are opened again for us.

Following the chanting of the hymn "O Gentle Light..." we sing the **prokeimenon**, short verses taken from the Holy Scriptures. On Saturday evening, for the Vespers for Sunday, we chant, "The Lord is King; He is clothed with majesty".

After the chanting of the prokeimenon, on the more important feasts there are **readings**. These are selections from the Scriptures in which there is a prophecy or a prototype which relates to the event being celebrated, or in which edifying teachings are set forth, which relate to the saint commemorated that day.

Following the prokeimenon and readings the deacon intones the **Augmented Litany, "Let us all say with our whole soul and with our whole mind, let us say."** The prayer, **"Vouchsafe, O Lord, to keep us this evening without sin..."** follows, and at the conclusion of this prayer the deacon reads the Supplicatory Litany, **"Let us complete our evening prayer unto the Lord..."**

On great feasts after the Augmented and Supplicatory Litanies the **Litia**, or **Blessing of Bread and Wine**, is celebrated.

"Litia" is a Greek word meaning "common prayer." The Litia, a series of verses chanted by the choir followed by an enumeration of many saints whose prayers are besought, is celebrated in the western end of the church, near the main entrance doors, or in the Narthex, if the church is so arranged. This part of the service was intended for those who were standing in the Narthex, the catechumens and penitents, so they might be able to take part in the common service on the occasions of the major festivals.

At the end of the Litia is the **blessing and sanctification of five loaves of bread, wheat, wine and oil** to recall the ancient custom of providing food for those assembled who had come some distance, in order to give them strength during the long divine services. The five loaves are blessed to recall the feeding of the five thousand with five loaves of bread. Later, during the main part of Matins, the priest **anoints** the faithful with the sanctified oil, after they have venerated the festal icon.

After the Litia, or if it is not served, after the Supplicatory Litany, the **Aposticha** (Verses with hymns) are chanted. These are a few verses which are specially written in memory of the occasion.

Vespers ends with the reading of the prayer of St. Simeon the God-Receiver, **"Now lettest Thou Thy servant depart in peace, O Master, according to Thy word, for mine eyes have seen Thy salvation, which Thou hast prepared before the face of all peoples; a light of revelation for the gentiles and the glory of Thy people Israel."** This prayer is followed by the reading of the Trisagion and the Lord's Prayer, and the singing of the salutation of the Theotokos, **"O Theotokos and Virgin, Rejoice!...,"** or the troparion of the feast, and finally the thrice-chanted prayer of the Psalmist: **"Blessed be the name of the Lord from henceforth and for evermore."** The 33rd Psalm is then read or chanted until the verse, "But they that seek the Lord shall not be deprived of any good thing." Then follows the priestly blessing, **"The blessing of the Lord be upon you, through His grace and love for mankind, always, now and ever, and unto the ages of ages."**

The conclusion of Vespers with the prayer of St. Simeon and the angelic salutation of the Theotokos indicates the fulfillment of the divine promise of a Saviour.

Immediately after the conclusion of Vespers during an All-Night Vigil, **Matins** begins with the reading of the **Six Psalms**.

Matins

The second half of the All-night Vigil, **Matins**, is meant to remind us of the New Testament period: the appearance of our Lord Jesus Christ in the world for our salvation and His glorious Resurrection.

The beginning of Matins immediately reminds us of the Nativity of Christ. It begins with the doxology or glorification of the angels who appeared to the shepherds in Bethlehem: *Glory to God in the highest, and on earth, peace, goodwill among men.*

This is followed by the reading of the **Six Psalms**, selected from those by the Prophet David (3, 37, 62, 87, 102 and 142) in which the sinful condition of mankind is depicted with all its weakness and temptations. The ardent expectation of mankind for their only hope, the mercy of God, is expressed here. Those praying in church should be listening with special attentiveness and reverence to these psalms.

After the Six Psalms the deacon proclaims the **Great Litany**. The choir follows the Litany with the loud and joyful chant of this hymn with its verses: **"God is the Lord and hath appeared unto us; Blessed is He that cometh in the name of the Lord."** It is affirmed that God is Lord and has manifested Himself unto us, and He Who comes in the glory of the Lord is worthy of glorification.

The **troparion** or hymn that particularly honors and describes the feast or saint being celebrated follows, and then two **kathismas** are read, two of the twenty sections into which the Psalter is consecutively divided. The reading of the kathismas, as well as that of the Six Psalms, calls us to ponder our wretched, sinful condition and to place all our hope on the mercy and help of God. At the conclusion of each kathisma the deacon recites the **Small Litany**.

The **Polyeleos**, a Greek word meaning "much mercy," is then celebrated. The Polyeleos is the most festive and solemn part of Matins and the All-night Vigil, expressing the glorification of the mercy of God, which has been manifested to us by the coming to earth of the Son of God and His accomplishing our salvation from the power of the Devil and death. The Polyeleos begins with the triumphant singing of the verses of praise:

Praise ye the name of the Lord; O ye servants, praise the Lord. Alleluia. Blessed is the Lord out of Sion, Who dwelleth in Jerusalem. Alleluia. O give thanks unto the Lord, for He is good, for His mercy endureth forever. Alleluia. O give thanks unto the God of heaven; for His mercy endureth forever. Alleluia.

With the chanting of these verses all the lamps and candles in the church are lit, the Royal Gates are opened, and the priest, preceded by the deacon holding a lit candle, comes out of the altar and goes around the church censing as a sign of reverence for God and His Saints.

On Sundays, after the chanting of these verses, special Resurrection troparia, joyful hymns in honor of the Resurrection of Christ, are sung. They describe how the angels appeared to the Myrrhbearing women when they came to the tomb of Christ and told them of the Resurrection of Jesus Christ. On other great feasts instead of these Resurrection troparia, the Magnification, a short verse of praise in honor of the saint or feast of that day, is sung before its icon.

After the Resurrection troparia or the **Magnification**, the deacon repeats the **Small Litany**, which is followed by the singing of the **Hymns of Ascent**, alternately by two choirs. There are three antiphons for each of the eight tones (the eighth tone has four); one group being used on each Sunday, depending on the tone of the week. Other feast days the first antiphon of the fourth tone is used. The deacon then says the **prokeimenon** and the priest reads the **Gospel**.

At a Sunday service the reading from the Gospel concerns the Resurrection of Christ and the appearances of Christ to His disciples, while on other feasts the Gospel reading relates to the events being celebrated or to the saint being glorified.

On Sundays, after the Gospel, the solemn hymn in honor of the risen Christ taken from the Paschal Matins service is sung, **"Having beheld the Resurrection of Christ, let us worship the holy Lord Jesus..."**

The Gospel is then carried into the center of the church and the faithful proceed forward to venerate it. On other feasts the faithful venerate the festal icon, and the priest anoints them on the forehead with oil and distributes the bread blessed during the Litia.

After the hymn, "Having beheld the Resurrection...," the 50th Psalm is read as well as other hymns asking for the mercy of the Lord, the Theotokos and the Apostles. The deacon then reads the prayer for the intercession of the Saints, **"Save, O God, Thy people...,"** and the priest exclaims, **"Through the mercy and compassion...."** The **chanting of the Canon** begins.

The canon is the name for a series of hymns which are composed according to a definite order. "Canon" is a Greek word which means "rule." A canon is divided into nine parts or odes. The first verse of each ode is called the **irmos**, which means "connection" or "link" and is chanted. With these irmosi all the rest of the canon is joined into one whole. The rest of the verses for each ode, called troparia, are now usually read, although they were originally chanted to the same melody as the irmos. The second ode of the canons is included only during Great Lent due to its penitential character.

The most noted composers of these canons were Sts. John of Damascus, Cosmas of Maiouma and Andrew of Crete, who wrote the penitential Great Canon used during Great Lent. The hymnography of these composers was inspired by the prayers and actions of some of the great Old Testament saints. Though in common practice they are now chanted only during Great Lent, each ode should be preceded by the Biblical ode upon which each Canon ode is based. The figures commemorated for each Biblical ode, which are found at the end of the Psalter, are the Prophet Moses (first and second odes); the Prophetess Anna, the mother of Samuel (third ode); the Prophet Habbakuk (fourth ode); the Prophet Isaiah (fifth ode); the Prophet Jonah (the sixth ode); the three Hebrew children (seventh and eighth odes); and the Priest Zacharias, the father of St. John the Forerunner (ninth ode).

Prior to the beginning of the **ninth** ode, the deacon proclaims: **"The Theotokos and Mother of the Light, let us magnify in song,"** and proceeds to cense around the entire church. The choir then begins the Song of the Theotokos, **"My soul doth magnify the Lord, and my spirit hath rejoiced in God My Saviour."** Each verse of this hymn alternates with the singing of the refrain, **"More honorable than the Cherubim, and beyond compare more glorious than the Seraphim, Who without corruption gavest birth to God the Word, the very Theotokos, Thee do we magnify."** Following this hymn to the Theotokos, the choir continues with the irmos and troparia of the ninth ode of the canon.

Concerning the general content of the canons, the irmosi remind the faithful of the Old Testament period and events from the history of our salvation and gradually lead our thoughts to the Nativity of Christ. The troparia recount New Testament events and the history of the Church, presenting a series of verses or hymns glorifying the Lord and the Mother of God, and also honoring the event being celebrated, or the saint glorified on this day.

On major feasts each ode is concluded by a **katavasia**, a Greek word meaning "descent," and the deacon proclaims the Small Litany after the third, sixth and ninth odes.

On Sundays, **"Holy is the Lord our God"** is then alternated with a few verses, and another special verse for the feast called the **Exapostilarion**, or "Hymn of Lights," is chanted.

Then the **Lauds** or "Praises" (Psalms 148,149,150) are chanted, along with the verses for the "Praises," in which all of God's creation is summoned to glorify Him: **"Let every breath praise the Lord...."** If it is a major feast special hymns in honor of the occasion are inserted between the final verses.

The **Great Doxology** follows the chanting of the Lauds. The Royal Gates are opened during the singing of the last hymn of the Lauds (the Sunday Theotokion) and the priest exclaims, **"Glory to Thee Who has shown us the light."** The doxology begins **"Glory to God in the** highest, and on earth peace, goodwill among men. We praise Thee, we bless Thee, we worship Thee, we glorify Thee, we give thanks to Thee for Thy great glory..." In early Church practice the singing of this hymn just preceded the first light of dawn.

In the Great Doxology we give thanks to God for the light of day and for the bestowal of spiritual Light — the light of Truth, Christ the Saviour, Who has enlightened mankind with His teachings. The Doxology concludes with the chanting of the Trisagion and the singing of the festal troparion. The deacon then intones the **Augmented and Supplicatory** litanies.

Matins for an All-night Vigil concludes with the **Dismissal**. The priest turns to the faithful and says, "May Christ our true God (on Sundays, "Who rose from the dead" through the intercessions of His Most-pure Mother, of the holy, glorious, and all-praised Apostles, of the holy and righteous Ancestors of God Joachim and Anna, and of all the saints, have mercy on us and save us, for He is good and the Lover of mankind."

The choir responds with a prayer that the Lord preserve the Orthodox episcopate for many years, as well as the ruling hierarch and all Orthodox Christians. The last part of the All-night Vigil, the **First Hour**, follows. The service of the First Hour consists of the reading of three psalms and of various prayers, in which we request that God **hear our voices in the morning** and that He guide our hands during the course of the day. The First Hour concludes with the victorious hymn in honor of the Theotokos, **"To Thee the Champion Leader..."** The priest reads the **Dismissal for the First Hour**, and the All-night Vigil comes to an end.

CHAPTER 7

The Divine Liturgy

The **Liturgy** is the most important divine service, for in it the most holy Mystery of Communion is celebrated, as established by our Lord Jesus Christ on Holy Thursday evening, the eve of His Passion. After He had washed the feet of His disciples, to give them an example of humility, the Lord gave praise to God the Father, took bread, blessed it and broke it, giving it to the Apostles, saying, *Take, eat, this is My Body, which is broken for you.* Then He took a cup with grape wine and also blessed it and gave it to them with the words, *Drink of it all of you: for this is My Blood of the New Testament, which is shed for you and for many, for the remission of sins.* And when they had communed of these, the Lord gave them the commandment to always perform this Mystery, *Do this in remembrance of Me* (Matt. 26:26-28, Lk. 22:19; I Cor. 11:24).

The Apostles celebrated Holy Communion according to the commandment and example of Jesus Christ and taught all Christians to perform this great and saving Mystery. In the earliest times the order and form of celebrating the Liturgy was transmitted orally, and all the prayers and sacred hymns were memorized. Eventually, written explications of the apostolic Liturgy began to appear. As time passed, new prayers, hymns and sacred actions were added in various churches so that the uniformity of its performance was lost. The need arose to unify all the existing orders of the Liturgy and to reintroduce harmony in their celebration. In the fourth century, when the persecutions of the Romans against Christians ended, it was possible to re-establish good order in the Church's inner life through Ecumenical Councils. **St. Basil the Great** wrote down and offered for general use one form of the Liturgy, while **St. John Chrysostom** composed a shorter version of St. Basil's Liturgy. These liturgies were based on the most ancient Liturgy, ascribed to St. James the Apostle, the first bishop of Jerusalem.

St. Basil the Great, who reposed in 379 A.D, was archbishop of Caesarea in Cappadocia in Asia Minor. He is called "the Great" because of his great ascetic endeavors and his literary contribution to the Church of numerous prayers and ecclesiastical writings and rules.

St. John Chrysostom was an archbishop of Constantinople. He was called "Chrysostom" (in Greek, "the golden tongued") for his unique rhetorical gifts with which he proclaimed the Word of God. Though he reposed in 402 A.D. in exile, many volumes of his sermons and letters remain to edify us spiritually.

The liturgy is described by various terms. "Liturgy" itself is a Greek word meaning "common action or service" and signifies that the Mystery of Holy Communion is the reconciling sacrifice of God for the sins of **the entire** community of faithful, the living and the dead. Since the Mystery of Holy Communion is called "**Evharistia**" in Greek or "the Thanksgiving Sacrifice," the Liturgy is also called the "**Eucharist.**" It is also termed the "Mystical Supper" or the "Lord's Supper" since it is customarily celebrated around noon, and the Body and Blood of Christ offered in the Mystery of Holy Communion are called such in the Word of God (cf. I Cor. 10:21; 11:20). In apostolic times the Liturgy was referred to as the *breaking of bread* (Acts 2:46). In the Liturgy the earthly life and teachings of Jesus Christ, from His Nativity to His Ascension into Heaven, are recalled, as well as the benefits which He bestowed upon the earth for our salvation.

The order of the Liturgy is as follows. First, the elements for the Mystery are prepared, then the faithful are prepared for the Mystery, and finally the very Mystery itself is celebrated and the faithful receive Communion. The Liturgy is divided into three parts: I) the **Proskomedia**, II) the **Liturgy of the Catechumens** and III) the **Liturgy of the Faithful**.

The Proskomedia

"Proskomedia" is a Greek word meaning "**offering**." The first part of the Liturgy derives its name from the early Christian custom of the people offering the bread and wine, and all else that was needed for the Liturgy. Therefore the very bread which is used in it is termed "**prosphora**," another word meaning "**offering**." This bread or prosphora must be leavened, pure and made of wheat flour. The Lord Jesus Christ Himself, for the celebration of the Mystery of Holy Communion, used leavened, not unleavened bread, as is clear from the Greek word used in the New Testament. The prosphora must be round and is formed into two parts, one above the other, as an image of the two natures of Jesus Christ, divine and human. On the flat surface of the upper part a seal of the Cross is impressed, and in the four sections are thus formed the initial Greek letters of the name of "**Jesus Christ**," **IC XC**, and the Greek word **NIKA**, which mean "Jesus Christ conquers."

The wine used in the Mystery must be red grape wine, as this color reminds one of the color of blood. The wine is mixed with water to remind us of the pierced side of the Saviour from which flowed blood and water on the Cross. Five prosphoras are used in the Proskomedia to recall the five loaves with which Christ miraculously fed the five thousand, an event which gave Jesus Christ the means to teach the people about spiritual nourishment, about the incorrupt,

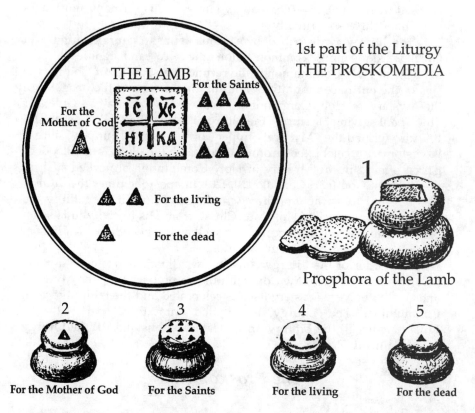

Prosphora of the Lamb

spiritual food which is bestowed in the Mystery of Holy Communion (John 6:22-58). For Communion only one prosphora is used (the Lamb), in accordance with the words of the Apostle: *one loaf, and we many are one body; for all have partaken of only one loaf* (I Cor. 10: 17). Therefore this one prosphora must correspond in size to the number of communicants.

The Celebration of Proskomedia

In order to prepare, according to the ecclesiastical Typikon, for the celebration of the Liturgy, the priest and deacon read the "entrance prayers" before the closed doors of the Royal Doors and then enter the Sanctuary and vest. Then going to the Altar of Oblation the priest blesses the beginning of Proskomedia, takes the **first prosphora**, the Lamb, and with the spear makes the sign of the Cross over it three times, saying the words, **"In remembrance of our Lord and God and Saviour, Jesus Christ."** These words mean that the Proskomedia is celebrated according to the commandments of Jesus Christ. The priest then cuts a cube out of the center of this prosphora with the spear and pronounces the words of the Prophet Isaiah, *He was led as a sheep to the* *slaughter, and as a blameless lamb before his shearer is dumb, so He openeth not His mouth; in His lowliness His Judgement was taken away* (Is. 53:7-8).

This cubical portion of the prosphora is called the **Lamb** (John 1:29) and is placed on the diskos. Then the priest cuts cruciformly the lower side of the Lamb while saying the words, "Sacrificed is the Lamb of God, that taketh away the sins of the world, for the life and salvation of the world." He then pierces the right side of the Lamb with the spear, saying the words of the Evangelist, *One of the soldiers with a spear pierced His side, and forthwith there came out blood and water. And he that saw it bare witness, and his witness is true* (John 19:34). In accordance with these words wine is poured into the chalice mixed with water. From the **second prosphora** the priest cuts out one portion in honor of the Mother of God and places it on the right side of the Lamb on the diskos. From the **third prosphora**, which is called "that of the nine ranks," are taken **nine portions** in honor of the saints, **John the Baptist, the prophets, the apostles, the hierarchs, the martyrs, the monastic saints, the unmercenaries, the parents of God, Joachim and Anna, the saint who is celebrated that day, and finally the saint whose liturgy is being celebrated**. These portions are placed on the left side the Lamb on the diskos in three rows of three. From the **fourth prosphora** portions are removed for the hierarchs, the priesthood and all the **living**, and are placed below the Lamb. From the **fifth prosphora**, portions are taken for those Orthodox Christians who have reposed, and these are placed just below those which were removed for the living. Finally, portions are removed from those prosphoras donated by the faithful as the names of the living and the dead are read simultaneously for the health and salvation and the repose of the servants of God. These are placed together with those portions taken from the fourth and fifth prosphoras. The Russian tradition is to use five separate prosphoras at the Proskomedia. Other traditions such as the Greek use one or two large ones from which the portions are taken.

At the end of the Proskomedia the priest blesses the censer and incense, and after censing the Star he places it on the diskos over the Lamb and the portions in order to preserve their arrangement. He covers the diskos and chalice with two small cruciform cloth covers, and over the two of them another larger veil called the "aer" is placed. Then he censes the Holy Gifts and prays that the Lord bless the offered gifts, remember those who have offered them and those for whom they are offered, and make the priest himself worthy for the solemn performance the Divine Mystery.

The sacred instruments used and actions performed in the Proskomedia have a **symbolic** meaning. The Diskos signifies the cave in Bethlehem and Golgotha; the Star, the star of Bethlehem and the Cross; the Covers and Veils, the swaddling clothes and the winding sheet at the tomb of the Saviour; the Chalice, that cup in which Jesus Christ sanctified the wine; the prepared Lamb, the judgment, passion and death of Jesus Christ; its piercing by the spear, the piercing of Christ's body by one of the soldiers. The arrangement of all the

The Nativity of Jesus Christ   *The Service of Proskomedia*

portions in a certain order on the diskos signifies the entire Kingdom of God whose members consist of the Mother of God, the angels, all the holy men who have been pleasing to God, all the faithful Orthodox Christians, living and dead, and in the center its head, the Lord Himself, our Saviour. The censing signifies the overshadowing by the Holy Spirit, whose Grace is shared in the Mystery of Holy Communion.

The Proskomedia is performed by the priest in a quiet voice at the Table of Oblation when the sanctuary is closed. During its celebration, the **Third and Sixth** (and sometimes the **Ninth) Hours are read** according to the Horologion.

The Liturgy of the Catechumens

The second part of the Liturgy is called the Liturgy of the Catechumens because the catechumens, those preparing to receive Holy Baptism and likewise the penitents who are temporarily excommunicated for serious sins, are allowed to participate in its celebration.

The deacon, upon receiving a blessing from the priest, goes out from the Altar to the Ambo, and loudly pronounces the words, "**Bless, Master**," that is, bless that the service begin and for the gathered faithful to partake in prayerful glorification of God. The priest in his first exclamation glorifies the Holy Trinity, "**Blessed is the Kingdom of the Father, and of the Son, and of the Holy Spirit, now and ever and unto the ages of ages.**" The choir responds with "Amen" ("so be it"). The deacon intones the **Great Litany** in which are enumerated the various needs of Christians and our requests to the Lord, at which time the

priest in the Altar privately prays that the Lord look down upon the
church and those at prayer in it and fulfill their needs. The Great Litany
begins by reminding us that in order to pray to the Lord one needs to
be "**at peace**," that is, reconciled with all, having no resentment, anger,
or hostility towards anyone. According to the teaching of the Saviour
we may not offer God any gifts, if we *have anything against our neighbor*
(Matt. 5:23-24). The loftiest good for which one should pray is this
peace of soul and the salvation of the soul: "**for the peace from above
(Heaven) and the salvation of our souls.**" This peace is that serenity of
conscience and sense of joy which we experience when we have conscientiously been to Confession and worthily partaken of Holy Communion, or that sympathetic concern for the welfare of our fellow men
when we have done a good deed. The Saviour bestowed this peace on
the Apostles during His farewell conversation at the Mystical Supper
(John 14:27). "**For the peace of the whole world**," asks that there be no
disputes and hostility among nations or races throughout the entire
world.

"**For the good estate of the holy churches of God**," is a prayer
that the Orthodox Churches in every country might firmly and unwa-
veringly, on the basis of the Word of God and the canons of the Universal Church, confess the Holy Orthodox Faith, and "**for the union of
all**," asks that all may be drawn into one flock of Christ (cf. John 10:16).

We pray "**for this holy temple**," which is the principle sacred object of the parish and should be the object of special care on the part of
each parishioner, so that the Lord preserve it from fire, thieves and
other misfortunes; and that those who enter it ("**for them that enter
herein**") do so with sincere faith, reverence, and the fear of God.

We pray for the **patriarchs, metropolitans, archbishops and bishops** because they are entrusted with the overall supervision of the purity of the Christian faith and morals; "**for pious rulers**," who preserve
the freedom of the Orthodox Faith and the general lawful order for the
peaceful life of all citizens; "**For this city** (or monastery)" in which we
live and work, and "**for every city, country and the faithful that dwell
therein**" we also pray in a spirit of Christian love, and for all the other
cities and their environs and all the faithful who live in them.

"**For seasonable weather, abundance of the fruits of the earth,
and peaceful times**": we pray for good weather so that the earth might
yield in abundance her fruits that are necessary for the nourishment of
all the inhabitants of these countries, and for peaceful times, so that
there be no enmity or conflicts among these citizens that will distract
them from peaceful and honorable labors; "**for travelers by sea, land
and air, for the sick, the suffering, the imprisoned and for their salvation**" — all those persons who more than others need divine aid and
our prayers.

We pray "**that we be delivered from every tribulation, wrath,
and necessity.**" Then we beseech the Lord that He defend and preserve
us not according to our deeds nor our merits, which we lack, but solely

according to His mercy: **"Help us, save us, have mercy on us, and keep us, O God, by The grace."**

In the final words of the Litany, **"calling to remembrance"** the Mother of God and all the saints, we entrust and surrender ourselves and each other to Christ God so that He might guide us according to His wise will. The priest concludes the Great Litany with the exclamation, **"For unto Thee is due all glory, honor, and worship, to the Father, and to the Son, and to the Holy Spirit, now and ever, and unto the ages of ages,"** which contains, according to the example of the Lord's Prayer, the doxology or glorification of the Lord God.

After the Great Litany, Psalms 102 (**"Bless the Lord, O my soul..."**) and 145 (**"Praise the Lord, O my soul..."**) are chanted, separated by the Small Litany, **"Again and again in peace let us pray to the Lord."** These psalms describe the blessings for the human race bestowed by God. The heart and **soul** of the Christian must **bless** the Lord, Who purifies and heals our mental and physical weaknesses and fills our desires with good things and delivers our life from corruption, and thus one must not forget all His **benefits**. The Lord is merciful, compassionate and longsuffering. He keeps truth unto the ages, gives Judgement to the wronged and food to the hungry, frees the imprisoned, loves the righteous, receives the orphan and widow and punishes the sinner.

These psalms are called the "Typical Psalms" and are chanted "antiphonally," with the verses alternating between two choirs. These psalms are not sung on the feasts of the Lord but are replaced by special verses from other psalms which relate to the events being celebrated. After each of these verses the refrain is chanted, **"Through the prayers of the Theotokos, O Saviour, save us."** The verses of the second festal antiphon are dependent on the feast being celebrated. For the Nativity of Christ we chant **"Save us, O Son of God, Who art born of the Virgin,"** **"Who wast baptized in the Jordan"** for the Theophany of the Lord, and **"Who art risen from the dead"** for Pascha. All are concluded with "save us who sing unto Thee. Alleluia."

The second antiphon is always followed by the hymn, **"O Only-begotten Son and Word of God, Who art immortal, yet didst deign for our salvation to be incarnate of the Holy Theotokos and Ever-Virgin Mary, and without change didst become man, Thou Who art one of the Holy Trinity, glorified with the Father and the Holy Spirit, save us."** This hymn sets forth the Orthodox teaching on the Second Person of the Trinity, the Son of God, Jesus Christ. He is the Only-begotten (one in essence) Son and Word of God, Christ God, Who being immortal, became human without ceasing to be God ("**without change**" — became **incarnate**) and accepted a human body from the Holy Theotokos and Ever-Virgin Mary. By His crucifixion, He with His death conquered our death, **"trampling down death by death,"** as one of the three Persons of the Holy Trinity, and is glorified equally with the Father and Holy Spirit.

The Small Litany and the chanting of the **Gospel Beatitudes** follow (Matt. 5:3-12). The Beatitudes indicate the spiritual qualities necessary for a Christian seeking the mercy of God: **humility of spirit** (spiritual poverty) and contrition concerning one's sins, **meekness** when drawing near the righteousness of God, **purity of heart, compassion** for one's neighbor, **seeking peace** in all situations, **patience** amid every temptation, and a readiness to endure **dishonor, persecution**, and **death for Christ**, trusting that as a confessor for Him, and for such ascetic struggles, one can expect a **great reward in Heaven**. Instead of the Gospel Beatitudes, on the great feasts of the Lord the festal troparion is sung several times with various verses.

During the chanting of the Gospel Beatitudes the **Royal Gates are opened** for the Small Entry. As the Beatitudes are ending the priest takes the Holy Gospel from the Altar, gives it to the deacon and comes out with the deacon, who carries the sacred Gospel through the north door onto the ambo. This entrance with the Holy Gospel by the clergy is termed the **Small Entry** to distinguish it from the Great Entrance which follows, and it reminds the faithful of the first appearance of Jesus Christ to the world, when He came to begin His universal preaching. After receiving a blessing from the priest, the deacon remains standing in the Royal Gates and raising the sacred Gospel aloft, he loudly proclaims, "**Wisdom! Aright!**" He then enters the Sanctuary and places the Gospel on the Holy Table. The exclamation, "Wisdom! Aright!" reminds the faithful that they must stand **upright** (in the literal meaning of the Greek word *Orthi* which is correctly, or straight) and be attentive, keeping their thoughts concentrated. They should look upon the Holy Gospel as upon Jesus Christ Himself Who has come to preach, and faithfully sing, "**O come, let us worship and fall down before Christ; save us, O Son of God, Who didst rise from the dead** (or, **through the intercessions of the Theotokos,** or **Who art wondrous in Thy saints), who chant unto Thee: Alleluia!**" The troparia and kontakia for Sunday, or the feast, or the saint of the day are then chanted, while the priest privately prays that the Heavenly Father Who is hymned by the Cherubim, and glorified by the Seraphim, receive from us the angelic (trisagion) hymn, forgive us our sins, and sanctify and grant us the power to rightly serve Him. The conclusion of this prayer, "**For Holy art Thou, our God...,**" is uttered aloud.

The **Trisagion Hymn**, "**Holy God...**", is then chanted, though for the Nativity of Christ, the Baptism of the Lord, Pascha and Bright Week, and the Day of the Holy Trinity, as well as on Holy Saturday and Lazarus Saturday, we chant, "**As many as have been baptized into Christ, have put on Christ: Alleluia.**" This hymn is chanted because in the early days of the Church, the catechumens received Holy Baptism on these days. On the feast of the Exaltation of the Cross of the Lord (September 14) and on the third Sunday of Great Lent (when the veneration of the Cross is celebrated) instead of the Trisagion we chant, "**before Thy Cross we bow down, O Master, and Thy Holy Resurrection we glorify.**"

The Appearance of Jesus   *The Little Entry With the Gospel*
Christ in the World.

Following the Trisagion the **Epistle** for the day is read from either the Book of Acts or the seven catholic epistles of the Apostles or the fourteen epistles of the Apostle Paul, according to a special order. The faithful are prepared for the attentive hearing of the Epistle by the exclamations, **"Let us attend,"** **"Peace to all,"** **"Wisdom"** and the chanting of the prokeimenon, which is a special short verse which changes with the day. During the reading of the Epistle a censing is performed as a symbol of the Grace of the Holy Spirit by which the Apostles proclaimed to the entire world the teachings of Jesus Christ. One should respond both to the censing and to the exclamation of the priest, "peace to all," with a simple bow, without making any sign of the Cross. **"Alleluia"** is sung three times with the intoning of special verses, and the **Gospel** of the day is read, also according to a special set of indications. This is preceded and accompanied by the chanting of a joyous hymn, **"Glory to Thee, O Lord, glory to Thee,"** since for the believing Christian there can be no more joyful words than those of the Gospel concerning the life, teachings, and miracles of the Lord Jesus Christ. The Epistle and Gospel must be listened to with particular attention, with a bowed head. It is good for people to familiarize themselves with the readings beforehand. Before the readings begin one ought to cross oneself and at their conclusion make the sign of the Cross and bow.

The Gospel is followed by the **Augmented Litany**, when the faithful are invited to pray to the Lord God with a pure heart and all the powers of their soul. **"Let us say with our whole soul and with our mind..."** In two of the petitions we fervently request the Lord to hear our prayer and to have mercy on us. **"O Lord, Almighty, the God of our Fathers, we pray Thee, hearken and have mercy — Have mercy on us, O God..."** Then follow the fervent petitions for the patriarchs, the metropolitans, the archbishops, the bishops, the ruling hierarch and **"all our brethren in Christ"** (all the faithful Christians), for pious rulers, for priests, priest monks and all the serving clergy of the Church of Christ, for the blessed and **ever-memorable** (always worthy of memory) holy Orthodox patriarchs, and pious kings, and rightbelieving queens, and for the founders of the holy church parish, and all the Orthodox fathers and brethren who have reposed, and are buried in the vicinity and everywhere. It is necessary to pray for the dead in the spirit of Christian love which never fails, all the more since for the reposed there is no more repentance after the grave, but only requital: blessed life or eternal torment. Christian prayer for them, good deeds accomplished in their memory, and especially the offering of the bloodless Sacrifice can evoke the mercy of God, lighten the torment of sinners, and according to Tradition even free them entirely.

We pray too for **mercy**, that the Lord will be compassionate towards us, for life, peace, health, salvation and the forgiveness of the sins of the **brethren of this holy temple** (the parishioners). The last petition of the Augmented Litany refers to those who are active and do good deeds in the holy, local church (parish), those who labor for it, those who chant and the people present who await of God great and abundant mercy. Those who are **active** and **do good deeds** for the church are those faithful who provide the church with all that is necessary for the divine service (oil, incense, prosphoras, etc.) and who contribute to the needs of the church and parish with their monetary and material goods for the beauty and decoration of the church, for the support of **those who work** for it, the readers, chanters, serving clergy, and those who help poor parishioners and provide help when other common religious and moral needs may arise.

The Augmented Litany is followed by the special **Litany for the Departed**, in which we pray for all the fathers and brethren who have reposed. We beseech Christ the immortal King and our God to forgive them all their sins, voluntary and involuntary, and to grant them a place of repose and serenity in the dwellings of the righteous, and, admitting that there is no man who has not sinned in his life, we ask the Righteous Judge to grant them the Heavenly Kingdom wherein all the righteous find peace.

The **Litany for the Catechumens** is then recited, in which we ask the Lord to have mercy on them and establish them in the truths of the Holy Faith (**"reveal unto them the Gospel of righteousness"**) and make them worthy of Holy Baptism (**"unite them to His Holy, Catholic and Apostolic Church"**). During this litany the priest opens the **Antimins** on the Altar, and the litany ends with the exclamation, **"that with us they also may glorify..."**; in other words, that they (the catechumens) might together with us (the faithful) glorify the all-honorable and great name of the Father, Son and Holy Spirit. Then the

catechumens are requested to depart from the church building: **"As
many as are catechumens, depart..."** Catechumens exist even today as

The Preaching of Jesus Christ

The Reading of the Gospel

people prepare to become Orthodox all over the world, pagans (in
China, Japan, Siberia, Africa), Muslims, and Jews — as well as those
coming into the Orthodox Church from the schismatic and heretical traditions of the Western denominations. They are all in need of the mercy
of God, and therefore we are obliged to pray for them. These words for
the catechumens to depart from the church building should also be a
warning to us, even if there are no actual catechumens among us. We,
the baptized, sin frequently and often without repentance are present
in the church, lacking the requisite preparation and having in our
hearts hostility and envy against our fellow men. Therefore, with the
solemn and threatening words, **"catechumens depart,"** we as unworthy ones should examine ourselves closely and ponder our unworthiness, asking forgiveness from our personal enemies, often imagined,
and ask the Lord God for the forgiveness of our sins with the firm resolve to do better.

With the words, **"As many as are of the faithful, again and again,
in peace let us pray to the Lord,"** the **Liturgy of the Faithful** begins.

The Liturgy of the Faithful

This third part of the Liturgy is so called because only the **faithful**
are allowed to be present during its celebration — those already baptized. It can be divided into the following sections: **1) The transferal of
the honored Gifts from the Table of Oblation to the Holy Table, 2) the**

preparation of the faithful for the consecration of the Gifts, 3) the consecration (transformation) of the Gifts, 4) the preparation of the
faithful for Communion, 5) Communion, and 6) the thanksgiving for
Communion and the Dismissal.

The Transferal of the Honored Gifts
From the Table of Oblation to the Holy Table

Following the request for the catechumens to depart from the
church two short litanies are proclaimed, and the **Cherubic Hymn** is
chanted: "Let us who mystically represent the Cherubim, and chant the
thrice-holy hymn unto the Life-creating Trinity, now lay aside all earthly
care, that we may receive the King of all, Who cometh invisibly upborne
in triumph by the ranks of angels. Alleluia."

The words of the original Greek for **"upborne in triumph"** mean
literally, "borne aloft as on spears." This refers to an ancient practice
when a nation, desiring to solemnly glorify its king or war leader, would
seat him upon their shields, and raising him aloft would carry him before
the army and through the city streets. As the shields were borne aloft on
the spears, so it would seem that the triumphant leader was carried by
their spears.

The Cherubic Hymn reminds the faithful that they have now left behind every thought for daily life, and offering themselves as a likeness of
the Cherubim, are found close to God in Heaven and, together with the
angels, sing the thrice-holy hymn in praise of God. Prior to the Cherubic
Hymn the **Royal Gates are opened** and the deacon performs the **censing**, while the priest in private prayers requests of the Lord that He purify his soul and heart from an evil conscience and by the power of the
Holy Spirit make him worthy to offer to God the Gifts which have been
presented. Then the priest, with the deacon, three times quietly says the
words of the Cherubic Hymn, and both proceed to the Table of Oblation
for the **transferal of the precious Gifts from the Table of Oblation to
the Holy Table.** The deacon, with the Aer on his left shoulder, carries the
Diskos on his head, while the priest carries the Chalice in his hands.

Leaving the altar by the north door, while the choir chants "Let us
lay aside all earthly care...," they come to a stop on the ambo, facing the
people. They commemorate the patriarchs, metropolitans, archbishops,
the local ruling bishop, the clergy, monastics, the founders of the church
(or monastery) and the Orthodox Christians who are present. They then
turn and enter the altar through the Royal Gates, place the precious gifts
on the Holy Table, on the opened Antimins, and cover them with the
Aer. As the choir finishes the Cherubic Hymn the Royal Gates and curtain are closed. The Great Entry symbolizes the solemn passing of Jesus
Christ to His voluntary suffering and death by crucifixion. The faithful
should stand during this time with bowed heads and pray that the Lord
remember them and all those close to them in His Kingdom. After the

priest says the words, "and all of you Orthodox Christians, may the Lord God remember in His kingdom," one must say softly, "And may the Lord God remember your priesthood in His Kingdom, always, now and ever, and unto the ages of ages."

The Preparation of the Faithful for the Consecration of the Precious Gifts

Following the Great Entry is the preparation of the faithful so that they might be worthy to be present during the consecration of the Gifts which have been prepared. This preparation begins with the Intercessory Litany, "Let us complete our prayer unto the Lord" for the "Precious Gifts set forth (offered)," so that they might be pleasing to the Lord. At the same time the priest prays privately that the Lord sanctify them with His Grace. We then pray that the Lord help us to pass the entire day in perfection, that is, holy, peaceful, and without sin, and that He send us a Guardian Angel to be a faithful guide on the path of truth and goodness, keeping our souls and bodies from every evil. We ask that He forgive and forget our accidental sins as well as our frequently repeated transgressions, that He grant us all that is good and beneficial for the soul and not those things which gratify our destructive passions, and that all people might live and work in peace and not in enmity and mutually destructive conflict; that we might spend the remainder of our lives at peace with our neighbors and with our own conscience and in contrition for the sins we have committed; that we be granted a Christian ending to our lives, that is, that we might confess and receive the Holy Mysteries of

The Lord's Entry Into Jerusalem   *The Great Entry*

Christ before our repose. We ask for an end to our lives which is peaceful, with peace of soul and reconciliation with our fellow men. Finally, we ask that the Lord deem us worthy to give a good, fearless account at His Dread Judgement.

In order to be present worthily at the celebration of the Holy Mysteries, the following are absolutely required: peace of soul, mutual love and the true (Orthodox) Faith, which unites all believers. Therefore, after the Litany of Intercession, the priest when blessing the people, says **"Peace be unto all."** Those praying express the same desire in their souls with the words, **"And to Thy spirit."** Then he exclaims, **"Let us love one another that with one mind we may confess...,"** and the choir chants, **"The Father, the Son, and the Holy Spirit, the Trinity, One in essence and indivisible."** This response indicates for us Who should be confessed in unanimity in order to recite the Creed in a worthy manner. Then comes the exclamation, **"The doors! the doors! In wisdom, let us attend."** The **Symbol of Faith** (the Creed) is then sung or read, in which briefly, but exactly, our faith in the Holy Trinity and the other main truths of the Orthodox Church are set forth. At this time the **curtain** behind the Royal Doors is opened and the celebrant lifts the Aer from the precious Gifts, and gently waves it over them in expectation of the descent of the Holy Spirit. The words **"The doors! the doors!"** in ancient times reminded the doorkeepers to watch carefully at the doors of the church that none of the catechumens or unbelievers enter. Today these words remind the faithful to close the doors of their souls against the assault of thoughts. The words, **"In wisdom, let us attend,"** indicate that we should be attentive to the truths of the Orthodox faith as set forth in the Creed.

From this point on, the faithful **should not leave** the church until the end of the Liturgy. The Fathers condemned the transgression of this requirement, writing in the ninth Apostolic Canon, "all faithful who leave the church... and do not remain at prayer until **the end**, as being those who introduce disorder into the church, should be separated from the church community." After the Symbol of the Faith the priest exclaims, **"Let us stand aright, let us stand with fear, let us attend, that we may offer the holy oblation in peace,"** directing the attention of the faithful to the fact that the time has come to offer the "holy oblation," or sacrifice. It is time to celebrate the Holy Mystery of the Eucharist, and from this moment one ought to stand with special reverence and attentiveness. The choir then responds, **"A mercy of peace, a sacrifice of praise."** We offer with gratitude for the mercy of heavenly peace granted to us from above the only sacrifice we can, that of praise. The priest blesses the faithful with the words, **"The grace of our Lord Jesus Christ, and the love of God the Father, and the communion of the Holy Spirit be with you all."** His next words, **"Let us lift up our hearts,"** summon us to a reverent presenting of ourselves before God. The choir responds with reverence in the name of those praying, **"We lift them up unto the Lord,"** affirming that our hearts are already striving and aspiring to the Lord.

The Consecration of the Gifts

The act of the Holy Mystery of Communion comprises the **main** portion of the Liturgy. It begins with the words of the priest, **"Let us give thanks unto the Lord."** The faithful express their gratitude to the Lord for His mercy by bowing to Him, while the choir chants, **"It is meet and right to worship the Father, the Son, and the Holy Spirit, the Trinity, one in essence and indivisible."** Praying silently, the priest offers a **eucharistic** prayer (one of thanksgiving), glorifying the infinite perfection of God, giving thanks to the Lord for the creation and redemption of mankind and for His mercy, in forms both known and unknown, and for the fact that He deems us worthy to offer Him this bloodless sacrifice, although the higher beings, the archangels, angels, Cherubim and Seraphim stand before Him **"singing the triumphal hymn, shouting, crying aloud, and saying:"**. These last words of the priest are said aloud as the choir proceeds with the described hymn by singing the angelic hymn, **"Holy, holy, holy, Lord of Sabaoth, Heaven and earth are full of Thy glory."** Then the choir adds to this hymn, which is called the "Seraphic Hymn," the exclamation with which the people greeted the entry of the Lord into Jerusalem, **"Hosanna** (a Hebrew expression of good will: save, or help, O God!) **in the highest, blessed is He that cometh in the name of the Lord, hosanna in the highest!"** The words, **"singing the triumphal hymn,"** are taken from the visions of the Prophet Ezekiel (1:4-24) and the Apostle John the Theologian (Rev. 4:6-8). In both their visions they beheld the throne of God surrounded by angels in the form of an eagle (**singing**), a bull (**shouting**), a lion (**crying out**) and a man (**saying**) who continually were exclaiming, **"Holy, holy, holy, Lord God of Hosts."**

The priest privately continues the eucharistic prayer which glorifies the benevolence and the infinite love of God, which was manifest in the coming upon the earth of the Son of God. In remembrance of the Mystical Supper, when the Lord established the holy Mystery of Communion, he pronounces aloud the words of the Saviour which He spoke upon instituting the Holy Mystery, **"Take, eat; this is My Body, which is broken for you, for the remission of sins"** and **"Drink of it, all of you: this is My Blood of the New Testament, which is shed for you and for many, for the remission of sins."** The priest then inaudibly recalls the commandment of the Saviour to perform this Mystery, glorifies His passion, death, and resurrection, ascension, and His second coming, and then aloud says, **"Thine own of Thine own, we offer unto Thee, in behalf of all and for all,"** for all the members of the Orthodox Church and for the mercy of God.

The choir then chants slowly, **"We praise Thee, we bless Thee, we give thanks unto Thee, O Lord, and we pray unto Thee, O our God,"** while the priest in private prayer asks the Lord to send down the Holy Spirit upon the people present and the Gifts being offered and that He might sanctify them. In a subdued voice he reads the troparion from the Third Hour, **"O Lord, Who didst send down Thy Most Holy Spirit upon Thine apostles at the third hour, take Him not from us, O Good One, but renew Him in us who pray unto Thee."** The deacon pronounces the twelfth verse from the Fiftieth Psalm, **"Create a clean heart in me, O God, and renew a right spirit within me."** Then the priest again reads the troparion from the Third Hour, and the deacon pronounces the next verse from the same psalm, **"Cast me not away from Thy presence, and take not Thy holy spirit from me."** The priest reads the troparion for the third time. Blessing the Lamb on the Diskos, he says, **"And make this bread the precious Body of Thy Christ."** Blessing the wine in the Chalice, he says, **"And that which is in this cup, the precious Blood of Thy Christ."** After each blessing the deacon says, **"Amen."** Finally, blessing the bread and wine together the priest says, **"Changing them by Thy Holy Spirit."** Again the deacon says, **"Amen, amen, amen."** At this great and sacred moment the bread and wine are changed into the true Body and true Blood of Christ. The priest then makes a full prostration to the ground before the Holy Gifts as to the Very King and God Himself. **This is the most important and solemn moment of the Liturgy.**

After the sanctification of the Holy Gifts the priest in private prayer asks the Lord that, for those who partake the Holy Gifts, it might serve **"unto sobriety of soul** (that is, that they may be strengthened in every good deed), **unto the remission of sins, unto the communion of the Holy Spirit, unto the fulfillment of the Kingdom of Heaven, unto boldness toward Thee; not unto Judgement or condemnation."** He then remembers those for whom the Sacrifice is offered, for the Holy Gifts are offered to the Lord God as a Sacrifice of Thanksgiving for all the saints. Then the priest gives special remembrance of the Most-holy Virgin Mary and says aloud, **"Especially for our most holy, most pure, most blessed, glorious Lady Theotokos and Ever-Virgin Mary,"** to which the faithful respond with the laudatory hymn in honor of the Mother of God, **"It is truly meet..."** (During Holy Pascha and all the twelve great feasts, until their giving up, instead of "It is truly meet..." a special hymn is chanted, which is the ninth irmos of the festal canon from Matins with its appropriate refrains.) The priest at this time privately prays for the reposed, and in beginning the prayer for the living says aloud, **"Among the first, remember, O Lord, the Orthodox episcopate...,"** that is, the most holy Eastern Orthodox patriarchs and the ruling hierarchy. The faithful respond, **"And each and every one."** The prayer for the living ends with the exclamation of the priest, **"And grant unto us that with one mouth and one heart we may glorify and hymn Thy most honorable and majestic name, of the Father, and of the Son, and of the Holy Spirit, now and ever, and unto the ages of ages."** After this he gives his blessing to all those present, **"And may the mercy of our great God and Saviour, Jesus Christ, be with you all."**

The Blessing of the Bread and Wine by the Lord at the Mystical Supper

The Consecration of the Gifts

The Preparation of the Faithful for Communion

This section begins with the Supplicatory Litany, **"Having called to remembrance all the saints, again and again, in peace let us pray to the Lord....For the precious Gifts now offered and sanctified...That our God, the Lover of mankind, Who hath received them upon His holy and most heavenly and noetic altar as an odor of spiritual fragrance, will send down upon us Divine Grace and the gift of the Holy Spirit..."** Then come the usual requests of the Supplicatory Litany, which ends with the exclamation of the priest, **"And vouchsafe us, O Master, with boldness and without condemnation to dare to call upon Thee, the Heavenly God, as Father, and to say."** The choir chants the **"Our Father...,"** and in some churches all those present sing this prayer together. Then follows the bestowal of peace and the bowing of one's head during which the priest prays to the Lord that He sanctify the faithful and enable them to partake without condemnation of the Holy Mysteries. At this time the deacon, while standing on the ambo, takes the orarion from his shoulder and girds himself with it in a cruciform pattern, in order to 1) serve the priest unencumbered during Communion and 2) to express his reverence for the Holy Gifts by representing the Seraphim who, as they surround the Throne of God, cover their faces with their wings (Is. 6:2-3). During the exclamation of the deacon, **"Let us attend,"** the curtain is closed and the priest lifts the Holy Lamb above the Diskos and loudly proclaims, **"Holy things are for the holy."** This means that the Holy Gifts may be given only to the "holy," that is, the faithful who have sanctified themselves with prayer, fasting and the Mystery of Repentance.

In recognition of their unworthiness, the chanters, in the name of the faithful, exclaim, **"One is Holy, One is Lord, Jesus Christ, to the glory of God the Father. Amen."**

The faithful who intend to come to Holy Communion must in advance attend the Vigil service in the church and read at home "The Order of Preparation for Holy Communion."

Communion

Then follows the communion of the serving clergy in the Sanctuary. The priest divides the Holy Lamb into four parts, and communes himself and then gives the Holy Mysteries to the deacon. After the communion of the clergy, the portions intended for the communion of the laity are put into the Chalice. During the communion of the clergy various verses of the psalms termed "Communion verses" are chanted, followed by various hymns relating to the feast, or the Prayers before Communion are read. The **Royal Gates are opened** then in preparation of the communion of the faithful laity, and the deacon with the sacred Chalice in his hands calls out, **"With the fear of God and faith draw near."** The opened Royal Doors are symbolic of the open tomb of the Saviour, and the bringing forth of the Holy Gifts of the appearance of Jesus Christ after His resurrection. After bowing to the Holy Chalice as before the very risen Saviour Himself, the choir, as representatives of the faithful, chant, **"Blessed is He that cometh in the name of the Lord. God is the Lord and hath appeared unto us."** Those of the faithful who are to commune, "with the fear of God and faith," make a preliminary bow to the Holy Chalice and then listen quietly to the prayer before Communion, **"I believe, O Lord and I confess..."** in which they confess their faith in Jesus Christ as the Son of God, the Saviour of sinners, their faith in the Mystery of Communion by which, in the visible form of bread and wine, they receive the true Body and Blood of Christ as a pledge of eternal life and the Mystery of Communion with Him. They beseech Him to deem them worthy of partaking without condemnation of the Sacred Mysteries for the forgiveness of sins, promising not only not to betray Christ, as did Judas, but even amid the sufferings of life to be like the wise thief, and to firmly and boldly confess their faith. After making a **full prostration** — if it is not a Sunday — the faithful step forward and go up to the ambo. To keep good order and out of reverence one should not leave one's place, nor is it proper to impede or embarrass others with a desire to be first. Likewise, one should not be overly cautious and fearful, but should step forward with gratitude and serenity of faith. Each should remember that he is **the first among sinners**, but that the mercy of the Lord is infinite. With one's hands crossed over one's chest one should step forward to the Royal Gates for Communion and, without making a sign of the Cross near the Chalice, receive Communion from the spoon in the priest's hands. After receiving, one kisses the side of the Chalice, again without making any sign of the Cross, so that the Chalice will not be accidently hit.

Children are encouraged to take Communion often from their earliest infancy, in the name of the faith of their parents and educators in accordance with the words of the Saviour, *Suffer the little children to come*

The Communing of the Apostles

The Communing of the Clergy in the Altar

unto Me and *Drink of it, all of you.* Children under seven or so are allowed to take Communion without confession, as they have not reached the age of responsibility or discernment.

Following Communion, the communicants step away from the Royal Gates to the small table set out specially in the center of the church, upon which are a mixture of water and wine together with some small portions of prosphora, which they drink and eat so that none of the Holy Gifts remain in the mouth but are washed down. After the communion of the laity, the priest puts all the particles taken from the offered prosphora into the Holy Chalice with a prayer that the Lord purify with His Blood the sins of all those commemorated through the prayers of the saints. He blesses the congregation with the words, **"Save, O God, Thy people** (those who believe in Thee) **and bless Thine inheritance,"** (those who are Thine own, the Church of Christ). In response the choir chants, **"We have seen the true Light, we have received the Heavenly Spirit, we have found the true faith, we worship the indivisible Trinity: for**

The First Appearance of the Lord   *The First Appearance of the Holy Gifts*
after the Resurrection

He hath saved us."** This means that we have seen the true light since, having washed our sins in the Mystery of Baptism, we are called the sons of God by Grace, sons of the Light. We have received the Holy Spirit by means of sacred Chrismation, we confess the true Orthodox Faith and worship the indivisible Trinity, because He has saved us. The deacon takes the Diskos from the priest, who hands it to him from the Holy Table, and raising it before him bears it to the Table of Oblation, while the priest takes the Holy Chalice and blesses the faithful with the exclamation, **"Always, now and ever, and unto the ages of ages"** and then likewise carries it to the Table of Oblation. This last elevating and presentation of the Holy Gifts to the congregation, their removal to the Table of Oblation, and the exclamation, are to remind us of the **Ascension of the Lord Jesus Christ into heaven and His promise to remain in the Church** *for all time unto the end of the ages* (Matt. 28:20).

Thanksgiving for Communion and the Dismissal

Bowing to the Holy Gifts for the last time, as to the **very Lord Jesus Christ Himself,** the faithful express their thanks to the Lord for Communion of the Holy Mysteries. The choir chants the hymn of gratitude, **"Let our mouth be filled with Thy praise, O Lord, that we may hymn Thy**

The Communion of the Faithful

glory, for Thou hast vouchsafed us to partake of Thy holy, divine, immortal and life-creating Mysteries. Keep us in Thy holiness, that we
may meditate on Thy righteousness all the day long. Alleluia."

Having exalted the Lord because He has deemed us worthy of partaking of the Divine and immortal and life-creating Mysteries, we ask
Him to preserve us in the holiness which we have received through the
Holy Mystery of Communion, that we may contemplate on the righteousness of God throughout the entire day. Following this, the deacon
intones the Small Litany, **"Aright! Having partaken of the divine, holy,
most pure, immortal, heavenly, and life-creating, fearful Mysteries of
Christ,"** and thus summons us to **"worthily give thanks unto the Lord."**

Having asked His help in living the whole day in holiness, peace,
and sinlessness, he invites us to devote ourselves and our lives to Christ
God. The priest, folding up the Antimins and placing it on the Gospel,
exclaims, **"For Thou art our sanctification, and unto Thee do we send**

The Last Appearance of   *The Last Appearance of the Holy Gifts*
the Lord at the Ascension

up glory, to the Father, and to the Son, and to the Holy Spirit, now and ever, and unto the ages of ages." And then he adds, "Let us depart in peace."

This indicates that the Liturgy has concluded and that one should leave the Church at peace with all. The choir in the name of all chants, "In the name of the Lord," that is, we go forth with the blessing of the Lord. The priest then comes out through the Royal Gates and stands facing the Altar in front of the Ambo and reads the "Prayer before the Ambo," in which he again requests that the Lord save his people and bless His inheritance, sanctify those who love the splendor of the church building, and not deprive all those who hope on His mercy, grant peace to the world, to the priests, to faithful rulers, and to all mankind. This prayer is a condensed version of all the litanies uttered throughout the Divine Liturgy.

After the conclusion of the prayer before the ambo the faithful devote themselves to the will of God with the prayer of the Psalmist "Blessed be the name of the Lord from henceforth and forevermore." Often at this point a pastoral sermon, based on the Word of God, is given for the spiritual enlightenment and edification of the people. The priest then offers a final blessing, "The blessing of the Lord be upon you, through His grace and love for mankind, always, now and ever, and unto ages of ages," and gives thanks unto God, "Glory to Thee, O Christ God, our hope, glory to Thee."

Turning to the people and signing himself with the sign of the Cross, which the people should also make, the priest utters the **Dismissal, "May Christ our True God..."** At the Dismissal, after the priest commemorates the prayers for us by the Mother of God, the saint of the church, the saints whose memory is celebrated on that day, the righteous ancestors of God, Joachim and Anna (the parents of the Mother of God), and all the saints, he expresses the hope that Christ the true God, will have mercy and save us since He is good and loves mankind. He steps to the bottom of the ambo and holds the holy Cross for the faithful to venerate and distributes the antidoron, the remainders from the prosphora which are cut into small pieces. In an orderly fashion the faithful proceed forward to kiss the Cross as a witness to their faith in the Saviour, in Whose memory the Divine Liturgy was celebrated. The choir chants a short prayer for the preservation **for many years** of the most holy Orthodox patriarchs, the ruling bishop, the parishioners and all Orthodox Christians.

The Liturgy of St. Basil The Great

The Liturgy of St. Basil the Great in its content and order is almost identical with the Liturgy of St. John Chrysostom. The only differences are the following:

1) The prayers which the priest reads privately in the altar, especially that of the Eucharistic Canon, are significantly longer, and therefore the chanting for this Liturgy is of longer duration.

2) The words of the Saviour by which He instituted the Mystery of the Holy Eucharist are as follows, **"He gave it to His holy disciples and apostles, saying: Take, eat; this is My Body, which is broken for you for the remission of sins."** And then, **"He gave it to His holy disciples and apostles, saying: Drink of it all of you: this is My blood of the New Testament, which is shed for you and for many for the remission of sins."**

3) Instead of the hymn, "It is truly meet to bless thee...," a special hymn in honor of the Mother of God is chanted, **"In Thee rejoiceth, O Thou who art full of grace, all creation, the angelic assembly and the race of man..."**

In addition to these, when the Liturgy of St. Basil is celebrated on Great and Holy Thursday, the Cherubic Hymn is replaced by **"Of Thy mystical supper, O Son of God,..."** and on Great and Holy Saturday: **"Let all human flesh keep silence..."**

The Liturgy of St. Basil is celebrated only **ten times throughout the year, on the eve of the feasts of the Nativity of Christ and the Theophany** (or on the feasts themselves if they fall on Sunday or Monday), **the first of January** (the day St. Basil is commemorated), on the **five Sundays of Great Lent** (excluding Palm Sunday), and on **Great Thursday** and **Great Saturday of Passion Week.**

St. Basil the Great

The Liturgy of the Presanctified Gifts

The distinguishing characteristic of the Liturgy of the Presanctified Gifts is that the Eucharistic Canon is not served during its celebration but rather the faithful are communed with "**Presanctified Gifts**," gifts which were consecrated earlier at another Liturgy of either St. Basil the Great or St. John Chrysostom.

The Presanctified Liturgy originated in the first centuries of Christianity. The first Christians took communion frequently, some even on weekdays. However, it was considered improper to serve a full Liturgy on days of strict fasting, as they were days of grief and contrition for sins.

Since the Liturgy is the most magnificent of all the church services, in order to give the faithful the opportunity to receive Holy Communion on fast days in the middle of the week, without destroying the character of the divine services of Great Lent, they were provided with the Gifts consecrated earlier. For this reason the service of the Presanctified Gifts was introduced into the services of Great Lent. The definitive order of this Liturgy was put into written form by **St. Gregory the Dialogist**, the Pope of Rome in the sixth century.

The Liturgy of the Presanctified Gifts is celebrated on **Wednesdays** and **Fridays** of the first six weeks of **Great Lent**, on **Thursday of the fifth week**, when the Great Canon of St. Andrew is commemorated, on February 24th, the commemoration of First and Second Findings of the Head of St. John the Baptist, sometimes on March 9th, the day commemorating the Forty Martyrs of Sebaste, if it falls on a fast day, and not a Saturday or Sunday; and on the **first three days of Passion Week** (Great Monday, Tuesday and Wednesday).

The Presanctified Liturgy is served following the Lenten Hours and consists of **Vespers** joined to the **Liturgy of the Faithful**, with the omission of its central part, the sanctification of the gifts.

One **kathisma** is added to each of the Lenten **Hours** so that the Psalter might be read twice during the week rather than the usual once.

After the kathisma the priest leaves the altar and reads the **troparion** of each hour in front of the Royal Doors with its corresponding verses, and makes appropriate prostrations while the choir chants this troparion three times.

In the **troparion of the Third Hour** we ask the Lord to not take from us, due to our sins, the Holy Spirit that He sent down upon His disciples.

In the **troparion of the Sixth Hour** we beseech Christ, Who voluntarily endured crucifixion on the Cross for us sinners, to forgive us our sins.

In the **troparion of the Ninth Hour** we beseech Christ, Who died for us, to mortify the sinful movements of our flesh.

At the end of each hour we read with prostrations the **Prayer of St. Ephraim the Syrian: "O Lord and Master of my life..."**

During the Sixth Hour there is a reading from the book of the Prophet Isaiah.

The Ninth Hour is followed by the Typica, and the **Beatitudes** are read along with the prayer of the repentant thief on the Cross, **"Remember us, O Lord, when Thou comest into Thy kingdom."** Then various prayers are read, followed by the Prayer of St. Ephraim and the Dismissal.

Immediately after this, **Vespers** with the Liturgy of the Presanctified Gifts begins with the exclamation, **"Blessed is the kingdom of the Father, and the Son, and the Holy Spirit, now and ever and unto the ages of ages."**

Up to the Entry the service proceeds in the usual order. After the Entry and **"O Gentle Light"** the reader goes to the center of the church and reads two **lessons**, one from the Book of Genesis relating to the fall of Adam and his unfortunate descendants, the other from the Proverbs of Solomon which exhorts one to seek and love divine wisdom. Between these two readings the **Royal Gates are opened** and the priest, holding a lit candle and censer, proclaims the words, **"Wisdom! Aright!,"** blesses the faithful with them and says, **"The light of Christ enlighteneth all."**

In response, the faithful, recognizing their unworthiness before Christ, the pre-eternal Light which enlightens and sanctifies mankind, make a **prostration to the floor**.

Following the second reading, the Royal Gates are again opened, and in the center of the church, choir members slowly chant these Psalm verses:

"Let my prayer be set forth as incense before Thee, the lifting up of my hands be an evening sacrifice.

"Lord, I have cried unto Thee, hearken unto me; attend to the voice of my supplication..."

During the chanting of these verses, the faithful are kneeling prostrate and the priest, standing before the Holy Table, censes.

Vespers concludes at this point with the Prayer of St. Ephraim, **"O Lord and Master of my life...,"** and the main portion of the Presanctified Liturgy begins.

On the first three days of Passion Week (Monday, Tuesday, Wednesday), after this prayer the Gospel is read. On other days the **Augmented Litany and the Litanies of the Catechumens and of the Faithful** are intoned as in a usual Liturgy.

During the **Great Entry**, instead of "Let us who represent the Cherubim..." the choir chants, **"Now the powers of Heaven invisibly serve with us; for behold, the King of Glory entereth. Behold, the mystical sacrifice that hath been accomplished is escorted."** During this hymn the **Royal Gates are opened** and the **Altar is censed**.

With the conclusion of the first half of this hymn, with the words "is borne in triumph," the Presanctified Gifts are transferred from the Table of Oblation to the Altar Table. The priest, with the Chalice, preceded by candles and the deacon with the censer, goes out through the north door on to the solea with the Diskos over his head, and silently bears them into the Sanctuary and places them on the Antimins which has been opened earlier on the Altar. Then the choir concludes the interrupted hymn, "With faith and love let us draw nigh that we may become partakers of life everlasting. Alleluia." Since the Sacred Gifts are already consecrated (transformed into the Body and Blood of Christ) the praying faithful fall prostrate during their transferal to the main altar. The priest then prays "O Lord and Master of my life..." after which the Royal Doors are closed.

Since at this Liturgy the consecration of the Gifts does not occur, all which relates to this sacred action is omitted. Thus, after the Great Entry only the three final portions of the Liturgy of the Faithful are celebrated: **a) the preparation of the faithful for Communion, b) the communion of the clergy and the laity,** and **c) the thanksgiving for Communion with the dismissal.** All are celebrated as during a full Liturgy with only minor

St. Gregory Pope of Rome Author of the Liturgy of the Presanctified Gifts

alterations in accordance with the significance of the Liturgy of the Presanctified Gifts.

The **Prayer before the Ambo** differs in this Liturgy. The priest in the
name of the faithful gives thanks to God, Who has deemed them worthy
to reach the days of this fast for the purification of the soul and body, and
requests that He give His help in accomplishing the good struggle of the
fast, preserve them unchanged in the Orthodox Faith, manifest Himself
as the conqueror of sin, and grant them uncondemned to worship the
holy Resurrection of Christ.

St. Gregory the Great of Rome and Archdeacon Peter

CHAPTER 8

The Most Important Actions During the Serving of the Mysteries and Reflections on Their Significance

For the inner power and significance of the Mysteries see the explanation of the tenth article of the Symbol of Faith.

Baptism and Chrismation

Before the Mystery of Baptism is celebrated one is given a name in honor of one of the saints of the Orthodox Church. In this rite the priest thrice makes the sign of the Cross over the candidate and prays to the Lord to be merciful to the person and, after joining him through Baptism to the Holy Church, to make him a partaker of eternal blessedness.

When the time arrives for Baptism the priest prays to the Lord to drive away from the person every evil and impure spirit which is concealed and rooted in his heart and to make him a member of the Church and an heir of eternal blessedness. The one being baptized renounces the Devil and gives a promise not to serve him, but rather Christ, and by reading the Creed confirms his faith in Christ, as King and God. In the case of the Baptism of an infant, the renunciation of the Devil and all his works, as well as the Symbol of Faith are said in his name by the sponsors, the godfather and/or the godmother, who thus become the guardians of the faith of the one being baptized and take upon themselves the duty to teach him the faith when he reaches maturity, and the responsibility to see to it that he lives in a Christian manner. Then the priest prays that the Lord sanctify the water in the font, drive out of it the Devil, and make it for the one being baptized a source of a new and holy life. He thrice makes the sign of the Cross in the water, first with his fingers, and then with consecrated oil with which he will likewise anoint the person being baptized, as a sign of the mercy of God towards him. Following this the priest three times immerses him in the water with the words, "The servant of God N. is baptized, in the name of the Father, Amen; And of the Son, Amen; And of the Holy Spirit, Amen." A white garment is put on the newly baptized, and he is given a cross to wear. The white garment serves as a sign of his purity of soul after Baptism and reminds him to henceforth

Holy Baptism

preserve this purity, and the cross serves as a visible sign of his faith in Jesus Christ.

Immediately after this, the Mystery of **Chrismation** is performed. The priest anoints the one being baptized on various parts of the body with the words, "the seal (the sign) of the gift of the Holy Spirit." At that time the newly baptized is invisibly granted the gifts of the Holy Spirit, with the help of which he will grow and be strengthened in the spiritual life. The **forehead** is anointed with chrism for the sanctification of the mind; **the eyes, nostrils, mouth, and ears** for the sanctification of the senses; the **chest** to sanctify the heart; the **hands and feet** for the sanctification of actions and the entire conduct. Circling around the font three times, the priest with the baptized and his sponsors symbolize the spiritual solemnity and joy of the occasion. The lit candles in their hands serve as a sign of spiritual enlightenment, and the cruciform **tonsuring** of the baptized symbolizes his dedication to the Lord.

Confession and Communion

Those approaching these Mysteries after a significant lapse of time

Receiving Holy Communion

should fast for several days in addition to the normal ecclesiastical fasts and attend the daily services in the church. For those who commune regularly and frequently and pray daily, additional fasting is not necessary. One should carefully recall one's sins, consider them with contrition, and pray that the Lord have mercy on one's soul. At a prearranged time one should come to the priest, who will serve the short service of Confession before an analogion on which are placed a Cross and Gospel, and repent before Christ Himself of one's sins. The priest, upon noting one's conscientious repentance, which consists of a full confession and the resolve not to repeat one's sins, will lay the end of his epitrachelion over the bowed head of the penitent and read the Prayer for the Remission of Sins, in which one's sins are forgiven in the name of Jesus Christ Himself, and will bless him with the sign of the Cross. Having kissed the Cross, the penitent departs with a peaceful conscience and prays that the Lord grant him to receive Holy Communion.

The evening before Communion, one should read at home the Prayers before Communion and whatever rule the priest has given. The Mystery of Holy Communion is celebrated during the Liturgy. All those who have confessed repeat quietly the **Prayer before Communion** with the priest, and making a bow to the ground (except on Sundays) with reverence, go to the Holy Chalice and commune the Holy Gifts, receiving in the visible form of the bread and wine the true Body and Blood of Christ. After Communion and the Liturgy conclude, in addition to the thanksgiving offered up during the Liturgy, there are special Prayers of Thanksgiving to be read. The ailing and elderly are communed by the priest at home privately after their confessions are heard.

Ordination

This Mystery is accomplished in the Altar before the Holy Table during the course of a Hierarchical Liturgy. A single bishop ordains one to the diaconate or the priesthood, but the consecration of a bishop is celebrated by a group of bishops, usually three. The ordination of a **deacon** occurs in the Liturgy **following the consecration of the Gifts**, to indicate that a deacon does not receive the power to accomplish this Mystery. A **priest** is ordained during the "Liturgy of the Faithful," just after the Great Entry, so that he who is consecrated, as one who has received the appropriate Grace, might take part in the sanctification of the Gifts. **Bishops** are consecrated during the "Liturgy of the Catechumens," following the Small Entry, which indicates that a bishop is given the right to consecrate others to the various ranks of holy orders. The most important action during an ordination is the hierarchical laying on of hands, together with the calling down upon the one being ordained, of the Grace of the Holy Spirit and therefore consecration is also termed the "Laying on of Hands" (in Greek, "Hierotonia").

The one to receive Ordination is first led through the Royal Gates into the Altar by either a deacon or priest. The candidate circles the Altar Table three times, stopping each time to kiss the four corners of the Table, and making a prostration before the bishop. He then kneels at the front right hand corner of the Altar, a deacon on one knee, a priest on both knees, and the bishop covers his head with the end of his omophorion, three times making the sign of the Cross over his head,

Ordination

and placing his hand upon him says aloud, "By Divine Grace (N.) is raised, through the laying on of hands, to the diaconate (or priesthood); let us pray therefore for him that the Grace of the Holy Spirit may come upon him." The choir responds "Kyrie eleison" (Greek for "Lord have mercy") and as the bishop bestows each of the vestments proper to his rank to the newly-ordained he exclaims, "Axios!" (Greek for "Worthy!"). This is then repeated thrice by the clergy and then the choir. Following his vesting the newly-ordained is greeted by all those of his rank as a colleague and he participates in the remainder of the service with them.

The consecration of a bishop is nearly identical, except that the prospective bishop, before the beginning of the Liturgy, stands in the center of the church and pronounces aloud a confession of the Faith and vows to act in accordance with the canons of the Church during his service. After the Little Entry, during the chanting of the Trisagion, he is led into the Altar and remains kneeling before the Altar Table. When the presiding bishop reads the prayer of consecration, all the bishops lay their right hands upon his head and over them hold the open Gospel, with the printed pages downward.

Matrimony

The Mystery of Holy Matrimony is celebrated in the center of the church before an analogion on which are placed a Cross and Gospel. The ceremony begins with the **betrothal** and is followed by the **"crowning,"** or actual wedding. The first is performed as follows. The

Matrimony

groom stands on the right hand side and the bride on the left. The priest blesses them three times with lit candles and then gives them to the couple to hold as symbols of conjugal love, blessed by the Lord. After a litany asking God to grant them every good thing and mercy and that He bless their betrothal and unite them and preserve them in peace and unity of soul, the priest blesses and puts on their right hands rings, which earlier were placed on the Altar for sanctification. The groom and bride receive these rings as sacred pledges and as a sign of the indissolubility of the union into which they aspire to enter. The betrothal is followed by the wedding or crowning. Here the priest prays to the Lord to bless the marriage and to send down upon those entering into it His heavenly Grace. As a visible symbol of this Grace, he puts crowns on their heads and blesses them three times together with the words, "O Lord, our God, crown them with glory and honor." In the epistle from St. Paul which is read, the importance of the Mystery of Marriage and the mutual responsibilities of the husband and wife are discussed, while the Gospel recalls the presence of the Lord Himself at the wedding in Cana. Those united in marriage then drink wine from the same cup as a sign that from this moment they must live as one soul, sharing their joys and sorrows. They then walk behind the priest, circling the analogion three times, as a symbol of spiritual joy and solemnity.

Anointing of the Sick

This Mystery is also called **Unction** and is served to aid in healing from weaknesses of soul and body. Ideally it is served by seven priests, but in cases of need it can be served by only one. Into a vessel with wheat is put a smaller vessel with oil as a sign of the mercy of God. Some wine is added to the oil in imitation of the mercy shown by the Good Samaritan to the man attacked by thieves and in memory of the blood of Christ shed on the Cross. Seven lit candles are placed in the wheat and between them seven small sticks wound around one end with cotton which are used to anoint the ailing person seven times. All those present hold lit candles. Following a prayer for the sanctification of the oil and that it might serve the ailing person through the Grace of God unto the healing of soul and body, seven sections from the Epistles and Gospels are read. After each reading the priest anoints the sick person with the sign of the Cross on the forehead, nostrils, cheeks, lips, chest and both sides of the hands while saying a prayer to the Lord that He, as Physician of soul and body might heal His ailing servant from the weaknesses of soul and body. After the seven-fold anointing the priest opens the Gospel and places it with the printed pages downward, as if it were the healing hand of the Saviour Himself, over the head of the sick person and then prays that the Lord forgive Him his sins. Then the sick person kisses the Gospel and Cross and, if possible, makes three prostrations before the priest(s) asking for his blessing and forgiveness. This concludes the Mystery of Unction.

Moleben

A Moleben is the term for a short service of prayers in which the faithful, according to their individual needs and circumstances, appeal in prayer to the Lord God, the Theotokos, or the saints.

The customary Moleben resembles Matins in its form, but in practice it is significantly shortened and consists of the beginning prayers;

Moleben

the singing of the troparion and refrains, "Glory to Thee, our God, glory to Thee...," "Most holy Theotokos, save us...," "Holy Father, Nicholas, pray unto God for us..." and others; the reading of a passage from the Gospels; the Augmented and Short Litanies; and finally, a prayer to the Lord God, the Theotokos, or the saint petitioned, concerning the subject of the Moleben. Occasionally these Molebens are joined with an akathist or the Lesser Blessing of Water. An akathist is read after the Short Litany before the Gospel reading, while the blessing of waters is served after the Gospel reading.

In addition to the supplicatory Molebens there are also special Molebens which relate to a particular situation: a thanksgiving Moleben for a sign of God's mercy; a Moleben for the cure of the sick; a Moleben on the occasion of a common trouble: drought, bad weather, flood, war, etc. There are also special Molebens to be served on New Year's Day, before the school year, on the Sunday of Orthodoxy, etc.

The Burial of the Dead

After his death a Christian's body is washed and clothed in clean, and if possible, new clothes and placed in a white shroud, preferably that garment in which he was baptized if he was an adult when this occurred, as a sign that the deceased, in his Baptism, gave a promise to lead a life in purity and holiness. He may be dressed in the uniform of his calling as a sign that he departs to the Lord God to give an account for the obligations of his calling in life. Across the forehead is placed a strip of paper representing a crown, imprinted with the images of Christ, the Theotokos, and St. John the Forerunner, with the inscription "Holy God, Holy Mighty, Holy Immortal, have mercy on us." It is a sign that the deceased, as a Christian, fought on this earth for the righteousness of God and died in the hope that by the mercy of God, and the intercessions of the Theotokos and St. John the Forerunner, he will receive a crown in Heaven. A cross or an icon is placed in his hands as a sign of the faith of the deceased in Christ, the Theotokos, or one of the saints pleasing to God. The body is placed in a coffin, and is half covered with a church covering as a symbol that the deceased was under the protection of the Orthodox Church. If the body remains in the home then it is put before the domestic icons with the body facing the exit. Candles are placed around the coffin as a sign that the deceased has passed into the realm of light, into the better life beyond the grave. Near the coffin, the Psalter is read, along with prayers for the repose of the deceased, and Pannykhidas are served. Until burial special prayers for the departure of the soul, which are located in the back of the Psalter, are also read. The psalms are read to comfort those grieving for the deceased.

Before the burial the body is transferred to the church for the funeral, and prior to the departure for the church a short service for the

Burial of the Dead

repose, the Litia, is chanted and during the actual removal we sing, "Holy God..."

The coffin is placed in the center of the church, with the body facing the Altar. The funeral service consists of hymns in which the entire destiny of a man is depicted. For his transgressions he is returned to the dust from which he was taken, yet despite the multitude of sins a human being does not cease to be "the image of the glory of God," created in the image and likeness of God. Therefore the holy Church prays to its Master and Lord that by His ineffable mercy He forgive the reposed his sins and deem him worthy of the Kingdom of Heaven. After the readings of the Epistle and Gospel, in which the future resurrection of the dead is described, the priest reads the **Prayer of Absolution**. With this prayer the deceased is released from any bonds of oaths or curses, and his sins for which he repented, and which despite repentance he might have forgotten, are absolved, and he is released unto the life beyond the grave in peace. The written text of this prayer is then placed in the hand of the reposed. The relatives and friends then give the body a last kiss as a sign of mutual forgiveness, and the body is covered with a white sheet while the priest sprinkles the body with earth in the form of a cross saying, *The earth is the Lord's and the fullness* *thereof, the world and all that dwell therein.* The coffin is closed and "Memory eternal" is sung for the reposed.

Following the funeral, the body and coffin are transferred to the cemetery and lowered into the grave with the feet towards the east, so that the person is facing east, and then a short Litia is said for the reposed.

Over the grave of a Christian a **cross** is placed as a symbol of Christ's victory over death and hell, like a large fruitful tree under whose shade the Christian finds rest as a traveler after a prolonged journey.

Since She has true faith in the immortality of the human soul, the future resurrection of the dead, the Dread judgement of Christ, and the final reward to be granted to each according to his deeds, the Holy Orthodox Church does not leave Her children who have reposed without prayer, especially during the first few days after death and on days of **general** remembrance of the dead. She prays for them on the **third**, **ninth** and **fortieth** day after death.

On the third day after death the Holy Church recalls the three day resurrection of Jesus Christ and prays to Him to resurrect the reposed unto a future, blessed life.

On the ninth day the Holy Church prays to the Lord that He might reckon the reposed among the choir of those pleasing to God who are, like the angels, distinguished by nine orders.

On the fortieth day a prayer is said that the Lord Jesus Christ, Who ascended into Heaven, might lift up the deceased into the heavenly dwellings.

Often the remembrance of the reposed, due to the love and faith of the relatives, is celebrated on every one of the forty days with the serving of Liturgy and a Pannykhida.

Finally, on the **anniversary of the repose** of the deceased, his close relatives and faithful friends pray for him as an expression of their faith that the day of a human death is not the day of annihilation, but a new rebirth unto eternal life. It is the day of the passing of the immortal human soul into different conditions of life, where there is no place for earthly pains, griefs, and woes.

Pannykhidas, or "Memorial Services," are short services which consist of prayers for the forgiveness of sins and the repose of the deceased in the Kingdom of Heaven. During the serving of a Pannykhida the relatives and friends of the deceased stand with lit candles as a sign that they also believe in the future, radiant life. Towards the end of the Pannykhida, during the reading of the Lord's Prayer, these candles are extinguished as a sign that our lives, like burning candles, must expire, more often than not without burning through to the expected end.

A Brief Survey of the Particulars of the Divine Services of the Yearly Cycle

After the creation of the world, God consecrated the seventh day for divine worship on earth (Gen. 2:3) and subsequently, through the Law granted to Moses on Sinai, this service was extended to include every day, for He commanded that **daily**, the morning and evening are to be consecrated by offering sacrifices to God.

Jesus Christ, when He came to earth to fulfill the will of the Heavenly Father, and the **Holy Apostles**, as the select disciples of the Lord, by their example and teachings, demonstrated to the faithful the utmost importance and necessity of establishing and preserving days of **general divine services**.

Since apostolic times the Orthodox Church in her daily divine services has united various sacred commemorations unto the glory of God from which have developed the **various daily services in the course of the year.**

On each day in the Holy Church's year, in addition to the weekly cycle, the memory of one or several saints is celebrated. Definite days of the year are dedicated to either the commemoration of particular events in the life of our **Lord Jesus Christ, the Theotokos**, or from the history of the **Christian Church**, or in honor of various **saints**. In addition, **fasts** of either a single day or several consecutive days have been ordained throughout the course of the year, and several days are set aside for the remembrance of the reposed. In accordance with these sacred days of the year special hymns and prayers have been composed and rituals established which are combined with the prayers and hymns of the weekdays. The greatest changes in the divine services occur on the days of great feasts and fasts.

The days of general remembrance of the reposed, which are termed "ancestor (soul) days," are as follows: the Saturday before Meat-fare Sunday, the Saturdays of the second, third and fourth weeks of Great Lent, the Saturday before the feast of the Holy Trinity (Pentecost) and the Tuesday after Thomas Sunday.

In addition, the Russian Orthodox Church has ordained that Orthodox soldiers killed on the field of battle be remembered on the **Saturday before the feast of St. Demetrios of Thessalonica** (Oct. 26) and on the day of the **Beheading of St. John the Forerunner** (Aug. 29).

CHAPTER 9

Great Lent

Great Lent is the most important and most ancient of the fasts which extend over more that one day. It reminds us of the forty-day fast of the Saviour in the wilderness, and prepares us for Passion Week and for the joyous Feast of Feasts, the radiant Resurrection of Christ.

The Holy and Great Fast is a time for special prayer and repentance during which each of us should beseech the Lord for forgiveness of sins through Confession and preparation for Communion, and then worthily partake the Holy Mysteries of Christ in accordance with the commandment of Christ (John 6:53-56).

During the Old Testament period the Lord commanded the sons of Israel to give each year a tithe (**one tenth**) of all that they possessed, and when they did so they received blessing in all their affairs.

In like manner the **Holy Fathers** established for our benefit that **a tenth of the year**, the period of Great Lent, be consecrated to God, so that we might be blessed in all our affairs and **each year** purify ourselves of our sins which we have committed during the course of the year.

Great Lent then serves as the God-ordained tenth of the year, for it equals approximately thirty-six days, excluding Sundays, during which we separate ourselves for a time from the distractions of life and all its possible enjoyments, and dedicate ourselves primarily to the service of God unto the salvation of our souls.

Great Lent is preceded by three preparatory Sundays. **The first preparatory Sunday of Great Lent** is termed the "**Sunday of the Publican and Pharisee.**" This Sunday's Gospel parable of the Publican and the Pharisee is read in order to demonstrate that only prayer with heartfelt tears and humility, like those of the publican, and not with a recounting of one's virtues like the pharisee, can call down upon us the mercy of God. Starting with this Sunday and continuing until the fifth Sunday of Great Lent, following the reading of the Gospel, during the All-night Vigil, the contrite prayer is chanted, "The doors of repentance do Thou open to me, O Giver of Life..."

The second preparatory Sunday of Great Lent is termed the "**Sunday of the Prodigal Son.**" In the touching parable of the Prodigal Son read during Liturgy, the Holy Church teaches us to rely on the mercy of God, provided we have sincerely repented of our sins. On this Sunday and the succeeding two Sundays, during the Polyeleos at the All-night Vigil, Psalm 136 is chanted: *By the waters of Babylon, there we* *sat down and we wept when we remembered Sion...* This psalm describes the suffering of the Jews during the Babylonian captivity and their longing for their fatherland. The words of this psalm teach us about our spiritual captivity, the captivity to sin, and that we should aspire towards our spiritual fatherland, the Heavenly Kingdom.

The final words of this psalm scandalize many with reference to *Blessed shall be he who shall seize and dash thine infants* (those of the Babylonians) *against the rock!* Of course, the literal meaning of these words is brutal and unacceptable for the Christian, for the Lord Himself taught us to love and bless our enemies and to worship God *in spirit and truth*. These words gain a pure and lofty significance with a Christian and

The Last Judgement

spiritual nature, for they mean, "Blessed is he who has a firm resolve to break, on the rock of faith, the newly forming evil thoughts and desires (as it were in their infant state) before they mature into evil deeds and habits."

The third preparatory Sunday before Great Lent is called "**Meat-fare Sunday**," because after this Sunday, of non-fasting foods, one is allowed to eat cheese, milk, butter, and eggs, but no meat or poultry. This Sunday is also termed the "**The Sunday of the Last Judgement**," as the Gospel passage concerning the Dread Judgement is read, describing the final reward or punishment awaiting us, and thereby awakening the sinner to repentance. In the hymns on Cheese-fare Sunday, the fall into sin of Adam and Eve is recalled, which resulted from lack of self-control and fasting, with their salvific fruits.

The last Sunday before Great Lent is termed "**Cheese-fare Sunday**," because it is the last day on which one can eat cheese, butter and eggs. During the Liturgy we hear the Gospel reading (Matt. 6:14-21) concerning the forgiveness of our fellow man for his offenses against us, without which we cannot receive the forgiveness of our sins from the Heavenly Father. In accordance with this Gospel reading, Christians have the pious custom on this day of forgiving each other their sins, both known and unknown, and those who have a quarrel with someone undertake every effort to be reconciled. Therefore this Sunday is also termed "**Forgiveness Sunday**."

The general characteristics of the divine services during Great Lent consist of prolonged services of a less exultant character. There is less chanting, longer readings from the Psalter and additional prayers, which dispose the soul towards repentance. At every service full prostrations are done during the penitential prayer of St. Ephraim the Syrian, "O Lord and Master of my life..."

During the **morning** hours, **Matins, the Hours** with certain insertions, and **Vespers** are served. In the evening, **Great Compline** is served instead of **Vespers**. On **Wednesdays** and **Fridays** the **Liturgy of the Presanctified Gifts** is celebrated. On **Saturdays the Liturgy of St. John of Chrysostom** is celebrated and on the first five Sundays the **Liturgy the St. Basil the Great**, which is also celebrated on **Great Thursday** and **Great Saturday** of Passion Week.

During Great Lent each Sunday is dedicated to the commemoration of a special event or person which calls the sinful soul to repentance and hope in the mercy of God.

CHAPTER 10

The Sundays of Great Lent, Their Significance and Basic Rubrics

The **first week of Great Lent** is distinguished by its special strictness and its lengthy services. On the first four days (Monday, Tuesday, Wednesday and Thursday) the canon of St. Andrew of Crete is read at Great Compline with the refrain between each verse, "Have mercy on me, O God, have mercy on me."

On Friday of the first week, at the Liturgy after the Prayer before the Ambo, the blessing of "koliva" (a mixture of boiled wheat with honey) takes place in memory of the holy Great Martyr St. Theodore Tyro, who granted supernatural help to Christians to help them keep the fast. In 362 A.D., the Byzantine Emperor, Julian the Apostate, ordered that the blood of sacrifices offered to idols be secretly sprinkled on the provisions for the city of Constantinople. The Great Martyr St. Theodore, who was burned alive in 306 for his confession of the Christian faith, appeared in a dream to the bishop of Constantinople, Eudoxius, and exposed the secret plot of Julian. He ordered him not to buy food for the entire week at the city market, and to instruct his flock to live on koliva.

On the first Sunday of Great Lent the **"Triumph of Orthodoxy"** is celebrated, which was established by the Empress Theodora in 842 A.D. in memory of the restoration of the veneration of the holy icons. At the conclusion of the Liturgy a Service of Intercession ("Moleben") is held in the center of the church before icons of the Saviour and the Theotokos, asking that the Lord confirm Orthodox Christians in the faith and bring back to the path of truth all those who have apostatized from the Church. The deacon reads the Creed solemnly and pronounces the anathemas, proclaiming that all those who have presumed to distort the true Orthodox Christian Faith are separated from the Church. He then intones "Eternal Memory" for all the reposed defenders of the Orthodox Faith, and finally, "Many Years," for all those who are living. This service is customarily done in the presence of a bishop.

On the second Sunday of Great Lent the memory of **St. Gregory Palamas** is celebrated. A bishop of Thessalonica who lived in the fourteenth century, he continued the battle against Western, Latin distortions of the Christian faith by teaching the importance of the deifying power of the uncreated Grace of God and preserving the true balance between immanence and transcendence with the doctrine of the

St. Gregory Palamas

relationship between the "essence" and "energies" of God. In accordance with the Orthodox Faith he taught that the ascetic endeavor of fasting and prayer, particularly the practice of the Jesus Prayer according to the teachings of the hesychastic Fathers, prepares one to receive the grace-filled light of the Lord, which is like that which shone on Mt. Tabor at the Lord's Transfiguration. In other words, if God wills, according to one's striving, one can partake of divine blessedness while still on this sinful earth. Thus the second Sunday of Great Lent has been set aside to commemorate this great Church Father, who made explicit the teaching which reveals the power of prayer and fasting.

On the third Sunday of Great Lent, during the All-night Vigil after the Great Doxology, the **Holy Cross** is brought forth from the Altar and placed in the center of the church for the veneration of the faithful. During the prostrations made before the Cross (which often contains a portion of the True Cross) the church chants, "Before Thy

Cross, we bow down, O Master, and Thy holy Resurrection we glorify." This hymn is also chanted at the Liturgy instead of the Trisagion.
The Church has placed this event in the middle of Great Lent in order
that the recollection of the suffering and death of the Lord might inspire and strengthen those fasting for the remainder of the ascetic
struggle of the fast. The Holy Cross remains out for veneration
throughout the week until Friday, when, after the hours and before the
beginning of the Presanctfied Liturgy, it is returned to the Altar. Thus
the third Sunday and fourth week of Great Lent are termed those of the
"**Adoration of the Holy Cross.**"

On the fourth Sunday of Great Lent **St. John of the Ladder** is
commemorated, the author of the classic ascetic text, *The Ladder*, in
which he indicates a ladder, or succession of virtues which lead us up
to the Throne of God. On Thursday of the fifth week at Matins, the
Great Canon of St. Andrew of Crete is read, along with the reading of

St. Mary of Egypt

the life of **St. Mary of Egypt**. The commemoration of the life of St. Mary of Egypt, who formerly had been a great sinner, is intended to serve as an example of true repentance for all and convince us of the ineffable compassion of God. On Saturday of the fifth week (Matins on Friday evening) we celebrate the "**Laudation of the Theotokos**," which consists of the reading of the Akathist to the Theotokos. This service was initiated in Greece in gratitude to the Theotokos for her numerous deliverances of Constantinople from its enemies. The Akathist is read here for the confirmation of the faithful in their reliance upon the heavenly Mediatress, who, delivering us from visible enemies, is even more an aid to us in our battle with invisible enemies.

On the **fifth Sunday of Great Lent** we commemorate our holy Mother **Mary of Egypt**. As mentioned above, the Church finds in her an image of true repentance and a source of encouragement for those engaged in spiritual endeavors, by virtue of the example of the ineffable mercy of God shown towards her a repentant sinner.

The sixth week, which directly precedes **Palm Sunday**, is dedicated to the preparation of those fasting for a worthy meeting with the Lord and for the commemoration of the Passion of the Lord.

On **Saturday of the sixth week** the **resurrection of Lazarus by Jesus Christ** is commemorated. This day is termed "**Lazarus Saturday**." During Matins the "Troparia on the Blameless" are chanted: "Blessed art Thou, O Lord, teach me Thy statutes..." and at the Liturgy instead of "Holy God" we chant "As many as have been baptized into Christ have put on Christ. Alleluia," for those catechumens who are baptized according to custom on this day.

The **sixth Sunday of Great Lent** is one of the twelve great feasts, in which we celebrate the solemn **Entry of the Lord into Jerusalem** for His voluntary Passion. This feast is also termed Palm Sunday. After the reading of the Gospel at the All-night Vigil, we do not chant "Having seen the Resurrection of Christ," but the 50th Psalm is read immediately, and after being sanctified with prayer and holy water, bundles of palms, flowers, and (in the Russian Church) pussy willows, are distributed to the faithful, who then remain standing until the end of the service holding these bundles with lit candles as a sign of the victory of life over death.

At Vespers on Palm Sunday the dismissal begins with the words, "May Christ our true God Who for our salvation went to His voluntary Passion,..."

Passion Week

Passion Week is the term for the last week before Pascha. It has this name because it is consecrated to the commemoration of the last days of the earthly life of the Saviour, His suffering, death on the Cross, and burial. **Monday, Tuesday and Wednesday** of this week are dedicated to the commemoration of the last conversations of the Lord Jesus Christ with the people and His disciples.

The specifics of the services of the first three days of Passion Week are as follows: at **Matins**, after the Six Psalms and the "Alleluia," we chant the troparion, "Behold the Bridegroom cometh at midnight...," and after the Canon is read we chant the exapostilarion, "I behold Thy chamber, O my Saviour..." On each of these three days we serve the **Liturgy of the Presanctified Gifts** with readings from the Gospels. The Gospel is also read at Matins.

Great Thursday

The service of Great Thursday is dedicated to the commemoration of **the Mystical Supper, the washing of the feet of the disciples by**

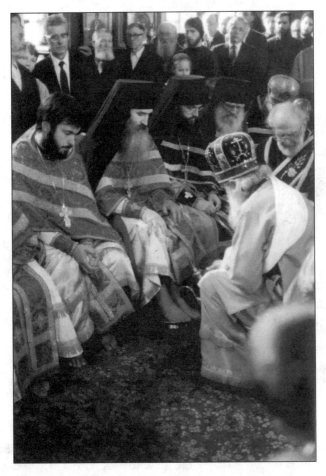

The Bishop Washes the Feet of the Clergy in a Cathedral Church on Great Thursday.

Jesus Christ, the prayer of Jesus Christ in the Garden of Gethsemane and His betrayal by Judas.

At Matins after the Six Psalms and the "Alleluia" we chant the troparion, "When the glorious disciples were enlightened at the washing of the feet,..."

The Liturgy served is that of **St. Basil the Great** and is combined with Vespers in commemoration of the fact that the Lord established the **Mystery of Communion** during the evening. Instead of the Cherubic Hymn and the communion verses, "Let our mouths be filled...," we chant the hymn, "Receive me today, O Son of God, as a communicant of Thy mystical supper..."

In the Moscow Cathedral of the Dormition and in the Kiev Caves Lavra on this day after the Liturgy, and in the Greek Church during Matins of Great Wednesday, there is performed the **Sanctification of Chrism**, which is used for the Mystery of Chrismation, and in the consecration of churches and Antiminsia.

Great Friday

The services of Great Friday are dedicated to the commemoration

The Tomb of the Lord on Great Friday

of the **sufferings on the Cross of the Saviour, His death and burial**. At Matins, which is served on the evening of Great Thursday (as all

Matins services of this week are held the night before the actual day),
the **Reading of the Twelve Gospels** takes place, the Gospels being
placed in the middle of the church. These are selections from the four
Gospels which proclaim the Passion of the Saviour, beginning with His
final conversation with the disciples at the Mystical Supper, and ending
with His burial in the garden by Joseph of Arimathea and the setting of
the military watch over His Tomb. During the readings, the faithful
stand with lit candles, which are symbols both of the glory and magnificence which the Lord did not lose during the period of His suffering,
and of the ardent love we should have for our Saviour.

On Great Friday the **Royal Hours** are served, but Liturgy is never
served, since on this day the Lord offered Himself as a sacrifice.

Vespers is served at the ninth hour of the day (3 P.M.), which is
the hour of the death of Jesus Christ on the Cross. In this service His removal from the Cross and His burial are commemorated.

With the chanting of the troparion, "The Noble Joseph, having
taken Thy most pure body down from the Tree...," the clergy take up
the **Burial Shroud** (an icon) of Christ lying in the tomb (called
"Plaschanitsa" in Russian, "Epitaphion" in Greek), from the Holy
Table as it were, from Golgotha, and carry it from the Altar, into the
center of the church, preceded by candles and incense. It is placed on a
specially prepared stand that resembles a tomb, and the priests and all
those present prostrate themselves before it and kiss the wounds of the
Lord depicted upon it, the pierced side and the imprint of the nails in
the hands and feet.

The Burial Shroud is left in the church for three days, from Friday
afternoon through Saturday and until the first moments of Sunday, in
commemoration of the three day entombment of Christ.

Great Saturday

The divine services of Great Saturday are dedicated to the commemoration of **the time Jesus Christ remained** "in the grave bodily,
but in hades with Thy soul as God; in Paradise with the thief and on the
throne with the Father and the Spirit wast Thou Who fillest all things O
Christ, the Inexpressible," and finally, **the Resurrection of the Saviour
from the grave**.

At Matins on Great Saturday, after the Great Doxology, the Burial
Shroud is borne out of the church by the priests, accompanied by the
chanting of "Holy God...," as at a normal burial service. The people all
join in following it while it is carried around the church in commemoration of the descent of Christ into hell and His victory over hell and
death. After it is brought back into the church, it is taken through the
open Royal Gates into the Altar as a symbol that the Saviour remained
inseparable from God the Father, and that with His suffering and death
He again opened the gates of Paradise. During this moment the choir
chants, "When the noble Joseph..."

When the Burial Shroud is again placed on the tomb in the center of the church, a litany is said and the prophecy of the Prophet Ezekiel is read, concerning the resurrection of the dead. The Epistle instructs the faithful that Jesus Christ is the true Pascha for us all, and the Gospel relates how the high priest with the permission of Pilate placed a watch over the Lord's tomb and sealed it.

The Divine **Liturgy** on this day is later than any other day of the year and is combined with Vespers.

After the Vespers Entry and the chanting of "O Gentle Light..." we begin the reading of **fifteen lessons** from the Old Testament, which contain all the foreshadowings and prophecies of the salvation of mankind through the Passion and Resurrection of Jesus Christ.

After these readings and the Epistle reading, the forefeast of the Resurrection of Christ begins. The choir begins to chant slowly "Arise, O God, judge the earth, for Thou shalt have an inheritance among all the nations..," while in the Altar and throughout the church, the black vestments are replaced with white ones. This change is a symbol of the event in which the Myrrhbearers, early in the morning "while it was still dark," saw before the tomb of Christ the angel in radiant vestments and heard from him the joyful proclamation of the Resurrection of Christ.

The deacon, now clad in bright vestments like an angel, goes out into the center of the church and before the Burial Shroud reads the Gospel which proclaims to mankind the Resurrection of Christ.

The Liturgy of St. Basil the Great then continues in its usual order. Instead of the Cherubic Hymn we chant the following, "Let all mortal flesh keep silence," and instead of "It is truly meet..." we chant, "Weep not for Me, O Mother, beholding in the tomb Thy Son..." The communion verse chanted is, "The Lord awoke as one that sleepeth and is risen, saving us."

Following the Liturgy there is a **blessing of bread and wine** for the nourishment of those praying. A few hours later the reading of the Acts of the Apostles begins in the Church and continues until the beginning of the Midnight Office.

An hour before midnight the Midnight Office is served during which the Canon of Great Saturday is read. At the end of this service the priests silently take the Burial Shroud from the center of the church and into the Altar through the Royal Gates and place it upon the Altar Table, where it remains until the Ascension of the Lord, in commemoration of the forty day abiding of Jesus Christ on the earth after His Resurrection from the dead.

The faithful now reverently await the hour of midnight when the **radiant, Paschal joy of the greatest feast, the Resurrection of the Lord our Saviour Jesus Christ** begins.

This paschal joy is a sacred rejoicing of which there is no likeness nor equal on earth. It is the endless joy and blessedness of eternal life. It is of this joy that the Lord spoke when He said, *Your heart shall rejoice, and your joy no man taketh from you* (John 16:22).

CHAPTER 11

The Feast of Pascha — The Radiant Resurrection of Christ

The word *Pascha* means "passover" or "deliverance" in Hebrew. The Jews, in celebrating the Old Testament passover, commemorated the liberation of their forebears from Egyptian slavery. Christians, on the other hand, in celebrating the New Testament Pascha, celebrate the deliverance through Jesus Christ of the entire human race from slavery to the Devil and His granting to us life and eternal blessedness. Due to the blessings which we have received through the Resurrection of Christ, Pascha is the feast of feasts and the triumph of triumphs, and therefore its divine services are distinguished by magnificence and an exceptionally solemn rejoicing.

Long before midnight the faithful in bright and festal clothing stream into the churches and reverently await the approaching Paschal Festival. The clergy are vested in their brightest garments. Prior to the actual moment of midnight, festive bells peal out the announcement of the coming of the great moment of the light-bearing Feast of the Resurrection of Christ. The entire clergy with crosses, candles and incense come out of the Altar and together with the people, like the Myrrhbearers who went very early to the tomb, circle the church and chant, "Thy Resurrection, O Christ Saviour, the angels hymn in the heavens; vouchsafe also us on earth with pure hearts to glorify Thee." During this procession, from the heights of the bell tower, as if from Heaven, there pours forth the Paschal peal. All those who have come to pray walk with lit candles, thus expressing their joy of soul in the radiant feast.

The procession pauses at the closed western doors of the church, as if at the opening to the Tomb of Christ. Here the highest ranking priest, like the angel who proclaimed the Resurrection of Christ to the Myrrhbearers at the tomb, is the first to proclaim the joyous verse, "Christ is risen from the dead, trampling down death by death, and on those in the tombs bestowing life." This verse is thrice repeated by the clergy and the choir.

Then the presiding clergyman proclaims the verses of the ancient prophecy of the holy King David, "Let God arise and let His enemies be scattered...," and all respond in answer to each verse of the psalm with, "Christ is risen from the dead...."

The doors are opened, and the congregation, as once did the Myrrhbearers and the Apostles, enters into the church, resplendent with the light of candles and lamps, and chants joyously, "Christ is risen from the dead...!"

The Resurrection Matins consist primarily of the **Paschal canon** of St. John of Damascus. Each ode of this canon concludes with the victorious hymn, "Christ is risen from the dead." During the chanting of the canon each of the clergy in turn, holding the cross with candles and preceded by candle-bearers, go around the entire church censing the

The Procession at Pascha

faithful and joyously greeting everyone with the words, "Christ is risen!" The faithful all respond loudly, "Truly He is risen!" The repeated procession of the clergy from the Altar commemorates the appearances of the Lord to His disciples after the Resurrection.

After chanting the hymn "...let us embrace one another. Let us say Brethren, even to them that hate us; let us forgive all things on the Resurrection...," all the faithful begin to greet each other saying, "Christ is risen!," and replying, "Truly He is risen!" They seal this greeting with a kiss and exchange Paschal eggs which serve as a meaningful symbol of the resurrection from the grave, the resurrection of life from its very depths through the power of omnipotent God.

Then the **homily of St. John Chrysostom** is read which begins with the words, "If any be devout and God-loving, let him enjoy this fair and radiant triumph..." St. John summons all to joy, "Ye rich and ye poor, with one another exult. Ye sober and ye slothful, honor the day. Ye that have kept the fast and ye that have not, be glad today...

"Let no one weep for his transgressions, for forgiveness hath dawned from the tomb. Let no one fear death, for the death of the Saviour hath set us free..."

And finally he solemnly proclaims the eternal victory of Christ over death and hell, "O death, where is thy sting? O hades, where is thy victory? Christ is risen and thou art overthrown. Christ is risen and the demons are fallen. Christ is risen, and the angels rejoice. Christ is risen, and life flourisheth. Christ is risen, and there is none dead in the tombs (for death is not a permanent end now, but only a temporary condition), for Christ being risen from the dead, is become the first-fruits of them that have fallen asleep. To Him be glory and dominion unto the ages of ages. Amen."

Immediately following Matins, the Hours and Liturgy are celebrated with all the doors to the Altar open. They were opened at the beginning of Matins and will not be closed throughout the entire week as a sign that Jesus Christ has opened the gates to the Heavenly Kingdom forever. At the Liturgy the first section from the Gospel of St. John the Theologian is read, which begins with the words, *In the beginning was the Word, and the Word was with God, and the Word was God...,* which is a description of the divinity of our Redeemer. If the Liturgy is concelebrated by many priests, then the Gospel is read in several languages as a sign that the "proclamation" concerning the Lord "went forth" unto all the people on earth.

Before the conclusion of the Liturgy the blessing of the Paschal bread, the Artos, is performed. It is distributed to the faithful on Bright Saturday following Liturgy, as a Paschal blessing.

Immediately after the Paschal Liturgy, and sometimes between Matins and the Liturgy, the Paschal bread, cheese, eggs and meat for the Paschal meals of the faithful are blessed.

After each Liturgy of Bright Week the Cross of Christ, accompanied by the ringing of bells, is carried in triumph around the church.

The Resurrection of the Lord

Indeed, all during the week bells are rung as often as possible. It all serves to express the joy of the faithful and to celebrate the victory of Jesus Christ over death and hell. To emphasize this joy the Holy Fathers instituted the rule that kneeling and prostrations are forbidden in church from the first day of Pascha until the Vespers on Pentecost.

The presiding priest celebrates Vespers on the first day of Pascha in his best vestments. After the Vespers entry with the Gospel, the Gospel passage is read which describes the appearance of Jesus Christ to the Apostles on the evening of the first day of His resurrection from the dead (John 29:19-25).

On the first Tuesday after Bright Week, in order to share the joy of the Resurrection of Christ with the reposed and in the hope of the **universal resurrection**, the Church holds a special remembrance of the dead. After the Liturgy a general Service of Remembrance and Intercession, or Pannykhida, is said, and following a custom of the early Church, the faithful visit the graves of their relatives on this day.

Paschal chanting is used in the church until the feast of the **Ascension of the Lord**, which is celebrated on the fortieth day after Pascha.

The Feast of Pentecost — The Day of the Holy Trinity

The Feast of the Holy Trinity is termed Pentecost because the descent of the Holy Spirit upon the Apostles occurred on the fiftieth day after the Resurrection of Christ. The feast of the Christian Pentecost includes two celebrations, one in honor of the **All-holy Trinity** and the other in honor of the **All-holy Spirit**, which visibly descended upon the Apostles and sealed the new eternal testament of God with mankind.

The first day of Pentecost, always a Sunday, the Church dedicates primarily **to the glory of the All-holy Trinity**; hence this day is popularly known as Trinity Day. The second day is dedicated **to the glory of the All-holy Spirit**, and therefore it is known as Spirit Day.

In celebrating the Holy Spirit the Church begins with the usual Vespers service on Trinity Day. During this service three compunctionate prayers written by St. Basil the Great are read while the entire congregation kneels. In them we confess our sins before the Heavenly Father and, for the sake of the great sacrifice of His Son, we implore mercy. We also ask the Lord Jesus Christ to grant us the Divine Spirit, unto the enlightenment and confirmation of our souls. Finally, we pray for our deceased fathers and brethren, that the Lord might grant them repose in a place of light and refreshment.

It is customary on this feast day to adorn the church building and one's home with tree branches and flowers and to stand in church holding flowers. This adornment of home and church with living plants is both a confession of the vivifying power of the life-creating Spirit and a dutiful consecration to Him of the first fruits of spring.

Feast of the Exaltation of the Cross of the Lord

The divine services of this day differ from others in that at the end of the Great Doxology at the All-night Vigil, as the **Trisagion** is being chanted, the presiding priest takes the Holy Cross, adorned with flowers, from the Altar Table and lifts it over his head. Preceded by candles, he goes out of the Altar through the north door. He stands before the Royal Gates and from there, with the exclamation, "Wisdom, let us attend!" carries the Cross to the center of the church and places it upon an analogion.

The troparion to the Cross, "Save, O Lord, Thy people...," is chanted while the priest, together with the deacon, completes a threefold censing of the Cross. Then all those serving venerate the Cross

The Exaltation of the Cross

with three prostrations while the verse, "Before Thy Cross, we bow down, O Master, and Thy Holy Resurrection we glorify!" is chanted. The faithful then come forward, make prostrations, and kiss the Cross. During this veneration the choir chants verses explaining and honoring the Crucifixion of Christ.

At the Liturgy the Trisagion is replaced with the hymn, "Before Thy Cross...," and St. Paul's Epistle concerning the Cross, which for those spiritually perishing is foolishness, but for those being saved is the power of God, is read. The Gospel of the day discusses the Crucifixion of Christ. Due to the commemoration of the sufferings and death of the Lord, this day is appointed to be kept as a **strict fast**.

This feast commemorates the finding of the Precious and Life-giving Cross of the Lord by the Equal-of-the-Apostles, Empress Helen (326 A.D.). From the seventh century this day was also considered the commemoration of the return of the Life-giving Cross from the Persians by the Byzantine Emperor Heraclius (629 A.D.). At both the finding and the return of the Cross, the Patriarch of Constantinople, in order to give the faithful gathered to celebrate the event an opportunity to see the hallowed object, raised the Cross aloft and turned it to all four directions, during which the congregation reverently prostrated themselves crying out, "Lord, have mercy."

Feast of the Transfiguration of the Lord

The divine services of this feast are special in that at the end of the Liturgy grapes and fruit, which have been brought to the church by the faithful, are blessed.

This feast is selected for the blessing of fruit because in Jerusalem, from whence our typicon is derived, grapes ripen at this time and thus they are especially set out to be blessed. The church, by blessing the fruit, teaches us that all things in a holy community must be consecrated to God as His creation.

Feast of the Nativity of Christ

The Christian Church annually celebrates the great event of the Nativity of Christ on the twenty-fifth of December (O.S.). In order to more worthily celebrate, the faithful prepare with a **forty-day fast** called the **Nativity or Philip's fast**, lasting from the fifteenth of November until the twenty-fourth of December. The eve of the feast is kept with an especially strict fast. Special food is set out only at the end of the day, consisting mainly of boiled wheat with honey or other lenten dishes, depending on the custom.

On the eve of the feast, if it does not occur on a Saturday or Sunday, the Royal Hours are served, and around noon the Liturgy of St. Basil the Great with Vespers. On the feast day itself, the Liturgy of St. John Chrysostom is celebrated.

The Hours which are served on the eve of the Nativity of Christ are distinguished by the fact that **Old Testament readings** are included as well as readings from the **Epistle** and **Gospel**. Therefore, to distinguish them from the usual services of the Hours they are termed Royal Hours. This designation also refers to the custom in the Byzantine Empire of the Emperor being present for them.

After the Liturgy a candle is placed in the center of the church behind the icon of the feast, and the clergy chant the troparion of the feast, "Thy Nativity, O Christ our God, hath shined upon the world the light of knowledge; for thereby they that worshipped the stars were taught by a star to worship Thee, the Sun of Righteousness, and to know Thee, the Dayspring from on high. O Lord, glory be to Thee."Yhis is followed by the kontakion of the feast: "Today the Virgin giveth birth to Him Who is transcendent in essence; and the earth offereth a cave to Him Who is unapproachable. Angels with shepherds give glory; with a star the Magi do journey; for our sake a young Child is born, Who is pre-eternal God."

If the eve falls on a Saturday or Sunday, the Royal Hours are read on Friday. On the eve itself the Liturgy of St. John Chrysostom is served, followed by Vespers. The glorification of Christ occurs after Vespers. The fast, which is required by the Typicon, is waived in this instance so that after the Liturgy, before the evening, one is permitted to eat a small amount of bread.

The All-night Vigil begins with Great Compline in which the triumphant hymn of Isaiah is chanted, "God is with us, understand, O ye nations and submit yourselves, for God is with us!" The frequent repetition of "God is with us!" expresses the spiritual joy of the faithful who recognize the presence of God-Emmanuel among them. The content of the remainder of the service can be expressed by the initial irmos from the Matins Canon, "Christ is born, give ye glory; Christ from Heaven, meet ye Him; Christ is on the earth be ye exalted. Sing unto the Lord all the earth, and in gladness sing praises, O people, for He is glorified."

Feast of the Baptism of the Lord

This feast is also called **Theophany** because on this day the Mostholy Trinity, and in particular the divinity of the Saviour, Who now solemnly begins His saving service, is manifest.

The feast of the Baptism of the Lord is celebrated in much the same manner as the feast of the Nativity of Christ. On the eve of the feast the Royal Hours, the Liturgy of St. Basil the Great, and an All-night Vigil, beginning with Great Compline are served. The distinguishing feature of this feast is the blessing of water which is performed twice, and termed the **Great Blessing of Water**, to distinguish it from the Lesser Blessing, which may be performed at any time in the Church year.

The first blessing occurs on the eve of the feast in the church, and the second, on the day of the feast, in the open air near a river, lake or well. In ancient times the first blessing was celebrated for the baptism

Water Blessing at the Jordan River

of catechumens and only later was joined with the commemoration of the Baptism of the Lord. The second probably originated from the ancient practice of Jerusalem Christians who, on the day of the Theophany, would go to the Jordan River and there commemorate the Baptism of the Saviour. Therefore, we still term the procession with the Cross on Theophany the "**Procession to the Jordan.**"

CHAPTER 12

Concerning Monasticism and Monasteries

In the first period of the Christian Church almost all the faithful led pure and holy lives as the Gospel requires. We find that many of the faithful aspired to the most lofty ascetic endeavors. Some would voluntarily renounce their possessions and distribute them among the poor. Others, such as the Mother of God, St. John the Forerunner, the Apostles Paul, John, and James took vows of virginity and devoted their time to continual prayer, fasting, abstinence and labor. They did not separate themselves from the world though, and lived with the rest of mankind. Such people came to be called **ascetics**, or those who undertook a special discipline (in Greek, *askesis*) in order to "train" for the Kingdom of Heaven.

From the third century when as a consequence of the swift expansion of Christianity the strictness of life among Christians began to weaken, ascetics began to withdraw to live in deserts and mountains. There, far from the world and its temptations, they led a severe life of spiritual asceticism. These ascetics who left the world were called **anchorites** or **hermits**. Thus the foundations were laid for **monasticism**, far from the temptations of the world.

Monastic life is a way of life which is only for a few, select persons, who have a calling, an irrepressible inner desire for the monastic life, by which they consecrate themselves entirely to the service of God. As the Lord Himself stated, *He that is able to accept it, let him accept it* (Matt. 19:12).

St. Athanasius says, "There are two forms and states of life. One is the usual life for mankind, **married life**; the other is the angelic and apostolic life of which there is no higher, **virginity** or the **monastic** state." The **Venerable Nilus of Sora** says, "The monk is an angel, and his business is mercy, peace and the sacrifice of praise."

Those entering the monastic path of life must have a resolute will **"to renounce the world"** and to deny themselves all earthly interests so as to **develop within themselves the powers of spiritual life**. In all things they must fulfill the will of their spiritual guide, renounce all possessions and **even give up their old name**. The monk takes upon himself a voluntary **martyrdom** — a life of self-renunciation, far from the world, and filled with labor and deprivation.

Holy Trinity Monastery

Monasticism in and of itself is not the goal, but it is the most effective means of attaining the highest spiritual life. The aim of monasticism is the attainment of moral and spiritual strength in order to save the soul. The monastic life is the greatest ascetic endeavor in the spiritual service for the world. The monk upholds the world, prays for the world and spiritually nourishes it and represents it; that is, he performs the ascetic feat of prayerful intercession for the world.

The birthplace of monasticism is Egypt, and the father and founder was **St. Anthony the Great**. St. Anthony established **eremetical monasticism**, a discipline in which each monk lived separately from the others in a hut or cave, giving himself over to fasting, prayer, and labor to support himself and the poor by plaiting baskets and rope. All were placed under one leader or elder, called an *abba* or father, for guidance.

St. Pachomius Receives the Monastic Habit From an Angel

During St. Anthony's lifetime another form of monastic life also began to develop. The ascetics gathered into one community where each would work according to his strength and talents for the general welfare, and all were subject to one rule. Such communities were called **coenobia** or **monasteries**. The abbots of monasteries began to be called **abbots** or **archimandrites**. The founder of communal monasticism is considered to be **Pachomius the Great**.

From Egypt monasticism quickly spread into Asia, Palestine, Syria and finally to Europe. In Russia monasticism came almost simultaneously with the acceptance of Christianity. The founders of monasticism in Russia were Sts. **Anthony and Theodosius** of the Kiev-Caves monastery.

Large monasteries with many hundreds of monastics came to be called **lavras**. Each monastery had its order of life, its rule or monastic typikon. Every monk was obliged to fulfill various tasks which, according to the typikon, were called **obediences**. Monastics can be either male or female, both having exactly the same rules. Women's monasteries (convents) have existed from ancient times.

Those who desire to enter the monastic life must first undergo a trial period to test their strength before they give irrevocable vows. Those undergoing this preparatory testing are called **novices**. If after a long testing period they prove capable of becoming monastics, then they are partially garbed in the robes of a monastic with the initial service of profession. At this stage they are called **rassophore monks** having the right to wear the rasa and kamilavka, so that they might still be more confirmed upon their chosen path to become full monks or nuns.

The full monastic profession comprises two degrees, the **lesser** and **greater form**, little schema and great schema. Upon entering monasticism itself, the rite of the **profession to the lesser schema** is performed in which the monk or nun gives the initial vows and is given a new name. When the moment arrives for the tonsure, thrice the monk gives the abbot the scissors as a sign of his firm decision. When the abbot

Iveron Monastery on Mount Athos

the abbot the scissors as a sign of his firm decision. When the abbot receives the scissors for the third time from the hand of the person to be tonsured, he then with thanksgiving to God cuts a piece of hair of the person, in the name of the Most-holy Trinity, consecrating him utterly to the service of God.

The person receiving the lesser schema is dressed with the **paraman,** a small, square cloth with a depiction of the Cross of the Lord and the instruments of His Passion, the **cassock and belt**, and the **mantia**, a long pleated cloak, without sleeves. Upon his head is placed the **klobuk** or kamilavka, with a long **veil**. Into his hands a **prayer rope** is entrusted (*chotki*, in Russian; *komvoskini*, in Greek), which is a black string of knots for counting prayers and prostrations. All of these garments have a symbolic significance and remind the monastic of his promises. At the conclusion of the ceremony the newly tonsured monk is given a **cross** and a **candle**, which he holds throughout the Liturgy until Communion.

The monks who take on the **Great Schema** give even stricter vows. Again one's name is changed. There are also changes in the garments. Instead of the paraman the person is dressed in the **analav**, a special cloth like a scapular with crosses and inscriptions, and instead of the klobuk the person receives the **koukoulion**, a rounded helmet with a veil that covers the shoulders.

Among the Russians, it is customary to call "schemniks" only those monks who have attained the Great Schema.

If a monk is elevated to the rank of **abbot**, then he is granted a **staff** as a symbol of his authority over the brethren, a symbol of his lawful position as a director over monks. When an igumen is elevated to the rank of **archimandrite**, he is vested with a **mantia** having "**tablets**" or **pectorals**. The tablets are rectangular sections from red or green cloth which are sewn onto the front of the mantia, two at the top and two at the bottom. They symbolize the fact that the archimandrite will guide the brethren according to the commandments of God. In addition the archimandrite receives the **palitsa** and **miter**. Usually **bishops** are chosen from the ranks of the archimandrites.

Many monastics have been true angels in the flesh who have shone forth as lights for the Church of Christ. Despite the fact that monks have separated themselves from the world in order to attain moral perfection, they exert a great and beneficial effect upon those living in the world. In addition to helping in the spiritual needs of their neighbors, monks do not hesitate to serve the temporal needs of those around them when the opportunities arise. In obtaining their own sustenance they divide their food with others. Among the monasteries there are those hospices which take in, feed, and provide rest for travellers. Often monasteries distribute alms for other locations, those in prisons, those suffering from famine and other misfortunes. But the **primary service the monks provide** for society is their **perpetual prayer for the Church, their country, the living, and the dead.**

St. Theophan the Recluse says, "Monasticism is a sacrifice to God from society; it devotes itself to God and comprises its defense. The monasteries are especially noted for church services which are orderly, complete, and lengthy. The Church is manifest there vested in all Her beauty." Truly monasteries are inexhaustible sources of edification for the laity.

In the middle ages monasteries provided a great service by being centers of learning and science and disseminators of Christian enlightenment.

Monasteries are the best expression in a nation of the strength and power of the religious and moral spirit of a people.

In Russia, Greece, and other Orthodox countries the people loved monasteries. When a new monastery was founded, the people would begin to settle next to it, forming a village. Sometimes these villages would grow into great cities.

On Pilgrimage

The love for monasteries and the holy places evoked among Orthodox people the custom of **pilgrimage**. In times when Orthodox

A Procession During a Pilgrimage at Holy Trinity Monastery, Jordanville, New York

countries flourished, many people, both men and women, old and young, with packs on their backs, a staff in hand, and a prayer on their lips walked patiently in all seasons of the year from one monastery to another. They often brought their troubles there and within the walls of a monastery found help, comfort and consolation. Many undertook pilgrimages to the **Holy Land,** Palestine and other distant places.

Our forefathers in the spirit were aware that monasteries were the seed-bed of faith and spiritual enlightenment, and were the **bulwark of Orthodoxy**, without which the Orthodox empires of old could not even have existed.

Orthodoxy, in the form of the **Church**, was the basis of **Russian unity**, which was a fruit of the religious unity. Orthodoxy established Russian **literature**, **historical studies**, and the **religious and ethical law**. Without Orthodoxy there would have been no Russian civilization.

Foolishness For The Sake Of Christ

We have yet to consider one form of the ascetic Christian life, the so-called **foolishness for the sake of Christ**.

The fool-for-Christ set for himself the task of battling within himself the root of all sin, pride. In order to accomplish this he took on an unusual style of life, appearing as someone bereft of his mental faculties, thus bringing upon himself the ridicule of others. In addition he exposed the evil in the world through metaphorical and symbolic words and actions. He took this ascetic endeavor upon himself in order to humble himself and to also more effectively influence others, since most people respond to the usual ordinary sermon with indifference. The spiritual feat of foolishness for Christ was especially widespread in Russia.

The Lord blessed Orthodox lands by sending unto them many ascetics, righteous men and women who instructed the people in struggle, patience, and submission to the will of God. The Russian Orthodox peoples endured their hardships with patience and hope in the mercy of God. Thus the long-suffering and humble soul of the Russian Orthodox nation was cultivated and given the strength for the most difficult, heroic labors in the name of righteousness and love of God.

CHAPTER 13

Bells and Russian Orthodox Peals

Bells are one of the most essential elements of an Orthodox Church. In the "Order of the Blessing of Bells" we read, "So let all that hear them ring, either during the day or at night, be inspired to the glorification of Thy saints."

Church-bell ringing is used to:

1) Summon the faithful to the divine services.

2) Express the triumphal joy of the Church and Her divine services.

3) Announce to those not present in the church the times of especially important moments in the services.

In addition, in some cites in Old Russia, bells summoned the people to gatherings. Also, bells were used to guide those lost in bad weather, and announced various dangers or misfortunes such as fires or floods. In days of peril to the nation they called the people to her defense. Bells proclaimed military victories and greeted those returning from the field of battle. Thus bells played a great part in the life of the Russian people. Bells were usually hung in special **belltowers** constructed over the Entry to a church or beside it.

Bells did not come into use immediately after the appearance of Christianity. In the Old Testament Church, in the Temple in Jerusalem, the faithful were summoned to services not with bells, but with trumpets. In the first centuries of Christianity, when the Church was persecuted by the pagans, Christians had no opportunity to openly call the faithful to services. At that time, they were secretly summoned either by one of the deacons or special messengers, or sometimes the bishop himself at the end of a service would reveal the time and place of the next one.

Following the cessation of persecutions in the fourth century, various means came into use to summon the faithful. More specific means were found in the sixth century when the sound of boards or iron hoops, beaten with hammers, summoned the faithful. Eventually the most perfect means of calling the faithful to the services was devised, **pealing bells**.

The first bells, as is well known, appeared in Western Europe. There is a tradition by which the invention of bells is ascribed to **St. Paulinus the Bishop of Nola** (411) at the end of the fourth or the beginning of the fifth century. Several versions of this tradition exist. In one, St. Paulinus saw some field flowers in a dream, daffodils, which gave forth a pleasant sound. When he awoke the bishop ordered bells cast, which had the form of these flowers. But, evidently, St. Paulinus did not introduce bells into the practice of the Church, since neither in his works nor in the works of his contemporaries are bells mentioned. Only in the beginning of the seventh century did the **Pope of Rome, Sabinian**, successor to St. Gregory the Dialogist, succeed in giving bells a Christian significance. From this period, bells began gradually to be used by Christians, and in the course of the eighth and ninth centuries in Western Europe, bells properly became part of Christian liturgical practice.

In the East, in the Greek Church, bells came into use in the second half of the ninth century, when in 865, the Doge of Venice, Ursus, gave the Emperor Michael a gift of twelve large bells. These bells were hung in a tower near Hagia Sophia Cathedral. But bells did not come into general use among the Byzantines.

In Russia, bells appeared almost simultaneously with the reception of Christianity by St. Vladimir (988 A.D.). Wooden boards and metal hoops beaten with hammers were also used and still are in some monasteries. But strangely enough, Russia took bells not from Greece from whence she received Orthodoxy, but from Western Europe. The very word **kolokol** comes from the German word "glocke." The Slavonic word is **kampan** which comes from the Roman province of Campania where the first bells, made of bronze, were cast. Initially the bells were small, and each church had only two or three.

In the fifteenth century special factories for bell casting appeared, where bells of huge proportions were made. In the bell tower of Ivan the Great in Moscow, for example, are the "Everyday" bell weighing 36,626 pounds; the bell "reyute" weighing 72,000 pounds; and the largest bell, called "Dormition," which weighs around 144,000 pounds.

The largest bell in the world at present is the "**Tsar Bell**." It stands on a stone pedestal at the base of the bell tower of Ivan the Great. There is no equal to it in the world, not only in dimension and weight, but in the fine art of casting. The "Tsar Bell" was poured by Russian masters **Ivan and Mikail Matorin**, father and son, in 1733-1735. Material for the "Tsar Bell" was taken from its predecessor, a gigantic bell which had been damaged in a fire. This bell weighed 288,000 pounds and was cast by the master craftsman, Alexander Grigoriev, in 1654. To the 288,000 pounds of base metal was added more than 80,000 pounds of alloy. In all, the **total weight** of the Tsar Bell is 218 American tons. The **diameter** of the bell is 6 meters, 60 centimeters, or 21 feet, 8 inches.

This amazing product of casting was never successfully hung for it was severely damaged in a terrible and devastating fire in 1737. Still in its casting form on a wooden scaffolding, it is not known whether or not it was ever hung from this scaffolding. When the wooden scaffolding caught fire, they started to throw water on it. The red hot bell developed many large and small cracks due to the extreme change in temperature, and a large piece, weighing 11,000 kilograms (11.5 tons), fell from the bell.

After the fire, the "Tsar Bell" lay in its casting form for a whole century. In 1836, the bell was lifted out and placed on a stone pedestal, the project of the architect A. Montferrand, the builder of St. Isaac's Cathedral and the Alexander Column in Petersburg. It stands on this pedestal now with the fallen piece of the bell leaning at the foot of the pedestal. Such is the fate of the largest bell in the world, the "Tsar Bell," which was never rung.

The largest working bell is the "Dormition" bell, located in Moscow, at the bell tower of Ivan the Great. Its pealing gave the signal

Czar bell

to begin the festive ringing of the bells of all the Moscow churches on Pascha night. Thus, the Russian Orthodox people loved the ringing of the church bells and enriched the craft with their innovation and art.

The distinguishing quality of Russian bells is their sonority and melodiousness. This is attained by various techniques:

1) An exact proportion of bronze and tin, often with silver added, the proper alloy.

2) The height of the bell and its width, the right proportions.

3) The thickness of the walls of the bell.

4) The correct hanging of the bell.

5) The correct composition of the tongue and its manner of being hung in the bell.

Russians call the clapper, the tongue. The Russian bell is distinguished from the Western European bell in that it is fixed in position, and the clapper moves and strikes the sides of the bell, which produces the sound. It is characteristic that the Russian people call the movable part of the bell the "tongue," enabling the bell to have a **living voice** and **trumpet**. Truly, with what other name, if not a talking one, can one call the bell?

On the days of great feasts the sound of the bell reminds us of the blessedness of Heaven. On the days of great saints, it reminds us of the eternal repose of the dwellers of Heaven. During the days of Holy Week, it reminds us of our reconciliation with God through Christ the Saviour. On the days of Bright Week, it proclaims the victory of life over death and the eternal, endless joy of the future life in the Kingdom of Christ.

Is it not a mouth that speaks when the bell tells us of each passing hour, and reminds us of the passage of time and of eternity when *there should be time no longer* (Rev. 10:6).

Announcing the glory of the name of Christ, day and night, from the heights of a church of God, the sound of bells reminds us of the words of the Lord, the Pantocrator, spoken through the Old Testament Prophet Isaiah, *I have set watchmen upon thy walls, O Jerusalem, which shall never hold their peace day nor night* (Is. 62:6). It is not by chance that pagans, when they heard the sound of bells, often said, "**that is the voice of the Christian God.**"

The sound of **one church bell** is something **exalted** and **solemn**, and if there are **several** bells in harmony with each other, then a more **magnificent sonority is sounded**. A moving peal of bells acts upon our inner feelings and awakens our souls from spiritual **slumber**. What grieved, despondent, and often irritating tones are evoked by church bells in the soul of an evil and impious apostate. The feelings of discomfort and weariness of soul are evoked by the sound of the bell in the soul of a perpetual sinner. But in the soul of the faithful, who seek peace with God the Lord, the church bell awakens a bright, joyous, and serene disposition. Thus a person can define the state of his soul by means of the sound of bells.

One can bring forth examples from life, when a man, exhausted from fighting life's bitterness, and fallen into despair and despondency, decides to take his own life. Then he hears the church bell. Preparing to commit suicide, he trembles, becomes afraid, and involuntarily guards himself with the sign of the Cross. It recalls the Heavenly Father, and new, good feelings arise in his soul, and the one who was perishing forever returns to life. Thus, in the strokes of a church bell there is hidden a wonderful power, which penetrates deeply into the soul of mankind.

Having loved the sound of the church bell, Orthodox people associate it with all their festive and sorrowful events. Therefore, the sound of the Orthodox belltower serves not only to indicate the time of divine services, but also to express joy, grief and festivity. Various forms of bell ringing, each with their own name and meaning, developed to express this range of feelings.

The Forms of Bell Ringing and Their Names

The manner of church bell ringing is divided into two basic forms: 1. the measured ringing of the bell to announce church services, and 2. ringing of all the bells.

Ringing to Announce Church Services

By the "announcement of church services" is meant the measured strokes of one large bell. By this sound, the faithful are called together to the temple of God for divine services. In Russian it is known as the "Good news bell" because it announces the **blessed, good news of the beginning of divine services**.

The "good news peal" is accomplished thus. First there are produced **three** widely spaced, slow, prolonged **strokes**, so as to sustain the sound of the bell, followed by **measured strokes**. If the bell is very heavy or of great dimensions, the measured strokes are produced by the swinging of the clapper from side to side of the bell. If the bell is of medium size, then its clapper is drawn sufficiently close to the rim by a rope. The rope is attached to a wooden foot pedal, and with pressure from the bell-ringer's feet, the sound is produced.

The "good news peal" is subdivided in turn into two types:

1) The **usual** or **hourly** peal, produced with the largest bell.

2) The lenten or occasional peal, produced on the next largest bell on weekdays of the Great Fast.

If the church has several large bells, as is usually the case in cathedrals or large monasteries, then the size of the bells corresponds to their significance: 1) the holiday bell, 2) the Sunday bell, 3) the polyeleos bell, 4) the daily bell, and 5) the fifth, or small bell. Usually in parishes there are no more that two or three large bells.

The ringing of all the bells is subdivided as follows:

1) **Trezvon** (Peal) — thrice-sounded, multiple bell ringing. This is the simultaneous ringing of all the bells, then a brief pause, a second ringing of all the bells, again a brief pause, and a third ringing of all the bells, i.e., **a simultaneous ringing of all the bells three times**, or a ringing in three refrains.

2) **Dvuzvon** — twice rung. This is the simultaneous ringing of all the bells twice, in two refrains.

3) **Perezvon** (Chain Ringing) — this is the ringing of each bell in turn, with either one or several strokes of each bell, beginning with the **largest to the very smallest**, and then repeating several times.

4) **Perebor** (Toll) — This is the slow, single peal of each bell in turn, beginning with the **smallest to the largest**, and after the stroke on the largest bell all the bells are immediately struck together; then this is repeated several times.

The Use of the Bells and its Meaning

Bells For All-night Vigil

1) Before the beginning of the All-night Vigil — the "**good news peal**," which concludes with the simultaneous ringing of all the bells, or the **trezvon**.

2) At the beginning of the reading of the **Six Psalms** comes the twice-rung, simultaneous peal, the **dvuzvon**. The dvuzvon announces the beginning of the second part of the All-night Vigil — **Matins**. It expresses the **joy of the Resurrection of Christ**, the incarnation of the Second person of the Holy Trinity, our Lord, Jesus Christ. The beginning of Matins, as we know, recalls the Birth of Christ, and begins with the doxology of the angels in their revelation to the shepherds of Bethlehem, *Glory to God in the highest, and on earth peace, good will among men.*

In popular usage, the twice-rung bell at the All-night Vigil is called the **second-bell** (the second bell peal after the beginning of the All-night Vigil).

3) At the time of the singing of the polyeleos, before the reading of the Gospel, the **trezvon**, the thrice performed, simultaneous ringing of all the bells, is rung, expressing joy in celebrating the event.

At the Sunday All-night Vigil, this ringing expresses the **joy and festivity of the Resurrection of Christ**. In some localities it is performed at the time of the chanting, "In that we have beheld the Resurrection of Christ..." Customarily in guide books, this peal is called the "**bells before the Gospel**."

In popular usage, the trezvon in the All-night Vigil (the bells before the Gospel) is called the "**third ringing**."

4) At the beginning of the Song of the Most-holy Theotokos, "My soul doth magnify the Lord...," occurs a short **good news peal**, composed of nine strokes of the large bell (customary in Kiev and in all of Little Russia).

5) On **Great Feasts**, at the conclusion of the Vigil, the **trezvon** occurs.

6) At Pontifical services, after every All-night Vigil, the **trezvon** is rung, accompanying the bishop as he leaves the church.

The Bells for the Liturgy

Before the beginning of the reading of the Third Hour, the **good news peal for the Liturgy** is rung, and at the end of the Sixth Hour, before the beginning of the Liturgy, the **trezvon**.

The Belltower on the Mount of Olives

If two Liturgies are served (an early one and a later one), then the **good news peal for the early Liturgy** is **simpler and slower than** the one for the later Liturgy, and it is customarily done not using the large bell.

At **Pontifical divine services**, the good news peal for the Liturgy begins at the indicated time. As the bishop approaches the church, the **trezvon** is rung. When the bishop enters the church, the trezvon ceases and the good news peal resumes and continues throughout the vesting of the bishop. At the end of the Sixth Hour, the **trezvon** is rung again. Then, during the Liturgy, the good news peal is rung at the beginning of the Eucharistic Canon, the most important part of the Liturgy, to announce the time of the sanctification and the transformation of the Holy Gifts.

According to T.K. Nikolsky, in the book *Ustav Bogosluzhenia*, it is said that the good news peal before "It is Meet ...," begins with the words, "It is meet and right to worship the Father, and the Son, and the Holy Spirit ...," and continues until the chanting of "It is truly meet to bless Thee, the Theotokos...." It is also the instruction in the Book *Novaia Skrizhal* by Archbishop Benjamin (published in S.P.B., 1908, p. 213.).

In practice, the good news peal for "It is meet..." is shorter, composed of twelve strokes. In southern Russia the good news peal for "It is meet..." is performed customarily before the beginning of the

Eucharistic Canon, at the time of the chanting of the Creed (12 strokes, 1 stroke for each clause of the Creed). The good news peal before "It is meet...," according to the custom of Russian churches was introduced during the time of Patriarch Joachim of Moscow (1690 A.D.), similar to the custom of the West, where they ring during the words "Take, eat...."

At the conclusion of the Liturgy on **all Great Feasts** the **trezvon** is rung. Also, after **every Liturgy served by a bishop** the **trezvon** is rung to accompany the bishop as he leaves the church.

On the **feast of the Nativity**, the **trezvon** is rung all the day of the feast, from Liturgy until Vespers. Also, on the **feast of the Resurrection of Christ —Pascha**.

The **good news peal** before Bright Matins begins **before the All-night Vigil** and continues until the **Procession of the Cross**, and the festive trezvon is rung from the **beginning of the Procession of the Cross** to its end and even longer.

Before the Paschal Liturgy, the good news peal and the trezvon are rung. During the **Paschal Liturgy** itself, at the time of the **Gospel** reading, the **perezvon** is rung, with seven strokes on each bell (the number seven expresses the fullness of the glory of God). This festive ringing of bells signals the homily on the Gospel of Christ in all languages. Upon completion of the reading of the Gospel, the perezvon concludes with the joyful, victorious **trezvon**.

During all of Bright Week, the **trezvon** occurs every day, from the end of the Liturgy until Vespers. On all **Sundays from Pascha until Ascension**, after the Liturgy the **trezvon** is rung.

On the feast day of a church, at the conclusion of the Liturgy before the **beginning of the Moleben**, the short **good news peal** and the **trezvon** are rung, and at the **conclusion of the Moleben**, the **trezvon**.

Whenever there is a **procession around the church**, the **trezvon** is rung.

Before the **Royal Hours**, the **good news peal** is usually rung on the large bell, and before the **Great Holy Week Hours**, the Lenten good news peal in rung on the small bell. As at the Royal Hours, so also at the Great Holy Week Hours before each Hour the bell is rung. Before the Third Hour the bell is struck three times, before the Sixth Hour, six times and before the Ninth Hour, nine times. Before the Typica and Great Compline, twelve times. If during the fast a feast day is celebrated, then for the Hours they do not strike separately for each Hour.

On **Matins of Good Friday**, when the **Twelve Gospel Readings of the Lord's Passion** are read, besides the usual **good news peal** and **trezvon** at the beginning of matins, there is a **good news peal** before each **Gospel reading**: before the first Gospel reading — **one stroke** on the large bell, before the second gospel reading — **two strokes**, before the third Gospel reading — **three strokes**, etc.

Upon conclusion of Matins, as the faithful carry the "Holy Thursday fire" to their homes, the **trezvon** is rung.

Use of the Perezvon and its Meaning

At Vespers on Great Friday, before the elevation of the Burial Shroud, at the time of the singing of the last sticheron of the aposticha, a slow perezvon, one stroke on each bell, from the largest to the the smallest, is performed. Upon the placement of the Shroud in the center of the church, the trezvon is rung.

At Matins for Great Saturday, beginning with the chanting of the "Great Doxology" and continuing through the procession with the Shroud around the church, the perezvon is rung the same for the carrying back of the Shroud, a slow perezvon, one stroke on each bell from the largest to the smallest. When they pick up the Shroud in the middle of the church and go with it to the Royal Gates, then the trezvon is rung.

The slow perezvon with one stroke on each bell, beginning with the largest, most powerful sound, and ascending by degrees to the most delicate and highest pitched tone of the small bell, symbolizes the "outpouring (in terms of humility)" of our Lord Jesus Christ for our salvation, as we sing, for example, in the fourth irmos of the Fifth Tone: "Foreseeing Thy divine self-emptying upon the Cross..."

As established by centuries of practice by the Russian Orthodox Church, in the central part of Russia such a perezvon could be performed only twice a year, on Good Friday and Great Saturday, the day of the Crucifixion of the Lord and His burial. Experienced bell-ringers usually follow this custom strictly and do not permit otherwise, so that the sorrowful sound pertaining to the Lord, our Saviour, would be reserved and distinct from the funeral bells of simple, mortal and sinful people.

At Matins on the day of the Elevation of the Cross of the Lord, during the week of the Veneration of the Cross, and on the first of August, before carrying Cross out of the Altar at the time of the chanting of the "Great Doxology," the perezvon occurs, during which they slowly strike three times (in some places, one time) on each bell from the largest to the smallest. When the Cross is carried to the middle of the church and placed on the analogion, the trezvon is rung.

Similarly to the perezvon, but faster and in quick succession, seven or three times on each bell, the bell is rung before the little blessing of water. At the time of the immersion of the Cross in the water, the trezvon is rung.

As before the blessing of water, the perezvon occurs before the ordination of a bishop. In general, the perezvon is quick, but sometimes on each bell there is a festive peal. In several places, such a perezvon is performed before the beginning of the Liturgy on the feast day of the church, or in other instances, for example, as we indicated above, during the reading of the Paschal Gospel.

The Use of the Perebor and its Meaning

The perebor, otherwise known as the funeral bell, expresses grief over the dead. It is used, as we explained above, in the reverse order of the perezvon. That is, slowly they stroke one time on each bell from the smallest to the largest, and after that they strike all the bells simultaneously. This mournful, funeral perebor must conclude with a short trezvon, expressing the joyous Christian faith in the resurrection of the dead.

In view of the fact that in several guides on bell ringing, one is instructed not to play a trezvon at the funeral service of the dead, and as this directive does not correspond to church practice, we will take this opportunity to give some explanation.

The slow perebor ring of the bells, from the smallest to the largest, symbolizes a man's growing up on earth, from small stature to maturity and strength, and the single, simultaneous strike on all the bells signifies that the earthly life of man is stopped by death, because of which all that is acquired by man in this life is left behind. As this is expressed in the hymns of the funeral service, "All mortal things are vanity and exist not after death. Riches endure not, neither does glory accompany on the way; for when death comes, all these things vanish utterly" (or as in another hymn, "yet one moment only, and death shall supplant them all"). Therefore, to the immortal Christ we cry, "Give rest to the one who has passed away, in the abode of those who rejoice." The second part of the hymn directly speaks of the joy of the future life with Christ. This joy is also expressed with the trezvon after the sorrowful perebor.

In the journal *Pravoslavnaia Rus'* (Orthodox Russia), Archbishop Averky, according to the custom of the occasion at funerals and Pannykhidas for the deceased, gave the soundly based explanation which, without doubt pertains to the bells as well. "According to our Orthodox custom, to perform Pannykhidas and funerals, bright clothing is put on. The custom of celebrating these orders of worship in black clothing came to us from the West, and is absolutely uncharacteristic of the spirit of Orthodoxy. Nevertheless, it is widespread among us. So much so, that now it is not easy to eradicate. For true Christians, death is a passage to better life, joy and not sorrow, as is beautifully expressed in the moving third kneeling prayer read at Vespers on the day of Pentecost, "Because there is no death, O Lord, for Thy servants when we depart from the body and come to Thee, our God, but a change from things very sorrowful unto things most beneficial and most sweet, and unto repose and gladness."

The trezvon, reminiscent of the Resurrection, gracefully acts in the soul of the Christian believer, grieving over the separation from the deceased, and gives it internal consolation. To deprive the Christian of such comfort has no basis, the more so since this trezvon has fundamentally entered into the life of the Russian Orthodox people and has become an expression of their faith. In this way, as the body of the deceased is brought to the funeral in the church, there is the mournful perebor, and as it is being carried into the church, the trezvon. After the funeral, upon carrying the deceased out of the church, there again occurs the perebor, concluding also with the trezvon.

During the funerals and burials of priests, hieromonks, archimandrites and bishops, a slightly different perebor is performed. First they strike the large bell twelve times, then follows the perebor; again the twelve strokes on the large bell, and again the perebor, etc. As the body is brought into the church, the trezvon is rung; also during the reading of the prayer of absolution — the trezvon. During the removal of the body, again the perebor is indicated, and upon the placing of the body in the grave, the trezvon occurs. In other places, the bells are rung according to the usual custom for funerals.

In the *Chinovnei Knige,* it is said that during the removal of Patriarch Joachim, there was a good news peal, alternately on all the bells (*Vrem. Mosk. Obshch. Ist. i drevi.* 1852, vol. 15, p.22).

Not long ago we had occasion to learn that there exists still one other form of **perebor.** It is one stroke on each bell, but beginning with the largest to the smallest, and then a simultaneous striking of all the bells. This was put on a record, *Rostovskie Zvoni* (Rostov Bells), recorded in Rostov on 1963. In practice we have not heard such ringing, and there are no directions about them. Therefore we are unable to indicate where and when this pattern is used.

There also exists the so-called "**beautiful ringing**" on all the bells. The "beautiful ringing" exists at cathedral gatherings, monasteries, wherever they have a large collection of bells. The "beautiful ringing" is composed of several bellringers in a company of five or more people. The beautiful ringing occurs on the great feast days, at festive and joyful events of the Church, and also for greeting the bishop of the diocese.

It is also necessary to mention the "**alarm bell**," which serves a social purpose. By "alarm bell" is meant the uninterrupted, frequent strokes on the large bell. The "alarm bell" is used to alert people in the case of fire, flood, mutiny, invasion by an enemy, or some other form of social calamity.

The "vetchevnie" bell was used to call all the inhabitants of ancient Novgorod and Pskov to the **vetche,** or popular assembly.

Victories over the enemy and regiments returning from the fields of battle were announced with the joyous, festive **trezvon** on all the bells.

In conclusion, we note that Russian bellringers attained high mastery of bell ringing and were famous throughout the world. Many tourists came from Europe, England and America to the feast of Pascha in Moscow, to hear the Paschal bells.

On the "Feast of Feasts" in Moscow, the bells of all its churches, numbering more than 5,000, were rung. Thus, whoever heard the Paschal bells of Moscow would never forget it. It was "a unique symphony," as writer I. Shmelov expressed it. This powerful, festive sound permeated to Heaven a victorious hymn to the Resurrection of Christ.

(The basic description of the order of bell ringing is laid down for the most part in *Practice of the Russian Church in Central Russia*. The description of practice was compiled and confirmed by the many events and daily practices of the Russian Orthodox people, by the very life of the Orthodox Church.)

Epilogue

In our own time of weak faith the dark powers of evil approach, battling against the righteousness of God. We, the faithful, must remember especially that none other than the monastics, by **prayer and fasting**, appear as the vanguard of the battle against the powers of evil. **For the Lord Himself said,** *This kind* (satanic spirit) *goeth not out but by prayer and fasting* (Matt. 17:21.) We must love these zealots of Christ, and we must help them by all means, begging their spiritual help.

We ourselves, knowing the great power of prayer and fasting, must pray every day and fast to the best of our abilities, in order to maintain fervor, to fortify our hearts toward good and holy resolutions, and to generate in ourselves spiritual strength, so that with God's help we may withstand the intrigues of the Devil.

In the words of Metropolitan Philaret of Moscow, "Let us not be deceived by the attractive appearance which ordinary, worldly honor possesses; let us not be enemies of the faith, behave scandalously, but let us do good deeds, and turn away from injurious overindulgence. In short, to fulfill only the most necessary ostensible obligations of a man and a member of society is to mearly whiten our sepulchers, which in the meantime, *are within full of dead men's bones* (Matt. 23:27).

"How many so-called, wise men of this world suffered and tortured themselves and others by striving to follow the good life?" says the same hierarch. "And who did they make blessed? Of course, their works are not for the understanding and activity of children, because their own understanding never completely escapes their struggle with doubts; their personal deeds do not correspond to their teaching (i.e., they themselves do not practice what they preach). Here we see man's insignificant importance. In contrast to this, there is the **great simplicity of God.** God does not say much. In His simple commandments are set forth the teaching of life, which for the wise are profoundly significant, and for children are easily understood. God's simplicity enlightens the ignorant and guides the educators; it purifies the souls of men and preserves civilization; it organizes temporal life and recreates it for eternity."

In all this one must not forget that the commandments of God will be active and redeeming for us only when Christian love towards God and neighbor reigns in our hearts. The Lord Himself said, *On these two commandments*, love for God and neighbor, *hang all the law and the prophets* (Matt. 22:40), that is, genuine and true life.

For, "It is possible to know true faith with only the mind and the memory," says Archbishop Innocent, "but poor, lifeless and fruitless is this knowledge. It is possible to know the true faith only by directing it by the principle of life, but this knowledge, although much higher than the first, and a necessity for perfection, is cold and dry; instead of delight, it often **produces the spirit of bondage to fear** (Romans 8: 15). Only the participation of a grace-filled heart makes the yoke of self-renunciation easy and the burden of the commandments light (Matt.11:30). Only the lively sensation in the soul of the heavenly and the divine links a man to Heaven and gives him a taste of the powers of the world to come (Heb. 6:5). Only holy love produces real unity of man with God and Christ, and therefore, a living faith and living hope."

Such living faith and hope, true life, we will find if we are in the **Holy, Catholic, Apostolic, Orthodox Church of Christ** and live the life of the Church, which is a unity of love; and in which invariably, by the promise of God, dwells the Holy Spirit, sending down His Heavenly gifts in the Mysteries of the Church, to strengthen us on the path of salvation.

Having such a priceless treasure, the Orthodox Church, we with full consciousness of that great joy, join our voices to the voice of our ever-memorable St. John of Kronstadt, whose many miracles witness to the truth of his words, both during his lifetime and after his death. He writes, "O Church of God, Holy, Catholic, Apostolic! You are so great, wise, true and redeeming!... Glory to the Orthodox Church! Glory to Christ God, its Most-holy Head, the only Head of the Church of God on earth." Amen.